PRAISE FOR *ICONS OF FRIGHT*

"*Icons of Fright* brings together 20+ years of interviews with the ghosts of horror cinema's past, present and future. Reading it captures the magic of wandering among the tables and through the bar of an epic, timeless horror convention— the thrill of recognition, the shared enthusiasms, the new insights. If you want to stoke those fires, you can't do much better than this book!"

– **Joseph Maddrey** (Author of *The Soul of Wes Craven*)

"Reading this book made us nostalgic for the glory days of horror websites, when fans had briefly wrestled control of the cultural steering wheel, asking the kind of questions fans would ask. And shining a light on lesser known icons that even the magazines wouldn't have the space to feature. This book preserves an era of horror fandom at its purest."

- **Josh Miller & Steve Scarlata** (*Best Movies Never Made*)

"A fascinating and fun time capsule of horror in the aughts. These *Icons of Fright* guys did their horror homework, and it shows!"

– **Tony Timpone** (Former Editor-in-Chief of *Fangoria*)

"Wildly entertaining! This remarkable collection of in-depth interviews with generations of horror icons spanning over twenty years will deeply satisfy both casual and obsessive fans. A must-have for anyone who loves the genre."

– **Craig Perry** (Producer of the *Final Destination* franchise)

"*Icons* gives you the same feels you had when you went to your neighborhood video store and spent two hours picking which four horror movies you were going to watch in your friend's basement on a Saturday night with stolen beer and pizza - and these interviews by Rob, Mike, Adam and Jason are all the kinds of questions that only lovers of the genre could give. Do yourself a favor and buy this book right now."

– **Scott Reynolds** (Writer/producer of the *Dexter* franchise & *Marvel's Jessica Jones*)

"An essential archive of some of horror and dark fantasy film culture's most influential and interesting voices. Written and curated by the fans, for the fans. It's slick, smart and tons of fun."

– **Chris Alexander** (Former Editor-in-Chief of *Fangoria*)

"Reading *Icons of Fright* is like stepping back into your most beloved video store (you know the smell, the sounds, and how much you felt welcome there), only all the talented folks who made the films on the shelves just happen to be there, too. And boy-oh-boy do they have a story or two to tell. Detailed, expansive, and when looked at in its totality, quite moving. Horror really is home."

- **Aaron Dries** (Author of *Dirty Heads* and *House of Sighs*)

"It's like a massive high school reunion of some of the most fun folks from favorite late night flicks."

– **Sandy King Carpenter** (Producer at Storm King Production)

"An essential archive of early internet genre journalism, a treasure trove of in-depth interviews by writers with undeniable, infectious passion for their subjects."

-**Matt Serafini** (Author of *Feeders* and *Rites of Extinction*)

"Long before scary movies hit peak online commercial viability, the *Icons of Fright* folks were already in the trenches, interviewing both the legends and semi- obscure characters of the genre. This book is a testament to the fact that it was, and always will be, the passion of the fans that keeps horror slithering and slashing onward."

– **Bill Shafer** (Owner/curator of the Hyaena Gallery)

Paperback Edition
ISBN-13: 979-8-9890130-5-0
Copyright © 2025

Published by Harker Press
http://HarkerPress.com
Book Design by Dustin McNeill

ICONS OF
FRIGHT

100 INTERVIEWS
WITH LEGENDARY
HORROR FILMMAKERS

MIKE CUCINOTTA - ROB GALLUZZO
ADAM BARNICK - JASON ALVINO

FOREWORD BY NEIL MARSHALL

ICON DIRECTORY

BEHOLD! THE GREATEST COLLECTION OF HORROR MOVIE INTERVIEWS EVER ASSEMBLED!

FOREWORD BY WRITER-DIRECTOR
NEIL MARSHALL

It's one thing to be included in this book, amongst such esteemed company, but it's truly humbling to be asked to write an introduction to such a weighty tome. Upon reading this book, one thing that immediately leaps from the pages is the entire *Icons* crew's clear passion for their subject matter. As long as I've known them, *Icons of Fright*'s love for the genre and the creatives behind it is nothing short of infectious. Rob's Blu-ray collection alone is a veritable shrine to the movie-gods! But here, within these pages, their professional respect for their guests is obvious, while their inner-fanboy is never too far away, and the combination makes the conversations all the more fun for it.

My first memory of meeting and hanging out with Rob and Mike was a trip to the dark side I will likely never forget. We were all in Dallas, Texas for Fear Fest 2 back in 2008. I was there to promote *Doomsday*, coming out just a few weeks later, and was introduced to Rob by our mutual friend and my then-wife, Axelle Carolyn. What do a bunch of movie geeks with a penchant for the dark-side do with a day to kill in Dallas? Visit Southfork Ranch, the home of J.R. Ewing? Sure, why not. Take a turn around Dealey Plaza and stand on the grassy knoll? It would be rude not to. Go and visit the grave of Lee "the Patsy" Harvey Oswald and take some selfies? Had to be done! Finding the grave wasn't easy, and not that surprisingly, we were the only ones there. We weren't there to determine his guilt or innocence, just to sample a slice of the other side of history, and take a few pictures because, let's face it, we're never going back there. The point being that we were all on the same wavelength from day one, and have remained good friends, through thick and thin, ever since.

Another, more recent, but equally fond memory, comes from my days living in LA, around 2018, when myself, Rob and a few other rebellious cinephiles formed a little collective based around the pure joy of watching truly terrible but utterly lovable 'BAD' movies. Not the kind of 'bad' that's just bad. I mean the kind of 'bad' that exudes the passion and sometimes misguided enthusiasm of the filmmaker, and makes the experience of watching just a hoot! Add in a few beers, some pizza, and a virtual live commentary from the gang we had some hilarious screenings, usually featuring movies from the 80's and more often than not, either 3D or sword-and-sorcery movies. If you know, you know. These screenings with Rob and the gang are a cherished memory, along with many other screenings, Q&A's, festivals, conventions, passionate debates, and other movie related encounters Rob and I have had over the years.

This book is a worthy tribute to the icons contained within, as well as the tireless dedication and years of hard work the *Icons* team has put into championing the cause of genre.

So kick back, dig in, and enjoy!

Neil Marshall

A FEW WORDS FROM
ROB GALLUZZO

It started simply enough. Mike said to me, "What if we started a website that was like Bravo's *Inside the Actors Studio*, but for the horror fan?" At that point, I had only recently met Michael Cucinotta through our mutual friend Vin Minichiello. Vin had worked with me at Tower Records and with Mike at Hot Topic. Funnily enough, long before Mike had met me, he came into my Tower Records and saw that I had curated an entire end cap of VHS movie picks. Among them, things like *Donnie Darko, Chopper, Dead Alive,* and *Opera*! At the time, he thought, 'Who is this Rob G guy that knows Dario Argento's *Opera*?' We became fast friends because back in that era, finding a kindred spirit that loved horror was a rarity! In 2004, *Fangoria* was still a print magazine that had an online message board. *Bloody Disgusting* was just beginning and *Dread Central* did not exist yet. And after taking a year long course in computer graphics and web design, I found myself in an awkward position of being unable to find a job to utilize any of those newly acquired skills. As soon as I met Mike, I finally had someone that would go to the East Coast horror conventions with me. Our interactions with horror celebrities in those days were brief, and not all that different from Chris Farley's *Saturday Night Live* sketch where he nervously interviewed Paul McCartney. We thought, 'How the hell do we make those interactions last just a little bit longer? Be just a little more meaningful?'

Since I couldn't land a job in web design, I decided I should get some practice by building a website from scratch. And in having these conversations with Mike, we both decided it should be a horror website that would give us a reason to have more substantial conversations with the genre folks we were meeting. After all, we truly and sincerely loved every single thing these people worked on and would often stay up late at our local diner discussing horror films. Alas, *Icons of Fright* was born in one of those diner sessions. That initial pitch he made set the precedence. We would be a long form interview web magazine. Given that we had regular day jobs, we would make it a monthly webzine, initially aiming for a minimum of four interviews per month. And maybe a few genre related columns mixed in for the fun of it. In March of 2004, we launched a little teaser page at IconsOfFright.com with an original Freddy Krueger art piece by Steve Ciancanelli. In April, we officially launched our first four interviews.

Looking back, our timing was quite perfect. Among our first interviews were names that people recognized like *Fangoria*'s Tony Timpone and *Friday the 13th*'s Betsy Palmer. But we were also suddenly seeing a handful of emerging new East Coast filmmakers like Dante Tomaselli, Stevan Mena, and Larry Fessenden. We were so lucky to loop in one of my lifelong friends Jason Alvino early in our inception. Jason and I had a background playing in local rock bands together, so we applied the same "promote the band" mentality to *Icons of Fright* because that's all we knew! For example, by our second year, he had created a mini-magazine version of the site that we printed out at the local Staples and handed out to a hundred fans at the Chiller convention in New Jersey. He came up with the quirky column, "Vault Of The Forgotten and Obscure," which harkened back to the wonder of picking up a VHS tape and marveling at the cover art. Adam Barnick was a New Jersey filmmaker that was already interviewing fellow directors for his own personal site. After discovering his short film, *Mainstream*, we sensed yet another kindred spirit, and he quickly became a part of our team. He would bring to us new and upcoming filmmakers such as Adam Green with *Hatchet*, or Scott Glosserman with

Behind The Mask: The Rise of Leslie Vernon. Our reputation grew quickly, and I think the reason it worked so well for that first decade was we always remained sincere. None of us thought that any kind of industry career could possibly emerge from having long, nerdy conversations with genre celebrities. We did it for the fun of it. And eventually, we were taken seriously and looked upon as fellow writers and peers.

Jason was the one that in early 2005 said, "You know who I want to find and talk to? Bob Clark." At that time, no one in any media was talking about this incredible filmmaker who defined the holidays with both *Black Christmas* and *A Christmas Story*. Jay's *Icons* interview with Bob helped raise appreciation of the underrated filmmaker with horror fans. It also inspired Tony Timpone to invite Bob to the next Fangoria Weekend of Horrors for a career long celebration, his first time being invited. Jay rekindled his love of special FX make-up and worked on the Los Angeles shoot for Paul Solet's short film version of *Grace*. I'll never forget Bob dropping by in the middle of the night to visit us on set, because he was a night owl! He captivated us with stories of all the raunchy things he had to cut out of *Porky's* and decided to hire Jay that night for his *Children Shouldn't Play With Dead Things* remake. Sadly, he and his son Ariel were killed a short time after by a drunk driver.

We went from requesting interviews either in person at the horror conventions or via MySpace to eventually being invited to press junkets for big studio releases like *The Omen* and *Orphan*. Mike and I had gotten into an early test screening of the 2006 movie *The Signal* and immediately brought it to the attention of Tony Timpone, who in turn, based upon our recommendation, invited actor AJ Bowen and co-director Dave Bruckner to attend their first Fangoria show. Bruckner would go on to direct the *Hellraiser* reboot and continues to be a much sought after genre director. When *Hatchet* was released in theaters, we put a call out to readers to come meet us at a Manhattan screening where we got up beforehand and gave away prizes by doing horror trivia. The theater and employees had no idea who we were or that we were doing this! We just did it! We always tried to make what we were doing with *Icons* feel inclusive. I had gotten an early screener of the beloved Swedish vampire film *Let the Right One In* and immediately noticed altered subtitles on the official DVD release. My screen-comparison *Icons* article about this was our first "viral" sensation, getting the attention of Roger Ebert, *Entertainment Weekly,* and other major trade publications forcing Magnolia to re-issue the disc. In other words, in a short period of time, we somehow managed to actually influence things.

A lot of horror sites exploded in the mid-2000's, and we were friendly with all of them, but we never considered it a competition. A lot of them were "scoop" based, trying to beat everyone to the punch of a new sequel or casting announcement. And while we did eventually loop in news bites into our site, the focus was always the long form interviews. That's what made our content timeless. Now, I look back at all the interviews within this book, and they are snapshots of that person in that moment in time. We remained honest in our love, and I feel that everyone who spoke with us instantly recognized that passion, which is why they felt comfortable to open up so candidly with us. A handful of these genre vets are no longer with us, and now I look back at their *Icon* interviews with both a sense of awe and pride. We had a lot of reverence for the keepers of horror history before us, and we hope that anyone reading this book will be inspired to continue to carry that forward. Or just be entertained! As an added bonus, we are presenting three long-lost *Icons* interviews circa 2008-2009 that have never before been published, as well as bringing *Icons* up to speed with three brand new interviews with modern horror "Icons." To everyone that contributed to *Icons of Fright* in any capacity, to anyone that gave us their time, we appreciate it more than you can ever know. You are the true icons.

Robert V Galluzzo

2004

TONY TIMPONE
BETSY PALMER
LARRY ZERNER
LAR PARK LINCOLN
FELISSA ROSE
ELLIE CORNELL
PJ SOLES
BRAD LOREE

TONY TIMPONE

Interviewed by Rob Galluzzo (4/04)

Having discovered *Fangoria* in my formative years, there's always been one person who has embodied the spirit of the magazine, and that's former editor-in-chief Tony Timpone. I first attended the Fangoria Weekend of Horrors convention when I was fifteen and I've always made it a point to thank him at the end of each one, every year, for helping put together such a great event. To most of us, he's the goodwill ambassador of the genre, so it made perfect sense for him to be our very first interview on *Icons of Fright*.

What are your first recollections of the horror genre?

I started out as a fan of the genre when I was just a kid, watching the Universal and Hammer monster movies and going to the drive-in to see movies of the late 60s and 70s. I just always had a big love for horror, science fiction, and fantasy. I also used to read comic books as a kid and I always had a passion for *Famous Monsters of Filmland*.

When I was in high school, I used to do my own fanzines. I used to go to the conventions and meet people like Tom Savini and try to interview them and then try to sell the articles to *Famous Monsters* or *Fangoria* or any publications like that. That was my dream, to work on a horror magazine. Sure enough, as soon as I got out of college, that was my first job and that's where I remain today. I actually like getting up in the morning to go to work because I'm doing what I always wanted to do, which is, ya know… editing a horror magazine, getting involved with horror projects, movies, and videos. It's all very fun and exciting.

How did you come to work for *Fangoria* and eventually land the gig as editor?

Well, it was mostly networking at conventions. And I think that anyone wanting to get into the business or anyone who does writing… that's what they do, they go to the conventions. And the horror personalities there are very approachable. They're all good people. They enjoy meeting their fans. And it's just a great place to network. That's where a lot of make-up guys get started. They'll bring their portfolios and show them around. And filmmakers hand

out their short films. Fango cons really are the place to meet people that can help advance their careers.

Tell us about your early experiences with *Fangoria*.

While I was still in college, I was writing freelance articles for *Starlog*, a science fiction magazine, because at the time, *Fangoria* used to be pretty much all written 'in-house', meaning that the editors themselves wrote all the articles, which was pretty unheard of at the time. So *Fangoria* was a very difficult market to break into for that reason because the editors, at that time Bob Martin and Dave Everett, for some reason just liked doing all the articles themselves. They'd write as many as four articles each per issue. I used to go to the science fiction conventions and Creation shows and meet a lot of the *Star Trek* and *Star Wars* people, and they were also very accommodating back then. I would interview these science fiction people and then sell the articles to *Starlog*, the science fiction magazine at that time.

Then I started meeting some of the horror people like Tom Savini and Caroline Munro. And I would sell those articles to a magazine called *Monsterland*. *Fangoria* didn't need them, so I went to the competition, *Monsterland*, which was edited by Forrest J. Ackerman, who was sort of my mentor in the business. I started doing a lot of writing for *Monsterland* toward the end of college, and when I got out of college, I ran into the editor of *Starlog* at a convention and told him I was just getting out of school and asked if there were any positions opening up.

A month later, he called me while I was working at my dad's deli to come in for an interview. I went in and got the job. I was originally going to start as an editorial assistant and I would've worked on *Starlog* and a number of wrestling magazines we'd published around that time, which wasn't too exciting, but I figured it was getting a foot in the door. But in the weeks leading up to my start at *Starlog*, Bob Martin who was co-editing *Fangoria,* decided to leave to go work on a rock magazine, and Dave Everett had no one to help him on *Fangoria*. There was a vacant desk in his office where Bob Martin used to sit, so as fate would have it, I got that desk and instead of that job of editorial assistant, I was going to be helping out Dave Everett. But then Dave Everett left after about a month, and I was pretty green at the time, being just out of college. The editor of *Starlog*, Dave McDonald, decided to be editor for about a year until I earned my wings and could become editor in chief. In that one month with Dave Everett, he promoted me from editorial assistant to assistant editor to associate editor to managing editor. I did writing, editing, and I enjoyed my job and was off and running.

With all the publications that *Fango* and *Starlog* press have put out over the years, is there any particular project or issue that stands out as something you're most proud of?

There are several issues I'm really proud of. *Fangoria* #100 and *Fangoria* #200 are probably my favorite issues. I was really happy with the way #200 came out and I've liked a lot of the theme issues we've done. We've done issues devoted to vampires, werewolves, dinosaurs, Godzilla. Some of the Godzilla issues I really liked because we always managed to get such fabulous pictures and that's another thing I grew up on. I used to love the Godzilla movies. I'd see all of those in the theaters as well. And we did a few specials. We did a magazine on Dracula when the Coppola *Dracula* movie came out and I thought that came out really good. We did a dinosaur magazine to tie in with *Jurassic Park* with a 3-D cover and I was really proud of the way that came out. We've done a Lovecraft issue. All those issues were a lot of fun.

Back in the late 80s/early 90s, there was another horror publication called *Gorezone*. Were you involved in that?

Yep. That was a *Starlog* publication and I edited that one as well. During that time, *Fangoria*'s circulation really spiked through the roof and we realized there were probably going to be a lot of rip-off publications that are going to come along and steal *Fangoria*'s thunder. We thought we should create our own competition to discourage these other people that were going to try to steal our subscriber

base. So, we created *Gorezone* to literally form our own competition. And it worked.

There were a few rip-off magazines that didn't come out or folded after one or two issues, whereas *Gorezone* lasted several years. I think it went up to #22 or so. *Gorezone* was a lot of fun to put together too. We put a lot of stuff in there that *Fangoria* didn't have like fiction, we had a make-up effects column, and a lot more independent and foreign film coverage. More reviews. It was fun while it lasted, but now we've folded a lot of those departments into *Fangoria* and on our website, so *Gorezone* lives in other ways. We're also starting a *Gorezone* video label to put out more independent gory horror films and so the title's going to live on that way as well.

By profiling films in production for the magazine, were there any projects that either met or surpassed your initial expectations or surprised you on release?

I would say the two remakes that came out this past year. *Dawn of the Dead* and *Texas Chainsaw Massacre*, I had low expectations going in because I didn't think they were going to be able to top the originals. But even though they weren't as good as the originals, they still stood out and were very effective in their own right. Ya know, I think they were much better then I anticipated and they did a good job of re-imagining the films. They didn't just slavishly recreate the magic of the original films, but they tried to do something different, so I respect that. *28 Days Later* was better than I thought it would be. I knew it was going to be good, but it was even better than I expected; it really scared the hell outta me and I thought that was terrific. That's one that really blew me away.

Speaking of zombies, fast zombies or slow zombies?

I think the fast ones are scarier. I love the original *Dawn of the Dead* and *Night of the Living Dead* but there's other social commentaries going on in those films. You have that in *28 Days Later*, but I think it also upped the scare quotient by making them faster zombies. I think they're scarier when they're faster.

In the 80s, you went on a crusade defending horror films. What do you think of the current state of horror films & how people view these films now?

Well, back then video was just gaining popularity. There were all these mother's groups and PTA groups that were always attacking horror movies and violent films. That whole generation of concerned parents used horror films as a scapegoat. So yeah, I was frequently called up on the carpet to defend the genre and the magazine. We were getting thrown off newsstands. There was always a lot of trouble. And even back then, I said *"You're going after horror films now but what's next? Are you going to go after TV and other movies"*, etc. etc. And sure enough, that's what happened. After they were done attacking horror, they would go after *NYPD Blue*, and starting ratings on records and tv shows, all the trouble with the MPAA. It was a real mess. It got worse and worse and worse, and all these censorship issues never really died. We're actually seeing a lot of that going on right now. But horror films haven't really been the target like they used to be. The MPAA has almost sort of been horror's best friend in the past few years. When you see what *Texas Chainsaw Massacre* and *Dawn of the Dead* got away with, it's unbelievable.

Do you think the MPAA has lightened up in recent years?

Absolutely. Just look at *Kill Bill* and again, *Dawn of the Dead*. It's amazing. I can't imagine those films getting R ratings, say in 1990. Look at what *Leatherface: Texas Chainsaw Massacre III* went through back then. The film was taken apart due to MPAA restrictions.

In a recent editorial, you mentioned how you desire more original films based on un-adapted books, as opposed to all of these current remakes. Can you tell us a few books you'd love to see adapted?

There's a lot of great Lovecraft stories that haven't been done yet. Guillermo Del Toro wants to do *At the Mountains of Madness*, and I think that would be wonderful. Um, there's some [John Skipp and Craig Spector] books that would make good movies, like *The Light At The End*. They were the splatter punks of the 80s. They also did a werewolf book called *Animals* that I remember liking a lot. So I think they're some good 80s splatter punk type books that would be really cool to see made into movies. There's some Clive Barker stuff that hasn't been done yet. Like *Weaveworld*. Christopher Fowler, Kim Newman (some of the British authors). They've done a lot interesting ones that would make good movies.

You published a book called *Men, Makeup and Monsters* and helped edit several other books. What led you to write that book and do work on the others?

I was approached by an agent who wanted to represent me,

and asked if I had any idea for books. So that was the first one I thought of. *Fangoria*, especially in the early days, was the bible of the make-up effects industry. Back when every kid wanted to go out to Hollywood and sling make up or latex. You don't get that as much anymore because of CGI. So many people were coming to *Fangoria* just to read these profiles on Rick Baker and Rob Bottin and Tom Savini. They were the gods of our readership during the 80s, so I thought it would be a good idea to write a book about all these make-up gurus who were inspiring the fans. We profiled twelve to thirteen of the top guys at that time. I got that book done, but it was a lot of work writing a book and editing *Fango* at the same time, so when the idea for other books came along, I decided to just edit them. I haven't written any other books since, but I've edited four others under the *Fangoria* banner.

How did the Fangoria Weekend of Horrors get started?

Well, pretty much as soon as I started here, I got involved with the convention because I was going to the conventions myself as a fan even before I started here. The first *Fango* convention was in 84, and then I got involved with producing the shows by late '85/early '86. I took a real active role to producing them, seeing them and booking the guests, and did everything it took to put on a big show.

How difficult is it to get genre professionals involved with the Fango Weekend of Horrors? How do you go about making your selections from year to year?

I try to bring people on board people that the fans haven't seen before. That's usually the big goal. To bring a guest you just don't see at other horror conventions. To get a Quentin Tarantino or a Jack Nicholson or Kenneth Branagh, just cool people. Guillermo Del Toro. They want to do these conventions because the magazine supports their movies in print. They want to meet the fans and press in the flesh and promote their new movies. I'm pretty much able to get most of the people I want to at the *Fango* shows because I work with these people on a daily basis in the print edition and they want to meet the people who support them at the theaters. A great place to do that is at the conventions.

The Fango Weekend of Horrors takes place on both coasts. Any differences between the NY and CA shows?

Yeah, there are. At the LA shows, sometimes you have just as many celebrities in the audience as you do on stage. Ya know, it's the company town where all the movies are made. You get a lot of people coming down just to hang out, even if they're not speaking on stage. It's not uncommon to see John Landis or Quentin Tarantino floating around the dealer's room when you're in LA. That always makes for a pretty exciting atmosphere. But the fans in LA are kind of jaded because they see these people on line at the supermarket. But when you bring Ron Perlman of *Hellboy*, to New York, it's a real event and the fans go crazy. They're not used to getting these people to come into their town.

The New York shows have moved to different locations throughout the past few years. What initially sparked the merger with Chiller for the most recent *Fango* convention?

It started out as competition for the *Fangoria* shows. Kevin Clement, who runs Chiller, used to be a dealer at the *Fangoria* shows years ago. So, he created his own show and it was a different kind of show, but it kept growing and growing and getting bigger and bigger. I went to my first Chiller show and I just could not believe the numbers of people that were turning up. And at the *Fangoria* convention, the attendance was starting to erode a little bit. It wasn't as big as it used to be.

So, we decided it was time to switch partners and try to reach a lot more people and the first show we did with Chiller, we thought we had three times as many guests than with the previous convention partners that we had, Creation. The experiment worked and we were happy with the numbers of fans. The conventions are very crucial to us because we're promoting the magazine, and our video and movie projects. So, the more people there, the better.

You've helped set up events in Milan, Italy and the Fantasia Fest in Montreal. How'd you go about setting up these other *Fango* related events? What were the experiences for those events like?

Well, those are different from the conventions because they're film festivals. Those are very exciting to work on because it's always exciting to see a lot of these films on the big screen. A lot of these movies don't get big screen exposure, so you go to a festival like Fantasia in Montreal or the festivals in Spain and it's amazing when you see these films this way and not at home on video. You have a chance to discover a new film before anyone else. Fantasia was the first place to show the original Japanese *Ring* in North America. Last summer, they had *Dead End* and *Undead*. Films that haven't even come out on tape yet. It's a great place to get a buzz going and get the fans excited about

upcoming films. It's exciting working with the studios to premiere these films in front of audiences of hundreds of fans who are seeing these movies the way they're meant to be seen and enjoying them.

Thanks so much for talking to us Tony!

Anytime. I'm looking forward to logging onto the website every day to see what excitement you guys have lined up.

BETSY PALMER

Interviewed by Mike Cucinotta and Rob Galluzzo (5/04)

Actress Betsy Palmer has had a long and incredible career working along side such established actors as Henry Fonda, Jack Lemmon, Anthony Perkins, Joan Crawford, and many more. She's worked in every medium from television to stage to movies, but most genre fans will recognize her as the mother of Jason Voorhees from *Friday the 13th*. We talked to Betsy about her huge body of work, her experiences on the original *Friday*, and her recent convention experiences.

Tell us how you initially got involved in acting.

Well, it all started long, long ago in a little town called East Chicago, Indiana, which is right out side of Chicago, and is next to Gary, and it's a lot of steel mills, oil refineries, it's a small town like that. And from the time I started school from a very young girl, the teachers were always encouraging me and sending me on stage whenever there would be a program. It seems I had an affinity for performing, for being out in front of people and I enjoyed it. I guess I was sort of a good at it too, I don't know. That was a long time ago. Then I went through all my school years they kept giving me more parts and things to do. Then, I went to business college in East Chicago after I finished high school. Most of my friends went away to a university or to a college, but I couldn't afford to do that, so I learned to be a stenographer.

My first job was with the B&O Railroad, and I was pounding typewriters. One day my parents and I were talking and they said, "Don't you think it's time you further your education?" I said I don't really know what to do, and my mother was a very pragmatic woman and she said, "Why don't you go into Chicago and take an aptitude test?" So, I sought one and went to the YWCA which gave the test for free, which was the same one Northwestern was giving for money and I took the test. About two weeks later I went back and they gave me the readings and they said that I should always be involved with people in personnel work of sorts and that I had a flair for the arts. The last thing I was supposed to be doing was what I was doing, being a stenographer for the railroad.

So my dad came home one night and brought a friend with him that he was working with who had come from New York who had been in the theater. So we got to talking about theater. He and his wife had graduated from The Goodman Theatre, which was the theatrical theater in Chicago. He said, "You should work with the man who teaches us, Dr. Itkin." So I thought it out and it was so expensive. I was going to have to work during the daytime to go to school, but Itkin taught at the university at night. So I signed up there and I sold shoes at Marshall Fields in Chicago and I pounded typewriters at WGN which gave me my first TV job, eventually. I went and I graduated after three years in 1949 and my first summer stock job came very, very easily. I went and auditioned for somebody up in Lake Geneva. I worked with Sally Burman and Tom Bosely that summer, we were all in the same company, and these two men were going to start the opera house, which was a wonderful little opera house in Woodstock, Illinois, and was going to do six months of winter stock. We'd do a new play every weekend. Paul Newman was in that group, and he married his first wife that winter, Jackie.

When did you go from theater to television?

I came back from doing the winter stock and I had finished the six months and I went over to WGN where I had worked in the typing pool just to say hello to everybody. My old boss said to me there, "How would you like to do some television?" I said, "Wow, that would be great." We, of course, didn't have a television set.

I hadn't been around a TV set, because people didn't have that many sets in those days. He said there was going to be a show with this band leader, who was well known and I can't remember his name. He was involved with this woman who owned a lingerie store on Michigan Ave in Chicago and she was going to sponsor a fifteen minute show for him to be the kind of master of ceremonies and I was going to be his "girl Friday." I've always been able to talk and love to talk, I was the one that talked about things and then there were girls who modeled lingerie on camera. I would describe what they were wearing, and that was my first television job I ever had. I wasn't paid any money, but I thought the experience would be good for me.

Then I did some more summer stock, the first summer stock that brought in the star system, and Imogene Coca was the first person I worked with. I worked with her and she said, "You've got to leave Chicago. You've got to go to either coast, New York or California, but you mustn't stay here. You have talent, you should go." So, I worked with Arthur Treacher, and I worked with Burgess Meredith and all of these big name people who kept saying, "You've got to leave Chicago." I still went on and did more summer stock, and I had a friend, Sasha, who was working for an advertising agency. She was offered a job in NYC and at that time I was doing commercials with Hugh Downes on a soap opera that came out of Chicago, we would do the commercials live. So, I went home and said to my parents, I'm going to go to NY. I saved $400 from my summer stock work and a few weeks later I went to NY with Sasha.

We went to a party at her sister Toby's house, her sister worked on *The Molly Goldberg Show*, she was the PA on the show. Her husband was Frank Sutton, remember he was on *Gomer Pyle*, well, in those days he couldn't get himself arrested. So Frank and Toby were having this little gathering and there was this man sitting in the corner with three other guys sitting around him. I heard him say, "Well, she'd be perfect for it." He motioned me to come over and he said, "Are you an actress?" He said, "On Monday go up to the Ted Ashley office and go and see this guy." I went in on Monday and told this man he sent me. They asked, "Do you have a southern accent?" and I said, "I sur' enuff do, honey," and I got the job. I was on a soap opera that originated out of Philadelphia. We actors would commute on the train everday to do this live soap. It was called *Miss Susan*. Susan Peters, who was the lead had been a starlet of films. She was taking so many painkillers that after a while she couldn't function anymore and the show lasted for about three or four months.

How did you get involved in working on some of the major drama hours of the time?

I needed a job and I ran into this guy, Peter, on the street. I told him I was on the way to an audition or maybe to be hired at a restaurant. He said I've got this show that is a half-hour live show at CBS that the Goodson and Toddson people, who I eventually worked for, were doing. Anyway, he said it's not an acting role, but it's job and you do it five days a week on TV. Well...it turned out to be the first *Wheel of Fortune*, and it wasn't anything like the show it turned out to be. I was on the original one and there was another one I did with Mike Wallace. The first major nighttime drama I did was called *Hollywood Screen Test* where they took an unknown person with a known person and you did this half-hour show live. The known person was Jackie Cooper and I was the unknown, which was very interesting because the first movie I ever saw was *Treasure Island*.

When did you first break into features?

My first two movies were John Ford movies. The first one was *The Long Gray Line* with Tyrone Power and Maureen O'Hara. The second one I did for Mr. Ford was *Mister Roberts*. That was before Ford left the picture. He shot our girl sequence in Hawaii, and Mervyn LeRoy wanted to reshoot it out in Hollywood and I wouldn't go back and do it. I wanted Ford's hand to be the touch of the scenes that we did. The third movie was *The Tin Star* with Henry Fonda and Tony Perkins. Then they put me under contract at Columbia Pictures before I made the first film and I was to do two films a year.

Is that when you did *Queen Bee* with Joan Crawford?

I did *Queen Bee* with Joan, or Joanne as I called her, and she and I stayed friends all of her life. I liked her and she liked me and I found her a very professional and wonderful person. I don't know about the kids except I know for me it was great.

We know she was wonderful with her fans...

She was a top, top actress. She was a MOVIE STAR. Big pictures. When I was doing *Friday the 13th*, well, you know she did *Whatever Happened to Baby Jane* when she and Bette Davis couldn't get themselves arrested. I kept saying to Sean Cunningham, "Are you sure this is the way Bette Davis and Joan Crawford made their comeback?" (laughs)

You also worked on a lot of game shows during the 50's and 60's, how did that come about?

Warner Bros was called one day by the *I've Got a Secret* people. Faye Emerson had been part of the panel and Faye was out of town, they wanted to know who was in town. The guy said, well, Betsy Palmer is, we have this big movie we want to promote. I was promoting *Mister Roberts*. The people fell in love with me when I became a regular and that was just before I did my first Broadway show.

So you were still doing stage at the time?

I never left it! I loved the stage. I always loved it. I don't think film is really an actors medium, it's a directors medium, and a producer and your cameraman and your sound man.... Everybody's got all of this going on. You can do a wonderful thing, but your best stuff can be left on the cutting room floor.

      I did all kinds of musicals, *Hello Dolly*, *The King and I*, *Gentlemen Prefer Blondes*, *Peter Pan*. Actually, Sandy Duncan, the Peter Pan who became very big, she played my Wendy, it was her first acting role. I did *Eccentricities of a Nightingale*, which was the last show that Tennessee Williams had anything to do with while he was still alive, and it was beautiful working with him.

Didn't you even do a genre play, *Countess Dracula*?

I did *Countess Dracula*, yes. It was a play that was written for me up in the Arena Theater in Buffalo. I did *A Doll's House* for them, and *Countess Dracula*. I played three different roles, I played Elizabeth Von Helsing, which is the doctor that tracks Dracula, I played Lady Alucard. Then I played the Countess. In fact, my first entrance on-stage was as Elizabeth and I had to change and I had to get to my Lady Alucard outfit. I was at the door thirty seconds later, pulling on my black gloves, and talking with a very deep voice. The audience didn't know it was me because I changed so quickly. Pretty soon, after two, three minutes you'd hear them whispering, "It's Betsy!"

You then went back to television in the early 70's...

Went back? I never left. I was doing *Studio One*. I did the *Philco Playhouse*, *United States Steel Hour*. I did the first *Playhouse 90* that was ever done where they had a show that was an hour and a half long with Jackie Gleason.

What was the live television experience like?

It was like working on stage. It was just great. That's why I loved it so much. You rehearsed for a week and then the crew would come in on a Sunday, then of course when the red light would go on the camera you were there. Sink or swim. Speaking of swimming...I was doing this *Studio One* and the side curtains caught fire. The drapery was on the hot lights and we couldn't stop the show...and oh, the water that they brought in was all over the floor, and you're running from set to set. It was like theater, absolutely like theater. There was no stopping.

How did this all lead up to *Friday the 13th*?

What happened was I was on Broadway, I did the last year and half of *Same Time, Next Year* and by this time I was living in Connecticut. I was driving home to Connecticut after the performance that night and my car just clonked out on me. It was Mercedes that I had for many, many years. I could never find anybody to fix it right and it finally just pooped out. I was on my way home and I didn't get home until five 'o clock in the morning. So I said to the universe, or god: "Universe, or god, whatever, I need a new car." I went out and I was looking and found a Volkswagen. I decided I was going to buy that. So, my agent called me on Friday and said, "How would you like to do a movie?" I said, "Great, I hadn't done a movie since the 1960's. Is it going to be in California?" He said, "No, it's going to be shot in New Jersey. It's ten days work and they'll give you $1000 a day."

      And that's it. I said that's great, I found this car I wanted to buy which was $9,999.99. (laughs) Then he says "There's only one catch. It's a horror movie." I said, "Oh no, I have enough of a hard time trying to convince people I don't just play games on television." You know, by then I'd been the girl on *The Today Show*, I'd always done other things other than being a dramatic actress, which is the only thing I wanted to be. But I had a knack for doing these other things and being myself. So I said, "Send me the script." So he sent me the script, I read it and I said, "What a piece of junk! Nobody is ever going to see this piece of crap." So, I called him back and said I'd do it.

You didn't think the movie would become as successful as it has?

Oh no! And I never met any of those kids! I only worked with that last girl, that's the only one I saw. We did it at a Boy Scout camp. The night I was driving up to see Tommy Savini, it was all just beginning for him too, I remember there was a sign that said Crystal Lake. I thought that was a good omen. I used to spend my summers at a Crystal Lake in Warsaw, Indiana with my dad and brother. Then they immediately took me to Tommy Savini's workshop and they started to make my head that night. I remember the night I finished doing all that fighting on the beach, and this of course wasn't in the summer anymore, we were into the fall. We would have snow sometimes. We had finished that sequence and I went up to the cabin to get out of my wet clothes. I said I want to get out of this stuff, and I never knew how they did it. I know Tom was the one that wielded the machete.

Was that all you in the fighting?

That's me. Yes.

How did you prepare for all the fighting?

I didn't prepare for the fighting. I mean, I was acting a role. I was taught the real method of acting where you do an autobiography for the character and you make a story happen before you come on stage. These people always have a life before you portray them. My story for myself about Pamela Voorhees was that she was in high school, and she and this boy fell in love and they were going steady. And in those days gals just didn't go to bed with guys. So I figured they did make love and she became pregnant. So she finally has to tell her parents and her father throws her out of the house. I had done a lot of work for the Salvation Army, they had a service for unwed mothers, so I figured she went there and had the baby. Of course, she had no education and didn't know how to earn a living. Then when Tommy was showing me some Polaroid pictures of his special effects, there was this one....I said, "Who is this?" He said, "That's Jason, your son." I said, "Why does he look so strange?" He said, "Oh, he's a mongoloid." I said, "Well, that wasn't in the script!" So not only did I have this child out of wedlock, but I also had a child that was born with a handicap. So, I got this job at a summer camp so he could be around other children, and that's how the job came to pass. But then those kids weren't watching my boy, my Jason, when they should have been! This is my story, the autobiography. It's why I killed all the kids! They let my boy drown. I tried to warn them! So there... now you've got the whole story about *Friday the 13th*.

What was it like working with Sean Cunningham?

Sean was very good. He really made this film happen. I remember, well sometimes when you're doing something

so hokey as this seemed to me, you'd kind of want to overact. Like put your arm up over your face and go "He! He! He!," and he wouldn't let me do that. He said, "No play it straight." And I did. I played her totally straight. I only saw it twice after it opened. Then I never saw it again until last year at one of those conventions. They were going to show the movie on Friday night and asked if I would come say a few words before the movie. I told them the story like I just told you. I said to one of the men, "Why don't you bring me back after the movie was finished. I'll go through the audience and say 'I'm sorry. I lost my head.'" They brought me back but they brought me back a little early and I had to see myself in that last sequence. I watched, and I forgot that it was me, I could see this character and it's a study of a person going insane. She comes so sweet, like she's going to save the day, and she loses it.

Any memorable experiences on the set of *Friday the 13th*?

That one sequence where I have to haul off and hit her. I said to Adrienne that night "Why don't we rehearse this scene, I have to slap you," because on-stage when you slap somebody, you slap them.

You try to catch it along the side of the cheek where the jawbone is very strong so you don't hurt them. Well, we started to practice and I hit her. She collapsed to the floor, crying, "Sean! She hit me." I said, "Well, of course I hit her, we were rehearsing the scene." He said, "No, no, no Betsy, we don't hit people in movies. We miss them." I said, "It's going to look like I missed her," he said, "Oh well, we'll put in a sound effect."

Any idea why the film became so successful?

You know, I was dumb, *Friday the 13th* is an excellent film. I am now called the Queen of the Slashers, and it was the first of the slasher movies. I remember there was a girl who called in on a radio show, and finally I said, "Why do you all love Mrs. Voorhees the way you do?" And she said, "Because we understand why you did it." So, there you go.

Did you film anything for the sequels?

I went in and they had to make a new head. I never saw the second one, I hear my head is in the refrigerator, and my head is surrounded by candles looking very ghastly. I might have done a little voice over, but that was it. If they have shown anything it's flashbacks. I never did anything else. All I ever made on that movie was $10,000. Everybody thinks I get all these residuals, I got residuals for two years and each year it was $15, not $50. $15, and I never made any money on them since.

How you heard about the action figure that's coming out?

I love it! You know I'm going to be dead and buried and live on through these crazy movies.

You're going to be immortalized in plastic.

Wow. Isn't that wild? Who would have ever thought?

Was it true you were invited back for *Freddy vs. Jason*?

Yes, actually. They approached me about a couple other ones, but they never wanted to pay me, they offered me scale. I guess they're cutting corners, saving bucks, after making billions. They said it was only two days, I said I'd work 200 days. Pay me what you pay the men! I said thank you, but no thanks. Then I hear they got someone to look and sound like me. Of course, all the *Friday the 13th* fans

tell me they knew it wasn't me. And anyway, the scenes were dumb. The first *Friday the 13th* was really a hunk of something I could act.

You took part in the *Friday* Reunion, what was that like?

I love it. I love going to these events. People are so sweet, it's really adorable. I'm accessible, I'm not a mean, grumpy person. It's great fun, but I like people and always have all my life. But it is the irony of it all that I should be known for two things I never really wanted to be a part of. One is a game show, because I never really liked to play games, never in my life. Of course that's what made me known, *I've Got A Secret*. Then to do a horror film which I never in my wildest dreams thought that I would ever want to do anything like that, and look what happened. You never know. Life is a ball, when it bounces right, it's a happy ball.

LARRY ZERNER

Interviewed by Mike Cucinotta and Rob Galluzzo (5/04)

Actor Larry Zerner is proud to be one of the many victims of Jason Voorhees from the *Friday the 13th* series. He played the lovable prankster Shelly in *Friday the 13th Part 3* and was responsible for introducing Jason to his trademark hockey mask. *Icons of Fright* spoke to Larry about his experiences on *Friday the 13th Part 3*, the *Fangoria* reunion, his commentary session for the upcoming *Friday the 13th* DVD box set, and about horror movies in general. Visit him at ZernerLaw.com.

What are your earliest recollections of the horror genre?

Well, the first movie I ever saw that I remember scaring me was this old '50's movie called *Them!*, which was about giant ants that lived in the sewers of Los Angeles. I remember seeing that when I was about five on television and it scared the crap out of me. And then growing up, I was a voracious reader of Stephen King and read everything he wrote four or five times. Those would be my earliest recollections.

Were you a fan of the *Friday the 13th* films prior to working on *Part 3*?

I had seen part one. Not sure if I saw *Part 2* then? Ya know, it didn't really have the type of impact that it has nowadays. It was pre-Jason and pre-hockey mask...

And you started it all pal!

I didn't. I was just... there. (laughs)

Overall, what were the working conditions like on the set for *Friday the 13th Part 3*? The movies tended to come out rather fast. Was it a rushed production or did everything run fairly smoothly?

This was my first movie, so I didn't have much to compare it to. But at the *Fangoria* convention, I found out a lot more about the shoot because I had talked to Gerald Feil who was the cinematographer and he was telling me they had a huge number of problems because of the 3-D.

So, our shooting schedule was twice as long as any of the other *Friday* films because of the 3-D. It was such a new process. I remember the first week of shooting they shot and ended up scrapping it and starting over again. It was actually the store scene. Everything took hours to light, so we'd do a shot and then they'd move the camera to get the reverse angle and it'd end up taking two or three hours before we'd get called back. But as an actor, I was fairly insulated from that. I just went back to my trailer... well, dressing room... in one of those mobile trailers and hung out.

What was it like for you to see *Friday the 13th Part 3* on the big screen for the first time with your friends?

It was trippy. I remember going on opening night and it was a Friday the 13th. August 13th. It was a sold-out house in Westwood. I had actually seen it before at the crew screening, but then seeing it with a crowd and hearing them react to the 3-D.

People would be yelling and it was just great. It's odd though because I think most people who see it now, see it on television, which is really just a different experience as opposed to seeing it in the theater, because the 3-D really just adds... a whole other dimension to the movie, I should say! (laughs) I would tell anyone who hasn't seen it, that if they have the chance to see it in theaters, go see it in the theaters because it's a much better movie. So many of the shots are made to be seen in 3-D and, on television, they're kind of pointless. The snake jumping out and the rats coming out just seem meaningless unless you're seeing it in 3-D and they're coming at ya. The scenes when the eyeball popped out or the arrow coming toward the screen, the audience in that first screening just jumped and started screaming and it was great.

It was sort of weird to see me up there, because you think "Hey, that's me! It's a whole movie," and you think "I was there!" and it was the first time I'd seen myself acting. Then the movie was over and I'm walking out and everyone's yelling "There's Shelly. It's Shelly! It's Shelly," so right there I had a little touch of fame and it was interesting.

Other actors that have portrayed Jason Voorhees in the past have been known to keep their distance from the cast in order to instill a bit of fear into them for the movie. Was Richard Brooker intimidating in his version of Jason to you?

Richard was very friendly. If you remember, in *Part 3* Jason doesn't really have a lot of interaction with us. We have no scenes together! For everyone else, except for Dana, there was pretty much just one scene. And you see him and you die. So, there was no chasing or fighting back. It was more like "Hey, who are you?" BANG, you're dead! So, he didn't need to instill fear. I would see Richard in his makeup and he'd be sitting in a chair smoking his pipe... and it was funny, him smoking his pipe in his Jason makeup.

You recently took part in a *Friday the 13th* reunion for the *Fangoria* Weekend of Horrors in January of 2004. What was that experience like and how did it feel to meet all of Shelly's fans?

It was fun! You know, I don't get recognized anymore. Maybe a couple of times a week, I'll get an e-mail and someone will ask me for an autograph or want to talk about the film. But it's not a big part of my life. It's not like I get any attention for it anymore. But then to go to New York and to be in this place and there's thousands of people there and they're all *Friday the 13th* fans and they all know Shelly and all the other actors, it was a pretty amazing experience. It was fun to go and play a movie star for a weekend, because I'm not an actor anymore.

It was just great to also meet the other actors from all the other movies, whom we're all sort of in this weird club where we don't know each other, but we have this shared connection. And we all sort of know it. I got to meet Adrienne King, Amy Steel, Lar Park Lincoln, Kane Hodder, CJ Graham, and everyone was great and it was just a lot of fun!

I had missed you at that Fangoria Weekend of Horrors convention.

I was there for two days!

The way they set things up was a bit of a nightmare and by the time I got in the room, some people had left for panels. So, I had just missed you.

Were you there Saturday or Sunday?

I was there on Saturday during the day and it was really busy and hectic.

Yeah, it was a very, very crowded area. They didn't expect that many people and I guess they just weren't equipped to handle that big a crowd. I heard the wait was an hour to get in that room.

Oh yeah! It took ME an hour to get in there! But it was worth it. Anyways, you recently recorded the commentary track for the upcoming *Friday the 13th* DVD box set with some of the other cast members from that film. What was that experience like?

That was good, too. I had seen Paul Kratka and Richard Brooker about two years ago at a screening in LA and we got together and spoke to the audience. But none of us had seen Dana in twenty-two years and it was great that she came down to do the commentary. And basically, we sat in a little room and watched the movie along with Peter Bracke, who's writing a book about the *Friday the 13th* series. We just tried to tell stories about what was going on and I hope the fans will like it. We were the only cast that Paramount asked to do a commentary. I think more because of a time thing more than anything else. So, there are some director commentaries coming up on the boxed set, but there's only cast commentary on *Part 3* and I just hope the fans like it.

I'm sure they will. I'd read that you did another film called *Hadley's Rebellion*?

Yeah, I had a very small part in that. I was 'Boy F' or something and spent two days on it. It was written and directed by Fred Walton who did *When a Stranger Calls*, but this was not a horror movie. It's... not a very good movie, either (laughs) ...and I don't think it was ever released in theaters.

I read that you were a contestant on *Who Wants to Be a Millionaire*. Is that true?

Yeah!

How'd that come about? Were you just a fan of the show?

I'm sort of a trivia buff and the way you get on the show at the time was you just call up a phone number and answer some questions. You have to get three questions right, put these things in the correct order, and if you get them all right you go into a pool of people and if you get picked you fly to New York. And that's what happened. It took a year of calling and answering the questions to get in the pool until I finally got picked. And then I got to New York and I was 18/100's of a second off the leader for the hot seat. So, I came in second. But it was a fun weekend.

Did anyone recognize you from *Friday* when you did *Millionaire*?

No! Come on, no one knows who I am. I mean, I told them because they asked "What do you want to talk about?" They ask you in your pre-interview that in case you get in the chair. "What is Regis going to talk to you about? What do you do?" So, I told them. I gave Jason his hockey mask. (laughs) But once I was on, I saw on the *Friday the 13th* message board people talking about it. I mean, I was on for like two seconds! But some of the people on the forum I guess saw it and mentioned it.

What'd you think of *Freddy vs Jason*? I know you said you were looking forward to it.

I liked it. I actually wrangled an invitation through a friend of a friend to the premiere. So that made it a LOT better! So, I was there opening night for the premiere and Robert Englund and Ken Kirzinger were there along with a bunch of other stars. So, I sat and enjoyed it. I thought the writers did a good job of combining the mythologies into one and it delivered. Overall, it was a good night. I got to go see the film and got to go to the after party, and they had a good spread so THAT made the film that much better!

It took them a long time to put that movie together. In all that time, did the filmmakers ever ask some of the old cast members to make appearances in the *Freddy vs Jason* movie?

No. And I had spoken to Adrienne King at the convention and asked if they spoke to her about it. Because when I saw the film, I was thinking to myself it would've been great if both Adrienne King and Heather Langenkamp showed up. I mean, those two *should* have had cameos. They should have put them in there somewhere. I think they missed a good opportunity there. But I asked Adrienne and she said they never asked her about it. I figured if they didn't ask her, they didn't ask any of us.

How'd you initially get involved with entertainment law, which is your current profession?

Well, acting wasn't working out. I took the LSAT. I did really well. I went to law school to figure out what to do and law worked out really well. I enjoy being a lawyer and I represent a number of people in the horror field and it's great. I do copyright law and represent writers and producers. If anyone needs a lawyer, come to ZernerLaw.com and contact me.

Thanks so much for talking to us, Larry!

LAR PARK LINCOLN

Interviewed by Rob Galluzzo (7/04)

Long before Jason duked it out with Freddy Krueger, he went up against the young powerful psychic Tina, played by the lovely Lar Park Lincoln in *Friday the 13th Part 7: The New Blood*. A huge horror fanatic herself, Lar has been in other genre films such as *House 2* and has appeared on an episode of *Freddy's Nightmares*. We caught up with her to find out more about her experiences on *Friday 7*, as well as hear what she's been up to lately.

What are your earliest recollections of the horror genre?

Well, I have to say I love scary movies and I always go back to Hitchcock. I love *Psycho*, the early Jamie Lee films, and *Carrie*. And no, I did not pattern Tina after Carrie. She was really messed up. Tina was just...confused! I personally liked the first *Friday*.

How'd you initially get involved in acting?

I have always known that I would be an actress. I had three major goals in life by the third grade. I'm always surprised that children today don't have clear cut goals like that. They seem to "flounder" and I believe that is due to the extreme amount of information we have today. I believe they think there are so many choices that they don't have to make any. Anyways... off my soapbox. Ha! I wanted to act, I wanted to teach (although not in a school) and I wanted to write. I kept written goals all my life and that is how I believe I've achieved them all.

You were in *House 2: The Second Story*, which featured such a great cast including Arye Gross, Amy Yasbeck, Jonathan Stark, John Ratzenberger, and even... Bill Maher. What do you remember about that picture?

Dyeing my hair! No, really. Why do we go to so much trouble to stay blonde and then we are dyed brown!? Ha! I had seen and loved *House*, so I was excited to be in *Part 2*. On the way to the final audition, my $300 car broke down, of course, and I am never late! So, I called my manager and he came to get me. I dropped him back at the office and he let me drive his Jag to the audition. I really pretended to be

a star! I nearly lost that job after starting because I had a tear on my eye and had to miss some days of filming. So, I was almost recast. Luckily, I recovered and that was good. The sets were fun, the big old house, the scenes with Amy... she's really cool and, of course, that cutie pie Arye!

Why do you think your character Kate ran off with that darned Bill Maher anyways?

The script said I had to! I don't know. Don't the bad guys always have to leave together?

What were your initial reactions to the script *Birthday Bash* (aka *Friday the 13th Part 7*)? Was Tina the role you were always auditioning for?

Yes, she was. I came in late to the casting process, largely because my agents weren't too excited about me doing more horror. *Friday 7* looked like a fun film to work on.

What were your working experiences like with the rest of the cast & crew? Were you able to keep in touch with anyone from the production?

I didn't really keep in touch. I ran into a few of the actresses at the salon. Of course, since then I have now met *Jason 6* C.J. Graham, whom I wouldn't mind running into more often! I was just trying to keep getting booked and working all the time. Overworking on any project is my Achilles heel, which I actually pulled during a marathon two years ago! I was in a wheelchair and four casts for the past two years. Life has its ways....

You had to fight Kane Hodder's version of Jason for a good portion at the end of the film. What were your experiences together like?

I was tired. I used to have severe migraines and all the crying and indoor scenes with smoke gave me a lot of headaches. Tina's intensity was needed and I just wanted her to appear "real" and not like a *Carrie* character.

The fire in the basement toward the end of *Friday 7* seemed like a real close call. I know you had said previously that you were nervous working so close to actual fire. What was it like working on the stunts for *Friday 7*?

Well, I learned a lot! I learned not to insist on trying a stunt. The fire scene did scare me, personally. I also don't recommend falling from a run onto a pier if you have boobs. God bless the real stunt people!

Overall, what were the working conditions like on set for *Friday the 13th Part 7*? Was it a rushed production or did everything run fairly smoothly?

It did not seem rushed to me. John [Carl Buechler] worked with me very graciously and never yelled or embarrassed me. I do wish I had a massage clause in that contract because Tina was so tense. I really ached at night!

Friday the 13th Part 7 sported probably the creepiest looking version of Jason out of all the *Friday* films. What'd you think when initially seeing Kane Hodder in full make-up?

This guy needs a facial!

Did you have any idea how well received the film would be among fans while making it?

Yes, I knew it was a solid story and that John was trying to make the story "stand alone." But no, I didn't realize the full impact until I saw it in a theater. I thought no one would recognize me, but I was chased by a group of fans afterwards.

What was it like for you to see *Friday the 13th Part 7: The New Blood* on the big screen for the first time with friends and family?

I first saw the posters popping up around LA and that was cool. Then I saw the trailer in the theatre while going to see other movies. It was really exciting!

You had admitted to being a huge *Friday* fan before working on *Part 7* and actually saw all the movies that preceded yours. Have you kept up with the series since?

No, I haven't. What the heck happened to the storyline!?

You recently showed *Friday 7* to your kids. What'd they think of Tina kicking Jason's ass? Do you ever instill some psychic fear into them?

Well, we don't say ass in our house! But they had friends starting to see it. I had the poster in my office for a long time and my youngest made me take it down because it scared him. But after he saw the movie, which they do not see often, he said I could put the poster back up! Mostly they said things like "Mom, why would you run up the stairs?" Like I was an idiot! They had fun with it. I suspect someone had shown them parts of it before.

You recently took part in the *Friday the 13th* reunion at the *Fangoria* Weekend of Horrors convention in NY; one of your first convention appearances. What was the convention experience like for you, and what was it like meeting all of your fans?

Aside from still being on a cane from my injury, I just loved it! I was so happy to meet fans and share stories.

You once mentioned that you'd written your own sequel to *Friday 7*. Can you PLEASE tell us a bit about the story you wrote and how you would've followed up the series?

Okay, I am waiting to still pitch the film. It can still work and actually bring the series together. We have a large adult audience that I believe would like to relive that first film. I wrote this script where Tina would come back with her telekinetic gorgeous daughter. The audience would feel the terror from both the teenager's side and their own immortality. The babes would be hotter. The guys would have brains and the series would get the respect it deserved!

At the *Fango* con, I had tried to convince you that Kane Hodder had, in fact, worked on *House 2* also. Do you believe me yet!?

I will if I go check the credits!

You've done a lot of work in television. Most notably in *Knot's Landing*. How different was it for you working in television as opposed to movies?

I like TV the best. The daily work is there, not too many all-nighters, and you get to see it sooner.

You fought Jason Voorhees in *Friday the 13th Part 7* and won! What do you remember about your work on *Freddy's Nightmares*?

THAT was so great! I was offered the role and made it my own personal *Twilight Zone*! There is a scene when I am running in slow motion. I ran in slow motion and they filmed it normal. That was interesting. And doing the scenes without the effects there was fun! I like the technical side.

Rumor has it you'd like to return to acting. Any prospects on the horizon?

I am out there trying. Making a comeback when you haven't gone anywhere is tough! Ha! I'm looking at a few independent films that are good and next week I'm in New York for the beginning of a publicity tour for my books. I have several in editing.

Anything else you'd like to share with our *Icons* audience?

Mostly I must say to all the people who have kept me going... no one person ever does it all. We need so many people to help the "stars" shine. I'm so grateful to those that have helped me, especially after the death of my husband.

Lar, thank you for being so sweet. You were one of the first people we knew we wanted to interview when we first started this site.

Thank you and all the fans so much for all the support. Now... I must go have an iced tea and play "Mom!"

FELISSA ROSE

Interviewed by Rob Galluzzo (8/04)

Felissa Rose portrayed the first version of Angela Baker, aka the Angel of Death, in the original *Sleepaway Camp*. Ever since a reunion with her fellow *Camp* alumni, she's back to working on a slew of independent horror projects. She's also been spotted around the set of the upcoming *Return to Sleepaway Camp*. Could this mean the return of the original Angela? We tried our best to find out. Here's the scoop on all the films she's worked on and is set to appear in.

What are your earliest recollections of the horror genre?

I can remember seeing the trailers for *Magic* and *The Shining* and they terrified me. They scared me so much that it wasn't until years later that I'd be able to sit through these films. Now, I love them and I've seen practically everything. I'm officially a horror-aholic.

You started out acting at a fairly young age. How'd you first get involved in acting and what were your early experiences like?

I can't remember wanting to do anything else. From when I was about three, I told my parents that I wanted to sing and dance. They took it seriously and by nine they got me a children's manager. I think it's really hard for a kid because rejection isn't fun, especially when you're under the age of ten. I loved performing, so the shows I'd do were a lot of fun, but the professional part was difficult. I remember crying when I didn't get a part in the movie *Annie*.

What were your initial reactions to the script for *Sleepaway Camp*?

Cool! I couldn't wait to get to the set and have fun! I was thirteen. I wanted to meet boys and get out of school for two months.

What do you remember about seeing *Sleepaway Camp* for the first time? Was it in a theater with a full audience or a small screening with the cast and crew?

I saw it in a theater with my eighth grade class. The movie theater was packed in my hometown and I think everyone was pretty shocked. I remember closing my eyes as the last shot appeared. I had never seen a penis!

After college, didn't you run a theatre production company? What can you tell us about that? Were you always interested in acting on stage as well as screen?

I was part of a theatre company in NYC, which my ex-husband ran and directed. That was great fun. We'd perform all over the tri-state area and I loved being on the stage. There's nothing like the immediate reaction you get from a live audience.

Jeff Hayes from *SleepawayCampMovies.com* was the first person to track you down and interview you since *Sleepaway Camp* came out. Were you surprised to learn of the film's cult following? What was meeting him like?

He blew me away when he told me to check out his website. I could not believe the interest this little horror movie had generated all these years later. Jeff became a very dear friend of mine and, when I first met him, I was like a schoolgirl. He came to my house with some of his friends and it was the first time in, about fifteen years, that I had even given *Sleepaway Camp* a second thought. Jeff surprised me with stories about fans he had met on the internet and he really gave me a chance to start a film career again. I owe Jeff a lot of gratitude and to this day, I feel like he's an angel... or my agent.

You were then brought in for the commentary session for the Anchor Bay DVD. What was it like for you, rewatching the film with director Robert Hiltzik and Jeff Hayes?

Pretty surreal. I hadn't watched it in years, and it was the first time I was in a room with Robert Hiltzik in seventeen years. It was like watching the film for the first time. I just wish I could have remembered more about the filming, but we got through the commentary as best we knew how and the reunion, with Robert, became the highlight for me. That day was really the beginning of my wanting to work on film and in the horror genre especially. Jeff's enthusiasm sparked my excitement and luckily, I got a second chance.

You had mentioned previously that you didn't see the sequels until recently, but you were offered the chance to reprise the role of Angela. Did you ever get to see the scripts from back then? We're curious how much the sequels might have changed since their initial inception.

I never saw the scripts, but the sequels were perfect for the way the genre had changed. By 1989, the horror genre was more campy and fun, so I think parts two and three were done perfectly. I love the way Angela is portrayed. I was very curious to see what had happened to the character. Even though she got rid of her "extra part," she had the balls I always knew she'd have under that quiet exterior.

Actress Pamela Springstein obviously approached the character of Angela completely differently then you did. How did you feel about her interpretation? And do you think you would've played Angela differently had you reprised the role for the sequels?

You can't really compare the two Angelas. They're totally different scripts. An actor takes what's on the page and interprets the words as best they can. Angela was written as an outgoing smart ass. Pamela was terrific. I'm sure all those years later it would have been fun for me to finally speak in that role! I was directed to just sit there with an intense stare so I did the best I could.

You took part in the *Sleepaway Camp* reunion at the *Fangoria*'s Weekend Of Horrors convention a few years back. What was it like to be reunited with your cast and crew from twenty years back?

It was so much fun. I really like the whole cast. We had a lot of catching up to do. The whole reunion took me by surprise, especially that there were people in the audience.

What's your fondest memory from the reunion?

All the people who showed up and told us about their first experience watching the film. I was overwhelmed by the amount of people and how they knew everything about it, more than I did.

Since that first convention appearance, you've made several more convention stops. What's the convention experience like for you?

Amazing. I absolutely love hanging out with everyone and talking about horror movies. I become fan girl and drift off to get autographs!

Any odd or memorable experiences from the con circuit? Either with a fan or another celebrity?

There are so many, but I think it's all the excitement people have for the films. I loved meeting Brinke Stevens, the Ladies of the *Evil Dead*, and David Hess. They're so nice. It makes it a pleasure to work in this genre.

Back at Flashback Weekend convention in Chicago, you hosted a screening of the original *Sleepaway Camp*. What was it like to see it on the big screen again? Didn't you bring a childhood friend with you whom had never seen the movie before?

I hate watching myself on screen. You're right, my best friend John, from high school came with me and he got a kick out of the film. It was like he entered another part of my life. Now he gets excited to hear all the stories because he actually witnessed the convention world. It's pretty trippy.

Dante Tomaselli's *Horror* is one of our favorite recent films here at *Icons of Fright*. How'd you get involved in that film?

I got in touch with Dante several years ago and luckily he had heard of *Sleepaway Camp*. We decided to meet and he gave me the part of the art therapist. He's one of my dearest friends now and I want to work with him for as long as he'll have me.

You've since formed a friendship with Dante and you're appearing in his upcoming *Satan's Playground*. What's the working experience like with him from film to film?

He's intense. The best director you could ever dream to work with. He's incredibly giving to the actors and makes the set really calming, which is hard to do since what we're filming is traumatic. Dante is so gifted and this film was by far one of the best experiences in my life. I really got to work on a character and give my all in every scene. He knows just how to drive an actor to the darkest places, with tons of compassion. This role is dedicated to my boyfriend that I lost last year, Trevor Goddard, so it was really emotional for me. I worked out a lot of personal issues on this set and I couldn't think of a better group of people to work with. An incredible cast and crew.

What can you tell us about your character in *Satan's Playground*? And how does this differ from what we've seen Dante do before? How does this differ from the other projects you've done?

I could go on for hours with this question so I'll do my best to sum it up. My character, Donna Bruno, is a typical NJ suburbanite who's just going on a little vacation with her family...boy does disaster find them. It's so cold, and dark and torturous. He really tells a tale of fright and heartache for this family in a way that takes us back to the horror days of the late seventies and eighties. I love it because it has the feel of such classics like *Texas Chainsaw*, *Evil Dead* and flicks of that era. He captures the trauma they go through and in his own way, it's stunning to look at. It doesn't have that glossy, CGI look. It's raw and evil.

You've worked with the Hitchhiker himself, Edwin Neal (of *Texas Chain Saw Massacre*), on a number of pictures. How'd you two become friends? Is it true you recommended him for *Satan's Playground* when Michael Berryman had to drop out over scheduling?

Ed Neal is a great friend of mine. We met in Kansas while shooting *Zombiegeddon*. He's such a terrific man, with a hilarious personality. When Dante found out about the conflict with Michael Berryman, he asked what I thought and I didn't have to blink. I said "Get Ed Neal if you can, he's fucking amazing."

You had a role in *Corpses Are Forever*, which also features Linnea Quigley, Brink Stevens and Don Calfa. What can you tell us about that project, and how was your working relationship like with those other fan-favorite actors?

Unfortunately, I was only there for a day, so I did my role and I left. Writer/director Jose (Prendes) was great to work with and the film is getting good response. I think it's coming out soon, so I'm excited to see a finished cut. It's very original and the cast is amazing.

You were in *Nikos* with Joe Zaso (whom by the way, was in *Rage Of The Werewolf*, a movie in which, at the last minute, I ended up playing a bounty hunter). What can you tell us about Joe and your experience on that film?

Good for you! *Nikos* was a bit of a disaster. The budget was low and there was too much to film in such a small amount of time. It's one of those experiences you go into with crossed fingers and hope for the best. I'm glad to have met Joe. He's fantastic to work with. Very sweet and very professional. All I can say is, thank God for him, or nothing would have gotten done.

What can you tell us about *Zombiegeddon*, another film with Brink Stevens, Tom Savini, your *Satan's Playground* co-star Edwin Neal, Robert Z'Dar, and Lloyd Kaufman?

That was fun. Again, I didn't get to work with anyone but Ed Neal, but I was excited to hear everyone was in it. I'll be working with the director, Chris Watson, in September on a film called *Slaughter Party*, a real family film.

I know you're sworn to secrecy on the upcoming *Return to Sleepaway Camp*, but as your co-star (I shot a cameo as a camp counselor), I think I'm entitled to ask some questions!

This is true... ask away, I'll do my best!

First, when did you know that Robert would make this sequel? Was it the night of the reunion?

It was Jeff Hayes' idea when he first came out to visit me. He's very ambitious and told Robert Hiltzik to get on it immediately. After several years, the script was done and on to camp we were.

Was it a surreal experience for you to be back at camp during filming for *Return to Sleepaway Camp*?

Oh yeah. Totally weird. Even though it's shot at a different camp, it felt exactly the same. Too strange for words. I think it's finally sinking in, a year later.

While I was there, I noticed you spending a lot of time watching the original *Sleepaway Camp* with the kids. What are the new kids like? Can "kids STILL be so cruel?"

They're worse. I think through the years the kids are smarter and torture each other much worse. I guess that's why the killings are more severe.

Overall, with Vincent Pastore and Isaac Hayes, not to mention the new kids on camp, there's a good solid cast lined up for *Return to Sleepaway Camp*. Being on set for most of the shoot, were you happy with the progression of the film and the actors' enthusiasm toward the project?

Yeah, I think the cast is great. Vinnie and Isaac really made the project a hundred times better. They're pros. We learned a lot from them. Everyone seemed enthusiastic, but I spent most of my time with the crew. All the actors were put up in hotels and I stayed on camp with the entire crew. I wanted to do that 22 years ago, so I finally got my chance.

Although it's still a little while away from completion, how do you feel about *Return to Sleepaway Camp*? Do you think it turned out the way everyone involved would have hoped it would?

I haven't seen any of it so it's hard to tell. When we were filming it seemed like they got great stuff. Ken Kelsh is the cinematographer and he's a badass. He did *Bad Lieutenant*.

You hopped onboard a project titled *Destination Fame*, which was written/directed by Paul DeAngelo (Camp Counselor Ronnie from *Sleepaway Camp* and *Return to Sleepaway Camp*). What was it like to work with Paul again after all these years, and what can you tell us about his upcoming directorial debut?

I did *Destination Fame* right before *Return to Sleepaway Camp*. Paul is the sweetest man and this is a great coming of age story. This film will be released soon and he did an excellent job.

What are some movies you've seen recently that you enjoyed? Both in the horror genre and in general?

I'm a huge horror fan. I've seen so much recently. Everyday I buy something new. I just watched *The Hitcher*, I love C. Thomas Howell, *The Vanishing*, *Village of the Damned*, *Don't Go in The Woods*, (cheesy but great) and *Deliverance* (craziness!) I've mainly been watching horror. Oh, and I just saw *Open Water*, a very good film but it got better for me at the end....I had no idea what was going to happen.

ELLIE CORNELL

Interviewed by Rob Galluzzo (9/04)

Most genre fans know actress Ellie Cornell as Rachel Carruthers from both *Halloween 4: The Return of Michael Myers* and *Halloween 5: The Revenge of Michael Myers*. But she also currently runs a production company with her husband called Mindfire Entertainment. They've produced the films *Free Enterprise, The Specials*, and most recently *House of the Dead*, in which Ellie also made an appearance. We caught up with her to hear about her *Halloween* experiences and what her company has been up to.

What are your earliest recollections of the horror genre?

I remember, as a child, a film called *Sweet, Sweet Rachel*, and a Kim Darby movie-of the-week called *Don't Be Afraid of the Dark*, about these creepy little guys who lived in her basement chimney shaft. Both films scared the pants off me, and yet I couldn't NOT watch them either. Horror films can be so fun for the fright experience!

Tell us about how you initially got involved in acting?

Acting was something I knew I wanted to do, even before I started kindergarten. It just kept being a recurring theme throughout my school years, it became part of my personal identity. I was never, however, a musical comedy gal. I remember being in a one-person show in grade school called *The Last Flower*. It was about being the last living thing on earth. It felt so cutting edge at the time, and such a privilege to do something so enjoyable and seemingly edgy!

Your first role in film was in *Married to the Mob*. Tell us a bit about working on that?

Married to the Mob was my first feature experience. I met Jonathan Demme through Bill Murray, who had become my friend when I lived in NYC, and he gave me the part of a pushy reporter who interviews Dean Stockwell's character. Blink and you'll miss it, but the experience was invaluable.

***Halloween 4* was your first lead feature film. What were your initial reactions to the script? Were you familiar with the films that preceded the fourth installment?**

I thought Alan McElroy wrote a good, scary script. The screen test was such a thrill, I had to wait an unbearable weekend and on Monday they gave me the role of Rachel Carruthers. I had seen bits and pieces of *Halloween*, which is a classic, but the plot line went astray in *Halloween III*.

You were only in a few short scenes with Donald Pleasence, but what was it like working with him?

Donald was a consummate pro, soft-spoken with a wonderful, quiet sense of humor, which you needed during night shoots!

You spent a good chunk of time with Danielle Harris on *Halloween 4*, which was also her first feature. What do you remember about your experiences together?

Danielle and I worked very hard, under some pretty tough conditions. The rooftop scene, for example. They had a roof built to match the real one, but it was still high up with barrel tiles to slide down! Dwight Little was a fabulous director who mentored Danielle and me. I learned a great deal from him. His insights were invaluable.

You had an on-screen rivalry with Kathleen Kinmont's character, Kelly Mecker. How'd you get along with the rest of the cast when the cameras weren't rolling? Did you stay in touch with anyone involved in the production?

We all got along beautifully. I try my best to get along with everyone on some level because you're all in it together, working long hours together. The crew on that movie was awesome and supportive. A good tone was set from the get-go. My co-star, Sasha Jenson, and I went on to do an *Afterschool Special* together for ABC right after *Halloween 4*... what a small world!

There's a story from *Halloween 4* that involved you injuring yourself badly during the infamous rooftop scene. What exactly happened there?

I slid down the tiles and got a slice down my torso. But no stitches, no guts, just a lot of sympathy from the crew and a panicky on-set medic.

What was it like to see *Halloween 4* for the first time on the big screen with friends and family?

I went to Westwood to go see it, with my agent at the time, the wonderful Philip Carr, and this line of people went around the block. I asked someone what the big fuss was, and they said *Halloween 4*. I thought I would bust out of my skin, I was so excited! It's a huge kick to have a first big job where folks actually go to see it. I'll never forget there were policemen at the back of the theatre, I guess there had been riot threats...

Were you surprised by the success of *Halloween 4*?

I knew Dwight was on the right track because he honored the script, he didn't order huge changes mid-stream, and the characters were ones you cared about. Sometimes simple is better.

What would you consider your favorite scene while watching *Halloween 4*? And what was your favorite scene to work on behind the scenes?

I thought the scene when I mow Michael Myers over in my truck was soooo cool! The audience was yelling "Hit him!, hit him!" so that was fun. The great part of that sequence was that, while we were shooting it, some fellas were bouncing on planks propped under the truck to make it look as though I'm driving for the close-ups. You gotta love the movies!

What are your thoughts on the radical direction the series COULD have taken, as implied by the shock ending of *Halloween 4* in which Jamie would've been a killer?

I'd go see it. Continuity is a good thing when the product's worth the keep.

Rachel has always been a fan favorite. Was she always scripted to die in *Halloween 5*? Is it true you agreed to come back only if they killed off your character?

No, but Rachel was scripted to have scissors shoved down her throat, which I wouldn't agree to do. I was reluctant to do the sequel because Dwight Little wasn't on board, and the tone of the story had changed.

***Halloween 5: The Revenge Of Michael Myers* is considered a very odd entry into the series. What's your take on that particular film?**

Obviously, what I took away from my *Halloween* experience was under Dwight Little's direction. I still get a kick out of Rachel in *Halloween 5* running through her yard wrapped in a towel, and getting Mr. Cornish to help her. I always think of Cornish Game Hens.

You worked with both George Wilbur's version of Michael Myers and Don Shanks' version of Michael Myers. What were the differences in the two Michael's you went up against?

I liked George's Michael Myers because I KICKED HIS BUTT for a while there! Don was a sweetie, especially during Rachel's death scene, which was less than pleasant.

Is it true you had a part in *A League of Their Own*, but had to drop out at the last minute? Which part were you initially cast in?

I have no idea where they wanted to put me, but somehow I ended up on the "A-list" of actresses to play for the USC coaches. I caught a fly ball from heaven, and next thing I know I'm interviewing with Penny Marshall because I can play good ball!

When did your production company Mindfire Entertainment first come together?

In the late 90's, two very funny knowledgeable movie nuts sent my husband and I a script that we fell in love with. We shot it during the rainiest January in LA history. It was renegade filmmaking at its finest.

The first feature film you produced was the cult favorite *Free Enterprise*. How'd you meet screenwriters Mark Altman and Robert Burnett?

We read their script and had tea at the Plaza with them. We

share a mutual love of the movies and working with good honest folks. Mark and Robert are the real deal.

Free Enterprise had an excellent cast including Eric McCormack, Rafer Weigel, William Shatner, Audie England, and Patrick Van Horn. What was the casting process like on that film?

Christine Sheaks is a casting genius. Eric got *Will and Grace* about a week later. Who knew? Christine did!

You had a little cameo as Robert's ex-girlfriend in *Free Enterprise*. How'd that come about? Was it a given that you'd appear somewhere in your production or was it Mark & Robert's idea?

Thankfully, Mark and Robert knew my work from the *Halloween* films and thought it would be a kick to dust off the ol' gear and put me back in the game.

Tell us a bit about your second production, *The Specials*?

A very funny script. I actually laughed out loud when I read it. That's rare.

How'd *House of the Dead* come together?

We worked diligently to acquire the video game rights from Sega. A script was written, a German director (Uwe Boll) came aboard, and we set sail....

Were you always keen on the idea of taking the role of Jordan Casper or did you just want to play a bad ass?

What housewife doesn't dream of playing a bad ass? I'd do it again in minute, but I'd shoot it in Los Angeles. Vancouver was chilly and damp, especially at five in the morning. The sun's coming up after a twelve-hour day and I have to get on a plane.

You made an appearance last year at the *Halloween* Returns to Haddonfield: 25th Anniversary convention. What's the convention experience like for you?

Surreal! We have such supportive fans! It was well organized and attended, as it should be.

I think just about every *Halloween* fan has at one point had a crush on Rachel Carruthers. Are you surprised by all of Rachel's fans and her popularity in the series?

I don't consider Rachel "crush" material, but rather a character you respect and pull for, attributes I'd take in a minute over the "flavor of the month" gals. I liked her, too!

You're going to work with another *Halloween* victim (PJ Soles) on the upcoming *The Second Line*. What can you tell us about that project?

It shoots in the Spring if our schedules line up... I might be in Prague but I'll find my way to Illinois!

What's up next for Mindfire Entertainment?

Our cups runneth over! I start *All Soul's Day* this week, fittings tomorrow, rehearsals the next day. Is this fun or what? *House of the Dead 2* starts in November. Check out the website, it rocks. And by all means check out *CFQ magazine*, THE magazine for horror, science fiction and fantasy enthusiasts and *Femmes Fatales* for the latest and hottest gals in the biz!

PJ SOLES

Interviewed by Mike Cucinotta and Rob Galluzzo (9/04)

Everyone TOTALLY knows and loves actress PJ Soles. She's been in the comedy hits *Rock N' Roll High School, Stripes*, and *Jawbreaker*. She's also appeared in genre films such as *Carrie, The Possessed* and *Uncle Sam*. But horror fans know her best as Lynda, one of Michael Myers' first victims in the original John Carpenter classic, *Halloween*. She'll be returning to horror by appearing in *The Devil's Rejects*, the upcoming sequel to Rob Zombie's *House of 1000 Corpses*. Here's what we learned from the lovely PJ Soles!

What are some of your earliest recollections of the horror genre? Do you remember the first films to scare you?

Anything Hitchcock... *The Birds* and *Psycho*. Films having to do with werewolves...

When did you initially decide to pursue acting? Can you tell us a bit about your experiences starting out?

I started acting in school plays in 6th grade when I lived in Venezuela. I played the witch in *Hansel and Gretel*, and my dad made me a special magic wand with a lightbulb, a battery, and a switch... my first real prop! It was a night performance and we had a huge fake oven that they pushed me into. My little brother, who was only three, thought that was the end me and started screaming. I was very proud of my performances because I beat out an 8th grader for the coveted weekend shows.

      I was in plays in high school, but it wasn't until I was in college that I spent some time in NYC and realized that people actually got paid to do this. Since I'd lived overseas for most of my childhood, I wasn't up to speed on a lot of things. But I went by the Actor's Studio and there was a "spotlight" position available, so I ran the spotlight on Joanna Miles and Scott Glenn for the summer. I got an agent and started doing commercials, which made it easy to not go back to college. My parents were living in Turkey at the time, and communication back then was not like it is today or else they would have marched me right back to studying languages to become an interpreter for the United Nations.

Were you a fan of Stephen King's work before going in to audition for *Carrie*? If so, do you still follow his books?

No, I had never heard of him. I don't think he was as well known in 1975. I don't read those kinds of books. I like biographies and non-fiction.

Tell us about the audition process for *Carrie*? Wasn't it a dual audition with George Lucas for *Star Wars*?

Yes. Brian De Palma and George Lucas shared a desk in an office and met every teenager in town. It was a massive line.... but it was worth it.

***Carrie* was one of your first feature films. What was it like working with Brian De Palma?**

I bet he hasn't changed. He was quiet and commanding. He knew exactly what he wanted from each set-up. You could see extreme delight in his eyes as he sat in his director's chair. He seemed like he loved the process and the challenge of telling through showing a story on film.

Despite the way the characters treated each other in *Carrie*, what was the working atmosphere like with all the other cast members? Did you manage to stay in touch with anyone from the production after the shoot?

We really became close right away - all of us. We had a lot of fun. I was especially close with Michael Talbott, John Travolta, and Betty Buckley. Betty and I remained friendly for a long time. But you know, she's a New York theater person and I'm an LA mother of two. Michael Talbott was like a brother to me, and he is the funniest man alive.

Did your friendship with John Travolta lead to working with him again on *The Boy in the Plastic Bubble*?

John recommended me for that film. He loved people that made him laugh, and when we would watch the dailies of *Carrie*, John would howl at my scenes. It really made me feel good. He is a genuine and caring person.

What do you remember about filming the infamous "blood bath at the prom" scene at the end of *Carrie*?

It took days, but it was fun because nobody knew how their characters were going to die until the day of their scene. De Palma kept us all in suspense and speculating. And I remember how intense and focused Sissy Spacek was... she is amazing!

You worked on a made-for-television horror film called *The Possessed* with Harrison Ford in the late 70's. What do you remember about that project?

That Harrison asked me and another actress out to dinner. We were having a great time until he started playing footsies under the table. I knew he was married with two young sons, and I didn't know what to think. That was the first time I realized I had a lot to learn about "show biz." Other than that, I don't remember even seeing it on TV.

What was your initial reaction to the script for *Halloween*?

"TOTALLY" cool. I couldn't wait to play Lynda.

You seemed to have a great on-screen friendship with Jamie Lee Curtis and Nancy Loomis. How'd you get along with them when the cameras weren't rolling?

We all had a blast, really. There wasn't time for anything else. Jamie got along with everyone - she was very happy and carefree back then. The set atmosphere had a constant focus on collaboration and effort and originality.

Debra Hill takes credit for writing most of the dialogue between the girls in the film. Did you get to improv at all with your lines? Was the "totally" thing always scripted or something you came up with?

I definitely added more "totally." I told John to tell me if I

became annoying. The scene in the bed was pretty much improvised. John asked me to taunt the "Shape" and then get upset... it worked out... totally!

You spent a lot of time with John Michael Graham, who played your on-screen boyfriend Bob. What do you remember about working with Mister Graham? Were the "love" scenes difficult or uncomfortable?

As with any love scene in a film, it is always the most unsexy thing to make it look like you are being intimate onscreen. You don't feel anything remotely sexual. Mister Graham and I spent only two days together, so I really didn't get to know him at all, although I chose him with John Carpenter during the casting session.

Even though you didn't share any scenes together, did you get the opportunity to meet Donald Pleasence?

Yes, we all ate lunch together on the set. He was reserved and polite. He didn't seem interested in conversation, but now I realize he probably didn't know what on earth to say to us giggling girls.

What was it like to see *Halloween* for the first time on the big screen? How'd your friends and family react?

It was great fun. I thought it was amazing, considering how quickly we filmed it. I was blown away by John Carpenter's soundtrack. My friends loved it. My family was upset that I took off my blouse - not exactly United Nations behavior.

Did you follow any of the *Halloween* series after the first?

I've never seen any of them except the original.

You've admitted to not being a huge fan of The Ramones until halfway through filming the cult favorite, *Rock 'n' Roll High School*. Looking back now, what do you remember most about them?

It stood out how shy they all were. I was amazed by that, because to me being "punk rock" meant you had to be brave, especially since they were forging new territory in the world of "rock 'n' roll." I assumed they would be confident and cocky. But I was happily surprised that they were huge film buffs, and they couldn't believe they were in one, especially a Roger Corman film!

How close are you to the character of Riff Randell?

Like I said, I grew up in foreign countries, so I had not experienced a high school life like Riff. But she was such an American girl in the script, so we merged. She has my heart and my energy. I just acted her out as written on the page. Oh yeah, and I bought all her clothes, but they were definitely Riff's and not mine!

You got to reprise the role of Riff Randell in a music video for The Donnas. How did that come about?

A friend of mine, Dave Besdesky, was working on the shoot, and the director said he wanted it to look like *Rock 'n' Roll High School.* Dave told him he could do better than that, that he could get Riff Randell to be in it! They called me and I went down the next day. It was fun, even though I barely fit in Riff's jacket anymore.

You worked on the comedy classic *Stripes* with director Ivan Reitman and a stellar cast. Was it a fun picture to be a part of?

Yes, it was a lot of fun working with Bill Murray, but Harold Ramis is the bomb!

Bill Murray is known now for his improvisation. Did he stray away from the script a lot during your scenes together in *Stripes*? And is it difficult to work with someone who's constantly making everyone laugh?

Yes, Bill changed everything all the time, but that was exciting. Our whole stovetop scene was improvised at 3 AM. It's not difficult if you're in character. Stella wasn't amused most of the time... until she fell in love. But seriously, Bill is very funny when he's acting. He's really more of a somber guy in real life.

You took a break from acting at one point. Were pursuing other interests and spending more time with your family motivating factors in this?

Raising my son and daughter has been the most important thing to me, but now they are older, and I hope to work more often. It's a long story!

Are you surprised that the character of Lynda from *Halloween* is a fan favorite?

She's the girl every guy wants to be with and every girl would like to be... "totally" fun!

Have you heard about the recent Local H album being named after you? Is it surreal to have a band with an album titled *Whatever Happened to PJ Soles*?

It is awesome. I saw them perform in LA. They are great guys and I am totally flattered. My kids think it's crazy. 'What do you mean what happened to PJ Soles? She's our mom, duh!'

How'd you get involved in *The Devil's Rejects*? And are you a big fan of Rob Zombie?

I auditioned. And I signed a *Carrie* photo to Rob Zombie at the casting session saying, "DEAR ROB, PLEASE LET ME SCREAM AGAIN FOR YOU. LOVE, P.J." I think that helped get me the part. Honestly, he wanted to cast 70's actors for the various cameos. Rob Zombie and his wife are extremely caring people.

What can you tell us about your role in the sequel and also about working with Rob?

I got to work with Sid Haig. He punches me out, but I LIVE! That is so rare in a Rob Zombie film. Rob is great. I hope to have a bigger part in his next film... he is a definite 100% pure genius.

BRAD LOREE

Interviewed by Mike Cucinotta and Rob Galluzzo (10/04)

If you don't recognize Brad Loree at first, it might be because you're used to seeing him in a certain white mask. Throughout his career, Brad's performed stunts on films such as *The 6th Day*, *Final Destination 2*, and *House of the Dead*. He was also the most recent actor to portray Michael Myers in *Halloween: Resurrection*. We spoke to him about his time in the business and he turned out to be one of the nicest *Icons* interviews yet, which makes us wonder... how can someone so darned nice play pure EVIL? Cue the *Halloween* theme.

Why don't you start by telling us your earliest recollections of the genre. Were you a fan as a kid?

Well, guys... as a kid, I honestly was never a horror film fan. I had never actually even seen a horror film until I was nineteen. It just wasn't my cup of tea. I'm a chicken shit, so being afraid was not my idea of being entertained back then. BUT when I was nineteen, I ended up dating this girl who *only* watched horror films. Because ya know, she wore the pants in the relationship. (laughs)

Ohhhh... (laughs)

We watched lots and lots of horror films. They were what they were to me. Having seen all these gory and violent films, I really appreciated the original *Halloween* for being suspenseful and for having a very minimal amount of blood and gore in it. So, that girlfriend and *Halloween* are my earliest recollections of the horror genre. Now, of course, I enjoy it a whole lot more.

You've been a stuntman now for years. What event from childhood made you decide, "I want to risk my life in front of the camera?"

It was sort of a vocation by accident. When I was thirteen, I went to see a Bruce Lee film called *Fists of Fury*. I then fell in love with martial arts and Bruce Lee. So, I joined the local karate school and my karate instructor there was a guy named Tony Morelli. Shortly out of high school, when I was twenty years old, I went to watch him win the World Kozera Kickboxing title. He became something of a local

celebrity here in Vancouver. The film industry was just starting to come up here a lot in the early 80's. Tony started doing commercials and then he started doing some stand-in work, so it was his influence. He sort of kicked open the door for me and introduced me around. And it was by following his example that I ended up becoming a stuntman because, as a world champion, of course they took him on very quickly. And it was through his connections that I became a stuntman. My heart was really in acting, but I didn't have the confidence for it.

Did you initially start out as an actor?

Well, I studied acting in school in my mid-twenties but again, I was really shy and too dissident to just go for it. And then it was 1991, I had done a day's work doing stunts for this TV show, doing some fights. One of the guys there just said to me, "You should really be pursuing this stunt work, because you're a good guy and you've got this athletic skill and whatnot." So, that's when I first got my page, resume, and headshot and started peddling my face around.

Is being a stunt-man a difficult field of film to break into? How was it for you first starting out?

When I was first starting out, it was a *long* process. There were not a ton of people that were aware of the life and living you can make as a stuntman here in Vancouver. The group that had the most power, as far as stunt casting, was Stunt Canada. And to them, it was a minimum of five year's experience before they'd even consider you for membership, except for someone like Tony Morelli, who was a world-class athlete. And today I see two skills - gymnastics and martial arts. If you are exceptionally good at either of those, I see people getting into the business and getting work very quickly, but that's today. Ten years ago, you still would've had to pay a lot longer dues than I see people today doing. These days, some kids come off the street and they don't know what it is to do extra work to pay the bills. They try getting some stunt work and they're off to the races.

You've been doing stunts for a while now. Was there any stunt that you may have been nervous to approach? Anything that might have been really difficult?

Well, in my career, I would say the scariest, most nerve racking stunt I ever did was doubling an actor on a show called "M.A.N.T.I.S." He was this android that jumped out of a window on the third story and, of course, lands on the ground unscathed and knocks out a couple of guards. I had to jump out of this eight-foot by eight-foot window from the third story down into an airbag, which is not the trickiest thing in the world. The tricky part was the floor below - the second floor jetted out from the level of the building I was in by about fourteen feet. It was like this concrete staircase. And it was a long jump as well as a high jump. It was also at night, and the way they had it lit, the window I was jumping from was just this black wall. I really had to run and jump and commit before I had any sight of my target, that being the airbag. So, it was a little unnerving.

Then on the rehearsals, I had my rain shoes and on the day we shot this, I had to wear this really funny costume with rifles on my back. This other stunt guy was supposed to do the gag, but he had turned it down and they had already bought the costume for him. So, I had to wear these very stiff, brand new, thick leather motorcycle boots that were two sizes too small. I was very nervous about clearing the railing below. During rehearsals, I was getting by it by about ten to twelve feet. But when we shot it, someone said I just got by it by about three or four feet. If I'd have fallen short, it would've been very ugly for me. But I made it and it was really great, and the director raved, but it was just one of those situations where, if something had gone wrong, it would've went really wrong. I've never had a coordinator ask me about allergies and blood type and all that stuff before doing a stunt before. (laughs)

You've done a lot of work on both shows and features. Are there any major differences between working on a television production as opposed to doing a big film?

TV shows don't have the money or time, so they have to get what they want on the day. I've been on features where you sit around for a week and don't do anything. I mean, like long hour days. Television's not like that at all. They have to shoot. They can only afford so many takes before moving on. Features have the money to keep shooting until they get their shots. So, it's definitely a time thing with television verses features. You get much longer days on features. And more days. Television's just a lot quicker.

Any point of your career that you consider a highlight or the most fun for you?

My favorite day on set, I would have to say was a stunt job I did on a TV production called *The Long Way Home* because I got to do both a stunt and a little bit of acting with Jack Lemmon. I think fondly about that because I was a huge admirer of his.

How'd you initially land the role of Michael Myers for *Halloween: Resurrection*?

I'd been working as a stunt double for a kids show on Fox called *Los Luchadores*. It was that show where these guys were Mexican wrestlers by day and crime fighters by night. The stunt coordinator left after about eight episodes and I was left to finish the last five episodes by myself as the coordinator and the double. So, we finished the thirteen episodes and I left to go find new work because they hadn't made the executive decision at the time to make more episodes. The first AD, a gentleman by the name of Brian Knight, had gotten an interview with the *Halloween* people.

And he decided the night before to do some research. So, he rented the first film, and he told me later that he thought, "Brad would be a good double for that guy." And then I guess during his interview the next day, they mentioned to him that they didn't have a Canadian stunt coordinator yet because they had to match him with the American. And they also didn't know who was going to be their Michael Myers in Canada.

And he said to the production manager, Tracy Long, "The guy you should talk to is Brad Loree." So, Tracy gave me a call. Her first question was "How tall are you?" I said "Well, I'm six foot and a half." She said "That's perfect! Can you come in tomorrow to meet the executives about doubling for Michael Myers?" So, I said "Yeah!" And I thought "It's kind of strange that Mike Myers is doing this horror film." But it turned out I just forgot the character's name because I hadn't seen the movie in years! So, I went in the next day and met with Malek Akkad, Rick Rosenthal the director, and a couple of the producers.

Rick had me stand against this wall and walk towards him, imitating "the walk." We did it like four or five times. And then he turned to the producers and said "Yeah, this guy'll be fine." And then they started talking to me about flying out to LA to get my head cast for the mask. So, I asked "Whoa whoa. Why do I have to fly out to LA to double an actor?" And they said, "No, Brad. You're not going to double the guy, you're going to BE the guy." And that's when I went "Ohhhh." So, it put a spin on me, because I just thought I was going to go back to do that *Los Luchadores* show.

That's awesome.

The gentlemen from *Fangoria* actually asked the producers, "How many guys did they go through before you met Brad?" and I was reading on and they said "He was the first guy we met and interviewed and we just went with him." So, that's how it happened.

When you were cast, you had mentioned having seen some of the films before. Did your memory of the early films influence how you were going to approach the role of Michael Myers?

Well, I do remember that the first one struck me as being very well done for its type of film. I remember being on the edge of my seat. I remember that guy (Nick Castle) being very scary. I had also watched the second one. And when I went to see the third one, of course, I was terribly disappointed like everybody else that there was no Michael Myers in it. And I stopped watching them after that. But after they told me I got the job, I got copies of all the films. I watched four, five and six, and I watched what the other guys did in their versions of the role.

I wasn't overly impressed with some of the previous Michaels. I was in Pasadena at that *Halloween* convention last October, and one of the guys admitted to the crowd during the panel that he didn't look at any of the other films. He just did it his way. And I just thought that was so strange. I remember just how eerie the portrayal was in the first one. So, I watched the first one over and over and over again and just tried to copy Nick Castle because to me, he IS Michael Myers.

I'd read that while you were preparing for the role of Michael Myers, you had also watched a series of different serial killer documentaries. Was there anything in those real-life serial killers that you might have brought into the role on *Resurrection*?

Well, I just wanted to try to understand a little better the serial killer mentality. And I had done some research. In fact, I'm reading a book right now on psychosis. I just wanted to have something to work with while I was playing Michael where he doesn't really view humans like you or I do, like normal people do. For psychopaths, humans are really just objects. They're not really people with feelings or emotions. I can't say I got a whole lot out of the documentaries. But some of the other *Halloween*'s I watched, I felt the other guys played Michael far too human-like. And it really took away the eeriness and scariness of the character.

What's one of the first sequences you filmed as Michael Myers? And what'd it feel like to put on the mask for the camera the first time?

I remember being super nervous. At the very beginning, when he first hands the knife over to the guy in the asylum and he's walking down the tunnel with all the lights and the character's going on about Michael Myers. "And now he's back!" That was the first thing we shot, and I just remember thinking to myself "Oh, I sure hope I do this walk right. Because if I don't, I'm going to get fired!" (laughs) Through the whole movie though, Rick was constantly reminding me to just take my time, nice and slow. I was perfecting it from the very first day to the very last day that we shot.

You were the one and only Michael to finally kill Jamie Lee's character of Laurie Strode. What was it like working with Jamie Lee in general? And how did it feel to have that honor of being the one that got her?

It was a real treat just to get to meet and work with Jamie Lee, because like most heterosexual males, I'm a huge fan! (laughs) But, no, she was really terrific, and I was really impressed with what a grounded, normal, and rational person she was. She didn't have any attitude at all. It was a real treat. And I feel kind of special being the one to finish her off. I'm sorry to see her go, but that's the way the story goes. And I'm sorry I'm not going to get to work with her again. But she was great and she set a real example.

Rick Rosenthal directed the second *Halloween* as well. Tell us a bit about your working relationship with him?

Rick and I got along very well. We're both hockey fans. He actually plays hockey down there with celebrity teams and whatnot. I thought he was a great guy, and I loved him, of course, because he was as responsible as anyone for me getting the job because he was one of the people that picked me. We got along great and he was a lot of fun. He kept his tension in check. For the most part, he was pretty relaxed and easy going. He was just really easy to work with. I think him and Busta had some moments, but I wasn't privy to them. Rick and I still email each other a lot and he was very encouraging in me pursuing acting because, like I said, I'd still like to do more of that.

Well, you mentioned Busta Rhymes. A lot of fans are very mixed on the character of Freddie Harris. What do you remember about working with Busta?

I've been hearing a lot about those mixed feelings myself. But I've got to be honest, Busta impressed me very much in that he's this really big rapper, but you wouldn't get that from working with him. I'm not too familiar with his music and that world, but apparently, he's quite big. He was just such a happy guy. Easy-going and friendly and a professional with everybody. And I certainly hope I get to work with him again because he was a lot of fun, a very warm person.

Tell me everything about Bianca Kajlich!

(laughs) Bianca! Oh, she's a darling. I absolutely had a huge crush on her too. I never told her that. She's from Seattle, which is a sister city with Vancouver and she was just remarkable. Very beautiful and very, very talented. I was really impressed with her, just watching some of the scenes that she did. She was great fun, although she was very afraid of me at first, even without the mask! I think she thought I was really Michael Myers. But then she kind of warmed up to me and we became very good friends. I think that helped get over her fear of me somewhat. And I certainly hope she comes back for *Halloween 9*, whether I'm involved or not. I'd like to see her continue. I just thought she was terrific.

Halloween 9 is currently in pre-production now. Anything you can tell us about it? We've heard you'd really like to reprise the role of Michael Myers?

Well, I do. The last thing I heard was from Paul (Swearingen) is that they're still trying to hash out a script that everyone's happy with. Um, I've heard rumors that people want to see Michael take on someone like Freddy or Jason, but that Moustapha wasn't interested in toying with the formula.

I don't think anyone's interested in Michael doing that.

We'll see. I just hope they do another one next spring and that they do it here in Canada so I can get another shot.

We're really rooting for you, man. We hope you get to do it again.

I really appreciate that.

What was your favorite scene in *Halloween: Resurrection*? Both to film and to work on?

Oh, I have a lot of them, but the one scene that comes to mind is when I'm following behind Busta dressed as Michael Myers. And then he turns around thinking I'm his workmate and he starts chewing me out. Instead of stabbing him, I just turn and walk away. I think I blew two or three takes because I was laughing so hard under the mask and it was noticeable. I couldn't help it. I just couldn't keep it together with him. I was really hoping that scene stayed in the film because I know we did a bunch of scenes that never made it into the film because they changed the storyline around a little bit.

Speaking of, there's actually a production still of Michael coming up behind Tyra Banks' character. Looks like you're about to off her?

Yeah, we originally shot it that I pull down a bunch of the cables hanging from the ceiling there in the computer room and I strangle her. For whatever reason, they decided to leave it more to your imagination. So, we just see her hanging from the rafters. But yeah, originally, we shot it with me strangling her with the cables.

What's your favorite kill in *Halloween: Resurrection*?

Favorite kill? I guess I have to say Jamie Lee because... well, it's Jamie.

And is it true that one of the first guys you kill in the film is now your roommate?

Yeah! A local actor named Brad Sihvon. He plays the guy who's setting up the cameras in the Myers house. He's the one I stab with the leg of the tripod.

The Spielberg fan!?

THAT's the guy. He's now my roommate. Good guy.

Is it true that you auditioned for Jason in *Freddy vs Jason*?

Well, when production came to town, the producer on *Freddy vs Jason* had seen somewhere an interview I had done on the set of *Halloween: Resurrection*. He felt I was somewhat articulate and put some thought into the role and that I was possibly the kind of person they wanted to play Jason. So, he was very on my side about doing it. And we had talked about it. But when I met director Ronny Yu, he immediately dismissed me as being too short. (laughs) Actually, when I was talking to you earlier about this TV show, where there was this other gentlemen that helped convince me to pursue doing stunt work, that was Ken Kirzinger. Who ended up playing Jason. He is one of my best friends. And he actually doubled Kane Hodder on *Friday the 13th Part 8: Jason Takes Manhattan*. When Ronny passed on me, they had this huge casting call where they had every giant six foot seven guy come in, trying to get the biggest, tallest guys in town. It somehow came back around to Ken and he ended up with it, which was awesome. I was really hoping Ken would get it if I didn't, and he did. It was fine with me because I didn't want to divide camps anyway.

You took part in the *Halloween* Returns to Haddonfield convention. Your first con appearance, I think?

Yeah, that was my first convention experience. I was VERY nervous when I got there, but I had a great time. And everyone was so friendly.

What was the convention world like from your perspective?

It was just a surreal experience to get to meet the fans. The people that put the convention on were terrific. It was great to meet Dick Warlock, too. He and I have since become really good friends. We keep in touch. He's been trying to get me to follow him around on the convention circuit. And I'd love to do more conventions. I've been to a couple of appearances since. I did an appearance a few weeks ago in Georgia at a theme park.

Thanks so much for talking to us, Brad.

Guys... seriously. Anytime!

2005

JUDITH O'DEA
BEN CHAPMAN
BOB CLARK
PATRICIA TALLMAN
DANIEL FARRANDS
DON SHANKS

JUDITH O'DEA

Interviewed by Mike Cucinotta and Rob Galluzzo (3/05)

If you're truly a horror fan, then the original George Romero classic *Night of the Living Dead* should be among one of your all-time favorites! And if that's the case, then you should know that the wonderful Judith O'Dea played Barbara. We caught up with her to reflect on her *Night of the Living Dead* memories, talk about her convention experiences and to learn a bit about her company O'Dea Communications. Read on, folks!

Are you a fan of horror films?

Not exactly. When I was around seven years old, I saw *House Of Wax,* the 3-D version starring Vincent Price. It scared the bageebees out of me! Science fiction, flying saucers, and things like that were more to my liking. I also loved the old MGM musicals and loved stories like *The Ghost and Mrs. Muir* and *A Portrait of Jennie.*

You grew up in Pittsburgh, but were in Hollywood at the time *Night of the Living Dead* was being cast. Who was it that thought you were right for the part of Barbara?

Pittsburgh was my home from sixth grade until I left for Hollywood in my early twenties. I think it was Karl Hardman who thought I might be right for Barbara. He called and asked if I'd like to come back to audition.

The role of Barbara is looked at differently by many people. Some think Barbara represented a change in the role of women in horror, seeing her as the roots of the strong, determined characters of modern horror, while others have criticized the character. Where do you see Barbara's place in the evolution of women in horror?

Wow, that's quite a question. I'm not quite sure how to answer it, except that I believe Barbara exemplifies honesty. How she got through her horror ordeal is probably the way many real people would. She wasn't a superwoman, but she wasn't a wimp either. She was just trying to survive the best way her unique soul could. And yes, that included a period of catatonia... a mental protection, if you will. It was a time for her mind to pull it together while her body waited. Then, when all looked to be lost, when the zombies were breaking

into the house, she snapped back into reality. It was time to fight back. And she did, until her death. If Barbara is remembered for her honest behavior in the "evolution of women in horror," then I'll be thrilled.

What was the toughest for you on *Night of the Living Dead*?

I really can't remember any time being really tough. Maybe the sitting around during set ups between scenes could be considered tiring. But, in all honesty, that was fun, too, for it was a constant learning period for all of us.

What was your impression of Romero, as a director?

I thought George was extremely creative. He was relentless and could go on forever. He was/is very dedicated to producing a quality product.

Did you ever think that "They're coming to get you, Barbara" would become such a memorable and quoted line from the movie? How many times have people come up to you and said that?

I never ever guessed the line would become so quoted. I couldn't begin to tell you how many times I've heard it. Let's just leave it at lots and lots!

Did you know in the recent zombie flick *Shaun of the Dead*, they homage that line, as Shaun's mother's name is Barbara and they say "We're coming to get you, Barbara?

Yes, in fact, it was my son who told me that. I went right out and rented the movie. It was really well done.

Duane Jones' character of Ben was unlike any cinematic hero seen in a horror film before *Night of the Living Dead*. What do you remember about working with Duane?

Duane Jones was pure class. Quiet, thorough, dedicated, and extremely intelligent. Working with him was effortless.

What was the first indication that you'd taken part in a cinema classic?

Oh, I don't believe that awareness came for a long time, some years really. It wasn't until friends and acquaintances continually sent screening notices and reviews from around the world that I began to feel we'd made something more enduring than originally thought.

When was the last time you've seen the film?

I saw *Night of the Living Dead* at a screening this past September in West Los Angeles at the Nuart Theatre. It was one of those midnight showings like the *Rocky Horror Picture Show*.

What would you consider to be one of your favorite scenes or moments from *Night of the Living Dead*?

One of my favorite scenes is when Barbara runs her fingers over a music box and starts it running. You can just catch a look at her eyes as the little doors open and close.

After *Night of the Living Dead*, we couldn't find any more credits for you, but we understand you continued to work in film. What other films or shows have we seen you in?

I worked for Warner Bros. upon my return to Hollywood. I did a picture called *The Pirate* with Anne Archer, Eli Wallach, and Franco Nero. But most of my work after *Night of the Living Dead* was on the stage doing a wonderful variety of musicals, comedies, and drama.

There was a much different Barbara in the 1990 Tom Savini remake, but again, some critics were harsh on that characterization. What's your opinion of it, and can strong women ever get a break in horror?!

I can understand why Tom made Barbara's character more commanding. Women were asserting their strength and equality in so many ways and venues in the 90s. It seems quite acceptable that Barbara should be so much more a leader and vanquisher in this version. I don't compare the two versions. Each stands on its own merit in its own time.

And as far as strong women ever getting a break in horror, I certainly would think so. We just have to get ourselves beyond the "scream queen" mentality.

You've attended conventions such as Horrorfind in Arizona. Have any fun memories you'd like to share?

The best convention memories for me are of the many and varied truly wonderful conversations I've had with *Night of the Living Dead* fans. It's really been mind boggling! I am continually amazed to meet so many fantastic people who still support and enjoy *Night of the Living Dead* so much.

Did you have a chance to meet up with any of your fellow *Night of the Living Dead* castmates at any conventions?

Yes, I've met up with my castmates at various times. And when we do, we rock! What a great bunch of people they are: Karl, Marilyn, George, Kyra, Bill, Jack, and Russ. Just the greatest! I only wish Duane and Keith were still with us.

Have you collected much *Living Dead* memorabilia over the years? What are some favorite pieces?

I think I have given more away than I have collected. Some favorites though are the few original stills I've managed to hold on to that were shot during production and an original movie poster that was given to me by a very generous fan.

Tell us about your company O'Dea Communications?

O'Dea Communications offers a variety of oral presentation coaching and training workshops, seminars, and multi-session courses for both the professional and non-professional speaker. My company vision is verbal, vocal, and visual communication excellence throughout global Corporate America. And my mission is to provide the finest oral communications training, consultations, and private coaching tailored to my customers' specific needs.

Tell us what you think made *Night* so special? Why do you think it connected with people so strongly?

Night of the Living Dead was more a horror docu-drama. It appeared real, even with its zombie storyline. And the fact that not one of the lead characters survived was a first at that time. I think the movie was also very special in that it paired a black man of strength and intellect with a white woman. It was their survival we cared most about. The racial element was never an issue.

BEN CHAPMAN

Interviewed by Mike Cucinotta (4/05)

This month, we're proud to present a legendary icon on *Icons of Fright*. Ben Chapman played the Gill-man in Universal's *Creature from the Black Lagoon*. And with his portrayal of the monster, carved himself a place in horror history right alongside Universal monster greats Dracula, Frankenstein, and the Wolf Man. He currently resides in Hawaii, and *Icon*'s own Mike C. caught up with him to hear about what went into the making of a classic! Read on, folks!

We read on your website that you were actually raised in Tahiti. Can you tell us a bit about your childhood there?

Yes, my mom and dad were dual citizens because they were naturalized. They were born and raised in Tahiti. I am also Tahitian. Dad left Tahiti as a seaman on a yacht, but became a Merchant Marine officer during World War 2. He had two ships torpedoed from under him. I was born here, meaning I'm a dual citizen. I carry French and American passports. I've been a citizen of both countries my whole life.

What brought you back to the States?

Well, Tahiti is French, and I was raised there in the 30's. With the war in Europe, the United States wasn't involved yet, there was no Pearl Harbor yet. So the French government asked all aliens to return to their respective countries. My mom and dad were put in a precarious situation. We owned property, that was our home, but they were American citizens. So even though they were born and raised there, and were also French citizens, the French government told them they'd have to go back to the United States. So, we emigrated up here and landed in San Francisco. I came up here with my older sister in 1940. Then my other sister came up, then my mom. We lived in San Francisco where I went to high school.

What did you do after high school?

I moved down to Southern California in 1948, I think. I always came from a show business family. While I was down there, I happened to be at a luau where my brother-in-law was. He was a famous musician. So, I went and watched the show. When the show was over, my brother-in-law got up there and said, "Now, ladies and gentlemen, before we go any further, we have a special guest in the audience who's one of the best dancers to come out of Tahiti." I'm sitting there looking around for this person. I'm going, "Wow, I wonder who this is." So he says, "With a little encouragement, we can get him to come up here to dance for us," and he points at me. I'd danced, but never on-stage. I was familiar with the music, so it wasn't something I didn't know. They started the music and I went up and danced, got a big hand, and came off. That started my show business career. From there it led to a movie called *Pagan Love Song*.

In the interim I lived in Santa Monica and Malibu. I had a friend who had joined the Marine Reserve in 1948. We were driving around one night and he said, "Benny, I got to go to the Reserve meeting, come with me." So, I go down there with him and a sergeant came up to me and explained what it was to be a Reserve and he said, "Why don't you join?" "Sure," I said. I'm an adventurer, so I joined. Come 1950 was the Korean War and they activated everybody. So, I wound up in Korea.

How long were you in Korea?

Let's see - we did the Inchon Landing August or September of 1950 and I came home the next year, March or April. I'm a member of the Aloha Chapter Chosen Few. A very famous Marine battle took place at the Chosen Reservoir in the month of November and part of December. It got down to forty below zero. The military said it was a bad situation and everyone should pull out – like a retreat. That's where there's a very famous quote coming from our commanding officer, General Oliver P. Smith, better known as Skinny Smith, of the First Marine Division, "Retreat, Hell!" The Marine Corp never retreats. So, they pulled out and left us up there alone. The Chinese came down with twenty divisions and they surrounded us. When they found out they had the USMC surrounded, the word was "No prisoners. Kill every one of them." So, we fought our way out and we did make our way out. I came back and was stationed out in Long Beach, California at the Naval Base down there. I finally got discharged in March 1952.

What happened after Korea and your time in the Marines?

I went back into the business, dancing, again in Hollywood. How it came about, I did this one big show at the Palladium in Hollywood. I usually opened the show. There was a woman in the audience who owned a hotel along with her brother. They were going to open a nightclub across from the Chinese Theater at the Hollywood Roosevelt Hotel and call it the Islander Room.

So, I opened up there, and one night my dancing partner, Tani Marsh, came in and said there are some people coming here from Universal Studios, and they want to look at us. They were doing a musical short for the Miss Universe girls of 1952. So, they came in and we did our show. In those days, nightclubs weren't anything like they are today. You did two shows a night and it was very nice. After the show, we all went up to the table where they were, and we sat down. They said to come down to the studio the next day because they liked what they saw.

We went in and it was going to be the dance troupe in the short. The director came up to me, you know... because I'm 6'5", and said, "Would you mind playing the Chief?" They showed the film to the executive at the studio and he asked, "Who's that young guy who played the Chief?" They said, "His name is Ben Chapman, his cousin used to be one of our stars." Now, I had a cousin who was a very famous star in the 40's named Jon Hall. He did *Hurricane* and a television show *Ramar of the Jungle*. In those days, it was a studio system where you became a contractee and they owned you. They paid you whether you worked or not. So, they asked me if I wanted a contract. I said, yes, but under one condition – that I could still dance, because you're not supposed to work anyplace else. So, they were thinking about bringing back the tropical movies that my cousin used to do and they would groom me to do it.

So there I am, under contract at Universal. I used to come in and say hello and walk around. I would go down to the casting office. I walked in one day and this woman named Jonni Rennick, a casting director at Universal, said, "Bennie, can I talk to you about something? Has the studio talked to you about this movie they're going to do about the Amazon and something about a creature? I believe it's in Brazil. There's going to be some swimming and I know you, Ben, you're half fish." I was a free diver. I could hold my breath for three to four minutes. Well, that's when I was young. (laughs)

I said, "I have no idea what you're talking about." She made a few phone calls and I came back the next day. She took me up to this office and told me to sit down. She was there talking and they would turn around and look at me, then look back. This one gentleman turned to me and said, "Would you mind standing up?" I stood up. He said, 'Now turn around.' I did and sat down. The gentleman who told me to stand turned out to be Jack Arnold, the director.

I came back the next day and was making, like $125 a week, and they re-wrote a new contract for me for $300 a week because I was going to have to do some stunts. Now, I didn't do the swimming because there was no place in Southern California that would have clear water. It was also going to be much cheaper to hire a second unit to go to Florida. Ricou Browning doubled me and Ginger Stanley did Julie. Those people you see under the water are not us, they're doubles. Ginger Stanley and Ricou Browning did the beautiful swimming scenes. Ricou went on to create *Flipper* and direct many swimming scenes in the movies.

Wasn't there also another double for the fire scene?

Yes, for the fire scene, that was done on the stage. They had a big pool and constructed part of the boat there. I wanted to do it myself. I said, "I can do that." They didn't want to take a chance in case I got burned. So, Al Wyatt did that. In fact, he was Rock Hudson's double.

I heard somewhere that Rock Hudson would bring people to see the costume and you would be hiding.

Yeah, they'd call me and tell me Rock was going to bring some people by the set. I would get in the lake. It was a man-made lake, only six feet deep. I'd get out in the middle of the lake and all I'd do is leave the top of my head and eyes, like an alligator. All you'd see is like a little rock or ball floating. They'd be pointing and I would start swimming in close, closer, closer until I could get into about three feet of water, but still only the top of my head showing. Then I'd arrange my feet and legs and arms so that I could spring straight up and go "ROAAARRRR!" They'd see this thing come out of the water. The studio said, "Don't do it anymore!" They were afraid someone was going to have a heart attack and they'd have a lawsuit, because it was frightening to look at.

Do you know why Universal decided to go with *Creature*, because it's kind of different from a lot of movies in the 50's. It seemed to be the era of the Atomic Age monster and the giant bugs.

William Allan, who was the producer, had this story for many years. Originally it was called *The Beastie*. He wanted to get this project done. He tried it before and it didn't work. Universal Studios, as you know, has a big following starting with Lon Chaney Sr. with the *Hunchback*, *Phantom of the Opera*. Then came the 30's with Boris and Bela with *Frankenstein* and *Dracula*. Then Jr. did the *Wolf Man* in the 40's. Now it was the 50's and they were going to give it one more shot.

Those others must have seemed hard to follow, no?

When I did get the assignment, it didn't dawn on me until I was sitting home, "Oh my God, we have to follow those guys. I don't want to be the first one to fall on his face." I sat down and tried to figure out what made the others so successful. They're all different, but there has to be a common denominator. It finally dawned on me - they all have *Beauty and the Beast*. They were all in love with women. I said, "Ah! That's it!" So, I went in the studio and was talking to Jack Arnold, and asked, "How do you want me to play him?" He said, "Just don't make him a cartoon." I told him about *Beauty and the Beast*, and that was fine. Even today you read reviews and they feel sorry for the creature, because [the humans], they were the bad guys.

You were acting in a costume; do you think your background in dance helped?

Yeah, because I used my body motion. I couldn't use anything else. You know, the tilting of the head, or whatever. The movement of the body. We got what we wanted - because there is a very famous movie, *The Seven Year Itch*, with Marilyn Monroe. Well, she has a thing about the *Creature* all through the movie. Just before the scene where, you know, her skirt blows on the grating, as she's coming out of the theater, on the marquee - *Creature from the Black Lagoon*, with a big standee of me holding Julie. Marilyn says, "I felt so sorry for the creature." We were very amazed because that's a 20th Century Fox movie and they usually only mention their own movies. We were very flattered.

What was it like to work inside the suit?

It was very comfortable.

What was the process you had to go through?

The foundation of it is like a one-piece body stocking. It zipped up the back. It was like a leotard. So, what they did was, each piece was molded separately. The lower part from just below the knee down, the feet, were like boots. They came up to the knees. Then they'd zip off the back and snap the dorsal fin closed. Same for the helmet. That's it, it's very simple. But it took a long time to get into. About two to three hours, because it had to fit like an outer layer of skin, because you don't want a fold that's not supposed to be there.

Was it hot inside the costume?

Oh yeah. I mean, if I wasn't in the water, yes. If I was working in the sound stage, I had a guy with a hose, and if I got too hot, I'd just walk up to him and he'd hose me down.

Did you have to do a screen test in the costume?

No, we took some photos, but not really a screen test. The Creature was very top secret. When they were constructing him, nobody was allowed in makeup. They didn't want anyone to see what he was going to look like until the day they released him.

What was the reaction to the costume?

People loved it, cameras were going crazy. They had all the press and the publicity guys there. I have a few pictures with Julie, and she had never seen me in costume before that. They told me later that she turned and asked, "Is that Ben?" I would look down at her and just go "Uhhhhgggghh!" And she kept asking me, "Ben, is that you?" I put my arm around her and thought she was going to have a heart attack.

How long were you in the suit for?

The longest was about fourteen hours. I couldn't take it off. I could take the hands off, but as far as the body suit, I could not get out of it. I had to watch my diet! Once I'm in, I'm in.

What was the atmosphere like?

It was interesting, it was fun. You got up in the morning and couldn't wait to get to work. It was like a big family. There are some shows you work on and think, "Oh, shit." We were all relaxed, there was never an ounce of ego on that set. I felt very fortunate that I had the chance to do it.

Why weren't you credited in the movie?

The reason they didn't credit me, and this is crazy, is the studio wanted to give the impression that it was a real creature. If you see the original *Frankenstein*, Boris doesn't get credit. It's a question mark in the credits. I looked at the studio and asked if they thought the people were that stupid, and they said, "You'd be surprised what people believe."

Do you remember the first time you saw the finished film?

It was up at the Pickwick Theater in Los Angeles. We went to see the movie - and there was a big, long line.

How well did the 3D work?

The only way you should see this movie is on a large screen in 3D. Those small screens, like at a multiplex? It doesn't work too good. But from the old big screen, that thing just leaps out. You actually do start ducking. If you have a chance, and they do it every once in a while, go see it. Recently at the Pantages Theater in Hollywood, a famous old theater. Julie went. She was the guest of honor. They had 750 people sitting outside who couldn't get in. They had to run it twice.

What keeps the *Creature* alive, so to speak, all these years?

The story still holds up today. The story is about trying to find out where man came from. When you play the movie today it's still just as interesting. Also, Julie and myself want to thank all you loyal fans of *The Creature*. Without all of you, we wouldn't be sitting here, and the Gill-man would've been buried and forgotten a long time ago. Julie said it, 'You know we're set in stone now.' And it's true, we belong to the Universal family. You know when they show *Frankenstein*, *Dracula*, *Wolfman*, you see the Gill-man. He will be there forever. We're very grateful.

You see the formula used a lot today too, don't you?

Yes, we were the first ones, we set the precedent. If you look at a lot of the monsters that you see today, they all have that scaly body, two arms and two legs. And that movie with Jon Voight, *Anaconda*, was a rip-off of *Creature*. They went right in with the boat and everything. All they had was an anaconda instead of a Gill-man. It was the same thing. We've been copied so many times. Some people think we'd get insulted, but I say no. If anything, I'm very flattered they would use my character.

There's another thing copied from *Creature*. If you remember, in the movie whenever the Gill-man was around, there was that special sound. You don't see him, but you know he's there, they're playing his music. There's a gentleman who made a movie that's one of the all time highest grossing movies, *Jaws*. You don't see him, but you know he's there. Steven Spielberg got that idea from *Creature*.

Which castmates have you reunited with?

Well, two years ago there was a *Creature* Fest in Tallahassee, Florida. Ricou Browning and Ginger Stanley were going to be there. Julie and myself had never been there - where the real lagoon was, and we'd never met Ginger Stanley. I'd met Ricou, but only because I'd be standing around while they were getting his suit ready. When we got there, the first day we had the press following us. One of the questions they had was, "Does it still look the same?" We had to explain that we'd never been there.

Did Universal do anything for the 50th Anniversary?

They brought out the Legacy DVD and they had a big to-do at one of the places. Me and Ricou were there talking about how much the studio has made over the years – millions. The least they could have done was put the four of us together for the 50th Anniversary for a celebration at the studio. It's not often you still have four of the major actors of a successful movie after fifty years.

Have you any favorite pieces of memorabilia?

Y'know, God gave us one thing, 20/20 hindsight. They made a bust of me to mold the head. Inside of that mask is my face, so it fits perfectly. They asked if I wanted it, I said, 'Ok, I'll take it.' I took it home, and I lived on the beach in Malibu. I put it in front of the house, in the sand, colored it, and put dark glasses and a hat on it. It looked like a guy buried up to his shoulders. So, we moved a couple years later, and I didn't take it. That thing today is worth a fortune.

Now the only merchandise I don't like is when they put teeth in him. It changes his look, makes him look menacing. When you look at him standing there, he's not menacing. He's different, but when you put teeth in him, I hate that.

BOB CLARK

Interviewed by Jason Alvino (5/05)

Legendary filmmaker Bob Clark set the standard for stalker movies with *Black Christmas*, cast the mold for coming-of-age comedies with *Porky's*, and will forever be part of the holiday season with *A Christmas Story*. Throughout his impressive career, he has shifted genres seamlessly, the spiritual predecessor to cinematic "jack-of-all-trades" like Robert Rodriquez. Some of you may not be familiar with his name, but you almost certainly know his work. And we're happy to report that, in addition to being a consummate professional, he's also just a really nice guy! We got the chance to catch up with him and talk a little about his past, present and future projects.

Can you tell us a little bit about your earliest recollections of movies? What made you want to become a filmmaker?

Oh, you started with a tough one there. (laughs) I grew up in Fort Lauderdale, moved there when I was seven years old, and I used to go to the theaters down on Las Olas Boulevard. I did like horror movies, but I liked all movies. I always wanted to be a writer from the earliest time I could remember. It wasn't until I got into college that I started to think about films seriously. I was a film buff, but not an addict, if you know what I mean. I wasn't crazy about films, but I liked 'em. So, I'd say it was probably at college, University of Miami, where I started thinking about making films. It's a long, long story but I got into films when I was an actor in the local Miami film industry of the mid-sixties.

Kay Gordon Murray and other famous people started with that. So, I was in a film and this crazy man said to me, 'We're gonna make a film over in Lehigh Acres,' and Lehigh Acres was a jungle community in effect, a community built on the edge of the Everglades. Charlie Brune, the man who owned a funeral parlor there, also had a movie studio. It was an amazing place, you had to drive across the Everglades to get there. Anyway, I did my first film for him, and nobody knew what they were doing, me included! The film never got out and the next one I did was *The Emperors New Clothes*, which wasn't too bad, it was just with local people. Charlie was a cross-dresser, his wife was a very butch lady, and they had three kids. It was a strange situation and I said, 'I gotta make a movie out of this whole thing!' (laughs)

Wasn't John Carradine in that movie?

Yes, John Carradine was in the movie. Of course, the movie was about a son of a senator who got out of the Korean war by cross-dressing as a woman. John was in it with Lila Lee, the silent film star, and it was an education. My editor's name was Hack... get it? (laughs) He was a local editor out of Fort Meyers. Nobody knew anything about filmmaking. My cinematographer was an ex-newsreel cameraman, nice guy. Nobody knew anything. I had *The Five C's of Cinematography* in my hands the whole time I was doing it.

So, you pretty much just learned it by doing it?

Totally. Completely. So, I figured, at that point, what I would do was become an AD. That's a nice position to be in to learn how everything works. It was interesting. But it was another four years before I started thinking with my friend Alan Ormsby that the next thing we were going to do was a horror film. That was just short of pornography to get a break in.

It seems like a lot of people say that. It's either pornography or horror movies if you want to break into the film business.

Independently in Florida, that's for sure! (laughs) That was part of devising *Children Shouldn't Play With Dead Things*. We got the script together and my brothers and Gary Gotch and Ken Gotch, along with their uncles, put up a total of $40,000. We shot it over eleven nights in a park in Miami. That's how my career started. There were two other horror films before I moved on and finally got my big break. Well, *Black Christmas* was picked up by Warner Brothers, but it was *Murder By Decree* that...

That's a personal favorite of mine, actually.

Thank you. It was like another world. I was a twenty-nine-year-old guy. I go to England, I meet John Gielgud, Tony Quayle, Frank Finlay. I already had Chris Plummer. I had to get (James) Mason, he didn't want to do it, so I drove to where he was shooting another film to talk him into it, and he did it. I had some of the greatest British actors in a four million dollar movie and something like fifty shooting days.

Were you a Sherlock Holmes fan? Is that what interested you in the project?

I had just read in the newspaper this theory about the possible source of Jack the Ripper and thought, what a good idea to put Holmes into it! Actually, I did watch all the Basil Rathbone and Nigel Bruce movies. I was a fan. I thought they were very well done.

Murder By Decree **is considered by many fans to be one of the best Sherlock Holmes movies ever made.**

I felt quite honored. It was a phenomenal cast. For a four million dollar movie, that's extremely fancy. Shooting all over London made it look unique. It had a nice opening in New York and good reviews.

Let's talk about *Black Christmas*. **That movie pretty much created the "slasher" genre long before** *Friday the 13th,* *Halloween,* **and even** *When a Stranger Calls...*

Oh yeah, way before THAT movie. They really did rip us off directly! (laughs)

What influences did you draw from if there was really nothing else like it before?

A script came to me. I often rewrite and work on scripts, and I did a tremendous amount of work on *Black Christmas*. I just drew on the imagery that I had. I had this idea from the beginning that I would obscure the killer and make him all the more frightening and ominous. My obvious influence

for say, *Children Shouldn't Play With Dead Things* was, of course, *Night of the Living Dead*. But with a more comic sort of turn. Other than that, all the other classic horror films from *Psycho* and on were in my consciousness, I suppose, but I can't say I took ideas from any particular film. I just took the story and my ideas of what I thought would be frightening.

Black Christmas **came out in 1974, but the Steadicam wasn't introduced until 1976. How did you film those scenes from the killer's point of view, especially the opening where he's climbing up the trellis and entering the attic window, with both his arms and legs in frame?**

If you get William Alexander's DVD, the Canadian DVD, of *Black Christmas*, they go into it in some detail. Basically, Bert Dunk, the camera operator, designed a camera rig that attached to his head! No one had ever done that before. Those are his hands climbing with the small camera. The moving shots when we were on the ground were just standard handheld shots. But the climbing ones were the unique style camera. When he looked up, the camera looked up. Critical Mass is the company that released the 25th anniversary edition of *Black Christmas* on DVD, and it's got some wonderful extras. It takes you through the old house! Art Hindle walked through the house and showed where what scenes were filmed where.

It was something he created specifically for the movie?

Yes, exactly.

Were there ever plans for a sequel to *Black Christmas*?

No, I never intended ever to do a sequel. I did a film about three years later, started a film with John Carpenter, it was his first film for Warner Bros. (which picked up *Black Christmas*). He asked me if I was ever going to do a sequel and I said no. I was through with horror, I didn't come into the business to do just horror. He said, 'Well, what would you do if you did do a sequel?' I said it would be the next year and the guy would have actually been caught, escape from a mental institution, go back to the house and they would start all over again. And I would call it *Halloween*. (laughs)

Was *Black Christmas* **directly responsible for** *Halloween*?

No, that's not really true. The truth is John didn't copy *Black Christmas*. He wrote a script, directed the script, and did the casting. *Halloween* is his movie and besides, the script came to him already titled anyway. He liked *Black Christmas*, and may have been influenced by it, but in no way did John Carpenter copy the idea. Fifteen other people at that time had thought to do a movie called *Halloween*, but the script came to John with that title on it.

When you were working on the script for *Black Christmas*, it was your intention all along to never reveal the killer's identity or backstory?

That's correct. It was bold and some people didn't appreciate it. When Warner Bros. bought the movie, they tried to talk me out of it and into making more of a concluding finish. As you probably know 2929 has bought the rights to *Black Christmas...*

Which brings us to the remake.

They are remaking it with Glen Morgan and James Wong. Glen has finished his script and did a sensational job of creating the backstory, I don't want to give too much away but, pursuing what was being implied in those phone calls... quite horrible things that happened back then. They should be shooting in the fall.

What would you like to personally see them do with the movie as far as a direction?

I don't want to get into that because I KNOW what they are going to do! (laughs) Taking it back to the backstory is a brilliant stroke though, at the same time still keeping it in the sorority house but learning more about what happened then. That's as much as I can say.

And aren't you remaking *Children Shouldn't Play With Dead Things* yourself?

I am indeed! I've written a new script for it. I did it for $40,000 with my college buddies twenty-something years ago and it's the only movie that I wanted to do more with. *Deathdream* had a modest budget, but I'm very proud of it. Oliver Hudson and company, they bought it last year. A lot of my movies are being remade! (laughs) They want to do *Murder By Decree*, but I won't let them. (laughs)

Anyway, I've added a new dimension to it, a new character. There's a ghoul that murdered fifteen people forty years before and that's what changed the island from a resort, a mansion island, to a horror island and he's brought into the story now. I thought, there's more fun to be had

with this. It's going to be very funny but quite horrifying too. We'll probably start shooting in September, maybe earlier, and are putting money together for it now.

Do you have a favorite genre or a favorite project?

Like Altman said, asking what's my favorite film is like asking who's my favorite child (laughs) That being said, I certainly have an enormous affection for *Porky's*. It has a tremendous history. It was odd because it actually has strong varied supporters. It was despised on one hand, but it had supporters like David Mamet, Arthur Miller, Norman Mailer... they all admired the movie. So, it had its strong core of supporters, but it also was so despised.

People also have many kind words for *A Christmas Story*, which I also have a lot of affection toward for many reasons, mainly because I tried for ten years to get it done. Someone bought the actual house where we shot and turned it into a museum. It had that many people come by just to see it. But those two certainly, and I have enormous affection for getting to work with Arthur Miller on *American Clock*. THE Arthur Miller. I grew up in theater and he's the playwright of America. So those three certainly, but there was no film I didn't have fun doing and enjoy working on.

Is there something you haven't done but would like to do? A pet project you haven't gotten to yet but hope to?

I have two, yeah. I have a science fiction film from an original screenplay I've written called *Lost in the Stars*. It's not *Star Wars*-type fantasy, it's more reality/fantasy. It's about a ship that was marooned on another planet where the denizens are quite horrible creatures. They captured this ship and get into all their tapes and computers and learn our history and turn themselves into the Roman Circus. When our rescue ship crash lands, the creatures have a Roman coliseum and they become the gladiators.

The other one is a western. Akira Kurosawa was a big fan of mine, of *Black Christmas* and *Murder By Decree*. In the early eighties, we tried to do a film together with me producing for him over there and it was called *Ran*. Kurosawa wrote the short version of it and I'm writing the longer version and I'm putting that together right now. It's an adventure story starting with Thomas Jefferson and his illegitimate children with his black mistress. She has children again herself, and they have the grandchildren. A blonde God who goes to Montana to the Montana war. It's really the whole early American history, not done as a Japanese film but somewhat in that style.

I think Science Fiction and Westerns are the only two genres you haven't dabbled in.

That's correct. I almost did Science Fiction but not quite. I started a Western, but I left the film.

Well, thank you, sir, for taking the time to talk with us. I'm personally a big fan, and this was a quite a thrill.

Thank you, it was a pleasure talking to you!

Unfortunately, Bob Clark never finished the films he was planning to make as Bob and his son Ariel were tragically killed by an unlicensed drunk driver in 2007.

In the years following this interview, we developed a friendship with Bob and were able to meet when he came to visit us on the set of Paul Solet's short film, *Grace*. Bob was so impressed with the special makeup and creature effects we (as Wicked EFX) were supplying for the film, he offered us an opportunity to handle a few gags for his remake of *Children Shouldn't Play With Dead Things*. It just speaks to Bob's kindness and generosity. Here is some never-before-seen concept art by Mike Carlo for those sequences:

- Jason Alvino

CHILDREN SHOULDN'T PLAY WITH DEAD THINGS!

THE LOST REMAKE CONCEPT ART

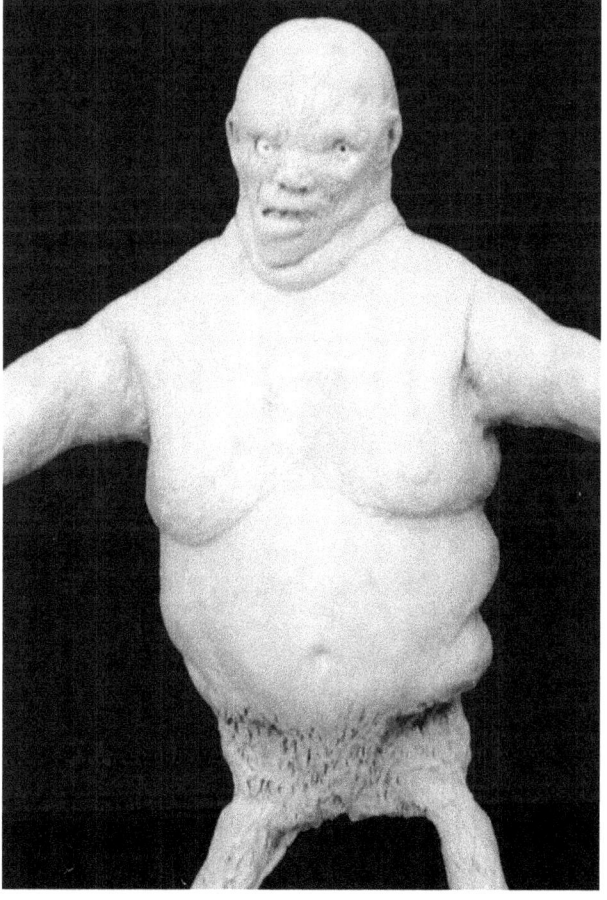

Children Shouldnt Play
With Dead Things . . .
Conceptuals

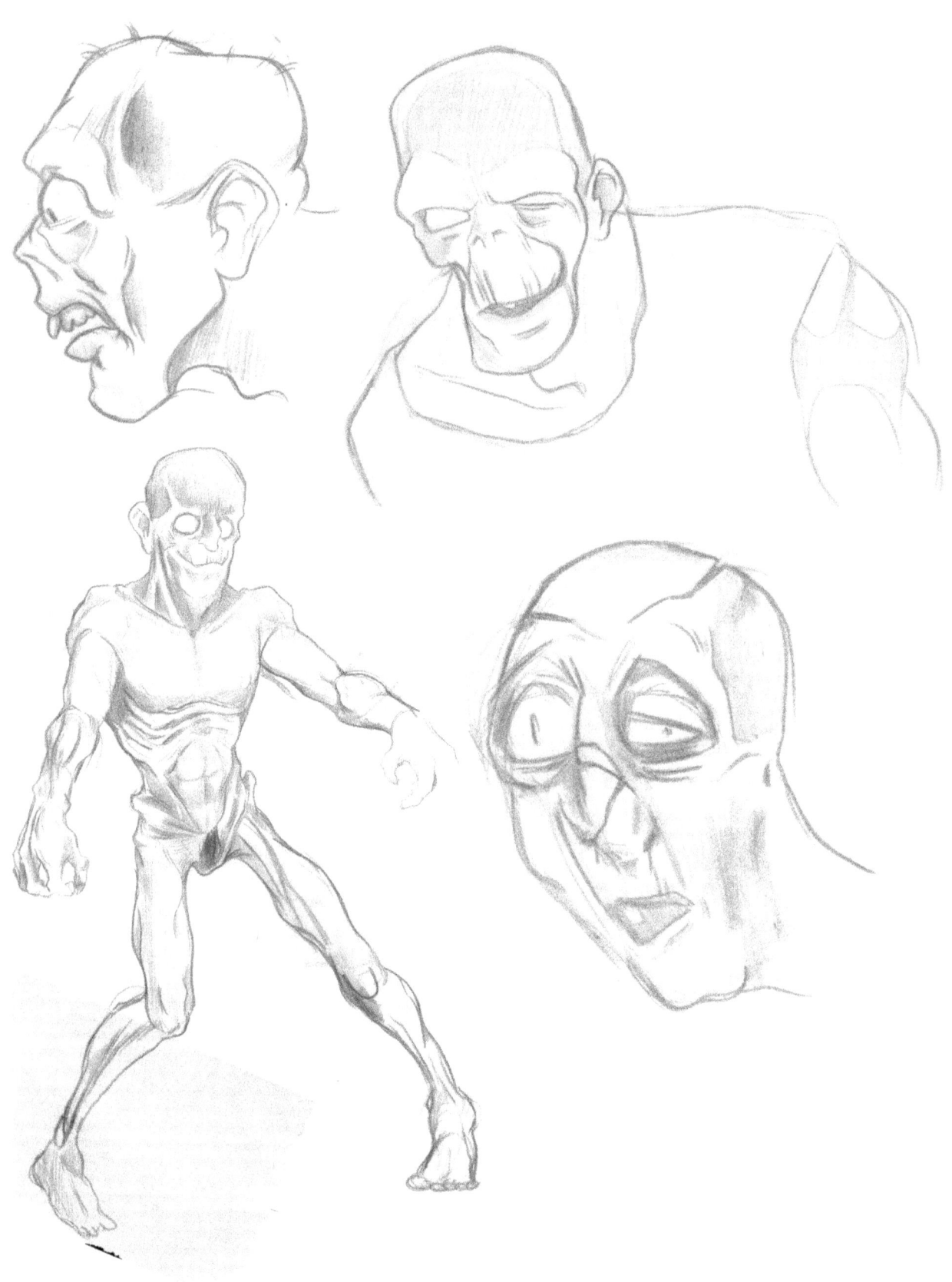

CSPWDT CONCEPTUALS

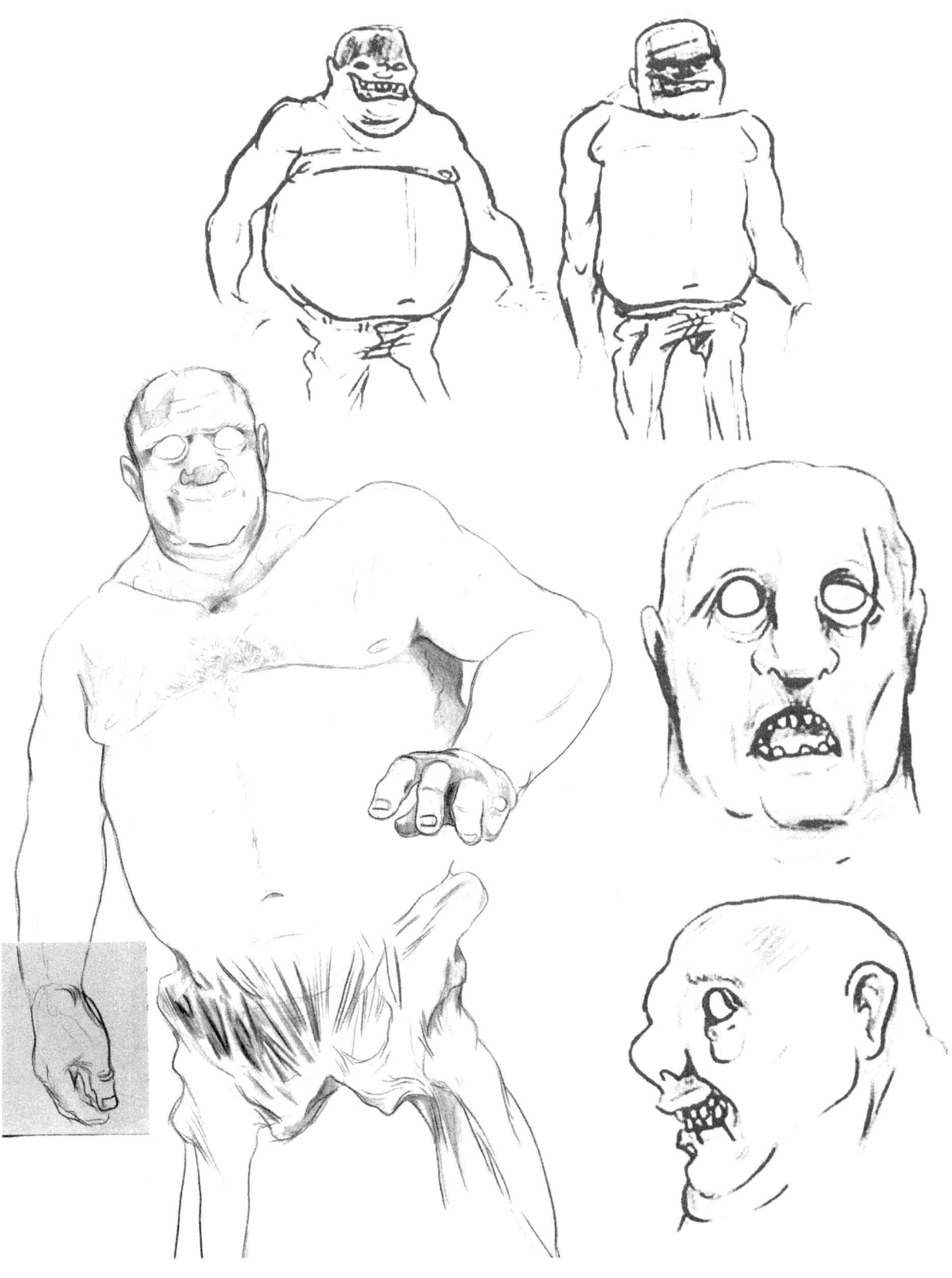

PATRICIA TALLMAN

Interviewed by Rob Galluzzo (6/05)

Many fans know Patricia Tallman from either her role as Lyta Alexander on *Babylon 5* or as the reduxed Barbara in the *Night of the Living Dead* remake. Most people don't realize she's risked her neck in dozens of productions from soap operas to television shows to feature films such as *The Long Kiss Goodnight, Creepshow 2, Army of Darkness*, and two *Austin Powers* movies. Read on and get to know the lovely and sweet Patricia Tallman.

What are your earliest recollections of the horror genre? What was the first movie to really scare you?

We went to the drive-ins as a family. My sister and I would be in our jammies in the back seats. I think my parents assumed we'd get bored and fall asleep, but we never did. I remember *The Hand* with Michael Cain. I had terrible nightmares about that one! There were a couple of Vincent Price movies that scared me pretty bad as well.

Do you remember your initial reactions to seeing the original *Night of the Living Dead*?

I hadn't seen *Night of the Living Dead* until I was in college. By then, it was already a classic. And at first, I didn't want to go because scary movies always freaked me out and had given me bad dreams! (laughs) So, of course I was pressured into going to a midnight show on campus and it was one of the scariest things I had ever seen. Terrifying. When I heard George was doing this remake in 1990, I thought "Why?" Because the original was so effective and scary. But it turned out it had to do with some copyright issues.

How'd you initially get involved in acting? From what I read in your bio, you started at a very early age with your father's radio show?

I have always wanted to act. When I was little, I used to reenact TV commercials and musical numbers for my family and the neighborhood. I played *Star Trek* with my Barbies and acted out *Dark Shadows* with my cousin. So, no wonder I ended up in horror and sci-fi!

You came to New York City to pursue acting after college and started out by doing both theatre and television work. How'd this all lead to you becoming a stunt woman?

I always wanted to be Errol Flynn. I had taken fencing lessons in college and loved stage combat. When I got to New York, I took period sword technique classes as a hobby. I met some stunt people in those classes, and it all went downhill from there!

Do you remember the first stunt gig you got and how you went about approaching it?

I'm pretty sure it was a soap opera. Although... hmm... I'm trying to recall...

Stunts in a soap opera?

Yeah. A soap opera and then I met some other stunt people. And usually, the way it is with stunts is you kind of apprentice with people that are already doing it. They teach you what you need to do, and if it looks like you show promise and can do the work and have the right attitude, then they'll give you more small jobs. So, I started with the soaps, which didn't have major stunts because of the budgets and how quickly they shot them. So, the stunts would mostly involve falling and small fights and things you normally wouldn't want to do with the actors. That's the kind of thing we did, and I was very good at fights. Because it's choreography—like with dancing. I actually subbed Tina Louise from *Gilligan's Island* in a really terrible movie called *The Pool*, falling off a balcony. And I had the right height and color to double for her. It was really exciting. I remember I had to just topple over this balcony and I fell into boxes, because it wasn't that high of a fall, twenty or thirty feet. I remember the stunt guys being very indulgent and sweet with me.

Has there ever been a stunt that you approached that you perhaps felt a bit nervous about doing? Or maybe even one that you're really proud of?

I am always a bit nervous. That's how you stay safe. You treat each stunt with respect no matter how simple it is or how many times you have done something like it. I am proud of doing the work, all of it, and the fact that stunt people I respect called me to work with them.

Was any project more difficult to work on than the others, due to the amount of stunts or workload involved?

My God, yes! There were a couple that left me thinking "Why am I doing this? This is crazy!" Probably the hardest was *The Long Kiss Goodnight*. It was a brutal environment, because it was so cold. We shot that in Toronto. And I was doubling Geena Davis. The stunts in that were very involved and I think I was the fifth stunt double brought in because the other ones kept getting hurt. That was tough.

Tell us a bit about your working relationship with George Romero, which started on his film *Knightriders*? Is that where you first met Tom Savini?

I auditioned for Chris and George in NYC for *Knightriders*. My boyfriend at the time knew George, so we both got an audition. I ended up with a much better part! I knew Tom also from this boyfriend. Tom taught a make-up class at C-MU, where I went to college. That's in Pittsburgh, where Tom and George lived. I got to know Tom better on *Knightriders* and see what a fine actor he really is.

I read you were in *Creepshow 2*. I love *Creepshow 2*! Can you tell me a bit about some of the things you had to pull off on that film?

Ummm, let's think back a bit now. The most colorful stuff for me was in Arizona where we did the Blob part of the film. (The Raft) We had a lot of water safety to do for the cast and the crew. The water was extremely murky, there was NO visibility. I did the part where the girls got eaten by the blob. Lots of nasty make-up. But I loved the area, the west. I love living in California now.

First and foremost, let me say you kicked so much ass as Barbara in the *Night of the Living Dead* remake. Now, how'd you get involved in *Night of the Living Dead*? Did you audition for Barbara initially or were you always a choice of Tom's for the role?

I had to audition. They were only seeing people in NYC, and I had moved to LA, so I sent in a video tape. My friend, Marty Schiff, shot my audition. He really directed it. He was in *Knightriders*. Tom has said he always wanted me for the role. I choose to believe him!

Your version of Barbara was, obviously, far different from the version portrayed by Judith O'Dea in the original. How exactly did you approach your Barbara?

I just constructed a character based on the script. The writer puts the black on the page, I fill in the white. I never wanted her to be the same as the original. What would be the point in that? The original was so perfect as it was!

Were you surprised to see such a different version of Barbara in the remake's script as opposed to the one from the original? Didn't George actually write the script to both the original and remake?

Well, I was really pleased that he updated it. He wrote for the time period when he did the first one in 1968. I wasn't interested in playing that girl. And when I read the new one, I thought "Ok! Much better!" (laughs)

There's a slew of phenomenal actors in the remake from Tony Todd to Bill Moseley, Tom Towles, and William Butler. What do you consider some of your favorite moments in the film? Both from your performance and maybe some from the other actors?

It's interesting you should say that because I think I take all the performances for granted. Everyone was great. It's the relationships I remember, our off-screen bond. They were all just remarkable folks. I should watch the film again and just look at the acting. I don't think I have ever done that. The movie is so scary, I don't enjoy it on that level! And I hate watching myself.

Do you remember much about the behind-the-scenes stuff on *Night of the Living Dead*?

It's really hard to have enough distance from a movie you're working on. I know that if there were a bad performance, then it was stick out like a sore thumb. And there was none of that in *Night*. Everyone was just so solid. I knew that when we were doing it. Here we are in this very surreal situation, where most people would not take it seriously, but everyone did take it very seriously. And was very creative with it. And also, everyone had a really great sense of humor during our downtime. There are times you work on something where you'll notice an actor does not want to ever socialize or have too much fun with it, who is always trying to be so serious. But we had a really good mix of both. When we were working, everyone was on top of it, well prepared, and well rehearsed. And when we had to wait for a long set-up, then we'd get goofy because it was the middle of the night.

Tony was the most serious guy. He'd often just kick back while we were waiting for a set up. And often, we just couldn't let him get away with that! The guy who lived in the house we shot in, I believe, really did have a hobby in taxidermy. The whole place was filled with real stuffed animals! Animals that were once alive and were now stuffed. We used all of them in the movie. All the ones on the wall were already there and they were really creepy. So, anyway, I would find a stuffed alligator or something and stick it on Tony while he was trying to sleep. But he was really a good sport about it. You go a little nuts when you're shooting all night, every night, six days a week. You just need some sort of comic relief.

Everyone was really great about that. The only sad thing is that I don't see everyone. Tony and I are the only ones that really cross paths at the conventions. I just saw Billy Butler for the first time in fifteen years. Katie was asking about him too. Savini, I still see and talk to. And George and Chris...

Speaking of, are you excited for *Land of the Dead*? Isn't it time George came back to the genre?

Oh, I'm sure the fans are absolutely thrilled. He created it, and he's the one who should be doing it! And I'm sure it'll be awesome because it's George! Of course! Some people asked if I was sad to not be in it, but I say "As what?! As grandma of the living dead?" You can only be a zombie hunter for so long. I do think it's going to be a great movie. George should really be doing more of everything. I think he's a phenomenal filmmaker.

Agreed. I love all his movies.

I know. I hope he gets the career he deserves with this film.

There's some great social commentary, both in the original and remake versions of *Night of the Living Dead*. I love your line "They're us. We're them and they're us." Followed by your sarcastic smirk and the "Having fun?" comment. What's your opinion of what these films are trying to say? Do you think this is perhaps the reason that Romero's original has become such a classic?

It's something that I believe we can do in the film and television industry; make people think while entertaining them. Sometimes if you show a subject, or an idea out of context, it gets into the brain easier. Like if you watching a show that takes place on a space ship, and you see a storyline about prejudice against an alien race, how wrong it is, some people may be able to get the point. They don't want to hear about how prejudiced they are in real life, but maybe we can get them to see it if we put it in a less threatening setting like sci-fi.

I get all tense when asked "What do you think George is trying to say?" I guess it's because I don't want to tell anyone what to think. It's each person's job to decide for yourself, think for yourself. It doesn't matter what I think. My experience of the film is completely different from what anyone else's could possibly be. You who didn't act in it have a much purer vision of it.

With Tom Savini involved, obviously the creature effects were going to be top-notch. (Which they were!) Any zombies or effects really stand out to you as impressive or memorable while working on the picture?

They were all so gross. I didn't want to hang out and see how it was being created. I wanted to experience it as an actor. So, I didn't hear all the stories about the people who wore the make-up. The person who was the zombie I shot in the head was a real townsperson who wanted to be in the film. He was just so scary to me. And he really got into it...following me around and whispering about how he was going to get me. Oh yeah...it was fun being me.

Greg Funk, who is a make-up artist and won an Emmy for his work on *Babylon 5*, was the graveyard zombie that I fight with and stab with the flower arrangement. I forgot about his make-up because we were working so hard on the action. He was so wonderful to work with because he understood completely all aspects of what was needed in the scene. I loved working with him. Maybe because of that, his make-up affected me the least.

I really feel that the 1990 version of _Night of the Living Dead_ stands the test of time and, in fact, was maybe a bit ahead of its time, considering the current crop of remakes. What were your reactions to first seeing it on the big screen and how do you feel about it now?

I was very proud of our work. I felt like the acting was as honest and real as we could be. The reaction from the audience was so satisfying. And people still talk to me about it. Yeah, I feel really good about it. Joe Straczynski said he wrote the part of Lyta for me based on seeing me in _Night_.

I feel a common mistake made in horror movies is that the filmmakers don't take the subject seriously enough. The actors don't try to be real. So, you don't end up caring about anyone and just wait for the next gross thing to happen. You don't go home with any message.

Didn't you recently get to work with Katie Finneran again, who played Judy Rose in _Night of the Living Dead_?

Yeah! That was so great. Because I got a call from this stunt coordinator, Doug Coleman. I've known him since he was first getting started, and now he's a huge stunt coordinator and second unit director. He just did work on _The Aviator_. And he was working on the new _Bewitched_ and called me out of the blue. "You know, I got this actress I think you'd be good to double." And I thought "Doug, you haven't seen me in forever. I'm not the same size!" But he still told me to just come down to the set to catch up. So, I went down to Culver Studios where they were shooting _Bewitched_ and he took a look at me and said "You'll be fine." So, I show up for a costume fitting a few days later and he told me the actor I'm doubling is Katie Finneran and I said "You're kidding! I haven't seen her in ten years!"

So, when she showed up, we were both in make-up at the same time and it was just so much fun. Awesome to see her again. So, in the movie she plays Will Ferrell's ex-wife. And the Nicole Kidman character, who's playing Samantha, gets angry with Katie's character and causes all these mishaps. I stunt for some of those mishaps. And it was fun, we had a great time. I hope everyone goes to see it, because I think it should be a pretty cute gag. And I know they were very, very happy.

I'm a big Will Ferrell fan, so I'm going to check it out for him. And now you, of course!

Oh, I love Will Ferrell. He was just so sweet, and really easy going. And very, very funny. At one point, I'm laying on the floor at the end of the stunt. With this huge light on top of me. I had been squashed like a bug. And it looked very dramatic. It was not a difficult stunt, but it was very technically involved from my end of it. So, he comes running over in character and all his friends come over and lift this light off of me like I'm the Wicked Witch of the West, and... the look on his face... was SO funny. Because he really was concerned, because it looked very dramatic and it looked very real. So, I look at his expression and started to laugh, which came off as inappropriate. But he was just so cute. It didn't ruin the take or anything, but it was just very, very funny. He was great with Katie too. Even from a fan perspective, I love that. When an actor you really love turns out to really be a nice guy.

You got to throw down with Ash in _Army of Darkness_ as the possessed witch. What was it like to attempt to kick Bruce Campbell's ass?

Well, I sure don't think I came out on top! Bruce is a hunk, he's totally fab, and he's funny which makes him irresistible. I wish I wasn't in so much pain at the time so I could have really enjoyed it. I was in make-up for over seventeen hours, had horrible contact lenses in (so I couldn't see), couldn't eat or pee, and was working two stunt jobs at the same time. I really wanted him to shoot me for real and get it over with.

So, while working on _Army of Darkness_, you were also simultaneously doing other gigs?

I did that a lot back then. There was a time when I was just working so hard, and I couldn't turn anything down. So, often I did what they call double-dipping. That just means that you're doing as many jobs as you possibly can all at the same time. I don't recall what I was doing at the same time. All I know is I was not sleeping! And it was tough! But that was a bread-and-butter job. And it was all union, so it went toward my pension and health plan.

Army of Darkness seemed like a fairly big production. Were there a lot of difficult stunts to perform on that particular show?

It was intense! The puppets were so cool. Stuntmen were flying all over the place. I was the army's only stuntwoman.

So, you were (pardon the expression) the she-bitch in _Army of Darkness_. Did you also come back as the S-Mart ghoul for the reshoots on the alternate ending after the film wrapped?

No, I was just the she-bitch. And I was in the army. KNB built all the costumes around my body for the skeletons, so I had my place assured!

You were the only female in the army?

Only stunt female in the army. They had a lot of skinny people cast for the skeletons for anyone with a skeleton like body. So, if it was a woman they didn't care. But in the stunt army I was the only female.

You instigate one of the most memorable lines in the first Austin Powers film. You're the waitress that gets punched before Austin says "That's a man, baby!" What can you tell us about working on the *Austin Powers* films? Are sets on comedies really as tense as people claim?

I thought everyone seemed to be having a really good time. Mike Myers was very sweet, and in character, he was adorable as Austin. It was all good. The stunt coordinator, Bud Davis, is a good friend of mine. We had fun. I loved my outfit!

      I got to see more of Mike's acting style on the second one. I was in the fight scene on the Jerry Springer set. Mike first did the scene as written. Once they had that in the can, he'd get creative. I was fascinated. He was so funny and Seth Green could keep up with anything Dr. Evil threw at him. I'd told my son, who was six at the time, that I was going to go to work with Dr. Evil and his son Scott. Julian said, in awe, "Scott Evil?!" Like he was a rock star!

You also have a huge fan base from playing Lyta Alexander on *Babylon 5*. Series creator Joe Straczynski apparently had the entire series mapped out when he pitched it to the networks. What were your initial reactions to stepping into the sci-fi world?

I loved the pilot script. I never thought I'd get the part. I was blown away. I didn't know anything about the series. I only had *The Gathering* script. And I knew it was very special. I love sci-fi. I read it constantly. I'm a total geek, squid, nerd.

Joe Straczynski is my favorite writer in comics today. What can you tell me about him from working on *Babylon 5*?

Joe was always easily accessible and generous with his time. Unless his door was closed and he was writing, his door was usually always open and it meant, "Come on in. If you have a question or want to talk." He was amazing that way. Our producers were right there on the set with us, so it wasn't

like they were in another building or another lot. They were always right there for us. Joe was always tight-lipped about what was coming next. We were kind of on a need-to-know basis. Because he didn't want to spill any secrets before we shot, which makes total sense.

With his writing in general, I tend to notice he has everything planned out way in advance.

Oh yeah! He's amazing that way. And so, there were times when you'd be acting, you'd say to Joe, "What exactly do I mean by this? I don't know what this means!" (laughs)

And did he ever just say "You'll see?"

Nah. He felt if he could trust you, then he'd illuminate you. But if it was something he really didn't want to let go of, well he would give you as much as he could and then we'd have to figure it out. I don't recall ever having too much of a problem with that. He would always give us enough as actors to make sense out of it.

You've made a lot of convention appearances in the past few years. What's the convention experience like from your perspective?

It's actually very draining. Doing the conventions is hard work. But most conventions, they try to treat you really well, but it's almost necessary because you have to put out so much energy. And you don't always get energy back. So, sometimes it feels like a level of energy is sucked out of you, because everyone wants a piece of you. That's why they're there! And I understand that and I know that going in. There was a point I had to stop doing conventions, because I didn't feel I was being as accessible and friendly as I wanted to be. The downside is people do make fun of the conventions. Some people can't separate reality from tv and sometimes that makes it very hard too.

Were there any people you've either bumped into or always wanted to meet at the conventions?

I've always wanted to meet James Marsters from *Buffy* and we have the same convention manager, but we always seem to miss each other. I haven't really had a chance to meet him. I mean, it's always fun to meet other actors, and most are very sweet. We're there for the same reasons, so it's like we're in the same little club. Last Chiller, I got to meet Glenn Shadix, who had done *Beetlejuice* and *Carnivale*. It was great to meet him because he's such an accomplished actor. And we talked a lot about *Carnivale* because I have some friends that work on that show. I love to meet other actors. Mostly they're really great, but there's a few that think they're too big for their britches, and that's hysterical! Who DO you think you're fooling? (laughs). And you hear these stories about these actors being really rude to the fans, and you think, "Oh, get over yourself." But most of them are totally cool.

You do a lot of work for an organization called Penny Lane. Tell us a bit about them and how you got involved?

I've been working with the kids from Penny Lane for about twelve years now. It's a home for kids who don't make it in regular foster care, they have been so abused, they just don't function normally. I run a program for them called "Be A Santa." And fans helped me build them a computer lab. It became a community project, with our community being fans from all over the world.

DANIEL FARRANDS

Interviewed by Rob Galluzzo (6/05)

Do we have any *Halloween* fans out there? If so, you're in for a treat. Because, as a fan myself, this has to be one of my all-time favorite interviews. I got the chance to talk to Daniel Farrands, the writer behind *Halloween 6: The Curse of Michael Myers*. And finally, he sets the record straight on what he had planned for his *Halloween* sequel, which should have been the ultimate love letter to the fans. He also worked on the *Amityville Confidential* documentaries for the History Channel. He gives us the truth on all of the above projects and more. Read on!

What are your earliest recollections of the horror genre? What movie just really scared the hell out of you?

Well, I'd definitely have to say *Jaws* because I was five. It was the summer of *Jaws* and, like everyone else, it completely terrified me. The even scarier thing about *Jaws* for me personally probably had something to do with the fact that it was actually filmed at the beach we used to go to. (laughs) So, it's pretty traumatic when you're five and you recognize the little huts on the beach. It was Martha's Vineyard, and we'd go out there in the summer from Rhode Island, which was where I was born and is very close to where *Jaws* was filmed. I really was way too young to have seen it. But I do remember begging to go see it.

Do you remember the first impression *Halloween* made on you? Which was the first one you saw and how'd you feel about the character of Michael Myers at the time?

I remember vividly. It was the first airing of the original *Halloween* on network television in the fall of 1981. And it was on NBC. And I remember sitting in the living room and we were one of the first families on the block to have a VCR, so I decided for some odd reason, I had to record this. I sat there through the first forty-five minutes or so of the film, and as it got darker and scarier, it seemed the rest of the family just disappeared and went to bed. And I was the only one left. The last man standing. (laughs) And I made it through the whole movie by myself, huddled in the corner of the sofa, with this remote control in my hand, because I didn't want to record the commercials, sitting there in absolute terror. I was twelve. That was it.

I felt like I had stared death in the face and survived it. *Halloween* was really a cathartic experience. People always use that analogy of a horror film being like a roller coaster, but I think that's true. Again, I had recorded it, so my fascination for it just grew. And I started writing scripts for my own horror films in junior high and high school. I became known as "Dan the Horror Movie Man." I made movies back then like *Halloween Party* and *The Halloween Hospital Massacre* and it went on and on from there.

Is this how you got into screenwriting? Writing a lot of *Halloween* related stories back in high school?

Absolutely. And a number of my own *Friday the 13th's* as well. It really wasn't much of a surprise to any of my classmates at my high school reunion that I actually went on to write one. Everyone just thought "Well, of course you did!" This was pre-determined! This was fate.

How'd you land the gig writing the sixth *Halloween*?

I came back to Los Angeles right out of high school. I didn't go to film school, and I didn't have any rich uncles in the business. I truly was just determined to work in this field. So, it really began in late 1989 or early 1990 through a chance meeting with Ramsey Thomas, who had produced *Halloween 5*. I had seen *Halloween 5* the night it opened, and I walked out of that theater with my two best friends, who remember this very well, and I said, "I'm going to write *Halloween 6*." And that was it. It was one of those crystallized moments where I just knew. I was going to make this happen. It was one of those things where, if you focus enough on something ... well, I suppose now I'd say, "be careful what you wish for." (laughs)

That's really how it began, it was this years-long journey of being absolutely focused on the goal. And doing whatever I had to do to get there. It wasn't stepping over anyone and it wasn't writing a spec draft of *Halloween 6* and bugging the producers because they don't respond to that kind of thing. There is a protocol for how these things get done in Hollywood so, even though I knew I'd be facing some stiff competition, I knew I still had to play by the rules while at the same time making sure the producers knew I was the guy to do this job! I went off and wrote several other things over the next several years. I had an independent film produced and, like all new hopeful writers, I just set about making my way.

Early on, I had sent Ramsey another script I had written. And he told me, "Hey, we're looking for writers to come in and take a crack at *Halloween 6*." This was in 1990, which to me was like, the calling. I prepared for weeks for this meeting. I literally researched every element of Halloween; not only the *Halloween* films, which I knew like the back of my hand. What I brought to the table was sort of a representation of the mythology and all this stuff that was hinted at in *Halloween 5*. Thorn, this ancient rune, and all of this Celtic lore that I felt could really be tied in to the mythology of Michael Myers. I really set about laying out the groundwork for what all of that means. And I kind of had an instinct that even they [the producers] didn't know what all of this mumbo-jumbo introduced in five was all about. It was like they dropped these hints in five of what may come, but as I learned when I went in and met with the producers, they really had no idea what any of this Man in Black business meant at all!

That's interesting. When I walked out of *Halloween 5*, I felt like they left a lot of questions open with almost no intention of answering them.

Well, yeah. They didn't and it's funny. When we filmed *Halloween 6* in Salt Lake City, where they had done 4 and 5, some of our crew came from those earlier films. I got friendly with some of them, and I asked them questions. And I remember asking what had gone on with *Halloween 5*? Why did certain things happen the way they did with that film? What were the director or writer's intentions? And the response I'd always get is... nobody knew. They were making things up as they went along. And the director of 5 from what I understand was very big into ancient superstitions and the idea of introducing some kind of black magic. So, I think

he would come to the set with these ideas about bringing some of the black magic to the plot. I had one conversation with one of the screenwriters, Michael Jacobs, and I asked him while I was writing the script, "Can you guys give me a hint here? I want to be true to what you had set up." And his take was, "We didn't know what any of it meant." There was really no answer as to what all this stuff about runic symbols and the man with the black coat and the strange cowboy boots was all about. This all came from the director of part 5. So, since no one had any idea, I was free to go my own path with it.

And I think one of the things that impressed Moustapha Akkad was that I came in with a ton of research. I literally made a binder with a big black cover and with the title *Halloween 666*, and it had the Thorn symbol replacing the 'A' in the *Halloween* logo. And for five years, he apparently kept this thing on his desk and used it as a reference for other people coming in with pitches. This is a big leap in time, because I was first brought in to talk to them in 1990 and there was a big legal battle in terms of who was going to pick up the distribution, which ended up being Dimension. And until that happened, there really was no development on the project. From my understanding, there were two other teams of writers brought in to work on the script initially. And apparently, neither of those teams worked out. And suddenly they really had a problem because they had a production date. There was no script. All they had was the mask! (laughs) But no script. There was a whole crew in Salt Lake waiting for this thing to go. So, I was brought in as a last act of hope and maybe desperation on the part of the producers, because they were looking for someone to crack this thing and to do it very quickly. So, that's when I got the call.

I was brought in, and basically grilled. "What is this? What is that? What's the story? How would you do it? We know you know this better than anyone else, so tell us. What should we do? We have no idea." Apparently, the other scripts didn't even address the issues of Thorn and the Man in Black. They just sort of forgot about those elements and went in a different direction entirely. And I think Akkad was committed to picking up the story that had been left off in *Halloween 5*.

The thing I liked about your take was that you really tried to explain and define Michael Myers and even bring out more about the mythology of Halloween itself.

Yeah. That was always my intent, but I think as the script developed and other people got involved, it just went too far in terms of attempting to provide an explanation of Michael Myers. My original take was never about the stars aligning. But the director wanted to create a real mythology for Michael, to explain to the audience: "Why does he kill?" and "why some years and not others?" And I was basically given one night to kind of come up with something. And I thought... "Well ..." (laughs) And he opted for that version. I didn't really agree with that take. I always felt Michael was, for lack of a better term, a sexual deviant. A child trapped in a particular moment in time. He's become so fixated on this event when he was a kid, which I think had a lot of sexual context to it and a lot of underpinnings of repressed sexuality to it. The original *Halloween* was very voyeuristic in nature, which was part of what made it so scary. It's something the audience can't quite put their finger on. But really what Michael does for the better part of the movie is just follow the girls around and watch them. He's a watcher. And I think, at least in my view of who the character was, is that he became utterly fixated on this particular moment in time [the murder of his sister] and for whatever twisted reason he had to continually replay that for himself. Even as an adult. That's why he escaped and had to go back and search out a girl who reminded him of a sister that once was.

It wasn't until the sequel [*Halloween II*] of course, where she [Laurie Strode] literally became the sister. But that was never the original intent. And I always thought it was much more interesting psychologically that Michael Myers fixates on a particular girl that excites him sexually. I think that's something that all of the sequels have missed out on. They always pushed it into a different realm. But the basic simplicity of that character makes it so much more frightening. And in a way, relatable. I really think the essence of it was this guy out there. With this crazy mask, who was unbelievably nuts and he will get to you. He doesn't care if he knows you, or you're related to him in any way ... the fact is that he will kill you. And that's the simplicity of the original *Halloween*, which worked so well. Even *Halloween: H20*, which proclaimed itself to be the definitive sequel, missed that sense of terror and realism. Well, that's just my opinion as a fan. (laughs) I do appreciate what you're saying though. I felt at the time, this guy's been burned and beaten and shot... how does he keep coming back?

He can't just be a man anymore; he's gone beyond that. He's mythical. He's supernatural. So, I took it from that standpoint that there's something else driving him. A force that goes beyond the five senses that has infected this boy's soul and now is driving him. In justifying why and how this guy keeps coming back, we came up with this idea that he's gone beyond being human. That he's controlled by something much

bigger than we could ever understand. And I thought that was a good launching point for future films, but unfortunately, they dropped all of that. And now he's just this guy in a mask who kills people on the Internet. (laughs)

Were there any parameters set up from the get-go? For example, did you know early on that Danielle Harris wouldn't be returning and that's why Jamie Lloyd died so early on in the film? Was that always your intention?

Nope. In fact, they didn't want that character in the movie at all. I had to push to really get Jamie to come back. And the way that I sold it was, she can literally be the bearer of the torch by passing it to the next set of characters ... in this case, a living baby.

I thought Jamie could be in the opening scene so at least we see what's happened to her and at some point in the film she passes on. Literally, the torch she passes on in this film is this child. And Mr. Akkad took to that idea right away. He thought it was a great way into this movie, with this baby, which Jamie would give birth to at the beginning of the movie. And I remember the way I got them behind the idea is by referring it to as *Halloween* meets *Rosemary's Baby*. And that somehow this child, this innocent, has something to do with continuing the bloodline of Michael Myers. And that's why no one's heard from Jamie in six years.

She's developed into a young woman, and they've incubated her, these people ... who really are there to protect Michael Myers; not so much control him. They kind of have these bizarre pseudo-religious beliefs, whether they're true or not. I saw this cult as a kind of Heaven's Gate group or secret society that has been steeped in their belief system for so long that they have really come to believe that the murders and the blood sacrifices are God's way of preserving a natural balance and order. And from the earliest days, it is true that sacrifices were part of what would evolve into our modern Halloween traditions. Whether these things are true or not really doesn't matter. You can't argue with true believers. But they look at Michael as sort of this avatar, a deliverer of these sacrifices. He may just be nuts, but these particular people see him as something far more. Ultimately, we thought most of the town of Haddonfield would be in on this secret society. We were saving that reveal for *Halloween 7,* but decided initially to center the cult around the staff of the Smith's Groove Sanitarium where Michael's been confined all these years.

So, in answer to your question regarding Danielle Harris, at first they didn't want the character and I sold them on bringing her back. And when I did, they went out very quickly and started looking at actresses for the role. And Danielle came into the casting director's office and said, "What are you doing? This is my part, and I'm going to play it. I am going to see this through." And they were shocked because they didn't expect that she would want to do the film. But of course, more than pleased that she came in and said "Hey, I'm in." So, that was the beginning of that. So, as I was continuing to write the script, I wanted to make the role juicier for her. So, the way I wrote it in the original draft, the one I was happiest with, was that Jamie lived until almost the end of the film. It was always agreed that she would not be the center of the action.

But she was there at the beginning, and then put out of commission for the majority of the movie. Basically, she's mortally wounded and ends up in the hospital. But by the end of the film, even though she's severely injured, she comes back for one last battle with the Shape. And she does it in a very heroic way. She did it in a way where she would fight Michael, not only to save her baby, but so that it would allow time for the other characters [Tommy, Kara and Danny] to escape. The idea was that Jamie would've shown up in the tunnels beneath Smith's Grove at the end of the film, the same place she had escaped from with help from the nurse at the beginning of the film.

Jamie shows them the way out. But by now she's so injured, she knows she's not going to make it. So, in a final showdown, she puts up this huge heroic battle to the finish with Michael Myers. She dies in the scene, but I thought that would be so fantastic not only for the character but for the audience. You know, she made it, not literally but figuratively. Jamie fights to the end. She lived and died a hero. That's the way it should have been done.

I would love to have seen that.

I would've loved to have seen it too, but they just decided they didn't want to feature the character that much. I think it eventually became an issue of money. And I can't blame Danielle for stepping down prior to production. I don't think anyone blamed her, even Mr. Akkad. But the studio just wasn't willing to pay her as a featured character. I think they wanted to pay her basically a weekly rate, which is ridiculous. I mean, she's on the poster for *Halloween 5*! She was the character the audience identified with. I remember we were all really disappointed when she dropped out, but we understood her reasons. So that began a whole new series of changes in the script and cutting back on everything to the point where all of the things I thought were exciting and special about it slowly started to disappear. It was really disappointing.

What can you tell us about the actress who did end up playing Jamie, J.C. Brandy?

J.C. was a real pro and a lot of fun. She had to go through a lot physically for the role, and it literally was freezing when she had to run around in the dark in this pouring rain wearing nothing but a hospital gown. It really was rough on her, but she was a total trooper. She really is a huge *Halloween* and John Carpenter fan. In fact, I remember she would come to me during breaks and point out all of what I thought were my cleverly-concealed John Carpenter references throughout the script. Like the "stomach pounder" Tim Strode refers to in the breakfast scene. That's right out of *The Fog* and J.C. immediately got it. I felt bad that the fan reaction to her was so negative. I guess it's never fun stepping into another actress's shoes, but I think all things considered, J.C. did a great job.

Any other notable actors we didn't see?

Well, the role of Tim's girlfriend Beth, I know one actress who auditioned... and one who I and Malek Akkad thought would be really good, and who was even willing to do the nudity at the time was Denise Richards, but the studio passed on her. They said she was "all boobs," and I thought, "Well, isn't that the point?" (laughs)

Well, one thing I hope was in your script from the beginning, the character of Tommy Doyle. Let's talk a bit about that because you started introducing a lot of characters from the original film, such as Dr. Wynn and Tommy Doyle. Where did that all come about?

That was always just me. One of the first things I pitched was, let's bring back characters we know. What I really wanted to do with this film was make it the one that takes all of these little threads... although it doesn't necessarily do it very well in the final version! But the original intent was to bring together all of these threads from the previous films; not only from the original *Halloween*, but also the characters and plots of *4* and *5*. And tie them together in this one film, so they're all existing now in the same universe. Whereas before it was about Laurie Strode.

And with this one, I wanted to bridge all of that. And initially, it was going to be both Tommy and Lindsay from the original film as boyfriend and girlfriend. And Tommy would have run this pirate radio station out of the college. It sort of evolved from there. Having the radio element obviously. But if I remember correctly I think the producers were more interested in having Tommy return as this really strange, reclusive guy. I mean, his arc is virtually the same as Jamie Lee's character in *H20*. He's a survivor of the original massacre who's been completely traumatized by this event. So, the turning point toward the end of the second act was Tommy having to stop running and confront his childhood boogeyman all over again. But again, as the script developed, we just kept losing more and more of that.

My original draft had all kinds of flashbacks to the original movie. Like when Kara and the little boy are screaming and pounding at the door "Please! Open the door!" It should have been this insanely déjà vu moment for Tommy. It's the same event all over again -- seventeen years later. And so there would have been flashes in Tommy's mind to his childhood ordeal. All of that stuff got kind of lost. But it was always my intent to bring Tommy in. He's a great character. I liked Paul Rudd a lot. And I think it was a great way to bridge the original movie with the sequels. The intent at the time was to make Tommy into the successor for Dr. Loomis. Have Donald [Pleasence] pass the torch to Tommy. There was a lot of torch passing in *Halloween 6* ... except no one could seem to hold on to it! And of course, he [Pleasence] unfortunately passed away. We thought what a great in if we've got this other (younger) character in Tommy who has become as obsessed with Michael as Loomis was.

We thought Tommy could bring this voice of sanity, a kind of modern Van Helsing, the fearless Michael hunter! I think that's what the last two films were missing was a character like Loomis or Tommy ... someone to track Michael and give voice to this evil within him and to provide a sort of moral core to the stories, as twisted as they may seem. The thing I liked about the early films was there was always this theme of good vs. evil.

Speaking of Donald Pleasence, as a huge fan yourself, was it a thrill for you to think while writing the script, "I am writing Dr. Loomis's dialogue!?"

It was so amazing that it almost paralyzed me. (laughs) I just couldn't wrap my brain around the idea that the Donald Pleasence was going to be saying these words ... my words. And they were never good enough. Literally, I would sit there for hours and days. And remember, I was under an insane deadline. I was getting calls every day. I had less than a month to write that first draft. Actually, maybe it was two weeks. So, it was an incredible amount of pressure but also the pressure of wanting to do this well. Knowing that one of my idols was going to be in this film. Knowing that these lines had to have a certain weight.

I had lobbied for so many years telling Mr. Akkad that I'm the one who can do this. And now it's like, "Ok, kid, go do it!" Here I was being asked to write for this incredible actor who had really been the lifeblood of this series and hundreds of films before. I just kept thinking, "How do I do this? I'm not worthy!" Finally, I just did what I thought was best. And I wanted to give Loomis an arc. Start him as a different guy. It starts with him in seclusion, and he's retired and he's kind of put the insanity behind him, but not really. Secretly he's been writing a book about Michael and is basically pulled out of retirement to hunt down his patient one last time. I thought that was a great way to start with him. Start him in a place of relative peace and end up right back in hell. The amazing and gratifying thing was that when Donald read the script, he truly loved it. He said it was by far the best *Halloween* since the first and he was thrilled to be a part of it. So, for me that really was the ultimate validation, and I will never forget it.

Unfortunately, he passed away a few months after the first shoot. After that, things began to devolve rapidly. My idea was always to end the movie with this incredible battle for Michael Myers' soul between the good doctor and the evil doctor and that was really what it was building to in the script. I had written the part of Dr. Wynn with the idea of casting a serious equal for Donald. I never thought anyone would get the reference to the original (except J.C., who got it right away). But I think it's great that the die-hard fans knew right away that it was supposed to be the same Dr. Wynn from the original movie. And I went back to that line where he says to Donald Pleasence, "He didn't know how to drive a car." And Loomis says, "Maybe someone around here gave him lessons." And I thought, let's literally go with that. Wynn and his staff really did give him lessons! And there was even a reference to that line in the finale of my original script where Wynn is sort of explaining to Loomis what's basically been going on under his nose all these years. And he says, "We even taught him how to drive a car."

I never imagined this secret society to be anything like the *Temple Of Doom* version they shot. I imagined it to be much more relatable, like the Satanists in *Rosemary's Baby*. The scary part of it is they could be the nurse, the guy working at the bus station, or the old lady across the street. And I thought that was a very scary idea. So, Dr. Wynn as I had written him, was a much bigger character and I had begged the producers to offer it to the actor I had in mind as I was writing. I actually wrote the part for Christopher Lee.

Wow!

This is perfect because you have two amazing horror character actor veterans. Two giants in one movie.

Wasn't he one of the people Carpenter originally wanted for the role of Loomis in *Halloween*?

That's exactly it! That story didn't come out until much later, but I'd heard Christopher Lee was offered the role of Loomis and he had always regretted not taking it. So, I thought, here's our opportunity to bring him into the series! And the reaction I got was pretty much, "He's too old. Nobody knows who he is. And it doesn't really matter." I thought "What the hell are you talking about!?" And now of course, a decade later, he's in *Star Wars* and *Lord of the Rings* and he's got a whole second career playing the ultimate bad guy.

Donald Pleasence, to me, deserved to be on screen with a contemporary. Someone in his league ... not the guy from *Lethal Weapon*! That was just another thing I remember being shot down and standing there thinking, "you can't be serious?" Knowing in my heart that this was absolutely the right way to do this. And then having it made very clear that I wasn't the one calling the shots.

Christopher Lee as Wynn? That would've been fantastic!

Can you imagine him being revealed as the Man in Black? He had the right persona and the right build. And those gaunt, glacial features. He was just the perfect person to play off of Donald. Imagine seeing those two on film together ... in what turned out to be Donald's final screen performance? It would've been insane. For horror film lovers and all the way back to the Hammer films. And all those amazing films that they had both done. It would have elevated this movie to a place where no *Halloween* film had gone before. It would've been a class act.

What exactly are the differences between the final theatrical cut and the now infamous Producer's Cut? Is the Producer's Cut more along the lines of what you originally wrote or is it more of a first cut of the film?

It was supposed to be the final movie. It was what they intended to put out. It was a final cut. It was mixed. Everything was done for release. But it tested very poorly, which I completely understand why. It was terribly made, in my opinion. It was one of those things, where time after time, and not to get down on the director [Joe Chappelle] because he was a really nice guy. But just because you're a really nice guy doesn't mean you should be directing a particular type of movie.

The original director attached was Fred Walton, who did *When A Stranger Calls*, but he had to drop out, I think again, over money. I never personally got the sense that Joe cared about making *Halloween 6* as scary as possible. He just wanted to put his own stamp, his own style, on it. He didn't want it to be the next in this ongoing series. He wanted his film to stand on its own, or so he said when I would question him about things like, "Why is there no pumpkin in the opening title sequence?" Or "Why is the *Halloween* theme being played on an electric guitar?" Or "Why is the guy's head exploding on the fuse box?" With all due respect, I just don't think he got what sets *Halloween* apart from *Friday the 13th*. To me, *Halloween* should be about the suspense and the build up. It's not about blowing people's heads up. I didn't get it. I still don't get it. I don't know why they went that route with it. I always liked the way I pitched it, and I think the way the executive producers saw it ... as very classy, classic horror/suspense film. There's nothing wrong with continuing a tradition if it works.

So, the producer's cut is technically the final cut, and it just tested really poorly?

Yeah. The director and another uncredited writer would basically take the pages I turned in and toss them aside and start over. Then I think it came down to that they only had like a week to shoot all of that new material. And remember, this is after Donald Pleasence had already passed away. They had to sort of cleverly take the footage they had and infuse the new scenes into that. Dialogue was literally playing against someone who was not there, which was just creepy. I thought I was seeing a ghost one day. I went onto the set and there's this old man walking around with a cane and I thought, "Oh my God, it's Donald Pleasence." No, that's his double. It was very bizarre.

It came down to an element of time. The director was shooting stuff that, in my opinion, didn't need to be shot. And the crew was there on the final night of filming until 3 AM, and they literally ran out of time and couldn't finish the movie ... so here's what you get. And that's why you see a mask with a needle lying on the floor at the end. Because there was no time to shoot a real ending. Again, I'm not pointing figures. I think Joe's a nice guy and has done well for himself. But I just don't think he had an understanding of what makes *Halloween... Halloween.*

You were at the *Halloween* Returns to Haddonfield 25th anniversary convention. What was that experience like from your perspective?

It seems with anything, over time, people become a lot more forgiving. You learn more and compare it to the other movies that come later. Which, in the case of this series, have only gotten worse rather than better in my humble opinion. We got a great reception, and we did the Q&A panel and got a standing ovation after the little lady who played Mrs. Blankenship (Janice Knickrehm) recited her entire monologue from the film! She had somehow remembered all of it, so for me that was such a thrill. And so flattering. I actually thought that was one of the best scenes in the movie, because it's one of the few scenes that were actually all of my words. And it was shot, more or less, the way I had envisioned it. Intercutting that modern celebration of the festival going on as the old lady talks about the dark origins of the Druid festival of Samhain. And how amazing it was that she remembered all the words. I really loved meeting all the fans too, because at heart I'm just one of them. I thought Tony [Masi] and his crew did an amazing job.

I remember the theatrical trailer, which I still have on my original VHS of *The Crow*, where the film is called *Halloween 666: The Origin of Michael Myers*. Isn't there a story behind the title you guys ended up going with, which was obviously *The Curse Of Michael Myers*?

Well, that was never really the title, which is the weird part of that trailer. The only connection there is that the script some other writer had written before I came on the project apparently was called *The Origin of Michael Myers*. My script had no title other than *Halloween 666*. That was it. No *Curse of* or anything. I think Miramax needed to put a trailer out and they just threw that title on it. No one on our team ever called it *The Origin of Michael Myers*.

The title for *The Curse* ... well, I'll admit that it was my title. I remember going into the production offices in my pajamas. We were in Salt Lake City and they wouldn't lend me a printer for all of the new pages I was rewriting at the time, so I literally had to go down every morning after working all night and to the production accountant's office to use their printer to print the script pages. And they'd get mad at me! I was like, "How are you going to do the accounting on this movie if there's no script?" It was pretty funny. So, I'm in my pajamas and Akkad walks in and I'm looking like death warmed over, and he's in his suit smoking his pipe. I remember he kind of looked at me and I thought, "Where the hell have you been?" And he says to me (in Moustapha voice), "We need a title, Daniel, for this movie. What will we call this?" And I said, "Well, you know. This movie is cursed. So, why not just call it *The Curse of Michael Myers*." And he says: "Oh, I like this! This is good!"

And I didn't think he really took me seriously. I was half-asleep and sort of joking. But that became the title. And let's face it: it works. Oddly enough, we later were accused of copying the *Pink Panther* movies. Those were called *The Return*, *The Revenge*, and *The Curse*. And I guess that's exactly what I was thinking. So, no, just for the record, we did not copy the *Pink Panther* movies, although that's kind of cool. But I liked the *"blank"... of Michael Myers* subtitles. Because *4, 5* and *6* really are their own trilogy.

You did an excellent job on the *Amityville* documentaries for the History channel, which ended up on the fourth disc of the recent *Amityville Horror* box set from MGM. How'd those projects come together?

My involvement in Amityville began with an earnest interest in discovering what happened in this house and what this family experienced there and where are they today? It was those questions that led to the idea of doing a documentary. That in itself was a year-long process to get through. And to get the people who hadn't talked about the story in twenty years to come out and talk about it again.

George Lutz hadn't spoken about this in years. How did you approach him and convince him that your intentions for the documentaries were good ones?

It was a process. Getting to him was difficult. Finding and tracking him down was difficult. He definitely lived much like Dr. Loomis at the beginning of *Halloween 6*; which was in seclusion for many years. When we met, George was living a very quiet, off-the-media-radar life. The events of Amityville just were not part of his life anymore. He was busy fixing old cars and computers when I came along and said, "Consider this." For the record, he's far from the money-grubbing miscreant that he's been portrayed as in different stories and books by all these people who think they're experts who know the truth. The fact is that if George Lutz cashed in, and with all due respect, he's an incredibly nice and generous and funny man, he certainly would've ended up better off than he has today financially. A lot of people made a lot of money off of the *Amityville* story, including and especially the producers on the new remake. And the fact is, George wasn't one of them. Most of the money the Lutzes made went to lawyers defending lawsuits and this continues to this day. George and his family were, in my opinion, victims of the media. Their story was hugely popular at the time. I don't know if you remember the whole hoopla surrounding that from the 70s...

Well, I was just being born then. (laughs) But I remember a lot about it growing up and seeing the original movies.

When it hit, I remember this was the type of book that kids would bring to the school yard, and everybody would be reading it. And everyone was creeped out by it. And the Lutzes were this sort of typical American family from Long Island. I mean, you know what it's like, you live there. It's very much suburbia and the Lutzes were hardly media savvy. There was no CNN broadcasting twenty-four hours a day. It was a very different time. Today, if a story like theirs hit the evening news, I guarantee there'd be a dozen William Morris agents hounding them for representation. At the time, though, all they had was a local lawyer and a friend that worked at a hair salon giving them advice. It sounds amusing, but that's really all they had. They had fled their home with little more than the clothes on their backs. They were living at Kathy's mom's house when the media grabbed hold of the story. They had a nineteen-year-old intern from the TV station that they came to trust. These were the people they were in bed with, so to speak. These were not the kind of people that knew how to go out and make lucrative book and movie deals. So, I think, and pardon the pun here, when you sign a deal with the devil, it's for life. You don't get your soul back. I think that's what happened with this family. They were taken for a ride by the movie companies and the publishers. My impression of George Lutz was that he was a bit guarded at first, but when a relationship took hold and a bond was developed there, it was great. When I explained to him the intent of my project and that I would give him an equal opportunity to tell the story the way it happened, his reaction was, "We'd love a chance to tell this our way. To confirm that no one in my family ever said it was a hoax."

The thing I loved about your documentaries is that, between the editing and writing, you truly left it up to the audience to decide what they thought happened.

It was an absolute conscious decision on my part to do it that way, because I knew I was never going to convince die-hard skeptics that ghosts lived in this house. No matter what I say or the Lutzes say or how credible this family comes across, I can't take that stance. All I can do is present to you the differing sides, the opposing viewpoints, of the story and let you, as intelligent people make up your own minds. All I can do is present the story as they told it. And it seemed to be the right decision. Because over the years, the more it airs, we always get the same reaction: "I really liked that you made me make up my own mind." And let me tell you, the truth of this whole affair is difficult to get to and

to present, even after all of these years. There were people involved with our own show who did want to skew it. And I stayed really firm about it.

Although it was low-budget and done for The History Channel, the one thing I'm proud of with those shows is that it represented my work, that it was my vision. We didn't get everything we wanted. Of course, looking back, I wish there were things we had done differently or given more screen time to. But I thought at the time that if this one fails, it'll be because of me and not because of a bunch of people I have no control over. It was really my opportunity to direct something, produce it, write it and do it more or less my way, with the guidance of a group of very supportive producers. And it was great. I'm glad people enjoyed it. It was good enough for MGM to want to include on their box set. And the reaction from the majority of the people I interviewed sent letters saying how this was by far the most accurate account of the *Amityville* story ever done. Finally, someone told it how it was. There was no blood dripping down the walls. It wasn't George Lutz attempting to kill his whole family with an axe or attempting to...

I've read interviews with both you and George on a few websites. Did you see the *Amityville* remake together?

No, I didn't see it with him, but he called me right after he had seen it. And he and his friends and family were laughing and trying to have a sense of humor about it, as George always does. I think it's the thing that's helped him most through all of this. He said, "Well... they got two things right: We moved into a house on Long Island... and we owned a phone." (laughs) "That's pretty much it!"

Any problems while making the *Amityville* docs?

Problems? We had many problems. There were people that would not talk on camera. There were several interviews we set up and people just didn't show up. Interestingly enough, there were people in the community who would say things to us off camera. But when we asked them to speak on camera, they wouldn't talk. You know, about things they've heard about the house. Things that allegedly have happened there that people don't talk about. Maybe it's just certain folks trying to add to the mystery and the lore of the place. It was just interesting to me that they wouldn't say certain things on camera because they claimed they would be ostracized from the community. I'm not saying the house is haunted today. We weren't allowed inside. The owner wrote a very nasty letter to the president of A&E accusing us of trampling on his lawn and banging on his door. We never got within fifty feet of the house. So, we were very respectful to the people of the town. We spent a lot of money there. And we just did our job. I can understand in a way what they're saying. They feel that anything they say on the subject is only going to bring about more negative attention, but I think saying nothing brings even more attention.

If you ever got the opportunity to do another *Halloween* film, what would you do, or what do you think they should do to follow up on the series and make it interesting? Since inevitably there will be another *Halloween*.

Right now, I believe there is talk about remaking the original *Halloween*. Which is going to cause a huge furor among the die-hards. But they did it with *Texas Chainsaw* and it made a fortune and people seemed to have responded fairly well to it. What I would do? Well, my first answer is I would just stop! Call it a day. And let Michael go to the old people's home for retired slashers! But if they really wanted to make one and do it right, the only story left to tell, in my opinion, is the prequel story and intersperse that with a modern story. But I already told that story in the comic books.

That's right! You did the comics! I loved those first issues.

Thanks. That really was my pitch for *Halloween 8*. Invariably, it's an honor and very sweet each time I get a call from the producers when they're going to do another movie. They invariably call me and ask what should we do? If we bring you in, will you pitch us something? So, alright, here's what I think you should do given the last movie. When the opportunity came around to do a *Halloween 8*, right after *H20*, first my answer was just don't do it! You killed him, so don't cheat the audience. But then I started thinking about it, and I knew they had Jamie Lee Curtis for five minutes in the movie as a cameo. And I thought, wait, this could be really cool.

What if we know we have Jamie Lee but let's not let the audience know we have her for five minutes, and make it the big twist ending? You can play this movie out like a traditional *Halloween* movie, and I pitched it as a sort of wraparound, that Tommy Doyle had been accused of the murders from *H20*. He's been locked up for it in Smiths Groove. He's been basically treated like Michael Myers. He escapes very much like Michael in the original film. And he goes back to Haddonfield where Lindsay is living, as a reporter. And he holes up with her and they spend this long night going through the records and journals of Dr. Loomis. And through this, they learn of what happened all those sixteen years while Michael was locked up in Smiths Grove.

And so, we get to go back in time, ala *Titanic*. Not quite that epic, but going back to that early story of why Dr. Loomis was so obsessed with his patient. What was Michael doing during all these years of silence? And what happened between Michael and perhaps some of the other people in the hospital? And then you book-end that with the Lindsay and Tommy story. And ultimately what you find out is that Michael Myers has come back for them, or so we think, but at the end of the movie, the mask comes off ...and it's Laurie Strode. It's even sort of hinted at at the end of *H20* ... after she chops off his head, she's looking pretty deranged ... and breathing in an awfully familiar way!

Wow. Which essentially is what you did with the first two issues of the Halloween comic books.

That was pretty much exactly my pitch for *Halloween 8*, which eventually I ended up doing for the comics. Because I thought, if you're going to get Jamie Lee for five minutes, make it the best five minutes of the movie. Give it that *Sixth Sense* type of ending. So, people could walk out and say "Holy shit. You have to see this movie. I can't tell you why, but just go see it." Of course they didn't buy it. So instead, we got Laurie Strode falling off the roof of a mental institution with a knife in her back. Talk about a less than glorious end for an unforgettable character. I kind of found that insulting, that that's the way she would die. I'm sure there'd be fans who would have hated to see her as the crazed killer ... but it makes more sense than sewing Michael's head back on! It would have taken the story full circle.

I had initially been against the idea of remaking *Halloween*, but I don't know. Maybe a restart would be what the character needs. The sister plotline started with *Halloween II*, so it'd be interesting to restart Michael's motivations and make him what he was in the original.

Yep. In a way, what else can they do? They can't keep doing these sequels with these gimmicks. It's getting ridiculous. They have to get back to the basics of what made this character so scary. But I don't know. I think I would give it a good ten years. Let it sit on the shelf again. Let the sequels sort of die away. And then maybe consider starting over. Then again, Hollywood is about the money factory, and I think they want to cash in. And now that horror remakes are huge, why wouldn't they give the biggest horror movie of all time the same makeover treatment? I don't necessarily agree with it, but these are business people and I can understand why they would do it. But it's like that old saying. Just because you can doesn't mean you should.

DON SHANKS

Interviewed by Rob Galluzzo (10/05)

If you're a *Halloween* fan, then we're sure you already know that Don Shanks played "The Shape" in *Halloween 5: The Revenge Of Michael Myers*. Don's had an incredibly long career as an actor and stuntman. We sat down with him for a chat and he told us about first starting out in the movie business, the direction the *Halloween* series could have taken, and how he's got another "killer" role in his future. Read on for the *Fright* exclusive interview with Don Shanks!

What are your earliest recollections of the horror genre? And what was the first movie you remember really scaring you?

Well, I believe it was *Frankenstein*, when I was a kid. I had heard about it but hadn't seen it. I was pretty young when it was on TV, and then there were a lot of the Boris Karloff and Bela Lugosi films. *The Black Cat*, some that don't get shown as much, but they were scary. I remember seeing *M* for the first time with Peter Lorre, and I thought it was so creepy. I've always liked horror films.

What exactly motivated you to get into the movie industry? How'd you start out?

Actually, I started out as a special effects artist!

That's how a lot of people start out! And break in.

Well, I was doing a play at the Salt Palace. And I was playing a man who was sixty-five, and I was twenty-two at the time. So, I had done the prosthetic make-up, put on a bald cap, and put the gels on. And someone came back to compliment the show, and tell me how much they liked it, as I started to peel this stuff off. And they'd say "Wow, you look a lot different!" I'd pull this bald cap off and they'd see I had long black hair. And so, they were asking me about the effects, and I answered all their questions, and then about two months later, I get a phone call saying that there's a movie company in town. And they need someone to simulate someone being tore up by a bear. So, I thought "Ok." I asked if they also needed any actors, and they said they needed a Native American. Well, they were calling us

Indians then. (laughs) So, I said "Well, I'm part Indian." "Well, this guy has to be able to wrestle a bear." "Sure. I can do that." (laughs) And that's how I got started in movies. And that was *Grizzly Adams*.

And then from there I went to another series, with some films in between those two series. I was always considered what we'd call an "action actor" because I did my own stunts. I wrestle the bears; I do the falls. When I was in the theater, I taught stage combat.

It's safe to say you know how to kick a lot of ass! (laughs)

Well, yes, but it was staging. And believe it or not, I did a lot of dance. I took four years of ballet. I'm a terrible dancer, but it's very good exercise. This all kind of led into the movies and doing stunt work, along with doing other stuff.

Would you ever consider yourself a daredevil for doing your own stunts?

No, I wouldn't. A daredevil usually doesn't know where they're going.

... whereas stunt work is a very prepared thing?

You have to hit marks. I can throw a dime down on the curb and turn a car over and land right on that dime. If they want me to stop on that dime, I'll stop on that dime. We hit our marks every time. A daredevil, they're skilled, but they don't know if they're going to stop or where they're going to go.

Was there any stunt in your career that you were really nervous to approach doing? Or even one that maybe you're particularly proud of?

I've never really been that nervous about doing stunts. You prepare them, but there are some times where you don't know if you're going to come home that night. Because things can happen. It's dangerous enough. Yeah, I'm proud of them all. From the smallest fight scene to the biggest high falls and burns. But they're all about doing what you're supposed to be doing as a stuntman. Technically I started out more as an actor and I worked my way into doing the stunts.

Do you think it was easier to migrate to stunts because you're a big fellow?

Well, they always need a big guy for the little guys to beat up on. (laughs) If I beat up on the little guy, it doesn't look very good. But it's being able to take the punches and doing what you know how to do. I was a martial artist and I used to wrestle. So, it all works into it.

How'd you get cast as Michael Myers in *Halloween 5*?

The stunt coordinator called me up and wanted to know if I was available.

Then you met with the director and that was it?

Yep.

When you worked on *Halloween 5*, you hadn't seen the previous entries in the series, right?

Well, I had seen them, but it was years before. And I'd only seen *Halloween* and *Halloween II*.

Weren't you told not to go back and rewatch them, in order to do your own take on the character?

Yep.

How'd you approach playing the character then?

What you have to do, especially when you don't verbalize anything, is you have to internalize the part. You get the script. You read what's supposed to be happening and you try to imagine what you're supposed to be doing. And when you think about that, it changes your walk, it changes your attitude. It puts you into that character without saying anything at all.

I'm a big fan of *5*! It was the second *Halloween* I had the chance to see on the big screen. One of the sequences I love was at the beginning after you fall into the shaft and float away in the river. I think on the DVD you mention how difficult it was to work in the water.

Going into the water, we were going into a river that was all snow melt coming down from the mountains. So, it was thirty-six degrees, a little bit above freezing. We're also doing it at night. So, you lose your core temperature very easily. And where I had to catch myself, there was a little bend there that led into a processing plant. So, you go through the turbines. I put on a dry suit because it was too cold for a wet suit. The thing I didn't take into consideration was the mask. When water went under it, it didn't really vent out. So, it got very difficult to breathe, you can't blow it out, and I have to hit my target because if I missed it, I would've been in trouble!

Did they already have the Michael Myers mask for *5* or did they mold it to personally fit you?

Well, it's molded to my face, but a lot of it is Greg Nicotero, who did the special effects. The original mold is his face, but my head's a lot bigger than that. So, there's pieces of him and pieces of me, but the inside of the mask is molded to my face.

Obviously, you worked with the late, great Donald Pleasence, and you both got a little physical. Overall, how can you sum up working with Donald?

Well, he was the consummate actor. There was that one scene where he's talking out into the woods because he knows that Michael's out there. And I had wrapped for the night, but he came to my dressing room, and politely asked me if I'd stay. I said "Sure." He was having trouble really getting into that scene, so he asked me to stand in the woods. He said, "I just need to know that you're out there. I don't need to see you. But by knowing you're out there, it'd help." Because he'd tried it in rehearsal, and he wasn't able to focus unless he felt Michael was out there.

Donald Pleasence also had some of the craziest, wackiest dialogue in that particular film. I know fans love Donald in *Halloween 5*.

He was the type of actor where I'd come on the set just to listen to what he had to say. When he comes in through the house, and he'd just be talking, he just has that presence. I've always said too, that if you want to watch a good actor, then turn the sound off and just watch his eyes and face. He was very subtle about everything and very understated.

You worked with Danielle Harris on *Halloween 5*. She was very young at the time, and you spent a majority of the movie trying to kill her! How difficult was it to work with such a young actress on such dark material?

She was a sweetheart. We were buddies. She already knew the difference between the movies and reality. It'd be late at night, we'd be sitting there, and she'd be up on my lap, and I'd say "It's ok. It's time to play the killer." So, she'd get into it and start screaming, but then after it was over, she'd start laughing. She knew the deal. She was like one of the guys. She wanted to be part of everything. Anytime something was going on, she was always there, so we looked at her as a little person. But then she could turn around, be scared or cry.

Speaking of, I heard you say at one of panels last night that the part where you remove the mask and cry, you did completely on cue. You can cry on cue!?

Yep. It was a very difficult shot. On the [extreme close-ups], you can't move a millimeter, so they had to put a brace on my neck to keep me still. They hold your head in place, while they set the lights, and the camera. You can't move at all with this type of shot. While you're sitting there waiting to do this, it gets very uncomfortable, and when they yell action, you have to cry on cue. And they asked me if I could, and I could.

Not many people can do that!

It just takes a little practice, but you can do it. Besides, that's what we get paid to do. Not as stunt men, as actors. (laughs)

Although it was scripted that Michael Myers took off the mask and cried, did you read into that scene in any particular way? Maybe when you finally saw the film?

What was being described to us while we were doing it, and they never told this to Danielle, Dominique was telling me the Man in Black with the black boots and silver tips...

You played him too, correct?

Yes, on several shots. The reason they were showing Michael's face and not the Man in Black's face is because, in *Halloween 6* when they're driving away and they do a flashback, it was going to be my face. And I was going to play both parts in *6*. But you'd never see them together. In the car during that flashback, you'd see them separately. Sorta like *Fight Club*.

Interesting. Was that character intended to be Michael's brother? I think you mentioned something along those lines on the DVD.

It was meant to be his alter ego, like his twin brother. The thing about when they do the incantation... the thorn, they get that split personality. Through the druids, they get eternal life. But it's bringing everything back to life.

One of the things that cracks me up about Part 5 is they arrest Michael, he's in jail... yet they don't take his mask off. (laughs)

Maybe they were too freaked to take his mask off. (laughs) Actually, we shot it one way where I was just in the shadows without the mask and I was just rocking back and forth, and they didn't think that worked. So they said, "Put the mask back on." But they did shoot it both ways.

There were a lot of subtle hints to things in *Halloween 5* that were never truly explained. Other people eventually took over the series and continued, but you mentioned at a panel that Dominique had a clear vision of what *Halloween 6* was going to be. This is the first I've ever heard that.

See, he was supposed to be writing the screenplay for *Halloween 6*. Because *Halloween 4* led into *Halloween 5*, and *5* was supposed to lead into *6* where everything was meant to be explained. When she touches him, she sees what he sees. In *Halloween 4*, she goes a little berserk in the end. But as *Halloween 6* was meant to go along, she was meant to become Michael. And she starts doing what Michael does.

If Jamie was the original intended killer for *Halloween 6*, then what part would Michael or the twin brother (the Man in Black) have in it?

The whole thing was that he was there to do the explanation. The Man in Black, that is. He'd be the one that could talk. And they had called me about doing *Halloween 6*. I went out, and started promoting the film, started doing conventions. And everyone wanted to know about the Man in Black, but I'm not supposed to tell anyone. So, when they got different people to do *Halloween 6*, they totally changed it.

Well, it took a good five or so years from 5 to 6, no?

I don't think it took that long. At least not when they approached me about it. Danielle was supposed to come back. And apparently, they went with the production group that they had on *Halloween 4* - the line producers, all the coordinators and everyone involved with *4*. So, the people involved with part *4* were back, which is why they got George (Wilbur) back. But it was nothing like what they told me it was going to be. At least what I was told by Dominique. Dominique and Moustapha had a little falling out.

Dominique definitely brought a unique vision to the *Halloween* series with *5*. And there's certain elements of the movie I really like. What was it like to work with Dominique as a director?

Sometimes he was... a little weird. (laughs). Well, he was French and Swiss. Those were his primary languages. English was his third language. It was in his interpretation. Sometimes you wouldn't be sure exactly what he was saying. There was one time where I'm doing the kill with Ellie (Cornell) and he's trying to explain what's happening and it sounded kind of... erotic.

Were you and Ellie weirded out by that?

Yeah. And I just hated to kill her character off the worst.

She's a fan favorite!

Plus, she's such a sweetheart! And a great character.

What was it like for you to see the completed film on the big screen?

It turned out very good. Most of the time I don't watch the stuff I do. The first movie I ever did, I got second card. It was kind of exciting to see my name up there. When I came on screen, I looked to the floor and never looked back up! I did a series for years, and I never saw it.

A lot of actors say they're uncomfortable seeing themselves act.

I see things I do that I become self-conscience about, that no one else is going to notice. As a matter a fact, about two weeks ago, I saw a movie I did in 1991 that I'd never seen before. But I watched it and thought, "Hmm... I did a pretty good job!" (laughs) I'll watch the stunts as a coordinator, but that's because I'm seeing technically how they're done

and if they're cut the right way. It doesn't bother me. But to watch myself in a performance, I have no desire to.

After *Halloween 5*, did you follow the rest of the series?

Oh yeah!

Any particular ones either before or after Part 5 that stand out to you?

You know, they were all good for their own reasons. It's just that *Halloween 6* was tough, because of what I knew it was supposed to be. And the character I was supposed to be (the Man in Black) was completely different and to me, it didn't make any sense.

A few years back, I had seen you meet up with the rest of the Michael Myers actors for the twenty-fifth anniversary convention in Pasadena. What was that experience like for you? Was that the first time you'd met all the other Michael actors?

It was fun. One time, Dickie (Dick Warlock) got us together for a show in Cleveland, but it was just a little show. It was more of a get acquainted kind of thing. When we did the twenty-fifth anniversary, we had a lot more fun with it.

What do you remember best about that weekend?

You know, I enjoy meeting the fans. I'm not crazy about doing the autographs and all that, but I love being able to sit and talk to fans. If they want pictures, I can understand that. Sometimes at these events, they line people up and send them through, but I'd rather talk to them. Find out what they like. And it gives me more of an idea what I'd need to do in the future as an actor and stunt person.

I'm sure you hear plenty of stories about people's various memories to various films you've done.

Oh yes. Here's a story for you. I just had my wallet stolen in LA. I was at the airport and there was this one policeman taking my report. So, he's got the preliminary, and he asks, "What's your name?" And I tell him "Donald Shanks." He kind of looks at me and asks, "Don Shanks?" "Yeah." "Did you used to have long hair? Were you... the Indian in *Grizzly Adams*?" And I tell him "Yeah." So, he tells me this story, "When I was six years old, my dad took me and my sister to a personal appearance you did, and you signed an autograph for us, but you sat and talked to us, because we had a bunch of questions for you, about the bear, etc. Every morning, I see your picture! It's still on my wall!" (laughs)

(laughs) How surreal is that!?

Yeah. I mean, that was almost thirty years ago. But it's examples like that, because you took the time to talk to them and years later, they have that story. That's what's nice about this event (Monster Mania) because they don't run people in. They're allowed to ask questions and be part of the panels. Maybe this is the only time a lot of these people get to ask these questions.

What's the next film you're working on?

I'm doing the new *I Know What You Did Last Summer*, which they're calling *I'll Always Know What You Did Last Summer...*

Didn't you have your own title for the movie at the panel the other night?

Who Cares What You Did Last Summer? (laughs)

How'd that part come about?

Well, we'd just worked on *Bloody Mary*, which became *Urban Legends 3*. I coordinated it and doubled several people in the film. They (the producers) thought, "Well, Don does all this stuff, why don't we just make him the killer?"

Excellent. And you kind of resemble the Fisherman from the other two films.

Well, I can't give anything away, but you'll see in the film that it's a little bit different this time. It's going to be a lot of fun.

2006

OZ PERKINS
JAMES WAN
LIEV SCHREIBER
JULIA STILES
MIA FARROW
JOHN MOORE
ADAM GREEN
STEVE NILES
GREG NICOTERO
LIN SHAYE
GARY SHERMAN
DAVID ARQUETTE
KEN SAGOES

OZ PERKINS

Interviewed by Rob Galluzzo (3/06)

Fright fans, you're in for a treat! We caught up with actor Oz Perkins, most recently seen in the gory horror, slap-stick comedy *Dead & Breakfast*. He talked to us a bit about his experiences in both film and television, his brother Elvis; a musician who fronts the band Elvis Perkins in Dearland, and of course shares with us a few stories about his father, the late, great Anthony Perkins. Read on and enjoy!

What are your earliest recollections of the horror genre? What was the first film you remember really having an effect on you?

It's funny because, like most people I'm sure, there are a couple of horror films that worked their way pretty deep into my unconscious as a child. It's what they are built to do, after all, and I think that the genre's unique access to our subconscious, our secret fears and unspeakable desires, is largely the reason that horror films continue to attract such persistent audiences. Because of my dad's notoriety in the genre, we got a lot of things sent to our house. This was in the days before swag, so I'm talking about the occasional courtesy Fangoria subscription.

I never saw the film of *The Exorcist* until I was considerably older, but I did form a pretty developed obsession with a small color photograph of Linda Blair not looking so good. I guess I must have cut it out of one of the magazines. All I know for a fact is that the picture lived at the bottom of my toy chest in our summer house in Cape Cod. And every once in a while, and probably on a more compulsive schedule than I am able to recall here, I would dig down to the bottom, past the headless action figures, past the random puzzle pieces, past the jagged wood blocks, to where I knew this picture was. Looking at it freaked me out, disturbed my sleep, in turn disturbing my brother's sleep and everyone else's sleep, but I kept at it for quite a while.

A director who wanted to do something with my old man sent him a copy of *Cannibal Holocaust*, which even my old man thought was too much and so he threw it into the outside garbage bin. My old man was often pretty disturbed by effective works of horror art. I know, for instance, that upon finishing the novel *Red Dragon*, that he

had to get it out of the house, had to physically walk it out of the house and get rid of it.

You come from a family with a background in the industry. Your grandfather Osgood Perkins, and of course your father Anthony Perkins. Was it always a conscious choice that you would pursue acting?

I think that, to some greater or lesser extent, all kids want to be seen and heard and felt and understood. Ultimately, the entertainment industry caters to that original, base desire. I have a great friend David Seltzer, who wrote among a great many other things, *The Omen*, and what David thinks is that if all parents everywhere could somehow become experts at making their children feel loved and good about themselves, that there would be no entertainment industry. There would be no need.

My parents did a very fine job of making me feel good and loved, but even the most willing and capable adults are going to let some things slip through the cracks. And, of course, some adults in the industry are there in part because they didn't get everything they needed as children. Nobody really gets everything they need anyway, but in the case of my family, we all went looking for some of those missing pieces in the dreamy promise of the business. In the same way that a person can inherit high cholesterol from their folks, the desire to be magnified in the eyes of those who see them can also be a hereditary trait. I guess I have some of that.

Can you tell us a bit about your educational background? Is it true you majored in English? How'd this lead you back into acting?

As a senior in high school, I wanted to be Stanley Kubrick. More embarrassingly, I also wanted to be Tim Burton. I wanted to be a film director. Nothing impacted me as much as seeing *A Clockwork Orange* and the sudden realization that someone actually made this movie. Someone actually designed it. It happened on purpose.

Also, the moment at the beginning of *Beetlejuice* when the camera tracks over the whole town, finally settling on the little local church when a giant spider crawls over the roof and the camera pulls back to reveal that we are looking at a model of the town built by the Alec Baldwin and Geena Davis' characters. That moment was also hugely impacting for me for the same reasons. I saw, in this case quite literally, the giant hand of the director reaching down and forming what we saw on the screen. I was very into that. So, when it was time to apply for colleges, I tried for early acceptance to NYU film school and was lucky to be accepted. I did a year there, and then two non-consecutive semesters at USC film school but got thrown off when my dad died in 1992.

As anyone who has ever lost a parent knows, and I've lost two, it's a uniquely mysterious and disorienting thing to have happen. For a million reasons. Fortunately for me, our family had a lot of great friends who were more than ready and willing to help move us all along. Among them was Mike Nichols who, in case anyone doesn't already know it, is perhaps the most intelligent man in the country, certainly among the funniest and absolutely in the top tier when it comes to unrestricted generosity. He recognized that I was a little lost and he offered me a job as his assistant on a film called *Wolf* that he was preparing to make. He already had a bevy of eager assistants, and so it was more like he was just bringing me along for the ride. I had nothing to do but watch one of the greatest American film directors work. After four months of that, I found that returning to a classroom setting was a little out of rhythm. I think I ultimately made a good decision when I chose to try for an English major instead of pursuing film school. I figured movies would always be there for me and that we could reunite sometime later. In the meantime, it seemed a better use of my youth to read a whole lot of all the great works of all the great authors, and to learn the very underrated art of writing a good paragraph.

Do you remember anything about the *Psycho II* shoot or director Richard Franklin?

For me, the experience of *Psycho II* was mostly all about the world tour we took with the film when it opened overseas. We would go to all of these incredible foreign cities like Tokyo and Sydney and my dad would show up at the

theater and smile and shake some hands. I remember that my brother and my mom and I would wait at the back of the aisle, and that I was always anxious that we would get out of there before the lights went down. They made a habit of showing the original shower scene at every premiere and at the time I had never seen it. I just knew that I wasn't yet ready to do that, I guess.

A couple of times I did have to bear the beginning of the Hermann score, and the screeching of the violins before the doors swung shut behind us on our way out and that was more than enough for me.

Speaking of, when was the first time you had actually seen the original *Psycho* film? And what did you think of your father after seeing it?

It's funny because I really only have the recollection that I managed to avoid seeing it for so long. It seems like I should have a strong impression of when that all changed, but my guess is that by the time it actually happened, it just seemed like no big deal. It's probably the kind of thing where I was so surrounded by it all the time, with little bits and pieces crossing over into my consciousness that by the time it was all assembled as the actual movie, it was already mostly known to me.

I will say that I do try to get out and see it whenever they show it on the big screen in LA. It is a truly remarkable thing, and without relying on the obvious bias, what my old man managed to do in that picture is still, in my mind, one of the most dynamic performances of the era. And it always takes me by surprise. It's one of those things like Brando in *On the Waterfront* where he's in a totally different movie. There's that great bit where Brando is putting on the ladies' gloves in the scene with the girl, and it's like he's moved on from the scene he was playing with her and has ascended into his own little private heaven. I think the scene in *Psycho* in the parlor with the sandwiches is a little bit like that, too.

After *Psycho II*, you didn't do any official acting until *Six Degrees Of Separation* and *Wolf*, both in the early 90's. How'd you come to be involved in those projects?

I really should get someone, maybe one of the minor gods at IMDb, to take *Wolf* off of my resume. That was just Mike saying, "Hey, you have a SAG card, how would you like to make an extra seven hundred dollars today," I'm actually in there twice, once as a dude with one line (hilariously dubbed by some other twerp) at Jack's publisher's office, and then again at the end I'm one of the mounted policemen who arrives after the big showdown. They used my actual voice for that one, but not an angle of my actual face. *Six Degrees of Separation* was another nice little piece of nepotism in which the author of the play, John Guare (the other smartest guy in the world) was a friend of my old man's and had met me at my dad's last birthday party in New York a few months before he died. They couldn't cast this part so they sent me the sides and asked me to film myself doing the little monologue. I had never auditioned for anything before but got it together to videotape myself doing the pink shirt bit, sent it to the casting office in New York and, curiously, got the job.

After another short gap, you came back to do a few comedies including *Not Another Teen Movie* and *Legally Blonde*. From your experiences, what's it like working on a production for a "comedy." All fun and games or more difficult than it appears?

Legally Blonde was the first job I got under my own power, meaning that I auditioned like everyone else and got the job because they liked what I was doing. I'm proud of that film because, for whatever reasons, a whole lot of people loved it. I get more positive recognition from that than from anything else and it's always a good feeling to know that audiences liked what you did. I didn't really know much about what I was doing, and on pictures like that there isn't that much attention paid to you if your name isn't above the title. That was fine because I found a niche, or a groove, and really just let the needle spin on the record over and over again.

The director and producers kept liking it and kept calling me in to do more coverage, more reaction shots so I just kept giving them more of what they wanted. I guess they like it plenty because they ended up sticking me in the money shot of the film, the moment where the camera pans up from her feet to her face when she walks into the courtroom, the moment that really cements the conceit of the film. And there I am, every time they use that shot in a promo. It's actually kind of the shot that made Reese Witherspoon into the huge star she is. I wonder how she feels about having to share that particular frame with my goofy mug all the time.

Secretary was one of my fave films of the past few years. What's the one thing that stands out to you about working on that picture?

That was a cool film to be a part of. They didn't end up using a lot of what we shot mostly because they were smart enough to know that the film was about Maggie and James Spader, and not about the colorful but distracting supporting players. I had a lot of scenes to do but almost no dialogue to say, which I took as a mini-challenge that no one but me needed to know about. I was really into Steve McQueen then, and I was hooked on how in movies like *Bullitt*, he gave his dialogue to other actors so that he could just react with those eyes of his. So, I just pretended like everyone else had my dialogue and went through the movie like that, sort of secretly summoning the ghost of McQueen whenever I felt like it.

Nobody knew anything about this and likely would not have given two shits if they found out, but it seems to me that little private games like that are part of what make acting interesting, especially when you have no lines and are going to be cut out of the final print anyway.

How'd you get involved with *Dead & Breakfast*?

They brought me on when somebody else fell out for some reason. I knew a lot of the people involved so I think it was a relatively easy thing for them to think of me. During that time, I still owned the house I grew up in near Woodrow Wilson in the Hollywood Hills and made a pretty regular point of throwing big, completely impersonal parties there. Supposedly, I met the director Matt Leutwyler there at one of those things. Of course it's possible, but those parties were like long Shakespearean plays with hundreds of extras, broken up by the occasional intimate scene with someone I actually knew by name.

***Dead & Breakfast* has a really interesting visual style, switching between comic book panels and actual film, and including musical numbers. Were you aware early on of the vision that director Matthew Luetwyler had?**

I might be wrong about this, but I want to say that the cartoon stuff was added pretty late in the game. I think Matt (the director) realized that Zach Selwyn's songs were so funny and clever that he had to use them somewhere. Films like that are fun because there is a no holds barred quality to everything so that everything that works ends up in the movie, no matter how far out. At the end of the day, everyone wants their little film to stand apart from everyone else's little film and when you are dealing with such a time-tested and re-tested genre like the zombie film, you want to make sure you really have something to add, component-wise. In this case, we had some cartoons and a dance number.

***Dead & Breakfast* features a pretty fantastic all-star cast. Ever and David Carradine, Jeremy Sisto, Erik Palladino.**

How'd the entire cast get along during the production and who caused the most trouble? Our bet's on Erik!

Almost everybody knew almost everybody else before the shooting began, so the production kind of played itself out like a long, bleary-eyed paid vacation. We were all up to no good all the time. The whole cast and crew lived in a town about forty-five minutes south of San Francisco, one of those American towns that has exactly one Panda Express, one Target, one In and Out Burger, you get the picture. And we were all shacked up in one of those faceless Courtyard by Marriotts where every ashen-faced real life zombie corporate salesman hangs his hat for a night or two on his way to some other dead-end destination or conference.

Introduce a pack of Hollywood types with all of their booze and weed that we had driven down to us from Humboldt County, tied to a completely ass-backwards schedule (we shot all nights, so everything was reversed. eggs and bacon at 7am for dinner, that kind of thing) and you can begin to see what was going on. We were mostly just wrong all of the time and the second floor where most of us had rooms smelled like Trenchtown, Jamaica with visibility rarely exceeding three or four feet ahead of your nose. The hotel staff was into it. It was a good time.

You start out as the quiet, sympathetic character in _Dead and Breakfast_, and then become the lead zombie villain. How'd you go about creating the character of Johnny?

On low budget movies like this, or on any fast-moving production like a weekly episodic television shoot, there is no time scheduled for rehearsals or for any exploration of character. There just isn't any time or money for that kind of thing. It is rare in situations like this that an actor gets to ask the director anything and so it becomes up to the actor to figure it out the best he can and to make a strong choice about what they are going to do, one way or the other. A strong but bad take on a part is always preferable to having no take at all. With no take at all, you've got nothing to work with. So, it then becomes about who to ask. In my experience, the deepest source for information about character comes from the wardrobe artist. The costume designer.

The wardrobe department has detailed conversations with the director about the characters so that they can weave who the character is into what he or she is going to wear. They have made time for this kind of conversation and meetings between the director and the various department heads are scheduled and budgeted events. Makes good sense. In the case of Johnny, Matt had told the costume designer that he saw him as the nerd who

gets constantly picked on UNTIL he becomes a zombie and then all of a sudden, it's like he's finally captain of the cool kids gang. I thought this was a great take.

Once you have one clear idea, the rest falls into place. Knowing what I now knew, I could make educated guesses what his reactions would be to given situations. Being picked on was nothing new to him and at the same time, plenty of the offending people were going to get theirs.

So, Johnny lives in that kind of "just about to snap" place because that is ultimately where the story is going to take him. In the opening scene, I'm driving the RV and I'm supposed to give Jeremy Sisto a look in the rearview mirror. And it's the kind of thing where some of the takes were just too much and you don't want the audience, four minutes in, to be saying "Oh, he's the villain." That's when an actor starts asking for more takes, or starts begging the director to "not use take three, please, I don't want the audience saying, 'I bet he's the bad guy' in the first reel."

Your brother Elvis is an accomplished musician. What can you tell us about his musical background and have you both always been supportive of each other's careers?

My brother is a great artist. He's a singer/songwriter (check out his band Elvis Perkins in Dearland) and he recently finished an album which is, I think, deeply great. I was lucky to play some drums for him on that album, and it is a great kind of unspoken way to communicate with someone, to play music with them. Elvis' music is something everyone's going to hear, and I bet it will be soon.

You've done a lot of recurring roles in television. (_Alias, Close to Home, She Spies_) What are the differences in your experience between work in films and television?

Making a film, especially if you have a good part in something and work a lot of days on like I did with _Dead and Breakfast_, is a very fulfilling thing and if you choose to be friendly, it goes a long way. I'm a naturally friendly guy and on most movie sets, unless there is some palpable fucked up vibe, a kind of spontaneous family forms around you and being friendly makes work very nice. The process of making a film is something that everyone on board approaches as a shared product, a communal experience with a beginning, middle and end.

Television, if you do these guest star things like I have, is less personalized, somehow less intimate, especially because you are in and out of there in a week and the regulars practically live together. People just don't like to make temporary friends, and there is usually an unspoken sense that a regular is, in a way, not someone you can really become friends with. Their friends are all the other regulars. When it comes to being at work, and there is almost an impenetrable membrane around them. And that's not to say it should be otherwise, by the way; these people are invested in their work and in the characters' relationships and they kind of have to be the serious and professionals. No time for being too cute, you know? Now, I have made some great friends working on television shows, but they were all short-timers like me.

For me, and I know it's a useless point of view to have in this day and age, television still feels disposable. I know that it isn't, but the work feels a little disposable, like a single-serving razorblade or something, and that I just did it because someone had to and why shouldn't it be me who gets paid to perform this service, to be the serial killer of the week or the defendant of the week, or both, or whatever the script calls for. TV feels like a business to me, a little impersonal or something, and that most television is made just to fill in the spots between the commercials. That's extreme, I know. I probably sound like a real asshole. I just feel a permanence in making a film, like it's an actual experience, like it's actually something I'm creating.

What can we look forward to from you in the future?

It's such a relief to have an answer for that. I'm supposed to shoot a movie this summer called *The Utah Murder Project* with Amy Smart in which I play a dirty LAPD detective who gets wrapped up in his soap-star girlfriend's disappearance and possible murder. Sounds like a lot of fun and I'm excited about that. Also, I'm developing a coming-of-age slasher film set in the 1960s (developing means bleeding out of my forehead writing the thing), which I hope to shoot sometime next year. It's actually going to be something pretty special, I think. I hope.

JAMES WAN

Interviewed by Rob Galluzzo and Adam Barnick (6/06)

Icons of Fright were lucky enough to get a few words with *Saw* director/creator James Wan! His first film has already gone on to spawn two sequels (with *Saw III* scheduled for Oct. 06) and introduced the world to our latest beloved movie maniac, Jigsaw. Not bad for a first flick! He's currently finishing up his latest film, *Dead Silence*, and is gearing up for *Death Sentence*, based upon the Brian Garfield novel. Read on!

What are your earliest recollections of the horror genre? Do you remember the first film that really scared you or had an impact on you?

The horror film that has had the most impact on me, because I saw it at an early age, is *Poltergeist*. I think I was six or seven when my parents took me to see it. The cool thing was, my mum was a big fan of horror movies and she didn't have a problem with me seeing scary movies. The downside was, ever since then, I have had a strange fixation and fear of all things doll/clown-like.

Can you tell us about how you first got into filmmaking as a career? Did you pursue film school, or did it start even before that with a camera in the backyard?

Ever since I was eleven years old, I had wanted to be a filmmaker. I think even as a kid, I appreciated and loved the medium of cinema because it allowed me to utilize every aspect of art to tell a story. I went to an art college where I focused on filmmaking, which, in my opinion, was better than film school, because as an art institution, they fostered creative freedom and expression. It was here that I met Leigh Whannell.

When did your working relationship with Leigh begin? How do you write together and what's an average day writing with Leigh like in terms of process, hours, etc.?

Leigh and I didn't really start collaborating until we left college. We have a great working relationship, one that is very collaborative. Our working method is very simple. I

would come up with a thought or an idea, pitch it to him, and then he would take my idea and expand on it. We would just bounce ideas back and forth.

How'd you raise the money for that *Saw* short film? And who are some of the people you were able to turn to and depend on when you were trying to get *Saw* off the ground as a feature?

Leigh and I spent a year hashing out the *Saw* script and then another year shopping it around in Australia. There was interest in the project, but we couldn't find anyone who was willing to put up the money for it. Our manager then took the script to an agent in LA, who ended up loving the script and wanted to meet with Leigh and myself. At this stage in my life, my day job had just run out and I was flat broke.

But we thought if we were going to go all the way to LA, we may as well shoot a little short to accompany the script. We scraped together whatever money we had saved, roughly four grand USD, and shot the short in two days and edited it in three. We had very little hope for it or the script, as we touched down in LA. Two days later, we got the film off the ground.

You and Leigh are filmmakers from Melbourne, Australia. How'd you get the management/representation necessary to get his script seen here in the states?

Leigh had been acting since he was a child and has had the same representation since then.

There are some name actors in *Saw*, not typically found in horror films; Danny Glover, Cary Elwes. Were these actors you specifically sought out for *Saw* or did they come on board based on the material?

Saw does have an unusual cast for a horror movie. Because the producers themselves put in their own money, they wanted a certain pedigree of name to help sell the final product. Even if the material was a bit gruesome for some, there was always respect for the script and the ingenuity of the storytelling.

Some directors in the horror genre have said that working with a small budget can sometimes work toward the advantage of the final film. Besides the fact that you had such a short schedule and a tight budget on *Saw*, was this an obstacle for you at all? What was an average day like on *Saw*?

Saw was a tough, tough film to shoot. I wished I had a bigger budget to do the script justice. My vision for the film was a lot more than the $700,000 price tag allowed. What this meant was that every day became a struggle for me to not lose my spirit over the things I wasn't getting.

What was the initial expectation for *Saw* in regard to how it would perform financially? Was there a shock factor for you when it became a huge hit? How did you spend the opening weekend and what was your reaction when you saw the first weekend's performance?

At that point, I was so green to the process of 'opening weekends', I had no idea what a good opening weekend entailed. I remember the Friday it opened, it started out a bit slow and it wasn't until the late showings that the number spiked dramatically upwards. Even then, I still had no idea what it all meant, until I caught up with the producers at the Four Seasons hotel and they explained to me how well it was doing. It went on to become one of Lionsgate's highest grossing films. And to think that at one stage, there was talk about releasing it straight to video.

When watching *Saw* with an audience, where you surprised by the strong reaction? What's that like for you as the director?

It's an incredible feeling. Especially for a first film experience. I feel really blessed.

You had mentioned at a *Fangoria* Weekend of Horrors panel how you were disappointed with the color transfer on the original *Saw* release on DVD, hence the "director's cut" that followed. What exactly were the differences that you supervised between the original DVD release and the "unrated director's cut?"

I was back in Australia when the first transfer was made, so I wasn't around to supervise it. It's a lot more normal looking than the theatrical coloring, where the hues were a lot deeper and more saturated. I went back and corrected this for the director's cut. Overall, the director's cut has the gore shots reinstated, color and contrast corrected, put back Charlie's music that were replaced by the songs, and tightened one or two scenes at the end of the movie. Because I had to rush to get it ready for Sundance, there were a few editorial things that I didn't get the chance to do, so I addressed them in the director's cut. I think for the first time the director's cut is a bit shorter than the theatrical release.

Speaking of, you've made a few convention appearances as of now. What has the convention experience been like from your perspective?

Really amazing. I've always wanted to go to a horror convention and I finally got the chance to, thanks to *Saw*.

What can you tell us about your latest film *Dead Silence*? Where are you at with it, production-wise? When's the potential release date and what's it about!?

It's a story about a young couple receiving a mysterious package with a ventriloquist dummy in it, and death is brought with it. Our protagonist then heads back to his hometown where he believes the doll is from. There's an old legend here about the ghost of a ventriloquist who takes your tongue if you scream in its presence. It's not a gore movie. It's a creepy doll movie. It's in the spirit of those old *Twilight Zone* episodes or Hammer Horror Films. Very old school. The only thing missing is Vincent Price or Christopher Lee!

Now, my producer Gregg Hoffman, whom was a close friend, passed away unexpectedly at the start of the year. It was a very difficult time for me. The studio was kind enough to allow me some time off, and we halted production out of respect for Gregg. In doing so, I think we might have missed a window we were hoping for, which is fine with me, 'cos I'm still working on it, but close to finishing it off. I realized not every film is made at the maniacal pace of the *Saw* films.

Has there been a drastic difference working with Twisted Pictures as opposed to Universal? Being a financially successful filmmaker, are you able to do what you want to do on *Dead Silence*?

Haha. No comment.

Can you tell us anything about your recently announced project *Death Sentence*? And how's *Saw III* coming along?

Saw III is coming along really well. We're in the midst of production right now. It's pretty crazy how efficiently the *Saw* films are all put together. The trickiest part is always the script and story, and how much thought and effort are put into them. It's so much easier to do a sequel to one of those slasher-killer on the lose type movies. *Death Sentence* is the next project I'm working on. It's a raw and gritty, 70s styled revenge thriller. After the more subdued and atmospheric *Dead Silence*, I'm going back to the kind of intensity that *Saw* was and more character driven. It's my arthouse movie with guns. I see this film as a natural progression to doing movies outside of the horror genre. I love horror films, but I think it's also good to try something different.

THE OMEN PRESS JUNKET

LIEV SCHREIBER **JULIA STILES** **MIA FARROW** **JOHN MOORE**

Interviewed by Rob Galluzzo (6/06)

The following are interviews from one of the first major studio press junkets that *Icons of Fright* was invited to participate in. It was a big moment for us, and a turning point to being recognized for our respect and advocacy for the genre. A remake of Richard Donner's classic horror masterpiece, *The Omen*, was always going to be met with skepticism from loyal horror fans. Rob had the opportunity to sit with Liev Schreiber (*Scream*), Julia Stiles, Mia Farrow (*Rosemary's Baby*), and director John Moore to delve deep into why 06/6/06 was the time to release a new version of *The Omen*. We'd like to acknowledge and thank the other journalists from that press junket: Dave Bourgeois, Dave Basner and Chris Steible.

LIEV SCHREIBER

What was your initial reaction to the original *Omen*?

I was a big fan of the original. I thought it was one of (Richard) Donner's best movies. It's just so creepy and there was something about the psychological quality of the film and the perspective. I remembered a feeling of… the perspective of the lone gunman on the bluff. I remember there was a scene where the doctor and Thorn are talking about how his wife lost the child and he shot the scene from four stories up looking down a stairwell, and it had the effect that A) feeling like you were privy to a conversation you shouldn't be privy to, and also B) the feeling that you were being watched and maybe we were the watchers. There was also a wonderful way in which the vulnerability of Thorn in that moment was shown. He was

allowed his privacy to have that very painful conversation. It wasn't a particularly violent film and yet it was really, really haunting and creepy.

I had read that, because of your love of the first film, you were a little skeptical of doing this remake. What was it about director John Moore that convinced you that you wanted to be a part of this film?

I think John definitely convinced me. And to be fair, I'm skeptical about everything I do. Always. John was able to convince me of the validity of the story and the value in updating it, and why it could be as effective now in 2006 as it was in 1976. I think there is no coincidence that genre films flourished in 1976, in particular films like *The Omen*; it felt like it was the tail end of the Vietnam War and during disturbing domestic violence in America. There was something being vented by that film, and I think the conditions are again like that in 2006.

So, it's quite relevant to what's going on in the world now?

I think so. Yeah.

In the original, Gregory Peck was a lot older of a character and it seemed like he came from a different kind of wealth than from where your version of Robert Thorn came from. Did you go back and look at his work from the original? After seeing his great performance, how did you prepare for your version of the character?

There's no way in a million years that I can run the risk of reproducing the quality of Gregory Peck's performance. Having been through that before with Laurence Harvey on *The Manchurian Candidate* and perhaps Orson Wells on *RKO 281*, I've certainly made my peace with playing these characters. If you respond intuitively and honestly to the story, you're going to make it your own. That's just the nature of acting. But there were things about his performance that I was influenced by. Part of that, and maybe I'm projecting over from *To Kill A Mockingbird*, but he brings a tremendous amount of credibility and dignity to the parts he plays. The idea of a guy who essentially is trying to be good against some very powerful odds stacked against him.

How was it working with Julia Stiles?

It was cool. We had done *Hamlet* before. And in that we had played brother and sister, so it was a little kinky this time playing husband and wife. (laughs) But it's always easier to work with an actor whom you've developed a shorthand with. And I think that went a long way for us.

How was it working with child actor Seamus Davey-Fitzpatrick as Damien? Did he have any understanding of what was going on in the film?

I don't know how much he understood, because I didn't feel it was appropriate to discuss it with him. For me, it was about what game we were going to play that day to accomplish what we needed to accomplish to film the scene we were filming. And that usually involved some inwardly painful version of 'Gotcha Last' where he would punch me in the stomach. And when John said "Action," he would continue from where we left off last, so it was fun. Probably more fun for him than it was for me. (laughs) You have to find a way with a seven year old kid to make it fun or you're not going to get through the day.

How was it working with Mia Farrow on this project?

Pretty great. Billie Whitelaw was so terrific in the original, but the minute she walked into that room and said "Hello, little one. I'm here to protect you," you knew it was bad news! There was something about Mia Farrow that she has this angelic, luminous beauty that sort of reeks of innocence. I thought she was a really great choice, playing along with the idea of the embodiment of evil taking on a very innocent face.

I thought you and David Thewlis, who played Jennings, had such great on-screen chemistry for the second half of the picture. Did you guys know each other before? How'd your on-screen chemistry come together so naturally?

I certainly knew him, I don't know if he knew me. The reality of that was the first week around David, I was on pins and needles. I had seen him a few summers ago in a film called *Naked*, and for my money that's one of the greatest film performances ever. I was just shocked and awed when I found out I was going to act with him. So, the first week I was pretty nervous, but then on this movie, these great actors just kept coming and coming. Pete Postlethwaite and Michael Gambon and Mia Farrow. It was just one after another, actors whom I'd admired and never dreamt of working with.

I was really excited when I heard that you were cast in this new version of *The Omen* because I knew you'd do justice to Robert Thorn and I think you did.

Thank you.

Do you have any personal beliefs about the whole current chaos in the world and what is said in the Book of Revelation? Do you see any connection there yourself?

Well, not being Catholic myself, I thought it was important to familiarize myself with the New Testament, in particular the Book of Revelation and also, to make a decision about who Robert Thorn was and what his background was. I thought it would be effective if you approached that character from the perception that he was a lapsed Catholic, so that he would have an emotionally charged relationship with Catholicism and then a stronger resistance to believing in it.

One of the things I really love about films like *The Omen* is the ten minutes after you walk out, and you have to think "Well, it's just a movie." I think it's an important thing to remember about films like these. I like the idea that it's so preposterous, because I think there are parallels today of ideas that are just as preposterous. It's important to support faith and to respect people's faith, but you need to draw a line at the loss of human life. That's the paradigm that this story explores, that I think is provocative and interesting.

Are you typically a fan of the horror genre?

No. Frankly, I can't really watch them because I get scared! I'm a sucker for films. I love films. And I buy into them very quickly. I like watching them with other people to see how they react because it's easier to separate the reality by thinking "Oh, they're scared too." For some reason, a lot of my work keeps leading to this genre.

JULIA STILES

Do you remember your initial reactions to seeing the original *Omen* and how that film impacted you?

Yeah. It stuck with me for a long time after I watched it on video. The imagery is really powerful. And also, I think a really good horror movie doesn't rely on the violence so much, when there's something deeper going on psychologically. Those are the types of horror films that really stick with you, and the original *Omen* is very much like that. Then, when I was thinking about doing this remake, I watched it again and there was a scene where Lee Remick is asking to see a psychologist, and you can feel that she's so tormented underneath, that it's suppressed. That moment was really interesting to me, and I really wanted to explore that more.

And you did a great job. How'd you feel about Mia Farrow coming on after you'd just worked with her in a play?

I was really excited to work with her again. On the one hand, it was wonderful, because she's a talented actress and I've learned so much from her. She's also just a wonderful person. But it was very confusing and strange, because we went from playing mother and daughter, to two weeks later, we're in Prague and she's trying to kill me. But it was great. We were in the rehearsal room while we were doing the play, and she burst in saying "John says hi!" My dad's name is John, my brother's name is John, so at first, I had no idea what she was talking about. I guess, she was on the phone with John Moore and she had just decided to do *The Omen*, which was a good indication to me that I was on the right track.

Lee Remick was a lot older when she played the character, and you're doing a younger version of Katherine Thorn. Did you try to separate yourself from what she did?

Well, I think there's no way I could've done her performance. I had to quickly get over the inevitable comparisons. There's no way I could compete. But John (Moore) instilled in me a sense of freedom to make the part my own. And also, the circumstances are different this time, and I think it works really well that I'm a young inexperienced mother. Because a more mature woman would be able to assert herself and be able to stick up for herself. And part of what I wanted to explore in the update was all the guilt and confusion my character feels, and how her first instinct isn't to be afraid of her son, but to doubt her own maternal instincts.

You mentioned before that you had worked with Mia on a play, and you were in *Hamlet* with Liev (Schreiber). Was it easier jumping into this production already having a bit of a rapport with the main actors?

Again, the circumstances were so different. Liev and I played brother and sister in *Hamlet*, and in this we're playing husband and wife. But what helps in knowing the other actor already, they can sense when you're "acting" with a capital A or being false. I really love working with Liev. I thought he made me stronger in the scenes we were doing, and of course, I learned a lot from him.

One of the most memorable sequences in both versions was Katherine's fall. You actually did that stunt?

I did. I was very nervous about doing it. Normally I'm a daredevil, especially on a movie set because I have this naive idea that everything is safe on a movie set and protected. But I had noticed that they had scheduled that scene for my last day of shooting. You always hear these stories about "the curse of *The Omen*" or just bad things always happening on the set of horror films, so I thought "Oh great. Last day, doing this stunt. We're tempting fate."

But I was rigged to a decelerator machine, so I would stand thirty feet up in the air, and they would drop me backwards down, and I'd actually hit the ground, but the machine lets you free fall and just before you hit the ground it sort of stops from hitting it with full force. So, the rehearsals I was terrified! But after a few takes, it became really fun. And it's a memorable scene in the original, but what's interesting is that it's totally different technology. The original, they put the floor on the wall, and Lee Remick was on a dolly track and rammed against the wall.

It's beautifully shot, with all the rose petals. It's very graceful for such a terrible thing!

That's all John Moore. His idea.

Can you tell us a bit about working with John? You were one of the first people cast. How'd he convince you that he could pull off a new version of *The Omen*?

Talking to him is what convinced me. I was very intrigued. I thought the script was great. The story was great. But when I met him, I asked him how he was going to handle everything, because the script was very relevant to a modern day audience. It made reference to different catastrophes that are happening these days and I asked how he was going to handle that. I was so pleased that he didn't give me a diplomatic answer. He was so bold and opinionated. I thought he'd make a good leader for this production.

Well, this is your first "genre" picture. Do you consider yourself a fan of horror films?

I am a fan of horror films that don't rely too heavily on violence, and focus more on psychological aspects or the story, which is why I'm such a fan of *The Omen*.

Any personal favorites?

Psycho is a perfect example. Even though most people remember it for the shower scene, which is a very violent act. The reason that movie is so great is because Norman Bates' psychology is so fascinating. Other favorites? *The Shining*. Again, an example of a strong character who's trying to understand what's going on in his own head.

MIA FARROW

Do you remember seeing the original *Omen*? What kind of impact did that film have on you?

Not much of an impact really. I remember Billie Whitelaw, I had seen her in some Beckett plays. So, for an actor of my generation, she was sort of iconic. She was like the original portrayer of Beckett plays in England. I remember being really scared by her performance.

Did you re-watch the original *Omen* before working on this remake?

No, I didn't. But I asked John (Moore) "Why me?" I loved Billie Whitelaw's performance and I loved to be scared by her! She was awesome in that original movie. And he said, great as she was, he didn't want this character showing her hand so early in the movie. Who would hire a nanny like that? (laughs) Let alone keep her on the payroll! So, my job, when I come in, is to convince the couple and the audience that I'm no threat!

You come into the film as a comforting character, but of course later on, you start to play it with such sinister glee. Acting-wise, was it fun to go from those two extremes with your character?

Really fun! The first scene I shot for the movie was out in the rain with the croquet mallet. (laughs) And after that, it was a real ice-breaker. It was like "Hi. Everyone. How are you doing? Oh, this is my mallet? And this is the car? Ok!" And after that, I couldn't embarrass myself further so it was completely liberating starting out with that scene.

I happened to just see *Rosemary's Baby* recently, and now seeing these two films, it's kind of eerie in a way. I mean, they are different films, but your character at the end of that film sees the baby and seems to be OK with the devil baby. So, when you were acting in this film, did you ever think back to *Rosemary*?

Not until I came to this press junket! (laughs) I didn't realize it was close. I was doing a play with Julia right before this film, and I got the call. And I thought that Julia had mentioned me. And for all I know, maybe she did. And then John said "I want you to do this," and "I want someone who's angelic." And then he mentioned Liev, and I think Liev is the Laurence Olivier of today! I was so focused on this play we were about to open, which was James Lapine; Pulitzer Prize winning James Lapine. Very demanding roles for all of us. So, I wasn't thinking at all of *Rosemary's Baby*. I mean, whole decades go by that I don't think of it. So, I didn't think of it at all! It was more like "Oh, cool. I'll go to Prague! And Julia will be there. And I can't wait to meet Liev! Awesome!" I brought two of my sons with me and Prague was just an adventure. Then, I get here and everyone's asking, "Are you the queen of the horror movies?" (laughs)

It's just kind of weird! It's almost as if that character in *Rosemary's Baby* has grown up a little bit and become this nanny! Maybe I'm straining to make some sort of connection there.

Well, I respect that! Rosemary was a victim. And this person is not. It was very different in coming to this role. I will say though, what is similar is the idea, the personification of evil. And maybe *Rosemary's Baby* was one of the first to have this notion of "the anti-Christ," being born to a woman. I just hope this is a good, scary movie. But the idea as a parent, and a grandmother, I think it's valuable to think of evil, not the way as I was taught, but as an influence. I was brought up a Catholic, and evil was the devil. A little character that sat on your shoulder and told you bad things. And you had the angel on the other side whispering "No, don't take that cookie!" And that's what the devil was. I think the dual nature of human kind is everywhere.

I think it's more valuable to think of evil as not as this little devil on your shoulder, but that the enemy is within. I'm in favor of genocide education. I have seven sons. Most of the aggression on this planet is coming from men, victimizing woman and girls. I'm going to the darker region of Sedan on the seventh of this month.

I tried to bring up all my children to be aware that this is a human component. It's within all of us, the capacity for terrible things. And it's about the decisions we make and it's about the responsibility within our family, within our society, within the human family. Ultimately, my personal feeling is just some higher order, and that we are accountable. It isn't so far-fetched to show an angelic looking child as the personification of evil. Not totally. There's the dual nature. It's misleading to think of evil as something else.

How was it working with Julie Stiles on a film production as opposed to a stage production?

I love her so much! I played her mom (in the play) and we had such a great time. And then we ended on a Sunday night and then Tuesday I'm in Prague up to no good! (laughs)

You played her mom, and then you tried to kill her in the very next movie!

Yeah! A few days later. I've gotten so fond of her, and she's become practically a family member. She and my son Ronin are really close. And I care very deeply about her and her boyfriend. It's always great working with her.

You spent a lot of time with Seamus (Davey-Fitzpatrick), who played Damien. What was it like to work with a child actor, while the content of the film itself was rather dark?

He was flying paper airplanes in the hallway and his best buddy was his stand in, who'd sometimes substitute for him

when there'd be shots of the back of him. He was a little boy of identical proportions to Seamus. And by the end of the movie, Seamus could speak fluent Chez, and because of his little best friend who was his stand in. They'd always be intensely into their games, so I don't think Seamus knew anything about what was going on in the movie. He was just so cute and so much fun. And so smart. I loved him and he has wonderful parents too. Maybe in ten years, he'll understand the movie. (laughs)

He's just a regular kid, with a lot of energy and he's super smart. I doubt he'll become an actor. I couldn't see him following with acting considering how smart he was. I worked with Freddie Highmore this year (of *Charlie and the Chocolate Factory*, *Finding Neverland*) on *Arthur and the Minimoys*. Brilliant actor! But little Seamus is still just a kid. A great kid.

Director John Moore seems to have a passion for this particular film. Can you tell us about working with him on *The Omen*?

I think he's just a really passionate guy anyway. And he's a fellow Irishman, so we clicked right away on that level. Well, when you'd do a scene and he liked it, he'd be behind the monitor screaming "Yes!" He's such an enthusiast. He's passionate about what's going on in the world, and the political situations. And he's a visionary. You've got to love him.

JOHN MOORE

What are your earliest recollections of the horror genre? Do you remember the first movie to really scare and have an impact on you?

The first movie to really scare me wasn't a horror genre picture, it was *Jaws*. The first time I really got scared witless was when I saw *The Omen*. *Night of the Hunter* and *Freaks* really disturbed me too.

How'd you get the gig to direct a new update of *The Omen* and were you skeptical at first of taking it on? Or did you know right off the bat that you could deliver your own vision for *The Omen*?

Fox, who I have made two other films with, called me about *The Omen* and I said yes straight away. Some might think it was foolish or weird doing another remake, but I didn't give a damn. It's *The Omen* for God's sake! I wasn't skeptical, but

I was a little nervous, but once we actually got into the nuts and bolts of making the film, that subsided.

Do you remember your initial reactions when you saw the original *Omen* and the impact it had on you?

Very much so. I saw it broadcast on television in Ireland in 1979, so I would've been nine years old. And I thought I was too old to be scared of the dark, but after that film, it regressed me a couple of years! (laughs) I was terrified! I really thought that they killed David Warner. This is the era before video where you could slow it down and see how they did it. And I had no concept of how they must have done that. So, I thought "Fuckin' hell! This is why no one wanted me to see this! Because they kill a man in the movie." So, yeah, you could say I was profoundly affected.

Well, let's talk about that scene in the new version for a minute with David Thewlis. (SPOILER) How'd you arrive at the way that death played out in the new movie? I assume you didn't want to do exactly what was done in the original, and instead mix it up a bit?

I struggled, because all the set pieces in the original are just so damned good. They all follow an excellent rule of perceived coincidence. It's interesting with all the killings in *The Omen*. When you break it down from a structural point of view, it is about a series of set pieces, of deaths. What I thought was very clever about the deaths in the original is that they all follow a rule that you could say are primeval methods. A beheading, an impaling, you have a hanging. In the new movie, you have an immolation, a guy setting on fire. I didn't want to "tech" up the killings. And I could have gone super-fucking cheesy. "Killed by computer!" (laughs) Know what I mean?

But the truth is, the ancient nature of the killings, not only are they more macabre, but they also echoed the notion that this has been going on for eons. Because they have a medieval sensibility. So, you see the original and think "Fuck. Donner's cracked it! He's done 'em all. What can we do?" For the longest time, I struggled with how to re-invent the beheading, because it is a signature moment. Coming along the timeline in the movie where it does, it became absolutely crucial that we reinvent it a bit. Because the film is faithful to the original, no doubt, and I think fans of the original would have seen it coming a mile away. Whereas, I think and hope, we found a way to just wrong foot you. Because you'll start to think "Wait a minute?! Where's the beheading?"

That was my favorite kill from the original film, so I was really paying attention for it, and I think you actually topped it with your update.

Thank you. What's fun about it is we did use a little bit of technology to help enhance it. If you look, Thewlis blinks a milli-second before he's beheaded. It is a dummy head but because we can green screen his own head, you're not on the dummy head long, whereas they had to for the original. They had to set up the dummy and cut its head off. This way we could have David stand up, blink and have the head come off, and then we put a green screen hood on a stuntman and he falls downstairs… headless. (laughs) Which again. Gives it real life, because he's still kind of alive as he falls.

It really punctuated that moment.

Yeah. I think David (Thewlis) is in the Guinness World Book of Records as the most beheaded actor in history. He's been beheaded on film four times! Guess who did one of his last beheadings? Dick Donner in *Timeline*. How ironic is that? So, I sent him his head, he's now got two of them. (laughs) (**END SPOILER**)

Speaking of, did you at any point get to talk to Richard Donner about *The Omen*?

Yeah. I just showed the film to Richard on Monday night (May 2006). I wasn't there, but the report was that he was very pleased. Look… I wrote a letter to the man, saying "This is a mark of respect. It's very much a hats off to you."

I wanted to direct because of *Superman*! I couldn't figure out how they made him fly and it drove me fucking bananas! This was before "How they did that?" comes out five minutes after a movie comes out! When Star Wars did it first, it was a whole event. "We're going to go behind the curtain!" But for *Superman* it drove me crazy. I'm eleven years old, and I know he's not flying! So, to me, Donner's always been a hero of mine. So, I wrote to him and asked, "With the greatest of respect, please have a look at this and let me know what you think." He said that he hadn't been frightened that way in a long time, so I think he enjoyed it.

How difficult was it to pull off a lot of the special effects shots in *The Omen*? And how'd you decide that you wanted to do a lot of it practically as opposed to CGI, which… I don't think I noticed any CGI in your version?

There is one CGI shot in the movie. And believe me, I know the FX world. I'm from commercials and I did two previous movies that were very heavy on CGI. And I was crapping myself doing it the old-fashioned way! It was almost as if we'd forgotten the skill set required to do this old school. Everyone was nervous. The producers were nervous. "What do you mean we're going to do it real? No, we're not! We're going to do it in Santa Monica on a bunch of hard drives."

Our make-up designer Fiona Cannon had worked with Matt Mungle before from WN creations. Mungle's one of the last great sculptor effects artists. We went to Matthew and said, "Look. We're thinking of doing this old-school. Do you think you can pull it off?" We knew that everything had to be top-notch, or we'd be laughed at. But Matthew was brilliant, and he did a great job. He made everything. He made the baby and the jackal. The impaling piece with all the glass and obviously the beheading.

A lot of remakes lately seem to be toned down and made into these PG-13 films. But *The Omen* was a hard R. You didn't shy away from any of the dark material in the original. Was there ever any pressure against making this version of the movie or was there little interference?

I happen to have a very good relationship with the studio I work with. But there's no doubt that there was pressure at some point to consider a PG-13, because movies these days are an expensive proposition. This one wasn't particularly expensive, considering mega-budgets. But to have an R, there's something bad going on in this country about that. An R is going to become as rare as an NC-17 before long if this keeps up, because the rules are so destructively prohibited. I don't know if people commonly would know this, but even if the trailer of *The Omen* was a shot of a tweedy bird sitting on a tree in a summer day for thirty seconds and said *The Omen* at the end, I can't show that trailer with any PG-13 movies.

You can only show that trailer with R rated movies. There's a watershed cut off, where you can't advertise your movie with a lot of the bigger programs before 9 o'clock. So, there are draconian rules about advertising R rated movies, and the reason I say it's very amendable, it's a first amendment issue. They're supposed to judge on content! Not on perception. So, if I have a tweedy bird sitting on a tree, you're supposed to look at that and say, "That's not offensive." Why can't I advertise before that time slot! There's a classic example in the movie. In one of the nightmare sequences, Father Spiletto drops a baby covered in blood. It's a toy!

It's a doll dipped in red paint, so it poses the ultimate perception question to the MPAA. Because they went back and said, "It's a hard R, because you've got a dead baby." It's not a dead baby, it's a toy painted red. But it's the perception of it. Then you get into the whole debate. Once you have humans telling other humans what's appropriate, it'll always be about personal taste and perception. And that's where the rating system sucks. (laughs)

But at the moment, there's so many successful Rated R movies, like the *Saw* films, *Hostel*, and *The Hills Have Eyes*; maybe there's proof that these films can be successful with that rating?

They're cynical. I think those movies are lamentable in many ways. They're what I call rip off movies. It should be half price. You should pay $5 bucks to see those movies instead of $10 because they're not really serious. And I'm not saying you shouldn't have fun, but now with *Saw 2* and *Saw 3*, it's getting pretty cynical. Now, of course, this is rich coming from a guy who just remade a horror classic. (laughs) But, I think I'll give you your $10 bucks worth. The story is so good. That's why we remade it.

The cast for the film is fantastic. How'd you manage to get everyone from Liev to Julia to Mia involved, and what can you say about your working experiences with them on *The Omen*?

The cast really are the film. If it's good, it's because of them. I really enjoyed working with them all, Mia especially. She is such a smart, engaging woman. I think they all got involved because the story is so damn good.

What are among your all-time favorite horror movies?

Definitely *The Omen*, the ones I listed above, and I used to love the Hammer films we were allowed watch on Saturday night, though some were a little campy. I would love to see M. Night Shyamalan do a straight-out horror flick.

ADAM GREEN

Interviewed by Mike Cucinotta, Rob Galluzzo, and Adam Barnick (7/06)

"Not a Sequel, Not a Remake, Not Based on a Japanese One. Old School American Horror." That's the tagline for writer/director Adam Green's genre debut *Hatchet*, which stars fan favorite Kane Hodder as the vicious Victor Crowley. After reading Adam Barnick's "First Look" review here on *Icons* and catching a clip at a recent *Fangoria* convention, we knew we had to bring you guys an exclusive interview with the guy behind what's soon to be an instant cult classic slasher flick! Read on!

What are your earliest recollections of the horror genre? The first films that scared you?

The first horror movie I ever remember watching was *Friday the 13th Part 2*. My parents were gone for the night, and I had an older brother who was very cool about showing me that stuff. For the most part I was bored, but then Jason came through the window at the end and I was scared to death by what he looked like.

All of us were scared by that moment!

And if you look at Victor Crowley, it's so derivative of that moment. The make-up was designed to be more of a cross between John Merrick (*The Elephant Man*) and Rocky Dennison (*Mask*), but the "feel" of Crowley is from what I felt when I saw that scene happen as a child.

My next memorable experience with horror was *The Thing*. When the monster was killing all of the dogs and they had to shoot them to put them out of their misery, I started crying and my parents said, "That's it! No more horror movies! You're not watching them anymore!" I'm a big pussy when it comes to animals getting hurt. Gut a man right in front of me and I'll cheer, but kick a cat and I'll tear your head off. Funny, but it still devastates me to this day when you hear the dogs howling and getting shot in *The Thing*. It kills me!

When did you first first get involved in filmmaking?

Let's see… I borrowed my uncle's video camera back in eighth or ninth grade, and I used to make these little horror movies called *Stone Cold Crazy*. I don't know why I called it that. (laughs) I think I just really liked the Metallica cover of the Queen song a lot.

I would have started even earlier, but my family didn't have a video camera or any means to get that kind of stuff. It was me and one of my friends, and the whole thing was just us holding our hand in front of the lens and chasing each other around so that it'd be like we were running away from this killer hand. We'd show it to our friends at parties and they just thought it was so funny. So, we made probably ten of them. They were only five minutes each. And they're horrible! But those were the first movies I ever tried to make. Then in high school, there was a communications class that you couldn't get into until you were a senior, but when I was a freshman, I told the teacher that I was going to get in as a junior and teach it as a senior. He laughed at me and said I wouldn't. But I was tenacious, and I kept bothering him every day. "I need to get in as a junior!" And sure enough, I did.

The first project they give you (which is the same in every intro class, I think) was to learn how to edit by making a music video. Everybody does little songs like "I Get By With a Little Help From My Friends," and they shoot their friends dancing and cut it together. But I did… fucking *Master Of Puppets*! (laughs) And it's got a guy buying drugs, doing them and overdosing, and having a bad trip, and maggots are on his arm and he pulls off his skin – it was this nine minute opus, and everyone in the class just thought "What the hell was that?!" And from what I hear they still show it to this day after the kids exhibit their videos. "Those were nice. But you have to see what this kid did in '92!"

That's awesome. '92? That was pre-"black" album, huh?

I think that was just as the "black" album was getting huge. A lot of people say they've given up on them since then, but I still like everything they do. I can't give up on *Metallica*!

Didn't you mention in your *Fangoria* panel initially starting out with make-up FX?

I had a job directing bad cable commercials when I got out of college. You must've seen them out by you. You know, the commercials with the store front and the cheesy graphics and the guy in front of his store shouting "We've been in business for X amount of years!" while his wife and three fat kids wave? Well, I started stealing their equipment at night, and the first short film I ever made was called *Columbus Day Weekend*. It had Jason and Michael Myers stalking the same campgrounds by mistake and then falling in love with each other. It was my first time trying to do effects. We put a chainsaw into someone's balls, and we did the whole belt sander thing from *Hatchet*.

It was very crudely done, but that's how I learned how to shoot FX. But I'm still really not that good with actually building effects. I couldn't build that stuff on my own no matter how much you paid me. For *Hatchet*, it was all done by professional artists. I just told them what I was looking for and what the shot was, and then John Carl Buechler and his team built them. My first real feature film stuff was writing my own comedies, shooting them, and acting in them actually.

What was it that made you want to follow-up your first film, a comedy, with a straight up horror film?

I just always knew I was going to make *Hatchet* since I was eight years old. I knew it was going to be this story. My first film (*Coffee and Donuts*) was made to be a calling card to show that I can write and I can direct, but I just needed some sort of budget. I made *Coffee and Donuts* for four hundred dollars and it went so far.

Disney/Touchstone ended up buying the rights and then Tom Shadyac's company (*Liar Liar*) produced a TV pilot script that I wrote. Unfortunately, the network that bought it was UPN and in the end, it wasn't "urban" enough for them and it never got shot. I don't know who didn't see that coming. I didn't. But in the end, that helped me "arrive" in Hollywood. I had gotten an agent, and I was getting paid because of *Coffee and Donuts*. Then I wrote *Hatchet* and the first responses I got were "This is never going to get made." And I'd ask "Why?" They'd say: "Well, it's "slasher" stuff and

people don't do this anymore. And it's really funny, but then the violence is way too intense. No one's going to get it."

How long ago was it that you first wrote the script, just so our readers get an idea of when people were telling you this?

I wrote the script in 2003 while I was waiting to get UPN's decision back on *Coffee and Donuts*. I think the big hit back then was *Cabin Fever*? So, the trend was leaning towards 'no more slasher in the woods' type stuff. My reps basically told me that *Hatchet* wasn't going to happen. Then I went and got Kane (Hodder) attached, and the producers and I made a mock trailer that you can see on our official website. We made that trailer for literally four dollars. That's what we used to get the horror community talking about the film and then it was a little easier to get the money to make it. So, I went to my industry connections and I said, "I got the money to make this now." And they said: "Well, your schedule is insane. You're never going to be able to do this in the time you have." But I did, and then they told me it'd never get into a film festival because it's a "slasher" movie. And then it got into Tribeca and was hailed as one of the top five hits of the whole festival. Now we have offers on it and all these great things are happening. It's a funny story, because sometimes it just takes someone to say "No" for you to say, "Oh really?" and get it done.

Do you feel that you kind of proved everyone wrong by overcoming each obstacle that people said you couldn't along the way?

It's not about proving anyone wrong or anything like that. It was always more about proving to myself that I could do what I said I would do. I mean, I am one of the 1% who actually finished what I started. I got *Hatchet* made. And it's a real movie; not a video that I shot for 25K and want to call a real movie. With DTV nowadays, there's fifty new horror titles a month being shat out. This is way above par with those. I definitely think, if anything, I'm just an example of how you don't really need connections if you have the ambition and are willing to work hard. So many people throw their arms up and make excuses for why some people succeeded and they can't. While they wasted their time being bitter, I went and fought my own way in. I don't care whether you end up loving *Hatchet* or not; if there's one thing you can take from what I've done, it's that you can do this, too. No one can stop you if you're willing to bleed a little along the way. Kids write to me all the time telling me they're inspired by my story. And if that's all the recognition I ever get, then I've made some serious ground as far as I'm concerned. I'm happy. But at the same time, I still have a lot to prove before I can say I've truly "made it." *Hatchet* seems to be doing really well, but I still have to wait to see what really happens with it. There's still a lot of people that can screw it up! I'm a big pessimist when it comes to dealing with "suits." You have to be careful. There are literally distributors that might have other projects like this in development that they've already spent a lot of money on, who might try to buy this just to shelve it, so it doesn't compete with their own thing.

The business side of all of this is strictly about money, not about making a good horror movie, so whatever happens with this is going to be based on what makes the most financial sense for them, and not necessarily what's best for the movie. I have nothing to do with what happens from here on out, so that's very scary! I'm just praying for that final stroke of luck so that this film gets the chance it deserves. The decision makers are insanely out of touch with their audiences, so you have to always prepare yourself for the worst case scenario.

Well, the first person involved was Kane Hodder, whom genre fans know as Jason Voorhees. How'd he get involved with *Hatchet*?

John Buechler actually got involved first. I went to his shop. Sarah Elbert (one of our producers) produced the *Friday the 13th* box set, and when she read the script for *Hatchet*, she said she could probably get it in front of a few people that have worked on those movies to get an opinion on it. Well, Buechler read it and agreed to meet me. I just thought he would tell me what he thought I should do, but instead he said, "I want to do this." So, I thought, "Wow." I'm walking around his shop and I'm looking at Michael Myers, and Freddy and Jason, thinking this is crazy! He helped me do the trailer. He did the young Victor Crowley make-up on my girlfriend, Rileah. (Who wound up playing young Victor Crowley in the actual movie, FYI.) So, he said to me "I can get this to Kane Hodder if you're interested."

Absolutely! So, they gave Kane the script, he really liked the character and thought it was cool. It's very different from Jason in the fact that it's not just breathing heavy and stalking people. It's very frantic, and crazy with a lot of screaming and emotion. Another thing that attracted Kane is that he got to play Crowley's father, who has a very emotional scene where he kills Victor Crowley by accident and cries on camera.

Was it always your plan to have him play the father?

When I knew he was interested in doing it, that's when I got the idea that it'd be cool to show Kane not in make-up. The fans all know what he looks like, but the average person just knows the hockey mask. It's funny how some people only look at him as a "stunt guy." All the guys who played Jason were stunt guys, and admittedly, some of them just did stunts, but he (Kane) definitely took the role very seriously, to the point of being psychotic about it. Which I always loved about him. He's just a dream to work with – he's so professional. He motivated everyone else!

He's always on time. He's always polite and considerate and he has great ideas and great enthusiasm for the work. When he saw the first cut of *Hatchet*, he called me about an hour later and said, "This is the best horror movie I've ever been involved with." And went on the record saying that to *TV Guide*. What else do we need right now after that? Robert Englund too was such a fan of it and was so happy with the script. Having Tony Todd show up today at the convention was awesome! I was surprised to see him. That was great.

What was it like for you as a fan to have all these genre people involved in your film? Kane Hodder, Robert Englund, Tony Todd, Joshua Leonard.

It was really surreal! I first met Josh Leonard at Billy Butler's *Madhouse* premiere because he was in that. I'd really only seen him in *Blair Witch*, and when I saw him in *Madhouse*, it was weird to see him in a role. It was so cool. We talked a little bit afterwards about the things he did to get into character, such as listening to *Ministry*. Things that I do! So, we became friendly, and I offered him a part blindly and he said he'd do it. That was it. He was the first one on board after Kane. Robert Englund and Tony Todd took a little finagling to get to, because of their agents. Only because everyone has a script they're trying to get to those guys.

It was really weird, the first conversation I had with Robert Englund. I couldn't really even talk because he was being so complimentary of the script and how big he thinks this is going to be. And I'm thinking "Who am I?" On set, standing between the two of them, Kane's in full make-up and Robert's to the other side of me, and I'm standing in between these two guys as they're discussing the make-up job and how big the movie's going to be, and I'm looking at people thinking "This is so fucked up?!" Which is where the acting comes in. You have to act like you're not impressed. You have to be able to step in when you want something to be the way you want it. It's really hard to step up and say it to them as a fan who grew up watching their work. You have to put on the acting hat and act like you're this important director and they're going to listen to you. (laughs) And they do! Most actors don't mind working with an unproven director if that director knows what he wants. Because when you have someone who's a pushover and doesn't really have a plan, then it gets frustrating, and it all starts falling apart.

How much direction did you have to give Kane? Did he bring a lot to the role personally or did you have a clear vision of Victor Crowley?

I always knew exactly who Victor Crowley was. It's funny with Kane, because you just give him a couple of instructions and he would just go with it. The first time we did the make-up appliance in the shop and we saw what he was going to look like, my first reaction was that he seemed a little too Jason-like. He came over and grabbed me by the throat. I told him "Victor doesn't do that." Victor runs frantically and twitches because he's just as scared. I think he had a bit of resistance to the twitching thing at first, because it feels weird to be running and limping like that. Victor is not methodical; he doesn't move normally. He's all over the place.

Then, the screaming and the yelling and all the other stuff he does. Kane needed nothing for that. I'd just say, "Scare 'em!" Everyone would start crying and running away freaked out. He's such a pro. I hope there are sequels because we have so much more to do with this character. The key that I've always found to successful "slasher" movies is you don't answer everything in the first one. You purposely leave some questions so afterwards people can debate it, which is already happening with *Hatchet*.

People are asking me "Well, is he a ghost?" or "Did he just never die?" or "Is he a zombie?" And I know all the answers to all that! But the whole idea is to slowly keep revealing that stuff. What I'm happy about is I already have it mapped out for three or four of these. It's not like "Oh, the film made money, let's figure out how to bring him back." Which is what they did with a lot of other movies back in the 80's. If it lives and dies with this one, then I'm totally fine with that, but if we get to do the sequel and learn why he's deformed, or why he might be a ghost? What'd Tony Todd have to do with it? What'd Robert Englund's character have to do with it? It's all tied in.

So, you built this whole mythology around *Hatchet*, the same way that a lot of the 80's franchises did?

Yeah, and that's what made the character scary is where they came from. Why are they like that? That's what I loved about the old "slasher" movies is that there was a reason these people were killing people. Not just that they're crazy.

You explained in your panel how the story for *Hatchet* and *Victor Crowley* stems back to childhood. Can you tell the *Icons* audience the origins for your film again?

Sure. I was eight years old and my parents sent me to summer camp. And the counselors on the first day said not to go near this certain cabin or else "Hatchetface" would come get us. So, I asked "Well, who is he?" and they'd just say "He's Hatchetface!" Well, "Why's he called Hatchetface? What's he going to do to us?!" "He's going to get you!" And I thought it was so stupid! (laughs) So, that night, all the kids were like "Do you think Hatchetface will really come and get us?"

So, I started making up this story, and I told all the kids, "There was this kid, and his name was Victor Crowley. He was deformed and his dad kept him hidden away. And his house caught fire, and his dad chopped down the door to save him, and he was pressed up against the other side and he got hit in the face. Now, if you listen, you can hear him screaming for his father in the middle of the night!" All the kids started crying and freaking out and the counselors threatened to send me home. (laughs) Ever since then, I knew I would make that a movie one day. It's funny, because it goes even further. My friend Ben was getting married to another friend of mine from high school named Mary Beth, and Ben's bachelor party was in New Orleans and it was Final Four weekend.

I'm not really into basketball or drinking that much, so I had nothing to do in New Orleans, because that's pretty much all there is to do. I wanted to go on the haunted swamp tours, but the guy there said "Well, we don't do them anymore because of what happened." This is all stuff that's in the movie. I asked, "What happened?" And it was some lame story about insurance. And I thought, Man! I wanted to hear something horrible!

So, instead, I went to see this jazz band play, and the drummer had been in a fire and had no hands. He had his drumsticks taped onto his hands with electrical tape and the guy was wailing on the drums. He was missing an eye too and was just all messed up. I'm watching this guy play and I'm thinking about the haunted swamp tour, and New Orleans and I'm thinking about my friend Ben marrying Mary Beth and that's kind of how *Hatchet* all came together. Because the lead guy is Ben, and then there's Mary Beth. Victor Crowley and the whole thing came together at once.

***Hatchet* embraces a lot of the things we've loved from earlier genre films. It seems intended to be a theatrical experience. Was that always how you intended it to play out and how difficult is it to explain to investors that this will work theatrically?**

The big thing that people responded to is that you can take all of the gore out of it, and it's still a fun movie. And that's been a big compliment from the people that have seen it. They usually say that I almost forgot for the first forty-five minutes that it was a horror movie. It opens with a big horrific death, but then it's funny with good characters and you almost forget it's a horror movie until Victor comes running out of the house (which is the clip we screened at the *Fango* panel) and you think "Oh shit! That's right, people are going to get killed!" That was the idea, to make it a ride. Even with the music, we keep going up and down. The music cue on the bus driving through New Orleans, give me "Splash Mountain," I want Americana-cheesy Disney type music. And the investors would ask "Shouldn't it be Marilyn Manson like you opened the movie with?" No! Do *Jurassic Park* and make it a big ride! I'm glad you recognized that because I had to fight really hard for it. Even with the comedy! A lot of people say horror and comedy don't mix. And they're right. It doesn't mix…

It doesn't mix when it sucks! The humor came out of those characters. It's forty-five minutes of getting to love these characters because they're fleshed out and hilarious, and then it all goes to hell. Is that the reason you decided to make that group so energetic and animated and fun? Because we usually don't remember the characters, say in the *Friday the 13th's*. (Even though I love all those films.)

That's one of the things we kept saying. There's been twenty-five *Friday the 13th's*, *Nightmare's*, and *Halloween's* put together, but you can't name one character besides the villain. You don't remember who anyone was. That was the goal with this. To make my ultimate "slasher" movie. I'd never go on record to say "This is the ultimate slasher movie," but for me, that's what this was.

Do you have a stand-up comedy background? Is that where a lot of your humor comes from?

If you can make people laugh, they'll stick with you. A lot of times with horror movies, people will go to see them, but they have this defense mechanism where they don't want to be scared. So, the whole time they're watching it, their arms are crossed, and they'll say "He's behind him. Oh, knew it. Called it. Called it." They're only doing that to

justify that they're not scared to everybody else. But if you can actually make people laugh with the characters, you're already hooked. If it's genuine humor, it's really hard not to get invested in the characters. That was really where I came from with that. My first movie was a romantic comedy, and then I did some stand-up for a while. I actually started doing stand-up comedy because I was scared of it. It's the one thing that scared me besides sharks. It was a dare. Can I get up there for ten minutes with just a microphone? I used to front a band, and people would ask "How do you get up in front of an audience with a band?"

It's pretty easy because you can't even hear me sing half the time with the whole band playing. But when you do stand-up, and it's just you standing there with a microphone, you're pretty much telling the audience, "I think I'm funny. Here I go…" I did stand-up for a good year and a half, but now I haven't had time to do it and I miss it. One of the guys who was part of my stand-up troupe was Andy Samberg who's now on SNL. All of the guys in our show are starting to blow up now, so it's wonderful to see. We did it at the Rainbow Bar & Grill on Sunset. Once a month, we'd all get together and go. And it was vicious! Some nights we'd steal each other's jokes right before the other guy went on just to leave them on the spot. I did it to Andy once, and then he came out with no material and had to work the crowd for ten minutes. And he kicked everybody's ass regardless! (laughs) You could tell even then that he was just brilliant.

Once you got the film going, did you still have to keep convincing the producers about your vision or were they more supportive?

They were supportive for the most part. They believed in me, that I really cared about the horror genre and didn't just want to make a horror movie for the sake of it. But at the same time, they questioned certain things along the line. "Can we have this many jokes? Is this too funny right now? Are people going to be able to swing back and forth from laughing and being scared?" "The gore?" They tried to fight that a bit. "Is it too much?"

In *Hatchet*, each death starts to top the next one. I mean, by the time we kill Marcus, OK, he gets his ribs crushed. In some movies that would've been enough, but no, then he gets his arms ripped off. And then he gets swung against a mausoleum and his head explodes. It keeps going! And people think "OK, stop killing him already!" The belt sander one was… (laughs) Well, let's not talk about it.

You spent a long time with casting. How'd you approach working with all these different actors with all these different styles?

Instead of rehearsing on set, my rehearsing is usually just a meeting. You just talk to them about it and get their input beforehand, so that you can adjust the script accordingly and then only have to worry about blocking and rehearsing stunts on set. I ask what they have in mind, and then I tell them what I'm looking for. But to sit and to block it out and make them memorize it and say it over and over again… that just ruins it. You only really get about three good takes with actors, especially with a joke. After they've said it enough, it's not funny to them anymore and they start to think it's stupid.

To contradict myself though, Tamara Feldman who played Mary Beth had to do a lot of crying and getting emotional. I learned early on that the key to her was to wear her out. So, there are some times, and she'll be pissed when she reads this, we weren't even rolling on the first few takes, because I knew I had to get her completely sobbing - a mess, to the point she couldn't even stand up anymore. And that scene at the end in the boat, I made her do it fifteen times and she couldn't even breathe by the end of it. To this day she's still my favorite actress who I've ever worked with on any set ever. She's so committed and just so f'n good at what she does. She really let me inside of her head and she was so willing to play and put herself out there. She never acted too cool for anything or got sick of the games I wanted to play 'make-believe' with.

For instance, when she had to discover the bodies of her family in Crowley's shed. She never worked with the actors who played her father and brother. So right before she saw the carnage, I showed her candid pictures of them and told her stories about the time they went fishing together or the time they spent Christmas at her Aunt's, etc. Some of the people thought what I was doing was sick, but she was willing to really go for it and make believe. After making her discover them and cry seven times, she actually hit me. But two minutes later she was hugging me. That's the caliber of actor I strive to work with. If anyone ever has the chance to cast Tamara Feldman and they wind up going with someone else, they've made a terrible mistake.

How'd you tap into each of the actors' fears?

Each one of them reacts differently to fear. Deon Richmond (who plays Marcus) would laugh whenever he'd get scared. And the way to stop that from happening was that the first time I said "Cut", Kane just kept chasing him for about five minutes. Then he put him in a headlock, threw him down

and said, "Is it funny now?" And he'd say, "No!" (laughs) We played pranks to get them scared.

There's a scene where Victor Crowley throws his hatchet at Joel David Moore and right before we were going to do it, we pretended that the stunt hatchet broke, and Kane starts yelling "I'll just throw the real one at his face. It's fine." Mind you, he's got one eye covered in make-up. "I can do it." This was all planned, but I went up to Kane and said, "I can't let you do this." And the medic comes over, and the first AD and we're all arguing with Kane, and Joel's off in the corner thinking "What the hell is going on?" Finally, Kane yells at me, "Don't tell me how to do my fucking job! I'm a stunt coordinator! Let me fucking do it!"

So, I say "Fine! Pictures up!" and Joel's like "Wait a minute!" Kane throws it at Joel, and we had a close-up on Joel's face. He was so terrified because it hit him in the leg, but it was a rubber hatchet! He was so scared that he believed he actually got hurt and he was limping away for a second before he realized it was a joke. That's the type of stuff that we did for everyone. And also, never letting them see Victor Crowley until the moment they saw him on camera. It really helped. Because you can get numb to it after a while, especially when you're up close and you realize its latex and rubber. Also, some of them didn't know when they were really going to die, because we convinced them that I changed the script. And the schedule was all mixed up. So, there'd be nights where we'd be shooting a dialogue scene and I'd yell "Last looks on make-up effects." And everyone would think, "Wait a minute." Is he here? And then you'd start to hear someone screaming in the woods. And the cast would all think "Is he here?" The whole time, they're acting on edge because they weren't sure if Kane was going to show up, meanwhile Kane was at an event in New Jersey. (laughs) They were so scared just because they didn't know where he was.

How'd you meet with your director of photography Will Barratt? Did you guys go to school together?

He's actually ten years older than me, but we were both working at Time Warner making cable commercials. Will had already been there for a while and I was his intern. The very first day we were working together I asked him, and this is when I had just met him, "You're not going to do this forever, are you?" And he replied, "What do you mean?" And I was all like, "We could steal this shit, and make our own stuff!" And two weeks later we're shooting *Columbus Day* and he's saying, "I can't believe I'm stealing this equipment." He's totally the responsible one. This married guy with responsibilities, and I corrupted the shit out of him. (laughs)

We came up with this name, ArieScope – because *Columbus Day* was supposed to be a total spoof of *Friday the 13th*, and our opening credits needed to look exactly like *Friday the 13th's* with the white letters and stuff. We needed a "production company presents." We're both Aries, so we thought of ArieScope. We never really intended to do anything with it, but it gradually became a real company, and we've now won two Emmy's and made three feature films. Another just got green-lit. And it's crazy, because with this company, we just wanted to make friends with the people we work with.

A lot of people have this philosophy in this business, "I'm not here to make friends, I'm here to make money and to make a movie." Well, we are here to make friends. We make that abundantly clear, to the point that a lot of our crew will work for free for us at some points. If we say, "There's no money for this," sometimes they'll say, "Doesn't matter, we're doing it anyway." They'll turn down bigger paying gigs to work with us. It's been so surreal the whole thing. I get to work with my friends every day. Not a lot of people get to say that.

Was it true that you'd written a script for *Cabin Fever 2*?

I did. I wrote that in 2004 for Lionsgate. It's one of the scripts I'm the most proud of. It's the whole *Halloween II* thing where it starts with the same shot where the first one ended. It's a lot like *Hatchet*, where it's very funny. My script is basically about a bunch of kids on an outward-bound trip and it's basically *The Breakfast Club* meets *Cabin Fever*. All these kids have to do outward bound because if they don't, they're going to fail high school. So, it's all the fuck-ups who don't really know each other who get stuck on this bus, and go to do this trip with the gym teacher. What was interesting is when I got to read the first draft of *Cabin Fever* after I wrote mine, there's a scene where Bert is driving away from the hillbillies and he's starting to get the infection. And in the original script, he has to swerve because a school bus full of kids is going the other way back into the woods. And I didn't even know that when I did my draft for *Cabin Fever 2*.

Unfortunately, I got in so much trouble talking about this the last time so I don't know what I can or can't say! Lionsgate are really the only people that can answer what's going on with that. Eli Roth and I both say, "We don't know," because we don't know. I don't think that he knew that they asked me to write one, and I also didn't know at first that he was going to be writing one. There was a point in the making of *Hatchet* where a journalist came to set and asked me a ton of questions about *Cabin Fever 2* and my

answers were really taken out of context. What was awesome about Eli was that the second it happened, he e-mailed me right away saying he knows my comments were taken out of context. It's happened to him before. Where he could have been a total dick to me and come down on me, he literally sent me an email that said, "Don't sweat it." And that was sort of how we first met. You'll hear people say bad things about other people who are having success in the industry, and I think that all comes out of jealousy. Eli's first thing got a huge theatrical release and was a big success, so some people like to try and talk trash. But he's a cool guy. He really is nice, and he has been nothing but awesome to me. If my films could have half the success his films have had I'd be thrilled. And anyone who tries to say differently is lying.

How hard is it to manage your personal life with work?

It's such a struggle but I manage. However, if my girlfriend were here right now, she'd argue that statement. (laughs) It's really hard because all you do is work, and it consumes you, because it's your hobby. You don't have time for other things! Even when you go to a movie, it's not the same anymore. It's not like you go to lose yourself in a movie. Your friends don't understand that you don't have a lot of time for everything. And when you start having success, they think, "Oh, well he just thinks he's too good for us now." It's not it. You just don't have time. Every fan that writes me a letter, I try to write back to every single one. Sometimes, I can get back to someone within five minutes, other times it takes me a month depending where I am. I try to do it! Sometimes in life you'll hear people say, "I don't care what other people think about me," and I think they're lying because I totally care what people think about me. I really try very hard to be around for everyone and to stay as accessible as I can. Between the hours you actually work and then trying to keep up with everyone, there's not much personal time left. But I'm getting better at it.

Then of course, the whole struggle thing in the years leading up to this part. Just three years ago I was working at a club where I had to eat the leftovers that they took off the tables to throw out. I would scrape it off the plate just to have food to eat. I was so poor. The cable commercial job paid well enough to get by before I moved to LA. And then my feature, *Coffee and Donuts*, got picked up over here, but when something gets picked up, you don't get money for it right away. It took three years for me to get any money from *Coffee and Donuts*. I came out here, thinking "Where do I start?" and I went to meeting after meeting, and everyone would say, "We love you. We love your voice. But we don't have anything for you. You have to sell something first." Nothing was happening. This town loves to say 'no' and will only say 'yes' if they have to because they're afraid to say 'no.' You can't go out because you have no money, and some nights I went to sleep in tears because I was so hungry both literally and emotionally. My parents would try as hard as they could to help me, but they didn't have a lot of money either. My dad was a gym teacher, and my mom was a Hebrew school teacher. It's really, really, really hard.

And its even harder cause here in LA, people around you tend to have or come from money. Even some of my friends that were also struggling. Their parents paid their rent and bought them cars, etc. But you can't get bitter or focus on that. You just have to do what you need to do. Everyone's story is different. This one was mine. And it still is to this day, because I'm always worried that it can go back to that at any moment! I finally bought a new car after three years of having some money. I thought, "I'm just going to keep driving the Camry! It's only twelve years old! I can get another eight years out of this thing!" (laughs) You're just too scared to spend any of the money.

Can you talk about *Spiral*, your follow up to *Hatchet*?

I didn't know anything about *Spiral* when it came along. And then Joel Moore who was the lead in *Hatchet* called me up and said, "I want to send you this script, just read it." It was something he and his friend Jeremy Boreing had written. It's so hard to be a writer when your last name is Boreing. (laughs) I had it tough because I was Adam GREEN, but he's Jeremy BOREING. You know that execs are coming up with their shitty "no pun intended" jokes before they even open the first page. Anyway, they gave me the script, and I read it, and I just couldn't figure out where it was going, because it's a drama. But at the same time, it's really fucked up and dark and scary. So, I told them I thought it was great. So, Joel said "Well, I wanted to direct it, but I don't feel comfortable being the lead and directing on this particular project, so would you want to do it with me?" I was in the middle of coloring *Hatchet*, and he suggested, "Come out to Portland for a month, and be the onset director, and you're just going to direct the actual production of the movie and then I'll take over in post." And my first answer was no. To co-direct something, you're just asking for problems. Especially… with Joel, he's got more ideas than anyone you've ever seen. He's A.D.D. and he doesn't even remember what he's saying half the time because his ideas just keep coming so fast.

It wouldn't be a big deal, except that all of his ideas are actually good. So here you are on set, two creative minds, one of which (me) is concerned with getting it all done on time and on budget and another (Joel) that could keep firing off new ideas by the second if you'd let him. It was definitely an experience, but we got along famously. In fact, as much as I'd still say, "no thanks" to co-directing, I bet that few people have ever gone into something like this and had it work out as well as it did for us. Sure, there's some shots we may not have agreed on and there's some stuff left on the cutting room floor that I would have kept in the film if it were only up to me, but we both have nothing but respect and love for each other and we know that we made a beautiful film. He and I will most definitely work on something again in the future. We just work that well together. *Spiral* is not a horror movie. It's a dramatic thriller. It's about relationships, art, jazz; it's nothing like anything I would ever normally do. And that's exactly why I did it. *Hatchet's* going to come out and everyone's going to say, "Ok. He does "slasher" movies" – but then I can follow up immediately with *Spiral* which is a 180 degree turn in every single way.

The horror fans who love *Hatchet* may not be into something like *Spiral*, and I'm embracing that. Already, I keep getting offered "slasher" movies and oddly enough, lately I even get offers for remakes. And I say, "Did you read the poster for *Hatchet*?!" You'd be surprised how many more remakes people want to make. They'll remake anything at this point. These days, you pitch the studios an idea and they ask, "Well, who was in the original?" Everyone wants remakes these days. And for the record, I'm not anti-remake. I thought *Texas Chainsaw* was sick. I loved *The Hills Have Eyes*. But I'm fed up with the fact that it's 90% of what they're offering us.

It's insulting to the Japanese that we think we can do all of their movies better! I can understand remaking a Japanese movie from fifty years ago. But they make them, and then the American version is out a year later. Has Hollywood lost that much faith in today's generation that they're literally scared to put out something new? Funny thing is with *Hatchet*, it's not even a new concept. It's a formula that is so old, it's new again. But it's completely original and that may scare some people up top.

Anything you would consider tackling as a remake, if you had complete control?

Absolutely. I actually took a meeting on one recently. It didn't work out that I'm going to end up doing it, but why I took it was because they said to just forget the original, because I didn't like the original, and go back to the short story it was based on, which was only seventeen pages long. The writer who wrote that short story, to get to work with him would've been great. I don't know if it worked out with a writer just yet. But I did go in for it and it was a remake, and I wanted to do it because of the people I would've gotten to work with. I always said I'd love to remake *Clash of the Titans* if you could have a *Lord of the Rings* budget. Now, they're doing it. Hopefully, they have the *Lord of the Rings* budget because if they don't, they just can't beat the original with cheesy CGI. Hmm… what would I remake? I'd like to remake *Weekend at Bernies*! (laughs)

You should write the third one and then reintroduce all the characters!

I've heard that Terry Kiser (Bernie) wrote a third one! He wrote a third one and can't get it off the ground just yet! Everyone says, "All he had to do was play dead." I thought he was genius in that movie. Because the trust that you have to have in other actors to fall and not flinch to catch yourself. I can talk about *Weekend at Bernie's* forever. I love that movie. (laughs) It's so great. He was the psychiatrist in *Friday the 13th Part 7*.

One thing we wanted to talk about, the *Hatchet* poster. It says right on there, "It's not a remake. It's not a sequel. It's not based on a Japanese one." But you also mentioned previously a disdain for movies focusing just on the brutality rather than story…

No, I love *Saw*. One of the best movies I've seen in years! And there's a moment in *Hostel* that I still clap to myself when I watch it, which is when Jay Hernandez starts speaking German to the guy, and the guy thinks about it and leaves. And you think it worked. And then he comes back and puts the gag in and you hear the chainsaw! I loved that! But right now, I think that studios think, "Oh those torture movies did well? Then hell, let's just be as depraved as we can be!" And they don't care who's in it. And they don't care about the story. I personally don't think it takes much talent or effort to torture someone for an hour and a half if that's all you're going to do. Anybody can think of that stuff. Even the deaths in *Hatchet*, as creative as they are, I'm not a genius because I can come up with them. A lot of people can come up with that stuff. I think everybody who's sitting here right now could probably do the same thing. But to come up with a fun story with good characters and dialogue and to execute a quality movie is very difficult. That's why, for my money, *Saw* and *Hostel* worked.

Sure, they were torture films, but they were built around great concepts. But some of the other stuff that's starting to float around out there, the knock offs, just give

me a break. No thanks. Give me some of the old days again when horror was still fun. *Hatchet* has some of the most brutal violence you'll ever see, but I'm proud to say it stands on more than just that. It's fucking entertaining. You'll walk out of it exhausted and smiling. Take the monsters and make-up FX from back in the day and push it way more over the top, mix it together with the dialogue and tone of the 90's slashers, and then remove the WB kids, lame acting, "who done it," and spoofy-ness, and you have *Hatchet*. It's like a *Friday the 13th* or *Halloween* on steroids. I cared with this film. I really, really cared.

STEVE NILES

Interviewed by Rob Galluzzo (7/06)

For years, writer Steve Niles tried pitching his horror scripts to unreceptive Hollywood studios. He opted instead to tell his stories via the comic book medium and won over legions of fans with such works as *30 Days of Night*, *Freaks of the Heartland*, and *Criminal Macabre* (featuring Niles' recurring character Cal McDonald). Now, practically all of his comic work is coming to the silver screen! And he's still churning out books with collaborators such as Rob Zombie, Thomas Jane, and Ben Templesmith. *Icons of Fright* is proud to present this exclusive interview with Steve Niles!

What are your earliest recollections of the horror genre?

Well, the first horror movie that scared me was *Night of the Living Dead*. Without a doubt. Because I caught it late at night. And I thought it was a documentary. I was probably around seven or eight and I had my mini-*War of the Worlds* moment, where it freaked me out so bad. (laughs) But even before that, I used to read *Creepy* and *Eerie*. I'd bring them to church when I was around five or six and my mom would take them away from me, because I'd be reading the horror comics in church. (laughs)

What was it that initiated your interest in writing and to follow that creative path?

I was just one of those kids always working on projects, making Super 8 movies. I thought I wanted to do special effects. At one point, I was building monster heads and doing some stop-motion animation, and really, I just got frustrated trying to make movies with my stoned drunken friends all the time. (laughs) So, I started working on scripts and I really enjoyed it. I was a huge, huge Richard Matherson fan, and he made writing really accessible. Just the way he writes, he's not intimidating at all. After reading *I Am Legend*, I really wanted to start writing. So, it was sort of a mixture of all of that stuff.

Do you remember what those early stories were about?

Oh yeah! The first story I wrote was about some kids that hide in the Washington Monument from zombies. (laughs) I was living in DC at the time.

Well, you have a long history of writing and initially you were trying to do it for films, how did that segue into writing comic books?

I started doing comic books in 1986-87. That's when I went out and met Clive Barker before the *Books of Blood* were released here. I wrote Richard Matherson this long letter and he ended up selling me the rights to *I Am Legend* for $100 bucks. So, I was living in my sister's basement and hiring artists that I saw doodling on napkins at restaurants. Just doing whatever I could to work. Clive gave me half the rights to the *Books of Blood*. He split them with me and Eclipse at the time. I had a company called Arcane Comics and that pulled me into this really weird area where I was editing for a few years. I was adapting Clive's stories and editing books. I had done a book called *M* and I had done *I Am Legend*, and I had done a bunch of the Clive Barker stuff such as *Rawhead Rex*, and I got sucked into this whole editor/publisher world for a while.

It took me a really long time to get out of that. Then this really bizarre thing happened. I was living in Pittsburgh, and I got offered a job at Disney. So, they called me, and I thought, *"They're hiring everybody at Disney,"* and they're active now with their video game division. They were trying to copy the old Disney model, which was to hire people from all over the place, all different artists and writers, put them in a room and you'll create magic. All they did was create an army of people who could play video games. (laughs) Because none of us knew how to make them, so we sat around and played them. But that's what got me out to LA.

I'd always been doing comics on and off during all that time, and so some guy at Disney convinced me to take some of my stuff out and pitch it. I pitched *30 Days Of Night*, *Cal McDonald*, and *Freaks Of The Heartland*, and all these scripts that I had at the time, and I just got "No. No. No. No." After that, I worked for Todd McFarlane and I was writing *Spawn: Dark Ages* and *Hellspawn*, and that's when we decided to do it just as a fluke. I did the first issue of 30 Days of Night for free. I just thought, "You want to put out a comic? Here's all these pitches that no one will buy!" (laughs) Let's do "three Act" comics. Three issues. One for each act. And the day the ad hit, things went nuts!

Let's talk a bit about *30 Days of Night*, because it's one of my favorite books. I always notice that you take certain genres and put a very unique twist to them. The vampire genre, for example, has been done to death, but you came up with a really kick-ass original idea. Mike C. doesn't read comic books, for example, but he has read *30 Days of Night*. So, what were the origins for that story?

It's the same thing as you! I've read a lot of vampire stories. I've read all the Anne Rice books and seen every one of the movies. I knew all the things that annoyed me and that were tired, and had already been done. Honestly, I'm so sick of the fucking romantic vampire! I really wanted just some vicious killers! Once I got into it, I started thinking about the hierarchies, and how it would work. And what their systems would be like, which is how I got that whole other twist in there with the other vampires showing up.

What about the whole Alaskan backdrop? The whole thirty days of night thing was something I never knew until I read your book!

I was living in Minnesota for a year, and I'd read those little human interest stories. And what caught my attention was every year, not only was it dark for this long period of time there, but alcohol was illegal during that period because the suicide rate was so high. I thought, "God, what a grim fucking setting that is! (laughs) Now, let's attack you with vampires!" So, yeah, I carried that idea around for years, thinking that's the perfect place for vampires.

Now, it's spawned so many different *30 Days of Night* comic books. But you did follow up your initial run with a sequel, *Dark Days*. Did you kind of have this whole story mapped out from the beginning?

No, actually! And you can dig this quote out, but I believe I said, "I will not do a sequel. I will not stretch this." I wasn't going to do vampires in Finland or go around the Artic circle and do the whole story over again. But I was talked into it.

Really? Because it felt as if you had this trilogy planned.

Once I started thinking about it, I got an idea of where I wanted to go with it. Because I didn't want to go back to Barrow. I didn't want to do the same thing over again. I just wound up liking Stella so much as a character. It just came out of me. I swear to God, that whole thing was outlined on one page, the whole series. It was a time when everyone was so excited about it. So, it was a lot of fun.

You had a pitch for it way back as a movie, then you ended up doing it as a comic, and now it's going to be a movie again. How does it feel that it had to go through this whole long cycle just to make it to a movie again?

I feel really lucky. I spent years pitching stuff and just got nothing. I can't believe that something exploded so big and now a bunch of my stuff is being adapted into films.

Are you nervous about the way Sam Raimi's Ghosthouse Pictures might approach the film?

Well, I know Raimi really respects fans, and he really respects the source material. I think he really learned that doing *Spider-Man*. The latest version of the script I read is absolutely very accurate to the book. And David Slade, who's directing and who recently made *Hard Candy*, when I had met him, he told me he bought the comics off the stands. And as a fan, he pursued the project, which is great. And he is fighting to make sure it's everything that the comic is. Because there were a few studios executives that had some creative ideas they tried to get in there.

I'm mad at Raimi for *Boogeyman*!

No, this isn't going to be anything like that. They've got Weta involved, and they've got a $30 million budget.

I hope they do your book justice!

You know, I just hope they keep it simple! It's a simple story! It's *Night of the Living Dead* in the snow.

Another character you've been with for a while is Cal McDonald from *Criminal Macabre*. Can you tell us a bit about the creation of Cal McDonald?

When I first started writing him, I tried to mimic Raymond Chandler. And all I was doing was really bad Raymond Chandler, but with no real plot. So, I started throwing in things I knew. Like drugs and monsters, and the character just literally started coming together. All those short stories were things I wrote while I was on tour with my band. I'd torment my friends with these stories because I made them read them. Because I had *Savage Membrane*, and *Guns, Drugs and Monsters*, and the first *Hairball* comic, they were in drawers for years! So, when people asked if I had any more from this character, I had tons of stuff!

Are there any plans for a cinematic interpretation of Cal McDonald?

Yeah, we're trying to figure out what to do with that right now. Dark Horse is going monthly with the comic. That was one of the problems. We were doing all these different comics, *Criminal Macabre* and *Last Train to Deathville*, and it turns out everyone was really confused! So, now it's going to be just called *Criminal Macabre* and it's monthly. First artist is going to be Kyle Hotz. Tim Bradstreet is doing all of the covers with Thomas Jane modeling as Cal and Chris Nelson modeling as Morlock. We just did a big photo shoot. And I actually have that '73 Nova that he drives. So, we took it into a shop and put it up on hydraulics so we could tilt it for different angles. KNB loaned us some monster parts and bodies and we staged the covers for the next few years.

Ben Templesmith is such a unique artist and you've collaborated him quite a bit. And I think he compliments your work so beautifully. So, how did you two end up working together?

We actually met on the *Spawn* message board. He posted his work up on there, and I was writing *Spawn: The Dark Ages* at the time and McFarlane was interested in having me taking over *Hellspawn*, because Ashley Wood and Brian Bendis were doing it. I pitched Ben, and we got that gig and that's how we ended up doing *30 Days of Night*. The thing with McFarlane is he has to approve everything, so we were literally on a break waiting on approval for a *Hellspawn* issue when IDW contacted us, because Ted Adams who started IDW was the one who hired us to work at McFarlane. So, he called us and said, "Is there anything you guys want to do?"

So, we did *30 Days of Night* and that was it. Ben's one of those artists I work with that I write the script, I throw it to him, and what I get back I love. I don't think I've ever asked Ben to change a single thing. Honestly, I think what Ben does so good is he's ballsy enough to make

comics dark. If you're going to do a horror comic, you're not going to do big, bright daylight. Make it a little murky, mysterious and hard to look at. It's what it's like in a horror movie sometimes. You squint to see what's coming from the woods. And he does that. He's one of the best horror artists out there right now.

Ok. One of my all-time favorite books that you ever did, *Freaks Of The Heartland*. There's something about that book, man! You have to tell me where that story originated!

I wrote it as a novella originally back in '89 or so. This little book. It had this totally awful ending. (laughs) It had a *Twilight Zone* ending, which tormented me for years. And then Mike Richardson, from Dark Horse, when the Cal McDonald stuff was starting to do well, had asked me about it. "Remember that novella you wrote?" And I told him, "Actually, I wrote a screenplay," where I fixed the ending. I finally wrote it the way I wanted to. Basically, in the novella, I told you where they all came from. And in the book, I realized it's so much better to let everybody's fears fill in that blank. Are they demons from hell? Is it radiation from the nuclear power plant? Whatever. You put it in there, whatever it is that you fear. The comic worked out so well, because that was one I wrote and had all these captions for, I mean, tons of captions, tons of narration. I had the kid's voice all the way through it. And then I saw Greg Ruth's art and I cut everything out except for the most basic captions.

I remember one of the things I loved about the first issue was that it didn't have a lot of text in it, but it told the story wonderfully.

He was doing the facial expressions! When a comic artist can get that stuff across without the words, that's what you hope for. As a comic writer, you're sort of attempting to erase yourself in the process, and *Freaks* is the closest I've come to that.

Nail and *Bigfoot* are your two collaborations with Rob Zombie. Both of you are credited as writers. Can you explain to us a bit about that dynamic?

Actually, we met because literally someone just shoved us in a room together. It was like, "You guys will like each other!" And we just stared at each other for a while and then we started talking. "Ok, I do like him." We both had all these ideas we wanted to do. I said, "I've got a Bigfoot thing." And he said, "Well, I've got a Bigfoot thing I want to do!" So, we came up with a plan. *Nail* was Rob's idea. So, Rob starts the idea off and then we'd play hot potato with it. We knew the general outline, so we'd pass it back and forth, until we'd get it done. The only subtle difference is if you notice is his name is first on *Nail* and my name is first on *Bigfoot*. That's how we trade off, because *Bigfoot* was my concept and that he played hot potato with. It's probably one of the real true collaborations.

Those are some of the things I can read, because I don't hear myself in them at all. It's been tossed around so much that there's characters in there saying dialogue that's not mine. It really works out well. We have a lot of similar sensibilities. We were both bound and determined to undo the damage done by *Harry and the Hendersons*! That was our mission. Now, we just signed the deal, Rob and I are going to be writing the script for *Bigfoot* with Rogue pictures.

Is he interested in directing *Bigfoot* as well?

I don't think so. He's still looking around for what he wants to direct next.

I'm a huge Tom Jane fan! So, can you give us one good Tom Jane story?

Just one?! Actually, I met Tom when he was promoting *The Punisher* and he came up to me and said, "I want to be fucking Cal McDonald!" And I thought, "Alright!" So, we just started talking and he said he had this comic idea he wanted to pitch me, and we went and had lunch, and it turned out we had so much in common. And the weird moment was when he asked where I was from.

I told him I was from Washington DC, and he said he was from Baltimore. So, he asked, "Do you know the music scene at all?" Well, yeah I was in a band called *Gray Matter*. And turns out, he used to come to my shows! He was thirteen years old and he used to come to my shows! I didn't believe him. So, he went back to his parents, and came back with the vinyl record that he obviously had played a million times. So, we've had a million of those bonding moments. We just totally get along.

If there was one superhero you could do, which one would you want to write?

Hulk. The Hulk! It's Jekyll and Hyde! It's perfect. I would love to do him. But the way he was in the 70's. Not talking and getting haircuts and shit. Now, I think he's on another planet or something. Yeah, that one I've always wanted to do. Hulk and Batman.

GREG NICOTERO

Interviewed by Mike Cucinotta and Rob Galluzzo (7/06)

You can't be a horror fan and not know the name KNB EFX. Founded by Robert Kurtzman, Greg Nicotero, and Howard Berger, the company has worked on just about every genre picture of the past two decades including *Evil Dead 2, Hostel, The Hills Have Eyes, Halloween 5, Land of the Dead, Kill Bill,* and much more. *Icons of Fright* was lucky enough to sit down with one of KNB's founders, Greg Nicotero.

What are your earliest recollections of the genre? Do you remember the first film to really impact or scare you?

Horror of Dracula! We had an old VCR, a reel-to-reel VCR when I was young, and my dad was really into gadgets, so I remember the first two movies that we ever recorded off television were *Horror of Dracula* and *The Time Machine*. So, to me, sadly, I never knew who Bela Lugosi was for a long time. When I saw six or seven years old, Christopher Lee was Dracula. Chris Lee is always Dracula to me. Between all the blood, and the contact lenses and the fangs, I loved it.

Was there any particular film that opened up your mind to the idea of special effects make-up?

Well, *Jaws*. I remember going to see *Jaws* back on June 21st; we went the second night it was out. And I remember looking at the lobby cards in the movie theater and seeing the shot of Hooper in the cage with the shark going by, and I was astounded in how cool that was. And I kept thinking "How the fuck did they do that? How'd they build a big giant shark that could eat people?!" So, between that movie, *The Exorcist, Planet of the Apes,* and of course, all of the Universal horror movies, I was always intrigued by monster stuff. I started reading *Famous Monsters* magazine around this time. I think *Jaws* and then later *Dawn of the Dead* were pretty much the two movies that did it for me.

Can you tell us a bit about when you started working with Howard Berger and Robert Kurtzman?

I worked with Howard on *Day of the Dead*, and we were shooting in Beaver Falls, and we needed a few extra people from LA. So, John Vulich had called Everett Burrell and Howard Berger because he had worked with them both at John Buechler's shop. So, they flew in and that's where Howard and I first met. When I moved to Los Angeles a year later, Howard had actually picked me up from the airport with Bob Kurtzman and we all decided to get a house together and we'd room together.

So, it was me, Howard, and Bob who had this rental house in Reseda, California together, and then Bob and I worked for Mark Shostrom and Howard was working at Kevin Yagher's and Rick Baker's, so we just kept working. It was really *Evil Dead 2* that really solidified our desire to work together. We decided on that movie, "Why are we working for someone else? We should just do our own thing." I sort of had the business acumen. Howard was the shop foreman and people person. And Bob was the creative guy. So, at that point in our careers, all three of us brought something very different to the table. It all started when I got a phone call from Scott Spiegel who had written *Evil Dead 2,* and he said, "Listen, I'm directing this really shitty, low-budget movie called Intruder. I've got no money, but can you recommend some kid working out of his garage to maybe build some of the effects stuff for me?"

I said, "Scott, I'll do it." And that was KNB's first job. We probably made a little over $200 dollars. I was working on *Phantasm II* and *Deep Star Six* at the time with Bob, and Howard was working on *Child's Play* at Kevin Yagher's, so we'd work on those movies – our day jobs during the day, and then go work at night on Scotty's movie. There was a six-week period where we never slept! We'd work all day at our day jobs and go work all night. It was so funny, but it was literally the genesis of KNB.

Well, going back a bit, *Evil Dead 2* is my personal favorite horror movie ever…

Mine too!

… and the DVD commentary is probably my favorite commentary on any DVD. I honestly can't watch the movie anymore if it's not with the commentary with you guys. (You, Sam, Bruce, Scott Spiegel)

You know, a lot of people have said that! Literally five people came up to me yesterday and said the only way we can watch *Evil Dead 2* is with the commentary with you, Sam, Bruce and Scotty, which is great. The commentary was great. At the beginning of the movie, with Henrietta sitting in the rocking chair and she rocks forward, and I had said, "Oh, this is a pre-shoot day," because I had had my video camera with me and I videotaped every day, it sort of ingrained the experience in my mind chronologically.

So, I start spouting off all these little tidbits, and I remember Sam covering up the microphone and asking, "How the fuck do you remember all this?!" (laughs) I said, "Sam, you forget, I shot six hours of behind-the-scenes video!" I remember stuff about that movie like it was yesterday. And it was really a fun commentary because I remembered so much of the technical stuff about it, and then to have the other guys bring up other stuff, it was just great.

At what point did you realize that you had made it; that this was what you were officially doing as a career?

I'll tell you, it was *Dances with Wolves* back in 1989-1990. KNB had been around for two years. All of a sudden, we were on set in South Dakota and we were puppeteering the buffalo with Kevin Costner. The movie comes out, and it becomes one of the most famous Westerns ever made at that point. I was really nervous, because I was terrified that we'd only be remembered for *Dances with Wolves*! I thought, "Jesus Christ, we've peaked in two years!" We've done a movie that was so well received. And I remember during the Oscars, they showed the buffalo hunt sequence which we had done, and I remember my mom calling saying, "They showed your stuff on the Academy awards!" And I thought, "Yeah, that's kinda funny." I always remember saying to Bob and Howard that I didn't want to peak after two years. We need to keep pushing and pushing. So, it was a really conscious effort for me personally because of that fact. I really was nervous that since *Dances with Wolves* was so well received that it'd be our biggest movie ever. Little did I know!

All three of us wanted so much just to push our company. Because we started off as a bunch of horror guys. We did *Halloween 5* and *Texas Chainsaw 3* and *Nightmare 5*, and to go from those low-budget slasher movies to *Misery* and *Dances with Wolves* within a year, was just too much.

I forgot about *Halloween 5*! Did you sculpt the mask to your face? I thought that was the story we heard or something along those lines?

No, Bob sculpted the mask. This is before the internet, so the only reference we had at the time was the John Carpenter *Cinemafantastique* issue, with him sitting there with a pumpkin on the cover. And there were a couple of shots of the mask, these tiny pictures that Bob used for reference. We got to location with this guy Mark Maitre, and the director (Dominique Othenin-Girard) says "Egh, I don't like the nose. We need to change the nose." So, Mark sculpted this nose and we put it on the mask as an appliance, to make the nose different. Don Shanks was just the stunt guy who wore the mask. We never fitted it on him or did a life cast.

I enjoy all the *Halloween* films, but *Halloween 5* stands out as such a bizarre entry.

It's a really different movie than all the other films, because Dominique was this really artsy guy. I had a few people come up to me that want to get a hold of people involved with *Halloween 5* for conventions (who normally don't do conventions) because that movie has such a different following than all the other films. It's just a really different movie.

Mike loves it because Donald Pleasence's version of Loomis in *Halloween 5* is "bat-shit crazy."

Donald Pleasence is the man! We had such a great time with him on that movie. It was the first time I'd met him, and we got to be really good friends. Because we did his make-up every single night. So, there'd be nights when I'd sit on set, and I'd start talking to him about *Fantastic Voyage* or *The Outer Limits*; all these great, great films he did. I'll never forget this one night, me, Mark Maitre, Donald, Danielle Harris – we all went out to dinner, and I look across the table and think, "I'm having dinner with Donald Pleasence. How fucking cool is that?!"

I also remember the day he died. I was in Vancouver working on *The Outer Limits* back in February or March of 1995, and I had heard on the radio that he had died, and I was really, really sad about it. I remember calling

John Carpenter, because they were really good friends and John loved him.

What was one of the most difficult gags you had to pull off for a movie? Was there anything that you were nervous you wouldn't be able to do practically but then managed to pull off?

Well, *Kill Bill* was a really intriguing process, because Quentin had very, very specific ideas in mind. And one of the things I'm most proud of, he wanted to do a shot where we cut off the top of Lucy Liu's head. And he said, I don't want her to look like the airport zombie in *Dawn of the Dead* and I don't want to use CGI. So, we have to figure out a way to make it look right. I was really nervous about how we were going to do it. He had this specific idea of how he wanted to be really close on her eyes, and then have a trickle of blood come down, and then pull back. I kept thinking "Fuck. How the fuck are we going to do that?!" So, I got together with one of my sculptors named Garrett Immel and we were sitting together brainstorming, and he came up with this great idea. Basically, he made an appliance that went on her forehead, but it was sculpted in forced perspective.

So, if you looked at it from a certain angle, it looked like you were looking across her head but it was actually sculpted in an oval shape. It's kind of hard to describe unless you see it, but it was one of those things where the director throws the gauntlet down and you have to sit there with your guys and keep throwing ideas out until you figure it out. And the fact that we were able to come up with this sort of really odd way to do it, I was really pleased that we were able to come up with a solution.

That's what directors do. "This is how I want it done. You guys figure it out." In terms of an effect, I wasn't sure about beforehand, I've never gone to a set with an effect that I was ever afraid would never work. You can't do that. You can't go to set with something you're not quite sure about. You have to figure it out. There are generally limitations, such as shooting it from certain angles. But I've always been really confident that everything we've ever done on set has been ready and prepared.

Would you consider yourself your own worst critic?

Yes. I want my company to be regarded as a company that delivers high quality work. Fortunately, we've been able to continue working for eighteen years! You can always go back and watch a film and think, "God, I would do that so differently now." Sometimes I feel like I want to shoot a movie, do the whole thing, and take what you learn from that experience, trash it and go and film the whole thing again. Rebuild everything. That's how Rick Baker does it and that's why his make-ups look so amazing. Because he'll sculpt the make-up and they'll bring an actor in and apply it. And they'll look at what they like and don't like about it, trash it, and then they'll start over. The difference is Rick Baker gets eight months to build stuff, whereas we get eight weeks to build stuff.

KNB has done a lot of work with Robert Rodriguez. He's unique in the sense that he works very much outside the studio system and pretty much does his own thing. What are the pros and cons of working with someone like Robert?

Well, the intriguing thing about Robert is he's still an old-school guy. He loves *The Thing*. He loves *Escape From New York*. He loves *Jaws*. His influences and the movies he loves are old-school movies. He's very much like me in that respect. But he plays by his own rules. When we were doing *Sin City*, it was one of those scenarios where the whole movie was shot on green screen, and we had all these character make-ups based on the graphic novels.

I remembered going into Robert's office and he said "I gotta show you this. These are some of the first finished scenes." It was a scene with Bruce Willis running through the woods, and the wind is blowing, and the snow is falling and he leans up against the tree and grabs his heart. He falls down on his knees and the snow moves as he falls into the snow. I was standing there when we shot that, and it was all done on green screen. But seeing it complete, my jaw just dropped. If I hadn't been there, I wouldn't have believed that that was not real. That's how impressed and amazed I was.

The way that Robert's brain works is really fascinating. I started with him on *From Dusk Till Dawn*, where everything was all done practically. He really wasn't a fan of CGI stuff, because he felt that at that time you'd have to stop, go over to a blue screen, and have separate set-ups and shoot all these elements, and later composite all of them together. Robert always felt that slowed him down. So, to go from that guy back then to the *Sin City* guy, where his movies are so visually driven by computer animation and make-up effects is incredible. I've watched him blossom into this filmmaker in the twelve years that we've been friends and it's been astounding. He plays by his own rules and is successful. There are a lot of people that play by their own rules, you just never hear about them because they don't do it right. But Robert does it right and he knows how to make good movies.

As a make-up FX artist, how do you feel about effects being done practically versus CGI? For me, CGI still looks like CGI. There's something about the old stop motion animation that I still like better.

There's a guy in LA named Shannon Shea and he and I are developing a movie that would have stop-motion (Ray) Harryhausen-type creatures in it. And there's definitely a charm to that. Listen, CGI – digital effects, there's always an even ground between the two. What happens when something is too overloaded with digital stuff that it tips the scales? Well, then it doesn't feel right.

I was watching *Hostel*, which you guys worked on, but Bob (Kurtzman) had done a lot of CG work in it as well, such as the backdrops in the train, etc. I had no idea that there was any CGI in that movie.

And that's the way it needs to be done. When you watch a movie like *Mission Impossible*, it just feels like you're watching a cartoon. I'm not bashing the movie, but you get to a certain point where it's too much. There's something about seeing an actor do his own stunts when you know that the actor was in genuine peril versus "Oh, it's just a digital effect." There's a really fine line. When we were shooting *Land of the Dead*, George and I had talked in the beginning about doing a lot of old school animatronic stuff and then augmenting some of it with CGI.

The headless zombie that flops over, we did a puppet head of it and then we did some CGI stuff, and I directed second unit on the movie, so I shot all the elements. So, there was a guy with a green hood on, and I put him through the motions and shot all the elements and plate stuff. So, there's a good example, because that gag was augmented by good digital work. All the head hits too. If you're on a movie where you have to shoot 500 zombies, and you have forty days to shoot the movie, to take a half hour to put a big blood bag on the back of someone's head, rig it all up, squib it, then do take two, verses have the guy just fall down and add a digital blood element that we could shoot later. You just have to be careful about it, because if it gets too lopsided, it doesn't feel right.

KNB handled all the episodes of *Masters of Horrors*, which to us is a dream list of directors…

Oh, for us too!

Was there anyone on the roster that you hadn't worked with before, or that you were excited to work with again?

Truthfully, the main reason we got hired on *Masters of Horror* is because we had worked with all those directors before. We knew Joe Dante. We knew John Carpenter. We knew Tobe Hooper. We knew Don Coscarelli because of *Bubba Ho-Tep* and *Phantasm*, so we had literally worked with all those directors except for Dario Argento. Dario's the only one we hadn't worked with. I had met Dario before, but I had never worked with Dario. And it was right after *Land of the Dead*, we had a conference call for *Masters of Horror* and we're talking about *Jenifer,* and he had a translator on the phone with him, so he would speak in Italian and have someone translate it to English. He spoke Italian to everyone except me.

When he talked to me, he'd say (in Italian accent) "Oh, Asia… she love you! How are you, my friend?" So, all of a sudden, he's speaking English to me and as soon as someone else would ask a question he'd go back to Italian. It was really funny! I was just really delighted to get to work with Dario. And we're doing the second season now, we're up to the fourth episode. We shot Landis'. We shot Tobe's. And we shot Dario's. Dario's second season episode was bloody, bloody, bloody! It's called *Pelts*. We're working on John Carpenter's now. Howard's in Vancouver.

The one episode you didn't work on was Takashi Miike's *Imprint*. Have you seen it yet?

I have a copy of it, but I haven't watched it yet. Everyone is telling me to be prepared. I loved *Audition*, because I didn't know anything about it. I remember people told me, "You have to see this movie". So, I just Tivo-ed one day, watched it, had no idea where the movie was going. That's the kind of stuff I love.

I recently watched *The Descent*, because Edgar Wright recommended it and said you have to see this movie. So, I bought it in London on DVD. Came home and watched it, and I had no idea what the movie was about or where it was going, and I loved it. That's what I try to do, shield myself from knowing what stuff is about before going in. Oh, I just have to say, Simon Pegg, Edgar Wright, and Nick Frost are three of the fucking greatest human beings. *Shaun of the Dead* is one of the best movies of the last ten years. They're doing another film called *Hot Fuzz*, which they're almost finished shooting. They sent me the script to read, and I dog-eared the pages of the script that I laughed out loud reading. When I was finished, the entire script was dog-eared. Those guys are fucking brilliant.

They are great friends of mine and I love them. And I made a joke a couple of years ago when I first met them and I said, "Every interview I do, I'm going to give *Shaun of the Dead* and *Hot Fuzz* a plug because I love you guys." I actually text messaged Simon last night, "Bub is here!" (laughs) So, I have to go get an autograph from Howard Sherman for Simon.

What's the convention experience like for you?

I'm really unassuming. Some kid in the elevator said to me jokingly, "Oh my God! You're a God!" And I said, "Let me tell you something. I'm as big of a horror geek as you are. The only difference is I'm sitting at the other side of the table." You don't realize, I went up to all the Cenobites before this show started and got all their autographs!

In the *Land of the Dead* special features, (John) Leguizamo calls you "*such a nerd.*"

I know! Well, I've known Johnny since *Spawn* because we did the clown make-up on that. Look, Howard and I have been blessed. Some people come over and say, "Dude, you

have the rock n' roll career of all careers." But these shows are so grounding, because they really make you realize how important the work that you do is to inspire and influence young filmmakers.

When I did my lecture yesterday, I had said that, "there are people in this room that will one day be the next Quentin Tarantinos." And I pointed to this twelve year old kid, who came to my table yesterday. His name is Paul, he was in the front row, and I said, "I may work for this kid one day." For me, it's all about those moments of inspiration. I remember the first convention I ever went to and all the stuff I bought, and the people I met, and it reminds me when kids come by my table and buy a picture that I was once that same kid. It really warms you. It makes me feel great that in my own weird way, I may be able to inspire people the same way that I was inspired by people like John Carpenter, Rick Baker and Rob Bottin. Someone asked me yesterday who would be the one person I'd love to work with that I haven't. And I said Rob Bottin. Between *The Howling* and *The Thing* and *Legend*, the man's a genius.

LIN SHAYE

Interviewed by Mike Cucinotta (8/06)

How can you not love the wonderful Lin Shaye?! She's appeared in dozens of films from *Dumb and Dumber* to *Kingpin*. Most recently, she appeared as Granny Boone in Tim Sullivan's *2001 Maniacs*. She's also going to be seen this summer in a little movie people seem to be talking about called *Snakes on a Plane*?! Read on for *Icons of Fright*'s one on one with Lin!

First, we always ask, what was the first horror film you remember seeing?

House of Wax, not the remake! Oh my god, the original *House of Wax* in 3D scared the living "you know what out" of me. And also, *Psycho*. Those were the two films that left imprints on my psyche. I would love to see *House of Wax* again in 3D, unbelievably frightening.

How would you describe your experience on *2001 Maniacs*?

Well, I met Tim on *Detroit Rock City* and we hit it off right away. He's an amazingly energetic, bright, terrific guy. When we did that film, he talked about *Maniacs*, but it seemed like the kind of thing where people say, "Oh, I have a project…" and it goes into the ozone and you never hear from them again. So, lo and behold, I don't remember how many years later, Tim called and said they'd actually gotten the money and would I be interested in playing the part of Granny Boone.

What is the role you were expecting to be offered?

You know, there's that part of you that goes, "A grandmother, wait a minute, I'm only eighteen!" Then as I thought well, "Granny" doesn't have to be a ninety-year-old lady at all, that's just what they call her. I read the script, and now keep in mind, I'm not really a major horror film fan. I'm not that into the genre, I mean it seems to be a whole culture that I've never been a part of, even though I've now done a fair share of horror films. Well, you read it and go "Ugh!" but it was with Tim, and Robert Englund's always been a great favorite of mine.

You did have role in the original *Nightmare on Elm Street*, as the teacher, right?

Right, the teacher, and I met Robert socially a few times and he's really an extraordinary guy. A tremendous actor in his own right, let alone what he did with Freddy Kruger. People don't know that he's a classically trained actor who cut his teeth on Shakespeare, a seasoned pro in many ways. I was really excited with the prospect of working with him and being his alter ego.

Now, didn't *Maniacs* have a somewhat bumpy start? Were you around for any of that?

Originally, Tim showed me some drawings and Granny Boone looked like *The Beverly Hillbillies* grandmother with the bun and glasses, and she was supposed to have a coonskin cap. That was all fine and good, and we started to have wardrobe prepping and everything, and the next thing I heard, the project was off.

I remember this, because *2001 Maniacs* had been announced for a 2001 release, right?

Yes, but the money fell out. So, Tim said we were on hold, and at the point you let it go, you don't know what's going to happen next. Now the irony is the sets we were supposed to use had been in one of the big fires and the whole area was burned down. There was a weird irony to that because if we had been filming, we would have been in trouble, or danger, at some point during that shoot. Then more time went by, and Tim was over here for dinner and he got the phone call in my kitchen that the money had come through, there was a new set of producers, Raw Nerve, and Velvet Steamroller, a young company trying to find viable investments.

They thought this sounded like a good one. So, the budget was going to be bigger, and they found this location that ended up completely inspiring the film. You know how they say everything happens for a reason? We ended up finding this living museum in Lumpkin, GA, a re-enactment museum. What they did was create a space, bring real Civil War buildings into the area and decorate them with 100% authentic dishes, rugs, bedding. It was really a fabulous place.

It makes the film look great.

Oh, you literally could not pay for those set pieces. They utilized all the real things there to enrich and enliven what we were making. And this helped us change the concept of Granny.

In what way?

Well, now you can't have this woman in a coonskin cap. Now we're talking "Southern Belle" here. So literally, on-set, the costume designer Wendy Moynihan, she was phenomenal. We walked into my trailer, we had the coonskin cap and all this stuff, and we said, "No, no! We got to look at different stuff. This woman is like a cross between Scarlett O'Hara and a black widow spider." So, she went and found skirts and petticoats, and sewed me into this fabulous costume with drapery skirts and this sort of off-the-shoulder blouse and necklace, and the sausage curls for the hair. She created this wonderful look for the character which I think was a wonderful counterpoint to the cannibalism.

What was it about Tim Sullivan that made you stick with *Maniacs* for so long?

Tim is just like a puppy with a rag in his mouth; once he gets a hold of something his passion is completely contagious. And his intellect too, in terms of what he was creating and wanted in terms of this movie. He really is a horror film aficionado. He exudes that and you catch it, not like a disease, but with absolute ease, because as soon as you catch it, you're on the train with him. I have tremendous respect for him. When you know what really goes into making a movie and the journey to get it on board, it's insane. How does any movie ever get made? And yet here's this guy who had this idea, along with Chris Kobin, and they just refused to let it die and let it get them down. It's so attractive to work with that kind of a package.

Where there any particularly fun scenes for you?

Well, they all were fun, but I think the dinner scene where I throw the biscuits and say the blessing, which was my idea and Tim was very open to that. We even came up with lines every once in a while, which were hilarious. I love the scene where we "put Ricky on a stickie." I would say everything was fun to film. Robert was a dream to work with.

What is Robert like on the set?

Full of energy, ideas, goodwill. Completely professional. Non-stop energy and a talker. The thing is everything he says is really interesting. He's had a lot of experience in his career, and a lot of opportunities because of Freddy, which he's eager to share with everybody, and with young actors. A real team player, always ready to go.

He seemed really into it. I think this is one of the best horror performances he's done in a really long time. It was good to see him dig in as Mayor Buckman.

Well, it was a really grand character, it's Shakespearean in size. He's like the ringmaster, and I hate to say broad, because people think broad means big, but it's grand.

But he never really went over-the-top with it, which could have been so easy to do with that character.

I felt so too, and he's very skilled with that and that comes from years of training and talent.

How about working with the rest of the cast, including a lot of young and new talent?

Giuseppe Andrews I worked with on *Detroit Rock City*, and he's one of kind. He's on his own plane, he's a really good actor. He played it very interesting, very straight. He was the handsome leading man of the town. I thought Wendy Kremer did a great job, a very brave performance. She's lovely. I think all the younger actors did a really amazing job. I mean, we had to rein them in a bit sometimes in terms of we being the older folks and the more experienced on-set, because they were all so excited to be there.

What were some ways you were able to help those guys out, being so experienced?

I think just focusing. They saw how much we focused, and I think that helped them automatically. There's time to be frivolous and fool and joke around, but then it's time to focus and do the scene. I think everyone really achieved that. There were no real "fuckups." Everyone tried their hardest to bring everything they had to for the scenes.

Do you know anything about some of the conflicting views on what the final cut of the film would be like?

A little bit, I mean, I think being that there were three different production companies involved; everybody had different considerations. Tim's idea was to create a vaudevillian horror film, slightly tongue in cheek. I think there was some difference of opinion on how funny the film should be, and how scary. Everybody put their two cents in so it took a long while for the film to get finished and edited appropriately. They did end up shooting some additional footage after we came back from Georgia which I think ended up being extremely useful. That was a fight scene between Jay Gillespie and Robert Englund. But you know, differences of opinion can be very creative, but conflict can be just destructive and cause some bad blood.

Speaking of re-shoots, I see you're credited with *Snakes on a Plane*, which just did some re-shoots.

Ah, yes! It's going to be the biggest hit of 2006! It's just a behemoth, it kept growing and growing.

I think the second anyone hears about it they instantly want to see it. What's your role in it?

I actually have a wonderful role. I play the Senior Flight Attendant, her name is Grace, and she's kind of the one who's seen-it-all, done-it-all and slightly cynical about everything, but you love her. I end up being a heroine, saving a baby from the snakes, and I end up getting it and I have wonderful death scene. I don't think I'm giving anything away, I mean, that's what it is, right? Let's just say I'm not the only death scene!

Were you working with real snakes?

Oh yeah! There were and I got to tell you, they are fabulous creatures and I'm not afraid of them. I find them very fascinating and beautiful. The little squiggly ones are kind of weird, but the bigger ones, wow. They had this 600-pound python named "Kittie" that was on set, Burmese python. It took ten people to hold her, and was probably one of the most beautiful living things I've ever seen. We had a fabulous snake wrangler, Jules Sylvester, one of the foremost reptile experts in the world in terms of what he does.

Now, I went into the snake room, which had this very peculiar smell and there were just cages and cages of snakes. He asked me if I wanted to hold one. I'd touched one before, and they're not slimy, they're like silk. They're so beautiful. So, I put my hands out and he laid the snake in my hands, a corn snake, it's not poisonous. He said their biggest fear is falling, and you have to make them feel safe. So, you end up almost doing tai-chi, they wrap around your arms, and you have to lengthen your arm so they don't fall down, and they seek warmth. It wasn't creepy, it was very pleasant. It was a real education and really very fun.

What's the feel of the film? Is it going to be tongue in cheek like *Maniacs*?

Well, what they realized is that they had this fan base going, so with the re-shoots they turned it into a hard R, so it's going to be much gorier, much scarier. David Ellis, who directed it, is a master of the scare. He knows how to do the boo, and of course it's going to be funny. Some of these characters are ridiculous. It is going to be a great time.

Have you seen any of the fan marketing?

Yeah, Wendy Kremer sent me a link with posters, cartoons, and that whole, "Hey it's like *Snakes on a Plane*" vernacular, it's very cool.

I want to touch a film you did a few years ago I thought was overlooked called *Dead End*.

Yeah, another great one, really. Unfortunately, the distribution companies don't want to be creative in terms of their marketing. That could have been a gem of a sleeper and doing midnight runs. I think it would have sold.

It was a very interesting movie, and I think you're right about the whole marketing, I'd seen the DVD and it never caught me until I saw it on television. How did that film come to be?

It was written by two French guys, from Paris and they decided to make this little horror film. I went in and read for it. I was so taken with the character and the script. We shot it for three weeks in Franklin Canyon, all night shoots. It was made on a shoestring budget, but it's so stylish. My son, who is sixteen, told me it was one of his favorite scary movies. When we saw it with audiences, they literally gasped, it makes you jump out of your seat. So, I'm thrilled it's getting around and developing a cult status.

I always recommend it to people. I think it will eventually find its audience.

I think it will too. I mean, it's interesting, I used to be known for *There's Something About Mary* and *Kingpin*, now it's Lin Shaye who did *Dead End*. It's great. It's starting to build its own steam. It did win a ton of awards in Europe. It won the Audience Award in San Sebastian, and in total about four best of show awards.

Were you nominated for anything, because you and Ray were fantastic in it.

Yes, I won Best Supporting Actress in Belgium at a festival.

Now, how did you come to work with those Farrelly Brothers so often?

I had a tiny role in *Dumb and Dumber*, Miss Neugeboren. I was sort of given the role, and it was the first thing they directed. I mean, Pete was so funny he didn't even know to say "Action!" in the beginning. He just liked my ideas. I came in thinking this woman looked like a French Poodle, and he loved it. Then I auditioned for *Kingpin* and again for *Mary*. That was how that relationship came about. I mean, they put me on the map. I've been acting since 1974, and the problem I run into occasionally still is being a "character actress."

The Farrellys hired me to play Magna and Mrs. Neugeboren, and I can safely say there's not another director in this town that would have hired me for those roles. The reason they did, Pete says, is I was the most creative actress who came in to read. Usually it's, "What does she look like?" So, often it's "nurse," "teacher," all those things. "Well, we want to use Lin somewhere, what do we got? Well, she's not the ingénue, she's not the leading lady, but maybe I will be at some point because I think I can carry my weight.

You did a great job in *2001 Maniacs* and *Dead End*, those are leading roles.

Thank you, those are leading roles. I think people are just getting to know the range I have. *Dead End* was probably the most screen time I ever had.

Is there anything else you've got coming up that you're particularly excited about?

Snakes is probably the most exciting. I did an episode of *My Name is Earl*. I'm going to be on the season finale. I did another thing with Jason Lee and Crispin Glover called *Drop Dead Sexy*, that's coming out on DVD. I hope that some of these films will find their way into a specialty theatrical release. Those are the two I'm most excited about.

GARY SHERMAN

Interviewed by Rob Galluzzo (8/06)

Icons of Fright recently got to spend some time talking to director Gary Sherman, the man behind the camera for *Death Line* (or as we know it in the US *Raw Meat*), the cult classics *Dead and Buried*, *Vice Squad*, and *Poltergeist III*. Gary tells us about his experiences on all of those films and more! Read on, folks!

What are your earliest recollections of the genre? Do you remember the first film to really have an impact on you and open you up to the world of horror?

Vincent Price's *House Of Wax* in 3D. I saw it when I was just a little kid, around five or six years old, and I went with my brother to see it in 3D. Basically, from the beginning with the guy with the ping pong balls shooting them out into the audience, I was scared. The rest of it just blew me away. I thought that was one of the scariest things I had ever seen and from that point I just got more and more interested in horror films. I grew up in Chicago, and there was this television program on Saturday nights called *Shock Theatre* with Marvin, who was a host in a black turtle-neck sweater and glasses that looked like coke bottles. They ran all the old *Dracula* and *Frankenstein* horror movies. All the *Hammer* stuff. *Wolfman Meets Frankenstein*. I was addicted to that when I was a kid.

My friend Nathan Herman, who actually ended up as a writer for *Saturday Night Live*, he went the opposite direction, he went into comedy. But Nathan and I would spend every Saturday night together since grammar school. We'd go over to one or the other's house and other kids would come too just to watch *Shock Theatre* every Saturday night. It familiarized me with all the old and great classic horror films.

Do you remember what it was that sparked your interest in the way films were made and that helped you decide that you wanted to become involved in filmmaking in some capacity?

Filmmaking came to me in a whole different way. I never knew I wanted to be a filmmaker. I knew I was an artist in some form. I had played music from the time I was a little kid, and I also painted and drew. I'd done sculpture. And at a very early age, I went to Saturday school at the Art Institute of Chicago and studied art and painting. I was really into it. Music was also a really important part of my life. All art in general. I was in search of a medium and ended up at the Institute of Design. It's an art school that allows you to just venture into every aspect of art in the modern world. I had discovered film. I found an old Arriflex camera in a closet at school and I just started shooting film. I had no idea that I wanted to be a filmmaker, until I discovered that Arriflex. I was working at a record company at the time as a session musician, to help me to work my way through school. And I was doing a session with Bo Diddley and I asked Bo if I could shoot some footage of him, and he said, "Sure."

That film ended up being my first movie, which was a documentary called *The Legend Of Bo Diddley*. It got sold to seventy-five television stations around the world and won a bunch of awards and the next thing I knew I was a filmmaker. It was all an accident. My first dramatic film was a little ten minute short that I shot called *Cry Angel*, which was a little horror movie. I just thought I could really get in touch with that sensibility of fear. I've talked about this a lot in other interviews, but I was really affected by a series of murders that took place when I was a kid in Chicago, and they really traumatized me. It was on the front page of the paper every day and I used to have nightmares about it. I suppose trying to fight off these fears and overcome this phobia that I'd developed about it was why I started to learn as much as I could about that aspect of life and serial killers and things like that. I thought the more I knew, the less fearful I'd be. It really just increased my fear.

That's interesting, because I think a lot of people are fans of the horror genre for the same reason, an attempt to conquer these fears.

I'm very in touch with my fears, and I understand my fears. Very early in my career, in segueing into dramatic and narrative films, I found that fear was an area I could really get into. When I started writing, I found that if I could scare myself, I could scare anybody. That's where "Scary Gary" was born. (laughs)

Your first foray into horror is the fan favorite *Death Line*. You came up with the story, and directed it in 1972. It's a film that, at this point, the story has been replicated dozens of times. What were the origins behind the story for *Death Line*? Weren't you living in London at the time?

I lived in London, yeah. I had a pretty successful commercial career going. And everyone kept saying to me, "Make a feature film. Make a feature film." The two industries, the commercial industry or the advertising industry and the feature film industry in England were pretty tight. Everybody worked in both genres. So, finally I asked, "Well, how do you get a feature film made?" And people told me, "Well, you have to write something." So, I thought, "What should I write?" I started working on different ideas, and I always liked horror and someone told me "I bet if you write a really good horror script, you'd get it made."

So, that's what I set out to do. I'm a real stickler for reality and research. I'm like a sponge. I need to learn about everything that surrounds me in my life. I started reading more and more about the London Tube system and I found out all this stuff about a hundred different companies that were involved in building the tubes. There were cave-ins and people were killed and it was a huge scandal. It wasn't until sometime later that they merged all the companies together and created London Transport.

I just got into the whole history of all of that. And then there was something else that I had read about which was a whole clan of people out in Scotland during the fifteenth or sixteenth century called the Bean clan. Sawney Bean, which was an old Scottish legend. I had read this book about Sawney Bean who was a highway man who had become so notorious, and the price on his head so high, that he didn't trust anyone. He took in his brothers and his cousins and all those that were involved with him, and put together this highway men mob that would rob coaches going from one place to another. But they became so notorious that they had to hide in these caves along the Scottish coast.

They had all this money, but they had nothing do to with it because they couldn't go anyplace to spend their money, so what they started doing was not only robbing these people, but they'd start killing them, and taking the bodies and smoking the bodies. They became cannibals. They ate their victims because they were starving and because they couldn't go anyplace to get food. It went on for generations. Then finally, I think it was during the reign of King James, he sent the army in, because they found a smoked arm floating in the water and they followed the tides back and went and found these caves filled with these cannibals. They were all taken back to Glasgow. The men were hanged, and the women were burned at the stake as witches. The whole Sawney Bean story always fascinated me. And suddenly I had the idea, why not put Sawney Bean and the building of the Tubes together for a story?

That's great. In fact, I believe that Wes Craven was also inspired by the Sawney Bean story for *The Hills Have Eyes*, which was a few years after *Death Line*.

Well, I'm not going to point any fingers. Lots of people did lots of things that were similar. *The Texas Chain Saw Massacre* has a lot of things that were reminiscent of *Death Line*. There were lots of films, even up to today that have resemblances to *Death Line*. And why not? It's like Picasso said, "Mature artists emulate. Immature artists steal." (laughs) That's what we all do. You usually copy from something that went down before.

I love Wes though. I love his work. He's one of the greats of our genre. But there are a lot of pictures I've seen that I think have stolen ideas straight from *Death Line*. My great friend Guillermo Del Toro, who I think is one of the great gifts to our genre, credits his whole career to *Death Line*. He's told me he first saw it when he was eight years old and that it inspired him. In every one of his films, he has at least one scene that's a tribute to *Death Line*.

In *Death Line*, about twenty minutes in, you've got this incredible shot – it begins with a rat eating a piece of meat and slowly pans left in a 360 angle to reveal a bunch of bodies and the whole underground set piece. How much prep went into achieving this shot and how difficult was it to pull off? It's one of my favorite moments of the film.

Well, thank you very much. The shot is eight and a half minutes long and it's the entire reel four of the movie, back in the days when films were reel to reel! I wrote it into the script. That shot is detailed moment for moment the way it takes place in the script. I had no money to make that film. We made it for pennies. Especially pennies based on today's budget!

That whole shot was done using a very primitive piece of equipment and an elemack, which was basically a studio pedestal, a hydraulic post on wheels. And you could drop on it, but you couldn't go up, because you'd have to pump it up with a pedal. So, there's no way to rise on it, it's only drop down. And then we put a mini-jib, which is basically a balancing arm with the camera on one side. We didn't have video assists back then. So, the operator actually had to be holding the camera on the mini-jib and a grip would work the arm to raise it lower as needed and it was on track.

Basically, the answer to your question is we spent one day setting the shot, lighting it, and rehearsing it. We laid the track and the track had to be covered with hay as we went along so you wouldn't see the track. Also, the camera does the 360 of the man's larder and then comes back up and through the window of the door and shows the door into the next room and then it goes out through the next door. We rehearsed all those tricks. At the end of the day, the producers came down to set.

Now, I'm pretty fast. I do a lot of set-ups every day, so the big joke at the end of the day was the producers asking, "Well, how many set-ups did you do today?" And I said "None." "How much film did you shoot?" "We never turned over." (laughs) They'd say, "You know, this is a low budget film! What'd you do all day?" "Well, we just rehearsed and lit and set the shot and we're going to do the shot first thing tomorrow morning. When this shot is done, it's going to be eight and a half minutes of screen time!" Getting eight and a half minutes of screen time in one day is not all that terrible! The producers kept asking me, "Well, what if it doesn't work?" I just told them, "Don't worry about it. It's going to work! I've seen it and it works." The next morning, we shot it, and the producers wanted the film daylighted so we could see the dailies on it by the end of the day. We went on to shoot more stuff, this being the following day, but the first thing we did was the tracking shot. When we finished shooting that next day, we already had the dailies from the tracking shot, and everybody just sat there in awe looking at it.

It's great. I watched it again recently, and even thirty years later, I'm in awe of it!

Well, thank you. I love it and I love doing stuff like that. I don't do a lot of that stuff today, because it's so easy. I mean easy in terms of the technology of doing it. I'm looking for more difficult ways to do things. (laughs) Using technology but in a whole new way. There's a lot of shots like that in *Poltergeist III* that had that kind of complexity. Most wouldn't notice them because they wouldn't realize how complex some of those shots were, which is the most successful way of doing it.

You had Donald Pleasence in *Death Line* and, of course, genre fans recognize him from *Halloween*. I love that he has a short scene with Christopher Lee. How'd that come about, and what was it like, in retrospect, to have these two legendary actors sharing a scene together?

Well, you know, I was in my early twenties when I made that film, and here I am in a room with one actor who's been in more movies than my life allowed me to see, in total! And another actor who was the highest paid actor in the world at the time. Christopher. Christopher was doing it as a favor for producer Paul Maslansky. He came in for one day and worked at scale to do this movie for us.

And Donald just loved the script. I was in awe, because here I am with these two amazing actors. The biggest problem was only that Christopher was 6 ft 7 and Donald is 5 ft 6. And I had to put both of them in a one-to-one scene together. And Christopher refused to work on his knees and Donald refused to work on a box.

I had to figure out how to put these guys nose to nose. That determined the way I shot it. In the beginning, Donald was the dominant character, so I started with close-ups of him and wide shots of Christopher. As Christopher gained dominance in the scene, the camera kept moving closer in on him and further and further away from Donald. Until Christopher sat down they were never in a two shot.

I love that scene. That's great!

It was pretty amazing to work with the two of them. We had a great time, and they were really great to me. They couldn't be more polite and understanding of a young filmmaker. I remained in friendship with Donald until he passed away, and I still have a friendship with Christopher. I haven't seen him in a long time, but we communicate. I have a very warm spot for those guys. They were real professionals.

Blue Underground put out a great special edition DVD of *Dead and Buried* a few years back, and I was actually just watching it with your commentary track. What was it like for you to re-visit that film, twenty years later for a special edition DVD? Especially considering the trouble you had during the making of it?

It was great. When you have trouble with a production like we did on *Dead and Buried*, I'm so far away from it at this point, that I don't have the emotion that I had back when it happened. And when I look back, I understand it was just business. And business is business and that's the way it worked. I'm still very proud of *Dead and Buried*, even though I hate the added scenes. I don't think the added scenes were necessary.

And also, you've got Stan Winston, who during principal photography had done all the special effects. Then, for them to bring in some cheapo special effects guys to do the re-shot added scenes, that was just the worst part. The acid up the nose scene with the doctor looks so fake and phony. I just really hate it. The fisherman getting his face cut up was also an added scene.

How can you compare those effects to the burned head in the car or the needle in the eye or the reconstruction of the girl's face? What Stan Winston did was great. Stan's just a genius. Stan was working with Zoltan Elek who actually did the applications on the set. Zoltan won the Oscar for *Mask*. We had these brilliant people, and this new production company just wanted more gore and brought in whoever for that other stuff. That I'm not happy about.

Also, that they added red in the film, because if you listen to the commentary, you'll know there was not supposed to be any red in the movie until Jack Albertson (Mr. Dobbs) starts to bleed, because he is the only one in the whole movie who's actually alive. So, he was the only one who could have blood. Once they put in the gory stuff, and changed things around, it ruined the flow. There are some continuity problems.

For example, the reconstruction girl, you see earlier in the film now before she's actually killed. *Dead and Buried* is what it is, and even with all the messing around, it's a film they couldn't ruin. The Blue Underground DVD is amazing. David Gregory, who produced the DVD for Blue Underground was probably one of the best DVD producers I had the pleasure of working with. They really care about their movies.

I was twelve when *Poltergeist III* came out, and although I wasn't initially aware of the problems throughout the production until much later on, I really, really enjoyed it. I have very fond memories of seeing it all the time on cable. How'd you get involved in that project and was it difficult or intimidating for you to write and direct the third movie knowing that you were following up two successful films?

First of all, I was approached to do *Poltergeist II* before Brian (Gibson). And for several reasons, I didn't do it. I had just written a pilot for NBC, and the pilot got picked up and I'd already committed to directing it. And also, I felt that the budget for *II* was a little over-inflated for what it needed to be. There were a lot of people involved in the production and there was a lot of money being spent that wasn't going to end up on the screen. And that's always been a real major thing for me. When I make a movie, I want the money on the screen, I don't want the money going into lining the pockets of all kinds of people, including myself. I think the idea is to take that money and give that money to your audience, and not keep that money for yourself. That's the way I've always been with all my productions. So, anyway, it just didn't work out when it came to *II*.

Vice Squad had been out there already, and it was a film that had gotten a lot of attention from other directors. I can't tell you the number of directors that contacted me after *Vice Squad* and just started talking to me about what a significant film it was. It was really mind boggling for me, but also humbling to get calls from Walter Hill, and John Milius and Martin Scorcese. John Milius had told me how he sat and watched it with Steven Spielberg and supposedly that's how my name got brought up for *Poltergeist II*. This is secondhand information, but that's what I'd heard. I wasn't available for it, so it just didn't work out, but when they decided to do *Poltergeist III*, they came to me first before they went to anyone else and said, "Would you like to do *Poltergeist III* and would you like to produce it, write it, and direct it?" The producers of *Death Line* were, at that time running MGM, and I had a long-standing relationship with them, so I said "Okay."

I had just done *Wanted: Dead Or Alive* with Rutger Hauer and they loved it. So, that's what I ended up doing. It started out to be a lot of fun to do *Poltergeist III* and I'd sold them on the idea that this was going to be the last film ever made that has no CGI in it. Not only no CGI, but I didn't want any opticals in the movie. I wanted no film tricks at all. I told them I think I can do the whole movie as a magic show and do every effect live on camera.

I watch it and am baffled by the visual effects in the movie, especially a lot of the tricks with the mirrors. Did you use pretty much everything you had learned on previous films about visual effects in *Poltergeist III*?

I used not only what I learned from my films, but I have a master's in photography and I went to a technical school, so you had to take scientific courses as well. I studied physics in college. Optics were always a big thing for me. Another thing, while working my way through school, I not only did it by being a session musician, but I also got myself a job at an optical laboratory once I got interested in film and learned how to use a lot of techniques that we don't use anymore.

All the tricks that were used to do special effects before CGI came along, which included manipulating film and using blue screen. I had a background in that, and I loved doing that stuff, and my career in commercials was really based on special effects because I used to do all kinds of special effects commercials. I loved the idea of doing long tracking shots and really manipulating the camera. I brought all of those things together to do *Poltergeist III*.

It was a film I was really excited about making until Heather (O' Rourke) died. (Carol Anne) It's the great unfinished film. I don't think anything could be more significant to a director than the film that he lost a star on.

It must have been so difficult. I had read that you and a lot of the people involved in the film didn't even want to complete it once Heather passed away.

I didn't want to complete it at that point. I mean, I loved that little girl. She was just so special. If I could've adopted her, I would have. If she could've been my kid, I would have absolutely loved it. She was just an amazing person and the sweetest little thing you could believe. When she died, I was in shock. I was a pallbearer at her funeral, and it was probably the worst day of my entire life. There was never a sadder moment in my life than that day. You know, it was hard. I didn't care about the film anymore. The studio said let's just bury the film. How can you release a film with a dead twelve year old in it anyways? I think it's awful.

And we don't have an ending. There's no ending shot. At the beginning, everyone agreed with me that we shouldn't try to finish the film. And then pressure from the board at MGM changed that. They pretty much said, "You finish the film, or someone else will." And I wasn't about to throw my footage over to someone else.

So, I wrote that little bullshit scene that now ends the movie. And we shot that little two second scene with a double, and the camera going back up through the window and the lightening striking the top of the building and… it's just… a bullshit ending. I hate it. And the rest of the movie, even after we shot that ending, the film was too short. So, I had to go back in and stretch and use scenes in the film that I had never intended on using.

There are scenes I wrote because the studio felt I needed to elaborate on certain things, and I knew those scenes would never end up in the finished film, and unfortunately they did, because I had to stretch the length of the film. I think I got seventy-seven or seventy-eight minutes out of the first cut and so, in order to bring it up to its delivery requirements, I had to just keep stretching. So, we stretched anywhere we could. Even on that seventy-seven minute version, we had stretched the opening titles for as long as you could possibly bear.

For what it's worth, I saw it at twelve and I loved it back then for the visuals and it left an impression on me. So, I hope that's worth something!

Well, thank you. It's my least favorite of all my movies. In fact, I don't think I've seen it since I made it. I remember every frame of it, I don't think I've seen it since it was released in the theater. I have the DVD, but I've never watched it. I've let other people watch it, but I have not watched it. I don't even know what the transfer on the DVD looks like. Mainly it's an emotional thing. I can't watch that film and think about directing Heather and losing her. It's pretty awful to lose someone.

It was a terrible tragedy.

It was. And I think she would've gone on to be a great director. Seriously. At twelve, she knew more about filmmaking than a lot of people out there making films today. That's what she wanted to do. That was her goal. She was going to stop acting because she wanted to direct. She wanted to go to film school. And I think the world lost a really good filmmaker.

I would assume that experience turned you off from filmmaking for a while?

Well, I had done *Lisa* right after, which was another horror story. The making of *Lisa* was the worst production nightmare I've ever gone through. And even after the production of the film, the release of the picture was an even bigger nightmare. I don't want to go into it all, but it was horrible. I did one film where my star died and the next film where the studio died while I was making the film. So, there was no money to release the film once the film was finished. And they forced me into doing stuff that I didn't want to do. I really felt like slave laborer on that film. Because they had taken a project I was very close to and a script that I really loved and they turned it into a piece of shit. And then didn't release it properly. And that's really why I decided to take a hiatus. I'd had my fill. Television had been very, very good to me over the years, so I just left the world of feature films and went back to producing television.

DAVID ARQUETTE

Interviewed by Rob Galluzzo (10/06)

Most genre fans know David Arquette from his portrayal of Dewey Riley, probably the most beloved character from the entire *Scream* franchise. He's also appeared in the giant-spider flick *Eight Legged Freaks*, the original movie version of *Buffy the Vampire Slayer*, and dozens of classic comedies. Now, he is making his return to the horror genre, but not as an actor. Instead as the writer and director of *The Tripper*! We caught up with David to discuss his directorial debut!

What are your earliest recollections of the horror genre? Do you remember the first movie to really scare you and open up your world to the genre?

The first horror film I remember seeing in the theatre was *Halloween* and, from the first scene when the kid puts on the mask and it is his POV, I was hooked.

You come from a large family, all involved in some way, in the entertainment industry. Was it always a natural choice to pursue acting or was there ever a point where you thought about doing something else as a career?

I got into acting in high school, although I had tried earlier but only got rejected. I had an awesome teacher, Ben DeBaldo at Fairfax, and he really gave me the confidence to pursue my goals.

I guess your first foray into horror territory was the vampire comedy *Buffy the Vampire Slayer*. How'd that gig come about? And how do you feel about Buffy now in retrospect, considering the cult following the radically different television series has generated?

I love that I was a part of that film. It had some great people in it and Paul Reubens became a lifelong friend, and Thomas Jane was also in it and he's now my brother-in-law. Both are now in *The Tripper*. So, shazam! Life is crazy. I also did two TV shows that were taken from movies, so when a movie I did became a TV show I felt I broke the curse. The two shows were *The Outsiders* and *Parenthood*.

I want to dabble into one of your comedy films briefly. I love *Airheads*. And you practically steal all your scenes in it! You worked with Adam Sandler, Steve Buscemi, Chris Farley, Michael Richards, and Lemmy(!), all in the same flick. What do you remember about that experience and working with those guys?

I had a blast on that flick. I was just stuck in this room, so I really had to milk it. I drew from some hesher friends of mine, most of whom you can't understand what the hell they are saying half the time.

What were your initial reactions to reading the script for *Scream*, at the time titled *Scary Movie*?

They originally wanted me to read for the part of Billy in *Scream*. I think that's what his name was, Skeet's character, but I wanted to play Dewey. Dewey at the time was written as this big beefcake guy, but I knew I could do something special with it and I really wanted to kiss Courteney Cox. Thank you, Wes Craven, in more ways than one.

How much of yourself did you inject into the role of Dewey? He's probably the most beloved character out of that entire series. Wasn't he initially scripted to die?

Yeah, Dewey and I are very similar, but people always call me Doofy from *Scary Movie* and that bugs me. I'm not so much like that guy except with my fascination with vacuum cleaners. I was supposed to die, but thankfully I didn't. If I think of how my life may have turned out differently if I had, I thank my lucky stars.

Did you have any inkling as to just how successful the first *Scream* film would become?

I think we all felt that while we were doing *Scream*, that we were part of something really special.

Any intimidation at first in working with Wes Craven on *Scream*? He is after all considered a master of the genre!

Wes is, by far, one of the greatest human beings I have ever had the pleasure of working with. He is so cool and never tries to intimidate. He actually sat me down at the end of *Scream 2* when I was going nuts in my personal life and said, "Get it together or you're going to lose Courteney and possibly more." He is a fantastic man.

I'll never forget sitting in screenings of both *Scream 2* and *3* and having the audience yelling for Dewey to make it. What is it about that character that you think has made him one of the most popular from the *Scream* franchise?

I think he was the geeky guy with a heart of gold that usually dies in these films, but he didn't. I was sad when Jamie Kennedy's character died in *Scream 2*. That just wasn't right.

Agreed! There's often been rumors of a *Scream 4*, especially in the last few years. Your name always comes up as a potential returning character. Would you want to jump in Dewey's shoes again should the opportunity present itself?

Are you kidding? I would love to do a *Scream 4*. I would hope that all of the original players were involved. Wes, Kevin Williamson, Marianne (Wes' partner), Neve, and of course Courteney.

Eight Legged Freaks was another movie of yours that developed a cult following. Didn't you actually coin that name from an improv during one of the scenes?

Yeah, I did come up with the name in a scene and I'm glad they used it, although I'm not sure if it hurt it at the box office. But ultimately what's better than having a cult hit?

Eight Legged Freaks also was an homage to all the 50's monster movies. Were you a fan of those types of films growing up? It was fun to see a big bug movie in theaters again when it came out!

Yeah, I loved watching those 50's films and waiting for Elvira to come back during the breaks.

Just so you know, the only other trailer at the *Fangoria* convention that got even close to the response that yours did was *Spider-Man*! The audience really seemed to love spider movies that year, I guess. Can you tell me about the origins of your latest flick *The Tripper*, which you co-scripted? Why a horror film as your directorial debut?

I learned a lot from Wes as I have already mentioned but I also watched him closely. I love how he made a whole audience jump. I wanted to do that. I had been thinking about *The Tripper* for years. I grew up in L.A. when Reagan was the governor and president, and my parents hated his politics. I remember the day I saw homeless people everywhere and my mom let me know it was because of his tax cuts to mental health. I also became a *Grateful Dead* parking lot crasher and made it up to an amazing concert, Reggae on the River, and it was there that I thought it would be great to see all these hippies massacred.

How'd you hook up with Steve Niles and Raw Entertainment? Were you already familiar with Steve?

Steve and Thomas Jane started Raw, and Thomas was instrumental in jumping aboard early on. Steve is a genius when it comes to this genre and his help has been amazing. I know the comic we have coming out is really going to kill. With him and Joe Harris, my co-writer on *The Tripper* and comic master, and the art of Nat Jones, how could it not?

You had a killer cast in *The Tripper*, consisting of Lukas Haas, Paul Reubens, Thomas Jane, Jason Mewes, Jamie King, Chris Nelson, to name a few. A lot of these actors you were friends with before making this movie. What was it like to be in control of a project with so many people that you've worked with on other films in the past? The flick looks like it must have been a blast to make!

It was a blast to make, and I must say Lukas is an incredible actor, so real, but he was my buddy and ultimately doing me a favor, as was Thomas and Paul. But Jaime King and Jason Mewes saved my ass. They both turn out performances that are unbelievable. I am so thankful to them. Chris Nelson, I had worked with as an FX artist, but I never forgot him and always wanted to work with him as an actor and I am so happy I went with my instincts.

Last question! Are there any horror films as of late that you've seen and really enjoyed?

High Tension rocked.

KEN SAGOES

Interviewed by Rob Galluzzo (10/06)

Anyone who grew up with *A Nightmare on Elm Street* probably has fond memories of Part 3, *Dream Warriors*. For me, it introduced my all-time favorite *Nightmare* character, Roland Kincaid as played by Ken Sagoes. Ken returned in *Nightmare on Elm Street 4* as one of Freddy's first victims. Despite his early demise in *4, Nightmare* fans all know that he's one of the few characters to go up against Freddy and survive for a sequel. We're now proud to share with you our exclusive interview with Kincaid himself, Ken Sagoes!

What are your earliest recollections of the genre? Do you recall some of the first films to really scare you?

Alfred Hitchcock's *The Birds*. And also, *The Mummy*. Those were my first memories. I remember a movie called *Blacula*. I was really young and my stepmom was watching a movie on television and it was *Blacula*.

***Blacula's* great! Can you tell us a bit about how you got interested in acting? When did you first become aware of the process of how films were made?**

First of all, I'm originally from Atlanta, but I came out here to LA and got a job at Universal Studios as a security guard. I got a chance to meet a lot of people. I actually met Alfred Hitchcock when I was very young. I got a chance to talk with him for ten or so minutes when I was on the lot, and I also saw Vincent Price on the lot. As a security guard, I would always find my way into the soundstages so I could watch different actors do their work. Those were my earlier days. Watching the pros really do their work.

What was one of the first things you did acting wise?

It was a movie with Jonathan Winters and I played a policeman, I remember that being one of the first things I did. Then, I got lucky and got another role, which was a role with Denzel Washington in a film called *The George McKenna Story*.

How'd you get the role of Roland Kincaid in *Nightmare On Elm Street 3*? Did you just go in on an audition?

It was really a fluke. I had just finished that role with Denzel Washington, and I didn't have a car. Well, I had a car, but it was broken down at the time. But I had had some tickets that I had to go down to the courthouse to take care of. My agent had called me and told me that he had gotten me an audition for the new *Nightmare on Elm Street*. Truthfully speaking, I was not familiar with *Nightmare on Elm Street*. I remember it was raining, pouring down rain that day, and I had to catch three buses to the audition. I read the breakdown of the character. The character they wanted was a young body builder, which was totally against what I looked like for anything. I didn't think I had a chance of getting it, so I wasn't even going to go.

The agent called back and told me at least go so you can get a chance to meet the casting director, because she's going to be casting other things. I had timed everything perfectly, I could catch the bus up there, run over and do the audition, and run back and catch the next bus. Now, when I tell you it was raining, that meant just crossing the street would get me soaking wet. I had an attitude! This really bad attitude, because I didn't want to be there. (laughs)

I get up there and the lady told me they were running behind, and the casting director wouldn't be able to see me for another forty minutes. Now I'm pissed again because I was going to miss the bus back. So, I waited. I had the bus schedule. And when they told me I was going in, I had ten minutes to go in and do the audition and run three blocks to catch the bus back home. That was all that was important to me, catching my bus. I went in with an attitude, and Chuck Russell thought I was coming in in character. (laughs) But I really didn't want to be there.

So, he said, "Well, do what you want to do. How do you feel? Just go with how you feel." And I just started cussing and throwing shit around. When I finished, Chuck just said, "Thank you" and I knew I didn't get the role. When I got home, they called me and said I had the role. (laughs) I just didn't think I'd get it because when I got there, they had all these guys that were in the best of shape. I walked in and felt like I was a little Rerun from *What's Happening!!*

That's a great story! When you got the role, did you go back and watch the other movies?

I did. I watched the other two movies. The first thing that Chuck Russell did was to bring us all together and everybody was very excited because I was going to be the first black guy to fight Freddy. Chuck told me that my character was a little different, because I didn't really have special powers. My power was strength and talking shit. (laughs) He had told me that if there was something in the script that as a black guy, I didn't feel I would say, to talk to him about it. So, a lot of the things that I said came from me, per se as opposed to the character. Not all of it was as written.

Does that mean you got to improvise with Kincaid a lot?

Not a lot. Some things, though. I know there's a part where I say, "Let's go kick the motherfucker's ass all over dream land." That came from me because, in real life, we call that jonzing. I was good at that. I was a standup comic as well. Some things Chuck would let me do and give me leeway on.

When you approached the character, did you prepare at all? Or did you pretty much act the way you did in the audition, which is yourself, just pissed off?

I prepared. Because the character was a little different from when I did the audition. I think it was the attitude that I had. I just wanted to go in there and catch the bus. That's all I wanted! Because of the description of the character, I didn't think I had a chance. I think the audition was at 4:30, and I had been on the street from 7am that morning. And it was raining while I was going from one place to another, so by the time I got there, I was pure attitude. I wasn't trying to act; I was just being myself.

But when I got the role, yes, I did prepare, because Chuck Russell and I talked and he explained to me what he wanted from the character. And this was also going to be the biggest role for me. I had no idea that Kincaid was going to be that popular. I had no idea. What was exciting about that was that I lived!

You lived in *Dream Warriors*!

I don't know if you know the history of being a black actor in horror films, but I am the first African American to ever survive a major horror movie and return to a sequel. That's in the books!

That's awesome, but I'm still angry about *Nightmare 4*. We'll get to that in a minute. I just wanted to know, I've met Robert Englund before and he's a super nice guy. What was it like to first see him in Freddy make-up for the first time? Was he intimidating or just his usual nice self?

For me, he was nice. He was not intimidating because of Robert Englund. He was intimidating because who he was to me. Robert Englund has always been a very generous and kind person. He made us feel comfortable on set. He was not an ego on the set, he made us feel really comfortable, at least when I was there. Because there were very, very long hours. At one point, we were in a warehouse in downtown Los Angeles that they had built, and it was very hot in there. By the end of the day, it was different personalities clashing together, but Robert Englund always kept his cool. Him and I were always cool when we worked.

The movie had a large ensemble cast, the "last of the Elm Street kids." Did you get some time to bond beforehand, so that your friendships would translate into the actual movie? Or did the production move fast?

What Chuck Russell did with us, before we went for principal photography, he got us all together and he brought us to a place in Westwood and we had lunch. Again, we met at a hotel and we all just talked. We got to know each other before we started shooting the movie. Rodney Eastman (Joey) and I became friendly right from the beginning. From the very first day, we became buddies. All of us became really close.

I remember Patricia Arquette, the first couple of times we got off set, she took me home a lot of the times. She drove all the way from where she lived to the hood to drop me off. (laughs) That was a big thing! Because we all looked out for each other. We don't hang out with each other, but we all kind of looked out for each other. Ira Heiden (Will Stanton) was always the playful one. Rodney was the one always in love. Heather Langenkamp (Nancy) was the big sister to everyone.

***Nightmare 3* is one of Laurence Fishburne's first roles. What was it like to work with him so early in his career?**

Laurence taught me physical acting. He immediately became a brother. I had no idea. This was the first role that I had done that I had to do some physical acting, and stunt work. He brought me to the side and told me how to do it, because we would do something and by the time we finished that scene on the first take, I'd be out of breath. He took me to the side and taught me how to deal with those things.

He knew this was new to me, because he had been in the business for quite some time before *Nightmare on Elm Street 3*. He would talk to me and tell me how important this character of Kincaid was and what it represents. After that, he recommended me for other roles as well. I see him periodically and he's always very gracious.

Do you remember how it felt to see the movie on the big screen for the first time with your friends and the cast?

Yeah, my family was at the first screening, we all went. And there were some parts in the movie that I was not aware of, and that actually scared me. I remember being with my California mom and family, and there was this part where a pig or something just jumps out at us and the whole audience jumped. And I remember her saying, "Well, this is a horror film!" (laughs) I almost pissed in my clothes! What was even more exciting was to see my name on the screen. It was there, and I was proud. My mother had never seen *Nightmare on Elm Street*.

How soon after *3* did they start putting *4* together?

You know, I have no idea. Because I didn't even know that I was coming back. True story. The next year when they were doing the new movie, my character was in the breakdown. So, I did not know if I was coming back or not. They never told me if I was coming back. When I signed on to do Kincaid, it was only for Part 3. Then, in the breakdown, they had my character because they were looking for that role to be cast. I just got a call that they're doing this, and this is what you'll get paid for this to come back.

I know comedian-wise, almost every comedian had me in their stand-up at the time. I remember one time; this was the weirdest thing, I get a call from an operator asking if I was Ken Sagoes, and I heard some foreign language on the other line. What it was, it was some dignitary in Taiwan that could not speak English, but who was speaking to a translator on the line through an operator here. She translated to me that they wanted me to say "Happy Birthday" to their son.

That's pretty wild.

I remember going "Ok," and just saying "Happy Birthday." That was probably one of the most memorable things I've done. The young man drew a picture of me, which I still have that he drew by hand and sent to me. There was a Kincaid fanclub in Taiwan. Never been there. (laughs)

For Part 4, you reunited with Rodney Eastman and Robert Englund, but Tuesday Knight ended up replacing Patricia Arquette as Kristin. What was that like?

Tuesday stepped right in. I missed Patricia, but Tuesday stepped right in. I'm going to say that there wasn't any difference with the character because I don't remember anything that happened out of the ordinary, except that I didn't know why she (Patricia) didn't come back. I never knew the reason.

I know that one of the jokes that was going around for me was that if you want to see Kincaid in the new movie, don't go get popcorn, go straight to the movie because he's getting killed that quick! Tuesday, we looked at her as another sister. Not another Kristin to me, but another sister who was playing the role.

Did you know from the get-go that Kincaid was going to be killed off right away in 4?

Yeah. This time it was Renny Harlin directing. He met with Rodney and I. He had already met with Tuesday Knight before he met with us. There was a day where he just wanted to meet with Rodney and I. I don't even think there was a script then, it was more of a treatment. And he told us we were going to be the first to be killed. He asked us how we saw Kincaid and how we saw Joey.

For my character, I don't know about Rodney, I only originally had three days on *Nightmare 4*. That's how quickly I was going to be killed off. But it turned out that I ended up working on it for two weeks. It took us a week to film that scene at the junkyard.

Speaking of Renny, *Nightmare 4* was one of his first gigs. It's common knowledge that he didn't always see eye to eye with the producers. Was any of that evident? Or did everything run smooth?

It was very smooth with Renny Harlin. I didn't have any problems with him. What I can say about New Line and Bob Shaye, the people who produced the movie, is that if there were any problems that were going on, they did not

127

allow the actors, at least from my point of view, to know that was going on. This is actually the first time I'm hearing that there were problems. I know that, just like Chuck Russell, he met with us before principal shooting began and he talked with us. The only problem I had was that I felt I was being killed too soon!

I just wanted to be there more. I also know there was talk that I was coming back to fight Freddy at the end. I don't know if you ever caught it. But if you pay attention, my character is the only one that says, "I'll see you in hell." I think it was supposed to be a set-up that I was going to come back and challenge Freddy Krueger with something spiritual or something.

That would've been great! When I saw _Nightmare 4_, I was a heartbroken eleven-year-old!

You know, by then, the Kincaid character was popular, and I was getting a lot of fan mail. People wanted to see a fight between me and Robert Englund. I don't know what actually happened. But those were among the rumors I heard. And that was the reason, I had to say that line specifically, "I'll see you in hell," which meant that I was going to return. But I don't know what happened though. No one ever sat me down and talked to me about it, I just heard that rumor. I wanted it to happen. And at the time, I was a young man that didn't know how to make it happen. If I had to do it all over again, I would've gone to them and tried to make it happen.

You could've showed them all that fan mail!

I still get a bunch of fan mail. I guess it's the new generation of fans that watch _Nightmare on Elm Street_. And as you know, next year is our twentieth anniversary.

Your character's dog in _Nightmare 4_ was named Jason. Was that done as a nod to the _Friday the 13th_ slasher?

There were rumors about that. I didn't know for sure. But there were rumors that they named Jason as a nod to _Friday the 13th_. I had heard that a lot on the set.

After _Nightmare 4_, you're listed as doing a lot of television work. Can you tell us, in your view, the differences between working on film as opposed to television?

Feature films? Well, for me, feature films are the bigger check. (laughs) But television has always been very quick. With feature films, you take time. I will say that the _Nightmare on Elm Street_ movies helped me as an actor, because a lot of the special effects are not there, you have to pretend that they're there. If you overdo it, you look like you're not acting or you don't know what you're doing. It taught me to be a better natural actor.

2007

SCOTT GLOSSERMAN

NATHAN BAESEL

DAVE PARKER

MIKE MENDEZ

DAVID J. STEIVE

CORALINA CATALDI-TASSONI

BILL JOHNSON

ROB ZOMBIE

JOEL DAVID MOORE

PAUL EHLERS

ZELDA RUBENSTEIN

ERICA LEERHSEN

JEFFREY COMBS

CERINA VINCENT

JOE LYNCH

TIFFANY SHEPIS

TOM WOODRUFF JR.

JOHN KASSIR

SCOTT GLOSSERMAN

Interviewed by Adam Barnick (2/07)

Expect to be hearing a lot more about director Scott Glosserman after you see *Behind the Mask: The Rise of Leslie Vernon*. Set in a world where killers like Krueger, Voorhees, and Myers are real and revered like baseball legends, *Vernon* is the story of a young slasher-in-training, letting a documentary crew cover his ascent to 'success'... all while deftly deconstructing why he does what he does. It's smart, it's funny, it's scary, it's one of the best-reviewed films you will find. Scott was kind enough to take a LOT of time to tell us about seeing this modern valentine to the genre archetypes through to fruition.

What are your earliest memories of the horror genre?

When I was around four or five, I saw the *Twilight Zone*, "Nightmare at 20,000 Feet" episode where William Shatner is the only one who sees the gremlin creature tearing apart the wing of the plane. I have felt terror in the twenty-some-odd years since then to be sure, but relatively speaking, it hasn't been worse than my state of mind after that *Twilight Zone*. Right around that time, my aunt took me to see *Time Bandits* because it happened to be playing, I suppose, and I guess the poster depicted a cartoon fantasy world or something. I was petrified by that movie.

And I remember watching some Hans Christian Anderson-type movie on TV about a scary-looking guy who kidnaps children by stealing them from their homes and stuffing them into his dog-pound, paddy-wagon-type thing. I cannot, for the life of me, remember the name of it.

For what felt like a long time, most things scared me – the walk up my neighborhood street, the older kids at school, the water at camp, the kids on the school bus. It was only after I began to understand the movies, how they're made, that they are not real, etc, that I emerged from that phase. Pretty soon, I was the only kid not falling for the campfire ghost stories. Seeking a greater understanding of the intricacies of horror helped to temper my fear. Perhaps *Behind the Mask* is a culmination of that?

I read you deconstructed *The Shining* as a college thesis. Was that the catalyst for one day doing a story that would examine genre conventions in detail?

My explication of *The Shining* was, in itself, a culmination of what I learned in a Conventions of Horror class taught by a professor named David Katz. Some of the principal conventions/themes/images/archetypes running through the horror genre (i.e.: the phallic weaponry, the closed hiding places being symbolic of the womb, the tunnel imagery representing rebirth, etc...) are best captured in *The Shining*. I further explored Kubrick's use of anticlimax to generate fear. Additionally, since Kubrick leaves nothing in the mise-en-scene unscrutinized, I enjoyed discovering all of his Easter eggs – pulling meaning out of his color choices, number choices, name choices, prop choices, and so on; even, perhaps, when there was no meaning.

The idiosyncrasies that led to the making of *Behind the Mask* were not premeditated. However, my knowledge of the academia of horror certainly played a part in us going forward with the development of the film.

After graduating, you moved to Los Angeles. Can you tell me about the early work you did out there to get by and make yourself known?

Rather than film school after college, I chose to work for a large talent/literary agency in Beverly Hills in order to observe and absorb as much as I could about the entertainment industry. Leaving felt as though I was walking the plank off the epicenter of Hollywood. I associate produced a friend's documentary. I also did some commercial acting, table waiting, soccer coaching, piano teaching. Mostly, though, I was writing, and when I wasn't writing I was doing anything

I could to feel as though I was in motion. That meant a lot of laundry and reorganizing of my bookshelves and closets.

How did you come across David J. Stieve's script for *Behind the Mask: The Rise Of Leslie Vernon*? What in it did you respond to right away?

My manager at the time, Andrew Lewis, had had David's script submitted to him for client consideration. I think Andrew knew I'd enjoy it because of my erudition in horror. I laughed throughout the whole read. I was at a diner on Pico Boulevard. I'll never forget. I thought to myself, this is so different from anything I'd read before, and the dialogue was so strong.

Can you talk about your collaboration with David and how you developed the script into its shooting draft?

David and I worked on the script for a long time. Structurally, we condensed his original iteration into two acts and we put a new third act on in order to add a twist and to pay everything off. The script, as it took shape, went from a marvelous running joke to more of a classic three-act story structure. Additionally, we infused some of the true academia of horror convention into the script and we cut back the caricaturing. So, the script became less parody and more satire. Another thing that really started taking shape was the development of the juxtaposition between the docu-world and the world of full horror filmic glory, which couldn't have been more different from each other.

As we got closer and closer to shooting, the script had to change to allow for certain locations that were the best we could do given our budget and time constraints. David was up in Portland, literally rewriting pages from the hotel while I was on the phone with him from a particular location on a scout, describing them!

You both really left no stone unturned in terms of intelligently, rationally explaining the moments that appear random or inexplicable in a genre/slasher piece. Thoughts on that?

We tried to strike a balance between imaginative, stream-of-conscious explanations for how something works or is done the way it is, and actual accepted academic theories for some of the prevalent conventions and archetypes common in horror. In context, with the right delivery, I thought both could be funny. Fortunately, we got some actors who were brilliant at pulling it off.

For the uninitiated, can you describe *Behind the Mask: The Rise of Leslie Vernon*? People who know really nothing about it might glibly compare it to *Man Bites Dog* or *Scream*, but it's really not close to either of those. It's its own beast completely. I'd call it a hyper-intelligent, entertaining meta-slasher that happens to be really funny.

Yeah!

Can you give me your take on it? What is the film?

It's interesting that you should bring up *Man Bites Dog*. What is unfortunate, but understandable I guess, some people have been very quick to say, "Oh I've seen this movie, it's *Man Bites Dog*. When they've read a log line or something. And the fact is, tonally…

It's not close at all.

That's right, it's apples and oranges. My film takes place in a world where Freddy Krueger, Mike Myers, Jason Voorhees all exist. Where you can get on a plane and fly to Metropolis. The movie is about an aspiring psycho-slasher. NOT a serial killer. Because the movie's not about the DC sniper or John Wayne Gacy, the audience is able to suspend their disbelief, go on this journey that if it were rooted in the real world, would be very disturbing and immoral. But rooted in the world of full filmic glory, it's nostalgic, and celebratory and fun! *Man Bites Dog* was brilliant and disturbing and raw and sure, I have used the shooting style as a template for the docu-world in my film.

But I've also pulled from Christopher Guest. *Spinal Tap* came out long before *Man Bites Dog*. The "mockumentary" style has been around. So, I took that mocu-style for the documentary world. It's about the LeBron James of horror. This guy (Leslie Vernon) is going to put them all to shame. He has given a documentary crew exclusive access to his life, while he plans his reign of terror upon this unsuspecting, sleepy little town called Glen Echo. All the while he's deconstructing for the documentary crew, and for the audiences, the true conventions and archetypes of the horror, specifically, slasher genre.

Part of it is in this *Blair Witch*ian docu-style perspective, where he's describing what it is he's going to do. And part of the film actually lives the world of John Carpenter, Sean Cunningham's late 70's/early 80's slasher films. What was so much fun was juxtaposing these two worlds. Everything from the acting to the dialogue, to the music and the aesthetic, was completely different between the docu-world and the "horror world."

In the docu-world, we had everything dry. And you played the comedy on the page, and didn't ham it up or overact. Very 'real,' as real as possible. The way Nathan channeled Leslie Vernon, he could have been an aspiring actor, or aspiring carpenter. He can take his acting, whatever sort of emotional transference he wants to take onto a scene and really demonstrate his full dramatic skills! But in context, it's hilarious because he's taking it so seriously.

So, I wanted my actors to play as truthfully as they could in the docu-world, because when we go to the "film world," we're in complete melodrama. All of a sudden you get some stilted, contrived dialogue. You get the rich aesthetic of a horror film. The angles of the camera become omniscient. In the docu-world all the shots were at eye level because a guy was holding the camera. When we go into the horror world, all of a sudden, we're gliding over a van, or coming down from the ceiling, and there's score, there's "horror score." We were meticulous about creating the theme song, about creating the iconic mask. All of this stuff was a labor of love for so many of us.

At the end, we also put in tons of Easter eggs. Really obvious homages, but also some extraordinarily subtle homages to horror films. So, people could re-see the film and try to identify all the little nuanced references in there. It's meant to be a very nostalgic celebration of all that we love about horror.

I liked you'd gotten the more flat-out 'geek' references out of the way early on, practically in the opening intro. This also immediately tells you what world we're in. But you didn't bathe in it like a lot of debut genre filmmakers do. And the film never "stops" to let us point at the archetypes and wink at them.

Exactly.

Was it difficult in shaping the performances to hit that balance, so those of us looking for the references completely acknowledge what it is, without doing something along the lines of *Scary Movie*? Those films stop dead so we can gawk at the reference. You were subtle.

Thank you! It's sort of a two-part answer. The first one is the movie is certainly not intended to be a parody. I think if you're doing a parody, everything is so blatant and over-the-top. Because (this) movie is a satire, it gets away with a lot more subtlety.

To me, when I'm watching *Pulp Fiction*, and someone tells me later that the two board games in the room where (Travolta) administers the adrenaline shot are *Operation* and *Life*… that's cool. When I make this film, I want to throw the *Hellraiser* box on a mantelpiece. You know? If people don't get it, they'll figure it out from a blog or something. I don't mean to draw attention to it. I could cast Robert Englund, and that's a more obvious homage, but I wanted to do the horror fan right by doing a whole spectrum of layered homages. Down to the color scheme in the library. I wanted the librarian to wear yellow because in *The Shining*, yellow was the color for death, and sacrifice. Not that I expected anybody to make that connection. There's so much different stuff.

We had one thing we built; you know one of those crossroads signs when you get out to Arizona, there's a post with street signs going every which way. Like thirty of them. (laughs) We spent hours building this. We had Cuesta Verde from *Poltergeist*, Nellis Falls from *Hills Have Eyes*, every friggin' street from like every horror film! I was so proud, so psyched about it. There's a scene where the filmmaker's van pulls up, and the headlights were supposed to shine on this street sign. The street sign fell over, out of frame…

To me, the more comprehensive my vision was, I can tell the prop master exactly what to get, the costume designer exactly what to do. It sort of gives everybody on set a greater sense of purpose. They've got more direction, and more autonomy. If you can articulate that vision in your head to everybody, even if you don't execute perfectly on what you're trying to do, the overall product I've learned will reflect, at least, a passion. That you didn't just phone it in. The more specific a director is about his vision, the better.

I think we as the audience do pick up, subconsciously, on the color scheme etc. If it's NOT there, you feel the absence of a mind behind it.

One example, which will be on the DVD release. Remember the high school scene (where Leslie points out the archetypes of high schoolers and their cliques and how it relates to his stalking)? I shot that scene in one take. We shot it five times, but it was supposed to be one shot. Leslie starts talking, and we had this ridiculous choreography with all these extras, the Communion girls skipping rope, the stoners, the survivor girl landing on her mark next to the tree. That was going to be my Scorcese/*Goodfellas* "going through the restaurant" one-shot. And we did the whole thing, and we nailed it! We nailed it like twice. I was so psyched!

And of course, we get into the editing room and that scene's four minutes long! It just drags out. There's a certain point in postproduction where you have to kill your babies a little bit. And so on the DVD, I'll show that scene uncut, completely choreographed. But I'm pretty sure ninety-nine percent of the audiences would watch that and say, "I see what he's trying to do, but I'm glad he cut it up!" There's too much air in it, it's boring. And as a first time filmmaker, setting out with those ideals and ideas is one thing, and executing them is another. But the fact that you set out with a specific vision, I think the end product is going to be elevated.

When you knew the script was ready, did you consider trying to interest studios, or did you decide to go the independent private investment route from day one?

Trust me, I spent a lot time trying to drum up interest from within the industry. And I simply couldn't. It wasn't as though people didn't like the script or thought it wasn't original, or fresh and interesting. They just didn't know what to do with it!

20th Century Fox, they know how make a broad comedy. And market it. And they know how to make and market a horror. But they don't know what to do with a hybrid. But every so often, an Edgar Wright comes around, and does a *Shaun of the Dead*. And it works. He nails it. *American Werewolf in London*, *The Howling*, and it just works! But it's not a commodity business the studios are into. That trickles down to the production companies because studios give them distribution. So, the production companies might acknowledge that something's cool or different or worthy, but that doesn't mean that they're willing to do it. And that's when you have to go out and find independent financiers.

And how did you attract investors to your project?

Initially, it was seed money from family. I was talking to the dean where I went to school about getting an independent study, getting students to work for free and I'd go in and lecture them on filmmaking and it would be a course credit. (I was) in the Berkshires trying to piecemeal friend's and friends of friend's vacation homes to shoot in, and same with outside of Washington DC. I had enough money to go out and basically get my friends to do this for free. Then finally, I got up to Spokane Washington, which they call "Spokanada," because there so many production and postproduction facilities that are a one-stop shop for filmmaking.

I gave these guys a budget and my script, and they came back and they wanted to make a million dollar film, they wanted to invest in it. I didn't end up going with them, but it gave me the validation and legitimacy to be able to go back to my private investors and say, 'hey look, if this company here wants to make this movie for this amount of money, let's raise like half and keep everything to ourselves. But I just need a little more money!" And this was enough to push them over the edge.

Turning to Nathan Baesel as Leslie Vernon. Everybody I know who's seen it so far has said it, right from his opening laugh, he's got us. He's charming and funny and scary. Can you talk about casting him, and your process of working with him?

First off, I should say that if more people than just my family get to see this, I think Nathan's going to be a movie star. Along the lines of creating subtle and not so subtle references to other films, you could say I pulled one right out of *A Nightmare on Elm Street* with the "introducing Johnny Depp" credit. I can kind of reference *Nightmare* by introducing my star, and I can take credit for discovering him. (laughs) Because he's going to be a freaking superstar.

What some actors don't realize is that when they come in and they've prepared an audition and they just rip it and they're really good, and the director says, "All right, now try to do it this way." Often times actors think they fucked up, but it's not true! They did such a good job that now the director wants to see if they can work with them!

Sure! You need to see if they can take direction.

Exactly! What you find, often times, is that actors are very good at one thing, which is OK, you can create superstar careers out of that. When Nathan came in to read for this role, he was able to just turn on a dime. He would take any direction you gave him, and he could do anything. The other thing was, I had preconceived notions of who I wanted, other people (figured I'd) want a guy who's intimidating at 2AM in the morning in an alley. Nathan walks in and completely changes my conception of this character!

When Nathan first felt the role, he saw 'let's start out really charming and then create this really maniacal metamorphosis.' He's telling me on the phone in a precall before we got up there, "I'll end up plucking my eyebrows out and just go crazy" and it's a true testament to Nathan's commitment as an actor. By the way, the guy had bare feet throughout the whole (finale) and got hypothermia and we never really even had the camera on his feet!

He's that passionate. He gets that into character, and that's what you get with him. I was so attracted to his charming personality, but I knew if he's the charming guy but he plays the role as truthfully as possible, then it's going to work in context and create even more humor. And he nailed it! He's just brilliant. He's got Harrison Ford's jaw and Jim Carrey's laugh and John Malkovich's skill.

We were in an ADR session out in Burbank, you're watching yourself, onscreen, do things like die and run. These are called "efforts." Like Angela Goethals has a scene where she's running through the woods, so she's got to (recreate the panting, grunts, etc).

You look totally silly when you do it, but we need the voiceover. Nathan's got to do his one scene, he's kind of gargling with blood. So, Nathan goes over to this little buffet table and takes a cup out. And he puts Coca-cola in there, and fills it with non-dairy creamer, this powdered crap (laughs) and mixes it up with some water and he pounds it! And then he walks up and does this gurgling thing… unbelievable! We were just in an ADR room! But the commitment he has is truly amazing.

Angela Goethals, another great choice. A counterpoint to Leslie, he's going to be the best slasher and she's going to be the best journalist. Tell me about working with her.

Angela, with the exception of our cameos (Robert Englund, Zelda Rubenstein) had the most experience of anybody on set, above and below the line. She's in *Home Alone* when we were all ten years old, she was in all of season 4 of *24*, *Jerry Maguire*, she's just been around! She went to Vassar, she's really, really smart. She's just so wonderful and professional.

The best testament to Angela's professionalism and superior talent was we shot a lot of this movie in this old barn, with tons of hay and a lot of dust. And we were always checking the gate. After you shoot, you have to check to see if dust got caught in the camera and the film is ruined. Angela is doing her big emotional scene where she's crying and we did most of these scenes in two or three takes but this scene was four or five, not because of Angela, because of the camera, and dust problems, and coordinating other things. And we checked the gate, and for the first time in maybe twenty days there was a piece of dust in the gate. We had to do that whole scene over again and do another five takes of it. Basically, she cried on cue, compellingly and believably, ten times in a row.

One of the reasons we were able to afford the production quality, the production value that we could, was that we shot with a skeleton crew on the docu-world days. A much tinier crew so that when we shot the library for instance, we could get the thirty to thirty-five people it takes to light a library and to use all the equipment. We also sped

through the mockumentary stuff, which was all dialogue-driven material, and I wanted to stay true to the two-camera setup, Todd's and Doug's cameras.

We basically shot it once with Doug's camera, where the cinematographer would play Doug. And once where he'd play Todd's point of view. And we ran through the scenes uncut. All the scenes are longer than what's seen in the movie. But what was so amazing was Nathan and Angela would run through five-seven pages of dialogue, and we would do it in two-three takes at the most. If they weren't as good as they were, we'd still be shooting this movie. (laughs) It was never because of Nathan or Angela that we had to 'fix' anything. It was, if anything, a technical issue. Or maybe a choreography issue.

One more thing I would say was the best piece of advice I got regarding casting was, "Just cast the best actors you can." That will make your life so much easier. That's what I did, cast the best actors I could find, and they just nailed it.

That answers one of the questions I had about whether Britain and Ben (the actors who play the documentary cameramen) were actually filming the DV footage or not. Every once in a while, I'd see one of them in the other's shot, I thought they'd really filmed it!

The DV scenes were shot on a DVX100a. We had a prop camera that they'd use in scenes. Jaron (Presant, the DP) would shoot as one of the cameramen, and we would throw the other actor in there as a cameraman. Not really show their faces much until the reveal in the "horror world." But we put them in so you'd know as an audience member that we're not cheating. We're in one or the other's point of view.

We came up with the shooting style for each of the guys too. One of them was going to be the archetypal jock; just center everything and shoot it straight on, locked off, just get everything. And the other guy was gonna be the arty stoner dude. He was going to "Dutch" all his shots and get some really artsy stuff. This was me trying to develop their personalities through their point-of-views and not through watching them. I thought could we, for the first time in cinematic history, actually develop characters through how they're shooting scenes, and what they choose to watch?

And of course, the answer is absolutely not. (laughs) Because I realized in post how often I wanted to cut to keep the pace moving, and for different reasons I wasn't going to hang on a shot long enough for someone to figure out what I was trying to do. I wanted to tell a story most importantly and I wanted it to flow, coherently and correctly. So, a lot of that had to go. But having had those sets of rules and parameters, I think the overall product was still elevated in a way.

And there's no B.S. in that. We're seeing, in the docu-world, only what the cameramen see. I figured the choreography was pretty tight. When they're going to see Stacy, it's shot from one camera, and we notice Ben in the background. Then you cut to that actual angle. They're matched so well that I wondered if the actors really shot this.

I'm glad you noticed things like that; I wanted it to be airtight. I wanted people not to be able to point out places where "we cheated." There's one scene where they get separated and Taylor shows up in her van with Todd, and you're like, "who stayed at the farm to shoot Leslie?" But if you look closely, Doug was there. They were still shooting, and Todd stuck with Taylor. There's a scene where they're at the van and Leslie gets angry with Taylor. And you see Leslie and you can glimpse a camera in the van through the window. At first glance you might think it's a mistake, but then you flip POVs and realize Doug is shooting from within the van. His composition is different and at an interesting angle. It's all a testament to my DP Jaron Presant.

So, you never ran two cameras at the same time on set.

The only time we ran two cameras in the docu-world was when we were locked off, for the "interview" environment. We did use two film cameras in certain horror scenes.

Britain and Ben, the cameramen characters. In early scenes we can hear them, but we really don't physically meet them until the third act. Did you have them on set? Or the lines just dubbed in afterwards?

They were on set the whole time, and the majority of the things that they said were scripted. But after a particular scene we'd record wild lines of theirs. But then we edited the movie together, if there was some space in a scene where we could fill in a line here or there, we brought Ben and Britain in to just improvise a bunch of lines. They're both improv actors, standup comedians. Early on in the shoot, they were able to get situated and comfortable, not having to do a lot of dramatic acting, but getting to riff! Then they both got opportunities to rip their dramatic stuff later, when we went to the "film world" days. They both did excellent work.

I have to bring up your noted genre/acting veteran trio making cameos. Robert Englund, Zelda Rubinstein,

Scott Wilson. Can you tell us about working with them and how they came on board?

You can't even imagine how excited I was to get all of them! Robert's role was written with him in mind. We always talked about how great it would be to get him to play the 'Doctor Loomis' archetype. We were certain that if we were able to offer him a role, we should absolutely offer him that one instead of the retired psycho-slasher. It would have been so telegraphed had we done that. Actually, he told us later on that he would have been turned off if we'd offered him the retired slasher role.

Getting back to that parody/farce depiction where we stop and point at the ironic horror reference.

Yeah, it would have been too on-the-nose. He respected the fact that we had too much respect for him then to offer him that role. He responded right away and jumped on board.

Scott Wilson was an acquaintance of mine through a mutual friend. We were already in Portland shooting, desperate to fill that role, and I called him and sent him the screenplay, and just begged him to come up for two days. Zelda, I'm not saying this as a joke, we didn't even know if she was alive!

I felt that way too, to be honest. When she shows up in the film I was like "Oh my God, it's her!"

Our casting directors tracked her agent down. And we offered her the role, it was a bit part. But when she accepted, we re-wrote tons of pages of completely expositional dialogue that went on and on. Which in itself was supposed to be funny, she's got the ridiculously expository dialogue, and she would not quit talking, but that was the point! She's the conventional harbinger of doom. (laughs) It was meant to be overly expository.

That matches the rest of the 'slasher world' though where the acting is amped up a melodramatic notch, the dialogue is stilted.

Right! Exactly! But going back to Scott Wilson and Robert Englund, it was amazing. When they got up there, it completely legitimized what we were doing. Everybody felt a greater sense of purpose when they showed up. "Oh my God, this is for real! This is an actual movie!" It did a lot for the morale and professionalism of what we were doing.

One guy showed up with the 1960's Time/Life cover of *In Cold Blood* with Scott on the cover to get an autograph! But from a business perspective, getting Robert Englund

135

was great for street cred in the horror world. Of course, the objective of this film is to do the horror fan right. But getting a guy like Scott Wilson, there's certainly an argument for the fact that this film, because of its cerebral, satirical nature, it might be accessible to a broader demographic of people who wouldn't normally see a horror film but who might see this because of its tone. Scott Wilson gives it the indie/arthouse street cred.

Obviously the DV/docu-world scenes are more free-form and natural. I was wondering how tight a script you were working from in those scenes.

It's a different style of shooting, but it's meticulously choreographed. Because when you're shooting any film, if you're going to do multiple takes and angles, and somebody doesn't do the exact same action, whether it's pouring a cup of coffee or crossing a room, than you can't cut it together and create continuity. So, it's meant to look free-form. It's meant to look "documentary," because that's the intention. But it's still rehearsed and choreographed.

But there are less setups and camera angles, and you do it less. We didn't have 'shot lists' per se for the DV. We knew that we were going to shoot two different points of views, and shoot the scene in the vernacular that these people would shoot it in. But in the "horror world" scenes, we had comprehensive, meticulous shot lists. It looks a lot more sophisticated, but I would say both styles were just as comprehensive.

The idea of switching back and forth from the docu-world to the movie/film world, was that part of the script from the beginning?

It definitely evolved. The opening scene of the first version of the script was a voiceover over a typical horror movie, in a death sequence. And then it went into a mockumentary. And the script ended before everything pays off as it does in horror films. But what we did was really take this from more of a glorified short film with a really good premise to paying everything off.

We condensed everything into two acts, we added that third act where everything goes to the "horror world." And then we interspersed some of the horror film scenes through the first two acts. That idea really took shape during the development process. In order to really create a three-act structure, a rising action and a resolve, and to create some real depth and conflict for characters, and of course to create something that wouldn't get stale before the movie ended, all of this stuff had to pay off. And the way to do that was to actually show Leslie Vernon "at work."

On the DV days, you've got the skeleton crew. On the 16 mm days, it's a fully crewed picture. But Jaron is still in charge of the cinematography on both. Can you talk about working with him and his approach to each style?

We were shooting two movies at once, but Jaron and everybody else got to do two different styles in one movie, which was such a thrill for all of us. I was a 'backpack.' Jaron basically carried me the whole way. It was so incredible just being able to wake up every morning, and go to our coffee shop, and go over what we were going to do that day with our shot lists and storyboards. Just like Angela with the acting, Jaron had so much more experience that I truly felt like I was in good hands. And Jaron really responded to the fact that I wanted to do things as geeky and meticulous as give the shooting styles characteristics (the way Doug and Todd shoot) and that I had a very specific vision about things like coming in on our 'horror shots' in a very Godlike omniscient way, just telling people 'we're in the horror movie now.'

And he is just such a perfectionist when it comes to the aesthetic. You talk to Jaron about the moonlight in *Halloween*, how it's Two Electric Blue, and the muddy greens in horror films, and how nothing is truly black! Even black has a color in horror. When you can have conversations with people on those types of levels, you know you're working with the right people. He really knew his stuff. I got his reel, he read the screenplay and we met.

One of my biggest pieces of advice would be, if you really know in your gut who you want, better not to be a penny wise than a pound foolish. Follow your gut.

You touched on a lot of the extra footage shot 'by the documentarians;' just how much is there? One of my favorite little moments is when you show clips of Leslie Vernon and Eugene (the retired slasher), with Scott Wilson's voiceover, and they're just hanging out skipping rocks at the lake. The student and the mentor just shooting the shit. Was that another scene that was cut down?

No, actually, we finished early that particular day. And we had time to kill, and I had Scott Wilson! And I just said to myself, "We've got to do something!" And there was this gorgeous ravine near the house, so we went there and turned the cameras on and just told them to hang out, skipping rocks. And we also shot them on the porch, talking.

How do you approach it as a director, in terms of the two distinct styles of the movie? And did you shoot about two weeks of each format?

We started film around day fourteen; I think we shot twenty-four days. One of the reasons why this film was such a good first film for me, as a director, was because I was able to demonstrate myriad skills in one film. I was able to show people (who might be looking at me for other projects) comic timing, as well as horror timing, tonally, in the same movie. I was also able to demonstrate a more improvisational, indie type of shooting. In the same movie, I was able to show say, a Universal executive that I knew how to shot-list and choreograph an action sequence.

Now although we weren't trying to compete with the cinematography of say, the *Texas Chainsaw* remake, we were certainly creating an homage to around 1981. I certainly wanted to demonstrate a wide spectrum of skills, so that I didn't have to do three films before someone gave me an opportunity to direct a comedy, or a horror film.

How did you come up with Leslie's look and costume? His "work uniform." I think of it like the movie, it's a balance of imposing and funny. When I realized what the mask was, it was still creepy. But humorous.

Thanks! Again, just like everything else, we were trying stay within the conventions of horror; and of course, what is so vitally important is the weapon of choice and the mask! We developed a whole backstory about how Leslie was forced to till the soil as a child using only a hand scythe, which was ridiculous but self-aware at the same time. So of course that's his weapon. (As for) the mask; a lot of the exposition of Leslie's back story ended up on the editing room floor. But if you piece together this story that Zelda tells in the library, Leslie is "The Boy, Returned." As a boy he was thrown off a waterfall and "drowned."

Since he was an undeveloped child when he died, his mask, and this was the brainchild of E. Larry Day, my visual effects and makeup guy, he went through a book of unborn fetuses and we honed in on a fetus-form face. This whole idea of a nondescript face with human features, but also sort of subhuman features. And I thought it came out really well.

Any advice for aspiring filmmakers?

I would say the barriers to filmmaking have all but evaporated. Everybody realizes it's a lot easier these days to pick up a camera, go out and shoot a film. But what aspiring filmmakers have to see is, they've got to see the bigger picture. You have to prepare and anticipate taking that content you've shot and actually preparing for the process of putting it onto celluloid, which is so comprehensive.

It took me two years to develop the script for *Behind the Mask*, and it's been two years since we shot it. Twenty-four days to shoot the film. So, people have got to develop a script that is airtight. That's certainly worthy and ready to go. And then the best thing you can do is get a postproduction supervisor on your film when you shoot it, so that person can plan out a roadmap so you can actually finish your film. So few films get finished because people make tremendous financial mistakes. I would map it all out.

NATHAN BAESEL

Interviewed by Adam Barnick (2/07)

Actor Nathan Baesel completed his Bachelor's Degree in Theater at UCLA. At The Juilliard School in New York, he was awarded the Liz Smith prize for voice and speech, and turned down the lead in a Broadway production to finish his final year of training. On television, he landed his first starring role playing Lewis Sirk, the one-armed deputy in ABC's sci-fi drama *Invasion*. While this role won him many admirers for his textured, affecting performance, his first leading, acclaimed role in *Behind the Mask: The Rise of Leslie Vernon* will win him even more!

Can you tell me what sparked the intention of becoming an actor? What lit the fuse?

I used to do church plays growing up with my family. Performances were always encouraged. Putting on Christmas shows at the house, things like that with my brothers and sisters. Before me, my two older brothers did drama productions in high school, and I just kind of followed in their footsteps. Acting in high school. But it wasn't until junior college that I knew it was something I wanted to commit myself to as a profession. Not only that I had an ability, but I also had a desire to commit myself to a life of poverty. (laughs)

I was still pretty much ego-oriented in my acting, doing it for my self-gratification. When I went to UCLA I had more of a profound realization of what acting could be. Doing a bit of a mind-shift from having it be an egocentric kind of act to one actually using my abilities to contribute to other people's experiences.

In terms of how the arts can enlighten the culture?

Yeah! Yeah.

And you came up our way, afterwards, to Julliard.

When I completed my (UCLA) degree, I felt like I had gotten a really great taste of what acting can be, and how it can be used to have an impact on an audience. But I felt like I was lacking in a facility. So, I knew I wanted to commit myself to a conservatory, some kind of intense training program

so that I could have a facility that would allow me to tackle many styles of acting, many styles of theater, and hopefully many styles of acting for the camera.

I was going to ask you overall if that helped you hone your craft towards all these different facets.

It did, in doing all of the voice and speech training; which is a huge component of acting; otherwise, we're just physically oriented. Without dialogue, we're dancers. That was something I just never had access to, that was tremendous; but also, being able to work on many different kind of styles of acting really just pushed my boundaries out. What I was capable of doing was so much more than what I'd gone into Julliard with, and I was really grateful to have been able to get everything out of it that I'd initially wanted from it.

After Julliard, did you come back to LA? I know you found a new 'home' with South Coast Repertory Theatre.

I stayed in New York for two or three months after I graduated. I got married on the day of my graduation.

Congratulations!

Thank you! I got married in LA and went back to New York and stayed out there for a little while. I felt like moving out to California was a good choice, especially if I wanted to raise a family, so we did.

One of my first (California) auditions was for a project at South Coast. I started a great relationship with the casting director. It's an incestuous group in a great way; they tend to use a lot of the talent that they like in multiple productions and with play reading and workshop opportunities there's lots of ways to get plugged into projects.

When you came back to California, you had a couple of guest spots on *The District* and *Cold Case*. Was this your first on-camera work other than in training?

We had some on-camera class work in our last year of Julliard. But really their focus was on developing us as theatrical actors. And I think there was a certain amount of wariness that they had about putting too much emphasis in training their students for film or TV careers, because that meant there would be less of a talent pool to draw from in the theatrical community, which is understandable. But I got out here and was really just trying to book any work I could get; I had done a couple commercials in New York.

Is that how you got into SAG?

Yeah, I got in SAG with my first commercial, a (laughs) Nintendo Gameboy job. Just got out here and pretty soon found myself getting confused, I didn't understand why I wasn't booking work and quickly realized it had really little to do with me.

Just the mundane grind.

It's just what happens, and I am still walking that line of trying to make adjustments in my performing to accommodate what I think people might be looking for in an audition, and just doing my thing! Doing it the way I feel comfortable doing it, or making a choice I think might be riskier. It might not be exactly what they're looking for, but I believe this is the way it might be best to play it, or the most interesting. The only thing you can really do is be truthful, and to make bold choices if you feel that's what is required.

Behind the Mask was one of those where I could see that they were wanting it to go a certain way, and I just felt like if this was a role that I was going to play, going to want to play for however long the shoot was going to be, heck, I want to make it as interesting for me as I can. So my choice making was unconventional.

That was an example of how they saw your choices and realized what you could bring to this!

Yeah! I think I kind of caused a mini-crisis, not even a mini, I think it was a total crisis because they had really envisioned it to be a much different kind of film, and I was making Scott rethink the whole tone of the movie! And fortunately, he was open to my efforts to convince him that it could work the way I was doing it.

Can you give us a general synopsis of *Behind the Mask: The Rise of Leslie Vernon* for the uninitiated?

I don't do nearly as good a job of explaining it as some people that I've read, but ... the main conceit is that it takes place in this alternate reality where we don't have serial killers like Ted Bundy and John Wayne Gacy; our serial killers, if you want to call them that, are Freddy, Jason, Mike Myers. These are our serial killers, but they're not even referred to as serial killers. Really there's not that kind of stamp that's placed on them. Most of the time they're spoken of with reverence. And so, there's room for comedy in a subject where there really shouldn't be if you were talking about it...

Yeah, nobody's comparing John Gacy to Hank Aaron.

No. But in this world, that's applicable. At least with the character that I play. And this guy, Leslie Vernon, has been training for years and preparing a legend, so that he can unleash himself into the pantheon of great psycho slashers of all time. And he intends to not just be a great, but I think to be the greatest. He has enlisted the help of a documentary crew to record this.

When it comes to the point where he is about to unveil his legend to the community, the documentary crew has a crisis of conscience, and shut their cameras off. At that point the film switches over into a traditional slasher pic, except the audience has been walked through so much of the process that they can anticipate the road that it's going to go down, with a few twists and turns here and there!

You said you caused the filmmakers to rethink the character after seeing what you were bringing to it in auditions. How did Leslie come across in the script you read? What was your immediate take on the character? What appealed to you about it off the bat?

Up until *Behind the Mask*, the only jobs that I was getting in film or TV were the bad guys (laughs) and I think why I was getting those roles was because, even though they do bad, I find that what makes a bad character more compelling is that there's enough of a humanity to them to ground them in something familiar, so that the audience isn't just steered in the direction of the duality of "here's the good guy, here's the bad guy."

Villains who sit home and clean their guns all day and nothing else.

Yeah! I enjoy creating characters, even good people that have other shades in them! So, for my bad guys, I like to explore their humanity. And with this guy, I felt like, yes, on the page he is the embodiment of everything that is evil. I think what would be so much more interesting and compelling and ultimately could be very funny without having to put any kind of over-the-top comedic spin on anything, I think you could cover all your bases by having the character be capable of dark and terrible things, yet in the next moment, be very charming and down-to-earth and relatable. So that's where I was coming from with him; you know, make a 'guy next door!' He's actually a pretty nice guy! He loves his job! A doctor saves lives, and he believes he has to provide a balance to the universe. He's somebody that takes lives.

Funny you say that, my take on Leslie in general was this was a respected, sort of, position in this world. He's going to pay his dues and work hard. The humor came out of the fact that his trade was fear and murder.

Sure! I reached a very good point during the shoot where I felt that there was something philosophically relevant about what he was doing. Something that was actually morally relevant about what he was doing, which sounds really bizarre and inhuman, but, in fact, in universal terms, he's providing a balance to the universe. You've got your Yin, you've got to have your Yang.

In terms of the metaphors, you've also got Scott Wilson as the mentor figure, as a killer in the film and he's a veteran of the screen, and you have the dual meaning with Robert (Englund), who's been performing for thirty years, most notably as one of these bad guys, what Leslie's going to become. You touched on finding where the humanity was in these characters; I wanted to ask you about playing, well any character for you personally, is the key to it finding something in the character you can relate to? Do you need to create these emotions or find something you've gone through that parallels the emotions? I'm curious about your process.

I think I try to steer away from having a preconception of where it needs to go. A certain scene, or a character overall. Because I feel like a lot of the answers are going to come in the actual exploration of it and then the collaboration. A lot of those questions will be answered. But sometimes there are choices that it feels like have the most potential for being mined, and developing interesting opportunities, so I do

make some overall choices sometimes that might aid down the line or offer the most potential to have yummy things to explore down the line. But it's different for every project and role. I think that's why I'm grateful I have the training and experience that I have. I have a lot to draw from, in terms of addressing certain problems that come up.

With *Behind the Mask* on a lot of the scenes, I would intentionally not memorize my lines. I wanted to have to be fully present to everything that was going on. From working with certain props or taking in my environment or interacting with the people around me, I wanted to try to force myself to be as present as possible, and so I didn't want to have my lines all clean and clear and well-rehearsed, and all my ideas set in stone as to how a scene needed to go. I wanted to get turned on by the things that were happening around me.

Is it a matter of if you got too much of the preconceived game plan, you might miss what's in front of you?

Yeah, that tends to be the case a lot! I was just doing an episode of *Without a Trace*, and my experience of *Invasion*… because *Invasion* was the first recurring role that I ever had, I'm up to episode seventeen, I didn't have to worry about my job 'ending' or if I 'did a shitty job,' that somebody was going to fire me. So, there was a greater level of ease. With my work on *Without a Trace*, once I had the job, I knew 'I had the job'! So, I could eliminate some of the stress and considerations. In fact, I can allow myself to, even encourage myself to 'screw up!'

You never know where it will take you!

You never know! I try to do everything that I can to ensure that I'm not controlling where it's going to go.

The documentary sections of *Behind the Mask*, they're really good for you then because they're a little more free form, playing an entire scene out as opposed to doing one shot for ten seconds.

That was a lot of fun.

Are these programs much more restricted because of the pace of TV, shots set up a certain way, etc.?

It is restrictive, but that's the form; that's the way it is, a very technical medium. *Behind the Mask* was great because it was both an opportunity to work in both a 'reality based' way, with the DV where we could play whole scenes through; and then work with film, which is more of a confined medium. I'm developing a little more rapport with that kind of process too. So, I got to have an opportunity to develop my skills in both mediums at the same time.

The filmic scenes, when Leslie Vernon's in silent-killer mode. Did they need you to be much more precise and set then, or does it just come across that way because that's the part that's shot more like a traditional movie?

I think it was more precise, in spite of the, I guess 'technical restrictions,' I didn't feel all that restricted, my attentions and focus were completely absorbed with the task that I had at hand, which generally was stalking and I went a little method with that. (laughs)

You mentioned in terms of not wanting to 'completely paint out your portrait' in advance, so to speak, can you talk about how you worked with Scott (Glosserman) in shaping this character?

I was given an amazing amount of freedom to do my thing. The thing that made the experience so great was it seemed to be Scott was really trying to do team building, with the auditions. And once he'd cast, because he was a first-time director, he trusted that the actors knew what they were doing. If there was a technical consideration that needed to be addressed, he'd step in, but for the most part, we were given license to play. It was a very liberating experience. I never felt confined, always felt free flowing.

What a great way to start out for your first big film!

Oh man! I can't tell you how incredible an experience that was, knowing it was my first film. You know that scene where Leslie is sitting atop that hayloft with Taylor?

Before the reign of terror?

Yeah, (Leslie's) saying, "This is like my Christmas" and he's crying, saying, "I'm so happy?" That actually was meant to be a funny scene! It was written to be a throwaway scene.

I was dropped off at the farmhouse that we were going to shoot at. They were doing location scouting, checking out the house, and I just walked around the fields for a few hours. Just sitting there with my thoughts, mulling over everything. I just felt so incredibly fortunate, realizing the best of what it is to be an actor, an employed actor; being able to put food on the table and feeling creatively fulfilled at the same time. Working my ass off but doing work I was so in love with doing. I felt like I had realized my purpose. (laughs)

That scene is basically the realization I had while I was walking those fields. I realized, "*Oh my God, this is that scene!*" And I talked with Scott, and he said, "Let's go for it!"

Was all your rehearsal generally in front of the camera?

The great thing about the role that I was playing was I was the focus; the subject of the documentary was me. And so, I didn't really have to worry about what other people were doing, because they had come here to document me and pay attention to what I was saying. That took a whole lot of the onus off me to have any considerations other than what was swimming around in my head, which is really selfish on one hand, but so was that character.

Sure! The magnifying glass is on you.

Really all I ever had to do was make sure I understood what the scope of the scene was, and a sense of what I wanted to do rhythmically in the scene, and a sense of what my lines were, and then we could just start playing! We would generally shoot the rehearsals and were usually able to knock a scene out in four takes.

Would Scott give you a direction to start it off with or just sort of let it run and see where you went, and then shape it to what he thought might be best?

Well, the great thing about the DV was, unless we were confined in a space like the van, we were free to move without consideration of falling out of frame or anything. We could just play a scene out, and if Scott wanted to jump in and take care of something, he could, but for the most part we were able to just play around with each other like kids in a sandbox, and have fun!

That was also really great about playing the character; he loves and has fun with what he is doing. So, it was really an opportunity to fuck around and the more excited and the more fun he was having, the better things would come across on film!

I wanted to ask about Angela Goethals as Taylor Gentry.

She was awesome.

She goes so many different places in this, and she's a good foil/balance for your character, with all those emotional notes she hits. Tell me about working with her since she's really the main person you get to act with.

She was just tremendous, as an actor and a person. It's funny, because the relationship that got built between our characters was mirroring the friendship between us personally. I think it's actually appropriate that it's coming out on Valentine's Day, because in a way, it's a love story in my opinion. She was just a total pleasure to work with. We just had a ball working on that thing, a labor of love.

We were getting a lot of work done in a short amount of time; but on the other hand, we were all doing work that was so enjoyable to do, and in our off times, we were enjoying everybody so much, spending all of our off time hanging out, getting drinks. It was a real fraternal kind of working environment. Angela was very giving too as an actor, open and available. So much of what happens on the screen was not in the script, just came out of what was there, what she was bringing, and what she was doing that made me feel I should do 'this', just a really good back-and-forth.

Because it's *Icons of Fright*, I am required to ask at least one question about Robert Englund, who plays Doc Halloran (Leslie's nemesis) in the film.

Robert's awesome! Really the only scenes we have together are in the library with Zelda Rubinstein, when I reveal myself for the first time, and at the end. He wrapped up all his stuff in three days at the most. We were all just so grateful that he'd signed on to do this film, it put such a stamp of legitimacy on what we were doing; the story we were telling could have been told without him, but simply because of his credit, and the associations built up with his fan base, and his associations with that character, it brought a whole new texture to the movie that we wouldn't have had otherwise. Same with Kane Hodder's cameo.

It's like meta-casting.

Yeah, it's not even that it necessarily makes it legitimized, it actually it takes it to another place conceptually. The night Robert got there he took us all out for drinks and paid for them all. We're like, "No! No!" Are you kidding me?" And he just said, "Hey, come on; let me take care of it." (laughs) I had a lot of reverence for him. His movies were really the only horror/slasher films I had seen growing up! I saw *Friday the 13th* for the first time right before I went to Portland to do the film, hadn't seen the *Halloween* movies all the way through.

I remember he finished one of his scenes, and then he waited around because there was a scene that followed it where Angela and I are up against the van, where it gets kind of tense.

I think it was kind of checking out what he'd gotten himself into. You know? And I think he was specifically checking me out. And he watched the scene being shot, and kind of pulled me aside afterwards and said, "It's really good, man. What you're doing is really good. Leslie's got a real volatility to him, where he can turn on a dime, that's great." And he told me, "You remind me of a young Anthony Perkins, has anyone ever told you that?" And I was like "NO!! THANK YOU!!" (laughs) "Oh my God! Robert Englund told me I reminded him of Anthony Perkins!" I think I called my wife right after that and told her that.

Leslie's body language when you're in masked-killer mode, I was just wondering if you could talk about your approach in those scenes. You did some interesting stuff in there. You've got a moment when you're going to make your first kill, where you rise up to your feet like a cobra. I was wondering where you came from with that aspect of the character.

Well, I wanted to try to put in visually some of the slasher conventions that I knew of, and obviously I wasn't as well-versed in them as Scott or the screenwriter David J. Stieve, but there were certain things like the 'sitting up when you think he's dead' that you see in all of those movies, it felt like the ones that needed to be in there, got in.

I was really stumped for a while on what the physicality for this guy in costume would end up being! I started going down this road of trying to conceptualize what his physicality would be, based on the fact that the character has created this boy; the legend he's created for this boy is that he was killed when he was ten or so.

I thought, well, he's a ten-year-old boy, there shouldn't be a masculine physicality, it should be a childish, impish physicality. And the first time I started shooting it as this 'boy', Scott stopped me and he's like, "let's do it again, but don't do any of that stuff that you were doing." (laughs)

So, I toned it down, we did it again and he's like, "all that stuff, I think it's too much!" I think he just needs to kind of stand there." (laughs) I was totally confused; I didn't know what do with him. Ultimately, I'm grateful that he pulled me aside and told me that. In retrospect, what I was trying to do was set my character apart from those other guys, and he was steering me towards the traditional which I think ultimately worked much better.

Once I started embracing the physicality of a powerful force, it really aided me on many levels, it was like *Batman*. My childhood intrigue with *Batman* was I felt like I was perfectly capable of being *Batman* because he has no "powers", he just trains and hones himself to the extent of human perfection. In a way, I felt like that's what I was able to do with Leslie. There's this scene where I'm dragging this body across the field, it's rather fluid despite the fact I'm dragging this 180 pound guy.

And you have to make it look effortless.

Yes! You know? He would be impervious to pain, he wouldn't be conscious of pain, that's another thing that served really well, because it was really cold and I had made the bonehead choice that the character didn't wear shoes. So, I'm standing in colder-than-freezing weather, standing on pebbles, rocks and mud. My feet were just… putting myself into the mindset of this character allowed me to just not entertain any of those thoughts.

Have you been to the festival screenings of *Leslie Vernon*? Can you watch the film objectively?

I was at Gen Art in New York and Screamfest in LA. I don't think that I can be truly 'objective,' but I'm not cringing. For the most part, I felt very much that I was doing the best job I was capable of doing at the time and so I don't really have any regrets. For the most part, I'm able to watch the film and really enjoy it. What's really surprising to me, after the number of times that I've seen it, I'm still able to enjoy it. I like watching it in front of crowds just to see the reaction.

The festival screenings have been really cool because people have been responding to completely different things. That's been really fun to see different audiences having completely different takes on the movie, appreciating completely different things. And something that has pleased me to no end is that even the non-genre-oriented crowd, people that steer away from horror films because horror films scare them. I'm one of those people. I'm really thrilled to see those people enjoying the film just as much as horror fans.

It is for the geek, there's a part of the film geared directly toward the geek; these are the people that will get the DVD and analyze all the little bits that were put in there consciously to please them. There are so many choices that were made, even in design, to please and excite the horror fans, you might not pick up on the first viewing. But maybe on a third or fourth viewing you'll still get more out of it!

There's also a quality about the movie; its humor and its humanity are for people that are horror and non horror fans alike. I hope this movie will actually create horror fans from those people who steer away from horror

films because of fear of them; maybe this movie will excite them in an intellectual examination of horror convention, and concept! And they'll go to see horror films to break them down conceptually. That's really exciting; to feel maybe we can be a part of turning people on to the genre who would never have done so otherwise!

This movie is an examination of deeper themes of things you might not think would be in a horror movie, and it happens to say "look, not all of these films are mindless murder fests."

There's some great benefits that have been mined from Scott's classes of 'horror convention' at Penn State! (laughs) He was approaching it from a reverential and analytical viewpoint, and I think that all of that makes it not just a love note to horror fans, but an academic endeavor as well.

Are you doing any more writing? I checked out the script you wrote for *Invasion*, great stuff. You had one part where you described the Varon's family scene as "Norman Rockwell with a five o' clock shadow." Dammit I wish I wrote that.

(laughs) I really enjoy writing, and that was something that struck me when on *Invasion*. I had a lot of time on my hands. I was being used (in early episodes) and I'd read enough scripts to get the gist of how they composed their stories rhythmically, and how the characters are going, I didn't know where they're taking the story, I'll use the information I had as a jumping-off point. And so, I just put myself to work; I enjoyed it tremendously, such a great creative outlet at a time when I had a lot of time on my hands.

By the time I actually finished it, it turned out that the episodes were going in a completely different direction, but it was fun to see some of the ideas I'd introduced in my script were introduced in some of the episodes they ended up doing. That was without any collaboration or consultation. It was nice to see I'd gotten my finger on the pulse, a little bit, of what the writers were doing. I really wanted to use it as an opportunity to meet with writers and pick their brains. Ultimately, I got to realize that's something that I want to explore more, other than the acting side of me.

Any ideas you're developing?

I have a script I've been mulling over, I actually wrote it out, but I've been feeling more and more pulled to work on it; that seems to be the one way people can stay working, producing their own stuff.

DAVE PARKER

Interviewed by Mike Cucinotta and Rob Galluzzo (5/07)

Ever since we started *Icons of Fright*, we've always wanted to talk to filmmaker Dave Parker. Well, this month we got to speak to Dave extensively about his underrated Full Moon debut *The Dead Hate the Living*, what it's like to work on DVD documentaries for some of the most iconic superheroes, and finally... we get to hear exactly what the hell happened with *House of the Dead*! He also speaks candidly about the upcoming *The Hills Run Red*, which marks his return to directing! Read on for the *Fright* exclusive interview!

Rob: What are your earliest recollections of the horror genre? What introduced you to that world as a kid?

Well, as a little kid, it was the cliché of a *Famous Monsters* kit. I started out liking dinosaurs, and then I got into *Godzilla*, and found *Famous Monsters* magazine and got into all the classic monsters. That's what got me into it. I watched scary movies as much as I could, but really, I was a bit of a scaredy cat until age twelve. (laughs) And then I saw *Creepshow* and that was like my gateway drug into the genre. Then it became every slasher movie and horror video I could find. As a little kid, I was always fascinated by monsters. The first time I got really in trouble over my love of horror was when I was in the second grade and my Mom and older brother were both reading *The Amityville Horror*. They told me about the book and the story behind it, and I decided for "show and tell" in second grade to bring in the book and tell them about the house where the devil lives. (laughs) I made a girl cry in class. That was my first inkling that, "*Wow, I can scare people!*", which was pretty cool.

Rob: At what point did you realize that so much effort went into making films? I know most filmmakers start with an interest in special effects, learning how the "tricks" were done. What was it for you?

The first two movies that really made me think about filmmaking were *Raiders of the Lost Ark* and *Creepshow*. *Creepshow* because it was so exaggerated, and I really noticed lighting and make-up FX and camera angles. With *Raiders of the Lost Ark*, it was just so fucking cool that I thought, "I want to do that for the rest of my life." It was picking up

Tom Savini's *Grande Illusions* and reading up on make-up and reading *Fangoria* magazine; that's what really got me into it. I thought, "Wow, I can do this for a living?" I thought it'd be like playing, playing with toys. Little did I know how difficult and how much work it is. I definitely was obsessed with Savini and Rick Baker's teams and how they did their FX. It helped me rationalize genre films to my parents. I'd say, "I'm studying it for the technique!"

Rob: You ended up writing and directing *The Dead Hate the Living* for Full Moon, but you were working at Full Moon for quite a while before that, right?

Yeah, I'd been there for about four or five years working on stuff. I moved out to Hollywood when I was eighteen, basically right out of school. The first thing I worked on was a movie for Jeff Burr called *Eddie Presley*, which was not a horror movie, but I was very stoked at that time to meet Jeff Burr and work on that movie as a props assistant. It was really low budget but it was my first taste of working on a movie. I kept working on some micro-budget productions and met the guy who did all the trailers for Full Moon. His name was Daniel Schweiger and he was cutting all the trailers and behind the scenes *Videozone* segments stuff for Full Moon. At the time, of course I had rented a bunch of Full Moon movies.

It was one of those things where I thought "Should I try to work for Full Moon, or should I try to work for Roger Corman?" It literally came down to the point where when I first moved out here, I didn't have a car, and Full Moon was in Hollywood, and I knew I could work there because it was close, whereas Corman was in Venice. So, I ended up working for Charlie Band and assistant cutting the trailers and behind-the-scenes stuff. It was a great learning experience. I got a lot of set exposure. I got to see how everything was done. At the time it was great, I was having a blast, even though I was working my ass off for no money. But at the time, I was learning while I earned something.

Later, Dan left, and it just seemed natural for me to take over his position. So, I did that for a couple of years, as the head of promotions. Cut all the trailers and shot all the behind-the-scenes videos and interviewed all the actors and filmmakers. As it always happens though when you're working for these low-budget companies, you start to think, "Well, I'm tired of working for no money and busting my ass. I want to do a movie." It came down to the point where I was really thinking of leaving and trying to get other work. That was always my goal, to make a feature and I figured at a place like that, it was a possibility. Push come to shove, Charlie finally said alright. They had a zombie movie, and I said I had to do it. And he gave me a shot.

Rob: Let's talk a bit about the inspirations for *The Dead Hate the Living*? Starting with that title, because I remember when it first came out, it was one of the coolest titles for a zombie flick!

I know. And if the movie was as cool as the title, I'd have a much different point of view.

Mike: I think the movie is as cool as the title!

(laughs) Well, thank you. The title came from Charlie. He took it from an old pulp novel or magazine. I think it was the short story from one of those *Weird Tales* pulp magazines. As Charlie always did, he made a poster and some artwork. It was this very EC Comics colorful artwork with the title. I thought, "That's the greatest thing ever! I have to do that!" It wasn't a zombie, but it had this science lab type of thing going on. When we were getting ready to do the movie, there was a script that did exist, but at that time, it was when Charlie was doing a lot of stuff in Romania. When that movie came around, their deal with Paramount was over, and the budgets were increasingly getting smaller and smaller and smaller.

The script that was designed for Romania just wasn't what he could do here. So, I pitched my idea. And I came up with basically a fan-boy wish list of stuff. I was so inexperienced at the time, I just thought, "Let me write what I know and what I've experienced working at this place. Try to make some kind of commentary on making low budget movies." Charlie was always pretty open and free on the creative level that way. He thought more in terms of, "We've got a cool title for the box, now can we sell it?" I worked on the original story with a friend of mine. Our original idea was way too ambitious for the money we had, so I had to scale it down. It became what the movie is now.

Mike: I wanted to ask about all of the references to all the older zombie movies, because no one was really doing zombies at the time.

We weren't the trailblazer of the zombie resurgence, but the thing that went through my mind was I was trying to be responsible with a budget. And I'd worked on enough low budget movies and knew people that worked on these no-budget movies to think, "Well, I know how hard it is to pull off something that was kind of neat." I didn't want to attempt a Romero-thing, because I knew we wouldn't have the budget to have a mass of zombies, and I didn't want gray and blue faced guys running around eating people. We didn't have the money or the time. I didn't want to tread on Romero's thing, I wanted to make it different from those.

A lot of the inspiration at the time… well, *Resident Evil*, the video game was big at that point, so I thought I'd make zombie "characters." At that time, Charlie was really into thinking about the Full Moon toys. So, it was one of those things where I guess we were trying to please so many cooks. I wanted to please myself, but I knew Charlie liked to make toys and cross merchandise. So, I thought I'd make as cool a zombie characters as I can. And then we'll be able to make toys and all this other stuff that never happened. I think if he had made a toy of one or two of the zombies, it would've done better than a *Shrieker* toy, or a *Ragdoll* toy. For better or worse, I wanted to pay tribute to the past zombie movies that I loved. The inspiration came from everything from *White Zombie* to Lucio Fulci's *Gates of Hell* and *Zombi*. I was really into that stuff and no one else, at the time, at Full Moon was remotely interested in those movies. I was the only one who was really into that stuff, which was funny because Charlie and his family lived in Italy and made movies in Italy. It really became this valentine pastiche of things I loved from all those zombie movies.

Mike: Is that something on the film you're not happy with?

It's not that I'm not happy with it. I think maybe it was just a little too fanboy-ish. Looking back at it now, I probably would've done it completely differently. But it's a time capsule. It's who I was at the time. And what I liked and was into. It's tough. I look at it now, and I think there's some charming stuff about the movie. I loved the experience of making it. I loved the people that I worked with. But, for me personally the biggest problem with the way the movie is now is it should have been edited tighter. I was really inexperienced as a director and, of course, because of budget, I had to edit the movie myself. And for a lot of first time directors, that can be hard. You get so wrapped up in the fact that you're getting to make a movie, you sort of lose sight of what you need and don't need. It is about forty-five minutes before the thing gets going and then I think there's some fun stuff in it. A lot of it comes from frustration of time and budget, but the movie still looks really good, especially for the budget that it had. The DP, Tom Callaway, who recently shot *Feast*, has gone on to shoot a ton of stuff, and he did a really nice job. And it looks different from other Full Moon movies. That was one of my biggest goals at the time.

Mike: That's one of the things I really liked about it when I came across it about seven years ago. There really was not a lot going on in horror then. And direct to video horror was really bad at the time…

I can't even remember what was coming out at the time!

Mike: I think the big releases from around 2000 were *The Rage: Carrie 2* and *Scream 3*.

I think it really did become that self-reflective era of horror, because *Scream* was so huge and so popular. And I think the first *Scream* is still a legitimate, good horror movie. What it did to the genre or what studios took from it became a dark period for horror.

Mike: I don't think you took from that though. You were doing something really different. And at the time, all that Italian zombie stuff was still really hard to find. You really had to be a fan to dig into it.

Yeah, at that time, I don't think Anchor Bay had released that stuff on DVD yet.

Mike: Exactly, DVD wasn't big yet at the time.

To me, that's what I thought was cool! No one was doing zombies like that. There were no maggots in anything! Since there was none of this type of stuff, I was a bit more influenced by European horror. Of course, the whole gateway thing was influenced by *Phantasm*. And again, *Creepshow* was such a huge influence which can be seen in the lighting scheme.

I wanted to make a living comic book. As cool as the title *The Dead Hate the Living* is, I knew it's not a title you take seriously. You can't make a serious, grim horror movie. It's a comic book title, so that's what we went for.

Mike: It had everything I wanted to see in a horror movie. You had these great creatures and they looked fantastic. You had the practical transformation…

That was the other thing too! Being very influenced by make-up FX, at that time, there were no transformations in movies anymore. No one would even attempt it. I wanted to bring back bladders! I wanted to take all those things I liked about horror movies at that time that people weren't doing. Movies then were just a bunch of teens running around quoting other horror movies. We were at least referencing obscure movies.

Mike: Besides me, who loves it and owns three copies of it, how did it do upon its release?

It did really well. I promoted it as best as possible. We were in *Fangoria*. *Rue Morgue* did a cover, and we got a lot of web coverage. To me, I never said, "This is the future. I am the future of horror," or anything. I just wanted people to see it! So, I talked about it as much as possible. At the time, there was still VHS and DVD together at the stores. I think it shipped 65,000 copies on VHS the first time out. And I think 15-20,000 DVD's. It certainly made its money back and more and did really well in that way. It rented well. It certainly got out there, it was on the shelves and that was exciting. So, Mike, what was it you liked about the movie that you owned three copies of it at one point?! (laughs)

Mike: (laughs) Well, like you said. No one was doing these homages to Italian zombie horror, and they were so hard to find. And then I come across this movie in the middle of Blockbuster Video, I rented it, watched it and I felt like it was made just for me. I didn't know anyone else who liked these zombies movies, or the way they looked. I loved the transformation scene. That was one of my favorite things about 80's horror movies. It just had this great energy. I loved the band *Penis Fly Trap*, and they had the theme song in there. Everything seemed to work for me, and I fell in love with it.

Rob: Dave Parker, I think you made *The Dead Hate The Living* specifically for Mike.

I think I must have. (laughs) Because I've never known

anyone to know obscure zombie movies and *Penis Fly Trap*. For me, that was very exciting, because I was friends with those guys. At the time, I was either going to do a movie for Full Moon or I was going to leave. I mean, the budgets had gotten really low. Everyone was struggling there. It wasn't a happy atmosphere most of the time. I just went out randomly and there was a party in Hollywood. It was a launch party for the re-release of *The Beyond* that Bob Murawski and Sage Stallone did.

It was this whole night where three bands played, and I was just going to stop in and say my hellos. But *Penis Fly Trap* played that show. And I just thought, "*Wow.*" I hadn't seen a band like that ever, and they were horror based. So, I loved them and ended up hooking up with them, eventually doing a music video for them. So, for me, the ego stroke of all time was to get a band to write an original theme song for you. It's something you think you're never going to get, and then they do that. That part, for me, was a thrill. I dug that song! They really came through and it was a nice bonus, which again Full Moon movies didn't have at the time.

Mike: Were you aware that Diana Cancer had been in *45 Grave* and on the *Return of the Living Dead* soundtrack?

Yeah! That was the thing! *Party Time*, being to me, the ultimate zombie theme and then to have her do this. And it was always a treat to see them play that song live. It always got a good reaction from the audience live, so that was cool.

Rob: The other thing that stood out for me besides the title was that cover image with that one main zombie.

Yeah, that's "Maggot!"

Rob: How much input did you have with the make-up crew on the look of the zombies? Because they were all so memorable and that one in particular, I remember loving. Is the front of his face cut off? I was always trying to figure out what was up with his mouth!

I don't know! Honestly, part of his look came from *Resident Evil*. If you look at *Resident Evil 2*, and it's not that he was in the video game or anything, but there was a character with a similar sort of exposed, no-nose. I thought, "Whoa! It's a creature, not just a rotted guy!", so that became part of the influence. And then I thought we need autopsy scars and the spinal cords sticking out. Since I was only going to have a few zombies in it, I knew they had to be designed to stand out. I thought things like, "What if the Incredible Hulk was a zombie?" (laughs) It became that big, hulking guy.

And then I wanted this really tall, elongated guy, because early on, there were these import *Dawn of the Dead* action figures, and they were sort of caricatures and elongated. So that's where "Gaunt," the really tall zombie came from. When I worked with the make-up people, I was really specific and we had gotten concept sketches done, so they knew pretty much what I was going for. Even the character of Eric, the actor, that make-up was inspired by *War of The Colossal Beast*. Again, little nods to things I thought were fun and cool.

The cover, Jamie Trueblood, who was one of the still photographers, his friend Brett Beardslee I cast in the movie. And Brett said, "You know my friend's a photographer. Do you mind if he comes down and takes some photographs?" And I said, "Sure. As long as I got some copies!" So, I started to get impressed with Jamie and I saw that photo from the cover, which looked different just as a photo, but it was a really interesting image and I thought, "That should be the cover! It looks like it could be *Famous Monsters* cover." Originally, I tried to convince Charlie to get Basil Gogos to paint that image for the cover, but of course we couldn't afford him. I was really getting into Photoshop early on, so I did a very rough color scheme of what I wanted using that picture. And we sent it off to Lee McCloud, who did all the Full Moon covers. And he painted the cover, and it came out gorgeous. The whole psychological thing of, is the character staring out at you, so when you see that box in the video store, it feels like someone's staring at you.

Rob: Mission accomplished!

A lot of people have complimented the box, which makes me pretty happy.

Rob: Let's talk a bit about Matt McGrory who, sadly, is no longer with us. Was this his first movie?

Yeah, this was his first movie. Matt had sent in his headshot for something else. I think he sent it into Full Moon just in general because they were doing weird movies and I assume his agency sent it in. I thought for our movie, we'd get a basketball player or someone who was really tall… I just didn't think we were going to get someone that tall! I saw his photo, because his headshot was of him standing next to a phone booth, and he towered over the phone booth. So, I thought if nothing, I have to meet this guy! I'll always remember it. He comes in and of course, he has to duck down to get in the doorway, and I'm thinking, "This guy is awesome!"

And then he starts talking and he's got this really deep voice. So, we start talking and I ask what he does, and he said, "Well, I've been a bouncer in Philadelphia and I've done a few things. I was in an Iron Maiden video where I played Eddie." And I was like, "Iron Maiden! Fucking Rad! Right on!" He also said he'd been bartending, so I asked him, "How do you make a Jack and Coke?" And he replied, "Well, I get some ice, put it in a glass, pour in the Jack Daniels and leave the Coke on the side." I said, "You're hired!" (laughs) And he was. Seriously.

You could never find anyone cooler than Matt. He was the nicest guy in the world. A complete sweetheart. He was the epitome of a gentle giant. I was very protective of him on the set. And I recall we would hang out at this bar, and obviously because of the way he looked, he was conscious of it, people would stare, but he'd sit at the end of the bar, and I'd go hang with him. He'd also gotten a bit of notoriety from The Howard Stern Show. But yeah, Matt was the nicest guy and he never complained about anything. The only time he complained was when he had to shave off his goatee. (laughs) And he didn't want to do that, but he did.

But in his real day to day life, he never complained about his situation in life. He really enjoyed his life as much as he could. After we did the movie, we kept in touch, because we lived down the block from each other. He told me he'd gotten a Rob Zombie movie, and I thought that was amazing and great. I'll never forget this one day, I hadn't heard from him in a couple of months, and he gives me a call and says, "Hey, I'm on set shooting this movie in Baltimore." He was just calling to say hi, and he didn't tell me what it was.

Literally, the next day I go online and there's a photo of him with Tim Burton and he's doing Big Fish. I called him back and said, "You son of a bitch! You're doing a Tim Burton movie, and you didn't even tell me?!" (laughs) And to me, Big Fish was his greatest role. In a lot of ways, that was Matt. I saw him about a month before he passed away at the Fango convention and we talked a little bit. I knew things weren't going too well because he wasn't moving around, and he was in a wheelchair. I was really sad to hear about his passing. He was a really good person, and he had a really good heart. He never said a bad word about anybody.

Rob: Is it an obvious homage that the main zombie in The Dead Hate the Living looks like Rob Zombie?

It was obviously… well a certain… Yes. (laughs) Of course. (laughs) Come on, if I said no, I'd be a fucking liar! But honestly…

Rob: Quite frankly, I thought he was in the movie for a very long time.

A lot of people thought he was in the movie. I'll tell you this though. The original concept came out of casting. I had it in my head for a while that I wanted to cast a musician. I wanted to cast a rock star. I tried to cast Alice Cooper. He turned me down. We gave the script to Dee Snider; he turned us down. I met with Blackie Lawless from Wasp for an hour and a half one day, which I thought was really fucking cool. He was into the movie, but he was going to Europe on tour, so he couldn't do it. When I was cutting the movie, I temp-tracked the transformation to a Wasp song. And then I thought, "Well, this guy is the king of the zombies. Why the fuck have I not tried Tom Savini?" I called him and he was into it, he wanted to do it. He told me to go look at his website, and at the time he had long hair, and he had a full beard, because he was trying to make a movie called Vampirates. So, he looked like Blackbeard…

Mike: We've heard about Vampirates!

So, from checking out those photos, I sort of got those images stuck in my head. But Charlie Band wouldn't pay Tom Savini. He wanted too much according to him, which was ridiculous, because having him in the movie probably would've added up to more sales. I mean, a zombie movie with Tom Savini at that time, it seemed like a no-brainer. So, we had a really hard time casting the role. It came close for us to start to shoot, and I decided to have this actor who had come in to audition for a couple of the other roles come in again because he was really a strong actor. He was young, but I figured maybe we can give him long hair and give him the look that Savini had… and… then it sort of became Rob Zombie. (laughs) Funny story. I remember there was a DVD store out here in the Valley called Daze Laser, which was the DVD place to go. And it was a big Laserdisc store before DVD, and I'd go there every Tuesday to go shopping for new releases. One day, I was there after the movie had just sort of come out. And Rob Zombie was there. I had a copy of the movie in my car.

I ran in, slapped the VHS in his hand. I really didn't say much, I just said, "Rob, I really just want you to check out this movie. Thanks for the inspiration. I think you're awesome." And I left. Of course, I never heard anything after that. But I don't know if he ever watched it and saw Matt and thought "Who's this big guy? I have to hire this big guy for something." I'm sure it had something to do with it. Rob obviously knows the movie, because someone talked to him while doing Halloween, and he mentioned, "Oh yeah, The Dead Hate the Living, that was Matt's first movie." So, I assume he watched it and remembered it. Hopefully, he feels flattered! The movie's probably not his cup of tea but I don't know.

Rob: It took me a while to realize you're in _Free Enterprise_, and I love that movie. Was a lot of the stuff that you did at "Full Eclipse" in the movie meant to be your real-life experiences at "Full Moon"?

Absolutely. The shooting of the girl doing the video intro, that happened. And there was more, because she took her top off right in front of us and we were shooting this intro for a Videozone. All that stuff… a lot of _Free Enterprise_, while it may be somewhat exaggerated, pretty much everything that happens in that movie happened in real life. In one way or another. Except in real life, I actually talk. (laughs)

But that Gene Simmons jacket was mine. Yeah, it's all based on real people. Anyone that's seen the movie and watched the documentaries knows. Rob Burnett and Mark Altman like to say it's loosely inspired by them… Bullshit. It's very close to them and our lives at the time. In a way it's a little time capsule.

Rob: Dare I delve into _House of the Dead_ next? (laughs)

Sure! Why not?! (laughs)

Mike: Oh, it's that time!!!

Well, when you're kicking someone while they're down, why not just go for the groin! (laughs)

Rob: Oh, we can't wait to talk about this one! How'd you get involved with _House of the Dead_ and… well… what exactly happened?

Ok, this is how _House of the Dead_ came about. I think we had just finished _The Dead Hate the Living_, and it wasn't released yet. A group of people, sort of the _Free Enterprise_ crowd of people who the movie was based on, we'd get together occasionally and watch stuff together. So, there was a day where we all got together, and it was about showing the work that you'd done. Some people had brought shorts. Or little things like, one of our friends did the _Star Wars_ spoof, _Troops_, so I brought _The Dead Hate the Living_ to show everyone, because obviously I wasn't going to have a big screening, because Charlie Band wouldn't pay for it. (laughs)

There was a movie before it, which was Mike Hurst's first movie called _New Blood_. It was a crime/gangster thing, I think. And it didn't really go over that well with the crowd. I was kind of freaking out and panicking, because here was this movie that had Joe Pantoliano and Carrie-Anne Moss. I just thought they were going to look at my movie and hate it. During that screening, I felt really bad for Mike, because I

don't think it's a bad movie, but people were getting up, and getting beer and fidgeting. So, we throw it on, and it hit for that crowd. All the references and jokes, they really got into it. And Mark Altman saw the movie there and he came up to me after and said, "Look, I think we're getting the rights to _House of the Dead_ and you have to meet on it! I think you know zombies so well that you've be right for it." I thought, "Are you serious? Great! I play this video game all the time and I love it. It would be fantastic." So, I was all excited.

A couple of months went by because it took them a while to get the rights, and they finally called me and I'm freaking out. They sit me down and they go, "You're our guy. You're going to write it. But here's what we want to do… It's got to be a WB type of cast. We want to set it during Spring Break. And ohhh, let's set it on an island, because wouldn't it be cool to shoot it on a tropical island. It'll almost be like a vacation!" Inside I'm thinking, "Oh fuck." "So, you don't want to adapt the video game?" And they replied, "No, no, no. Because they're getting ready to do the _Resident Evil_ movie and it's too similar with the bio-viruses and outbreaks and gothic settings." And I just thought OK. Here I am though, I just did this little movie, and they tell me this one's going to be a five million-dollar theatrical movie. And it's going to be all cool and impressive. So, what am I going to do? Turn it down? So, I thought OK, let me take a crack at it.

So, I write the first draft, and at that time the reviews for _The Dead Hate the Living_ came back, and I read what people didn't like and what they bitched about, so I was consciously writing with that in mind. No film references. Now I'm going to write a serious gory zombie movie with action. And there's a budget, so I'm going to write cool set pieces and good gore stuff and go nuts with it. Treat it seriously. Still under the restrictions and hitting the points that they wanted, which was young cast, on an island. I convinced them not to do spring break because no one's going to care about that. I was the one who did suggest a rave. But I suggested "the rave to end all raves." It was going to be "Burning Man." It was going to be this big, decadent festival. Of course, it would be at night. So, I turn in the draft, and I'm fairly happy with it. It's a first draft and it's pretty rough, so obviously there's going to be some more work to do. And I wait to get notes back.

Two weeks later what I do get is a new draft, written by Mark Altman. And I read it. And… I'm horrified. I'm fucking horrified. There's all this in-jokey film reference stuff. He's changed all the dialogue, the situations, and I just thought it didn't work. I went into the office after reading it for another meeting to talk about doing another re-write, because I contractually owed it to them. I sat down and said to them, "Guys, I don't know if I'm the right guy for this job, because your draft is so completely different from what we originally sat down and talked about. I just don't get this. I don't think this is cool." They were like, "No, no, no. We want you to do it." So, I went back and spent another three weeks or so rewriting their draft, not losing everything he had in there, but getting rid of a lot of the campy dialogue and things like that. And for me, that was it. I turned it in, and I got paid. It took them about a year to actually get the money to start making the movie.

I really didn't hear anything. I'd get random updates like, "Oh we're meeting with these people" or "We're close to getting the money." Then I heard through a friend of mine that worked at an FX company that they got the script in to do a bid on it. And… it was the draft that Mark Altman had written. They didn't even use or send out the draft that I had rewritten the second time. They were just sending out Mark Altman's draft. And I knew there was nothing I could do. Then he told me they got financing, and because they were a low-budget company, it wasn't always a sure thing that I'd get to direct it or anything. They got the financing, but it's coming from the director, and at the time… I'd never heard of this guy. So, I thought… well… all right.

Mike: Nobody knew! (laughs)

Nobody knew at the time about Uwe Boll, and they went off to shoot. It was one of those things where they were shooting it in Vancouver and I asked, "Cool, well, can I come?" And they were like, "Yeah! Well, if you want to fly yourself out and put yourself up, you're more than welcome to. And you can come to set." And I didn't have the money for that. So, thanks a lot. They went and shot the movie. I got to see promo footage several months later that they had for a sales market.

Rob: I think I remember them showing that at a *Fangoria* convention. And it didn't look all that bad.

It didn't look all that bad. Some of it was ugh, because well, the Jurgen Prochnow character was fine. But originally, here were the things. When I wrote the script, it was set in the tropics, like *Zombi* was. Then they went and shot in Canada. Well, they didn't change the script, so the island they're going to still has a Spanish name. The character that Clint Howard ended up playing was written for a black Jamaican guy, so that got totally changed. Then I saw the footage of "the rave," which looked like fifty people during the day. Of course, because no one had probably ever been to a rave, so they didn't know what it was supposed to look like.

So, that's all I saw for months and months. Then the internet stories started popping up about how the director was going to put video game footage in the movie. And I thought… you're… fucking kidding me! I just couldn't believe it being true. Some website asked me, and I said, "I think it's the worst idea a director could ever do. And here's the director's personal email and here's Mindfire's email. You should write them and tell them." I didn't hear anything for a while after that, but I later got invited to a screening at the American Film Market, where they were screening the movie for the first time. And I went with a friend of mine, who I actually named the main villain in the movie after. We sit there and watch it. And I was horrified and so embarrassed. And I was struggling from some of *The Dead Hate the Living* backlash, because places like the IMDb, people were tearing it a new a-hole.

Mike: They don't like anything on the IMDb!

They never asked if I wanted to take my name off this thing, and then there it is, first up and then Mark Altman's name. I'm watching this thing, and I'm seeing the video game footage, and I'm seeing the performances, which suck. And I'm seeing the action, which is insane gonzo. Just horrible. It's watching a horrible disaster car wreck and knowing that you are the only person connected to the movie that ever gave a shit about a zombie movie at all. That actually appreciated them. And having your name attached to this thing. After I saw it, I understood why he used video game footage because he was so fucking incompetent that he didn't know how to shoot out of sequence. So, he used them sometimes as transitions into other scenes because the guy was so clueless. It was the worst.

After that screening, I walked out of that theater, completely depressed and bummed. And there's Uwe Boll, whom I'd never met before and he's standing outside the theater talking to people. Mark introduces me. This is the first time I've met this guy at all. He's standing there in a *Batman* emblem T-Shirt and he's just… a big German dork. He asks the worst question he possibly could've asked me. He says, "So, are you happy?" (laughs) And I stood there for a second trying to think of what to say, and I just looked at him and said, "Not really, man." And I walked away. And that was the last time I ever talked to him. Then the movie came out in theaters, and everyone pressured me to go. My friends were like, "Come on, your movie is in theaters! Opening night, you got to go! You're being over dramatic! It can't be as bad as you think." I'm not an idiot, but I figure "Ok, let's go." We hit Burbank. And the show was sold out. Well, who knows, maybe we'll do ok? We get into the theater, and I sit there again. Twenty minutes go by and I start seeing people getting up and walking out. Continuously. Just start getting up and walking out. Finally, I left. I walked out. Then of course the end of the year "worst" list came out. And it's a clean sweep. *House Of the Dead*! 2003! The worst fucking movie to come out that year! (laughs) But yeah, it really hurt. It hurt me. Professionally I don't know if it hurt me because the movie did make money. Lionsgate did well with it on home video and DVD.

Rob: They did well enough to make a fucking sequel!

Yeah. And that was the thing. It psychologically fucked me up. Especially with my writing. I really wanted to do this. I love the genre. I love these types of movies and now I'm connected with the worst movie of the year. And the fans are not going to cut me a break, because they don't know the whole story. So, it was a bum period. And it really sucked. The fact that the movie is so worthless, it's just a sad waste of money. God, there's so much more I can say… The house itself looks like a fucking shack! Everything about it! The poster was ok. That's probably the best compliment I can give about it. The only time I started to feel better about it, and I hate to say this, because I don't hate Mark Altman – I can't stand Uwe Boll though. He's the worst filmmaker in the world.

Mike: Well, where does the blame fall but on him?

Well, the other thing that made me feel somewhat vindicated is when Mark Altman started making all these movies that Anchor Bay released, like *All Souls Day*. When *All Souls Day*, which was the first one in that string of releases that they (Mindfire Entertainment) did – was another zombie movie. It was solely written by him, and it felt like *House of the Dead*. The writing, the dialogue. It all felt like *House of the Dead*. Ok, if people see this, they're going to clearly see where that movie came from. And progressively every other movie that they've released, Mark Altman has had his hand in. I think now, I hope people can see where the blame lies in those films. At the time, when you're a little younger and struggling and trying to start a career, going through that experience, it's really damaging to the spirit. I should've sucked it up and moved on, but it was tough. Eli Roth had called it the *Gigli* of horror. It was just a horrible, horrible thing! I'm not the only screenwriter that has had that happened to them, where they have their name attached to something they're not happy with. Much better screenwriters have had the same experience. And… now that an hour has gone by… (laughs)

Rob: Well, let's focus on the positives! You're making your grand return to directing…

Yes, I got out of director jail!

Rob: Yes, so tell us a bit about coming back with *The Hills Run Red*. Did you write the screenplay as well?

No. Since *House of the Dead*, I've been working on DVD documentaries and doing all the documentaries for much bigger films. Like *The Usual Suspects*. We did the twentieth anniversary edition of *Valley Girl*. And I did the features for *X-Men 1.5* and *X2*. And *Spider-Man 2*.

Rob: I just have to tell you. Not only am I a horror fan, I'm a comic book geek too. And I was just telling Mike, with *X-Men 2*, *Spider-Man 2*, and the *Superman Returns* DVD's, I spent a full day with each just watching the special features you put together. They're among the best documentaries on superhero DVD's.

Oh thanks, man.

Rob: Obviously, you're a big comic fan too. So, what's it like working with all this behind-the-scenes footage for the making of some of the most iconic comic characters? I still can't believe you worked on the *Superman Returns* documentary, which quite frankly might be a tad better than the movie itself!

You're not the only person who has said that! It's pretty wild. Certainly, with the *X-Men* movies. 20th Century Fox put out *X-Men 1* on DVD with very little extra on it. So, when Bryan was doing *X2*, Bryan and Robert Burnett have been friends since college, and Rob had gone on from Full Moon and worked on NBC cutting promos, and he got to work at this company that was really at the ground floor for DVD features. He did a lot of Disney stuff like *Tron*. That company also did *Lord of the Rings*.

So, at the time he was doing *Lord of the Rings*, Bryan said, "We're going to do a *Usual Suspects* Special Edition and I want you to do it." So, that's how that started. When they were doing *X-Men 2*, Bryan said they were going to do a *X-Men 1.5* before *X2* comes out and then you guys will do the *X2* DVD. I thought, "Oh my God! This is amazing. I can't believe it!" I was doing these small movies and DVD stuff for those, and then to get these big ones.

What's great about doing these DVD's, and not just for Bryan's although Bryan's have been probably the most inclusive in detail documentaries. For me, not only was it getting to work on movies I'd love, but also getting to see the process of how these movies are made and to really get an insider's view that you normally don't get unless you're on the set every day.

Getting to work on *Spider-Man 2's* features was a dream because I love Sam Raimi, so getting to work on that and having him see that stuff was great. In some ways, I've been very lucky. The people I've gotten to work with, and a lot of DVD producers are like this, Robert and Charlie De Lauzirika have been the two main DVD producers I've worked with. They're both, of course, big movie fans. They love movies.

Despite what the budget for a DVD might be, we want to give the most to an audience that we can possibly give. Our thing was always that we've got hundreds of hours of footage, so don't give someone a thirty minute documentary and say, "That's it!" Give them everything and more than the studio would ask for. We're really doing it for people like us. We're such DVD collectors ourselves, that we really try to do documentaries that we would want to see if we were buying the disc. We approach them as telling them a story. Even if the documentaries are separated, if you watch them all through there is a focus that goes through them to tell a story. Even though we don't always have the urge to direct our own features, we look at these documentaries as we're making feature-length documentary films.

Rob: That's exactly what they are!

Because we don't get to make our own movies at the moment, for us, it's what keeps us interested and excited about doing this stuff. In a way, we do get to make movies. The process in a way is just as time consuming. *Superman Returns* was such a great experience in a lot of ways. Just to be involved in the return of this iconic character was just great. I loved *Superman 1* as a kid. These movies make me feel like a kid again when I see them, and that's what's so cool about getting to work on them.

And it was exciting. There were times where I couldn't believe I was there. And it's just me and Rob really shaping this stuff, really having the trust of the director. Really showing the process and making it as much of a personal experience as you can convey in the time we have. It's still long hours. There are many twenty-four-hour editing sessions, but what's great about it is Rob was on the set of *Superman Returns* for eight months.

I was on the set of *The Chronicles of Narnia* for five months. For us as filmmakers, it was like the best film school you could ever go to. The professors are Sam Raimi, Bryan Singer, Ridley Scott. Those are the types of advantages to

come from it. It's really fulfilling. Also, these titles, you get to walk into a store, and they have 300 copies there and it's being seen around the world. I wish the *Masters of Horror* documentary that Mike Mendez and I had done had been seen as much as those other documentaries. (laughs)

Rob: I'd heard about that! What exactly was the story with that? It was a horror documentary you did that never came out. Was it a rights issue?

What really happened with that was the company that made it, which was Flix Mix, they were connected with Universal – they went out of business. Universal still owns it. It's probably one of those things where they don't even realize that they have it. I know Mike Mendez and I would love to see it get a legitimate release someday, but would we have to re-title it now with the *Masters of Horror* series? We would love to get that out there.

Rob: Would you say your experiences the past few years doing docs and behind-the-scenes have influenced how you'll approach your next feature?

Absolutely. Like I said, it literally was like going back to film school and learning from the ground up by watching these guys. And even though the movie that I'm going to do is a much, much, much smaller movie, the process is still the same for a director. And what those experiences taught me were the importance of preparation before you get on the set and direct it. And working on the script. And storyboarding. And casting it right. Really bringing together the right team of people on the technical side and in front of the camera to execute it the best you can. Now, of course with all the editing experience I have now, I think I'm a much better editor than I certainly was. You learn not to fall in love with your material to a point where it's detrimental. The key to a good director is really assembling the right people to convey what you're trying to put on film. Or… capture on digital now. They say if you cast it right, half your job is done. But you have to pick the right director of photography. The right screenwriter. The right FX team. It's all a major part of it. And then it's about managing the ship and guiding them to give you the best work possible.

Rob: What can you tell us about the recently announced *The Hills Run Red*? And what prompted you to make a return to the director's chair?

Well, what prompted me to return to directing was that somebody asked me! (laughs) It was pretty easy. What happened was, the company that's financing the movie, they've produced three movies themselves over the past couple of years. They're a New York based company and they did *Flesh for the Beast*, *Shadow: Dead Riot*, and they did a co-production in Japan called *Death Trance*. The movies themselves on a dollar basis did really well, and they were happy with that, but they weren't so happy with the talent they got behind the camera at the time with those movies. They were still learning about the process. This go around, they wanted to come out to Los Angeles and find a great team, so they wouldn't have to micro-manage every aspect of the movie. They wanted to find people that had vision and could bring to the table the things they wanted. Daniel Schweiger, whom I worked with at Full Moon, knew one of the producers Carl Murano and he recommend me and Rob to him. So, they came out and met with us.

We made a presentation and showed them the office and what we had to offer. They saw my reel. They had two projects. They said, "Yes, we'd like you to do *The Hills Run Red*." So, we've been working on refining the screenplay. They had a screenplay they brought to us. We read it and made notes and they were very open to us changing the screenplay and making the necessary changes to make it more effective. That process went on, and then they came and asked for a promotional teaser for the Cannes Film Festival. They'll have a booth there because it's a sales market along with an actual festival. That was this past month. We came up with a teaser idea. Moreso for the tone and feel the movie was going to have, as opposed to something specifically from the movie. We wrote a script for it, storyboarded it and shot that little promo in early April (2007) in Hollywood at the Vine theater. It was a tough seventeen hour day. We had a small amount of money to pull it off, but we had really great people working on the crew. It seems to have come along really well and they're happy. Next thing is we're moving very quickly into pre-production on the actual film.

Rob: Awesome. Congrats!

Thanks! And it's nice. It was a really good feeling going on to that set, because it was really the first time I had directed since *The Dead Hate The Living*, so it had been seven years. It was proof that all of the stuff that I learned since that movie had really stuck. It was a much more confident directing style for me. It was different than it was before. There were no questions about how things were going to get done, and we got everything done. We even got extra stuff that wasn't storyboarded. I can't wait for everyone to get to see it, which will be a little taste of what's to come. Hopefully the feature will be its own thing.

Bryan (Singer) said it was like *Peeping Tom* meets *Who Killed The Great Chefs Of Europe*. Which… (laughs) Well, OK, there you go. I haven't seen *Who Killed The Great Chefs Of Europe* so I don't even know what that means. It's going to be very serious. It should be very brutal, but it's not the trend that's going on now with "torture porn." We're focusing on good characters, a good story that isn't generic that doesn't just go down one direction. We're trying to surprise people with it and give people a twist so it's not predictable. We're really focusing on the script. Are the characters interesting? Is it involving? And does it deliver? That's where our focus is.

MIKE MENDEZ

Interviewed by Mike Cucinotta and Rob Galluzzo (7/07)

Mike Mendez is the director behind *Killers, The Convent*, and *The Gravedancers*, the latter of which was one of the more impressive horror films shown as part of After Dark's 8 Films To Die For. We recently caught up with Mike at his place to talk about his entire film career and check out his amazing collection of toys, figures, and memorabilia. Read on for our *Fright* exclusive chat with Mike Mendez!

What are your earliest recollections of the horror genre?

One of the first horror films I saw, not sure if it was the first, but I do remember going to a double feature of a re-release of *Halloween* and *Motel Hell*. And that left an impression! I know I'd been to a fair amount of horror films previous to that, because I remember really liking a film called *The Children* that came out and it had a score by Harry Manfredini. I liked that quite a bit. In the recesses of my brain, I have all these nameless horror films, which I actually don't know what they were. I was five or six and kind of unaware of what movie titles were.

I have a feeling that whatever they were, they were probably Italian, because they were like nothing I'd ever seen before and there were these weird exploding heads and this whole visceral thing that would just terrify me! I went through a lot of phases. The phase of being too scared to cope, where I was so horrified about it, I couldn't watch. To getting to the phase of wanting to see these movies. I remember wanting to see *The Howling* and also *An American Werewolf In London* because I was really big into werewolves, but I had to close my eyes during the scary parts, which is why jump scares were the worst for me because you couldn't close them fast enough and you'd always see something you didn't want to see! It's funny, I'd close my eyes during the scary parts, but it still wouldn't deter me from seeing it.

I notice here you have just about every Jason figure that's ever existed! Big *Friday the 13th* fan?

I have fond memories of *Friday the 13th Part 2* and remember just loving that. I thought that was amazing and so scary. To me, when I was nine, *Friday the 13th Part 2* was cinema. That was just great fucking filmmaking. Similar things that were out at the time, like *Gandhi*, bored the crap out of me! (laughs) But *Friday the 13th Part 2*, now that's how movies were made. I briefly went into a period where *Friday the 13th Part 3* in 3D scared me so much that I couldn't see it theatrically. I saw it years later in 3D and it was like a religious experience. There are only two movies I wasn't allowed to see. My recollection, I think Barbara Walters said you shouldn't take your kids to see *Alien* and my dad heard that. I don't know what the fuck he was thinking, because he'd take me to see *Cannibal Ferox* if it was playing but someone on the TV said, "Don't see *Alien*," so *Alien* was the one movie I was not allowed to see. I went with my seventeen-year-old brother to go see *Return of the Living Dead* in theaters and they gave us shit about me not being old enough to see it. His friends were eighteen or nineteen, but I was denied access! By the time *Return* came out, this was no longer scary for me, this was just a good time!

Can you tell us the history of how you got into filmmaking? Where did your interest in films begin?

Well, I was somewhat lucky in that I had a very film savvy family, at least my dad and my brother were. My dad was an immigrant from El Salvador who sold restaurant equipment, but the reason he wanted to come to the United States was that he wanted to be a film actor. That was his first motivation, but he'd never done anything about that. We had a Mexican restaurant on Hollywood Blvd. So, we were exposed to Hollywood through the most outsider way you could be. It wasn't like any of us were in the industry, but I grew up outside of the Walk of Fame, and I'd go to the Chinese Theater every week. So, film loving was certainly an integral part of my roots. It's what we did. We weren't a sports family or a family that was heavily into functions. We went to the movies.

And from that, that started my brother on a path that he wanted to be a filmmaker. I think Steven Spielberg probably was what really cemented that for him, and it became his dream to go to UCLA film school. Now, because that was his dream, it never really felt like it was my dream. I felt like I'd be copying him. So, I actually got very interested in the make-up FX side of it. I think it's also partially the reason for my love of toys. I was really into sculpture. Not that I'm a good sculptor myself, but I have a tremendous appreciation of it. So, for the longest time, I was interested in being a writer, and also, slowly because of my love of *Fangoria* magazine and *Gorezone*, it turned into wanting to be an FX artist.

My heroes became Rob Bottin and Kevin Yagher and Rick Baker. It started for me when I was about thirteen or fourteen and when you're thirteen, it's a really expensive hobby! Making masks and prosthetics. I'd spend my allowance on alginate, which isn't the most exciting thing to spend your allowance on! (laughs) Back then, the make-up FX guys were like rock stars to me. So, my brother, in the meantime, was following his film dream. He quickly started to lose that dream and lose that focus. For me, what started the filmmaking craze was that it just seemed logical.

We were one of the first families in my neighborhood to have a video camera and my brother made movies, and I loved toys so much that I'd take that video camera and start making really bad stop-motion things with my action figures. My parents later sent me to an all-boys Catholic school, so there weren't too many fun things to do. We weren't drinking, smoking dope, or getting laid – that came later. (laughs) But in the interim, we thought, 'Why don't we get everyone together and start making films?' At that point, we were all into *Monty Python*. We did skits for school, and made up a club we called *The 8 Ball Club*, which now later in life has a more dark connotation. (laughs) Back then, we thought it sounded cool.

We made films like *Teenage Mutant Ninja Nazis* or *Poltrygeist*, long before the Troma one. They were for fun! And since I was the FX guy, I'd always worry about the blood and rigging of these FX. By college, we'd made twenty-five short films, so the only thing that made sense to me at the point was making movies. So, really over the span of a night I decided that I should be making movies. I never looked back ever since. I dropped out of college and got any job I could as a production assistant and started showing off my films until I could meet someone who'd want to do something with me. I met a guy who wanted to make an independent film called *Killers* and that's how I got my first film off the ground.

Killers was your first feature length film. How difficult was it for you to make that film?

Killers was a real hard film to make, because I was twenty-two at the time, I just dropped out of college at that point. I met this guy who made this film called *Tears of Heaven*. He spent something like $350,000 on it. And he directed it and starred in it, and it was a piece of shit. He couldn't do anything with it, you couldn't even cut it together. So, we had this stack of short ends. So, he had the idea, "You know, sometimes I think I should just make another movie with this stack of short ends." So, I convinced him to let me direct it. We wrote the script together, myself and this guy Dave Larsen, who unfortunately has passed away since.

He was also twenty-two at the time and we basically did the film with credit cards and family loans and whatever money we could muster. We had a stack of short ends of 35 mm film, we bought a little more, got a crew of maybe nine people together and shot this thing. I'm sure lots of people do that, but to our surprise it got into Sundance. For me at the time, it was a total whirlwind. Here you go from being unemployed, making these little films and music videos for garage bands, but it took me to a level at age twenty-three that was suddenly in the professional world.

I got an agent at ICM, who was Robert Rodriguez's agent, and I was meeting everyone in town. I got money to write my first script, so it was a huge jump for me, but again it all started with nine people over twenty-four days with no money and no PA's. I was getting lunch for everyone and directing the film at the same time. (laughs) The first pass at it, I think we spent $125,000 for a 35 mm feature film, which is kind of unheard of these days. I don't think you could do that if you tried. It was very hard, but obviously very beneficial. And it really is what started this crazy ride that I'm still on.

What's with the availability of your first film, Killers?

This company called Alpine bought it, and they released it themselves on VHS. You can find it at Hollywood Video and a few places like that, but they cut the shit out of it. They cut out all the real gory and more violent, disturbing aspects of it. But they did a great job of selling it foreign. So, it came out theatrically in Germany. It came out theatrically in France. And it came out on video and DVD everywhere else. But this was before DVD really got started, so there's mostly only these VHS copies of it.

This movie started to become a cult hit in Europe, so that led to them making a double-disc collector's edition DVD. So, when I would go to Germany people would tell me that they're big fans of mine and I'd think, "What are you talking about?!" because over here it was only on a video shelf somewhere, maybe if we were lucky! When we made my second film, *The Convent*, I remember we went to a film festival in Germany and it was weird; they thought I was Darren Aronofsky or something! They thought I was this real filmmaker from the US and I didn't have the heart to tell them any differently! (laughs) I must always thank the Germans for their support of the Mendez films! A lot of people tell me they love the film and that they can't get it anywhere, and it's true, they can't. The best you can do is that German double disc DVD. So, I'm trying to get the rights back, because I think it's high time that I released the film on DVD again.

You just mentioned your second film, *The Convent*. It's an independent film. I want to know how you went into early meetings and pitched to people, "Ok, I've got this new film, and it opens with this young girl running into a church and blowing away a bunch of nuns!"

You know? That was the crazy thing! No one really fucking looked twice! Or said anything, and that's the reason I did it. At the time, all these doors opened up for me. I was this twenty-three-year-old kid in Hollywood taking all these meetings for all these big projects, like *Species 2* or *Idle Hands*. I couldn't find anything I really liked that I could be passionate about. It was studio stuff, but it was all crap. And so, the company that released *Killers* said we have to do this other movie, and one of the secretaries here has a treatment.

So, I asked what it was about, and they told me, "Well, it's about a group of kids that break into a convent and then bad stuff happens." At first, I thought it wasn't all that original or exciting! I asked, "Well can I put some demonic nuns in it?" And they're like, "Sure!" And I added, "Well, can we blow them away and make them explode?" And they're like, "Yeah! Sure!" And honestly the reason I did it is because they pretty much said I could do whatever I wanted! I had to do it for a certain amount of money with their people, of course. I only had a certain number of days. But providing that I delivered them a horror film, that's all that mattered. And of course, the last thing I made was a horror movie with the film! I wanted to make an 80's style comedy. Thankfully, when you're dealing outside the studio

system and it's just guys that are contractually obligated to make a movie, they really don't care what it is that much. I told them the opening I wanted to do, and they loved it. In the original idea, she just comes in with a gun and starts shooting everyone, but then Columbine happened, so I felt very badly about it.

So, my solution to it was, "Well, it's bad if she just goes into a school and starts shooting people. But if she goes into a church, and takes out a baseball bat, and then beats them, and then pours gasoline on them, lights them on fire and then shoots them, you no longer think of Columbine!" (laughs) By some fucked up logic, it's true. It's so outrageous and so ridiculously violent, you can't take it seriously. I've only had one complaint ever from a Catholic who wrote us when the movie was about to come out that "God is going to kill you all!"

She never even saw the movie; she just wrote us this freaky letter about how God will strike us all down for our sins. The biggest complaint we had was for our portrayal of Satanists. (laughs) It was so under the radar, no one caught onto it. Of course, because of that opening, you'll never see it at Blockbuster, you'll never see it on cable. But I kind of like being a cult director. I like that audiences can find your film and that it can grow over time. Sometimes, I think that's cooler than being in Blockbuster. The people that have seen *The Convent* had to go seek it out! Had to hear about it from a friend or read about it somewhere.

What I loved about *The Convent* and what I didn't expect was the way you infused humor into it. Knowing you now and having met you a few times, it makes total sense to me. It's your type of humor. Was it always a conscious effort to make this funny?

Yeah, we never intended to make a serious movie…

You think you might go in a serious direction from the opening. I mean, you kill a bunch of nuns! But then it gets funny...

Even the opening is so outrageous that it's supposed to be funny. Some people complain about that with *The Gravedancers*. It's that they don't know what to do with the comedy. But I don't know! I like comedy. I like to laugh at real life. I like hearing audiences laugh. I like *Gravedancers* more as a film, but I love watching *The Convent* with an audience, because people are laughing and having fun with it. When people are scared, it's very quiet, and I get freaked out, wondering "Are they into it?!" The most natural thing to me is to write some comedy. Or take scary things and make them funny. I often find myself fighting myself against that. But I have one more script in the vein of *The Convent* that I'd like to make called *Dead Stuff* that is just the goriest comedy ever. That'll be fun, but I wanted to try to make something that more people would want to see. *Gravedancers* was my blatant attempt to make something "mainstream." Something that I still like and can get into, but something more commercial and accessible than anything I've made before, because I just like making my weird little films. It's a balance I'm always fighting within myself.

How'd Adrienne Barbeau get involved in *The Convent*? Because she hadn't been in anything for a while?

Honestly, I think she hadn't done anything in a while because no one was asking for a while. And I'm happy that we kind of re-started the resurgence of Adrienne Barbeau, because she went on to do *Carnivale*, and now *Halloween*, which is great. People should have the good sense to hire her because she's awesome. We had within the budget for one kind of actor to play that part. And they were trying to push Lynda Carter on me, which would've been great. Or Morgan Fairchild, or even Linda Blair, and they all would've been fine! But I really wanted Adrienne Barbeau. It was a great experience, and I feel fortunate to call her a friend, and I look forward to working on another movie with her.

Thank you for putting her in *The Convent*, because growing up in the 80's, I think we all had a crush on her.

I think we all did! She was always the bad ass chick! You didn't want to mess with her, which is funny, because when you meet her, she's fairly petite. But she still has this presence, which is perfect. I've always really liked her. She read it, liked it, and did it. It didn't take much convincing. It was harder convincing Coolio! (laughs)

Bring us through the process of getting this second independent film of yours out there? How'd you go about getting this film out on DVD?

It was easy and difficult. The good thing is that because my first film was at Sundance, my second film got into Sundance. Which is kind of funny, because Sundance is known more for more arthouse fare. They're not really known for the schlocky genre thing, and my thing was a celebration of all things schlocky! But they loved it. So, we premiered at Sundance, and we hoped a big company would buy it and put it in theaters.

I only found out recently that the production company had offers to put it out theatrically and they chose not to because it wasn't enough money. Lionsgate came around, finally after about a year and picked it up. It was a long journey, but what was cool about *The Convent* and what I didn't appreciate until later on was that it played every festival. It must've played at thirty or forty festivals around the world. So, even though it wasn't selling, I was going to Japan, I was going to Spain, and France and Germany and Brussels. All over the globe to tour with it. The short answer is it was painful, but I was getting a wonderful reaction from the fans at all these festivals. It won awards in Italy, and Adrienne Barbeau won a Chainsaw Award. But it was a solid year before it ended up on DVD.

What were the origins of *The Gravedancers*? How did you get introduced to that script?

I finished *The Convent* somewhere towards the end of 2000. On my doorstep, I got this script on Halloween for *The Gravedancers* and I just fell for it. It was everything that I wanted to do for my next film. I didn't want to do another schlocky picture because then that's all I'd be known for.

I really wanted to do something with a little more substance. What I liked about this script was it was very much an homage to *Poltergeist*. And *The Haunted Mansion*. I knew I could inject my visual style into it, and it got really crazy by the end. I liked that it wasn't just one thing. It had this arc, this evolution that started at one point and ended at another point. Some people hated that about the script, that it had different arcs. I still get that as a finished film, people think it's tonally inconsistent, but that's weird to me. I don't know how people can't follow that arc.

Well, that's how most ghost story pictures work, though. That's the format of *Poltergeist*, for example.

Yeah, it's definitely an escalation. I loved this script. It had been at Artisan for a bit, and they dropped it, and I opted to make it, which took way longer than any of us thought it would be. I'm tenacious. I see something that I want to do and that's all I focus on. It took five years from that point to get it financed. It was a solid year to option it and get the script out. And then another two years to get someone to finance it. We made the trailer because it was set up at Fox, but they didn't want me to direct it, so I made the trailer, which is on the DVD, as proof that I could make it.

So, they let me do it, but then we were doing it with this other company that was supposed to have the money to do it, but then they didn't. The whole thing fell apart, but thankfully we had the trailer. So, we shopped it around and finally got it to an independent company, who sat on it and let it sit around for two years before we actually made it! It wasn't until *Saw* and *The Grudge* were hits that one weekend that they were like, "Oh, let's make it now!"

The unfortunate thing was that everyone and their mother decided to make a horror film once *Saw* and *The Grudge* were successful, so when we were finally done with ours, now we had to compete with eight-hundred other horror movies, as opposed to if we had done it earlier. It was a process, but it was a script I immediately fell in love with.

When you finally started shooting it, were you relieved to finally be making it or was there pressure?

It was kind of a relief just to get it done, because we had waited for so long. We were trying to get it made for $15 million dollars and then $10 million, and then $6 million, and finally we were at $2 and a half million. The production company actually wanted us to stop and go make it in Romania six months after we were scheduled to. We just knew we had to do it now. It wasn't more pressure; it was more relief.

The cast was great. Can you talk about finding the right people for *The Gravedancers*?

Sure. Tcheky Karyo I met in Japan. We were at a festival together and Tcheky was in the jury, and they had all these other movies. The rest of the jury looked at me like, "Who farted?!" after watching *The Convent*, but Tcheky loved it and got it. Thankfully, he wanted to work with me. Wonderful person that he is, stuck with us, because he was attached to it for a long time. Clare Kramer came to us through auditions. We just liked her and thought she was great. Dominic Purcell we got through a meeting, but it was before *Prison Break* was a reality, so we just happened to catch him in the nick of time.

That was lucky, although funny enough, they didn't advertise the fact that he was in the movie. You figured they would! And Josie Maran was someone we cast very last minute. The production company had cast her something like three days before we started shooting. But she was great.

What was it about a ghost story that made you want to make this kind of horror movie?

Right when I read it, we were coming off of the "friendly" ghost phase. Well, not friendly, I should say the "troubled" ghost. The ghost where something was unsettled. And they came back to make the wrong things right! That's fine. I mean *The Sixth Sense* is a brilliant movie, but everything started to become a clone of it. I wanted a reason to make ghosts scary again, because I haven't seen a ghost even try to harm anybody in years! *Poltergeist* was certainly the model. Ghosts are inherently scary to everyone. I don't know why, I don't believe they even exist, but they're scary. One of the things I really wanted to do was explore atmosphere because it feels now like a lost art form.

The thing that a lot of horror movies don't do these days is take the time to build up that suspense, which is what you do in your movie. When you finally get to the point where you see that first ghost in the corner of the room, it's a shock! It's a great scare.

It was very important to me. It was probably a reaction to all the criticisms I got for *The Convent*. As much as people loved it, a lot of people fucking hated it! I'd hear people say, "It's not scary, it's stupid!" So, I thought, "Fine, I'll make a fucking scary one next time, dicks!" (laughs) I wanted to make people jump out of their seats. I wanted to make people tense and then have that release. When we were at Tribeca, I can't tell you what a relief it was to see all those heads jump up. I felt like I did my job. I miss atmospheric films.

The one thing that always takes me out of a movie is the usage of CGI with ghosts. I know you dabble with it towards the end, but it's well done. Most of the stuff in your movie is practical. Was it a choice on your part to opt towards practical ghost effects? To me, it's more frightening when a ghost is physically there!

That was the thing. I had this dream a long time ago that I was walking up the stairs and I turned around and there was this very tall thin creature following me with a grin on its face. And I just woke up in a cold sweat and it always kind of stuck with me. I think when people see ghosts in real life, from what I've been told, you would see a person just sitting there, and then you'd do a double take and they're gone. You certainly have never heard someone say, "Oh yes! It was glowing blue. And it was pale. And drifting off the ground!" I've never seen a ghost, so I don't know!

But from most stories you hear and what you'd imagine, you would see a real thing there for a moment and then it's gone. I thought it'd be scarier to just see someone there and then have them be gone. The smile always seems creepy. An angry dog, you know what it wants. But a freaky, skinny ghost just smiling at you. What the hell does it want?

Does it help the actors when there's a ghost physically there?

It depends. Dominic always thought the whole thing was goofy, so he just wanted to react as little as possible, I don't think he wanted to scream, so for him it didn't matter. But for Clare, it helped quite a bit, and I think it freaked her out. I love practical stuff. But I had this idea for how I wanted the ending to be. If I could've done the whole thing practically I would've, and in fact, I actually tried to do it.

The big head at the end, even though I get accused of using a CGI head, it's not CG! That's a big puppet. We did it like *Star Wars* in front of a green screen and moved the camera past it and had a fan on it to look like wind. We did it old school, but everything around it has an ethereal glow and is CG, so everyone assumes the whole thing is CG. We couldn't afford to destroy a set like I would've liked to! The biggest criticism I get for the movie is the ending, which I think is funny, because it's my favorite part.

Being that you're not a fan of CGI yourself, what kind of instructions did you give the people that created some of those effects?

I don't believe in CGI really unless you have Peter Jackson money! I think wonderful things can be accomplished with CGI but for low budget filmmaking, it's horrible! So, my instructions were basically, "Use as little CGI as possible!" (laughs) I told the graphics guys that I don't like CGI, which probably offended them, but they promised it'd look great. So, I was always trying to shoot as many practical elements as possible. But when you're trying to blow out a wall with spectral energy, there's only so much you can do.

At that point, it all still worked. Maybe because you build everything up until that point?

Well, that's how I feel. To me, that big head and that ending is the final drop of a roller-coaster. You have to suspend your disbelief. People say, "Well, it was scary up until that point." But the thing is it wasn't really trying to be scary by that point. By that point, I'm just having a great time, I'm just having fun. I hope the audience is too. Some of them get it, some don't. I knew going in from the arc of the script how it was going to be. So, I made it for the people who would appreciate it. And for those who didn't, well... my apologies!

When did After Dark get involved and when did you know you were going to be part of that fest in theaters?

We showed it at AFM, which is a film market back in November of 2005. This was much more painful than *The Convent*, because we screened the film, and a lot of people liked it. We had people circling it, like Lionsgate and New Line and all these companies. Towards the end of November, the town started shutting down and it hadn't sold. So, January came, and we thought "Ok, is this going to sell?!" So, then February, March, April, May! The movie was up for sale for nine months! At this point, I knew everyone had passed on it. Lionsgate was talking about releasing it, but that required the production company to put up a certain amount of money and they weren't willing to do that. So, when that happened, out of the blue, like a knight in shining armor, Courtney Solomon showed up with the After Dark fest. Of course, we were skeptical at first! We all thought, "You want to do what?!" (laughs) You want to release eight movies for one weekend? And only one weekend? But the more we talked to him, the more we thought this guy was really onto something.

This was kind of revolutionary and exciting! We were very quickly approaching the point where it was going to be a direct-to-DVD movie, despite our hopes. We didn't feel it deserved to be, but then Courtney showed up and said, "This is a way to get it into theaters." To its credit, it's been great in terms of how it's out there. I can download a HD version of *The Gravedancers* on my Xbox right now and that's pretty impressive! That doesn't happen to movies often, especially a movie like we did. It played in 500 theaters and the DVD release was huge.

We bought the last two copies at the Best Buy by us!

Well, thank you very much! It ended up being the best seller of the After Dark films, and I don't know exactly why. But I'm not going to complain about it!

Is that your wife Oakley at the beginning of both *The Gravedancers* and *The Convent*?

Yeah, *The Convent*, I purposely cast her for that. *Gravedancers*, I didn't want that opening in the movie! But I wanted to give her a part in it, so it worked out. One of the reasons they were ok with letting me put my wife in the opening was that they thought it would endear me to have that be the opening. But no, I fought tooth and nail to get it out, because it doesn't have anything else to do with the movie! It was just something the foreign sales market wanted. But I did like the idea and since it was forced on me, I was happy that she was in it. And now, it feels like we must do this on *Dead Stuff*. She doesn't die at the beginning of *The Convent*, but I like the idea of killing my wife at the beginning of every film. Some people think it's morbid, I think it's sweet!

DAVID J. STIEVE

Interviewed by Adam Barnick (7/07)

Behind the Mask: The Rise of Leslie Vernon is no stranger to *Icons* readers by now. One of the most acclaimed horror films in years, its recent theatrical release brought even more positive critical notice. But where does a success story like this begin? In the mind of writer David J. Stieve! David has several new scripts making the rounds and is also the subject of an upcoming doc on the struggle to make a career in imagination come true in Hollywood. Join us as we look into Leslie Vernon's origins, explore a potential follow-up, and learn what it takes to bring life to characters on the page!

What are your earliest memories of the horror genre?

I was probably five or six. I was with my older sister, Christine, and my two cousins Julie and Lori. I was the baby brother that got to tag along. They were watching *Frankenstein*, the Karloff version, and I was scared out of my mind. I thought it was the boogeyman; this guy's 7' 5 tall, bolts sticking out of his neck. I was absolutely horrified. And they were scared, but bonding and screaming as girls will do.

I remember very clearly being afraid of *Frankenstein*, which is ironic because now the novel's my favorite literary work. There's something very mythological about, even in Karloff's incarnation of the monster, the idea of, "What are we, as men, capable of creating; what evil are we capable of creating?" I don't know if it's the chicken or the egg. Do I like *Frankenstein* so much because of that earlier experience, or was I just predisposed to like that? The second memory, if I can cheat and get another one, was from the first R-rated movie I ever saw. I remember another babysitting event, my Aunt Vicki was in charge of watching me and my sister and two cousins, and she took us to *Blade Runner*.

Oh wow!

First R-rated movie I'd ever seen, first nudity I ever saw.

That's formative… "*Welcome to dystopia!*"

Oh, it was just spectacular! There's something obviously very, very dark and brooding about that, but that night we got home, and one of our neighbors found out we'd just come home from this movie, we're all amped up, and she came down and was pounding on all the doors and rattling the windows and scaring us when we were inside the house being babysat.

Good way to start as a kid. Come home and brood about the human condition for a few hours.

There's a very *Frankenstein* component to that film actually! With the androids and "What does man create?" Clearly, I have an obsession there.

You had a formative period working in a movie theater as well. When did you start working there?

The Orpheum? That was when I went to college, University of Wisconsin. My college job: that was sort of the one constant I always had. Spent countless hours there. It's a beautiful old movie palace; one of the original Orpheum Circuit movie palaces; red velvet ropes, chandeliers, the works. To be able to bring *Behind The Mask* there is closing a circle that's so satisfying.

Did they show newer films or classics and indies?

It was an independent but first-run theater. We had all the Hollywood hits but would get some independents. The manager was a guy named Jerry Fladin. He had a good eye for films but was also a great businessman. So, he had to find a mix of putting audiences in the seats but also showing the films that he loved.

You went to college for your English degree but eventually turned to screenwriting but were always out to tell stories.

I am part of the *Star Wars* generation, the idea that you could go to a theater and be a part of something that was so unbelievably escapist and spectacular, but still have a heart to it; very much a student of the Spielberg/Coppola/Lucas era. I think those movies were very grandiose but had a very real human element to them, and an emotional pull to the stories.

I had always gravitated towards storytelling, but it wasn't until I was in college that I had that soul-searching moment of "What am I going to do with myself?" I thought I was going to write the Great American Novel and it just wasn't working. I had sort of a light-bulb-coming-on moment while I was at the Orpheum; I worked at a video store in high school and the Orpheum in college… the answer was plain as day. I was always around films; I loved the medium of it; I love that it's a combination of the visual and the written format. I really respond to the fact that cinema and filmmaking, it's the youngest art form, with storytelling being the oldest. Starting with cave art, up through theater, musicals, film. It's sort of only 100 years old but the global reach it has… it's overwhelmingly enticing for me to be involved in that medium!

Were there initial authors that sparked that love of literature? Writers in general you admire?

Again, Mary Shelly had a pretty profound impact, I loved F. Scott Fitzgerald, still do; there's a very strong, melancholic sort of gravitas to Fitzgerald that appeals to me. I did the usual dances with Hemingway and Shakespeare. I appreciate the beauty of that and the greatness that are those works, but I think Fitzgerald is the author I responded to the most.

So, when you were wrapping up college, that was when you decided you would go into screenwriting?

I foolishly thought writing a script, since it was shorter, would be easier than writing a novel. The joke was on me! I backed into it thinking it would be a better way for me to finish a story, and I realized very quickly I did not know the first thing about formatting, structure, about how you refine everything you need to say down to dialogue and action, where you don't have the luxury of free verse or description or an omnipotent point of view. Obviously, it's a lot harder to express everything that way, and fit it into 110 pages, widely spaced.

How did you start teaching yourself?

I started reading scripts, and the first book I ever bought and read was Lew Hunter's book *Screenwriting 434*; quickly progressed through all the gurus, the Syd Fields and the Robert Mckees, and all those guys. I took a lot from all of them. I'm a very "traditional story structure" kind of guy, inspired heavily by that. I came to Joseph Campbell a lot later. I know that's almost become a cliché, everybody has their Hero's Journey turn, but I happen to believe that's accurate. There's a lot of mythology there to be mined; again, it goes back to it being a very old art, storytelling, just in a new medium. You can never stop learning, you have an obligation to read everybody who's done it before you, and especially if they're taking the time to offer any words of advice. Doesn't mean you have to follow it verbatim, but I appreciate the effort of someone taking the time to put their thoughts down. "Hey, I've written screenplays as well, maybe you would benefit from my experience."

Were there particular screenwriters you came to admire?

Randall Wallace (*Braveheart*) hit me at the right time and age, when I was trying to decide what I was doing; that script really hit me. Obviously, Charlie Kaufman; he's hard to follow sometimes for me, but I appreciate the lengths that he goes to to get his ideas out there. Robert Benton, who wrote *Nobody's Fool*.

Modern-day, I watched *West Wing*, *Sports Night*, anything that Aaron Sorkin is doing, I'm there. Same thing with David Milch. I would have watched *Deadwood* for another seven years. David Chase. I whole-heartedly believe *The Sopranos* is the best writing for a TV series that will ever be. I love those guys. I don't mean to be putting down anybody who writes the big blockbusters, or the smash hit series, but there's a deeper mythology with those guys.

I think what each of those guys did is… they knew what they wanted to say, they knew the characters inside and out, and they just expressed them and sort of let them do the work.

And it's really not about, "Is everyone going to get this?" It's not, "If there's people out there that aren't going to get this, how do we fix that?" That's out the window with those guys! With them, they're like, "You know what, if people get this, great; if not, I'm sorry, they're going to have to run and catch up." And there's something I respect about that.

They're not being elitist about it; they're not SO avant-garde that nobody follows it. But there are a lot of moments where you're watching those guys where you miss stuff and you think OK, I'll pick it up later, or it'll somehow come back into the fold later.

Do you have a specific writing regimen?

It's changing, it has changed very recently, partially because of the success of *Behind the Mask*. I've been able leave my day job and pursue writing full time. I had been working as a talent agent, called AKA Talent, for seven years. And that was a great job! I never had any interest in being a starving artist living out of his car.

It was a way to learn more about the business though.

It was, and the experiences, and relationships that I formed and the wisdom that I gained, being able to be on sets, around actors and directors and producers, and to see what goes on behind the scenes…all of it helped me as a writer. The downside of that is that you're working sixty to seventy hours a week, so writing is relegated to the part time job, the nights and weekends. I recently was able to flip the switch and reverse that polarity; and writing is the focus now. So, my habits are going to have to change. This has been my first week "off!"

It's weird, without the same pressure; it's different, and you really have to tap into that commitment and motivation. Obviously, it's a luxury to say that writing is my full time job.

Was *Behind the Mask* your third screenplay?

Behind the Mask was the third full script that I wrote that I let anybody read. I had a couple of disasters I worked on before those that never got finished. To keep up the *Frankenstein* mythology here, writing a script is a lot like building the Frankenstein Monster, to some degree. You're putting a lot of parts together; you have to assemble it correctly. But there has to be a secondary level, this infusion of life.

Anyone can kind of put a corpse together, if you know what I mean. But there's that lightning bolt that makes the body sit up off the table. With a story, you can put the pieces together, but if you don't have that mythology, the story's not going to live. So, there were a lot of "discarded corpses" in my case. When I got to the point where I was saying, "This is a finished script, ready to go," then *Behind the Mask* was my third.

Was there a general idea that Leslie Vernon seeded from?

Oh, I could give you a whole separate interview on that topic alone (laughs). I wish you and I could sit down with Scotty (Glosserman) and Nathan (Baesel), because there's definitely a real sort of profound thing that's going on with this story.

The original inception of it was, I was talking to my father on his birthday; this was in May of 2001. For anybody who's decided to pursue a career that's off the beaten path, you have to sometimes combat that sense of resistance from people: "When are you going to kind of get rid of this dream and get a real job?" So, I had that conversation with my dad, explained what's going on and how I'm trying really hard, etc. And he's being supportive, but you always hear that sort of underlying, "When's he going to give up this crazy dream and really lock in?" And I got off the phone and was mulling that over; and *Halloween* was on TV.

So, I'm watching it, which I love, and I'm lying there that night thinking of the conversation I'd had. It sort of melded into my thinking, "Am I doing the right thing? How am I going to get started as a screenwriter?" And it crossed over into the idea of, "I wonder if a guy like Michael Myers has moments like this. Did he have moments of doubt? How did he decide to do what he does?" It was funny; like, "What does a guy like this do on a Tuesday afternoon? It can't always be killing; it's not always Friday the 13th. What does Jason do on Tuesday the 10th?"

And it crossed into this thing; if there was a guy who aspired to be the next Freddy or Jason or Michael, what would he do? And what would be a funny way to showcase that? So, I thought maybe if a documentary crew followed him around, you could see behind the scenes; but it's really about this artist's struggle! To follow his bliss and do what he wants to do, find his calling in life! It's amazing to me how layered it gets, Nathan's talked about this in earlier interviews. There's the moment where life's imitating art.

You're talking about the hayloft scene. Where Leslie Vernon tearfully contemplates his life's work coming to fruition, just before his first big slaughter.

And there's Nathan the actor, going through the same emotions. And there's Scott the director, me the writer, going through the same emotions. There's been this layering that's so rich, the cycle keeps repeating. So that's where it originated, in "How do I pursue my career?" and molded it into this form of Leslie Vernon. Obviously, it went through many versions and rewrites but found its way to Scott in 2003. 2002 it was a finalist in Slamdance (Screenplay competition). Then it got to

Scotty and we worked together on revisions. It was another two years before it went before the cameras in 2004.

Can you talk about your writer/director relationship? It was also a writer/co-writer relationship in this case.

The story was there, I knew what Leslie was about and what he was trying to do. Scott brought to it a more detailed knowledge of the slasher genre. He got the story I was trying to tell, got the symbolism, but he helped me shape it more into its final form.

I had the basics; the biggest conversion it went through was initially the story ended where Leslie disappears from the bedroom to go make his first kill. Leslie's like, "You've seen what comes next!" and there was a little epilogue to say what Leslie did, and he comes back the following year, etc. The point I was trying to make was this was everything that happens before a slasher film, and we've seen slasher films a million times, there's no point to actually show it.

When Scott and I were working on it, it just became clear it needed a third act. And what would the third act be? It's classic speechwriting; tell them what you're going to tell them, tell them, and then tell them what you told them. And essentially that's what we were missing. Now we've told them everything he's going to do, let's play it out. How are we going to do that with a twist and a hook that's interesting?

(SPOILER) The domino finally fell for me, when I realized Taylor would be the virgin, that was the final hook for me. That all of this has been an elaborate setup, not for Kelly, but for Taylor to be the survivor girl. The documentary was actually part of his luring his survivor girl in. When that fell into play, the floodgates just opened. (END OF SPOILER)

Was it originally all depicted in the documentary style, with no cutaways to the "film world?"

There were flashbacks in the original script, but it was more comic. There was a scene where Leslie explained how he always gets stuff thrown at him. He told a story about how he had this girl trapped on one side of a dining room table, and there's an entire dinner setup: knives, forks, plates, glasses, all that stuff. And Leslie explains, "And what does she do? She picks up a handful of spaghetti and throws it at me. Not the knives, not the bottles…" There were funny moments where he'd deconstruct the genre that you'd seen a million times, and you'd see it; it was scripted that we'd cut away to a "horror film" and you'd see a

comedic moment but cinematic and shot in 35mm. So those moments were there.

When Taylor has that moment where she says "We can't stand here and let this happen," and she throws the cameras down, I wish I could take credit for that, I honestly don't remember if it was my idea or Scotty's idea, again it was like this universal truth; there's something so good about it that you're like, "Oh my God, when she grabs the documentary camera, that's literally her throwing herself out of the documentary world." It just worked.

I think those moments come whether you're ready for them or not. Those are the things, as a writer, and a director too, you just have to pay attention; to watch for those. Those pure moments that bubble up on their own.

This film always had a good subtle balance of showing off the "movie world" it takes place in, and the opening sets that up well with the reporting on Haddonfield and the Elm Street house, touring Crystal Lake's campground etc. Was it ever more overt in the drafts you had?

It was always one hundred percent intentional that this was set in a cinematic world. We never ever wanted it to be… I got to tell you, I'm so tired of the *Man Bites Dog* comparison. I appreciate that film, but that is about a 'real guy' who is a serial killer.

When you really look at *Behind the Mask* the two aren't really similar.

The comparison is valid, but it's always been very clear to myself and to Scott that this is homage to those 80's slasher films. It's the total opposite to today's pop sensationalism.

If there was really a killer in a hockey mask that killed thirteen people in a campground, that would be 24-7 news, every day, for a year, until they caught the guy. In the slasher world, as soon as the nightmare's over and someone sends Jason to the bottom of the lake, everyone wipes their brow and goes, "I'm glad that's over!" (laughs)

"Let's put this behind us!"

And then the next year it happens again and everyone's like, "This can't be happening!" It's the total reverse of what would happen in real life. We always wanted it to be in that world. Taylor has tapped into something; she's the misunderstood one. She's like, "Nobody is paying attention to this!"

And so, they investigate.

Right. So, whatever we could do to keep it in the cinematic world, that was always the goal. We never wanted to be confused with the real world.

I think I'd read in an earlier interview with you that this was the type of world where, say, Leslie Vernon could call Leatherface on the phone if he wanted to. I liked that you never got that overt though, that's what I mean.

Oh! Again, there were earlier versions of the script with more comedic tongue-in-cheek moments. There was a scene early on where Leslie is getting his house ready and Taylor asks what's going on and Leslie's like, "I'm having some friends over for poker!" And of course, Freddy and Michael and Jason all show up… in their street clothes. Having a reminiscent conversation about how they all got started in the business, and how Leslie was a persistent, pushy newcomer always sending them demo tapes.

It was funny, but obviously the biggest hurdle to clear there is we wouldn't have ever been able to use all those characters in one movie. In the long run, what we went with worked.

You can still discuss all those things, just with Eugene!

Yeah, Eugene was an amalgamation of all the killers…he is Jason and Freddy and Michael; it was implied in one of the earlier drafts, this would be good trivia for you, that Eugene's character was actually the killer from *Black Christmas*, one of the first slasher films.

Billy!

Obviously, we couldn't directly use a character, so we created the archetype. Which is Eugene. But it was implied early on in earlier script drafts that he was the guy from *Black Christmas*.

Yeah, I remember you did hint in the film that he was of the time before the 80's slasher franchises.

There's a lot of what Scott Wilson brought to the character. What a joy and a pleasure to see him, he got it. This is an actor who has had a remarkably successful career that nobody knows about! He's not a marquee name.

He's an under-the-radar legend.

Yeah! He's worked with the best of the best. You can listen to him sit and tell stories for hours! And he's the most humble, down-to-earth guy. But he gets it; "You know, I've had a hell of a career, but I can walk into a restaurant, and nobody will know who I am!" There's sort of a 'Eugene' quality to that! In Eugene's world that was intentional; nobody wanted to be known.

When did Leslie Vernon begin shooting?

We started shooting in October 2004 in Portland.

How was that for you? You got to stay involved with the picture all the way through, which doesn't happen often with writers.

I was absolutely spoiled. I should be so lucky to be this involved again. I wasn't up there for the whole shoot; just for the first couple weeks of preproduction and then I had to come back for the day job; and then I ended up going back for the last two weeks of shooting.

I don't know that I can truly convey how groundbreaking and earth-moving it was to be on a set, all these professional people scurrying around, because of something that I had this notion of two and a half years ago. People now running around gainfully employed. Worrying about "How are we going to make this happen?"

I'm trying to think of a relevant example from the plot… there's a grain silo in the script; it should be up on the set, and we're like "We don't have a grain silo, how can we make this work?" Seeing professional people really have to physically manifest what I had imagined was mind-blowing. You're crossing over from the imaginary world of "I want to be a screenwriter one day," to all of a sudden.

Now you know what it takes to build a grain silo.

Right! Scott and I were on the set, and Betsy Goslin (our propmaster) came running up to us, flustered. We had written (for an upcoming scene) that Leslie was carrying a bucket. She was asking, "What kind of bucket?" And she goes into this stream-of-consciousness thing where she's like, "I don't think it would be plastic, that seems kind of fake and Leslie's more of an organic guy, and really true, so a more wooden bucket with straps on it maybe."

And Scott and I agreed, wooden bucket. And she scurries off. But the next day on set there's this perfect wooden bucket. She showed up with it on set and it was overwhelming. I typed, "He's putting apples in a bucket," years ago, and that consumed Betsy's world for the last eighteen hours! Just a very poignant specific instance of what I'm talking about, I made the imaginary real to some degree… not me, I'm not going to take credit for it, Scott and Betsy and everybody that worked on that movie did it.

You started that ball rolling though, defining the terms of that world.

It's so validating and earth-moving to me, that I had made that transition. I don't know if I'll get that feeling again.

I noticed in the DVD extras you were tweaking the script to better adhere to the locations in Portland. In those scenes, are you writing at the set?

Yeah, doing guerilla rewrites on the fly. The other thing that's helped shape me as a writer, being on that set, was that I can only take these characters and ideas so far. At some point I have to turn this abstract concept over to these professional people and everybody else puts their stamp on it.

When I saw how hard Scotty and everyone was working, Nathan and Angela, what everybody brought to it, their dedication to those roles, whether they were in front of the camera or behind, it was kind of overwhelming in a different way. I liken it to sending a child off to college; I can only imagine this must be a similar feeling. I've done the best I can to raise this child; I have to let them go. Very helpful and instructive to see that other side of it, which was you have to trust that you do enough, that I gave Angela and Nathan enough to work with. I think I did, they took what I'd done and took it so much further, way beyond whatever I had imagined.

Talking to Nathan (Baesel, who plays Leslie Vernon), he'd mentioned that his take on the character in the auditions made Scott re-think his approach, I'm not sure if it was down to re-thinking what Leslie would be like physically, visually, or attitude, but I'm wondering what your opinion was on where they went versus what was on the page.

I remember very clearly in the discussions after the casting, when it was down to the final choices, I remember all of us repeatedly coming back to the fact that Nathan had a very different take on it. He brought such a different texture and layer to it. Vulnerability and confidence; naiveté, and wisdom. There was something so very powerful and subtle, yet creepy, about what he did where maybe another guy was more "plowing straight ahead" a la Jason.

I remember we all really liked his take. I think that there were a lot of things Nathan brought to it that weren't necessarily on the page, the way it was shot (the DV-

documentary scenes), as they all got more comfortable with it, they got to play with it. I know Nathan's said he knew the core of the scene, what was supposed to be expressed; so, it wouldn't have mattered to me that he followed the dialogue word for word if he hit broader strokes. More often than not, they did go with the dialogue. But Nathan had the character, so whatever he was going to do would have been fine.

Here's a good question: why do people think screenwriting is easy?

(David laughs)

I mean even in the business, not just the guy off the street. I know people who want to write or sometimes write who don't read screenplays, don't work on them regularly. You know? What's your take on that? People think it's a craft that is not a big deal. Know what I mean?

I do, I have a very clear opinion about that. I think because screenwriting or any other creative endeavor like acting or singing, these are all very creative, freeform sort of enterprises that there isn't a societal norm for. Where this is what you do: you go to this school for X number of years, you go to pre-med, you go to medical, residency and then bam! You're a doctor. Or you go to law school, pre-law, you're a legal aid and then you get your own practice. Even professional sports! There's a structure there that society's established very clearly. Little League, college teams, minor league teams, pros, etc.

When you're talking about screenwriting, or singing or acting, these are all viewed as very free form, "Either you've got it, or you don't." And when people watch a movie, especially if they're watching a formulaic story that's been done a lot, I think people think, I can do that! I understand, and I've seen this story a million times! I know what's going to happen.

It's so easy to look at what's up there and say, "There's nothing so difficult about this, I understand instinctively how to tell a story: you introduce the characters, make them go through a bunch of shit and then you resolve it." And people think that can't be that hard, but it's absolutely not true.

And I did the same thing! "I can't write a novel, maybe I can write a movie! I know how to write a movie." But the layering and subtlety of how to write good dialogue, or how to construct a scene, or how you watch the rhythm and pace of your script. How you make sure you're not losing your audience halfway through act two, which is the longest stretch of the desert to get through.

How do you deliver a payoff in the third act that's satisfying? How do you make them care whether someone lives or dies at the end? How do you wrap the story up and send everyone out of the theaters feeling that they got their money's worth and are satisfied? That there's been some closure, good or bad, laughing or crying? There are so many layers of that. It's a craft; something you have to learn, like woodworking or heart surgery or being a professional baseball player. For me, I wouldn't just show up at Dodgers Stadium and say, "I want to play for the Dodgers!"

"I saw some great games last week and I've played a couple of times!"

Yeah, "I'm on my company's softball team, how hard can this be?" (laughs) People don't respect the creative process, especially the screenwriting process, because it just looks so effortless and flawless when it's done, on the screen. When you're seeing 110 minutes of it, it looks so easy. More and more people are trying it; everyone can be a filmmaker now. Anyone can get a camera and shoot something, nobody's stopping you but it's hard to do it well.

There's a new documentary about screenwriting coming out called *Dreams on Spec* that you're part of, which follows three screenwriters struggling through the business of Hollywood. I was thinking there are so few good movies, about writing. It's not very cinematic unless you're going inside the writer's head. But I was intrigued by this, since it looks to be about the writing life.

It is. And Daniel Snyder did such an amazing job with what he calls the "Greek Chorus." He got all these icons of filmmaking and screenwriting to echo, or to cut away from, the three main stories, which are myself and two other writers. One of them doesn't necessarily encounter the success they want, and kind of packs up and quits, and one of them, it's sort of left open that that person is still working at it and still might get there someday.

And then Dan just happened to connect with me and I'm the "success story" of *Dreams on Spec*, it's just remarkable timing and coincidence and fate that that happened. Daniel did an amazing job of capturing how hard this is. Anyone who's interested in it who watches the movie, they're either going to come away from it thinking 'There's no way,' or 'I can probably do that if I just sort of do what that guy did, or learn, or work hard enough.'

A more realistic look at what it takes.

Yeah! It takes people into a world that no one understands. Screenwriting isn't this mystical process; it's just pounding it out on a keyboard and thinking it out and rewriting and revising. There's a very concrete, tedious, difficult process to writing scripts. And when you see a vision of that, like *Dreams on Spec* gives people, it demystifies it. And then what you do with that new knowledge is up to you.

I know you have scripts in all different genres going around or about to go into production, but would you write, or do you have plans to write, another horror film?

Well, then you're treading into sequel territory. If there is any kind of scoop, it's not really a scoop, but I can tell you and your readers that there is a definite idea for what's going to happen to Leslie Vernon next, that's been the goal all along. There are a lot of what-ifs, and things to have to happen right in this business for that to ever come to fruition, but certainly if there's going to be another horror movie coming from me, my biggest impulse, of course, is to relate what happens to Leslie next.

Obviously, the focus of that or the metaphor involved there, as it happened with Nathan as an actor or Scott as a director, or me as a writer, it's how do you handle that "freshman phenom/rookie of the year" type thing! That's the symbolism at play; how does Leslie handle his success? And of course, you have the whole genre-specific constructions and conventions of a horror sequel. There are specific conventions involved with every killer that comes back. How the town reacts, who the people are that survive, and who fills what role coming around again…so there are all these very specific genre expectations for a sequel that are ripe for the picking but there's obviously the metaphor of how does Leslie as the 'artist' handle his fame, does he handle it well, does he burn out too quick, keep himself in check, does he do it right? There's a very rich soil to till from a storytelling standpoint. Depending on how the DVD does, etc. that's the impetus.

Days Like This is a bank heist film; that's the farthest along as far as production goes, we're actively trying to cast that. It's an independent film again, trying to get a name interested in the lead, which helps with the people putting up money. It's on a different level than *Mask*, significantly bigger budget; it's been quite a whirlwind to be part of that process. That's sort of out of my hands really, in terms of the storytelling. The script is essentially done and that's what we're making offers on. Once we get to the point where it's cast, or if it's cast-contingent and we get a specific name, everyone wants their rewrites and things like that; but that's what we call a high-class problem. (laughs)

CORALINA CATALDI-TASSONI

Interviewed by Mike Cucinotta, Rob Galluzzo, and Adam Barnick (7/07)

Icons of Fright is proud to present an exclusive interview with actress/musician/painter Coralina Cataldi-Tassoni. Coralina made her genre debut in Lamberto Bava's *Demons 2* and later worked several times with Dario Argento in *Opera*, *Phantom of the Opera*, and *Mother of Tears*. She recently sat down with us to discuss everything from her music to working with Argento to making her first convention appearances! Read on for what we consider one of our best featured interviews!

Rob: What are your earliest recollections of the horror genre? The first films that impacted or scared you?

Hmm… scared me? *Deep Red* was a movie that had an impact on me and scared me. In a positive way.

Mike: What do you remember about that one that affected you so much?

In some crazy way, I felt like I related to that movie. It spoke to me and gave me this crazy feeling as if my life was similar to how that movie made me feel. Even as a little girl. It gave me this sense of foreseeing what I'd become as a person. I know, that sounds odd. (laughs)

Mike: Is that because it flashes back to childhood?

The feeling that *Deep Red* gave me was the feeling that I've always had inside of my life. The spirit of the movie is kind of how I felt at the time. And it also kind of told me who I'd become one day. The kind of mind I'd grow up with. I loved the music, which was a very, very important to me as well, because I'd watch that movie on TV at night, and I remember my mother was sleeping in the other room and after the movie was over, I went over to my father's piano and started recreating the same notes I'd just heard from the score. In Italy, you could catch *Deep Red* at 3PM in the afternoon on TV. But I caught it late at night, which made things even better.

Rob: Now, you were born here in New York, but moved to Italy when you were young. Did you start your acting career at a young age too? When did acting begin for you?

I was born into a family of opera singers and my father was an opera stage director. He had an opera company here in New York, so when I was at the tender age of three and a half, I was given my first little singing role in one of the operas he had put on with his company, so I slowly started working with his company doing singing roles here and there. It kind of started that way.

Mike: And when did you make the transition to film?

I thought I was going to be a rock star. (laughs) Music was really my passion. But then I started doing theatre, and figured what the hell? I started auditioning, but my agent kept sending me mainly for commercials. Now, do I look like the commercial kind of girl?! It was only natural I never got cast. But, I finally got cast as the lead in a short. I actually thought they would not cast me because I went into the audition with a bad attitude. I was tired of trying. It actually worked out great because I kind of let go that day. I was convinced I would not get cast for this. Chance had it, the role they were looking for was a girl that had a bit of an attitude. Well, I got cast, and it was shown on national TV. And this short, called *In Cerca D'Amore* (*Searching for Love*), so 80's! It was in theaters as well. From then on, it started happening, and then I met Dario Argento. And once again, going back to *Deep Red*, I felt as if I called for all this to happen. I thought Dario was the only one doing something in Italy truly different.

Rob: What was your first meeting with Dario like? Was it intimidating at all considering what a fan of his you were?

I met Dario in this club, and I was a big fan of his, but I did not tell him at first that I was an actress because I had such an admiration for him that I did not feel it was appropriate. I just told him I was studying at the University of Rome, which I was. I was trying to study psychology, and later he saw this short film that I was in on TV, and he asked, "How come you never told me you were an actress?" I really just wanted to be his friend! After he saw the short though, I got cast in *Demons 2*.

Rob: What do you remember about the experience of doing *Demons 2*, besides being in a tremendous amount of make-up for a majority of the time?

It was great. It was such an honor. Movies like that are shown in major movie theaters there. So, it was a really scary thing for me, and I remember the night before I was sitting on the edge of my bed, and I started crying a little bit! I thought, "Oh my God. How am I going to do this? This is a big deal." I remember that very vividly. I wanted so bad to do a good job. And I think it went well, right?

Mike: Can you explain to the *Icons of Fright* audience how Argento is viewed in Italy, and explain why you would be feeling so nervous to work on a movie with his involvement? He's almost like a rock star out there, right?

Yes. I'd say he's a mixture of Spielberg and David Bowie! You walk around with him and you're walking around with Bowie mixed with Mick Jagger. Yes, he's a rock star. But he's very humble. He's great with the fans. He always gives his time with them and signs autographs. People love him. When we did this last movie, the news would announce where we were shooting and what we were doing. It's on Italy's national news. He's very important to us. Even to people that are not into horror, in Italy Dario Argento is Dario Argento.

Rob: Now, for *Demons 2*, your character is memorable because of this extensive make-up you wear. A lot of people often say how uncomfortable it is to undergo so much make-up. Was it uncomfortable for you, or were you just so excited to be a part of the movie?

I had a blast. I felt like it couldn't get better than this. It was my first movie with these great icons, right? Giving me this huge responsibility. Yes, it's tough, it's a lot of hours, but it's my work! So, I thought it was great.

Rob: Can you tell us a little bit how you initially got involved with *Opera*?

Once again, Dario called me. He had me in mind for this. I remember meeting him with the producers in the lobby of a hotel and, basically, he introduced me by saying this is going to be Julia in *Opera* and the producers said, "Great!" And that was it! I was in.

Mike: Considering how nervous you were to be working under the direction of Bava for *Demons 2*, a production Dario was involved with, what'd it feel like to know this time around you were going to be directed by Dario himself for *Opera*?

Well, I cried before *Demons 2*, can you imagine how I was before *Opera*? (laughs) Well, Dario and I at that point had a friendship, and I knew he gave me this part and wrote this for me, and I felt comfortable delivering this role for him. It's nerve-racking, even today. Even with this last movie (*Mother of Tears*). There are two things I have to remember and keep in mind when I'm doing this job. Of course, Dario Argento and my fans. That's an obsession I have. To do a good job for both of them. Dario and the fans.

Rob: In terms of working with Dario, I wanted to talk about your death scene in *Opera*. The way it's built up, it's very artistic with a series of close-up shots of the dress you're working on and so forth. Did you have any idea that that's the way the sequence would be cut together, or did you just have to trust whatever he told you?

No idea. You read it in the script, but you never have a complete picture of it. You have an idea of what it'll look like, but it's definitely not the same as when you're sitting there and seeing it in the movie theater for the first time. It becomes so different.

Rob: How difficult is it to die in an Argento movie?

That's what it's all about! For me, to be killed by Dario Argento is an honor. It's a moment of love, the moment that I come to life. Not only does my character come to life, be it Julia or Giselle or even Sally, but I as a human being come to life. I'm given that eternity that I'm so obsessed about. You know, you want eternal life or immortality. And what better way than to be killed by Dario Argento and thus be immortal. And then your character becomes immortal and it's great.

Phantom Of The Opera, I don't get killed and I remember asking him, "Do I get killed?" and him saying, "No, in this one you don't get killed." (laughs) But that's ok. It's great. You wait for that moment of death, and you build your character contingent to that moment as well, so you hope the contrast works.

Mike: So, Dario often plays the killer in his movies. He's the hand in the glove. What's that like? Not only is he directing you in these scenes and directing your death, but he's performing it as well.

It's all about the love making! That moment. He's always there. He created that moment. He wrote it. He created that moment of love, so who better than him to perform it.

Rob: One of the things I find interesting about you is that you have a lot of creative outlets. You work on music, you work in films, you paint your own art. Would you say those all reflect different aspects of your personality? What does each creative medium mean to you?

When you're an artist and you're not working or doing something, you're not that fun to be around! So, I always have to be doing something. I think they're all very codependent with each other. My music, my acting, my art. They live codependently happily together. I think they all are intimately connected. Music is very important. When I'm acting, I feel a sense of music, I feel a sense of rhythm. I am in a painting. Everything one does is connected. When I paint, I can't paint without my music. When I am acting, I am choosing different shades and forms as if I am creating a painting. For me, it's all the same. Like life, it's all one.

Rob: I just read about a movie you did called *Ghost Son* that Lamberto Bava directed, but I haven't heard much else. Can you tell us a little bit about *Ghost Son*?

It's in theaters, I believe, still playing in Rome right now. It stars Laura Harring from *Mulholland Drive*. It's a very small cast. Oscar nominee Pete Postlethwaite…

Rob: Great actor! Great cast.

Yes. John Hannah from *Sliding Doors* and *The Mummy*. And Mosa Kaiser who was the little girl in *Hotel Rwanda*. And that was pretty much it. We shot it in South Africa. It was the day before my birthday. I remember Lamberto emailed me and said he was looking for me. "Where are you? Call me!" And I called him, and he said, "Do you want to come to South Africa to shoot a movie?" (laughs) So, I said YES! That was a great experience. The crew was incredible. The movie's quite interesting. It's a love story with a psychological twist.

Mike: I've always been curious with the process of filmmaking in Italy. Because you just mentioned this international cast working on an Italian film. How do language barriers play into all this?

Many are shot in English. A lot of the times, the Italians speak enough English to be able to be working. Dario speaks it. Lamberto speaks it. But there is also an interpreter. With actors, it might be hard. The actors you see, sometimes they might not know what's going on. For example, on *Phantom of the Opera* with Julian Sands, we shot it in Hungary, and on set everyone was speaking Italian and Hungarian and I felt bad for him! It's situations like that where you feel bad, because what can they do other than sit in the corner and read a book! It's tough on the actors, especially. I have dual citizenship, and I can speak Italian fluently, so for me it's really good, because I can speak both.

Rob: Does that mean you get to dub both your Italian and English voice for some of these movies?

Sometimes. *Demons 2* is not me. *Opera* is not me in English. *Phantom of the Opera*, although it's a British accent, that is me. And *Mother of Tears* will be me as well.

Mike: That *Phantom of the Opera* is interesting…

That's an elegant way of putting it. A lot of people don't like it.

Mike: Well, it's just so different for Argento!

Well, why not? It was a very courageous decision. He had his vision for his *Phantom of the Opera*. He gave it his little comedic sense and said this is how I want to do it. Good for him. I enjoyed it. I'm surprised more people don't enjoy it.

Mike: Perhaps a lot of fans confuse it with *Opera*? Because they both have a very similar theme?

Sure, it might be a similar name, but how many directors write and keep similar themes? I can't complain, right? Keep doing movies on opera and keep calling me! (laughs) Because also it's a world that I am familiar with. So, when I would go on set on *Opera* or *Phantom of the Opera*, I really felt like I was going home. The smell of the wood, even the stench of the costumes. Backstage memories of my childhood. While actors were going on set, I felt like I was going home. And I'm sure these are some of the reasons why Dario thought of me for these movies as well, because it was such a familiar sensation.

Rob: How quickly did *Mother of Tears* come together? From the first time you heard about it to actually filming it? A lot of people were surprised when he announced the third *Suspiria* movie.

The truth is I kind of knew about it for some time. It's really hard to keep these things close to yourself, but out of respect and care and gratitude that I have towards him, even though I already knew he was considering me, I kept the news to myself. I did not even tell my mother! It was tough keeping it a secret, but I couldn't say anything. That's an Italian superstition. I did get the call when they were about to start the movie, but I kind of knew that this might happen. The beauty of it was that when we were shooting this, and after my death scene, there was this very intense moment where I went to thank Dario for giving me this opportunity, and he says, "Just like Julia, this was written with you in mind." I was covered in blood, so I figured I could get a little teary eyed without him knowing. (laughs) It was a great thing to know that he knew already that he wanted me for this role. It's not a huge role, but a pivotal one for the movie. I'm hoping that the reason he gave me this is because where it is positioned in the movie, it's important that I deliver. So, I'm hoping you guys like it, and I hope I delivered! If anything from this movie gets cut, all I can say is I put so much devotion into this character of Giselle.

Rob: We've seen a lot of photographs of you in this movie, and it seems that a lot of terrible, terrible things happen to you in this movie! Care to comment on that at all?

Well, shall I comment on the fact that too many photos online cheapen my work and Dario's work? Because it's too much shown. You take care of little meticulous things in your acting so that when the fans see it, they go, "*Wow!*" But if they've already seen it in a picture, it takes the "wow" out of it. But yes, the death scene we hope; well, you've seen a lot of it already!

Mike: Are you surprised by the buzz the film is getting here in America? It made the front page of *Variety*!

Yes. And the great thing was we were all in LA when we saw that. Imagine, you come from Italy, you're in LA and you pick up the *Variety* at the news stand and see *Mother of Tears* on the cover!! Let's hope it sees a decent release here. But I'm having a great time promoting it.

Mike: I'd love to see an Argento movie in the theaters here! These are big, big movies there!

Oh, in Italy, people go nuts! They'll show it in a downtown Loews theater and people really get into it.

Rob: You just made an appearance at the *Fangoria* show in Burbank and then another appearance at the New Jersey *Fangoria* this year. What's the convention experience been like for you? Have you been surprised by the fan base?

Yes. I mean, at first, I didn't know all this was going on here in the U.S!

Rob: There's a lot of horror nerds out there! You're surrounded by a bunch right now.

I love them all! It's great! Horror fans are just incredible for many reasons. I can go on and on about that. But yes, I was completely pleasantly surprised. I had no idea what we were doing out there had such a big impact here. To go to LA and have directors that have worked on major movies that know your work and love your work. It feels like *The Twilight Zone*, but it's great! Once again, I am an American. So, to come back after having worked in the Italian genre is great. I feel like I came back to my own country after having won the war overseas. (laughs)

Adam: Who in terms of painters and musicians do you connect with? Who interests you and why?

I really don't connect with a lot of painters. I can see certain artists and appreciate them, like Munch or Modigliani, but mainly music and musicians have an impact on my art. First as a child I fell in love with Giacomo Puccini as my favorite opera composer. And then when I was eleven or twelve, I started getting into punk rock; Sex Pistols, Patti Smith, Lou Reed. But I still love opera, and now opera and rock are one to me. It's all music.

Adam: Can you talk a bit about your process for painting? Do you prepare at all for what you're going to paint or are you completely guided by your original emotion?

I'm completely guided by my original emotion. Exactly. I just go by how I'm feeling. What music I choose to play, which will understand me in that particular moment. It might sound like I am contradicting myself right now but... it's not what I choose, the music kind of chooses me. What's going to talk to me and do something to me. I choose a piece of music, put it on the stereo and I just go. It's really about the music and how I'm feeling. All I paint is autobiographical. All these figures or human presences are people that are in my life or in my past life, or even visions of people that I will see in the future. I'll meet new people and think, "God, I've painted you!" So, it's all about how I feel. It's all I know really. It's all I really have.

Rob: What's your relationship with Asia Argento? What's she like as a person? What's she like to work with?

I've known her since she was a little bitty person! She was in *Demons 2*, I'd be sitting in the make-up chair and she'd be there with her camera taking pictures. She was always so interested in everything. Very interested in things and people and life. She's a very hard worker. Great memory. She'll pick up a script and just memorize it so easily. We've known each other for a very long time, so when we do scenes together like in *Phantom Of The Opera* or *Mother Of Tears*, there's this very unspoken protectiveness we have for each other. We'll do a scene, but then we'll talk about our personal life, but also then give each other ideas about how we're going to do the scene. We're accomplices when we work on these things. Unfortunately, I don't get the chance to talk to her or see her as much as I would like to. But every time we see each other, it's like reconnecting with your high school friend.

When we reconnect, we're still close friends. Also, I would like to add that Dario Argento does have another daughter named Fiore Argento. Fiore which means flower. She's a fashion designer. Very similar to her father and a great, great girl. Everyone often talks about Asia, but there's also Fiore out there. She's in the first *Demons* and *Phenomena*, but she is really a talented fashion designer. She's very elegant and eloquent. Just had to mention her!

Rob: Thanks so much for your time, Coralina!

Thank you for the great interview and all your support. It is truly appreciated.

171

BILL JOHNSON

Interviewed by Mike Cucinotta and Rob Galluzzo (8/07)

When it comes to horror icons, Leatherface is definitely one of the best! We are therefore honored to feature an extensive *Fright* exclusive interview with actor Bill Johnson, who took over the role in Tobe Hooper's *Texas Chainsaw Massacre Part 2*! Here in his first full length online interview, he talks about working with Tobe Hooper, Jim Siedow, Bill Moseley, Dennis Hopper, and goes into great detail about the making-of the cult classic sequel! Read on!

What are your earliest recollections of the horror genre? Do you remember the first films to really scare you or have an impact on you?

I was probably ten or eleven watching TV and Boris Karloff as Frankenstein's monster is on the slab in the lab and opens his probing, rapacious eyes for the first time, and it is instantly clear that Satan has suddenly been released from eons of penury in hell, is alive and well in Frankensteins' creation, and is now free with carte blanche to make the world bend over, grab its ankles, and bark. I had nightmares after that.

Can you tell us a bit about starting your acting career and what it was that led you to follow that particular path? What was it like for you first starting out?

I was introduced to acting in my final semester of high school by an awesome teacher, Leo York, who introduced me to acting and speech. Up until this time, I was clueless about what to do as a career. But, voila, Leo York shows me something I liked and could do, yes! With no previous experience, within a month I went to the Statewide Speech Competition and won a statuette for doing a speech of Marc Antony's from *Julius Caesar*; and thus, the doors into a brave new world opened up for me. After high school and some community theater, I sent out applications and got an acting scholarship to Lon Morris College in Jacksonville, Texas, which has an excellent drama department. I later finished up at UT Austin with a BFA in acting. I started out after college by touring in the US with two national children's theatre troupes. I did that for two years,

came back to Austin in 1975, and got in local commercials on TV and radio, industrials, and tons of live stage plays including many original new plays. I also did improvisation groups, street theatre, student film projects, indie films, and eventually Hollywood films that were shooting in Texas, such as *Texas Chainsaw Massacre 2* in 1986.

Starting out is always a lot of dealing with the unknown, doing lots of free gigs for "the experience," and a lot of hit or miss on getting hired. I've been lucky and had some nice roles, met great people, and done something worth doing. And I now enjoy live performing in Austin and am heading toward the Poetry Slam competition. And still lots of indie films happening here in Austin and one in particular I'm proud to be in is *Fall to Grace*, which doing very well in online downloads from the Jaman website. It's rated #28 in the world for downloads and rated even higher for North America.

Do you recall the first time you saw/experienced the original *Texas Chain Saw Massacre* and what effect did the film have on you?

I hadn't seen it until the day before I auditioned for the role of Bubba for *Texas Chainsaw Massacre 2*. That's when I first saw Gunnar, Jim, Edwin, Marilyn, Paul, John, and Tobe tear it up. It was eerie, very deeply disturbing, unsettling, unnerving, and inspiring.

Leatherface is an extremely physical role, but unlike a lot of the other "slashers," the viewer is almost always aware of his emotions, mood, and his level of intellect,

especially in your portrayal. What did you rely on and do you remember using any particular techniques to help convey that?

Maybe the simplest thing might be to say, I endeavored to do the best job I could. I went for ensemble acting. As always, I decided to rely on the director and cast, but also on twenty plus years of acting experience and my training in most all venues of performing, which by now is mostly at the unconscious level. I wanted to be in a deeply meaningful personal relationship with every person I had a scene with. I took my inspiration from Tobe, Kit, Bill Moseley, Jim Siedow, Caroline Williams, Dennis Hopper, Lou Perryman, and Ken Evert.

Was there any particular direction from Hooper that you remember being of help to your performance?

Tobe conveyed a multiplicity of meanings by his mood and the other intangible forms of communication he used besides his words and rhythms all through the filming, and that was a tremendous help. Any play is pretty much about the writer and that was originally Tobe and, for this particular film, Kit Carson. So I got into Tobe and Kit as much as I could. Tobe was a man of few words, but got a lot of mileage and meaning with the ones he used. Kit loves words and to talk, so he was another great source of collaboration as we had in-depth discussions that were interesting and enjoyable. They were tremendously valuable, these kinds of high quality conversations with the playwright, who was also an accomplished screen actor, which rendered extra richness and value.

Were there any ways in which you referenced Gunner Hansen's previous performance in the role to help you build upon your portrayal of the character?

Nothing deliberate or planned on my part, especially since this sequel was quite different in style and form than his *Texas Chain Saw Massacre*. If this film had instead been a long running stage play, I would have had time to develop, solidify, and tweak a more complex characterization of Bubba and would have worked in some of the strokes that Gunnar applied to his canvas in the first film, which would have been a lot of fun too.

We had a new script from Kit, a new world, and essentially a new Leatherface, the one at home where he was at the bottom of the pecking order, the younger brother who gets hazed by his older brothers on a daily basis. I just wanted to keep up with daily events as they were unfolding during principal photography. Kit was rewriting every day.

The new information stream was kind of like being in fog. You can see things clearly enough close in around you, but beyond that, one must wait for signs and portents or just fly blind and run the risk of hitting an iceberg. So, things developed on the fly, lots of improvisation and last-minute adjustments, and luck, the "happy accident."

The chemistry between your Leatherface and Bill Moseley's Chop-Top is one of the most memorable aspects of *Texas Chainsaw 2*. Fans just love the work you both did with those characters. Can you talk a bit about your working relationship with Bill Moseley?

Thank you, it was a lot of fun playing together with that fine cast and especially Bill Moseley. I felt we had a sympatico right away. Bill was fun and easy to be around, we always found something engaging to talk about. We played a whole lot of gin rummy in the air-conditioning in our dressing room away from the hundred-plus degree Texas broiling summer heat while waiting to be called to the set. As you know, generally speaking, the percentage of time an actor spends in film acting is about ninety-plus percent of it waiting to do it.

We made up a lot of stuff about the special world of the film while waiting in the air conditioning, playing cards, listening to music, and making up lyrics. We created a family tree and family history. We even created the typical Sawyer Family daily life. We got into each other's modus operandi, got into a groove, and just went for having a lot of fun. So, when we got on the live film set, we were already into the daily chainsaw family life, scintillating to the rhythms of our chainsaw daily world, and had a lot of non-verbal communication happening. It brought out a texture, depth, and complexity we otherwise would not have had.

Originally derided upon its release, *Texas Chainsaw Massacre 2* has developed a strong following, especially in recent years. Any thoughts on why horror fans initially rejected it and why they have recently come around to it? Essentially, fan interest is why a special edition DVD was in demand.

Yes, the critics did initially have an unfavorable response. They were pretty conservative, but were probably just a reflection of the times back then. At that time, there was no internet to track fan response, but *Texas Chainsaw Massacre 2* has withstood the test of time. So, I don't know if I can really accept that the horror fans actually rejected it, but if they did, it may have been influenced by the critical brouhaha of the day. I just pulled some "Top 10" film stats from the internet for 1986. Look at the field, *Texas Chainsaw*

2 was way out on the extreme end of the continuum of what people were watching, it was way out there in comparison. *Texas Chainsaw Massacre 2* was released without a rating (already making the film a kind of outcast), lots of blood and violence (for 1986) mixed with very edgy comedy. They were attracted/repulsed and frightened by Tobe's work. And, in the end, the fans' enjoyment of this film, the fans' demand for more background about the creative team, called forth a re-release of the DVD and I'm so happy about that.

A lot has been said of Leatherface's burgeoning "sexual maturity" in *Chainsaw 2*, suggesting you were portraying him with the mindset of a young teen. Where did this come from? Was this scripted, or did you bring it to the table? What does one do to get into that state of mind? It seems so complicated!

Much of it showed up spontaneously. I think it was implicit in L.M. Kit Carson's marvelous script. Kit and I talked a lot about the script and characters, so it got fleshed out, so to speak. And Tobe had definite strong visions and feelings about how the "ice-tub scene" should go when we shot that scene. That night was a "fasten your seatbelts, because it's going to be a bumpy night" experience. The first "crush," besides seeming like a hugely complicated situation, is totally a major event for a young man and no different for Bubba, who had been kept inside a lot and kept a lot of himself inside himself.

So he was a little slow to mature, but he eventually got there. When he did, he was a runaway bullet train and the only dating skills he had was stalking, so for Bubba the course of true love was definitely not going to run smooth.

You know, all the hanging out me and Moseley did in the dressing room, keeping from going stir crazy and cabin fever, going over family history, grooving and headbanging to music, etc, all that stuff that Bill Moseley and I were doing while waiting to go onto the film set was so similar to what we imagined that Chop Top and Bubba did while waiting to go out on one raid or another. Chop Top and Bubba listened to Stretch's music show on K-OKLA and planned, schemed and fantasized, got cranked up and ripped out of there with blood lust and bad intentions. I recall reading an interview of Gunnar's and he stated to the effect that Leatherface of *Texas Chain Saw Massacre* killed anything that moved. However, in Part 2, for this, my Leatherface, now known as Bubba, there were distinctions and differences in the movement of others. Some kinds of movement were far better than others, for example: the delicious moves of Stretch (our fave), moved in fine ways that did not recommend to kill her but instead to thrill her.

If only Bubba could get a handle on these new overwhelming geysers of sensations roiling and revving up from the depths and steer that over in Stretch's direction, drive up to her lair and into her heart, bigtime, yeah! Then little by little, little Bubba could experiment, learn and through trial and error become Stretch's "friendly stranger" like the *Ides of March* sang about on K-OKLA. It seemed like Stretch, on her awesome radio show, was talking directly to Bubba and playing special music just for him. Bubba was in love with love and love was Stretch. Bubba is a romantic, which definitely is not an acceptable Sawyer Family trait. So, Bubba decided to break ranks and go for the girl. Well, what family doesn't have its ups and downs?

Speaking of Dennis Hopper, there's got to be at least one wacky Dennis Hopper story you can share.

If Dennis was not scheduled to shoot a scene, he was away from Austin doing pre-production on the film he was directing, *Colors*. I didn't see him very much, however, my evaluation of Dennis was that he was not so much wacky, as he was outré, orbiting outside of normal channels, which is the perfect purview of the artist. Dennis has played some wacky characters, but that is only acting. I recall one time when me, Moseley, and Hopper were getting our makeup taken off at sunrise after another grueling night. We were sitting in our makeup chairs all in a row and Bill Moseley was on a superb comic roll. He had us howling in convulsions. And I, sitting next to Dennis, out of the blue, spontaneously spouted a line of Dennis Hopper's character, Billy, from *Easy Rider*, I said, "….yeah, he's Captain America, and I'm Billy!" Without missing a beat, Dennis immediately chimes in, "We're headliners, baby. We played every fair in this part of the country. For top dollar!"

I thought, "Wow, here Dennis is well-nigh exhausted at the end of a long hard filming day in Texas hundred-plus degree temperatures and is now trying to unwind. He's then blindsided by a blast from the past while recovering, distracted by laughing his guts out, and Dennis spontaneously completes a bit of obscure dialogue from decades back in his past, after he's memorized zillions of words since *Easy Rider*." No flies on Dennis Hopper, he's as sharp as they come.

The years before *Chainsaw 2* weren't all that kind to Tobe Hooper. I imagine he had to be under so much pressure with this sequel. Did you get that feeling from him?

Tobe was a rock, even though we all knew the film studios were putting punishing pressure on him to go faster and faster, by many unsavory film studio underlings and methods. Despite all that, Tobe was an engine of industry. He seemed to be enraptured with his process and he was rock steady and inspiring. He took care of us and protected us. He knew exactly what he wanted to do and why. And Tobe remained so, despite the tremendous, repeated, and escalating real world pressures levied upon him by the film studio. One night, Tobe rightfully chewed out the "B" camera team when they were making an incredible racket while, at the same time, Tobe, the principal director was trying to film a scene in principal photography. I thought Tobe was heroic.

Did you feel any pressure stepping into the role?

Luckily, I was probably too naïve, not knowing of the cult status of the original, to feel pressured. I felt excitement, opportunity, and thrilled out of my mind. I just wanted to have the greatest time ever pouring myself into this experience leaving nothing remaining, to use it all up. The pressure I felt was to commit full-out until the end of filming, despite the myriad obstacles that come with the territory.

What expectations did you have about the film before making it, regarding both what it would be like on set and also regarding how it would turn out?

Yeah, great question and I started to go there, but found out real soon that to do anything but to stay focused in the present moment was a recipe for disaster and regret. So, I stayed out of the future, stayed in the present, stayed in character and stayed in my trailer preparing for my next scene until called.

You've done plenty of convention appearances throughout the last few years, sometimes reuniting with some of the cast and crew involved in *Texas Chainsaw 2*. What's the convention experience like from your perspective?

The convention world is the living definition of the fantastic unfolding of life's colorful pageant. I'm grateful and feel delighted to be a part of all that, meeting fans, talking with them, panel discussions, reconnecting with fellow cast members who are very talented and specially gifted friends. How perfect. And, on top of all that great stuff, is getting the electrifying pleasure of meeting stars of many genres, great artists, icons, is perhaps beyond description. What a privilege to meet them, speak with them, talk shop, have fun, network. It's a dream come true. All you far out fans, you make all the difference!!! I feel deeply indebted to each and every one of you, and I'm looking forward to meeting you at a convention in the near future.

ROB ZOMBIE

By Mike Cucinotta w/ Mike Bacon of Fri. Morning Quarterback (8/07)

Intimidating as it might have seemed and certainly not without a little hesitation, Rob Zombie has taken on the seemingly impossible task of reinventing *Halloween*. Here he talks candidly with *Icons of Fright* about what it takes to bring new life and a new sense of sheer terror to an aging horror series.

How'd the opportunity to direct *Halloween* present itself?

It came up in a weird way. After I finished *The Devil's Rejects*, I met with a lot of different people. Other remakes came my way that I didn't have any interest in, other original stuff too, different things. I took a million meetings, kind of worked on some projects a little bit. Then they started turning into things I didn't want to be associated with. One day I got a call asking if I wanted to meet with Bob Weinstein because he was in town, I think, for the Golden Globes. Ok, I'll have a meeting, but this is the last fucking meeting I'm doing. I'm sick of having meetings because they never amount to anything. It's just a lot of chit-chat. So, I went and met him at his hotel and we started talking and he just threw out "*Halloween.*" Dimension owns the rights to *Halloween*, and he wanted to know my take on *Halloween*. Not as a remake, just in any sense. They had *Halloween* and they didn't know what to do with it essentially. I know they had tried several times to make a *Halloween* movie and it failed, so that's basically how it came to me. Just out of the blue.

So, you get *Halloween* as your project, and it must be great considering you're a huge fan, but also consequently you have to reinvent *Halloween*. Did you have a moment where you thought, "What have I gotten myself into?"

Well, at first, I didn't know if I really wanted to do it because I was not really keen on the idea of making a remake. I just said, "I don't know, I'll think about it," sort of thinking that I was going to call them back later and say no. But I left there, and I thought about it for a couple of weeks. And then I kind of starting feeling like, "Wait a minute. Why am I assuming that this is a bad idea? This could be an incredible idea.

I'm taking the completely wrong attitude." And I started working on it thinking, "Yeah, I'm totally going to do this." I started envisioning how you could do this. I looked at it and thought Michael Myers is a great character. He's one of the few modern day iconic monsters. There are only about four or five modern day monsters. They very rarely pop up and present themselves in a classic way. So, I thought, "Shit, I have to do this movie. This could be so great."

How much free reign was given to you to make it yours?

One hundred percent. I wouldn't have done it any other way. That's what they wanted. Bob Weinstein said, "We want you to take it and run with it!" If there was only one thing he kept stressing to me more and more, which became his catch phrase was, "Make it more Rob Zombie!" (laughs) He wasn't worried about protecting the franchise, he wasn't worried about anything. He just wanted me to take it and run with it. Once again, it was a very rare situation, so it was very difficult to say no.

Was it difficult to make it? You had a lot of time between *House of 1000 Corpses* and *The Devil's Rejects*. *Halloween* was announced last June (2006) and it's just now coming out in August (2007)

The biggest hindrance to me was I made the mistake… well, I had seen *Halloween* a million times, but I had never seen it with the thought that I was going to remake it. So, I watched it again and again and again, and it actually started doing more harm than it did good; it started fucking with my head because I had the same thought that fans have. How can you possibly do this? How can you change this? So, I had to stop watching it and stop thinking about it and just start spinning it off in my own direction. It wasn't that difficult.

It was harder towards the end, because the beginning of the movie, doing young Michael Myers life was easy because it hadn't existed before. People look at the first movie and go, "Oh, he was a normal kid!" We don't really know any of that. He doesn't say anything, and we don't really get any insight into him. That's just people projecting that onto what they see. So, I thought, "Ok, that's good. I can run with that because that's pretty much a clean slate." And then everything with Dr. Loomis in the early days of Smiths Grove Sanitarium was also a clean slate. I could pretty much do whatever I wanted there. It was really when I got to the third act of the movie where we got to Haddonfield that I wanted to retain some classic elements. Make it different but retain classic elements. The best way I can describe it for people is that it's like *Batman Begins*. You're keeping Wayne Manor. You're keeping Batman. You want the Batsuit. You're probably going to have Alfred as the butler. You're going to keep some of the classic things, but the way you want to represent it is completely different.

What did you want from your cast? What did you want for your Loomis, and your Laurie, and your Michael Myers?

The main thing I wanted from everyone at all times was to be real and to take it seriously. Because one of the problems you have sometimes… you know… horror fans love horror. But there's a whole section of the population that not only doesn't love horror, they don't even care about it at all. Sometimes, that's an actor you have, so they come into it thinking, "Oh I know what these movies are like. You know, it's going to be kind of campy." They have a preconceived idea of what kind of acting you want for a horror movie. But no, I don't want that. I want you guys to play this as if it's a true story. Dead serious. A real thing. This whole movie's going to live and die on the acting. It's not about bad acting and the special FX. I want this whole movie to be compelling because you guys are giving amazing performances. Not because there's a big guy in a big mask walking around.

How beneficial was it for you that some of the main cast members had never seen *Halloween*? I know Malcolm McDowell had never seen the original.

It was great that they hadn't seen it, because I didn't want them to imitate what had come before them, because well… the people in the original didn't imitate anything. That was just their fresh take on what they should do. If people start imitating, then it would get weird. You don't want to watch someone do a Donald Pleasence imitation or something.

And there's no reason that they should, because someone like Malcolm McDowell is a great actor. I wanted Malcolm McDowell to be Malcolm McDowell, not to be imitating someone else. For the most part, the cast had either not seen the movie, or had seen it so long ago that their memories of it were so vague. So, it was never really a factor.

What about for someone like Danielle Harris, who not only had seen the original, but had been in other *Halloween* sequels?

Casting Danielle was a different case. A lot of people had approached me to be in the movie that had been in the other movies. And I said, "No offense, I think you're great and I'd love to work with you, but I don't want you in *Halloween*." Because if you start seeing people that are in cameos, the movie does not play as a serious movie. It plays as a joke, and I didn't want that. Danielle Harris came in and read, I wasn't there that day, but I really was thinking I wasn't going to cast her because she had been in *Halloween 4* and *5,* and I didn't see that as a plus, I saw that as a minus. Yeah, the fans would love her, but I didn't want to devalue this movie by saying, "Hey look. It's a wink-wink nudge-nudge homage to another movie." I didn't want to play it that way. It had to live and die as its own movie. But, to her credit, and this is the greatest compliment I can give, is that she was so great that I cast her even though I didn't want to cast her. So, she knew that. I've told her that many times.

From outside looking in, the cast is excellent. Did you have some of them in mind going in?

It was a little of both. I mean, all the older actors I wanted. I knew I wanted Tyler Mane for Michael Myers. I knew I wanted Malcolm McDowell. I knew I wanted William Forsythe and Dee Wallace. Really, the only people that I cast in casting sessions were the three girls, Laurie, Annie, Linda, and the three kids, young Michael Myers, Tommy Doyle, and Lindsay Wallace. Those are the only people that came in and read. But everybody else, I knew who I wanted but I didn't have… a ten year old in mind. Young Michael Myers and Laurie Strode, I knew I needed fresh faces that were not identifiable to any other films.

Scout Taylor-Compton's performance, from what I'm hearing, is supposed to be really, really strong.

It's phenomenal. She's amazing. And that was the greatest thing, because she was the only person that I wanted. Tons of people came in. People that were recognizable from other things, people that weren't, but Scout was always my number one choice. So, I always fought for her. I wanted her to be Laurie Strode, I knew that she would be perfect.

Going back to Malcolm McDowell, I was just wondering what he brought to the table considering what a great actor he is?

Malcolm's a strange actor because he always has that vibe to him. Even when he's the good guy, he seems like he's the bad guy. I don't know. He's got that innate sinisterness about him. But in a very likable way. Like in *A Clockwork Orange*, no matter how bad he is, you think, "I kind of like that guy!" What was great about *Halloween* is we created more of a character arc where younger Loomis is more idealistic. He's a child psychologist who starts working with this kid. And I kind of took the approach with it, I tried to pull from real life. Vincent Bugliosi is just a prosecutor, but then he gets the Manson case. So now he's the world's most famous prosecutor and that's going to change your life. Now, he's forever linked to Charles Manson. Forever.

And that's kind of the way I wanted to take it here. Dr. Loomis crosses paths with Michael before he ever does anything. And then he becomes part of Michael's life, and they become so intertwined that Malcolm starts one way and ends up another way. He starts out very idealistic and sort of becomes this cynical guy that knows that everything he did was basically a failure. It's interesting to watch his character evolve.

Donald (Pleasence) often said he loved the character of Loomis and would keep playing him. How'd Malcolm feel about the character?

I think Malcolm would do it again. Malcolm seemed to have a blast. He was enjoying every minute of it. I loved Malcolm. That was one of the greatest things about this movie. I've always loved Malcolm, whether it was *Clockwork* or *If....* or *O Lucky Man* or *Caligula* or *Time After Time*, I was always a big Malcolm fan. And to get to work with him, and to have him be the coolest fucking guy you're ever going to meet was just great. What more could you ask for?

Speaking of innately sinister actors, what about Brad Dourif? You see him on screen for five minutes and he's innately sinister.

That's the funny thing. I like casting people like that. I cast Brad as the Sheriff, he's the good guy. I cast Danny Trejo as kind of like the sympathetic kind of guy, not as a tough

guy. I cast Clint Howard as the serious doctor. I was trying to cast people opposite what they normally are. And Brad's great, what I love about Brad is he comes across so earnest in his performance. He really sinks in and he really, really thinks about it. He doesn't just show up and say his lines, he really thinks about it, and you can see it in his eyes. It's something that you may not even notice on set sometimes, and it's sort of like that X factor that only certain actors have, but there's just a whole other level to the look in their eye and you really buy into it. That's Brad. Brad's really brilliant. I really enjoyed working with him. Dee Wallace was another one who was a pleasure to work with.

She's a sweetheart. I've met her at conventions.

I never wanted her to leave! (laughs) You know, I just wanted to keep sticking her in scenes because she's just so great. She's another one, she's made a million movies, but she's just incredible. It's just a big love fest going on. (laughs)

You've got Sybil Danning in this too!

I met Sybil for *Grindhouse*. Because my original plan for the three Nazis was to have Sheri, Sybil, and Dyanne Thorne (Ilsa) as the three Nazi women. But Diane didn't want to do it, for some reason. That was a bummer. Um, but that's where I met Sybil. And I was already in production on *Halloween* at that time when I stopped to do the *Werewolf Woman* thing. And she said, "Oh if there's anything in *Halloween*, I'd love to do it. Anything. Anything!" And there really was only one kind of part left, she plays a nurse in the sanitarium. It's one brief scene, but she came in and rocked it.

Considering how active you were with your blog on MySpace, it seems like we were all getting our news and information from your MySpace blog. Was any of the feedback you were getting on the internet influential while you were making the film?

It was not influential in any way whatsoever. It really can't be, because the people that are commenting have no idea what they're commenting on. They're commenting on a movie that they haven't seen, or a movie that isn't even made yet! So, it's completely useless information unfortunately. And um, when I was working on the film, in pre-production on making the film, I didn't look at anything online or anywhere, because I didn't care. Because you're so focused on what you're trying to do, that it just doesn't matter. The only way to make your movie is you have to have a vision for what you want, and you have to be so single-minded that you don't give a fucking shit what anyone thinks. It's the same thing with casting. Certain people in the movie, nobody wanted me to cast them, and I had to fight to cast them. It went on for months sometimes, but I wouldn't let go of it. And now that it's done, it's like, "Wow, that person's fucking amazing. Thank God we cast them!" Because that's the way it goes. That's the director's job, you have to be put on the blinders and get ready to fucking fight the fight.

Expanding upon your MySpace blog, there was a lot of concern from fans that telling the backstory might take away from the mystique of Michael Myers. But as a fan, I always craved for more of that story to be told.

Yeah, and I mean, truthfully all that kind of talk to me is meaningless, because people's only frame of reference is that original movie. So, that's why they think it's that way.

Even John Carpenter put in a few extra scenes in *Halloween 2*. Such as him carving "sister" in the wall of his room at Smiths Grove…

I think it's totally fascinating. I don't think it demystifies the character. First of all, nobody knows what I did. (laughs) People say I don't want all that explained. Who ever said I was explaining anything? The funniest thing about the internt is one person will say, "I heard this…" and then that sends a hundred other people off on a tangents about why that would be a bad idea. Well, that's not true to begin with, so I don't know why they're all getting bent out of shape.

I mean, the thing with Michael Myers, I didn't want to explain anything. Because that is sort of the great thing about him. I wanted to get glimpses of his life, but everything that would make him that person is completely unexplainable. You can't go, "Oh this happened, so he's like that." No, the whole point was I wanted to set him in a more lower-class situation because it doesn't matter if he grew up in a rich family or a poor family, he's still fucking psycho! The environment doesn't matter. Friends don't matter, because he's a fucking psychopath and I just found that interesting. Good boy from nice house goes bad, it just didn't interest me to do the same stuff that had been done before. Anyway, that stuff people have created. In the first *Halloween* movie, all we know is that through the POV of a clown mask, a kid goes in and kills his sister. He walks outside, two people drive up, one guy pulls off the mask and says, "Michael?" That's all we know! Maybe they're the next-door neighbors? Maybe he was beaten by his father? We don't know anything! Anything from that movie is pure speculation put on by the fans. I mean, we don't know anything. It was my job to fill in the blanks as I saw fit.

Retelling the story to satisfy both purists and fans who wanted more, and your own vision.

Yeah, and what I thought was fascinating, or what's fascinating to me, is we get to see Dr. Loomis in the original after the shit's hit the fan. He's worked with this young boy, he's failed, and now all he wants to do is keep him locked up. Well, I thought, how great it would be to see Dr. Loomis while he's still optimistic about Michael Myers. And slowly he realizes this is hopeless. That's what I thought was great. Donald Pleasence would hint at these things, but we never got to see them.

I know, and I always wanted to see that stuff.

A crazy guy in a nightgown jumps out into the rain and drives the car away. That's all we got. The other thing that drives me crazy, I'm always comparing and contrasting the films, but I fucking love John Carpenter's film. But the problem is when I compare and contrast, people think I'm insulting the movie. No, I'm not. I'm just telling you how mine's different.

Has he, John Carpenter, seen the final product yet?

No, as of now, no one's seen the final product except me. Well, and the editor.

What was the dialogue like with Carpenter when you started working on *Halloween*?

Oh, it was pretty simple. I called him the day before the news was breaking, because I knew the next day it was going to be in Variety or something. I had known John for about ten years, so I called him up, "Hey, just wanted to tell you I'm doing this *Halloween* remake". And he said, "Hey, great! That's cool. Go for it. Anything else?" (laughs) He's a mellow dude. He was just like "Cool!"

The music in *Halloween* is almost as iconic as Michael Myers himself. What were you looking for from Tyler Bates' new score?

Tyler was in the same boat as me essentially. Because the music is just as iconic as anything else. And we weren't really sure, because as I was shooting, he didn't really start the music. He kind of dabbled with it, but he didn't start until late in the process, because we weren't even sure if the John Carpenter themes would work. You know, because they're so familiar and they're so associated with the movies you've already seen. I don't know. I thought maybe when you're watching this movie, they'll seem out of place. Who knows? I mean, we eventually did use all of them. All the classic stuff. He went back and rescored them but played them pretty straight. We didn't want to make it big and bombastic and rocking and techno-ey or any horseshit like that. We did it on purpose so it kind of sounded old. If anything had a weird synth thing, we'd use some old junk. We wanted it to sound authentic. And when he composed new music, it was the same thing. We wanted to make it sound like maybe there was a piece of score we never heard from back then. The score is pretty cool.

How'd you decide on the songs? And how integral to the film are they?

Well, the songs that I picked that I used, they don't play as score. It's not like *Devil's Rejects* where "Freebird" plays as a score element. The songs are all pretty much background things on the radio and things like that. What I like about putting songs like that in the movie is it just grounds the world in reality. And also, what was nice is that there's almost no sound in Smiths Grove Sanitarium. It's so sterile. And when Michael gets out, the first place he goes to is this huge truck wash where they wash eighteen wheelers and that's when he has his altercation with Ken Foree's character. The guys are washing the trucks and blasting music. And it was just like, from the world he had been trapped in for fifteen years, he steps outside and just explodes in this world of sound. It was just a way to contrast the isolation that he'd been living in for all those years.

Can you talk a little bit about the recent reshoots?

Basically, that's been blown out of proportion. Every movie on the planet Earth has additional shooting. Sometimes you hear about it, sometimes you go back and shoot for two days. Sometimes people go back and shoot for eight weeks. Reshoot half the movie. We shot for about six days. We weren't done with the movie.

We screened a rough cut in New York and it did really well, and Bob Weinstein came up to me after the movie and said, "Rob, the movie scored great. I really believe in this film. If there's any stuff that you felt you didn't get the first time, or that you feel you want to go back to get to add into the movie, I will give you the money to go back and do that." And that was it. He never told me what to shoot. He never even suggested anything. He just said, "If there's anything that you feel you can do to make this movie better, I will support you in that." And truthfully, there were things. Making a movie is like a crazy jigsaw puzzle. And it's not until it's done that you get to see it and say, "Shit. I wish I had that piece. And that piece there."

For *The Devil's Rejects*, I didn't have that opportunity to go back and do that, but luckily on here, I did, so I took it. One thing I wanted to do was restructure the timeline of the movie. So, I actually went back and reshot some scenes that were played in the daytime, and I reshot them at nighttime. Different things that I had to restructure. There were a couple of new things, certain characters to me felt like they didn't resolve themselves. One of them in particular was Danny Trejo's character. And that was it.

What an amazing thing as a horror fan, as a horror aficionado to take a crack at remaking one of the greatest horror films ever made…

Oh, it's totally surreal. Totally surreal. I've had a bunch of surreal moments in my life like that. One of them was about a year ago when I was on stage playing *God Of Thunder* with Ace Frehley. I was thinking, "This is so weird! I was like this goofy kid that worshiped Kiss in the 70's and I'm on stage doing this song." Ace Frehley's on stage with me doing this song, and the other Kiss guys are standing off stage and I'm thinking, "This is fucking weird! This is like some bizarre dream." *Halloween* was the same thing. You're on set… shooting *Halloween*. And I'm in Pasadena, shooting a lot of it on the same streets that Carpenter shot on. This seemed like I had a weird *Halloween* dream. I never lose that feeling of how insanely cool it is.

People are touchy about *Halloween*. But what can you say to sway fans of yours that this is OK. Because remakes have a long tradition in horror. You're a horror fan, so you know that. The Universal monster movies were remade by Hammer in the 50's. And *The Fly* was remade in the 80's. There's good stuff there…

I think so. To me, remakes are sort of about passion and intent. I mean, obviously. When someone goes, "Who do you like better as Dracula? Lugosi or Christopher Lee?" I was always like, "Fuck, man. I love them both. They're both fucking awesome." You know, but you can tell when something is quickly remade for a buck. This was not that case. I really believed in this. And being such a big fan of the original, and like many people, just watching Michael Myers degenerate through seven sequels until you're like, "What? That's what it's come down to?" I really wanted to take that character and when he comes on screen have people go, "Wow. Michael Myers never looked so fucking bad ass! In thirty fucking years." It really mattered to me. I really wanted it to be great. I took it totally seriously. People thought I was only doing it for money. No. I could've gone on tour and made ten times the money I made making this movie. It wasn't about money. It was just about really wanting to do it, and I think that's when movies work. I mean, you can tell! You can tell.

You love these movies. I think it's the first time in a long time that a remake has been in the hands of someone who loves these movies!

The thing with remakes is, no matter how good the remake is, nothing… nothing can make you love something more than the original because it's something special to you. I mean, same for me. No matter how great the remake of *Dawn of the Dead* was, it's never going to be as special to me as the experience of seeing the original *Dawn of the Dead* in a packed theater at midnight while I was in high school. That was a mind-blowing experience. And that's no insult to the movie, it's just there's so much emotional baggage attached to these films for some people. And I totally get it. But that doesn't mean that it shouldn't be done. If that was the case, *Nosferatu* would be our only version of *Dracula* that we would have seen for the rest of our lives. There's nothing wrong with doing it, you just have to do it with the right intent and not just to make a quick buck. Which obviously is what goes on a lot. We don't have to bullshit each other. Even if a hundred remakes are bad… you still have to always… I always liked the guys with the hope… "Well, maybe this is the one that fucking everyone's happy about." I don't care about everyone else's movies. I tried to make this awesome.

A reboot of the series was really the only way to go and to be put in the hands of someone who cares about it like yourself was a great move.

I would never have done a *Halloween Part 9*. *Part 9* probably would've went direct to video anyway. What are you going to do? I felt like by *Part 8* it was *Abbott and Costello Meet Frankenstein*. A once great character had become a punch line for someone. Abbott and Costello make a joke about Frankenstein or Dracula. That's what Michael Myers felt like to me in *Part 8*. Then Hammer does it with Christopher Lee and Peter Cushing and you're like, "Fuck yeah, man." (laughs) Those are things that made me think this is totally the way to go.

Were you a fan at all of the whole "Thorn" story line?

I couldn't give a shit about that. No. They ran out of things to do. It was almost, well let's shoot him into space. Let's have him fight someone else. (laughs) It becomes ridiculous after a while! It happens with everything. Ok, *Jaws*. I love it.

Jaws 2. I can deal with it. *Jaws 3*. *Jaws …4*? What's happening here? (laughs)

Have you made your peace with Michael Myers, or would you take it further when this movie does well? Or would you leave it the way Carpenter did?

I'm done with it. No matter what this movie does. If this movie was the biggest movie of all time, I still wouldn't come back. Because I wanted to make a single great film and that's all I was concerned with. And the way the horror genre works, it doesn't matter what I did, they would find a way to make *Part 2*. Ya know? If we exploded Michael Myers into a million pieces, for *Part 2* he would regenerate himself maybe. He'd be living in an underground laboratory as a secret government project, and they would reassemble him! (laughs) The thing I didn't want to do. I didn't care about restarting a franchise, because that's how you get into trouble. That's how you make crap. You just really have to be concerned with making a great film for everybody, because really that's all anyone really cares about. You don't want it to end and set it up for *Part 2*. That's a cheat.

Well, let's hope there's not too many sequels and that this can stand on its own.

They're not even talking about it. That's what I liked about Bob Weinstein. He wanted to reinvent it and do something different and wasn't ever talking about firing up a franchise. He was always focused on making one solid movie. Because already by now, they'd be planning *Part 2*, if they were thinking that. And they're not. That's what I like about this. The intentions all around were really in the right place.

Is this theatrical version going to be your final version? Will there be a double disc DVD with an alternate version? Director's cut or something?

You know, what was really funny about this movie is that we did not get into any trouble with the MPAA. We got an R rating super easy. And I was totally baffled by it. And I don't know if it's because there's been such an onslaught of harsh films, that this didn't seem so harsh. I have a feeling it's because, I actually think we got away with more because it was Michael Myers, and it was like… a monster. As opposed to a human hurting another human. You can blow a zombie's head off, but if you blow off a normal guy's head off, it's a problem. They make these weird rules. So, I think we got away with a lot because they thought of Michael Myers as "Oh, well he's like a monster." You know?

JOEL DAVID MOORE

Interviewed by Rob Galluzzo (9/07)

Who better to play the unlikely hero in a horror film than funny man Joel David Moore?! He's appeared in several comedies throughout the years including *Dodgeball* and *Grandma's Boy*. He'll next appear in James Cameron's *Avatar*. But on September 7th, he'll go up against Victor Crowley in Adam Green's *Hatchet*. We spoke to Joel about working on *Hatchet*, as well as re-teaming with Adam on *Spiral*.

Do you remember your earliest recollections of the horror genre? What films had an impact and scared you first?

Yeah, I think back to the *Friday the 13th's*. Those were the ones that were out growing up. I also have a very vague memory of seeing *Halloween*. I'd watched part of it recently though and I thought, "I don't remember any of this!" (laughs) But I remember being scared shitless of Michael Myers and the idea that someone can just walk into my house and follow me. While I'm trying to run as fast as I can, he's still always three steps behind me the whole time. I think that's where our dreams come from. The whole trying to run away from someone, and you can't run? I'm positive it comes from when we were eleven years old, watching these movies. (laughs) They'd run and run and run, and then it'd cut to Jason walking. And they'd run and he'd still be right behind them, or in front of us at some point, it's just so ridiculous. Makes no sense!

You're saying those films are responsible for a whole generation of common nightmares between us!

Yeah! I don't think there were nightmares like that about not being able to run away years before all those movies. Before that, nightmares probably involved not being able to eat or depression or something.

(laughs) So is it safe to say that you're a horror fan though?

Yeah, I am. I am. I enjoy horror movies a lot and some of the movies in my top twenty favorite movies are horror films. So, I am a fan of the genre and I have been. I knew I wanted to do a horror movie and, in the search for one, I feel that I found one that had its own notch in the pole. *Hatchet* was something that was different. It was funny, but also a throw-back to these old 80's "slasher" films that I really enjoyed. I appreciate from the very beginning how Adam Green would say, "We're going to do this real! It's going to be just like that old shit! We're not using CGI. All the kills will be real! We'll use prosthetics! The monster's going to be Kane Hodder, man! He was Jason!" Just his passion and energy towards filmmaking in general, but also his wisdom in trying to find the niche for this genre and for bringing back old-school American horror interested me. The buzz has revolved around that now.

How did you get involved in *Hatchet*? Did you know Adam Green beforehand or did you just come in to audition for the part of Ben?

I didn't know Adam. I just was up for the role, and I really wanted to do a horror movie. The role was sort of for a guy like… umm… like a Chad Michael Murray type. That's the best way to describe it. (laughs) That's nothing against Chad. He's a beautiful man and.. I'm not so… (laughs) Maybe we'll have drinks one day as one beautiful man to one ugly man. But it was sort of written for that kind of a guy. The good looking jock. But I went in for it and Adam saw me and probably thought, "Wait, this guy should be funny. And should maybe be an underdog" of sorts. Not necessarily great with the ladies. There's a different type of energy involved if the guy's a good looking, macho guy trying to get the girl. That is the type of guy that gets the girl. I'm not the type of guy that gets the girl.

182

Hey, you have your fans! Once you were cast as Ben, how much did you add to the part? Being that you weren't the initial "type" for it. Was there room to improvise?

Yeah, there was a lot more awkwardness in my version of Ben, I think. And it was really cool because they put a cast of comedians around me. So, I had Deon Richmond, who steals the movie. Mercedes McNab and Joleigh Fioreavanti. And then of course, your classic actors like Richard Riehle and Patrika Bardbo and Joel Murray, who are all so funny. Of course, the tour guide was played by Parry Shen; he did all those magic tricks and weird stuff like that we had never seen before. The first time we saw them was right on set that day. It was crazy to watch him do that stuff! We didn't know that any of that was going to be in that character, so it was fun to actually respond to all of the comedy going on as it was going on.

Well, you are surrounded by a cast of very, very lovely ladies. Can you talk a little bit about working with the ladies of _Hatchet_?

Ummm. You want to know the behind-the-scenes love-shit, don't ya, man?

No, I just want an excuse to say they're all hot, just in case they're reading this. (laughs)

They are all hot. Not only are they beautiful, they're fantastic actors. Tamara Feldman, who plays the lead Marybeth and my love interest in the movie is just perfect for this part. She's very innocent, yet she's on a journey and she has to "man-up" and really get into the fight and try to find her brother and her dad, although she knows something is going on and something is wrong. She still plays it in such an innocent, vulnerable way, and still deals with me hitting on her the whole time even though we're being chased by a monster. On and off set!

One of my favorite stories that Adam Green always tells is one night when Robert Englund was talking to Kane Hodder about his Victor Crowley make-up and Adam was just standing in between them thinking, "Holy shit. I'm in between Freddy and Jason on my own movie!" You grew up on a lot of the films those guys did, what was it like to work with them?

Well, it was part of what gave me security in climbing into the project, because I knew he had talked to Tony Todd, and I knew that Robert Englund was getting signed on. And of course, Kane was already attached as Victor Crowley, so bringing the horror trifecta of horror icons to the movie was a good business move, and I knew it was going to draw

in a new audience, as well as an audience that has wanted something like this for a while. There was something that was really special about that, and just being able to work with these guys, or even do Q and A's with these guys is crazy. Because I'm a nobody in that world! You've got people in the audience asking about specific, tiny little scenes from movies twenty years ago and I just sit and listen.

Those guys are rock stars at the conventions!

Oh totally. And they make a lot of money doing them to be honest! I want to be a horror icon. (laughs)

Kane Hodder is notorious for getting very into his roles. How intimidating was he when he was Victor Crowley?

He was… That guy is a scary dude. (laughs) I'm a tall guy. I'm not afraid! I'm not afraid of dudes. But that guy is 200 and some odd pounds of scary. (laughs) But it was great because, when he was in his prosthetics, he'd hide it. No one could see him as Victor Crowley, so there was this great advantage that he had on the rest of the cast to get them real scared. Him and Adam talked about this from the very beginning. Kane said he didn't want anyone seeing him as Victor Crowley. He was also the stunt-coordinator, so the guy basically does everything.

When he coordinated, he'd put on a huge trench coat and hoodie on to cover himself up completely. He'd coordinate the stunt, then walk behind a tree to take all his stuff off and come out and scare the shit out of everybody. It was fun to see the difference in what he was having to do. Playing the professional guy, making sure everything was safe and taking all the precautions, and then literally chasing us to our deaths. Throwing hatchets and ripping people in half. (laughs)

There's a bit of a story that ties into the T-shirt that your character Ben wears in _Hatchet_, which will tie into the premiere in Boston on the 4th. Can you tell us the significance of Ben's shirt?

Yeah, it's the shirt for Newbury Comics which is this place in Boston, and Adam was a fan of theirs and he knows the guys that work there. And told them, "Look, I want you in this movie in some way. I want to represent Boston." He told them they'd be in there somewhere, but little did they know that they're actually basically in every frame of the movie. (laughs) Implanted on my T-shirt. It's ironic too, because this weird looking smiley face is represented in every shot while people are headed towards their bloody deaths.

Speaking of those bloody deaths, this is pretty old-school hardcore stuff! Anytime Adam shows clips at a convention, it always gets a standing ovation. How much of a thrill was it to be there to see it get executed on set, but then seeing it on the big screen later with an audience and hearing their reactions to seeing practical FX in a horror movie again?

I really think this is what drove the movie to have a theatrical release. It was the audience, it was the people that came to Tribeca, it was the people that supported the screenings Adam had. They've done a number of festivals and people from all around the world have come out to support. They were all very excited and obviously fulfilled, because everybody who sees the movie tells a friend, "You have to go see this!" The buzz behind it is crazy for a shoe-string budget independent movie. And I think that's ultimately what's going to drive people to the theaters and be able to give *Hatchet* the success that it needs to go down in history as trying to be an honest throw-back to a lost genre. I guess it's making its way back, but we're the front runners on that.

There's an infamous *Hatchet* story involving you and vomit. Can you elaborate? And explain how dedicated you were to Adam Green and *Hatchet*?

First of all, it's still acting, even though it's comedy and horror, and I read the script and said, "Are we doing this throw-up moment? Am I actually vomiting?" And he said, "Yeah, yeah, yeah, it's going to be cool. We'll get you some stuff to spit out." And I said, "Nah, fuck that. I don't want anything. I actually want to vomit." So, we had made the decision before we even started shooting that I was going to do it. So, when the time came, granted everything is so frantic and there's so little hours to shoot at night. Adam said, "Hey, it's totally cool if you want to fake it." And I said, "No way!" I'm not going to go down as that guy that fakes throwing up in this kind of a movie.

When everything's supposed to be real and there's no CG or anything, I'm doing it. So, I sat and I literally drank six or seven bottles of water, which doesn't seem like a lot, but when you're doing that within a ten minute span, it's both the grossest and hardest thing to do. I greased the pipe with a pinky, he called action, and I ran around that corner and just… projectile vomited! So, then after that, I told him "Ok, we got the master. Let's get a close-up."

Now that was the hard one. Because when you get everything out of your system, you're kind of done. Your system is like, "Ok we got it! It's done!" But I wanted it to look good! I wanted Ben actually throwing up and to see

the way Tamara reacts to it. Adam was, of course, stoked but thinking, "Are you serious? You want to do that again?" It was a process to get me there. I drank more water. My stomach is already turned from throwing up. I got back into it and was having a little trouble the second time around. I was greasing it, throwing the pinky back there, it didn't work. And uh… (laughs) the special FX guys came over and said, "Ok, we're going to hand you something. And I guarantee this will make you throw up." They came back a few minutes later and put something in front of me. And literally, I looked at it, smelled it, and all I had to do was let it touch my lips and and I was ready! They called action, and I projectile vomited! Literally, so hard and so far that it hit the cameraman's feet. It was all over his legs, and this particular cameraman, BJ McDonnell always wore shorts, even though it was freezing cold in the middle of the night. He was always hot because he'd always have to carry this 100-pound rig. So, it just drenched his legs. It was disgusting! (laughs)

Any idea what they put in that concoction for you?!

The special FX guys came up to me after and told me it was half OJ and half clam-chowder. But the FX guy said, "It didn't really matter what it was, because once I told you that whatever you were about to put in your mouth was going to make you throw up, I knew that was going to push you over." When he started to bring it over, I was already gagging.

Wow. Unbelievable.

Totally disgusting. Whenever you're out for the night, you should try half-OJ, half-clam chowder and see how it feels.

I'll consider it. (laughs) Next time I'm out with Adam Green perhaps.

I'll make up a name for it. Put a little vodka in there and you can sell it as a drink. "*Hatchet* on the beach?"

So, you went on to work with Adam Green again shortly after *Hatchet* on *Spiral*. What was it about your relationship with Adam that made you want to work with him again?

I think it was the collaboration. Adam takes charge and is so structured in everything that he's doing. He does his homework. He's so passionate, but he also involves other people in that passion, and he allows people to create and have their own life and tell their own story. People are able to throw in their own ideas with him. We had talked about working together again anyways. I had written a short story that me and my producing partner Jeremy Boreing wrote the feature script to. He took that and actually got it funded. So, I talked to Adam and said, "Look, do you want to co-direct this with me?" I co-wrote it, co-directed, produced it and played the lead, so there was a lot that I had in front of me. And I knew that Adam and I were a great collaboration in creativity. So, I asked him to be a part of it. We brought on him and Cory Neal, who produced it. We were walking into another very hard shoot, but it was a good experience because it's such a beautiful film and we're very proud of it. It's 180 degrees from anything I've ever done before. I've done predominantly comedies all the way up until this. This is about a neurotic, out of touch painter who becomes infatuated with his subjects and who may or may not kill them. That's for the audience to go figure out. It's very Hitchcock-ian and character driven and that's what we set out to do. And I believe we accomplished that.

Is it true that you did a short between *Hatchet* and *Spiral*?

I did, yeah. It's sort of what made me more confident in creating *Spiral*. I did a film that my co-writer Jeremy wrote. It was called *Miles From Home*. I played the lead and directed it. It got accepted into South By Southwest. So,

from the success of that, we were able to go right into *Spiral*. And we knew we were capable in our filmmaking abilities to take on a bigger project. We didn't go from a short film to a $20 million dollar movie. We went to a very small, art house suspense movie. We weren't getting in over our heads, but I think people can see from the outcome of *Spiral* that it's a beautiful film and we've very happy with the way that it came out. Hopefully many more will come from these crazy brains of ours.

I hope so, man. Last question, *Hatchet* opens September 7th, 2007. What do you hope audiences get out of it when they go to see it in theaters?

I hope that audiences get out of it what the audiences that have seen it so far have gotten out of it, which is just a fun, exhilarating ride following these characters and going through some craziness. This is a callback to what people traditionally like about horror and the genre, which has been lost in many ways over the past few years. This really brings everything back around and calls attention to what has been lacking in horror. I hope this is the start of something new and something fresh. Oh, and it's very funny.

PAUL EHLERS

Interviewed by Mike Cucinotta, Rob Galluzzo, and Jason Alvino (9/07)

Here on *Icons*, we're huge fans of obscure cult classics! So, it came as a pleasant surprise to us when we learned that Paul Ehlers, the actor who portrayed "Madman Marz" in the 80's slasher gem *Madman* lived right here in New York! We caught up with the man behind the make-up who scared the pants off of us as youngsters! Check out our conversation with Paul about all things *Madman*. Jason even gets to debate with him the true meaning of the infamous "refrigerator" scene! Read on!

(*This interview is dedicated to* Madman *director Joe Giannone who passed away unexpectedly on December 10th, 2006.*)

Rob: What are your earliest recollections of the horror genre? What was your first exposure to horror films?

God's honest truth, the boogeymen in *March of the Wooden Soldiers*. When I was really little, man, that was freaky! Robert Wise's *The Haunting* was another one. I haven't seen anything since that has evoked that feeling as that movie did. I'd like to think it's more for the mastery of what he did and how he set it up, rather than the fact that I was just younger. I know that movie still works. *The Haunting* was a little later, but when I was really young, I loved a lot of TV stuff. I loved *Thriller*, Boris Karloff would sometimes host that and it's where I first heard some of Jerry Goldsmith's music. Of course, *The Twilight Zone* too.

Rob: When did you start an interest in film?

When I was making Super 8 movies with my best friend Kenny; we were into espionage, and we'd watch every spy show. None of them really hold up that well anymore. But back then, when you're impressionable and you're a kid, you say, "Ok, I'm going to go into espionage like James Bond." We'd do spy movies. We'd go to Kennedy airport wearing suits and bringing plastic guns; here we are about thirteen or fourteen years old (laughs). We'd shoot scenes there. Looking back at that, we could never get away with that now! My friend Larry at the time, his Super 8 movies were all horror because he was a Hammer and Universal monster fanatic. I used to occasionally be in his films too, I remember. He did things like… *I Eat Your Guts*. (laughs)

But yeah, film was an intricate part of my childhood, as well as drawing. I used to draw my own comics and my own monsters. When I got involved in *Madman*, I did some original drawings for Marz, what he could look like with the eye gone and the nose gone, and it was all really cool. We had a guy, I think named Rich Alonso, who did the mask for Marz and he did a casting of my head. I had this beard forever at the time, and I didn't remember what I looked like without it until this guy shaved me to do a head cast. I remember at the first read-through, I was telling everyone, "This isn't what I really look like! I usually have a beard and I look a lot different!" When they did the scene where the townspeople dragged me out, they put a beard on me. I made sure the cast saw me with it so I could say, "See? This is what I really look like! Don't I look so much better?" (laughs)

The famous stories regarding the face of Madman Marz, we're on the set and we get a package in and it's Marz's left hand. We get the hand, but only the left hand comes in. That's lovely, but where's the rest? We only had the left hand, but we had to shoot. So, I would do the best acting that I could do with the one hand. Everywhere where that hand is coming around trees is because that's all we had!

The famous foot thing too. I was barefoot and they took a shot of me walking towards the camera and I heard the crew laughing behind the monitor, which of course is never a good sign. The problem was I have nine and a half inch feet. I've got little feet. So, Madman had these little graceful feet marching along, so we had to order feet. They were funky feet, they looked like flippers. They were fused, which is ok if he's meant to be inbred. You see them in a few shots, but if you look at them, they're pretty disgusting. God rest him, my best friend Joe Giannone, the director of *Madman* who passed away back in December (2006). We were very saddened and surprised to lose him.

Jason: How long and difficult was it to shoot *Madman*?

We were way over-schedule. They originally planned to shoot for a month, then it became two months. Then it became December, and we started in October?

Jason: Did you have breaks?

It was pretty much constant. We were there on the location in Fish Cove, which they scouted out and found; it was a conference center with great cabins, and an old-style kitchen. We filmed that whole movie at night, so it's really night in all those shots. I'd get up around 4-4:30pm as it was getting dark, I'd go in for make-up. A couple of hours in there, they'd hot glue the feet on me. We filmed at night, over and over again, and we'd break at midnight for lunch, which was always freaky.

Jason: Going back, how'd the movie come about and how'd you get involved in it?

I knew Gary Sales, who was the producer on it. Joey Giannone, the writer and director, and Gary had gone to school together at Richmond College. I was visiting a friend of mine, and I was out a lot that weekend and Joey was there, busily writing the script to *Madman*. He was so secretive about it. He wouldn't talk about it a lot, but we did talk about horror films a lot. This was a couple of years before we made it. These guys wanted to make real serious films.

They figured let's make the horror film first and make the money, and then do the serious films. So, he asked me what I thought worked in a horror film. He knew I was an illustrator and a designer, so he said maybe when they were getting ready to do the film, I could do the one-sheet poster for them, which I said I'd love to do. He then kind of went off, and they did what they did, and I remember they got an office on 7th Avenue in the city, and back then it was called The Legend Lives company. Originally that was going to be part of the title, but at the time Frank Sinatra was doing a tour, which I believe was called *Frank Sinatra: The Legend Lives*, so we couldn't use that. I heard something was going on with this other movie shooting at the same time called *The Burning*.

Rob: The story with *The Burning* was that it was based on the same thing that inspired *Madman*?

The filmmakers didn't know each other, it just so happened that they were both scripts about the "Cropsey maniac." The freaky thing that nobody knows about; when my son was in elementary school back when we were living in Queens, he had a friend who's dad played the Cropsey maniac in *The Burning*, Lou David. It was really odd picking up our kids from school and it's like, "Hey, there's Cropsey!" and "Hey, that guy played Madman Marz!" (laughs) "Do you know who these guys are?" (laughs) All I know is there were a lot of changes made on *Madman* early on.

Rob: So, how'd you get cast as Madman Marz?

The story I tell everyone is that they were still trying to find the right guy to play Marz. They'd seen a huge guy, but he didn't work because he couldn't move well. I had done a lot of martial arts work and made swords and knives and axes. I remember I was talking to Gary and Joey; I know they didn't have a guy to play the part and they asked me how I saw him and I started discussing how I saw Marz and I was discussing how he would move and how he would walk. They look at each other and ask, "What are you doing for the next few months?" And I said, "Get out of here! You want me to play this?!" Here we go, fan-boy time. Yes, I went to film school. Yes, I was working as an artist. But here was a horror movie, man. And they wanted me to be the monster! It was the coolest thing ever. I went out of my mind with excitement.

Mike: Can you tell us about working with Alexis Dubin aka Gaylen Ross?

It's funny. When we had the first meeting with the actors, we were all sitting down having dinner. And I was sitting with Alexis Gaylen. You know Alexis Gaylen? (laughs) She was with those dead guys in Romero's movie. (laughs) (*Editor's note: Gaylen Ross did* Madman *under the name Alexis Dubin for unknown reasons.*) And I remember I was talking to her about something really serious, trying to be sexy without my beard. And I'm eating French onion soup with cheese, and as I'm talking to her, the cheese remains in my mouth, but three-quarters of it goes down my throat. And she's going on about being so excited to working on the film, and I'm trying my best not to choke to death. That was a great start. A nice weird, embarrassing moment right off the bat.

Mike: Was she really referred to as Alexis on the set?

Yes, she was Alexis Dubin. I never quite understood that.

Mike: *Dawn of the Dead* was big at the time, no?

It was!

Rob: But you knew obviously that it was Gaylen Ross from *Dawn of the Dead* though, right?

Yeah, everyone knew. But we were all cool about it. We figured there must've been a reason for it. She was great and always nice. I never had trouble with her, ever. She was very kind, and I have a cute card that she gave me for my birthday on Halloween which she signed as Alexis.

Jason: When you became involved in the project, was it was already financed?

It was financed. Everyone was pretty much on a salary by the week. Locations were all picked out. It was just about ready to go when I got involved. We all appeared in Fish Cove, which is kind of in the Hamptons. When you're heading out to Southampton, there's a cut-over that says North Sea and its inside that part of the island. The place was terrific. The woods were not huge, but they certainly made it look that way and we were able to get a lot of great stuff out there.

Madman's house was in East Quogue. We didn't have to dress that house at all! I don't think they added very much to it at all. Except the basement was actually the basement to the Fish Cove house. That they did dress. I remember we had this rat scene with Marz in the basement and I was talking to the guys about rounding up some brown or gray rats. So, they come in with white rats instead and I ask, "What, did Marz work in a lab?!" (laughs)

"This isn't working guys!" We thought, "What should we do?" So, we threw some dirt on them, but dirty white rats didn't look right either. I came up with a safe solution. We kind of painted them gray. So, they became this gray/white rat thing, which was ok. I light this candle and the rat comes over and sticks his face right in the fire. That really happened. (laughs) We were sick people. I still am a reasonably sick person. (laughs) I had a lot of fun with the film. We had a lot of kids coming around. What a camp! Twenty-seven counselors, three kids! (laughs) These were very gifted children, of course. Maybe these kids could levitate people or something?

Rob: You were initially scheduled to shoot for a month, but then the shoot lasted a few months. Overall, what was the shooting experience like? Since it was an independent production, were there any production snags? Or was it fairly smooth?

Umm, the hand thing was just one thing. A few things would occasionally go wrong. We didn't have a lot of stunt people, so since I used to do martial arts, I used to come real close to people's heads with the axe and the actors didn't know that. They thought maybe it was a filed axe. Oh, and the hot tub! There were probably these weird communicable diseases floating in that hot tub. I'm sure if you turned off the lights, the water would glow. (laughs) The camp was kind of in off season, so they weren't cleaning it.

Jason: Was there more stuff shot for *Madman* that we didn't see?

Yes, there was more shot. I would be on set but not constantly, but I know that Joey wanted to shoot the "madman at home" sequence. There's a scene I know he shot where he does this wonderful Michael Myers-style sit up, turns to the camera. Then there's a scene where he's got this box, and he's playing with dolls and stuff. It's the only time where Joey said talk but make it unintelligible. So, I was holding the dolls and growling something bizarre. It was really freaky, but you know what? It slowed down the pacing. It's probably a good thing it didn't get into the film, but it exists somewhere. I don't know where, but I would love to see it!

Jason: I have to talk about the refrigerator scene. How the hell did that come about?

I don't know! But we all kind of laughed at the time and Joey said…

Jason: Was he serious about it at the time, though? Was he like, "*No, really. Hide in the fridge*". (laughs)

She was little! So…

Jason: But you were right behind her! You saw her go into the refrigerator. She threw the food out while you were right around the corner!

But I went to the sink and took a drink. You didn't see that. (laughs)

Jason: I thought it was brilliant, but because of the mentality of the scene. Ok. You see her go into the fridge. You're Madman Marz. You've seen people in desperate situations do desperate things. Hide in bathrooms, hide in closets, hide under beds. And all these things are acceptable. But… you witness this poor woman hide in a refrigerator. So, maybe your brain just shuts down for a minute. You couldn't believe what you were seeing!

(laughs) And thought, "You know what? I'm going to go back outside, pretend this never happened and just wait for her. Because I know she's going to come outside." And you literally stood in the door frame of the cabin and waited for her to get out of the fridge. And then killed her!

You know what? I like that. I like that explanation. (laughs)

Jason: It seemed embarrassing for both of you!

I think Marz was smarter than anyone assumed. She went in the fridge and as you know…

Jason: She didn't just go in the fridge! She removed the food from the fridge and threw it over her shoulder, and you were there! Right around the corner. You weren't even running! You were taking your time! Because you knew!

Because I said to myself, "Where is she? No one would go in the refrigerator!" (laughs)

Jason: You heard her screaming! You knew it. You had to have known!

You have to understand why! When you throw out a refrigerator, you have to remove the door from the refrigerator, because children will go inside it, close it, and be locked in and smothered. I figured this stupid bitch went into the refrigerator and closed the door! I don't even have to dirty my ax!

Jason: I thought about that. But it's obvious that there was no latch. I like my idea of your mindset. That you just couldn't believe what you were seeing. You are a professional madman. You've seen everything! When you go hang out with the other madmen later, you'll say, "You'll never believe what happened to me today. A woman hid… in a refrigerator!" (laughs) Even for things that are funny, like the refrigerator scene or the hot tub scene, I think the opening for *Madman* is absolutely brilliant for a horror film. It's the campfire, it captures the essence of the story it's based on. The other brilliant thing is the car hood beheading. That was a smart kill.

Yeah, I know Joey was trying to think of unique ways to do the kills and make it more suspenseful.

Jason: How was that set up? The beheading scene?

They built this engine around her head, it's wonderful. And they built this prosthetic neck. I love when they start the car, and you hear the sounds. It's fabulous.

Jason: And I love the fact that Richie, that SOB that started the whole problem, he lives! He gets away!

I know. To be tortured with it for the rest of his life. What would happen to a kid like that who sees all those things?

Jason: When you guys were making the film, obviously there were a few slasher films that came before. At the time, there were tons of horror movies being released in the early 80's. Was there an anticipation for *Madman*? Or a thought that this was going to make money and do well?

Everyone hopes that, but you just never know. I remember at the time, we went into the office with whatever reports were coming in from *Variety* and it was all very exciting. But you just don't know.

Jason: How soon after wrapping was *Madman* released?

It looks like we were the first trailer shown on TV in January of 1982. I remember we were at a New Years party. Someone said, "It's *Madman*, it's the trailer!" We all got very excited.

Rob: When did you shoot it? 1980?

Let's see, we shot it in 1980, started in October, wrapped in December of '80. All through '81, they were working on the movie. Sometimes it's written that it came out in '81, but I'm pretty sure it came out in January of 82.

Jason: When I was younger, my brother and I were too young to watch horror films, but we were obsessed with them. We would watch trailers on TV, get completely freaked out and we'd dare each other to say "Madman Marz" at night! (laughs)

That's so cool.

Jason: The funny thing is I used to watch the trailer for the movie, and then make up what I thought the movie was about based on the trailer, because I couldn't see it. So, I had my own story for what *Madman* was about. For years, it freaked me out.

That is wonderful. You don't really know if it's going to be good, you hope. I was excited about it and my friends were excited about it. We all went to the opening at the Rialto on Broadway in NYC. Everybody I knew was invited. I was with one group of people and I had lost a lot of weight since I did the film.

Jason: I like the fact that there was no explanation given as to why or how you do these things. At the end, in the basement, it's bodies of the people you killed and then it's your wife and kids. That's it! There are no other bodies down there! So, Richie pissed off Madman Marz so bad that he started to manifest himself again and kill more people because of Richie! Max has been telling this story this whole time! Why wouldn't Madman come out the first time he told the story? It's because of Richie!

I don't think I ever asked Joey why Richie lived!

Jason: It'd be one thing to say Madman in the woods, but to throw a rock and say, "come and get me," you're just asking for it!

Mike: Maybe this is a punishment for Richie. All these early "slasher" movies are in essence morality tales. Richie has to go on and live with this guilt.

Rob: What was the climate for horror films at the time *Madman* came out in theaters?

It was at that time we were sweating out ratings. We were very happy when we resolved that. That was a big deal at the time because of the audience we'd be getting. I remember they tested it at a few places. We had a test screening in Philadelphia, and I drove down with a good friend of mine named Larry. I remember it was playing at a multiple screen theater. I took pictures of everything, the marquee and the poster in the lobby. I sat in the front and turned around and started taking pictures of the audience.

The guys sitting behind me said, "Why are you taking pictures of the audience?" And I said, "I'll tell you when the movie is over." We're running the film; I take pictures of the credits including the "Introducing Paul Ehlers as Madman Marz." (laughs) The film ends, the credits roll, and the guys behind me stand up and like wise-asses say to me, "Alright, why were you taking all the pictures of the audience"? And I said, "Because I… am Madman Marz." The guy goes, "Oh, bullshit!" And they all walked out. (laughs)

Jason: How was the film received when it first came out? You didn't get any coverage in *Fangoria* at the time, right?

We didn't. I think they mentioned us with a small picture. I don't know why we didn't get more coverage. And the thing that I always think is unfair is that writers today group us in with all the *Friday the 13th* clones. And that's fine, but we were one of the very first to come out.

Mike: You were shooting it in 1980, so it couldn't have been that far behind when *Friday the 13th Part 1* and *2* came out.

Yeah! In fact, we almost beat them out, but we had slight money problems and couldn't get it out in time.

Jason: Didn't *The Burning* come out early too?

The Burning beat them out, but we were very early on in this, apparently. That's why I don't find it fair to see reviewers refer to it as a *Friday* knockoff. The film looks good, the film was shot well, it's lit well, it's edited well. I think all of that is there. For a low-budget, the effects work very well. I think a lot of it works on a lot of levels. And I think people may be a little too hard on it. But then there's you guys who look back on it with fond memories and put it in a different category.

Rob: For us, there were so many movies from that era, but I don't remember the killer's name in something like *My Bloody Valentine*. But I have fond memories of films that have an interesting back story. And once you hear the legend of Madman Marz, you never forget that! It's just so memorable!

Mike: When did you start to realize that this movie had a cult following and was starting to make a come-back? You did a convention appearance recently, and then there's the DVD with the commentary, and you just did another interview.

Several years back, Joey called me and told me it was coming to DVD, and I was surprised. Anchor Bay was doing a lot of re-issuing of this kind of stuff, and he said, "They actually want us to do a commentary for the DVD." Larry and I love stuff with commentary and learning about movies, so I thought it was nuts! I thought it was so cool. We met in the city; I hadn't seen the producer Gary Sales in years. So, it was him and Joey was there too and Tony Fish. I'm sorry that Joey's gone because he's never had the chance to sit down and talk about a lot of this. It's great that there's a lot of re-interest in the film, because when I heard there were fans, I couldn't believe it. You know, I've never been too computer savvy.

But I remember when the DVD came out, my friend Linda, a neighbor down the block who happens to be a librarian would print me out all the reviews from people all over the world and I just couldn't believe it. I kept sending them over to Joe. I sent him a stack of reviews and he really was fascinated by the fact that it had this impact.

There was thought of "Would we re-do it?" "Should we do a sequel?" There was a sequel written and I read the script to it back in the day. We were prepared. But I like that we have the one distinction in horror for not having a sequel. They were ready, however. The title may have been *Hunt The Madman* if I remember correctly. It had to do with a motorcycle gang and some nastiness. Think about that for a little bit! I say we're ripe for a remake. I'd love to see that.

Rob: I'd love to see it as a combination remake/sequel. A new film that could play as a sequel, but that could retell the story and be fresh as a remake to a new audience.

I think it'd have to stand on its own. I wouldn't want people to have to see the original to see a new one. You can keep it pure; you can keep it simple. It's something I've been thinking about a lot.

Rob: Any last words for our *Icons* audience about *Madman*?

I have fond feelings for the film, I always have. I think it's underrated. And I certainly think the time is right to bring Madman Marz back.

The *Icons of Fright* crew with Madman Marz himself!

ZELDA RUBENSTEIN

Interviewed by Mike Cucinotta (10/07)

Zelda Rubenstein is best known for her role as short-in-stature, strong-in-mind psychic Tangina Barrows from the *Poltergeist* series. As the original film celebrates it's twenty-fifth anniversary with a new remastered DVD, Zelda chatted with *Icons of Fright*, as well as several other horror publications, for a roundtable interview about the blockbuster 1982 film, as well as some of her work since.

Russell Trunk: This was your first spotlight movie. How was the role presented to you back then?

It was by audition; I was actually screen tested several times before I was entrusted with the role and I do not know who my competition was.

Tangina's declaration of, "This house is clean" has to be one of the most famously spoken-too-soon miscalculations in film history. All these years later, is it ever a burden to have your name associated with that infamous quote?

No, it's neither a burden nor a pleasure. People identify me that way and they also easily identify me on the street because of my short stature. So, I get picked out in many ways and it's in no way a burden.

Rick Bently: In this day and age, movies are made with a lot of high-tech computer effects. Can you talk about the special effects? Was it low-tech or cutting edge stuff?

The special effects were added after I had finished my role. I only worked six days and since this was my first real role, I kept my mouth shut and ears open and let things play out. I'm not a technology maven, I couldn't give a rat's behind about technology. It's a necessary evil...

Could you talk about Tobe Hooper as a director?

I don't think I can because, during the six days that I worked, Steven Spielberg primarily took over the helm. Like I said, I only worked six days and I don't know what happened the other days. It was a year before I saw these people again.

Can you talk about working with Steven for those six days?

Oh, he's magnificent. His image gets on the screen. What I found is that what he wants to show is what gets up there the way he wants it. There's no deviation from that. I don't know the man well, I love him dearly, he was very influential in handing me a career. I'd love to work with him again. I mean, as far as I'm concerned, he's the best film director I've had so far.

Gabriel Debeitra, *FEARnet*: Coming off of *Poltergeist*, what was it like working on the film *Anguish*?

I loved doing *Anguish*! *Anguish* was shot in Barcelona, Spain. Everything was done to make the Americans involved in it very comfortable, both on screen and in our time free. Bigas Luna is a magnificent director, and we all had a very good time. I'm still good friends with Michael Lerner, who was the male star in the film. It was just a wonderful experience. It was my first work experience abroad.

Would you be willing to go back for another *Poltergeist*?

Oh, of course, but you know we don't have the little girl. We lost Carol Anne (Heather O'Rourke) in 1988 and that's the end of the series.

Edward Hill: What was the impact after you got this role, and then you saw your performance a year later. How did you react? What was the impact?

Well, it was very traumatic when I saw the film at a screening for cast and crew, I practically had to be carried out of there because I realized it would change my life. It did cost me a fourteen year relationship that I was involved in because neither one of us knew particularly well how to handle this. But I feel, looking back, hindsight is great. It was a fabulous experience. I didn't know many people because I only worked six days and I didn't socialize with anybody from the film. There was an attempt to connect all of the unfortunate things that happened to some mystique, and I never saw any of that.

You're talking about the rumors there really were curses...

Yes, that is what I'm talking about. I'm very pedantic and I don't believe in any of that. I believe there are phenomena we don't understand because we have no way of measuring them. I don't believe there was any kind of a curse going on.

How did each *Poltergeist* in your role with the special effects differ? Did it become easier with each film?

Well, every one was different. I like the first one best of all, then the third one. I was least content with my role in the second one.

Chris Haverman: You said Steven primarily directed you during the six days you were working there. Was Tobe around at all?

Tobe was there all the time. As I saw it, and I was not an experienced person at the time, it seemed that Tobe set up every shot, and Steven made adjustments to every shot. I was very happy for his input.

Eric: When you were first making *Poltergeist*, did you have any idea it would become such a big hit, and that twenty-five years down the road you'd be still doing interviews for it? What do you think makes it so enduring?

The first script was very good. Steven Spielberg, Michael Grais, and Mark Victor wrote a magnificent script. That's always the basis of everything that's going to be good in a film. He picked people that were in a position to support that script, and I'm just so thrilled that I was allowed to be a part of it. It was a new experience to me and, like I said, I only worked six days, but I learned so much.

There's been so many ghost movies over the years, and *Poltergeist* is still at the top of the class. What do you think it is about it that makes it "the ghost movie" of the last twenty-five years?

It's hard for me to say. I know that my role was one that was very sympathetic. I'm always surprised when people say it's a horror film. There were some astonishing things in it that you don't normally see, but I think the thing that made it so memorable was the quality of the acting. JoBeth Williams is so fine. I was brand new, I'm glad I was picked to do it, otherwise I'd still be doing it under a streetlamp.

Russell: What kicked in within you that made you realize you were an artist and destined to act?

I had an epiphany one night, overnight, in my sleep. I don't know what the epiphany was. As an artist, I had no idea what my discipline would be. I went into work that morning and I quit my job. I had no idea what I would do after a two week notice was worked out, and then serendipity happened. I met an agent who sent me on a couple of interviews and within two weeks I got my first job on *The Flintstones*, because of this most unusual vocal instrument.

Since *Poltergeist*, primarily your other big role was in *Picket Fences*, which I imagine had to be a very pleasurable experience for you?

Yes, I was there for two years as a regular in the cast. I loved doing the role of Ginny Weedon, she was a few bubbles off plum. I fit into that very well. I have since learned that I am basically a comedian, which has been very helpful in getting along with this society if you're different from most folks.

Can we expect to see you doing a routine some day?

No, I'm not a stand-up comedian, I'm a life comedian.

On *Picket Fences*, did you expect that your character would meet her demise by falling into a freezer?

No, no. Not at all. I was not invited back for financial reasons. The two main leads required a salary increase and they took it out of me. I think by doing that it changed the whole homeostasis of the series, and I don't think it improved it.

Mike C – *Icons Of Fright*: So, Zelda, what kind of preparation did you do for the role of Tangina, did you explore the world of psychics? And since this was your first role you had, what did you know about developing a character?

I developed the character under the Ficus tree in my living room. I did not know how to develop a character, but I decided to do something as it looked like a really good opportunity. So, I hid under there and developed an equilateral triangle in my mind. The base of the triangle was her knowledge, one side was her life as a boring Odessa, Texas housewife, and the third side was her dream of becoming a dealer in Las Vegas. I kept her dead center in that triangle, and those were my guidelines. I don't know where I got them from, but those were my mental image. That's how I developed the character. After I screen tested, I didn't hear back for weeks, and she'd gotten so big inside me that I would have been ready to perform her under a streetlamp on the street.

What about the rumors that multiple endings had been shot for *Poltergeist III*?

The ending that I did was what I saw on screen. If there were other endings, it must have been done because Gary Sherman wasn't happy. Gary's a good director, and he's also remained a good friend.

Tim Claudfelter: Do you get people coming up to you on the street expecting you to know about psychic phenomenon?

Just the crazy ones (laughs). No, but shortly after the film came out a lady came up to me in the market and said, "Please come to my house, it has things wrong with it." I had to let her know that I wasn't who she thought I was. I found that rather amusing.

Steve Barton – *Dread Central*: Up until *Poltergeist*, haunted house films were in a shambled house, in complete states of disarray. This was a normal house with crazy stuff going on in it. Another thing that made the movie special was the family dynamic. Can you comment on how that dynamic was on set?

The set dynamic seemed very normal. I did not have a lot of experience to rely on. I think the brilliance of the script is what made it so terrific. It was written in a way that everybody was just a few bubbles off plum and worked well together. It was an exceptional phenomena. The other two sequels did not have that.

And where do you go from there?

That's what I asked myself. I feel I've been given a rare opportunity to work with the best in all disciplines.

Tony Farnella: I heard you had an eerie situation on *Poltergeist III*, where you found out your mother had passed away?

Well, my mother had been ill for five weeks following open-heart surgery. She was alive, but not with us, for those five weeks. I knew she was dying. I went home every weekend to Oakland, California, and I did not have that experience. The director did. Gary Sherman was taking pictures with a still camera, I think they were Polaroids. Over one picture, there was a very diaphanous shadow, and it scared a few people. If that was her spirit, it didn't bother me. I had a superb relationship with my mother.

How do you feel about the current state in Hollywood?

The tendency is to worship the beauty and forget about the depth. There are some very good performers in Hollywood, and some very excellent writers. I love the work of Paul Haggis. Among my own personal friends, I feel are some of America's best directors. I think Hollywood wouldn't be in such bad shape if they had a few good scripts and they could get off the body image.

You mentioned earlier how you're an artist. What scripts get your creative juices flowing?

Romantic comedies! I'd love to do a romantic comedy that would show how different people can really have a fine relationship, as I do in my own personal life. I love films that allow people to be people.

Emily Christiansen: Could you expand upon what your first impression was when you got to the *Poltergeist* set?

I thought it was OK. I could function there. I didn't think it was too different from the strange jobs I've had in my life, like when I was traveling abroad. I was excited by it, and I loved the opportunity.

Anything else you took away?

Yes, I should keep my mouth shut and ears open because I have an opportunity to learn. I was made very welcome by everyone, the children, Craig T. I felt very much at home, this is my world.

How would you feel if they remade *Poltergeist*?

I don't know if I would be invited to be involved in any way. It's very rare that the sequel is better than the original or the second issuing. I just saw a film, *3:10 To Yuma*, and thought this was a better film. It depends into whose hands the direction falls. I don't see why they would remake it.

David Marlett: What do you do for Halloween?

I hide. I go to a hotel and I stay there until the next day! I feel very vulnerable at Halloween, that people who might come to the door might not have candy as their intention. I don't answer the door if I'm stuck at home, but I usually manage to go elsewhere.

Any personal experience that has led to that?

Just caution. I love children, and people, but not everyone has good intentions.

You said you feel "highly sensitive" regarding the psychic world. Besides the story of your mother, did you ever have any other experiences in that realm?

Well, I do have one, I don't know why it happened. While I was filming *Poltergeist*, I was in an auto accident. I was driving a little Beetle at the time and, just as the two cars impacted, I felt my deceased father reach into the roof of the vehicle and grab me like a puppy by the back of the neck and pull me out. That was as close as I've had to any extraordinary experience, personally. I mean, I'm sensitive. I stood in front of my mirror once and I felt something pulling at the hem of my dress, and there was no one present with me. I'm aware that things happen, and we have no way of measuring these things.

Russell Trunk, again: Is it true you filmed a scene in 1995's *Casper* as Tangina being shot out of chimney yelling, '*Don't go into the light*'? I read about this on the internet...

I never did *Casper*. I think I was booked to do it, and there was a strike going on, and I would not cross the picket line. I am from Pittsburgh, and we do not cross picket lines. The internet lies!

David Marlett: What scary movies do you like?

I don't particularly like to watch scary movies. Basically, I'm a gentle soul and I don't go out to scare myself. I like films that tend to be uplifting. Some of the scariest things are living through the 21st century with the administration we have currently. That's scary. The nightly news! I keep my TV at home tuned to CNN and it's hair-raising. Absolutely hair-raising. We live in a time that it's just miraculous that we find ways to survive.

ERICA LEERHSEN

Interviewed by Rob Galluzzo (10/07)

Genre fans already recognize actress Erica Leerhsen from her appearances in *Book of Shadows: Blair Witch 2*, as well *The Texas Chainsaw Massacre* remake. She also stars alongside punk legend Henry Rollins in Joe Lynch's directorial debut *Wrong Turn 2: Dead End*. She was kind enough to chat with *Icons* about all of her genre work, and set the record straight on some of the trivia facts listed on her IMDb page. Here's what she had to say!

What are your earliest recollections of the horror genre? Do you remember the first films to scare and have an impact on you as a kid?

Children of the Corn. That was the first movie I remember seeing and being completely petrified and having to go sleep in my mom's bed. I think I was eight?

There's something weird about kids killing their parents! I remember that it freaked me out when I saw it, too.

Yeah, but it was actually the weirdest thing. I used to get freaked out just by the opening scenes of movies like that. That shot of the corn and the diner. I remember those two images and it was just too much for me. Just with that, my imagination went crazy. Because your imagination is so active as a kid, it's weird. I just lost it with that. And it was the same with *Gremlins*. I was petrified just by the commercials! The commercials freaked me out so much, I actually had to go see the movie just to face my fear.

What was funny about that is I remember they tried to sell it almost as a kid's movie. And then all these parents take their kids to see *Gremlins*, and a Gremlin gets blown up in the microwave and a little old couple gets mowed down. (laughs)

It actually made me feel better to see the movie because I developed such an intense fear. I remember my mom bought me a Gizmo doll, partially to get over my fear of the commercial! (laughs) I had to conquer it, because I couldn't sleep. My imagination was far crazier than the actual movie probably was. When I saw the figures of the *Gremlins*, I had

to embrace Gizmo and accept that he was a "good Gremlin." (laughs) It was this whole psychological process just to get over those commercials.

So, were you a fan of the genre after having conquered your fear of Gremlins?

I definitely got into them. I come mainly from a theater background, I was always intrigued by the Shakespeare play *Titus Andronicus*, which is really a horror movie. They made a movie of that with Anthony Hopkins. But it's probably, well, not the first horror play, but those themes date back to the Greeks that have Oedipus pulling out his eyes. That kind of stuff always appealed to me. And I think that's the root of horror. Film has been around for such a short time if you really think about it, in terms of the whole scope of history.

Compared to theater.

Yeah. But yeah, I did get into things like *The Shining* and other horror films like that. I can't go for gore when I watch horror movies, though. I still go towards the kind of films where your imagination creates the monster.

Well, you and Joe Lynch are on opposite spectrums in that regard.

Yeah, I know!

So, you mentioned theater before, and I thought I read you went to Boston University, was it?

Yeah.

When exactly did your interest in acting and the making-of films begin? What was it like for you at the very beginning to pursue this career?

I wasn't really that interested in making films, to be honest. Until I was about twenty-five, all I ever wanted to do was theater. My goal was to be in off-Broadway plays and work with Tony Kushner, who wrote *Angels In America*. That was my ultimate goal in life. I did always have an obsession with Woody Allen movies from a young age. I was very into his films, but I wouldn't say I was a film buff at all, I was a Woody Allen buff. And I ended up working in theater and I got *Blair Witch 2*. That really started my interest in working in films. When you get thrown into being one of the leads of a movie when you've never done a movie before, except for student films, you learn so much. So much of acting in film is experience and getting in front of the camera and realizing what kind of muscles you have to develop to be a film actor. And so, then I started getting much more interested in film after that experience.

I started studying with film acting coaches and just started developing that aspect of acting for film. I mean, I've always been specifically an actor, and I see that as my job. And it's funny because a lot of people ask me all these film questions. A director I met with recently had me watch all these other movies, because he felt it would be valuable. But as an actor, I think your job is to preserve your own view of life and tell a human story. Not a story that's necessarily been told before by another actor.

It should be your own take on that particular character. I know, for example, when someone is hired to do a sequel, they're not always required to watch the movies that came before because some directors just want an actor's own fresh take on the material.

Exactly! I think that's part of the actor's job. It's more of a director's job to know everything about film. It is useful to know about cinematography and film, you end up learning a lot about that from working on the set. But it's your job to preserve the authenticity of your expression.

You just mentioned *Book of Shadows: Blair Witch 2* and obviously that's the first time I discovered your work. I really like that film for what it is. As its own horror movie, I dig what director Joe Berlinger tried to do with it. I'm not sure exactly what people were expecting in terms of it as a sequel, but it was an effective horror movie. I was curious what you remember about that whole experience in retrospect, especially since it's been so long since the whole *Blair Witch* craze?

Well, it was a crazy experience. We didn't even get a chance to read the script until we already had the offer for the role, because it was so secretive. And it was just so exciting getting the role. It was so competitive. Like I said before, I had never done any film or TV before, and to go through the audition process, it was all really exciting to me.

When I read the script, I saw the nudity and then we were all asked to sign off on it, but you're coming from the perspective of, "Oh my God, I just got this amazing opportunity." So, we all signed off on it. Then later on, it sort of became interesting because I think if there are problems with that movie, it wasn't the directing. It was the script.

Did they change the script a lot during filming? Because I thought I had heard that there were a lot of tweaks and adjustments right before it came out.

Yeah, there were tweaks afterwards and while we were working. I just think that it all culminated in a whole orgy type situation. It's really a tricky thing to do in a horror film, because… I don't know. Sometimes when you involve sex… the mythology of the *Blair Witch* had nothing to do with sex and then to make this sequel about a sexual experience… To me, if I were to analyze what I didn't like about the script, it would be that.

Because it wasn't originally in the first movie, there was no point of reference for it in the *Blair Witch* story, so it almost became something that could be funny. Whereas if it was a movie on its own about people not knowing what they were doing and having a crazy bacchanalian experience. But to bring the bacchanalian experience into the *Blair Witch* was a little bit far-fetched to me.

Joe Berlinger is mostly well-known for his documentary work. He did the *Paradise Lost* films, as well as that recent *Metallica* documentary. Since *Blair Witch 2*, you've worked with a number of directors including Woody Allen as you mentioned before. Do you recall any difference in Joe's directing considering he came from a documentary background?

I actually loved that. Because that's very close to my interests in acting. I study real people all the time. I watch a lot of documentaries and a lot of forensic file type shows and real true-crime stories. I'm very interested in true crime. So, I loved Joe's approach. And I think he's a great director, because he's interested in the truth as a human experience, which is really what I think we're all after. Especially in terms of film where you don't need to project. There's no skill required to project to a large amount of people. The camera's right there.

You just have to be as real as people are in real life. And so, I love working with a documentary director.

One of the things I wanted to ask about *Wrong Turn 2*, it obviously incorporates the "reality television" angle. It's not prominent for the entire movie, it's actually more part of the first act. Were there technical issues for shooting the "reality" footage? Did you have to adjust your acting for portions that are meant to be part of "reality" television?

Uh, no. Because the whole time I was playing a character on a reality show. I didn't play it that I was coached to act a certain way on a reality show. I just played it as me, Nina being herself in that situation. Because I had actually been on an audition for *The Real World* with someone. I went on a date with someone, this is over ten years ago, on an audition. I remember they didn't tell me anything, we just tried to be as realistic as possible and give a real reaction. I mean, that was probably the third *Real World* or something? It was before the whole "reality" thing took over television. But yeah, they just wanted us to be ourselves. So that was my remembering of my one "reality" TV experience.

So, you were always Nina, it didn't matter which camera was capturing it.

Right.

How'd you initially get involved in *Wrong Turn 2*, what attracted you to it and what can you share with us about the character of Nina?

The role attracted me. I love playing women who get a chance to use their brains and physical strength, which really isn't a common thing. You usually see someone like Jodie Foster getting those opportunities. There just aren't that many roles for women where they're allowed to be really powerful. So, that appealed to me first and foremost. And then, the fact that the action sequences were really cool to me, I thought that there was a lot of opportunity for good fights, and it really was an action/horror movie. I really felt that it did a good job of fitting into that genre. Having some really funny action movie lines. It kind of reminded me of an Arnold Schwarzenegger movie in the horror genre. (laughs)

It's funny, when they first announced that there was going to be a sequel to *Wrong Turn*, it wasn't exactly the type of sequel that everyone in the horror community was excited about. But then Joe Lynch got attached as director, and it's obvious to anyone that meets Joe either at a screening or at a convention that he's totally one of

us; absolutely loves and respects the horror genre and has an enthusiasm that can only be described as contagious. What were your initial reactions to meeting Joe and working with him on this?

Well, it was so great to work with someone who was so excited about what they were doing. I mean, he had a childlike innocence about it, but at the same time, a knowledge of horror movies compared to no one I had ever met. It was this oxymoron, sort of. To be that innocent and have that much knowledge about something, which is unusual. I liked the fact that he wanted the characters to be well rounded. He wanted us to do some acting work beforehand and give him a list of all our characters favorite songs. I actually really like that. I found that to be really appropriate for this movie, because it's such a pop-culture type of movie, so it really is important what kind of music these people listen to. It's an important part of all of their personas.

Nina has an interesting arc. She comes off as this strong character at first; we slowly begin to discover that she's somewhat broken. A bit lost. She's this girl from Brooklyn that's got problems. How much of that were you able to create or incorporate? How much of yourself were you able to put into Nina to really flesh her out as a character?

To me, I end up in my characters because I have to draw from my own experiences to relate to the character's experience. So, I'm always in every single one of my characters. And really, I kind of based Nina on this girl my husband now had been dating. Just sort of a very angry person, who came off as very intimidating at first. I was intimidated by her. And then, you found out later that underneath it all, she was really, really vulnerable and kind of childlike and maybe hadn't met the challenges of growing up as well as other people have, you know?

She sort of stayed a little bit immature. So, I kind of based it on someone I knew, actually. Well, that I knew from the outside. I created the soul of who I figured out this person was. She inspired me, this girl, who in real life is a stylist, but seems on the outside to have it all together, but then you get underneath it and there's a lot of vulnerability there and a lot of anger. I usually base characters on people I've seen. It's almost like I take pieces of different people and put them all into a stew.

One of the film's strongest points was the addition of Henry Rollins to the cast. Everyone loves Henry. Was he intimidating to meet and work with at first? What was it like having Henry on set?

Yeah, he is intimidating. I'm a little bit of a... I don't know how to say it. I'm a theater nerd. I would freak out when I would meet some obscure person from theater. Sometimes the most famous people, I don't actually get that intimidated by. It actually helped me, because I was able to talk to him as a regular person. I did see his show, and I knew of him, and I knew his music. But I tried not to focus on the fact that someone is so famous when I'm having to deal with them and work with them. Having worked with Woody Allen, I actually had to learn that. To not put someone on a pedestal, because then it can actually interfere with the work. So, I did my best to keep Henry on a human level.

It's interesting. You mentioned before you weren't a huge film buff, but you loved the films of Woody Allen. I love a lot of them too. So, was it odd working with him for the first time?

Yes, that was one of the most difficult things. It was so surreal to me to be working with him that it was almost overwhelming. I was so nervous around him. You're just sort of enamored by him. And then, it actually helped, because I worked with him three times now, so by the third time it was like, "Ok, that's just Woody." (laughs)

What's one of your favorite Woody Allen movies?

Um, *Crimes and Misdemeanors*. You know, it's funny because I tend to go more for his dramas, even though everybody always wants him to be funny and will say *Bananas* or *Everything You Always Wanted to Know About Sex*. I mean, I love that movie...

Sleeper **is my favorite! I love** *Sleeper.*

I'm such a drama obsessed person, I'm realizing in terms of my interests in film and theater. I tend to gravitate towards that genre. So, my faves are *Crimes and Misdemeanors* and *Hannah and Her Sisters* and then later *Husbands and Wives*, and of course *Annie Hall*. That's more of a comedy.

Well, one of the things missing from the *Texas Chainsaw Massacre* **remake was the dinner scene, which is one of the most famous scenes from the original. But alas, you didn't escape the dinner scene in** *Wrong Turn 2***, which goes quite over the top. Can you talk a bit about filming that scene and the horrible things you had to endure? I cringe every time you pull at the barbed wire they use to tie your hands down.**

Really? Oh good! (laughs)

It's bad enough you're tied down with these people, but the fact that you have to tug and struggle against barbed wire? Gets me every time. What was your experience shooting that scene?

It was incredibly disgusting! Actually, I couldn't eat Indian food for six months after and it's one of my favorite foods...

Is that what the entrails were? Indian food?

Yeah! Yeah, it was so disgusting. Actually, someone, one of the family members was getting sick in their costume because it was so hot, and they were kind of throwing up, and that was making me start to throw up. I was almost throwing up that entire scene, for real. There were a couple of times where Joe said cut and thought that I was actually throwing up, and he came over to me and said, "Are you ok?" But I really was about to throw up. So, it was so disgusting, I couldn't even deal with it. People were leaving the room!

Actually, crew members were also leaving because of the family praying. They were offended by the praying. It was a really heavy, heavy atmosphere where everybody was just gritting their teeth and trying to get through it. It wasn't fun, it smelled disgusting. That's the thing you wouldn't know about these movies if you didn't do them, that that fake blood is disgusting and it's not exactly the cleanest environment. Hair and make-up are doing their best job to keep everything clean, but it's not. You're on a dirty set in a dirty warehouse and there's this disgusting Indian food, people are throwing up, their costumes are uncomfortable. It has real elements of torture.

Which is why the scene is so effective!

Yeah. I'm not going to lie. It does help with your acting. (laughs) You don't have to work as hard when you're actually grossed out. I'd never been to the point where I was almost throwing up in a scene like that.

Let's talk about the *Texas Chainsaw* **remake, because obviously a lot of genre fans know you from that. Judging from the making-of featurettes on the DVD, it looked like you guys had a blast making the film.**

We did.

When they first announced it though, I remember people were livid! They didn't want it to be remade. But then when it came out, most fans seemed to be OK with it. Even though you guys had a great time making it, do you

remember there being a sense of intimidation or pressure to remaking *The Texas Chain Saw Massacre*?

Yeah. I remember people really not having high hopes for it, in terms of the feeling from the horror genre fans. And the country in general, nobody thought the movie was going to do well. Everyone thought it was just going to be another of the millions of sequels. So, there was a real pressure to try to do things different from the original, and not just copy it. For instance, a lot of people were talking about the *Psycho* remake that Gus Van Sant did and how we didn't want to do that. When a movie is so great like *The Texas Chain Saw Massacre* is, the original inclination is to just copy it. But that's specifically why I watched it once (again) before we started. I got the images in my head. I didn't want to get the original movie too much in my head. I almost wanted the character to be a dream-like subconscious reference to that movie, but not be the girl from that movie.

The script for the *Texas Chainsaw* remake, I have to say was amazing. Scott Kosar, who wrote *The Machinist*. It really all goes back to the script. You can have the most amazing director, the most amazing cast, but if the script doesn't set up these characters and what they have to endure, especially in a script like this - You can do the best acting in the world and it won't work as well. I thought Scott did a great job because he set up Erin to be really good with her hands. Like she'd been in juvenile detention, which obviously wasn't in the original. Not to say it improved the original, but it gave Erin just this one little character detail which ended up making sense why she could hot-wire the car in the end. It wasn't just like, "Here comes this hot chick suddenly hot-wiring the car."

One of the remake's benefits was that it wasn't the same characters, it wasn't the exact same story, but it definitely tried to keep with the spirit of the original.

It did and the script worked in and of itself. It was a well written movie, which was allowed to take a lot of different ideas because it was a remake. But in and of itself, it stood as a well-written piece, which is why I think it turned out so well.

I can't say the same for *Texas Chainsaw: The Beginning*, but that's just my own personal opinion.

That's why I always go back to the script on any movie. I would love to do another movie with Scott Kosar. I love the way he wrote the character of Pepper. He put in just enough detail to make her three-dimensional. And to make it make sense, like when she panics at the end. You know she's going

to panic, because she's been unable to stomach anything the whole time. It has the elements of the character's destiny. That's so important and underestimated. Because we can get so into special FX nowadays, that sometimes writers forget to create people.

I've seen Andrew Bryniarski, "Leatherface," at conventions and I will say it… he's intimidating as hell. I'm scared to go near him. I often heard rumors that he was very physically imposing and threatening during filming. Is there any truth to that?

(laughs) Oh, he was. I bet the people in *The Beginning* said that too.

I don't think you die on camera! Like you don't physically see Pepper die.

Right, you don't.

So, you lucked out!

Yeah, but that was an incredibly scary scene to shoot. Andrew did all of his own stunts in the original remake. I don't know if he did in *The Beginning*. He was jumping off of the van and chasing me! He was jumping off this six-foot jump in this costume and I just kept getting so scared that he was going to land on me. I had to just trust that when I jumped out of the van, he wasn't going to be on top of me. I mean, if I had stopped, he would've run me over. You know what I mean? He couldn't see or really breathe in that costume.

He kept saying he couldn't breathe when we were shooting that scene, and no one was really helping him. (laughs) Because he has a tendency to scare people on the set. So, I was literally just running for my own safety, and I was so lucky to have a stunt double pop in and get attacked at the last minute and have to go down and scrap all of her legs up. Yeah. I jumped out of the way at the last minute, and she took over for me. I didn't have to actually handle him, I just had to get out of the way, which was scary enough!

There are several things listed about you in the trivia section of your IMDB page. So, let's play a quick game of True or False? Let's set the record straight so people can fix your IMDB page.

(laughs)

True or False – Your birthday is on Valentine's Day?

True.

True or False – You sang in your high school choir?

Um, true. (laughs) I don't know how that's on there.

I know, very random! True or False – On the set of *Book of Shadows: Blair Witch 2*, there's a scene where you do a witch chant and rumor has it, the "god of the underworld" chant was so powerful, you passed out. Any truth to that?

Uh, false. I hate to say. That did not happen.

Now we're getting to the bottom of things! True or False – You first auditioned for the goth girl role in *Blair Witch 2*?

True.

Lastly, True or False – On your audition for *Texas Chainsaw*, you screamed so loud that the police were called in by other people in the building.

True.

Wow! Only one falsity on your IMDB page.

Oh, there's another false thing on there. People say I was born in Ossining. I was born in New York City.

JEFFREY COMBS

Interviewed by Rob Galluzzo (10/07)

It's hard to be a genre fan and not be impressed with the constant contributions of thespian Jeffrey Combs. He's appeared in everything from *House on Haunted Hill* to *From Beyond* to *The Frighteners*, as well as several Full Moon movies such as *Castle Freak, Doctor Mordrid*, and *The Pit and The Pendulum*. He is a frequent collaborator with filmmaker Stuart Gordon, most recently on *The Black Cat*, and together the duo created a true *Icon of Fright* in Dr. Herbert West from *Re-Animator*. We're proud to present a candid, casual conversation with Jeffrey.

Oh, Jeffrey! Such a pleasure to get to talk to you. I'm such a huge fan of your entire body of work.

Well, I hope not all of it! Some of it sucks!

Listen, I grew up in the 80's and 90's on a lot of the Full Moon stuff, so I loved it all.

Where are you calling me from?

I'm in New York, sir.

Good man!

Considering your huge, impressive body of film work, and of course the fact that you're very recognizable in the horror genre, I was wondering if you could tell you your earliest recollections of the horror genre? Do you remember the first films to scare or have an impact on you in terms of introducing you to the world of horror?

Yeah, yeah, I do. The very first movie, I went to a matinee, because dude, I'm old enough where I saw things pre-VHS. The only time you could watch movies was on TV on the few channels you got in black and white with commercials and totally cut up, but we didn't know it at the time. Or you'd go to the movies and catch a matinee. And there was a movie, I think it was called *The Brain That Wouldn't Die*? All that I remember is that at the end of the movie there was this woman head, and all they did at the time was cut a hole in the table. (laughs) Just like we did on *Re-Animator*! Only there wasn't a pan with blood in it. They didn't even bother

with that. They were so cheeseball that they just cut a hole for her head, and then they had wires on her head and the camera slowly dollied into a real close-up of her face and the whole time she was saying, "Kill me. Kill meeee. Kill meeee." (laughs) And it just rocked my world.

I can see that having an impression on a young Jeffrey Combs!

I just walked home going "*Oh... (pause) FUCK!*" (laughs) I'm scared. That is my idea of... that's a nightmare. Then I watched some movies years later...

It's a whole different effect when you watch it as an adult, of course.

Yeah, it's not the same thing!

You're back in *Return to House on Haunted Hill*! Were you surprised that the character of Dr. Vannacutt was brought back for the sequel?

I was surprised that it was eight years after the fact! The first movie did really well, and it's a nice movie. Bill Malone did a great job with it. But usually with sequels, they're kind of fairly right away. Except in my career with the *Re-Animator's*. (laughs) The three of those spanned over twenty years, I think. But typically... look at *Saw* for God's sake!

They crank those out once a year! (laughs)

I was a little surprised when they called. But I owe that to

Victor Garcia, the director. Because he insisted that Dr. Vannacutt be part of it, because he felt that he was the face of the house, you know?

I saw in a recent interview you mentioned that in the first film Dr. Vannacutt is somewhat of an enigma. And now in the second, it's fairly the same, although I understand you did film a branching scene with dialogue?

One of the branching scenes I did dialogue in.

I'm curious, as an actor, how do you build a backstory for someone like Dr. Vannacutt when there's not much of a backstory there? Did you apply any kind of process when it came to returning to this character?

You know, it's real strange when you don't have dialogue, you are kind of flying by the seat of your pants a little bit more. And I have to be honest, it's almost more difficult because you have nothing that you can hang on to that you can sort of bring it around. From a technical point of view, I kept thinking of the old 30's movies. Even when I did the first *House on Haunted Hill*, just the whole look.

The thing is, when you get in there and you're surrounded by the whole look and the costumes and everything, it really informs you about who you are and where you are. I just kind of leaned back on technique and I look at Vannacutt as my homage to the old mad scientists from the 30's. It was my idea a long time ago to give him one of those little mustaches. Those pencil-thin Errol Flynn mustaches, because he's from a different time. Bill Malone wanted that too, an homage to the movies he grew up with. I think Vannacutt resonates with people because they can go, "Oh yeah. I know what movie this guy's from."

Director Victor Garcia has a history in special FX make-up. I believe the attention garnered by his short film is what got him this job?

Great short. *El Ciclo*. I don't know if you've seen it?

No, I haven't seen it yet! What was your experience like working with him as a first-time director on a feature?

Well, I didn't get a sense from Victor that he showed any kind of tentativeness or worry about this being his first film. He's very emotionally pleasant. This is sort of an important thing for directors, but I don't think that he's flustered very easily. Because there's always something that comes up.

You have a game plan but it's kind of like war. You have a plan, but after the first shot is fired, or the first take

is made, throw it away because things just start coming in that just change things around. And this was an especially complicated project because it wasn't like you'd just shoot a scene and then be done with it. Then you had to shoot variations on that scene.

And if it's complicated for an actor to have to do all of these off-shoots, imagine what it's like logistically for a director who has to concentrate on all of them for all of the actors. It is a phenomenally daunting task, yet Victor seemed to have it all in his head, which was amazing to me.

It's a really interesting idea for this DVD, having this branching version where we can pick different directions the movie can go in. I'm looking forward to it.

And I'll tell you, when I was shooting it, that wasn't really articulated to me. So, I showed up and I thought I was done! I thought, "Good, I'm done with that take," and then they'd go, "No, no, no, no, wait a minute!" And I'd think, "What are you talking about?" (laughs) Then I realized how brilliant this was. There are ninety-six permutations.

Jeffrey, I'm such a huge fan of different points in your career, I just wanted to delve into a few of my personal favorites for a bit if you don't mind.

Go baby!

I just watched *From Beyond*, your second collaboration with Stuart Gordon. Great movie. It's often been thought of as somewhat of a "lost" cult classic. How do you feel about the fact that it's recently been re-released and restored as the director's cut that Stuart always intended?

Well, finally! Huh? (laughs) It's always been sort of a curious thing. Once Empire Pictures crashed and burned and all the body parts and pieces of the company got gobbled up and held and possessed by other companies and other companies, finally it wound up at MGM.

But MGM's library is so vast that they didn't really see this acquisition as something that was worthy of their attention, until years later. And I would imagine it was because of a growing query from people. "Hey, where is this From Beyond movie?" I'm pleased that it's out there. Um, but ... for me, I enjoy the movie, but it's not as near and dear to me as *Re-Animator*. In some ways, it was less of an enjoyable experience for me, because the nature of the role is the victim.

I was just about to mention that the character of Crawford is for the most part a victim in *From Beyond*, which is different from your other character work at the time.

I was playing the Dan Cain role, basically. I was playing the one that was basically reacting to what everybody else was doing. "Hey, you can't do that! No, I can't. Don't go! Wait!" So, all of a sudden, from being the driving force in *Re-Animator* who had a dark sense of humor, there's very little of that for me in *From Beyond*. Those are harder roles for me to play!

You eat eyeballs in it! You do all sorts of crazy stuff!

Oh, great! Oh joy, oh joy. I get to eat an eyeball. Thanks for bringing that up! (laughs)

Sorry! (laughs) We just mentioned Stuart Gordon, and I'm also such a fan of his. He's always doing interesting things. Since you guys have worked together so often, what's your relationship like? I imagine you've developed somewhat of a second-hand as director/actor at this point?

We have. And he's a great friend of mine. I have a tremendous fun time with Stuart. We laugh a lot. We have our own little in-jokes and it's comfortable. Stuart and I both come from a theatre background where the philosophy is, once you have a group of actors that you know and trust and can count on, then the actual problems are solved if you keep them in your troop and re-use them. Because you can go and solve other problems because that one's taken care of. Kind of like Orson Wells did with all those actors in *Citizen Kane*, they all came out of his theater group where he directed many plays. David Mamet is like that. Lots of people have that philosophy. And then there are others that don't! Stuart and I will go at it! We will disagree with things. Certainly, we've done that in the past, but it's never seemed to affect us. It's all towards the work. It's nothing personal involved in it. He can drive me nuts! But he can make me laugh too.

He is a tenacious man with his vision and in some ways, maybe I'm a bit of a temper on him sometimes too. It's like, "Stu! You're not going to do that much blood? Come on!" And he's like, "Yeah, sure. It's great." "But… it doesn't make sense!" I never win!

Well, you have to try at least, no? As I said before, I grew up on a lot of the Full Moon stuff. I love *Castle Freak*. I particularly love *The Pit and the Pendulum*. What stands out for you from that Full Moon era and those films I just mentioned? Did you shoot some of those in Romania or something?

Well, *Castle Freak* was shot in Italy.

Italy, ok.

As was *Pit and the Pendulum*. In fact, both of those movies were shot in the same castle! Literally a castle that Charlie Band owned. In a small village between Florence and Rome. And about once every two or three years, he would come up with the notion that maybe another movie could be shot in this castle. Because it's an all inclusive place. There's many, many rooms and many levels to it and bedrooms. You could live and work in the same place.

So, you'd have your own room and bathroom and then breakfast, lunch, and dinner in the big kitchen. Or you could go out to a restaurant or café if you wanted to. My memory of all those, *Castle Freak* and *From Beyond* and *Pit and the Pendulum,* are all that they were shot in Italy and the wonderful time that I had there, really for the first time spending an extended period of time overseas in a different culture. So, my memories are more about where than what. Isn't that funny?

Yeah, it makes total sense though. Speaking of *Pit*, *The Black Cat* was probably my favorite episode of *Masters of Horror* Season Two. I've heard that you've always wanted to play Edgar Allan Poe and you did an amazing job. What is it about Poe that appeals to you as an actor?

Well, I hadn't always wanted to play him. It was maybe three or four years ago, I read a lot of historical novels. Or biographies of people. And I was thinking, "Who would I like to portray in history?" And you know, that's kind of difficult! I was reading some things, and I came across a biography of Poe and I started reading it and I realized, "Oh my God, has anyone ever done his life?" His life, he's like the American Van Gogh. He is a tragic artist. Self destructive. Mercurially brilliant. And he would lacerate people in his editorials, because he was a critic. A poetry critic and he was scathing. We cut it from the scene (in *The Black Cat*) but it was there. A portion of it is there where he lacerated someone in a review, because that was sort of his day job was as an editor for a weekly newspaper. He was the editor, he was the critic, he was all these things. He lacerated this guy's newest publication and then ran into him on the street the next day and asked to borrow some money from him.

Wow!

If you watch in *The Black Cat*, in the bar scene, a guy named Griswold comes in, who was a historical guy, and he asked him to pay for his bar bill. And the guy says, "After what you wrote? Are you kidding?" But that's true! That's Poe. He was a dreadful alcoholic, but he was deeply in love with and devoted to his wife who was sick. He was just so complicated and so vulnerable and hungry for stability in a life that had none. We think of him as the great American writer, yet in his day, he couldn't rub two nickels together.

And writers that were huge in those days, we don't even know their names now. Part of his problem was he saw the total injustice of that. "What's a guy got to do? What do I have to do?" He got some fame in his life, but it was truly tragic and self-destructive. So, I went to Stuart and said, "Has anyone ever done a story about Poe's life?" And that was the last I heard of the idea. Maybe a year went by, and Stuart came to me and said, "Would you like to play Poe?" They came up with this brilliant idea of dove-tailing biographical details of Poe's life into one of Poe's stories.

Brilliant script by Dennis Paoli and Stuart for that!

Brilliant script! Brilliant melding of two things. It's great.

It's one of my favorite things that both you and Stuart have done, I really loved it.

Mine too! I was just talking to Stuart yesterday actually, and we had just finished shooting that a year ago.

Wow. The only other Poe project I think I heard about was that Michael Jackson at one point wanted to play him in a movie years back. Thank God, you beat him to the punch on that one!

I heard that! That's odd! I heard that Sylvester Stallone wants to do a Poe movie.

I heard that too. He's got a Poe script.

Whether he wanted to direct or perform, I don't know?

I think he just wanted to direct. I don't see him as Poe.

I don't either. But I'm just pleased that I got to try my hand at it. I think it has a beautiful look and it really is something to be proud of.

In the past few years, there's been a lot of talk about *House of Re-Animator*, the fourth official *Re-Animator* film. What intrigues me is the plot details that have surfaced so far. In a recent interview, Stuart Gordon said that the two problems with it are one - because of the political angle, it's a difficult film to convince financers to invest in and two - by the time it might get made, the current President will probably be out of office. My question to

you is, considering your deep affinity for the Herbert West character, how do you personally feel about putting him in a political satire?

Well, this is one of those things where Stuart and I still have an on-going difference of opinion on! Because my argument was, "Fine." I love the idea of Herbert getting put into a political story where the President or Vice-President is dead and can't be, so I resurrect him, bring him back and chaos ensues. I love that sort of idea! But where we sort of veer away from each other is that Stuart wants to do it right on the nose. Like an impersonation of George Bush and Dick Cheney and all of them. I just thought, firstly *Re-Animator* has never been a political vehicle, and you've got a long way to go to convince me that it should be!

And two, that's fine now, but in two years I don't know if it's still relevant. Then as it came closer and closer, you have to write this thing, then you have to shoot it, then you have to post, then you have to release it before an election day, it became even more and more clear to me that it shouldn't be an impersonation. It should be like *Dr. Strangelove*. Have a dynamic where there is a President and a Vice-President that are running roughshod over all of our liberties and freedoms. But don't have it be so obvious. When you see *Dr. Strangelove*, none of those people are particularly recognizable as anyone that's ever been president. And yet, the point is made about power. Absolute power and corrupting absolutely. And so, that's sort of been my take on it. He is right. People are weary about financing it. They don't want to go there. I'm not so sure that horror and politics are a mix…

Yeah, yeah.

I told Stuart once, "*If you want to be Michael Moore, do a documentary!*"

There's nothing wrong with subtle social commentary in a film, but I agree that it shouldn't be blatant.

I think you make your point better if it's oblique. People will maybe see it rather than if you throw it in their face. You don't want to split your audience!

You mentioned in a previous interview that *The Frighteners* was the best experience you've had on a movie. It's a terrific film I felt was vastly underrated. I love Peter Jackson. What was it about Peter as a director that set him apart from all the other directors you'd worked with to make that particular film one of your favorite experiences?

I would just say that Peter Jackson comes really prepared. I don't ever remember seeing him look at a script or a storyboard. But he knew what he wanted. He knew how he wanted it to look. He had such a sense of poise and simple ease on the set that he made the job that he was doing look effortless. He's very collaborative. Not stuck with just his ideas. If you came to him with something, he was totally and completely open to it and that portrayal of mine is both of us. It's Peter and I working together. I remember nights of giggling. I'm just thrilled that we had such a good time. I had really high hopes for that movie, but its distribution and release were ill-conceived.

Well, I think now it's found its audience and people that are fans of Peter's have gone back and discovered it, along with his other crazy horror movies. I think it's starting to catch on as one of his best films.

And I think that Michael J. Fox is terrific in that movie!

Oh yeah! It's one of the best things he's done.

It's one of the best things that he's done and at that time, that movie should never have come out… I'll never forget the date. It was July 19th! (laughs)

It was supposed to come out around Halloween that year? But it got pushed up to summer, right?

We can thank Sylvester Stallone for that.

Oh, what did he have coming out that year?

He had *Daylight*.

Oh…

It went over, and all of a sudden it wasn't going to be ready for summer release, so the studio thought we need to find something that can fill that slot. They were looking at these terrific dailies from New Zealand. Let's just move this movie forward! And we all thought, "Great, man! We're a summer release!" (laughs) "We're going out in the summer!" But it's not a summer movie, per say. It's very epitomical of Halloween. It's a perfect Halloween movie! And then whatever ad campaign they put together for it was goofy. I always say that they promoted it as a live action *Casper* movie with Michael J. Fox being funny. Well, that may be true for the first half of the movie…

But then it gets dark!

But then it corkscrews down and then you're splitting your audience. Because the hardcore horror fans are going to stay away in droves, because it's light, right? Besides, they're going to the beach or the lake or something. It's July, dude! So then the other half, the date movie people say, "Let's go see that!" They enjoy it for about forty-five minutes and then it goes some place that they didn't expect. So, you're not pleasing anyone. Peter doesn't fit into the cookie-cutter genre of things.

All his films are vastly different!

I don't think the studios know what to do with that. They don't know what to do with complexity and nuance.

You were in Ryan Schifrin's film *Abominable* and you shared a great, humorous scene with Lance Henriksen. Probably my favorite scene of the movie!

Right. We did *Pit and The Pendulum* and then another movie that shall remain nameless.

What was it like to reunite with Lance for that?

I love Lance. I just spoke to him recently on the phone. He's a terrific spirit. We had a terrific time on *Abominable*. We just worked together for one night. He'd never seen me do something like that before. He was going, "*Damn! What are you doing?*"

Yeah, I had Ryan explain the whole Darwin Awards to me because I love that little speech.

Well, the curious thing about that, and this hardly ever happens for me, I did a cameo for Ryan in that movie. It was just that scene in the store, where the guy comes in, buys some supplies, and I tell him what happened on the mountain. And that's all I did.

Then, about a year later —a year later!— Ryan called me up and said, "We're going to add a scene to the movie because we think it needs it. There's a spot where we want to bring you back and we're going to have Lance there. Would you reprise your role as Buddy the clerk?" I was thrilled to do that. So, there's actually a year difference between those two scenes I did in that movie!

Wow. Ryan's a really good guy and in fact, the first time I met him, we had a long conversation about you and Lance! Because you guys are two of my favorite actors, so I told Ryan, "Tell me everything about working with Jeffrey and Lance!" (laughs)

(laughs) It's a long way off, but there's a potential project where Lance and I might work together again. Maybe next year, but we'll see.

Of course, you and Stuart Gordon have now tackled Lovecraft and Poe multiple times. So, what's next for you two? Any other stories or authors you guys want to tackle?

I don't know! I don't think so. We haven't really talked about what we would do together next. It's kind of a curious time right now. I just talked to Stuart yesterday and right now it's really a quiet curious time. There's weird dynamics out here because of potential strikes next year. A lot of people are not going forward with things until that's all figured out, so it's kind of a quiet time right now. There's the possibility of a couple of movies next year for me but not with Stuart. I don't know what Stuart and I would potentially do together again? It's an actor's life for me!

You work consistently. You've worked in television and movies, you've done some voice over work as well. You're consistently busy. Do you have any advice for aspiring actors? Any advice you can offer to other actors?

Being busy, even though from your perspective it seems I work a lot, well I do, fortunately. But my biggest problem is keeping myself occupied when I'm not working on a script or role. I've not always been successful at that. But I would say the most vital thing that has kept me chugging along here is training and a philosophy of versatility. Any young actor should not jump in his Volkswagen and drive to LA and hit the ground. It can happen because there are no rules, but there are tendencies.

And the tendencies are that the better trained people are the ones that have more longevity. So, if you can do plays and get as good a training as you can, do that. I went to college; I didn't come to LA until I was twenty-six, twenty-seven. I just didn't think I was ready, and you know what, I was right. One of the things that I did was that I created a foundation for myself in theater, so that when I came to town and they said, which they always do, "Ok, thank you very much!" and you leave and you didn't get the gig, at least I had in my mind the idea that I was good because I did all that other stuff. I can go back and survive by doing theater if I had to, because I had a base of confidence there. If you have just confidence without any sort of justification for it, pretty soon you're going to get burned out. So, just keep training and just keep doing plays. Learn from others. Find pace-setters. Find people that you say, "How do they do that?" or "I admire that," and learn from them. And be reliable! Because no one likes somebody they can't count on.

Do you still do work in theater?

I haven't in a while. I directed for the first time a couple of years ago *Richard III*.

How'd that go for you?

It was quite a challenge for me, but it turned out very well. It was a nice little equity company near where I live, but boy, it can really take it out of you! I enjoyed it, but I didn't really want to turn around and do that again. But my thinking was I should try that so that maybe I can have that experience for when I maybe direct a movie one day… Can you hold on one second? Someone's trying to call, could be an emergency.

Go ahead!

(short pause) My dentist.

(laughs) When are you due in?

Next week.

Last question! You do a lot of these appearances both at the horror conventions and the *Star Trek* conventions. I'm curious, what is the convention experience like from your perspective? I'd imagine you bump into a lot of people that you've worked with in the past.

Yeah, that I love. I love that. To see old friends. That happens even more so with the *Star Trek* conventions that I will go to, because it's a bigger world. There are so many character actors that I've worked with long before I ever did science-fiction from when I was doing theater. These are old friends! You lose contact, but what's nice too is when you have friends in common and you get to catch up while visiting conventions. It's really quite lovely. It's just nice to sit down and have a drink with an old pal.

Jeffrey, thank you so much for your time. I really, really appreciate it and it was such a pleasure to talk to you.

Alright Rob, nice talking with you!

JOE LYNCH

Interviewed by Mike Cucinotta and Rob Galluzzo (10/07)

Very few filmmakers display such an open affection for the horror genre as director Joe Lynch. All it takes is one conversation with the guy to realize how seriously he loves our beloved genre. It also becomes quite obvious that he's a walking encyclopedia of horror history. He just completed directing his first full length feature *Wrong Turn 2* with Henry Rollins and Erica Leerhsen. We got to chat with him extensively about his entire career thus far. Read on, fiends!

Rob: What do you remember being your first introduction into the world of horror?

I remember bits of my mom taking me to see *Dawn of the Dead*. She told me we went to see that one and I think that's awesome. I remember flashes of really bad Tom Savini make-up or entrails or something. So, there's those flashes and obviously seeing things like *Star Wars*. I don't know where my mom's thinking came from, or her babysitting skills, but she would always bring home horror films for us to see. I know she was such a big fan of them, and she would always talk about them to us. She'd go to the library and rent them for free and bring home stuff like *Return of the Living Dead* or the *Tom Savini Scream Greats*. She would always buffer that *Scream Greats* video with the other horror films, and she would always buy us *Fangoria* magazine to allow us to see that it was all fake and that we could enjoy it on that level. Honestly, that's where I first became interested in making movies, because I wanted to be a special FX make-up artist. I'd think, 'Wow, look at all these magicians doing all these crazy things' with make-up, and camera tricks and sleight of hand. Seeing *Blood Beach* and all the Empire movies. All the New World stuff. All the Cannon stuff. My mom would bring that stuff home in droves, and we'd ingest them greedily. I basically grew up with horror in my blood from the beginning.

Rob: Well, you had an awesome mom growing up, because we had to sneak around our parents to rent these movies!

That was what was so cool about the "mom and pop" shops back in the day, was that really, they didn't give a shit. We used to go to this video store in Port Jeff Station called 2020 Video and they would not care. They were excited when I came in because the people behind the counter were also horror fans. So, I'd come in and be like, 'So, what'd you think of *Deady Friend*?' And they'd say, 'Awe, that movie sucks. But if you hate that old bitch from *Throw Mama From The Train* and you want to see her take a basketball to the head, then that's the movie you want to see!'

So for me, I'd pay attention to what affected the older kids, and then I would want it. I remember the day they were like, '*I Spit On Your Grave?* Little dude? You can't watch this… but ok, we'll let you rent it.' They were just pounding me with these horrible things! I bet in retrospect they were probably thinking, 'Let's try to fuck this kid up! Let's warp him and turn him into a serial killer or something' like *Dexter*. Their plan was thwarted because I obviously went in a different direction.

Rob: That's so funny! I had this "mom and pop" video store up the corner from my block, and this punk rock dude with a Mohawk used to work there and he'd let me rent anything. I remember renting *Henry: Portrait of a Serial Killer* at like, fifteen!

Exactly! I remember the day that came out on MTI. There was a thing in *Fangoria* that said it was coming out in October and I was like, I gotta go. (laughs) I was there the day of. The lady behind the counter was like, 'So, you want that *Henry* movie, huh?' 'Yes, I do!' She was totally cool about it! Every time I went in there, I thought I'd get busted. I was always waiting for them to say, 'Waaaiiit a second.

You don't look twenty-one!' (laughs) They never said that though. They were just always very cool.

And also, I think they knew that I was seeing it on a level that wasn't just to see fucked up shit. I was enjoying this stuff on a level a horror fan should. And it's a very objective level. The kind of level that you can appreciate the sort of violence and gore and suspense and the shocking stuff from a distance, because it's safe danger. We all like to be threatened but we don't like the repercussions of that, which is what horror's so great at doing! Giving those threats, making you feel a little bit in danger and then realizing, 'Oh it's ok. It's all over. We can turn off the TV now.' I think the people at the video store were getting a thrill by the fact that I was so into the horror genre on more than just a base level.

Rob: Horror opened the floodgates into how you got into films and filmmaking, but where did it all begin with you? Was it an interest in special FX make-up?

I knew I wanted to make movies when I got the issue of Joe Dante and (*Gremlins*) Spike on the cover of *Fangoria*. I remember reading this article with Joe in it and it'd go to Chris Walas and I was just enthralled with everything Chris did. Because not only did he do *Gremlins*, but he did *The Fly*.

I just thought he was awesome. It was between that issue of *Fangoria* and the *Tom Savini's Scream Greats*, which was basically a documentary about Tom Savini's work that I became so fascinated with it. I literally did that trick he teaches in his book where you take a razor blade and you file it down, take mortician's wax, put it in your palm, fill it up with blood and if you hold it right, and race the razor across your arm and squeeze the blood, it really looks like you just whacked your wrist! I did that in front of my mom, and it freaked her out for the first two seconds, and then she'd say, 'Oh Joe, you're crazy.' Make-up FX is where it started. Also, since I was a little kid, I was always acting. Plays and little things around town. I got really close to being cast as young Ron Kovic in *Born on the Fourth of July*. I made it to the fourth round of auditions or something like that.

I just loved movies so much that I just wanted to be enveloped in them in whatever capacity I could. If it was acting? Great. If it was special FX? Great. I always knew what directors did, but it wasn't until I saw Frank Darabont and Chuck Russell's *The Blob* remake from 1988, that I realized, 'Wow. A director does this and a director does that,' and this is how he tells a story. Ever since I saw that film, I became obsessed with what it takes to be a director. What does it take to tell a story visually with all these different components? You have acting, you have story, you have editing, you have camerawork, you have special effects, you have production design. How does all of that come together?

Before I went to film school and I was reading things like Robert Rodriguez's do-it-yourself exploits, I just thought to myself it would be better if I knew how to do everything on set. Literally everything from getting the producer a coffee all the way up to calling the shots as a director or a producer. Every facet. Every unit. Every single aspect of the filmmaking process, I felt I needed to know. It also started with writing a lot. I've always been writing a lot ever since I first read Stephen King. So, I've always been writing short stories. So, there was that component. When I was ten or eleven, I learned how to hook up two VCR's together and I learned how to edit that way. So, I would take scenes from *Lethal Weapon 2* or *Mad Max* or *Halloween II* and I would re-cut, re-mix them with music. Just to learn what it was like to change things, using just manipulation of images. And then with shooting, I had one of those VCR shooting cameras and I'd just experiment.

Our generation lived in an age where it was starting to become more feasible to do things at home. You didn't have to work in the industry to be able to cut things together or shoot things or make make-up FX. It was all starting to come home slowly. Now, you can make an entire feature at home with home-made stuff. Back then, you were just seeing what was available to you. So, by the time I got to film school, I honestly was only going for the facilities. I lived and breathed film way before film school or high school. I was the film nerd in school that watched every single movie. So, when I got to film school, I had already done a commercial that I shot and cut and did everything for my dad's shop, because he's an audio customizer.

I made a little music commercial that was on MTV right before I even got to school! So, I thought, 'Alright, I'm going to film school to make my parents proud, that finally, someone in our family went to school,' but mostly it was for that film camera, and so I could get to use the flatbeds. It was for experience, because I knew what I wanted to make. I didn't need some film theory class to tell me the finer points of existentialism. Fuck all that! It's good to know all that, its great knowledge, but that's not why I was there. I didn't need to find a voice, I was already screaming at the top of my lungs and waiting for the opportunity.

Rob: Obviously, you directed *Wrong Turn 2*, your first full length feature film, but before that, you have a long history with music videos and short films. How difficult was it after school to go through that process of breaking in as a director?

I have to admit, I was extremely lucky when I got out of film school. A good friend of mine Yaniv Sharon, we were partners in crime in school. He's a guy that loves that kind of crazy, schlocky horror movie stuff. Not just the serious stuff, but when I say *Toxic Avenger* and he says, 'What's that?' You just want to open his whole world up to the world of Troma. So, my entire senior year was educating Yaniv on Troma. So, when we got out of school, I got a call from him saying, 'Dude, I got a job at Troma. Do you want to jump onto this movie with me?' I had been a Troma fan ever since I saw the first *Toxic Avenger* film in 1986 and I always had the biggest respect for Lloyd (Kaufman) because good, bad or ugly, he made a movie and millions of people saw it. So that to me, I admire the shit out of that guy.

So, I thought, 'What could be a better summer camp than to go and make a film under the offices of Troma?' At the time, after then and even now, they're the purveyors of true independent film. They're making it, they don't care what you think. They're not catering to a demographic; they're just making what they want. Thinking what they know that the fans want and putting it out there. At the time, they were making *Terror Firmer*, which I thought was the most brilliant movie idea ever. It's a Troma movie about making a Troma movie? I'm in! So, I went to work on that. And it went from me being a grip, to being an actor on that, to being a co-writer on it, by the third week, I was a background director, and then at the end Lloyd said, 'I'd love to hire you as one of our writers.' From there it just kind of snowballed and I worked at Troma for a year. While I was in New York, I made more music videos. I worked on *Uranium* on Fuse. And then coming out here to LA to do a bunch of stuff. Honestly, the thing that I think people responded to, and what anyone would respond to with anyone in this position is the amount of passion you put forth.

It didn't matter what job I was on in any given shoot or any given gig. If you show you're excited about being there and you want to do it, not just as a "paying the bills" kind of gig, or "getting your foot in the door," but doing it in a sort of lackadaisical kind of way, no one's going to care. But if you're showing that, 'Hey, I'm a PA on this thing? I'm going to give it my absolute all.' Without looking like a total brown-noser because no one likes those dudes. It was a very storied affair to go from film school to here, but I just counted every single opportunity as a step up, no matter what it was. If the music video cost me $200 bucks?

The fact that it got on *Headbangers Ball*, to me was a step up. Or working as a shooter on G4 when I came out here, the opportunities that I had and the people that I met from that job? All a step up. If you have a goal, which to me was to make a feature, and you push through and focus on it, and show everyone how much passion you have about it, eventually someone's going to notice. With me and *Wrong Turn 2*, I think part of the reason I got it is because Fox saw a music video I did for *Strapping Young Lad* which was my love letter to *The Evil Dead*. I put the band in the house from *Evil Dead*.

Rob: Wow, you did that video? I didn't even realize.

They saw that and thought, 'Oh, he must know about horror.' But the other half was me being in the room and telling them, 'I really want to tell this story.' I love the horror genre and this to me would be a dream come true. That's not to say I'll never have this opportunity again, I hope I still do, but it was that kind of passion and showing them that I know and can do everything on a set that convinced them I might know what I'm doing.

Rob: Was it intimidating for you to go in for *Wrong Turn 2* considering it was a sequel to another successful film? Didn't you pitch your version of the opening scene?

Oh yeah! Look, when I got offered the film, well, it wasn't an offer, it was 'Would you read the script and can they put you on a list,' and from what I'd heard, the list was pretty fucking long and I was at the very bottom of it. So, yeah it was totally intimidating. It was my first studio meeting too. Since then, I've done a bunch of them and I actually really enjoy them, because I get to meet new people and talk movies and geek out, but this was my first meeting, and not only that but it was my first meeting at fucking Nakatomi Plaza! (laughs) So, I've got a cine-boner walking in thinking 'Yippie Ki-Yay, Motherfucker!' And yet, I still had to do a job and be passionate about it.

When I read the script, I thought, 'Ok, it's not the best script in the world but there's a blueprint there for some really great shit to happen, and I can have a lot of fun with this, if they let me do it.' Not only that, if they let me do it the way I want to do it. I went in saying exactly that, but I went in extremely prepared. Because I had nothing to lose! I knew I was at the bottom of the list. I knew there were guys above me that were probably way more qualified and probably had way more experience under their belt, but I don't think anyone really had the kind of passion I knew I was going in with. So, I knew that I had to make a good impression.

For that opening scene, my friend Luke, who got me the job, said we got to go in there and wow them. So, I said, 'What if we storyboarded the entire first scene, but let me do the kill the way I want to do it?' Because in the script, it just cut to black right before she gets killed and just goes to the title. It's such an old gem to do that. I remember reading the script and thinking, 'Are you fucking kidding me? You can't do that!' You have to show something.

I thought, 'Well, what do I want to see?' So, that's what we boarded. I went in, sweating my ass off and freaking out. I had a twelve-page bible with everything about the film from the look to the editing to the cast to how I wanted the deaths to be, down to the rust on the trucks. To be able to go in there and show them the definitive vision that I had for it, I think threw them a little bit, because they weren't expecting anyone to come in with any kind of interest or passion at all maybe, but here it is. I open up this huge billboard and it has every shot in the opening scene. It was intimidating, but I knew I was prepared. At that point, when I walked out, I knew I did the best I could. It's really up to red-tape bullshit or politics that would prevent me from getting this job.

Rob: Once you got hired, you went through the script and put your own personal touch on things, right? I felt like every kill came from you. Each death sequence was memorable and seemed to have your stamp on it.

Yeah, I'm not going to poo-poo Al (Septien) and Turi's (Meyer) work because, like I've said before, they gave me an amazingly positive blueprint where I could go off and say, 'Ok, this death. Seen it before. Let's try something different, something creative.' The order that the people got killed in, I thought, 'Why not make further changes here so we can thwart people's expectations?' They gave me a lot of leeway with the deaths, they gave me a little less leeway on the dialogue.

There were certain things I fought my ass off on changing, but you have to pick your battles with that sort of situation. On an independent film? You have a lot more creative say. In a studio film, where you have to get the ok on everything and from multiple people, it's a lot harder to push things through. So a lot of times, a lot of the little things I tried to do, I actually had to do on set because it's easier to just kind of do it on the day and say there it is. Like the "shit ghost" joke. That was never in the script. But I knew I wanted to do it.

So, on the script I'd throw out lines, and I'd tell Steve Braun 'Shit Ghost!' And he's like 'What?' It'd take a second to process and then he'd say, 'Oh, that's good!' What was great was that the Fox executive was on set that day and even he goes, 'Oh, that's good.' So, it was hard for me in certain respects because there were a lot of things I wasn't allowed to change, and at the same token they trusted me

enough, especially with the deaths and the visual style of it, where they just allowed me to go for it, as long as I brought it in on budget. That was my biggest thing. It had to be in on time and on budget.

I would call them up and say, 'What do you think about tying up the vegan with razor wire and feeding her entrails?' And then there'd be this long pause on the phone. Finally, 'Can you do it on budget?' (laughs) That would be it! They'd process it for a minute and then ask if I could do it with the money we had. And we would always do it. I don't think we ever went over budget to do to anything like that.

The only thing we went over budget on was because we went overtime on one day, but it was nothing we could control because it rained every day on that set. There are certain things you can control and there's certain things you can't control. I think Fox gave me a lot of leeway and I'm very thankful for that.

Mike: Working with the freedom of knowing you were going to have an unrated DVD, was it liberating working with that kind of freedom?

It was and it wasn't. I didn't want to go so overboard that it would turn into a total comedy. I didn't want *Meet the Applegates* or…

Mike: Did you just say *Meet the Applegates*?! You've seen that as well? I love that movie. (laughs)

(laughs) Oh, me too. I just watched *Hudson Hawk* the other day. (Both by director Michael Lehmann) and I went, 'I wonder if Michael Lehmann knew what the fuck he was getting into even with *Meet the Applegates*?' After *Heathers*, you must be like, 'Let's change the world! What are you doing next?' 'A movie about a family that turns into bugs.' 'Alright! I guess!' (laughs) That kind of freedom was extremely liberating because I knew at the very least, it would have a home. For DVD's and most media today, content is king. So, as long as we could put it on camera and put it on film, I knew that it had a home somewhere. I knew that at the very, very least, it would be presented as a deleted scene, or on an unrated cut. Knowing that, it was just a matter of making those phone calls to see if I could do it on budget. At the very least, I know that the gore hounds will be very happy with it.

Rob: The whole "reality-television" angle to the film, did you see that as a welcome challenge, incorporating that style to the film?

Oh, I love playing with different video and audio medias. I love crossing platforms, as opposed to crossing streams or crossing swords. (laughs) I love all that stuff, if you've seen any of my music videos, I love playing with the form of breaking the fourth wall or using video in different ways. When I read the script, I know some people don't like the idea of doing a reality show, but to me I thought it was a major advantage because I got to use all of the typical stereotypes that reality shows use and employ them into a horror film.

It's an old gem to use a reality show in a horror film now. There's *My Little Eye, Halloween: Resurrection*. There's a ton of them. But I also thought here's a great way to get the broad generalization that all these horror films have when you have an ensemble cast. The black guy. The bitch. The skater-stoner dude. The annoying guy. Everyone has an archetype, it doesn't matter what kind of horror film you're watching, every character falls into one archetype or another.

Here it is, by page seven, the audience knows everyone and every archetype. So, that allowed me to go, 'Ok, good. I got all that bullshit out of the way.' I can actually spend some time in the first act on some backstory and some characterization, and I worked with the writers on that. I, at least, wanted you to follow these characters and fall in love with them just a little bit, or in Jonesy's case tolerate him a little bit by the end.

That was so important to me, because if you don't have characterization at all, then you just have body bags waiting to be opened and just let the blood spill out. So, being able to do that was incredibly invigorating to get all that shit out there. Wait, what was the question again? I'm sorry. (laughs)

Mike: No, you answered it, pretty much. But what does a wet Henry Rollins smell like?

He smells like power! (laughs) And gruff sweaty balls!

Rob: Let's talk about Henry Rollins because he's so freakin' great in this movie. One of the things you point out on the DVD commentary is that he comes into the movie with four pages of dialogue, rocks it, and then has nothing left to say for the rest of the movie. He just puts mud on his face and becomes Rambo!

Pretty much!

Rob: Obviously, you're a big fan, but how good was it to have him on board for this?

He was my rock! Literally. He wasn't on set everyday but every time that he was on set, the entire cast and crew had a great time. Not saying that we didn't on other days, but it felt like 'Special Guest, Henry's here today!' And everyone just had their A game on. Just having him there was a total morale booster and just pushed everyone further, but working with him was a fucking dream.

Look, I know Henry from his music, so in working with him as an actor, I wasn't expecting him to be as prepared as he was, and to bring in the amount of thought that went into his whole process. I'm usually throwing geeky references out with total abandon, so I don't know if anyone's going to get it or not. But when I told Henry things like, 'I want Dale to be Jeff Probst from *Survivor* and then when shit hits the fan, I want him to be a cross between Rambo and Toshiro Mifune, the samurai.' And he'd go, '*Yojimbo*, got it. Done.' He just instantly got why I said Mifune, because more than Stallone does in the first *First Blood*, Mifune uses his eyes. His eyes are his acting. Henry really has to carry the rest of his performance based solely on his eyes and how he reacts in silence, and he totally got that.

If you ever read the book he put out, *A Dull Roar*, he chronicles the entire production of *Wrong Turn 2*, or at least all the days he's on set. And you can tell how much fun he's having, aside from the fact that he had to deliver literally four pages of dialogue in one whole scene, he's used to that though. I said to myself, who better to roll off this dialogue then someone we like and want to listen to, which is Henry. Anyone who's ever listened to his spoken word or seen him live or watched his TV show, he's got a very engaging voice. To me, on a very base level, I just thought it'd be great to hear these words coming out of Henry's mouth. If the rest of the movie, he doesn't do as well? At least I know I've got them for this part. And really, that's why I've always felt they've misused Henry in the past. It's always been, OK, he's good for a laugh or for people to say, 'Hey, that guy!' I wanted to get Henry and really push him into a character and really let him develop and make the character his own. Even he said this to me, it's one of the proudest things he's done, because he felt he really did great work on this.

It wasn't just a job. He had fun doing it, he felt he did the marines proud, and that was one thing he was very, very adamant about. That the character was true to the marines. Ask any marine about *Scent of a Woman* and they'll laugh in your face. He wanted to make sure it was very true to form so that the fans would like it, but also that the marines would like it too. And he had a great time! Everybody had a great time with him, and I would work with him again in a fucking heartbeat. He was just so great to work with.

Always rolled with the punches, literally. Always just there and willing to do whatever I needed. I felt the same way, whatever he needed I was there for him as well.

Mike: Did you want Henry Rollins in this film or was it a studio decision? Who was responsible for him being in _Wrong Turn 2_?

Oh, the second I read the first ten pages, I was in Tokyo and I wrote this on my original script that I printed out to read while I was there. I wrote 'Henry Fucking Rollins.' But at the time, I thought he would never do this movie. I had thought, 'Sure, he did _Feast_, but he wouldn't want to do another one of these movies.' But I always felt it'd be great to see Henry do a kick ass movie again. I suggested it to Fox and they said they had to check his "star-meter" or whatever and see how attractive he is to investors.

Not that that makes a difference because it's Fox, but all that stuff does get taken into consideration. So, you put a list up, and I had Henry on my list. When I talked to my casting agents, I said, 'Look, I don't know if he'd ever do this, but I need Henry Rollins or a Henry Rollins-type.'

And we had some amazing actors, some guys that I'm a huge fan of come in. But I always knew in the back of my head, I gotta at least hold out for Henry. And Henry came in, we sat down and talked, and I told him, 'The one thing I don't want is Henry Rollins in fatigues.' And I instantly felt the life of the room get sucked out because the producer and the executive were standing there thinking, 'Oh no. You really fucked that up.' But I said, 'Wait, let me finish!'

The reason why I went to go see _The Chase_ was because Henry Rollins was playing a cop in it. And I thought that was great casting. Five minutes after he was on screen, I forgot it was Henry Rollins. So, I had faith in him. It took a little bit of convincing for the studio, but they saw it too. Obviously when we were on the set and they saw him do his big speech, everyone came up to me and said, 'We made the best choice in the world.' It took a little coercion, but I knew I wanted Henry from the day I first read the script.

Mike: It's funny that you mentioned _The Chase_ because I was telling Rob earlier that _Wrong Turn 2_ is Henry Rollins' best film since _The Chase_.

Oh, well thank you very much! That means a lot to me, because I'm a big fan of _The Chase_! I like what Adam (Rifkin) did with that movie. It's fun, it's fucked up. Who doesn't like a car chase with cadavers falling out of a truck? (laughs) It's brilliant! I've always liked Henry in it. What's funny is my grandmother always watches that movie because it used to always be on HBO every other day. So, when I called her up and said, 'Guess who we got? We got the guy from _The Chase_! The cop!' She was like, 'Oh my God, I love him!' She doesn't know Henry Rollins from a hole in the wall, but she knows that dude from _The Chase_ and she was thrilled. I'll have to tell my grandmother at home what you just said, she'll be thrilled to hear that quote.

Rob: You started out having a big interest in special FX as a kid, and _Wrong Turn 2_ is heavy in practical FX. Who did that work on this film and what was it like to work with the FX crew to pull off a lot of these kills you had envisioned in your head?

Well, originally, I didn't know the parameters of the budget or the schedule, so when I first went in after I got the gig, I was thinking, 'Holy fuck, I'm going to work with Stan Winston! This is going to be insane!' But they had never mentioned him in the past, because he was a producer on the first one, so they never mentioned him, so I just thought, 'I wonder how involved he is?' So, I go in and ask 'Is... Stan involved?' And they said, 'Unfortunately, no.' That broke my heart for thirty seconds, but I figured I have friends at KNB and I'm really good friends with the guys that do the _Alien_ movies, so I came to Fox and said, 'Look, I have two of the biggest FX companies in the world who both said they would love to work on this film!'

And they said, 'Well, because of tax breaks and everything, we have to do everything in Canada.' I thought OK. Instantly, I thought Bill Terezakis. Because I had read about Bill in _Fangoria_ and online about all his work, especially on _Freddy vs Jason_. When you think of New York filmmakers, instantly a name like Scorcese or Spike Lee will come up. For me, when someone says, '_Canadian Special FX artist?_' Instantly, I think of Bill Terezakis or Todd Masters, you know? I wanted Bill from the get go. We went up there and tried a bunch of shops, but Bill and I just hit it off like gangbusters from the fucking first thing we said to each other. I think it was like, 'Hey you!' and 'Hey, fuck you!' and we just started saying 'fuck you' to each other and thought OK, it's a match made in heaven.

And everything that I would explain to him like the "snorri-cam" death, the ax in the head that was attached to the camera, that was a gag that was in my head for years, because I've always said to myself, 'God, I've seen that shot done so many times. Why doesn't someone do something different with it?' Because really, horror is about expectations and diverting expectations. And I know that at the very least I wanted to try to take a convention, which in this case was a shot like this that you've seen in every movie from *Requiem for a Dream* to *See No Evil* and do something where the audience wouldn't expect it.

So that gag was incredibly important for me to get from the get-go. And when I explained it to Bill, he was just like, 'That's fucking cool!' He instantly got it, and he started jumping in and adding things to it and suggesting how we could do it. Or even the ax wound scene at the very beginning. I explained to him, 'I want these entrails to come flying out of her vagina!' He just ran with that. The rapport we had was just like two geeks who discovered each other reading *Fangoria* in the lunchroom. We both had an unbelievably mutual affection for the genre.

We both had total respect for each other and each other's work. And we both pushed ourselves. Bill and I would have conversations for like two hours every Friday night just going over at first nothing, and then thinking, 'Aren't we supposed to be going over work?' It ends up us just going over the things that make us sick. We would send each other emails with the most repugnant shit trying to find the right balance for the "Baby Splooge" character. The most absolutely God-awful images, and we were sending them with love. (laughs) That was the kind of weird, fucked up relationship I had with Bill, and really he went all out for us, more then he even had to. He believed in the movie; he believed in us and I really think it's some of his best work.

Rob: I know the original script didn't really tie much into the first movie, but how much did you want to incorporate elements from the first *Wrong Turn*? Or homage it to make this officially the sequel?

Well, to me, a good sequel is one that can stand on its own, it can have its own voice, but at the same time it has to really satiate the fans need for a reason. There has to be a reason that we're watching a sequel. For me, usually when there's a two or a three attached to it, that leads me to believe that this is the next chapter.

I don't want to see a total rehash. I don't want to see a name only or a title only or a number only sequel. And really, when I read the first draft, there were barely any ties to the original film. In the draft I read, no offense to the guys, but they even mixed up the names for "Three-Finger" with "Saw-Tooth." I was reading it thinking, 'Wasn't 'Three-Finger' the one that lived at the end of the first one?'

There was an old man in the script, but it wasn't supposed to be the one from the first film. I even asked, 'Is this supposed to be the old man from the first film?' And they said, 'No.' Well, it should be! Because there's no reason

why it wouldn't be. I wanted to make sure that there was at least some story and character ties, because I knew I was not going to be adhering to Rob Schmidt's visual style with this.

He did the 70's homage with *Wrong Turn*, I wanted to do an 80's homage with *Wrong Turn 2*. I wanted to make sure that at least when fans watched this, whether they like it or not, they're going to say this definitely feels tonally and stylistically different from the first film. Say like how *Aliens* is to *Alien*, but as long as there are little things in there, like the old man from the gas station from the first one is here, and obviously "Three-Finger." If you look closely, some of the clothing from the first film remerges on some of the characters in *2*. Little things like that are only going to make people go, 'Oh, I get it!'

I knew they were going to package the two films together. I want people to watch both of them back-to-back. So, by the time they get to the end of it, for example, when they realize in part *2* that the old man who was in the first film was really in on it the whole time, it's going to completely change the way they watch the first film again. Basically, I gave you another viewing on it, because you get to go back and go, 'Fuck me! That old man was in on it the whole time!'

Mike: That bastard!

I'm sorry, but that to me is a good sequel. Because then you can watch them together and feel like you're part of a bigger story. And I really think there is more of a story to tell too. So, I'm hoping that if the movie does well and Fox goes ahead with a *Wrong Turn 3*, that they'll at least respect the first two films and make sure that there's a tie so that someone could say it was all part of our grand scheme. The *Wrong Turn* trilogy! (laughs)

Rob: When everybody heard that Fox was going to do a sequel, fans didn't seem that interested or thrilled. But over the the past year, you've gone to horror conventions and shown clips, and I feel that your enthusiasm has just completely sold everyone in the horror community that this was in good hands. What's it been like for you to go out there, meet fans and tell them, 'Look! This doesn't suck. I tried to make a good movie for you guys!'

Oh my God, it's been… this year alone… I thought last year was an amazing year. Actually, getting the movie, making the film all in a year, I thought that was amazing. But actually having the finished film and liking it, which is a big thing for me. Because I hate all my own work. You guys know, you are your own harshest critic sometimes, and if you're not, you should be. The film was finished around December and to have this film done and under my belt that I could say I liked and was proud of, and then going to all the conventions, I mean I grew up going to these conventions. And I know what it's like to see a filmmaker that is genuinely excited about their project, and then see filmmakers that are genuinely not excited, or who just don't give a shit, or just there for the quick buck or whatever.

I've been to those, so have you. You know what it's like when you go to a New York convention and hear Sam Raimi get up there and talk about *Darkman* and everyone flips out. Then you see Abel Ferrara get up there and talk about *Body Snatchers* and you think, 'Oh, really?' It was so amazing to go out and for once be on the other side of it with me not just being the fan, although I still was, at the front row of every panel, raising my hand, 'Excuse me, Mister Tony Todd, I have a question!' (laughs) That line is completely blurred to me.

People are like, 'Aren't you supposed to be in the back with the guests?' Fuck that. Why? I'm here to hang out. It's been amazing.

Rob: I love that we were all about fifteen years old and going to the same *Fangoria* shows in New York. We'd be waiting on the same lines to meet the same celebrities. And in this past year, between filmmakers like you and Adam Green getting up on stage, you're the only two guys that reminded me of what it was like when I was a kid. Filmmakers that were very excited to share their movies!

I've seen Bruce Campbell get up there and flip himself on stage! I remember Ron Underwood doing a panel for *Tremors*. You can just tell that they're genuinely excited about it. I know for a fact that Adam (Green) is very proud of *Hatchet*, no matter what shit he gets for it, or no matter whatever accolade he gets for it, he is proud of his movie. I feel the same exact way. I am extremely proud of what I got to do. Is it perfect? No fucking way! No way is *Wrong Turn 2* by any stretch of the means a perfect film, but for what it is and for the influences I had on it, I know I did a successful job on it. So, why not tell people?

Plus, if the film was theatrical, it'd be a lot easier. People are smart enough to think that when a film is theatrical, then it must mean that the studio loves it and when the film is direct-to-video, then the studio doesn't love it. There are so many online critics out there on the IMDb message boards who think they know the whole score. 'The reason *Wrong Turn 2* is not in theaters is because the studio thinks it sucks!' That's unfair. I hate to say that, but that's

an unfair stigma that doesn't apply to this film, especially over the fact that Fox actually did consider putting it out theatrically. It didn't mean that they didn't like the film and that's the reason it didn't go out. It's just that financially it didn't make sense to put a horror film out in the summer, especially after the walloping they got with *The Hills Have Eyes 2*. For me, I felt it was an awesome, ambitious challenge to spend the next couple of months, going out there, meeting fans and just saying, 'Hey, I'm really proud of my movie, I think you'll like it, because I'm one of you guys.

Look, we all have different tastes, but if you like splatter movies and you like 80's horror like I do, you're going to really dig this movie and you might want to give it a fair shot.' When it was announced before I was even hired, I did the same thing. I thought OK. It was only after I got to see the possibilities with it and then to be given the reign to do what I could with it. Horror on video is changing in a big way, because you have films like this, and you have Anchor Bay supporting films like *Behind the Mask*, even though it got a limited theatrical release which was bunk in a way, the film obviously is catching an audience on video. Besides, all the films that influenced me are ones that I saw on video. So, I felt like it was the perfect opportunity to pay tribute to those and also get away with as much fucked up shit as I could, because I knew that I would have this unrated DVD to show it all.

Mike: Being that *Wrong Turn 2* focused on the other relatives of the mutants from the original film, were you ever tempted to re-title it *Wrong Turn Too!*?

My original title when I went into Fox was *Another Wrong Turn*. Part of it was because "2" sometimes scares people off. I thought here's a way I'd be able to do my own thing, and the title will help people get it. If you called *Aliens Alien 2*, I think it would've had a different effect, but the fact that it's called *Aliens*, you get the sequel, but you also feasibly say that is a different movie than *Alien*. I figured if it's called *Another Wrong Turn* that could work. Believe me, I contemplated the *Teen Wolf Too*, with the T-O-O. (laughs) I definitely did. I thought, 'Hey, they're making it as well.' I got the understanding that Fox wanted to make sure it was right next to the first *Wrong Turn* in terms of the boxes at Blockbuster, so obviously *Another Wrong Turn* would not have allowed that. I tried, I tried for the T-O-O. I swear. I thought I'd have Jason Bateman fly in with hair everywhere. (laughs)

TIFFANY SHEPIS

Interviewed by Rob Galluzzo (11/07)

One of the busiest actresses working in our beloved genre has to be Tiffany Shepis. With over fifty credits to her name, a majority of them in horror, she's established herself as a fan favorite! *The Hazing, Abominable*, and *Ted Bundy* are just a few of the many credits on her resume. She's also the lead the After Dark's *Nightmare Man* from writer/director Rolfe Kanefsky. Read on for our *Fright* exclusive chat with Tiffany Shepis!

What are your earliest recollections of the horror genre? Do you remember the first films that scared you or had an impact on you and opened you up to the world of horror?

Yeah! First things first, *Children of the Corn*. My mom would not let us watch it in the house, which is weird because she had no problem with *I Spit on Your Grave*. (laughs) No problem with *The Toxic Avenger*. But for some reason, *Children of the Corn*, we were not allowed to watch. My brother was five years older than me, so anytime my mom would go out of town, we would just have bad B-movie night. It'd be everything from USA Up All Night to the early Troma stuff. We would even make movies as kids and then watch our own.

You started acting fairly early and most people know that you did work at Troma. My question is how difficult was it in the beginning to get into acting? Especially being a young actress in New York?

I think I did a commercial and I'd mess around at school and people would say, "Oh, you should do movies!" We would make our own little neighborhood movies and try to kill everyone in the neighborhood. But it was kind of a far off shot to be an actress, I never had any aspirations like, "I'm going to move off to Hollywood and do films!" It was just things that we'd do around the block. Then I went to a school in Manhattan and it was one of those weird schools for actor kids, I guess? The reason my parents put me there was because I wasn't doing well in any school! One of these kids had an ad for Troma and they were casting for *Tromeo and Juliet*. I knew the name, obviously, because my brother

and I would watch their movies every weekend. So, I cut school and went to the audition. From that minute on, I was hooked. Before that, it was more like, "Ah, we'll make movies around the house!" But from being on that set, I realized that this was it. I can't be anything else. Granted, I was so young and it was my first movie and you can always have that kind of excitement at that age, but this was it. Thankfully the horror genre is real loyal and allows me to continue doing it.

I know a lot of the same people we know got their start at Troma. Actually, it's funny, pretty much anyone from the east coast gets their start at Troma! Rolfe (Kanefsky) I believe worked there for a while…

Yeah! He worked on *Troma's War*!

Yeah, and even Joe Lynch worked with Troma. Yeah, Joe Lynch, who's my *Thirsty* co-star. Also, Trent Haaga, who I just starred in *Bonnie and Clyde vs Dracula* with started at Troma.

We'll get to those! But I really want to talk to you about *Nightmare Man*, which is opening in theaters as part of this November's After Dark Fest 2. What can you tell us about *Nightmare Man* and who do you you play in it?

I play a character named Mia. I know it sounds kind of typical, but some friends are throwing a party at a cabin, and my best friend's getting married to this douche-baggy guy that I don't like. Some underlying tension between her and I, you're not sure if there's some lesbian thing going

216

on there, but there's some tension! I'm kind of the crazy friend that brings the young boyfriend with me. Basically, this crazy chick comes knocking on our door screaming, "Someone's after me! Someone's after me!" We get a call from her husband that tells us not to listen to a word she says because she's nuts.

So, it's one of those, "What do you do in that situation?" things. Do you believe the husband? Or do you believe the chick that there's someone after her? And, of course, all hell breaks loose. That's my character and the story in a nutshell. That project was our baby, you know? Rolfe wrote it with me in mind and I've worked with Rolfe several times. When I read the script, I thought "Fuck! We need to do this!" And then we made it, and we were all jazzed about it, I told Rolfe, "Please don't give this away like we do with everything else!" (laughs) But it did nothing for a while. Everybody's pretty much seen it.

It's screened at festivals. I thought it easily could've been a midnight college town release! But it just didn't have the right promotion behind it. So, I kept pushing Rolfe to not give this movie away. And then of course, we delayed it, and we still hadn't given it away, and I said, "Wait. Don't take me seriously, man! Sell this movie!" (laughs) "Put this out on shelves!" But thank God to Rolfe for waiting, because we got into the After Dark event, which is actually a really funny story! He doesn't usually go to Comic-Con, but he went and I was showing up, which is why he stuck around. And he called me and said, "Hey, I gave my movie to the After Dark Film Festival!" And I thought "Way to go! You just lost $60 bucks on a press kit. Nothing's going to happen with that!" (laughs) I felt like an awful friend because I wasn't being supportive and I don't even know why. I figured these companies get really, really big movies. But After Dark picked it up and that's pretty rad, because that's the best we could've asked for! A theatrical release in 350 theaters? For this movie, that's huge.

That's awesome! And I remember it being the first film announced. I was so happy for you guys!

Yeah, I know! I was at a convention when I heard it, and I announced it to everybody and then thought, "Wait a minute, I probably shouldn't announce this because it's probably bullshit! It's probably some lie to fuck with Rolfe!" (laughs) I didn't really believe it! You know, 350 movie theaters in the grand scheme of things is small potatoes for Hollywood, but for the indie B-horror film, that's huge!

From what I understand about *Nightmare Man*, it's very different from things you've done in the past in the sense that Rolfe crosses different horror genres in it. Meaning, it's got the "slasher" element to it, it's got the cabin in the woods, the supernatural element. Does that factor into why it's one of the films you hold close to you?

Yeah, I think it's really different, and I hold it in personal high regard because I like my performance in it. If you've seen any of my movies, it's not often I get really cool shit to work with. I may get a really cool death scene like in *Abominable* and I love that movie, but I really didn't have much of a character. So as far a character piece and a chance for me to say, "Hey, look! You know, I don't just have a great ass!" (laughs) "I can actually deliver lines!" I was really jazzed about that and that's why I hold *Nightmare Man* close to me. Rolfe is one of my best friends, so he knows how to write for me, and he knows what I'm good at.

Since you guys have worked together so frequently, is it safe to say that you have developed a shorthand or easy way of working together on these projects?

Absolutely. I mean, he knows how I work, I know how he works. I think in all the years of working together, we've only gotten into one fight, and it was over something stupid in *Nightmare Man*. It's working with your best friend. It doesn't get any better than that. And that's why I like the genre in general, because almost every time I get to work with someone, it's another friend of mine. It's a fairly small, tight-knit unit.

I tend to notice the horror community is very supportive of each other. Amongst both filmmakers and fans. It's rare to see that in other genres of film.

They are for the most part! There are a few that are kind of douchey. But for the most part, I'd say ninety percent of them are super supportive and I think that's because we have to be! When you don't have $40 million ad campaigns out there pushing your movie, you have to go through word of mouth, and you have to go through your friends. So just because I went and supported *Wrong Turn 2* doesn't mean that no one's going to see my movie. You know what I'm saying? You have to support your buddies and hope that they support you back. I think that's why everybody's so close, because they all know how hard it is to make a film. They know how hard it is to get one out there. Plus, it's fun! It's fun to be around people that enjoy the same thing that you do. Who wants to drag along their shitty boyfriend or girlfriend who doesn't like these movies? (laughs)

You mentioned *Abominable* before. One of the funny stories that writer/director Ryan Schifrin told us was about your audition. You were one of the last people that they saw, and when they met you, it was almost an instantaneous thing that they knew they were going to cast you as Tracy, and you knew you had that part. What do you remember about that?

(laughs) You know, I don't remember much of it, but I do remember walking in and saying something to the effect of, "You guys… know you're going to cast me." (laughs) "So, let's just cut out the middleman here!" It was just one of those things that was just like, it's not often that I get auditions for a movie. And this was a group of people that I really didn't know, I'd worked with (cinematographer) Neal Fredericks before and I knew that he referred me.

I walked in and I looked at them and they looked at me, and it was just kind of this weird connection. It was great, because the Schifrins have become such great friends of mine. I was super jazzed! At that point, I think I knew that Jeffrey Combs was involved, and I thought, "I need to be in this movie! There's no other way around it!"

As a genre fan, I don't remember if you directly had scenes with some of these people in *Abominable*, but did you get a chance to talk and meet with Jeffrey Combs or Lance Henriksen or Dee Wallace?

Um, I actually never met Jeffrey, ever! Even after all the conventions I've gone to, I've never met him or worked with him or anything. I'd gotten to work with Lance Henriksen in another movie called *Dark Reel* and he's a pretty fun, rad dude. Dee Wallace, I've met a few times in passing at conventions and, actually, I think at the Schifrin's house. (laughs) In that movie, it was really weird because there were all these great people in it, but none of them really had scenes together.

Another film that I really like you in is *The Hazing*, which is another film you did with Rolfe. What stands out for you about that movie now in retrospect? Besides that amazing silver outfit!

Well, the silver outfit, of course. (laughs) But, fucking Brad Dourif, man! That guy is just cool! My biggest memory from it is that he actually came to my house. He came to my shitty apartment in the Valley and went over his English accent with me, so that I could nail it down, like the way he speaks.

I'm thinking, "This is a low budget movie! What are you doing?" (laughs) But he was just very cool, he came over and helped and he made me all these tapes for reference. He's

just this rad guy and working with him was awesome. *The Hazing* was a super close project for me, because that's how I met Rolfe. Years and years earlier when I had a distribution company, he came to us with the script for *The Hazing* to produce it and I loved the script. I thought, "Man, I want to produce this movie, I want to play Marsha. We need to make this film!" But our company was really new and really young. We were only able to come up with $100,000 dollars, but we knew that movie couldn't be made for that. Rolfe and I just stayed in touch and, finally, he was able to get it off the ground. And still, even after being friends with Rolfe after all these years, I still had to work my ass off to get that part!

I heard you had to audition several times!

Yeah! I came in and they're like, "She's not innocent enough." I come in to do innocent and then they're like, "Well, she's not tough enough." Are you kidding? I went in for it seven times. I came to find out years later that I wasn't even the first choice for it. I was the first choice to Rolfe, but the producer wanted this other chick, and she turned it down. Yay for her! It all worked out though. It was a really cool project that I really wanted for a very long time, and I was super happy with the way it came out. I still get tons of emails all the time from that movie, mostly about the silver space suit. (laughs)

Right after that one, you did *Corpses*, which I heard was a bit of a difficult experience for you guys?

Oh boy. (laughs) There were so many fucking problems on that movie. I just wrapped *Abominable*, which I was pregnant on. When I was on *Corpses*, I was pregnant. Everything that could've gone wrong went wrong. Like the producer stole a bunch of money, there was a bunch of nonsense. Whatever. I still think it was kind of fun, if you go into it looking for just a cheesy, corny zombie movie. If you go into it seriously, you're going to be disappointed with it. We actually heard from Jake West, and he was like (in British accent), "You know, I watched *The Hazing* and I was so excited… and then I watched *Corpses*." (laughs) Yeah, man. It was a downer that we had to go through that experience, but that's the world of moviemaking. Sometimes you get these million-dollar budgets and sometimes? Not so much.

You did the *Ted Bundy* movie from that company that did a series of serial killer based movies like *Dahmer* with Jeremy Renner, *Gein*, *Gacy*. *Ted Bundy* was the only one I thought was fairly decent.

Well, it had Matthew Bright directing it! And despite Matthew Bright's craziness, he's a genius! (laughs) If you've seen *Freeway*, that movie's awesome! It was really sick and really fucked up, and I was super jazzed to be a part of that. But it was weird because after it came out, I got a lot of hate mail from people saying we glorified *Ted Bundy* and that he's some type of fucking hero in our movie and it shouldn't be comical. It's true. The man killed lots of girls in terrible ways and none of that's funny. But the fact of the matter is, when you think of the time that that happened, shit… it was funny because someone goes, "Hey! Why don't you hop into my car, and I'll drive you down the street to my place!" and the girl goes, "OK!" That's fucking weird that that shit used to happen! I'm sure it still happens today, but not like then when people were just so trusting.

If I remember correctly, I didn't think *Bundy* glorified anything. It just told the whole story from start to finish. I liked at the end we see him sobbing like a baby in the electric chair. It ends exactly the way it happened in real life and shows him for what he was, right until the end. You know what I mean?

All I know is we got tons of letters from people afterwards. I thought, "Hey, what're you bitchin' at me for? I'm the one that kicked his ass! You should be rooting me on!" It was a weird movie. It had a small theatrical run in art-house theaters, and it did ok. It was what it was and it's unfortunate that Matthew's not doing more stuff these days.

Well, I saw the trailer for this the other day, and I think the title says it all… *Bonnie and Clyde vs Dracula*. And you're Bonnie!

Dude! I am! And I am so excited about that movie! We shot it last July in Kansas City, Missouri. And it's… fucking *Bonnie and Clyde vs Dracula*! That's really it! The first half of the movie is basically a Bonnie and Clyde on the run movie. They're on the road, pulling off heists, and it's awesome! Because these kids in Kansas City really pulled together and made everything look 1930's. We had real cars. And then the whole thing switches. Because one of my guys gets shot up, I have to go to this spooky mansion to get a doctor, the only doctor in town, and it turns out he's housing Dracula there! What gets better than that?! (laughs) You know?

I'm sold!

The funny thing is, when we were shooting it, we all thought, "Man, I really want to see both of these films." I don't know how it's going to play all together, but both parts of the movie were just awesome because they were two separate different things. I got that and found out Trent Haaga, my old Troma

cohort who hosted all the East Coast Troma segments while I hosted the West Coast segments, was in it too. So, we never actually had any scenes together in anything before. We were in a few movies but never had any scenes together. Sure, we had met, but only on brief occasions. He ended up playing Clyde and when I got there, he was in full garb. He had the hat on and his gun. He looked so bad ass. I thought, "All right, this movie's going to be good." (laughs) I saw the trailer the other day and I was blown away.

You've worked on so many movies varying in budget and quality over the years. Are there any wacky experiences that just completely stand out where you thought, "Only in show business would this happen!"

Shit! Not that I can remember off hand, but every movie's different, man. Every movie you have a whole different group of kids. And especially since my budgets do vary so much. (laughs) It's ridiculous from the $5,000 budget movies where I think, "Oh my God, did you guys really just pay me two grand and the movie's being shot for five?" to the $5 million dollar ones, so you get a whole slew of different people. It's just the people that you meet. It's always pretty interesting, because the people shooting them are usually fans. That's sometimes kind of strange because I'm a free agent. So, people tend to email me directly or occasionally go through my manager and I end up in the middle of nowhere, Idaho getting off a plane thinking, "Jesus Christ, is this person going to be a wacky, weirdo serial killer that's like 'Sure, the movie shoot is this way!'" There's always spooky thoughts going into some of these things, but nothing, knock on wood, weird has happened to me! (laughs)

***Nightmare Man* will be playing in theaters in November as part of After Dark Fest 2, followed by a DVD release early next year. Is there anything about it you specifically want to tell *Icons* readers? Why should they see this movie when there are seven other films to die for competing with it? What's this have that those other flicks don't?**

Ummm… Tiffany Shepis! With a hot bra and panties and a crossbow and a shotgun! Naked demon rape… do I need to say more?

You know what? I don't think any of those other films have those things going for it.

Exactly! I definitely know they don't have Tiffany Shepis in them, and I really doubt that any of them have naked demon rape. Nothing against the other seven! I want them all to do well. I just want mine to do a tiny bit better.

CERINA VINCENT

Interviewed by Rob Galluzzo (10/07)

Icon of Fright is proud to present an interview with actress Cerina Vincent, who made her debut in the horror genre with *Cabin Fever*. She's also appeared in *It Waits* and most recently opposite Erik Palladino and Jeffrey Combs in *Return to House on Haunted Hill*. We had a casual chat with her about all of the above and it became quickly obvious that she's just as sweet as she is beautiful. Read on for our *Fright* exclusive interview with Cerina Vincent!

What are your earliest recollections of the horror genre? Do you remember the first films to really scared you? What was your introduction into the world of horror?

My introduction into horror was when I was about nine, I went to a slumber party and the parents of this girl decided that it was smart to rent all three *Poltergeist* movies! We watched them all and it scared the crap out of me. It really turned me off horror! I was scared to death of everything!

I can see at nine that being traumatic!

I was young, and I remember I got braces and I was scared they were going to attack me. That just put things in my head for years! (laughs) So, that was my first experience with horror and it kind of turned me off of it because I was a wuss. Then I started working in the genre and, of course, now I have a whole new appreciation for it.

Is it safe to say that you stayed away from horror for a couple of years because of *Poltergeist*?

Yeah. Because I really didn't sleep for a few days. I thought about that movie for years! Totally.

Can you explain a bit about the origins of your acting career? Because I read that you started out as a singer/dancer and also became Miss Nevada Teen in 1996. How'd that all lead you into acting and was that a difficult transition?

Well, my mom was a ballet teacher, so we had a dance

studio in the back of our house. I grew up dancing around her studio when I was two or three. I would sing and make up skits with my cousins and all that kind of stuff. I wasn't the best dancer, there's no way I could've gone into that as a career like my mother did. At twelve, I was in a theatre ensemble and I did plays and musicals, which is how I started singing. Then I started doing local commercials and, at sixteen, I entered the Miss Nevada Teen contest for some reason, and I went on to Miss Teen USA. Basically, you're there for a full month shooting a TV show. That broadened my horizons and made me interested in TV and film. After high school, I came out here and it just sort of happened.

It sounds like a very natural progression for you.

Yeah, it was.

You're in *Return to House on Haunted Hill* where you play Michelle. Your character has a lot of ulterior motives that aren't always exactly clear throughout the duration of the movie. What can you tell us about your character of Michelle and what part does she play in the *House on Haunted Hill* sequel?

Well, Michelle is very self-involved and selfish, which... I guess means the same thing! (laughs) She uses men to get what she wants, I think she'll use anything to get what she wants. I feel like she was probably raised very poorly. She's untrustworthy. The role was actually a challenge for me, to be quite honest. I'm obviously not the lead of the film, but I still wanted to make her somewhat likable. It was hard because everything I pretty much said was kind of bitchy.

(laughs) And I don't think she's supposed to be likable. It was fun, and the character has a few interesting little twists. There's some backstabbing. She's in it for the money. Have you seen the branching scenes yet?

No. I only have the regular DVD, and the branching option is only on the HD-DVD! I think that's such a cool idea. But I only watched it as a straight-forward version of the film.

Yeah, I think that's what makes the film interesting and more fun. It was confusing as an actor. You look at your role and figure out, "Ok, at the beginning of the script I'm here. By the end of it, I'm here." You figure out your arc, and if you're shooting out of sequence, you try to make sure you're staying within your arc. When you shoot branching scenes, or navigational cinema, as it's being called, there are added scenes that maybe are different than what your character would do in the regular script. It's challenging, but it makes it a lot more fun and interesting.

It sounds like such a challenge to have to do a scene and then have to do a completely alternate version of it right after. Did you have any problems doing that? Or was it well prepared in advance?

I think it was a challenge for everyone because we weren't sure what we were doing when we were shooting it. We couldn't exactly understand how this was all going to work? But now in hindsight, it's really cool. It was confusing in the moment to shoot it. Because you shoot a movie out of sequence as is, and then you have to think, "Wait, is this scene before branching? Or after branching? Do I have my gun? Do I not?" It's confusing for everyone, including the prop people or wardrobe. Everyone. So, it was definitely challenging but totally worth it. I think it adds a little something to the film and makes it a little more interesting.

Did you watch or familiarize yourself with the first movie before you went to work on the sequel?

I hadn't seen it in a while, but when I got this role, the first thing I did was re-watch the first one. I actually didn't see the original, which… perhaps I should get myself together and watch it since I haven't yet!

Director Victor Garcia comes from a background with special FX make-up and after doing a short film, this was his first feature length movie. What was your working experience with him like considering this was his first big project debuting as a director?

Ok, first of all, before I even walked on the set, I'd heard all these great things about Victor. When I met him, all the things I heard were indeed true and I'd seen his short film and he is indeed extremely talented. But what's also awesome about Victor is that he's just a really cool guy and a really good person who has a really big heart. I'm excited for him! I think just doing the short with a couple of actors and then getting thrown onto a giant movie studio production and having to direct a ton of us in the film, I'm sure it was overwhelming. But he did a really good job and we all really worked together to try to make it work.

I know you have a very brief scene with Jeffrey Combs, but what was it like to meet and work with him? He's so beloved in the genre and such a great actor! In fact, he's one of my favorite actors.

Jeffrey Combs is again, so talented but also a really cool guy and a smart man. Down to earth and funny and warm. I did a brief scene with him in the movie, but I've also seen him around at some of the horror conventions. I just really admire him as a human being! Even though we didn't get a chance to really act together much, it was an honor to be in the same scene with him because I really do admire him.

It's been about five years since *Cabin Fever*…

Oh my God! I'm getting old! (laughs)

Oh come on! No, you are not! Looking back in retrospect, what about *Cabin Fever* stands out for you now when you think back about it?

I mean, honestly? Everything! It's one of those… It's rare when you do a job, and it changes your life. I've done so many projects that no one has seen, and then so many projects that aren't that good. But *Cabin Fever* was just one of those things that from the moment I got the script, I remember everything about it. I remember the audition, I remember first meeting the cast, first meeting Eli.

I remember the first day of shooting. It was one of those films that was just fantastic from the start. I had no idea what it was going to be! But Eli did. (laughs) He knew. He said this is going to be huge and change your life. I didn't quite understand that while we were shooting, but he was right. It was a huge success, and it did change my life. And I'm really, really grateful for that. I mean, if it wasn't for that movie, we wouldn't be having this conversation right now. It was that movie that got me known in the horror genre and got me horror fans and that's why people want me in their horror movies! I'm grateful for every aspect of it.

The film was shot in twenty-four days in North Carolina, which is a fairly short period of time to shoot a movie. Compared to other films you've worked on, was it difficult because of the budget and time constraints? Or was it a blast? Because it looks like you guys had a great time.

It was a blast. It's always difficult. It was freezing cold, so things like that made it hard. At one point in the production, the crew went on strike, so we were down for a day and didn't know how we were going to finish the film. There are always production hurdles like that, but it was just an all out great experience. I mean, I've done some other films where disasters happen and you just can't wait to get off the movie!

And you can't wait to get over the project, because of the people involved. *Cabin Fever* was great, but of course we had obstacles. I remember the dog that wouldn't work. Then we got a new dog, and it turned out to be an attack dog and we were all scared. But in the end, it was all worth it. Obviously.

One of the things that completely freaks me out is the idea of catching something. Especially if it were something like a flesh-eating virus. You obviously have one of the most infamous scenes in the movie when you shave your leg. Can you talk about the making of one of the most gruesome scenes in the movie? Do you remember anything from when you guys shot that?

Oh absolutely. I remember every detail! But yes, me too, one of my biggest fears is catching something. That's what I really loved about the script. I thought it was interesting that the monster wasn't a monster, the monster was a virus. The leg shaving scene was incredibly difficult to shoot, but it was one of those things I was excited about because I knew it was going to be a cool scene. I was sitting in a bathtub in the middle of a soundstage at 4am, it was [freezing cold] in the water, and I was naked.

The bathtub was dirty and bloody and disgusting! It was very awkward to shoot. It was obviously a very emotional scene, but it was also very technical, the reveal of the prosthetic. I remember disagreeing with Eli saying, "When we shave our legs, we look at our legs! Women look to see where they're shaving!" And he said, "I know! But… we're not going to be doing that here. You have to be so in your own zone, and not paying attention." And I thought, "Well, wouldn't it hurt?" And so, it was hard to shoot! Just to get the acting right and the emotion right.

Technically, it was difficult because of the position I was in and the fact that it was cold, and I was naked, and everyone was watching! But it turned out really great.

What a great pay off though when you see that scene with an audience and hear the reaction! I cringe!

Yeah, and that's obviously the editor and Eli. (laughs) And the make-up. A lot of people went into making that scene.

After you finished *Cabin Fever*, you and Jordan Ladd went on to shoot a few shorts with David Lynch for his web content. What was your experience like working with David? I know Eli worked with him for a very long time.

Yeah, that's true! It was amazing. Amazing! Eli introduced us to him, and Jordan and I got coffee at Lynch's house. David was like, "You know what? I want to shoot something with you guys!" I didn't really believe it! I couldn't imagine why he'd want to work with me! (laughs) But it was true. I remember Eli called me said, "Ok, you're going to shoot something with David tomorrow." And I'm like, "Tomorrow?! What are we shooting?" "I don't know. He'll get in touch with you and give you your lines and script." He faxed over these pages, this scene that made absolutely no sense to me. (laughs) It was brilliantly written, but I had no idea what any of it meant and I called my acting couch and was working with her until midnight, and then went in the next day and did it with him. He said, "That's great, Cerina! Now, do the whole scene completely monotone. I don't want you to move at all!" (laughs) His direction was just fascinating to watch. You just trust him, and he has such a warm heart and he's very hands on; he's everything you think that he would be. He's just a genius and a really cool human being. That goes down as one of my favorite things I've ever done in this business.

You were also in a horror movie called *It Waits*. Your character of Danielle has quite an interesting story arc that she goes through. Plus, you have a monster to deal with, literally! How did you approach working on *It Waits*? It was a lead role for you, and the majority of the film weighs on you.

I'm really grateful for that film, because it was my first lead. It was pretty much me in that movie, with that monster and that bird. (laughs) Um, it was a lot of work. Psychically. We shot in Vancouver and it was freezing and we were shooting nights and I was really sick the whole film. I'm grateful for that film because it gave me the opportunity to show that I can carry a film and how hard it is to do that, and how much work goes into that. I really took a lot away personally from that experience. I worked really hard, and it is what it is. It's obviously not brilliant or life changing. (laughs) But it was a life-changing experience personally for me.

Well, the coolest thing about the movie, besides you of course, was the creature design! Please tell me you took pictures with that thing?

Oh, I did! I did. I need to find them. But they did a fantastic job with the monster. They spent a lot of time and a lot of money on it. It was really cool in person. It was really scary in person. If you could've been on set and seen what that monster looked like in the dark, in the rain, in the middle of a forest, it was really cool.

You've done several convention appearances throughout the past couple of years. What's the convention experience like from your perspective?

I had heard that these conventions existed, but I had no idea what they were or how to get involved! It just sort of happened. So, the first one was shocking to me. I'd never been to a convention before or seen anything like it. I think there's a lot of people and a lot of actors that have mixed feelings about going to them, but I like it because you get so caught up living in this city, living in LA and this business and auditioning and almost getting parts and then not. Booking parts and having them be recast. It's hard! So, for one weekend, you can go away and remember again why you are working, and remember why you are in this business and that's having a chance to meet your fans. There are some times when I feel completely insignificant, and it is a really hard business and it is hard to get from A to B, or B to A. So, when you get to go and have conversations with the people that are actually the reason why we work, it makes me happy. It makes me feel this is the reason why we do this, which is to meet these people.

Last question, what scares you and what are among your favorite horror movies?

Oh, good question! Well, *Poltergeist* scares me.

Never got over that one, did you?

No! My favorite horror movies of recently? – and it's not because I know Eli, but it's *Hostel*. 1 and 2. I think they're great. They're a lot of fun. I'm really happy for him and I really thoroughly enjoy those movies. *The Shining*, obviously, is fantastic. That goes down as one of my favorites, and again I really enjoyed the two *Hostel* movies.

In real life, my fear is bugs! In any form.

Special thanks to Tracy Galermo!

TOM WOODRUFF JR.

Interviewed by Mike Cucinotta (12/07)

Next time you watch *The Monster Squad*, try to imagine the Gillman holding an Oscar. That's because the man in the suit is Academy Award winning effects wizard Tom Woodruff Jr., who over the last thirty years has been on the forefront of practical visual effects. As a kid, he taught himself how to use greasepaint in the bathroom mirror after seeing *Planet of the Apes*. As an adult, he trained alongside some of the biggest names in the effects industry. He would then sculpt, design, and even perform some of the most memorable creatures in modern horror movie history.

Not too long ago *The Monster Squad*, in which you played the Gillman, finally came out on DVD and was a hugely successful release. Were you surprised at how well *The Monster Squad* DVD sold? It almost immediately sold out everywhere.

Yes, I was surprised. I knew a lot of people were very interested in the movie and a lot of that was because it wasn't available. Had it been out on DVD, I think people would have picked it up and not caused such a stir. It was one of those things that was unavailable, which made people want it even more. I know, as Fred Dekker has said, it wasn't a hugely successful movie when it first came out. We all thought it was great, but it wasn't a hit. But still, you've seen far smaller movies come out on DVD. It was a situation where the ownership of it kind of got shuffled around and it didn't happen for so long. I think that helped it to age, you know?

So, what were your some of your earliest memories of the horror genre?

Well, my earliest memories were of the Universal monster movies. The original *Frankenstein*. Not so much *Dracula*, which always kind of bored me for some reason. I always liked the imagery of being in the basements of the mansions and the castles, but for me it was always *Frankenstein*, *The Wolf Man*, and *Creature from the Black Lagoon*. And I remember from when I was a kid, *Abbott and Costello Meet Frankenstein* was a very cool movie because it played all the Universal monsters for real. They didn't make fun of the monsters, it was just really well done for the time. It was funny but it still had some good monsters in it.

When you first caught the Universal movies, was it back when they were finally getting replayed on TV?

Yeah, it would have been probably the mid to late 60's. I was able to see them on TV when I lived back east and would always get things like Chiller Theater. They would show a lot of crap, but every once in a while, they'd show a real classic. When they showed the Karloff *Frankenstein*, I remember that was a big event for me, to have to wait until Saturday.

Did you have a favorite horror host on TV?

No. It's funny because I wasn't much into the hosts. I can't remember the guy's name out of New York. A guy with dark glasses trying to be cool and mysterious and shadowy. I would always want to get through that stuff and get back to the movie.

So would these have been the movies that inspired you to get into special effects?

For me, it became more of a career goal when the *Planet of the Apes* movies came out. I remember picking up *Famous Monsters of Filmland*, this was before I'd seen the movie, and seeing pictures of the John Chambers makeup and thinking, "This is what I want to do." It was amazing seeing that in a magazine at the time.

Were you the kind of kid who went home and had to try this stuff out?

Yeah, I put down *Famous Monsters of Filmland* and picked up the yellow pages and started looking for theatrical makeup. But I lived in a small town and there wasn't any to be had. There was one store in a neighboring town, so of course, at age twelve, I immediately had visions of my mom taking me to the store and expecting bins of makeup and all the tools and the right pieces of the puzzle to put together. She finally drives me over to this drugstore and it's a small case of grease paint and a few boxes of crepe hair. But I bought it. These were the tools, this was what I needed.

Also, it was difficult to get information. I went to the school library and checked out a book on makeup and started to learn how to work with crepe hair and how to apply grease paint. I started to learn the basics about shadows and highlights. At the time, there was something about having to dig for all that information. You really have to be motivated; it wasn't easy to find at the time. There certainly weren't any DVDs or instructional videotapes like we have today. You had to be motivated to find information and I treated it with a lot of respect, as this was a real craft, and there were all these volumes of material that had to be learned. And I think because I was on my own, I really dug deep for it. I remember reading about a *Life* magazine photo essay on Maurice Evans from *Planet of the Apes*, so I went to the library, looked through all the microfilms and finally found it. I went through all that stuff, trying to dig up as much information as I could.

You finally got all this information together and the tools that you could find. What were some of the projects you did to learn your craft before you became a professional?

I spent a lot of hours just with greasepaint, a magazine that Dick Smith put out in the 60's, and some traditional stage makeup, learning how to paint wrinkles. Standing in the bathroom looking in the mirror for hours and hours, putting paint on my face and just seeing how I could make it look like three-dimensional work, which was great for stage. And certainly, playing around like gluing hair to the back of my hands, trying to make finger nails out of wax and rubber. Trying to learn how to sculpt and do latex appliances.

I remember the first big disaster was talking my dad into doing a life cast of me and not having the right tools and just using modeling plaster, which is a horrible way to do it. It heats up and locked into my eyebrows. Of course, my dad, he's suddenly thrown into the middle of this thing, and I'd given what I thought was good information, but it was all wrong. I had the guy stuck with trying to get me out of this

with a minimal amount of pain. But still, it's all a learning process. Once I finally had a life cast of my face, that thing was like gold because I had to go through so much to make it. And I remember learning to sculpt and make molds, ordering foam latex from Paramount Theatrical Supplies in New York. I remember coming home from school and there would be a box sitting for me from Paramount and knowing there's a whole kit of foam rubber inside that I'd spent weeks of allowance on just to get a little one-quart kit of foam latex. It was like this rare commodity to have. Then trying to learn how to cook foam in my mom's oven in the kitchen, it was just crude steps taken to understand the medium.

Were you always planning on taking this professionally or was it a hobby for you at the time?

It's funny, I don't remember that there ever was a difference for me. Since I was a kid, it was that and making movies. I remember my dad teaching me how to use his regular 8mm movie camera when I was ten or eleven years old, and I started making movies. I mean, it certainly was a hobby, but I never thought of it in terms of, "Here's my hobby, now what do I want to do for a profession?" One just ran into the other, it seemed like a natural progression.

It sounds like you were working with your dad a lot, so he was encouraging?

My parents were great, and I think that was really important. Really important aspect. They were parents who really didn't understand anything about the art or the world of movie making, except as my dad said, "Hey, somebody's out there making these things, so why not you?" And they had no idea what was necessary to get into the business, certainly living at the other end of the country it could have been a million miles away. But they knew I had this intense desire and intense interest, and they supported me. They were always encouraging me to move forward with stuff and keep trying. I remember they turned the basement of the house over to me, and I set up a little shop. I had a place to make masks, a place to do stop-motion animation, and a place to set up a projector and an old bedsheet to project my movies. That was my whole life growing up.

How and when did you start to get yourself there? You grew up in Pennsylvania, how did you get from there--

I made a couple of stabs at it. When I graduated high school, as a graduation present my parents brought me a ticket to come out to Hollywood for two weeks, just to fly out and see what it was like. My sister and I flew and being out here in Hollywood, not knowing anyone, not knowing where to go, completely on our own, it was intimidating as hell! At this point in time, I'd been writing letters to everyone. I had letters from Gene Roddenberry, letters from people on the *Planet of the Apes* TV show.

But some my favorite letters are from people like John Chambers, who would write and send me little critiques of pictures of my work that I would send him. So, the idea was that when I graduated high school, I'd come out to California for two weeks and meet John Chambers, who was busy in the middle of a project and I didn't get to meet with him during the first week. Then some things happened, and we had to cut our trip short and I didn't get to meet him. And he always felt bad about that, so he made sure, a few years later when I drove out to California with a friend just to spend the summer, I got meet him. And he had me on my days off from work meeting everybody in town. That's when I met Stan Winston, when I met Tom Burman, and these are people that I ended up working with and who helped shape the path that I ended up on.

Had you done any professional work close to home ?

Yeah. It wasn't professional in the sense that it was a paying job, but there was money for materials. When I was in high school, I was doing school plays and community theater. Then in college, I was doing a lot of the productions. And every once in a while, we'd do a show like *Sleuth* that would allow me to do some kind of foam latex appliances. Or *Dracula*. Little pieces here and there beyond basic make up.

So, when did it turn into a job or a career?

After that summer, I went back and finished college. I came out here right after I graduated in September the following fall. And the town was in the middle of a miserable writer's or actor's strike. From what I was told at the time, it was the biggest one that ever hit. I remember John Chambers said, "Boy, bad timing. I know makeup artists who'd been working for twenty years that are losing their houses." I remember hearing that at the time and thinking, "Wow, is the business that fickle?" You know that you could be established for twenty-five years, be established and suddenly lose everything because of a strike. I thought what a horrifying career choice, but then I also thought well maybe some of that is decision making on the part of the person who's losing their house. It did open my eyes to being financially responsible and not to take for granted that it would be an easy task to move out here and start a career. So, I lasted for a few weeks, ran out of money, and went back home again.

About two years later, I'd gotten married and saved up some more money. My wife and I moved out here for a final time and made it work. I was out here six months, and I just took a job anywhere. I was selling cameras in North Hollywood because it was something I'd done going through college, I'd put myself through college doing jobs like that. Then again, on my day off I'd just keep making the rounds of all the different makeup effects places. Then finally after about six months, I'd gotten a job offer and never looked back. It's always been about moving forward since then.

Do you remember what that first movie was?

Yeah, my first movie was *Metalstorm*, a Universal 3D movie. It was also Kelly Preston's first movie too. And it was great! It was fun because I got to do everything on that movie. I had a portfolio of things I'd done on my own, makeups and miniature work and stop motion models, but I'd never worked in a shop or studio before. So it was starting at the bottom and literally like sweeping the floors. And then, over the course of one movie, over four or five months, I was taught how to make molds and how to sculpt things. Then I was moved into the foam room, so I was able to make appliances and paint them, then I was on the set gluing on appliances and puppeteering some of the creatures. In the space of five months, it was a gigantic learning experience, learning every aspect from beginning to end.

And that was a Charlie Band low-budget movie, so I guess everyone had to pitch in in some way, right?

Oh, absolutely, it was never ending hours and very little pay, but the enthusiasm was completely unchallenged. You just get going on and on.

Now, your first credited work in special effects was on *Chiller*, the Wes Craven TV film, right?

No, actually, it would have been *Metalstorm*, and from that I went to work with Tom Burman on *The Adventures of Buckaroo Banzai*. Those were uncredited because it was credited to Burman Studios. But man, what a great experience that was too, to be working with the guy who was right there through it all with John Chambers on *Planet of the Apes*. A great history.

That must've been a huge difference to go from *Metalstorm* to a big budget film like *Buckaroo Banzi*...

Well, I don't know if it was a step up, but it was a step forward. Here was a guy who'd been around for what, for me, were really substantial movies. To be working for the guy who worked on *Planet of the Apes* to me was a huge thrill and experience.

How did you develop a relationship with Stan Winston and how was it working for his company?

When a show would end, there was nothing to move onto. You were basically freelance, out on the street again. John Chambers had sent me over to see Stan, and Stan saw my book of pictures—oh, you know what was really helpful with Stan was that I had been working with a couple of guys from *Metalstorm*; Shane Mahan and John Rosengrant. While we'd separated after *Metalstorm* and gone our own ways, they'd both ended up at Stan's working on the TV series *Manimal*, remember that?

Oh yes!

So, they were working over there and I'd finished at Burman's. They had Stan look at my book again and he brought me in. I did a couple of weeks on a series that didn't go anywhere. Still, I knew who Stan Winston was. I'd read all about him growing up and the very next thing we started was *The Terminator*.

So, you worked on *Terminator*?

Yeah, I was on the first *Terminator*.

Did you design or build anything?

Stan had us sculpting designs for the endoskeleton for Cameron to look at. He then combined elements of them all into a single design. I sculpted things like the neck, the spine, and the pelvis, and ended up going on set and puppeteering. I was the guy reaching up through the neck of the Terminator when it's walking around the plant.

Puppeteering, now that's interesting. I guess you have to have kind of an acting aesthetic for that.

I think a lot of that came from my interest in and experimentation with stop-motion and having the fundamental understanding of performance, things like body language and expression to pull off a character.

How did all this lead to something like *The Monster Squad* where you're now in a suit...

Well, it was just such a quick step because I love being on set and puppeteering. Once we finished *Terminator*, we did

Aliens. We went over to London to do that and I remember being kind of dissatisfied with the look of the stuntmen wearing the alien suits. The alien suits weren't that detailed because they were only meant to be seen in really extreme lighting conditions, a lot of shadows, a lot of sidelight and stuff. I was watching these stuntmen thinking this wasn't the way I expected it to end up looking. Even though it looked great in the movie, I still thought I could do this, that I could get in a suit and do this. I remember one night when we were done in the shop, putting on one of the alien suits and doing different body poses and positions for still shots. I looked at them later and thought they were an improvement over what I'd seen on set.

It was only when we were back in the states and gearing up for *Monster Squad* that I went to Stan about trying to do the Gillman. Here was a role that didn't rely on an actor or a guy who has any kind of experience delivering lines on set. It's a silent role and I thought maybe this was the one to go for, and Stan was supportive of it.

Who ultimately made the decision to put you in the role? Was it because you were on the make-up team, or did you have to audition?

I didn't have to audition, which was a break because I hate auditions. I've gotten through twenty plus years of doing this without having to do an audition. I think it was because, well, the decision was made not just by Stan, but he was a voice in it because he's the guy behind the creature stuff. I'm sure he did have to have Fred Dekker's approval, and he got it. There was never an audition process, just the next thing I had a body cast done and they started sculpting.

Did you participate in sculpting that suit?

I didn't, it was done by Steve Wang and Matt Rose. I was working on the Frankenstein appliance design at the time. So I worked from Stan's drawing and got the Frankenstein makeup going, and then when I got to set ended up playing the Creature.

It must have been a challenge designing these classic monsters, and yet having to avoid the Universal look for copyright reasons.

Well yeah, exactly, when the project first came our way and we saw the script for the first time there was some plan, at least to some degree, that we were just going to capture the look of the old Universal movie monsters, which for a guy who grew up loving that to have the opportunity this early in my career to pay homage and do our own version would have been a hugely satisfying job. But ultimately the licensing issue emerged, and we had to change them all so they didn't look like the original.

But that had to be hard, what do you go to change?

It's subtle stuff. I remember on Frankenstein, he didn't have eyebrows, he had a big forehead, like the Universal, but he didn't have electrodes, I didn't put them on his neck. He had a scar across his forehead, you try to do things that are reminiscent without necessarily making it look like the Boris Karloff makeup, but with things are indicative of classic Frankenstein.

So, now you get on set and you get to be the Gillman. What did you have in mind for the performance?

At least for me, it was playing "for real," because I remember that's what was cool about *Abbott and Costello Meet Frankenstein*, the monsters were still played for real. So the comedy was not about making fun of what you're doing, but letting the monsters be real and having the comedy come from the situation.

What about interacting with the kids?

There really wasn't a lot of interaction between me and the kids. There certainly was action with Fat Kid, but I was more involved with the stuntmen who played the policemen who try to stop the creature when he's coming out of the hole.

The film wasn't a hit theatrically, as you've said, but it has developed a cult following. Do you remember when you first started getting a hint that it was gaining an audience?

No, I never did. It came and it went. There was no real awareness of whether it was financially successful or not. It was just something that we did and then moved on to different things.

What was the first horror convention you did?

As a guest, it was after *Tremors*. Universal sent us to New York to do a *Fangoria* convention. I'd gone to a couple as a kid. As a kid, I'd gotten on a bus to New York City to go to a *Famous Monsters of Filmland* convention and that was unbelievable. Again, a small kid coming from a small town where the only monster fans I knew were me and a friend who sat in basement reading *Famous Monsters* and scouring the TV Guide hoping a monster movie was going to be on. Then to be in the middle of a convention and see people like

Peter Cushing and meet people like Forry Ackerman, who I never thought I'd meet. Seeing real makeup appliances and Don Post's masks, the dealer room, it was unbelievable. And that was always my impression as a kid seeing through fresh eyes like that. Going back as a guest was fun, but it could never quite capture the magic of being a kid.

What was the first time you remember having a fan come up to you who recognized you and knew your work? What was that like for someone who grew up being a fan?

That's a good question because I don't remember the first time because, for whatever reason, I always end up seeing things through another's perspective, other people's eyes. So when I'm at a convention as a guest and people come up to me, I try to make sure that if there are questions they might have that they want to ask, I try to pull those questions out of them, I try to make myself as approachable as I can. I remember what it was like to be on the other side, meeting Peter Cushing and wanting to ask him questions but thinking, "Ugh, he's probably been asked that question a hundred times." But I don't care. For me, if I've been asked something a thousand times and some kid comes up to me and he hasn't asked it, I'm just as happy to let that be the first time I've heard the question. I just want people to be able to ask questions and have their picture taken, and satisfy them the same way I was when I was a kid.

At conventions, have you ever run into any of the guys who've played the Universal Gillmen?

I used to collect autographs of guys in monsters suits, so I have autographs from Ricou Browning and Ben Chapman. I finally met Ricou at a show a year ago back east. I met him and just started talking and he turned out to be a great guy. I mean, you go to these conventions and do a little Q&A thing, so I had to go see Ricou Browning. It's just great to see the real guy tell all these stories.

Hopefully you'll get a chance to meet Ben Chapman sometime soon. He's a great guy. We did an interview with him a few years ago when we started, and he's got some great stories. Ok, so after you did the Gillman, your next suit work was *Pumpkinhead*?

Yeah, that's right.

Ok, now there must been a lot riding on that, and there must have been a certain amount of trust put in you because we're talking Stan Winston's directorial debut. So, did you design any aspects of the creature at all?

All I remember is it was probably the high point of my career because everything was taking off. I'd proven myself in the suit stuff. Stan had complete faith in us, so he turned *Pumpkinhead* over to us as a design element. It was actually Alec Gillis, me, John Rosengrant, and Shane Mahan. We designed *Pumpkinhead* and the makeup for Haggis the witch completely on our own. It was like your parents turning over the keys to the house and saying, "Ok, we'll be back in three months," and every day was just an amazing day at work. You felt like nothing is going to go wrong with this movie. Not that it wasn't hard work, you just knew that everything we built was going to be used the proper way because there was a director involved who knew and understood the importance to make our stuff on-set work.

Pumpkinhead is interesting. What were you looking to or drawing inspiration from when designing him?

It was mostly from cadavers and dead bodies. We definitely wanted it to have the feeling of something that had been dead and also something that was partially human, but more evil and monstrous. Not in a science-fiction way, but more of a folklorish kind of way, a legend that was brought to life.

Any particular old ghost stories or legends?

No, growing up we all share the same ghost stories and local legends.

I'm thinking back, and I remember him being a huge creature. Was this a suit creature or a puppet? I mean, I remember him being so big. I always thought he was a giant puppet.

No, it was all me in a suit. I mean, I'm 6'2", I got a little bit of height because my head was in the neck of the creature. We also had leg extensions, so we probably added about a foot and a half for a couple of scenes where I was walking. For scenes where he was shot from the waist up, I was always walking on platforms.

For performing him, this has to be a lot different than the Gillman, because not only are you creating an original creature, but you've got to strive to be truly intimidating.

We also had to get the feeling that it was a creature born from a dead body, a regenerating thing. That was the point where I tried to work in those Ray Harryhausen-type moments, always trying to look toward his stuff. I incorporated a lot of his idiosyncrasies into not just *Pumpkinhead*, but things I've

done since then. There are times where I'll try to put a lot of that body language into a performance.

How did you get involved in the *Alien* series?

By the time *Alien 3* rolled around, Alec Gillis and I had formed our own company Amalgamated Dynamic, which we did shortly before Stan's second feature that he directed. The final movie we did with Stan was *Leviathan*, which was another creature suit thing, and Stan was going off to direct his second feature.

You were the creature in *Leviathan*?

I was the creature in *Leviathan*.

That's another good movie, I really like that one.

Yeah, that's a funny one too, because it was the summer of three underwater movies; *The Abyss*, *DeepStar Six*, and *Leviathan*.

Underwater, that had to be tough. You guys were working with a lot of water in that. Was that ever an issue?

Well, there was amazing photography that was shot on a dry soundstage. We were in Rome, and they would burn these flares that would produce this ash that would kind of float in the air. When you shoot it, if you're well lit, and shooting slightly slow motion, it looks like underwater sediment.

Wow!

And we actually built these little bellows into the footpads of these suits so when you'd walk on this fuller's earth, this kind of dusty ground, it would blow the dust away and it looks like you're walking through silt on the ocean floor. And they'd hang fish and stuff like that. It's kind of a cool effect. And I got to do the creature stuff for that. When we did the final sequence, we were in Malta, and there was this huge outdoor tank that was built so that the horizon of the tank lined up with the horizon of the sea. I had to do some water stuff and we all had to get certified as divers. It's always an adventure doing these thing.

So after we finished that, Alec and I started our own company and shortly after that we got the call from 20th Century Fox to see if we'd be interested in going to London to do *Alien 3*, We'd already been through it once before with Stan and Stan was not available for *Alien 3*. He was their first choice, obviously, and had won an Academy Award for his work, but he was on another project. So, we filled in with David Fincher directing. We were back to one creature instead of a horde, so I was able to do that role.

Now, the *Aliens* were these iconic creatures by this point, so were you redesigning any aspects of it?

Yes, we re-designed it quite a bit from *Aliens* in that it was now a full-body suit. In *Aliens*, it was kind of an impressionist suit that worked in those lighting conditions. Fincher's approach was wholly different from Cameron's, you know, in the way he was capturing images on film, so it had to sustain more close-up scrutiny. So we had to do a full sculpted body suit that I had to wear. For the most part it was a single body suit.

What do you use to keep that sort of thing from becoming incredibly heavy? I mean, the Aliens look like they're made out of metal.

Well, a lot of that is the finish, and a lot of the body suits are pretty light. They're pretty tight, like a lighter version of a wetsuit. Certainly the heads get heavy with all the radio controlled elements, and there are times when a head can weight eight to ten pounds.

That doesn't seem like a lot of weight except my head's down in the neck of these creatures so I have eight to ten pounds kind of cantilevered out, sticking out past my head another foot, foot and half, and that adds a lot of stress and strain. And some of them are very heavy. There was a gorilla suit that we built to be completely realistic, like you see in a zoo. Because of that, my head is way down in the neck and we have a radio controlled face with radio controlled eyes and thirty-seven servo motors in the head. If we packed that suit up with batteries and radio control gear so I can walk around without an electrical cable attached in any way, it's seventy-five pounds between the head and the body that I'm carrying around.

Alien 3 has been known to have been a difficult movie to make. Did you feel any of that on your end?

Yeah, some of it, some because the difficulty was that the script wasn't 100% locked down. We went to London, started building and then some substantial script changes were coming in and they'd already invested in moving us all to London. There were six of us together including Alec and me, so we kept building things. You know, *"Here's some elements that haven't changed, so we'll need these dead bodies."* We just kept working. But the time frame that we had to finish it was changed because now shooting was not going to start as early as expected. So, we slowed it down a bit so as not to eat up all our resources. It definitely extended the workload in terms of time.

I watched that documentary for *Alien 3* from the boxset and it just seemed like such a nightmare. That poor David Fincher, man...

He bore the brunt of it more than we did. For us, it mainly impacted our flexibility. We had to make sure we weren't burning up money. It didn't affect us artistically, it affected Fincher artistically. I remember Sigourney Weaver would come over to our shop a lot because she loved the artwork. And for us it was very inspiring to have her come over and remind us that it was art. I don't think a lot of us had looked at like that. We looked at it as something we liked to do, but it is art. It is a practical form of art.

And you continued with that series too, so they keep coming back to you. How do you feel that you grow with the creature every time? If you want to make changes, do they let you?

They do, and there are some changes we make from time to time. Like in *Alien 3*, we took four extruded-looking appendages and removed those because the alien is now running on all fours. It got in the way of the head, and in *Alien: Resurrection*, we put them back on. On *Alien vs Predator*, we went back to a darker color palette, more like the original, the first one. So, we kind of change around things, but you don't change things for the sake of changing them. There is an artistic temperament you have to keep under control, because the truth is H.R. Giger did such a remarkable design job that you're not going to improve it. You can alter it and change it, and we do from time to time for practical reasons, but to change something when it works so well is foolish.

How did *Aliens vs Predator: Requiem* work out for you?

It was great. Every time we get to work on one of these movies, it's great to have the same kind of enthusiasm and energy you had three or four years previously. You pull everything out of the box again, and you reinvent some things and try to show something fresh. But the truth is they are still very effective movie monsters. The fans should be very pleased with it. It's a good story, I mean, technically we were on Earth last time, but it was such a remote part of the world that it didn't impact us the way this one does. We're now in hometown America.

You're still doing creature work today when a lot of stuff has gone digital. How do you keep up?

It's funny because for the longest time we were busier and busier because of digital. Digital certainly opened up the ability to put stories on the screen on a scale you never could have done before. *Starship Troopers* was a perfect example of that, a huge movie and ninety-five percent of the creature stuff was digital and gorgeous. The thing is that, without digital, that movie wouldn't have been made. Still, there's still that five percent where you needed the contact so we had quite a bit of work in that movie even though in comparison, it was small in quantity it was still substantial.

We still had three full size warrior bugs, and the whole head for the front section of the brain bug. A huge amount of work. What's happening today is that is becoming much more "corporatised" in that effects are becoming more like production line techniques where there are hundreds of people involved. Don't get me wrong, I'm not knocking the art, there are things in the digital world that are amazing. Still, there's almost an overreliance on it as a crutch and a tool to fill up time on-screen that doesn't really move you anymore.

We've seen the cloudy blue-ish, gray, murky CG world. To do it right is an accomplishment. Doing something on the level of King Kong or Gollum is a huge accomplishment, these are standout examples. If everyone was churning out that level of work, there'd be no reason to keep our shop open. But what doesn't work to me is the proliferation of CG creature effects that have no real-life counterpart. There's no interaction with an actor. I know audiences are aware of it, that they're watching something that appears to out of a high end video game, and not a totally immersive environment.

I would never want to knock CG, a lot of people like to, but I'd almost rather see a cheap creature than a cheap CG effect.

Well, that's what directors are saying to us. They want to go back; they want it to look like it did in *Aliens*. *AVP* was a great example. We had a ton of practical stuff and there was digital that was really good in that. And a guy like John Bruno, a visual effects supervisor who understands both worlds, he can pull on both. He is the right guy to supervise visual effects.

He's got the burden of tying together the look of all the visuals, and a lot of time these guys don't have a practical visual effect experience. So, what they have in their toolbox is digital effects. I think it'd be a horrible position to be in

to suddenly realize that I don't have enough time or money because of studio needs and what's the digital answer. I think that's what's contributing to an overall mediocrity in creature effects.

So what do you think will be the next big stuff is? Are they going to come to the realization that they have to merge both the digital and the practical?

Yeah, people are doing it now. And we've been doing it for years. I mean, *Jurassic Park* was a perfect example: people don't realize that when you time out all the dinosaur shots in the first film, more than half of them were animatronic dinosaurs. You know it all worked together perfectly. We did a movie *Jumanji* with a digital lion overlapping our practical.

Thank so much for taking the time to talk to us, I mean, you must be so busy with everything--

Yeah, but I remember how hard it was trying to find information and if I can contribute to getting the right information out there then I enjoy doing it.

Special thanks to Ian Holohan!

JOHN KASSIR

Interviewed by Mike Cucinotta (12/07)

Hello, kiddies! For seven seasons, three films, and an animated series, John Kassir voiced that grinning ghoul the Crypt Keeper on HBO 's T*ales from the Crypt*. *Icons* recently participated in a roundtable discussion with John just as the show's seventh season was released onto DVD. During his *Crypt* years, John worked with some of the most talented actors and directors in Hollywood and more directly with many of the most important FX artists in the business. Without John's dead-on performance, it's doubtful the Crypt Keeper would have become as widely recognized a horror and worldwide pop culture icon.

Did you ever get to work with the directors on the wraparound segments?

Yes, occasionally we got to. There were certain episodes. Kevin Yagher directed most of the wraparounds which was, of course, a lot of fun. Most of them were written after they started working on the episodes, and sometimes the directors would come and talk to us about what they wanted in terms of the episode. I would improvise along with everything that was written. There were a few times when we'd go down to the set, such as when Arnold Schwarzenegger directed an episode. I would normally record the voice first and the puppeteers would choreograph to the voice, similar to doing a rock video or something like that. But if you wanted a conversation with another person on screen, they would have me off-camera talking directly to them so we could get better timing and to add to the fun.

With all the horror icons from the 80's and 90's being remade with big budgets, do you see them taking the *Tales from the Crypt* franchise and doing something really bad with that?

The partners, which were Joel Silver and Robert Zemeckis, really were passionate about it. They wanted it done right. Of course, it was also a playground, bringing in great directors and great actors, but they were even careful about who they selected for that. They wanted this show to have somebody who really knew it. I grew up on *Tales from the Crypt* comic books, so this was a dream come true. I thought it was just going to be something for just freaks like myself, but it turned out to be something people really enjoyed. I still have people in their twenties and thirties coming up and saying to me, "This was the only show my parents would watch with me as a family." So, I can't imagine them in any way, shape, or form taking the franchise that they paid a lot of money for and destroying it somehow. I would be less surprised to see the franchise come back as a series again the way that *Twilight Zone* or *Outer Limits* came back. With new directors and stars from today. I would see that happening above and beyond anything else.

You said you grew up with EC Comics, so what kind of horror did you grow up with? Have you always been a horror fan?

Oh, I've always loved horror. I used to rush home from school because while my mother was making dinner, back in Baltimore, they used have "The Twilight Movie." A lot of days they would have these horror movies, especially the Universal classics.

I mean, even today, *Abbott and Costello Meet Frankenstein* is one of my favorite movies ever. Then, of course, I liked the original *Wolf Man*, and would collect the models. I had a whole set of them. *Tales from the Crypt* comic books were something, obviously, back then that mothers were outspoken about how they thought comics were causing juvenile delinquency. It was highly politically incorrect back then, even more than it is today. But I loved those comic books and saw the humor in them. So, when I auditioned for *Tales from the Crypt*, I just thought it was an amazing opportunity. I didn't know it was going to end up being so widespread.

Where did you find the voice of the Crypt Keeper, what was behind the process of developing him, was it the same voice you'd auditioned with?

Yeah, the way you hear it today is pretty much how I auditioned. The auditions were kind of exclusive. I'd come off of being a popular stand-up after winning *Star Search*, and it was known that I did a lot of characters in my act. They were looking for somebody who was a combination actor/stand-up/voiceover artist. I've always described him as being a cross between Alfred Hitchcock, Henny Youngman, and Margaret Hamilton. They had the auditions, and I think there was only ten of us at the most, and we were invited down to Kevin Yagher's studio. Kevin was creating the look of the creature. As most of you probably know, he also created Chucky and Freddy Krueger.

The Crypt Keeper had gone through all these generations of looks. Some had noses, some had teeth, but what you see today is what he settled upon when I went to read for him. I took a look at him, and there he was with his nose rotting off, and these gleeful mad eyes, and holes in his throat. I had some copy and I improvised off of it and I said, "Be careful what you AX for, you may get it." The next day he brought me in to do it for Richard Donner and Joel Silver and they loved it. Of course, once we started shooting the episodes, if you listen to the very first season, the puppet was their first generation mechanically, so we had to slow it down and make him more ominous.

Do you have a favorite *Tales from the Crypt* episode?

The last season was one of my favorite seasons, the seventh season. Just based on the fact they were trying do something a little different with it. Originally, the season before was supposed to be the last season. The last episode of the sixth season starred yours truly and it went along with Priscilla Presley, Lou Diamond Phillips, and Rory Calhoun. It was a great episode. I play this nasty flim-flam audience, and of course at the end the Crypt Keeper is watching the screening going, "You know I liked the other actors but this one's a real Robert Deadford." So that was a real fun episode for me.

One of my other favorite episodes was the Walter Hill episode, one of the first few episodes, called "A Man Called Death" which had William Sadler as an executioner who loses his job and goes around killing people who deserve it. In the end, he gets caught and fried in the electric chair. This last season when we got picked up, they tried to breathe some life into the show and take it to London to give a different feel. It was exciting. Some of the actors that were on the seventh season were Ewan McGregor, Eddie Izzard, Daniel Craig, and all these other people who were not well known in the states. They were already talented actors who had started their careers in London. Very few of them had been introduced yet to the United States, it was great to see that transition take place.

I noticed that on the first three seasons on DVD, you did all new Crypt Keeper introductions, but you haven't done that since. What was the reason behind that?

I'm sure it probably just had to do with time, or that they were trying to do something to have more variety to it. Like this one we have a narrated virtual comic book. I think they were just trying to do something different because maybe they thought, "Been there, done that." A lot of times they decide to do these things at the last minute. All of sudden, somebody goes, "Hey, we really want to get this out by such and such time," and they don't have as much time to put it together. The *Tales from the Crypt* episodes are obviously the most important thing on the DVDs. I mean, two generations of people have only gotten to see it once it came to network television, on Fox or Sci-Fi, so they've never seen the unedited versions of it. So, I imagine a lot of it had to do with those elements. I think mainly they were looking for some variety, not to overload the DVD.

I still think that Christmas album you did was a classic, with songs like "Deck The Halls With Parts of Charlie" and all that stuff. I love that. Can you talk a little bit about that since Christmas is coming up?

I love that album. I think it is, out of everything that they've made, other than the episodes themselves, I thought that was the finest product that they made. I thought that the guy who wrote the music and the guy who wrote the lyrics did such a great job. And we had so much fun recording it. We could cut loose on that too. My father-in-law used to play that in surgery, he was a surgeon, and he would play it while doing surgery. I'm not sure I'd want somebody performing surgery on me while he was singing "Deck The Halls With Parts of Charlie," but I just thought it was really a great album.

When I showed up, they already had the musical tracks down so that all I had to do was my performance. I've actually been kind of disappointed that they don't do a widespread release of it. I'm sure it's still available online or whatever, but it was like the perfect stocking stuffing. It was one of those things that if you were on the checkout line you'd grab it and get a couple. I can't tell you how many people have told me they enjoyed that particular Christmas album. I just thought it was funny and clever. It's such a great holiday to make fun of. You know, the first episode itself was a Christmas episode where a demented Santa Claus comes to kill people, so I just thought it was perfect kind of item. I'd like to see it have a reemergence. I think Dr. Demento plays it every year when he plays Christmas stuff.

What are your biggest fears?

Oh gosh, let me see. My biggest fear... yeah... you know, heights unnerve me. Although I did go skydiving once. I did a tandem sky-dive and I had to use a reserve chute on my first sky dive, and I might say my last sky dive. The first chute's center panel came loose. Someone was trying to tell me skydiving wasn't for me. I guess in terms of fear, I'm not afraid of death. I don't think we're afraid of death so much as we are not accomplishing what we want to accomplish. Large crowds of people scare me. I love going to places like Disneyland, but not if it's crowded. I guess I have a fear of being trampled by large crowds of people.

So, what happened with the third *Tales from the Crypt* **feature film,** *Ritual***?**

I don't know exactly what happened to *Ritual* in terms of its release. I think that what happened was that it was supposed to be released with Miramax and when the guys there left it was part of the library that was meant to be released. Since other people took over, it didn't get out. They took that movie along with others in the library and a lot of others just ended up coming out through a video release. It was no reflection on the movie itself.

Was there ever talk of giving the Keeper his own show?

Oh yeah, there was, of course, the cartoon *Tales from the Crypt Keeper*, which was fun. I kept telling them to do a live action show for the kids in the vein of *Goosebumps*. Prior to *Goosebumps* coming out, they thought it wasn't appropriate for kids of that age. Nobody died in the cartoon, kids would learn their moral lesson, and they would move on. Of course, we could have done that live action too, and you would think with the success of *Goosebumps* that would have been a great opportunity. They have very often talked about doing some kind of horror talk show with the Crypt Keeper as the host. Obviously, it's a little difficult doing the puppetry and the voice at the same time, but with my history as a standup comedian, it wouldn't be too difficult. No disrespect to Johnny Carson. I know they have been talking for many years to try to get together a horror channel, but they're always so hush-hush about it. Of course, that would

open the door to having something like that. You know the Crypt Keeper was on Jay Leno, we've done that thing before, it's just about finding the right market for that.

I would feel remiss if I didn't ask you a question, outside of *Tales***, about a certain commercial you did back in the 80's for** *The Legend of Zelda***. How many people have asked you questions about that?**

Very rarely do I get asked. A few people at signings have brought the actual game with them. That commercial was a trip, that was the first game of its kind to come to the United States. That was an amazing game with all the different tiers you could go into. The commercial, I had no idea that being cast was going to be such a big deal. They were like, "Ok, this is the game, and you're going to be the guy who is stuck in the game. We're going to do a take on *Eraserhead* and your hair is going to be stuck up."

So, I was like that sounded really cool, and I was still playing in comedy clubs. That morning my alarm clock didn't go off. I came in like maybe a half hour later and the director was furious. She thought maybe I was one of those actors that just showed up whenever I wanted. I was unshaved because I just wanted to get there on time. They just threw me in the clothes, unshaved, which kind of added to the look of the whole thing.

Of course, as soon as we started shooting everybody started to relax and the director just cut me loose and I improvised. I mean, they told me what they wanted me to say. They would put the cameras staring up at the ceiling and I would run around saying all this stuff. Then they showed me a piece of the game and I would imitate it and they cut it all together. Then it was over, I mean I showed up at 9AM and it was over by 12PM. I just thought it came out great, one of the most fun commercials ever. And there's been a resurgence for it, it showed up on YouTube and people showing up with the game after all these years. Long time ago... And hey, I look the same there, guys. Ok, maybe a little less hair sticking up!

Special thanks to Anna Wu!

2008

AJ BOWEN
ZACHARY LEVI
DICK DUROCK
GUNNAR HANSEN
KEITH GORDON
NEIL MARSHALL
TOM HOLLAND
CHRIS SARANDON
WILLIAM RAGSDALE
JONATHAN STARK
AMANDA BEARSE
STEPHEN GEOFFREYS
JULIE CARMEN
TOMMY LEE WALLACE

HILTON GREEN
CHRIS HENDRIE
ANDREW LONDON
LEE GARLINGTON
KURT PAUL
JULIETTE CUMMINS
DONOVAN SCOTT
KATT SHEA
CYNTHIA GARRIS
LARRY FESSENDEN
TUESDAY KNIGHT
JEREMY KASTEN
MICK GARRIS
TOMAS ALFREDSON
BRUCE CAMPBELL

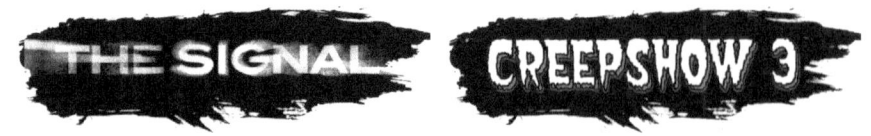

AJ BOWEN

Interviewed by Mike Cucinotta (2/08)

This winter you're going to be introduced to a whole staple of new talent when *The Signal* releases. We sat down with one of the leads from this amazing new film, actor AJ Bowen, who plays Louis, another victim of the strange transmission wreaking havoc in the city of Terminus. It's no surprise with a film as strong as *The Signal* is that some huge genre fans were behind the making of it, and AJ is no exception. Here we got to geek out over *USA Up All Night*, *Sorority Babes in the Slimeball Bowl-O-Rama*, and about what an incredible collaborative effort *The Signal* was.

What are some of your earliest memories of the horror genre? What draws you to it?

I have two sisters that are a lot older than I am. One is nine years older than me and the other is twelve. When I was four years old, we lived in an apartment complex and my sisters babysat me a lot. Specifically, I remember one time getting taken to this house party with the two of them while they were babysitting me and there was this movie that was on that all these high school kids were watching, and I was forced to watch it. It scared the hell out of me, and it was *Happy Birthday to Me*. It has such a profound impact on me that I haven't gone back and watched it since, but it really screwed me up. Probably really close to that same time one of those sisters was babysitting me by herself and she took me, as punishment, to see *Mommie Dearest*. I know that is probably not a horror movie, but I remember it probably being the most frightening.

That scared you, eh?

It did! As a child of the 80s, I remember there were a couple of these channels, this was before Fox, so we still had a couple of those city channels. All day long on Saturday, they'd play these movies. As a kid I was fascinated by genre movies like *Just Before Dawn*, and the early *Friday the 13th's* that would play on TV. I remember the first time I went to stay away from home and my friend's mom was more liberal with what she let him watch and I got to watch *Halloween* over there. And then I had to walk all the way back home! I was hooked at a very young age.

Did you have a strict upbringing? Were you allowed to watch horror movies? Or were they a forbidden fruit?

You know it's funny, I wasn't allowed to watch horror movies, but I was allowed to watch any movie with blood and guts as long as it was patriotic. I was allowed to watch *Rambo*. I was in the theater to see *First Blood*. I saw a double feature with *First Blood* and *9 to 5*, which I'm sure was very formative. I was allowed to watch *Alien* and I was allowed to watch all the Gallagher comedy specials for some reason. But if it involved tan lines, boobs, and slashers, I wouldn't have been allowed to be a part of it.

Well, I'm a fan of Gallagher as well as horror so... Those old city channels, I think those helped expose people to older horror films and they're now mostly gone. Do you recall the early days of VHS?

Absolutely, VHS, Betamax! We had a Betamax player. Whenever we'd go to the video store, before there were Blockbusters, there was a place called The Movie Stop and I would look through all of these old videocassettes. I remember there were some movies you could look at the box and know you couldn't get it, and you're trying to sneak a look while your parents aren't looking. There were certain movies that just from the box had an impact on me. I remember specifically they had a double feature tape with, and I can't remember the second, but the first feature was *I Spit on Your Grave*. There was a whole line of videos like that, like the old *Faces of Death*, I was so fascinated by them. And I would catch a few clips of them here and there, like at other people's houses. Those video stores were almost like those old TV stations back in the day, like you'd find such gems there and they're so hard to find now! You're in New York, right?

Yes.

I remember the first time that I went to Kim's Video. It was a similar experience. Going up to the second or third floor and finding all those movies, like all the old Troma films. It was a fascinating experience.

Would you have been a fan of USA Up All Night?

Hell yes I was! Big fan! Big fan of Linnea Quigley. Actually, Up All Night was the first time I saw *Sorority Babes in the Slimeball Bowl-o-Rama*.

Is that a favorite of yours, too?

I love that movie! That's one of those movies that was very different after I saw it as a "grown-up." There's something really weird about these kids being stuck in a bowling alley, and I like the gore of it. I didn't remember as a child how goofy the genie looked. I remember it being scarier, but I still love it. There's just a certain quality to all 80s films, not just genre pictures, there's such a higher entertainment value for me. I don't know if I'm biased...

It almost seems as if there was a little more of an effort made. Even in low-budget movies, even bad movies…

My buddy Ti West and I were talking about *Teen Wolf*, this completely ridiculous set-up and plot, totally unrealistic, but there's a shot in that movie, a really long tracking shot where Boothe and Michael J. Fox are walking down the street. It's a really effective amazing shot that would never happen today! There's a lot of photography in those older films. Everybody still knew how to do their job, and whatever the outlandish plot contrivance was, they would still try to execute it the best they could.

I think they really catered to those of us that were younger in the 80s. I mean, every movie was like, "Let's go with Louis Gosset Jr. and get my Dad who's stuck in the middle east and fly F-16s!" or, "Hey, we'll start a monster club and all the monsters that come to town will just happen to be the ones we like." I miss that!

Is there a horror movie that you've gone back to that just didn't hold up in sort of a humorous way, and is there one that does hold up and is an all-time favorite?

Oh man, you know what as a kid I really, really was freaked out by the first *Halloween*, and that always holds up, but you know speaking specifically, I'm just going to throw this out there, and I catch a lot of shit from my friends for this: I love *A Nightmare on Elm Street* and I love *Friday the 13th*, but you know in this day of red and blue, if you have to pick one… I lean toward Jason. I always have. I think that goes back to being a kid and catching some of the movies on local TV.

Friday the 13th Part III, I remember being so freaked out by that movie, specifically the biker dude that gets his hand chopped off. I went back and watched it two nights ago and it was so anticlimactic. That was almost disappointing. Then there are other movies like *Black Christmas* that totally hold up for me. Several of the *Halloween* sequels don't hold up. I was pretty scared by *Season of the Witch*. I went back and watched that, and I was scared about it but for a different reason. The music is still amazing. I got to be honest, most movies for me that are genre movies, they usually still hold up. Because they captured something, even if they don't scare me in the same visceral way. Mostly nothing does. There's still such a reckless abandonment and joy I find in them.

What about the original *Black Christmas*, you mentioned that as holding up. What is it about that one that makes it one of your all-time favorites?

I think what catches people who don't know a lot about it is how innovative it was. There are so many elements to other subgenres in that one film. You have the guy in the house, the babysitter, the sorority slasher film, the nameless monster in the house, you've got that "who-dun-it" element. You don't know who it is and there's this paranoia about it. It was so innovative in that respect! A lot of people don't know that it came out in '74 and would think that it was a rip-off of *Halloween*. Not to take anything away from *Halloween*.

Black Christmas was just amazing though because you were getting all these point of view shots as the killer. What made it so drastically different was that you never knew who it was, you saw Billy for two seconds in the doorway, or knocking shit around in the attic. He would lurk. What held up for me now is there was such a development of all the characters. Bob Clark did such an amazing job with sound design too.

There's some shots where there's two people having a conversation in a scene, but you can hear through the audio another character having a conversation on a phone that completely develops her story. It was just done with such care. My favorite thing to do is just set that up with *A Christmas Story* and watch both. And they both start and end almost the same way, with a house at Christmas in the snow. In *A Christmas Story*, there's a lot of color, and a fuzzy warmth to it, and there's Christmas music playing, it's really heartwarming. Juxtapose that with *Black Christmas*, there's no music, there's some carolers far off, instead you hear the wind, and it paints a completely different picture. I'm a sucker for any movie being in the cold, well, except for *Alien vs Predator*. I think *Black Christmas* is so watchable. That's the one horror movie that a lot of people I know still haven't seen, and I get a lot of enjoyment taking it over places and showing it to people. That movie is like *Halloween* or *The Texas Chain Saw Massacre*. If someone hasn't seen it, and you throw it on, almost without fail people love it and are freaked out by it. This film was... that phone conversation at the beginning!

It's very unsettling.

Oh, it's terrible. It's still very effective. I'm amazed that they got away with that. If you think about it, it's not really dated by any plotline. It's still so relevant, it's still so frightening.

Is there anything in the genre that you like now?

Actually I was talking to someone, and I made the mistake of stating that we're in a dire place for horror, and I don't think that's accurate because that kind of shits on people who are doing right by it. I meant more of the studio system, they're always six months behind what people want and they stay too long on things. There was a movie, I know you guys got to talk to some of the people involved in, I came into it late on, but this fall I finally got to see *Behind the Mask: The Rise of Leslie Vernon*. I felt like I was watching a Christopher Guest film about horror. I really loved that. I got to hear Scott Glosserman speak about his film well before I saw it, we were at SXSW together, and he had an infectious love of the genre. And I thought that guy, Nathan, I was blown away by him! He really held that movie down. I thought it was a really interesting take. I'd watch anything that guy does.

Now I'm completely lost in the geekiness. We have so much to talk about. When did you start to get into acting, after all this horror movie watching you did as a kid?

It's funny, it wasn't something I actively thought I could do or would do. As a young teenager, my buddy who showed me *Halloween* for the first time, we watched horror movies every weekend and would go out and try to make really terrible, terrible short films using stuffed animals as monsters. It was

something I wanted to do, but never thought I could. I'd done a little bit right before I graduated high school, so I auditioned for Boston University, it was awful. I was really, really bad. I still have the rejection notice on my wall. So, I ended up at University of Georgia because in the state of Georgia they have a scholarship where if you're in state, they pay for your school.

It was by default I ended up at Georgia and it just so happened Scott Poythress was there, Justin Welborn [AJ's *The Signal* co-stars], Jacob Gentry. All of these guys that ended up being people I work with now, we met there. So, through a state of attrition, we started learning about film, about acting. There were some of us that wanted to be editors. This just happened naturally: Ben Lovett the guy who composed the score for *The Signal*, he wanted to compose scores, like randomly.

We ran into someone who wanted to do every specific job. So, we started doing short films together. I did end up in New York, and auditioned, and did very little, I did a couple of plays up there. I ended up continuing to show up and do small parts with my friends, then I decided, well, I'm twenty-five years old, I'm going to go out to LA and see if I can do it. So, I went out and started booking immediately. I'm making it sound like I had an agent or something, I still don't have an agent. But I started finding auditions and taking them and getting cast a lot. I assumed it was because I had a beard. You know everyone else looks like a soap opera actor, so I get to play all the other interesting roles. Almost immediately after I got out here, I got an audition for... probably the best movie that's ever been made, *Creepshow 3*.

Ah! I have to ask you about *Creepshow 3*, because I rented it and if I don't ask you about it, I can't write it off on my taxes. (laughs) So... let's talk! What was that like and did you have any idea what you were getting into?

No, I didn't and that's what was kind of awesome about it. I felt like I was auditioning for something really important and special. I was doing a play at a rep theater in LA, and this play was having all sorts of problems. Finally, a friend of the director stepped into a role and he happened to be a casting director. He asked me if I wanted to audition for it, and said, "Well, it's a horror movie so you probably won't like it," and I said, "No, it's my favorite genre. I want to make horror movies." I didn't recognize any of the other people auditioning, and I did like three or four auditions and I kept reading, and then I got a call and I said I'd love to do it. Then we came to the first table read, and we weren't allowed to know anything about it.

Really? This was all secret?

Yeah, like I had the pages, but I wasn't allowed to take them with me. I could look at it for a few seconds and then I got to go in and try to do something on the spot. So, we went for the first table read and it was very professional, really nice. I mean, they had Starbucks coffee, man! That was the first time I found out that it was *Creepshow 3*, and it blew my mind! I own the first two and I was just really surprised. It was right around that time I'd heard about *Day of the Dead 2: Contagion*, but I hadn't seen it. So, I read the script and we shot the movie at Universal's backlot. Obviously, I'm not looking at it through rose-colored glasses, because it was a really awesome experience to shoot a movie right after you move out to LA on Universal's backlot and have a trailer.

I get to shoot my part in the house that was the house from *Best Little Whorehouse In Texas*. As an actor, you can't really shape a film. I can't be responsible for the writing or the editing or basically whether the movie is successful. The only thing I can be responsible for is my specific performance in it. My goal was to do as much with what I had. I spent almost all my time talking to myself without anybody reading the lines to me. Any day as an actor that you can say you shot a movie at Universal and that you can walk into a Best Buy and pick up a DVD that you're in, there's a lot worse places you can be. A lot of actors who haven't done it would kill to have that opportunity. I will say that it was a very auspicious beginning. I think it's so funny because I love the genre so much and I'm fan of George Romero and Stephen King and I was like, "*Son of a bitch!*" The other thing that was really tricky about it was that directors Jim (Glenn Dudelson) and Ana (Clavell) are really nice. They cast me when nobody else would, but I got to be honest, I didn't watch the whole movie. I watched part of my part and behind the scenes and was amazed.

I guess with the reputation of the previous two films...

You know, if they hadn't called it *Creepshow 3*, people would have looked at it and thought, "Hey, an anthology," but then when they tried to do the animation in the beginning, the *South Park* style animation, I think there were a lot of choices made that guaranteed you were going to be eviscerated for this. You know, calling it *Creepshow 3*, not really having The Creep, then doing a behind-the-scenes where they sort of admit with pride that a production assistant wrote one of the stories. I can't vouch for that film. But when you're just an actor, the trick is to find talented people that you know you can work with.

And maybe talented people you knew you could work with. That's kind of what happened with *The Signal*, isn't it? You did work with all those people.

The way it worked out was I was living out in LA, and Chad McKnight, the guy who plays Jim Parsons, lived in LA. Chad and Jacob Gentry met on Jacob's first feature *The Last Goodbye*, and I did a day on that, very brief. Jacob came out to LA for the DVD release of *The Last Goodbye* and we were just talking about film and horror movies. Jacob mentioned that *The Signal* was going to be a horror film and I said I would love to do it, love to come back to Atlanta. So, six or seven weeks go by and I get this conference call that I might be able to be in the movie. They talked about it and then called me back that I was now allowed to be in the movie and I got out of a play I was doing and flew back.

We did a reading of the script. That's also when I met Anessa (Ramsey), but everybody else had worked together or wanted to work together. So, I spent Christmas at home, did a week of rehearsal to work out the kinks in our performance and also develop our relationship with each other. And I highly recommend that, if you're shooting an independent film and you don't have a lot of money to do it.

At the time, there certainly was no ambition to make a movie that was going to come out in theaters. Of course, you don't ever make something without hoping, but from their end, they were trying to make sure they had a movie that would turn a profit so they could get money to shoot another movie. But the wheels just kept not coming off, and we kept saying to each other, "We might have fucked up, we might have actually made something that doesn't totally suck here," and the rest is history.

Ok, now here's what blows me away about this movie, and it's probably one of the things me and Rob were initially taken by. The acting is definitely superb. You and Anessa, everyone is fantastic. I want to ask specifically about your performance because you're in all three acts. They're all very different. In the first, you have to be intimidating and terrifying, the second you have to be scary and hilarious. How do you do that as actor? How do you keep the character together in your head?

Basically, you try the best that you can. If you get lucky like we did, you have a really solid script, and try to keep your head down, stay out of the way and not fuck the script up. This was kind of every actor's dream, to play these fleshed out characters. I think that was a great benefit. And I think a lot of the time, Dan Bush, Dave Bruckner and Jacob [the directors] don't get enough credit for helping the actors do the work that they did. Most movies if I'm going to be playing the typical villain, which we tried very hard to ensure that Louis wasn't a typical villain.

He's still very sympathetic in a way...

That was the hope, the goal. But, if I'm going to do that in most films, I'm going to be playing what is essentially "Leatherface," "Jason." There's one dimension, one note to it. But when you're doing a film that has three specific tones by default, you're getting an opportunity to show different angles to it. So, in that regard it wasn't that difficult. The thing that's difficult is when there's a poorly written script, and you have to try to figure out how to show all these angles without them being there. Also, when we shot *The Signal*, we shot it mostly in chronological order, which is another rarity for film.

Very helpful for the actors, though. In terms of creating a character it was just a nice change of pace to play somebody who feels more than one thing. That's kind of the goal. If you're going to do it professionally, you hope to do what we got to do. It's fun, I got to play a monster, I got to play a scorned husband, a guy who's losing his mind. I got to play comedy, a guy who's trying to hide a body and act like its business as usual. I think we're real lucky that it's a genre picture where the actors, directors, and writers cared about the characters to try to make them actual human beings. I can't really take credit for that. It was a privilege, a total fucking blast.

Let's talk about the guys who directed, because they did such a fantastic job. You said they helped you out a lot. Give me an idea how they worked? Were they left very independent of each other or were they always throwing stuff off each other?

I would say there was nothing, aside from the budget and lack of studio involvement, that was independent about this project. Not one thing. Nobody was left to their druthers on this. It was a true, I hate to say this, but it was almost like this socialist experiment. The greater good always won out. We were very fortunate to have developed relationships with each other because that made it possible. And the way that it worked with the directors was the same way. All three were always on set, all the time. It just worked very naturally. It seemed like an unspoken thing that whoever's transmission it was, they weren't running the camera. But when you watched the movie, it looks like one person was running the camera. It looks like one person edited the movie. That means that they were far into each other's head. They

collaborated on the script, and it changed a couple of times, and they still ran with it. When we first started promoting the film, people would ask if it was tough working with three directors. And I guess if it were three directors who didn't know what they were doing or didn't get along or were assholes, it probably would have been a nightmare, but it was the easiest thing in the world to do. It helped so much because there was such a democratic process to find out what the best idea was.

Everyone had a stake in what the best way to tell it was. I think having three directors gave the actors a lot more say too because it became more of a community effort, a community experience. Our line producer, our AD, all these guys had an equal hand in the telling of it. So, it would basically be a huddle. We would huddle over it, talk about it for a few minutes about how to do it and shoot. Specifically, there's a moment in act two, there's a continuous shot, a non-effects shot. I don't want to talk about how we did it, we just... did the trick.

Which shot is this?

It's the hallucination, when Louis is seeing Anna, it's obviously Anna, but he's seeing Mya there. The easy way to do that is to shoot a two-shot, cut away. Show Louis, show them. Cut it together. But we didn't want to do it that, we didn't want to cheat it that way. So, we banged heads for forty-five minutes, practicing it like we were going to be running a play. Once we got it down, we did it a few times and got it, and did it all in one take. We did that a couple of times in the movie.

Have you been surprised about the response the film got when it first started screening at Sundance last year?

Yes and no. It's hard for me. It's a little tough for me to be unbiased because they're my best friends. I'm a fan of theirs, I like watching their stuff. But once I saw the cut that was sent off to Sundance and how it had come together, I started thinking I actually thought we had a good shot of getting into Sundance. I would say aside from Scott, I've probably watched more horror movies than anyone who worked on it. I'd seen so many, and I thought this is good enough to get in. Other movies that haven't been as good have gotten in. I wasn't sure if people would respond to it. The best thing for me has been getting to travel and watch it with different audiences. It's almost like a different movie each time. For example, I'm not aware of how violent it is, because I worked on it, you know? So, I had no idea that it's remotely scary, but when we played it at Sundance people were freaking out over it. I had no idea people would see Louis as a "bad guy" except for a couple of moments. I was able to fight for it and say, "Hey look, his wife is having an affair." I don't think that any of us had any idea that people would like it enough to tell their friends to see it. Or that it would strike a nerve with anyone.

I thought that it would eventually find its audience, and I wasn't aware that it would have as many people interested in it. I thought it would be a cult movie on a shelf somewhere that you had to hunt for and find, and it still might very well be. But the response has been very humbling and that was a little bit of a shock. Going to all these film festivals, that's a little bit of a shock, having people want to support it. People who have nothing to gain from supporting it other than being something they had a good time with.

So, are you ramped up for the theatrical release, and curious to see how horror fans are going to react to it?

I have no idea, I'm curious if people are going discover it, because there's been some movies that have come out that I thought people were going to discover and not. It's been a while since we've had a movie along the lines of *The Blair Witch Project* that captures the collective conscience. At this point in time, having the number of people who have already seen it is more than we were expecting.

Any plans to work with the guys from *The Signal* again?

Always. They're my family. We're kind of like the low-brow *Good Will Hunting* of the horror genre. We know each other and we went off and did this thing. I'll always work with these guys. Like, I talked to Anessa three times yesterday, I talked to Jacob. It's tougher now because I don't think we're going to be able to shoot a $50,000 movie again because the budgets go up and it makes it tougher to hire some of us who aren't exactly a viable box-office draw. That makes it a little trickier, but we'll go off and work on our own, but I'm guessing every couple years, get back together. I think the time is getting nigh to get together and bang heads together. We're like a boyband and we want to get back together and work on a new dance routine and go on tour, but we're working on our solo projects right now.

Anything else on the horizon?

Well, I'm in the middle of writing a script that's not a genre picture. I'm writing a Western with Jacob. I'm also writing my own script, a Coen Brothers style film, set in Athens, Georgia in the 80s. And hopefully if everything works out,

I'm going to get to work with my buddy Ti West on another genre picture. (*House of the Devil*) I mean he loves horror films, obviously. He makes them, so I hope he likes them!

So it seems like you've had your hands in all aspects of filmmaking, have you given any thought to directing?

Certainly. I mean, if you're just an actor, unless you come across a pie-in-the-sky scenario that *The Signal* is, you're not in control of the story or the quality. You're a tool for the director and producer, a necessary tool, but a tool. But I'm more interested in storytelling, so I'd like to be in more control of the content. And I've always written, and I'll continue to write. Eventually I'd like to be producing and directing my own things. All aspects of the filmmaking process interest me. I certainly will continue to produce more of the stories I want to see that aren't being represented, the stories that I love and as soon as feel like I know enough of what I'm doing on a film set and someone throws some money at me, I'd direct. I'll just go off and do my own remake of *Sleepaway Camp II*.

We've ended where we started. Is that an old favorite too?

I love 'em, and I'm not going to be a purist and say I love the first *Sleepaway Camp*, fuck *II* and *III*. I actually really love *Sleepaway Camp II*. I like the first one, but I love *Sleepaway Camp II*. That movie and *Jason Lives*, I think people need to shut up when they talk about *Scream* revitalizing the genre. I like *Scream* too, but if you want to get a couple of movies that are self-aware in a fun way, *Sleepaway Camp II* is fucking hysterical, and it's got great gore! I loved what they did with Angela. And *Jason Lives*… that's another one because they shot that in Georgia and I was a Cub Scout at the camp they shot it at.

That's awesome, and I want to thank you, and all the guys from *The Signal* for talking to us!

ZACHARY LEVI

Interviewed by Rob Galluzzo and Joel David Moore (2/08)

In February of 2008, audiences will be treated to the psychological thriller *Spiral*! The project reunites *Hatchet* director Adam Green with actor Joel David Moore, who stars and co-wrote the script. We got to speak to one of the stars of *Spiral*, Zachary Levi (TV's *Chuck*). His buddy Joel Moore decided at the last minute to sit in as a guest *Icons* contributor to help us interview his friend. Below are the unedited results!

Rob: Hello, Zac and Joel!

Zac: Hey Rob! This is Zac's voice and obviously the other voice is Joel's voice.

Joel: (in cracking teenager voice) I plan on sounding like a teenager the whole time. Can you hear the difference?

Rob: (laughs) Zac, I saw *Spiral* a couple of months ago with Adam Green, and I already spoke to Joel in September for *Hatchet*. I don't know if you guys know this, but I was asked to interview you both because you guys are being referred to as "the next Ben Affleck and Matt Damon."

Zac: Well, we like that!

Rob: (laughs) I thought it'd be fun if Joel helped me interview you this month.

Joel: That that'd be great! And Zac, just to let you know, *Icons of Fright* put *Spiral* in their TOP LISTS for the year.

Zac: Oh, wow thank you very much, Rob! That's fantastic!

Rob: I loved it. I told Joel before; I picked both *Hatchet* and *Spiral* for my top list. I love *Hatchet*, but it seems like for everyone involved in *Spiral*, it's a better movie in terms of Adam's directing, Joel as an actor or even Will Barratt as a cinematographer. On all counts, it's just a great movie, and great work from all of you.

Joel: We're really happy with the way that it turned out, and we're so happy to be able to have Adam and Will involved in

the process. They were a big part of the movie. There was no other way to do it.

Rob: Joel, you've known Zac for a while before *Spiral*, so how'd you guys first meet?

Joel: Well, Zac and I met in LA about five years ago and just really hit it off and we've been best friends ever since. We've always looked for something we could do together, and we had talked about forming a production company very early on. Years and years before we actually formed the company. And so, after making *Spiral*, we decided that we were going to start a company and since then we've gone on to produce a couple of features and have been very excited about the future prospects of the company.

Rob: How'd Zac become a part of *Spiral*? I know you wrote the movie, Joel, so did you have him in mind for the character of Berkeley?

Joel: We wrote the movie for him. I mean, we wrote the movie for us. And I think that shows in the chemistry between the characters, even though we're not playing ourselves. You can really see that there's a lot of chemistry between us just because of our relationship off screen and I think that that bleeds through to these characters, even in the awkward situations that they're in. Mason and Berkeley have an odd relationship but they're necessary for each other. They're people who need each other, even if it's not in the most healthy of ways.

Zac: They're people who need people.

Rob: It's funny, because the last time we spoke, the way you described it is that the title *Spiral* is significant in that Mason is not only spiraling out of control, but for a part of the movie spiraling into control. And I always felt that Zac's character was the one who kept him balanced. Zac, what'd you think of the story when you first read the script? Did you know anything about it?

Zac: I knew a little bit about it because I obviously knew that Joel and Jeremy (Boreing) were writing the script. I feel like I had maybe recognized a couple of scenes, but they were more along the lines of the earlier initial premises that they'd been kicking around. When they first handed me the script, my first reaction was "*Wow*." I didn't realize two of my best friends who I thought on a whole were very untalented actually could write a script.

Joel: (laughs) Jerk.

Zac: (laughs) No, it was great. It was an incredible little script. At that point, there were no plans to make the movie, as we made it. I was just kind of waiting to see what they were going to do with it. They had told me as they were writing the Berkeley character that they were drawing upon me as a muse in some ways, and I took that both as a compliment and an insult, I suppose… because Berkeley can be such a douchebag. (laughs)

But I was excited to see what was going to pan out with it. We had a lot of irons in the fire with various scripts and ideas. It's interesting to watch Joel and his career, and for Joel to watch me in mine. The meetings we keep getting as the years go by and as our careers etch their way up. One week, I'd go in and have a meeting with some executive at a studio and literally either the next week or even a few days later, Joel will go in and talk to the same executive or vice versa. I remember one time, Joel went down to Fox and two days later I ended up sitting in the same office talking about the same stuff we were working on.

Joel: The other nice thing is now that we've had the company, we're able to take a lot of these meetings together and sort of power punch them. Like… *Thundercats*. Wait, which was the one where they joined forces?

Zac: That was *Voltron*.

Joel: Yes, like *Voltron*. (laughs)

Rob: One of the biggest thrills for me in the past year after seeing *Hatchet* and *Spiral* was to see everyone involved go on to other great projects. I remember when *Chuck* premiered, I turned to my friends and said, "Hey, that's the guy from *Spiral*!" And they're all like, "What? What are you talking about?" I'd seen Tricia Helfer in an episode of *Supernatural*, same goes for Tamara Feldman (from *Hatchet*). Obviously, Joel getting to work with James Cameron now. It's just great to see everyone involved in both films all over the place now.

Joel: Well, it's great. We wrote the film for Zac, but we were hoping for Ryan Reynolds. But that didn't work out.

(laughs)

Joel: And it really worked out well that *Chuck* came out. And Zac was actually hoping that DJ Qualls would play the main part in *Spiral*. (everyone laughs) That didn't work out either. So, his second choice was Jon Heder. Again, didn't pan out. So, I played the part.

Rob: (laughs) I see, I see. Well, I'm glad you guys ended up in those roles. Joel, is there anything that you've never had a chance to ask Zac that you can put him on the spot right now and ask him about? Anything, it could be personal or about working on the movie?

Joel: Yes. Why… can't we be together, Zac?

Zac: We've been over this and over this. But I think he asked, do you have a question you've never asked me before?

Joel: Oh, oh, oh! I thought, I thought he said ask him a question that you ask him every day.

Rob: Oh, ok.

Joel: Um, yeah. I want to know what Zac's interpretation is of his character's relationship with Mason? Because it's a weird relationship, it's really awkward and strained in many ways and there's obviously a history between the two. I just want to hear your thoughts? Why does Berkeley feel like he has to keep Mason around him?

Zac: Well, I think the first thing is that the two characters I find to be kind of the same guy in a lot of ways. I think that they're both isolated and Berkeley hides it better and surrounds himself with women and fake friends, whatever the case might be. We kind of discussed this as we were shooting and even while you guys were writing, it's implied through the story that Berkeley and Mason have known each other for quite some time, and this isn't the first time that Berkeley's had to bail Mason out.

Maybe they were childhood friends. I feel like Berkeley keeps Mason around for the same reason Mason keeps Berkeley around, which is that they are two kinds of loners in their own very different ways. Berkeley kind of fashions himself a father figure for Mason in some ways, and I think it's his way of feeling better about himself by taking care of another individual, albeit in a kind of shitty way sometimes. I feel that Jeremy and Joel did a really incredible job of creating characters that were interesting and colorful without being caricatures.

And I know that Joel and Adam (especially with Berkeley) in the first sit-down talks, when we first were reading some scenes, one of the biggest things was they didn't want Berkeley to come off jokey in any way. They wanted the comedy to play just out of the relationship. That's tough for me sometimes. I really like getting a laugh and making people laugh! So, that was a fun step for me and I appreciated that that's where Joel and Adam wanted to go with the character, because that's where I also wanted to go in the sense of my career, not always playing some jokester.

Joel: As a co-director and the co-writer, there were certain aspects of Berkeley's character that we wanted to come across as not a caricature. Zac is so naturally talented as a comedian that at first, when we were going through the scenes, there was a lot of "making the joke" instead of letting the joke happen. And because it's so natural, it was never about it being too much. It was always about letting the situation be the joke or whatever was surrounding the scene was what led to the joke. It was a very slight shift, because we're dealing with someone who's incredibly talented at the thing we've written into the script for him. There is a comedic side to Zac's character, but it always had to be based in a reality.

Zac: Rob, do you see how we do that? You give Joel an opportunity to ask me a question, and we turn it into just a, a patting-of-the-back fest. I might as well have just played with his balls right there.

Joel: I'm actually giving him a massage right now.

Rob: (laughs) Zac, I hope you know that every single thing you guys say is all going in this interview. Word for word. Don't worry, all the ass kissing and patting of the backs will be intact.

Zac: (laughs)

Rob: Zac, let me ask – what was it like for you in particular to work with two directors, Adam and Joel, who were both coming off another picture together and whom already had somewhat of a working relationship together?

Zac: I thought it was fantastic! For me, I love working with people that I know, and especially people that I know really well. Because when you get a job and you're on set, hours can be long, and the better the communication levels are, the faster things can move. Especially if you all think alike and see things similarly. While we didn't obviously always have that, for the most part as a collective, we all kind of saw the end results in the broader strokes. Being able to go to Portland and take on an eighteen day schedule, yeah, it was a little nutty in some respects, but I knew going up there that if anyone's going to pull it off in eighteen days, it's us, because we know each other and we know what to expect from each other.

And we bring out the best in one another. So, I thought it was great. It was truly an adventure from one end of the spectrum to the other. To all just kind of migrate north to Portland for the month between Thanksgiving and Christmas and stay in this little hotel. It was like the craziest, coolest adventure, from top to bottom. And Adam Green, I was really looking forward to working with him, because of how much Joel had spoken so highly of him, and the experience he had on *Hatchet*. And Will Barratt as well and BJ McDonnell and Lewis Fowler and Dustin Pearlman, our camera guys that we brought over from *Hatchet*.

Joel: Adam being involved in this project was not, "I need help. I can't handle this, let me bring on a co-director." It was something we had talked about during *Hatchet*, about working on something together and he's the first person that I called. I said, "Look, I want to do this movie, and I want to play the lead, we just worked together and we worked together famously. Let's do it again. Let's make another movie together this year." So, it was very much two people collaborating and not one person asking another to be involved.

Rob: Joel, how difficult was the editing process, because if I understood correctly, the original cut of the film was a lot longer?

Joel: The movie was a lot longer, and I took the reins on editing it.

Rob: So, how difficult was *Spiral* to edit? The movie as it is feels complete, but did you have to lose anything that that you filmed that just didn't fit in?

Joel: No. Not at all. We just trimmed a lot of fat. It's funny, the first version of the movie was two hours long and we knew we had to cut a half hour out of it, so we did a bunch of stuff collaboratively, and took notes on it and decided what we were going to cut out. We ended up taking out a ton of scenes that we actually wanted in the movie. And then, I went back and trimmed the fat out of all the scenes. I was new at this as well; I had never edited a feature before. And I guess I didn't know how much fat you can trim out of the scenes. You just take pauses here, or a beat there. And all of those pauses; if you're taking a couple of seconds out here, a couple of seconds out there out of every scene, that adds up to minutes and minutes!

The first pass, I took ten minutes out. So, doing that, we were able to then add some of the scenes that we wanted back into the movie because of the fat that we had taken out. That process slowly allowed me to put everything that we wanted back into the movie. The scenes that didn't make the movie didn't have to be in the movie. We didn't lose any part of the story. We didn't lose any part of the relationship. It was a terrifying process. Because at the beginning, I thought we're going to have to lose half of our movie to get this to an hour and a half. As time went on, it really opened itself up to let us put everything we needed back in.

Rob: Zac, what was the most memorable aspect of making this movie? Whether it be filming a particular scene, or just a night that stood out from the eighteen day shoot?

Zac: Um, you know, it's a tough question, just because I felt like so much stood out. I think anytime you go and try and pull off what we pulled off, not like we're moving mountains. But in some ways, we're moving little mini-mountains when you consider the budget and the time frame, and resources that – I don't know! The one particular moment where I just stood there and was taking everything in. It was the last day of shooting, and I was wrapped. We were getting these last shots, it's a scene that's in the beginning of the movie where Joel is walking down the street and looking into the café.

We had the rain towers set up, I'm just standing there, and I was watching everybody do what they do. And aside from my executive producing role, which to me was a lot of fun, being able to take care of people and make sure everything was running as smoothly as possible. I just had a moment to stand there and take it all in. To reflect on eighteen days that we had to shoot this thing. There was a blizzard day! We were shooting up on this hill, the roads were iced over and we thought, "Well, I guess we're not going to be able to make our film." Because we didn't have one single day to spare.

We were coming right up against the Christmas holiday. But sure enough, we got this incredible snow day right on our day off and then it all melted away, and we continued uninterrupted. I felt providence looking over us. Just thinking, "Wow, we were meant to come out here and do this, for whatever reason." Whether it's for some young kid who gets to see this in some theater and watches it and goes, "Why don't they make movies like this anymore?" Or for millions of people who hopefully go and rent it on DVD and say, "Wow, these guys really are the new Luke and Owen Wilson and Wes Anderson," in Jeremy and Joel's respect. For being our age, and at this point in our careers, I feel we pulled off something that few people actually pull off. A lot of people talk about it! Even we talked about it for a long time and didn't end up doing anything until Joel had some epiphany while taking a crap and that led us to Portland!

Joel: It really was interesting the way we put this movie together. It's really hard to put a movie together. Everything we've produced since has been put together outside of us and we've come on in some fashion beyond the funding of the film. We put this movie together piece by piece. Small chunk of the budget by small chunk of the budget. And we went to family and friends and relationships with people that we knew that were new to financing films. We said, "Look. Just give us a shot. Let us prove to you we can make a good movie." And we didn't know if we were going to make a good movie! (laughs)

Rob: You were hoping!

Joel: Because we were so attached to it, we actually didn't know if it was a good movie until other people saw it and we thankfully weren't wrong when we were finished with the movie and got the final cut and sent it out there. We got into the festival that we wanted to get into, the Santa Barbara Film Festival, and ended up winning one of the top three awards at the festival.

The Gold Vision award, which was the perfect award for us, because it encompasses everything about the film. The award was for outstanding achievement and visual work, and that was what we were trying to do. The style we put into it, and the creative aspects we put into it was the most important thing. We didn't want it to feel like a "whatever" movie that was just going to go straight to DVD and just be what it is.

Rob: Joel, I don't mean to keep harping on this, but most people are familiar with your work in comedies (*Dodgeball, Grandma's Boy*). I can't wait for people to see your performance in *Spiral,* because it's so different from everything you've done and it's fantastic. I just wanted to know if you personally have a favorite scene or a piece of work from *Spiral* that you're most proud of?

Joel: Um… I'm very proud of the piece as a whole. To deconstruct it is tough! I think that one of my favorite moments in the movie is the long, steady cam shot that Adam and I wrote on the fly, because we were trying to figure out how to shoot the scene. The camera is a character in this movie. And it's something that we knew from the very beginning. We had written our shot list and developed the style of the movie to show that the camera is almost an on-looker looking at this crazy man's life and the experiences that happen to him.

One of my favorite moments in terms of the camera being its own character, is when after Amber walks Mason home, Mason walks up into his apartment and is freaking out, and there's one long four-minute camera move of him coming through the apartment, looking out the window to see her, backing up to look at something that people don't know what it is. And he sort of freaks out watching this. The camera turns and reveals he's looking at these paintings of another woman. This woman that he was looking at, the waitress in the beginning of the movie. And I think that tells so much about this movie, because it doesn't cut.

It's an awkward feeling. It's like watching the *BBC Office.* You just get that uncomfortable feeling because there is no cut, and you're watching and following and he goes to the window, and he looks up and is staring at something and you don't know what it is! Finally, it turns to reveal and it continues on him moving into the bathroom. And it's just this moment that sets the tone for the rest of the movie. We deliberately made a movie that is slower in pacing because that's how it was written. That's the movie we wrote! To go against that wouldn't have made sense.

That sticks out to me as a moment that I'm proud of as a director. We wrote this long shot list, and a lot of times you get into making the movie, you can't use your shot list. We ended up using a lot of our shot list, and that was just a moment that we had to figure out because of the

setting of the loft - how do we get the whole shot off? It ended up being a very cinematic move.

Rob: Awesome. Well, my last question for both of you and, honestly the main reason I wanted to talk to you both, was to talk about *The Tiffany Problem.* Any comments on this year's AurieScope Halloween short?

Joel: (laughs) Adam Green and I talked about doing a short this year and we were on a plane, and he's like I got this idea about this guy who can't give up trick or treating on Halloween! We sort of answered back and forth about what jokes we could throw in and we figured out about 700 jokes, and we had to get that down to however many made the cut.

Rob: Well, I know it's a tradition for Adam Green to do an annual Halloween short film.

Joel: Zac literally just got off set shooting *Chuck,* shot his scene and had no clue what the hell was going on! (laughs) We put a wig on him, told him to wear these pink pj's, walk in, point to a bunch of people, look at her, and walk out. And he just made part of that up. We gave him the gist of what was going on, but he made a lot of that up. A lot of what we did on that short, we just kind of made up on the fly. We did it in six hours, the whole thing and it was a couple of days before I was leaving to New Zealand to shoot the rest of *Avatar,* so it was pretty fun. Zac was a sport. He was probably delusional after shooting a fourteen hour day having no clue what we did. He probably woke up the next morning thinking, "Did I just shoot a short film with Adam and Joel? What happened?" (laughs)

Rob: Zac, do you remember wearing the wig and dress?
Zac: Wait, what film is this?

Joel: Ha! It's this short, *The Tiffany Problem.* You were in it.

Zac: Oh, I was? (laughs)

Rob: Yeah! It's on YouTube, we'll send it to you. Thank you so much to both of you for your time, I appreciate it.
Zac: Absolutely.

DICK DUROCK

Interviewed by Mike Cucinotta (2/08)

Back in the 70's and 80's, if you turned on the TV, you just might have caught actor Dick Durock on one of his many bit parts and not recognized him. That's because the role he's best remembered for had him wearing eighty pounds of green latex. That's right – Dick played everyone's favorite leafy green superhero Swamp Thing, not just in two films but also for three seasons on USA Network's early 90's TV series. Dick sat down with us recently so we could dredge up some old memories from the swamp.

Swamp Thing: The Series **is finally out on DVD! It's endured after all these years.**

I still do get fan mail, and surprisingly a lot from Europe.

Really?

The Netherlands in particular. Yes, it still has a following.

How did it get this following in Europe?

I haven't got a clue. I know there was a girl in England that I was in touch with, gosh, ten, twelve years ago. It was huge in England. They had a whole national *Swamp Thing* fan club. I regret not taking the opportunity to go over there and say "hello" at least. You never know, telecommunications, everything is so universal now.

Sure, but that was much harder in the early 90's, not that it was the dark ages. You played Swamp Thing in this and two films, which almost never happens. What kept them bringing you back, besides the fact that you're great in all of them? Did they actively seek you out?

Yeah, and there's a good reason for that. This is something that hadn't been done in the history of motion pictures before where you had a guy in extensive makeup, eighty pounds of latex, working the entire day, every day, twelve hours a day. This was unusual and unheard of. I think I had them over the barrel because they knew I could do it, to start with. Believe it or not, there are a lot of guys who have claustrophobia with any sort of enclosure like that. They had a known commodity and they didn't have to pay major league price to get the lead.

What are some of the differences between working on the features and working on the series? We've all heard that series television shoots a lot faster.

And that's the major difference!

How did that work out for you, especially with the costume and makeup?

Well, the makeup and costume, I got used to that. The first time it took about four hours to put it all together, the second two hours, and by the time we got to the series we had it down to forty-five minutes.

That's great!

It was by far the best makeup and best costume, and I'm talking about the series. The hard part for me, not being the heavily trained or schooled actor, was just absorbing that you had to do ten pages of dialogue a day. You know, at the end of the day, a production assistant might come by and say, "Ok, here Dick, here's the show we're shooting tomorrow," and hand you another ten pages you had to start learning it. That was tough for me. That'd be tough for anyone, I imagine. Again, with the series, it's time. With the feature, you shoot one, two pages a day, but we were doing ten.

You'd already visited this character twice before. Was there anything you wanted to bring to Swamp Thing for the series that you hadn't before? Anything you were looking to do differently?

You know, a lot of times you don't have that luxury because

you do what the writers write and what the directors want. What I tried to do from day one, I thought the most important thing was to stress this guy's humanity, his vulnerability, to make him something more than just a green killing machine. Here's a man trapped in this miserable situation, but still trying to maintain his humanity as much as he can. And you know, to get a little sympathy for him.

This series had a different feel than say, _Return of Swamp Thing_, which was very comic book, almost campy. It seemed like they tried to make this more serious in tone.

They tried in _Return of Swamp Thing_ to make it comedic and campy, and it's tough to make that work. I think they kind of gave up on that idea and got back to the darker side of the character as he was written in the comic book.

And some of the stories in this series were kind of dark. You had Peter Mark Richman playing a character who used to be a bird, a very tortured character. These are really interesting stories, and they used _Swamp Thing_ almost as an observer.

That was intentional too. Because the guy is in the swamp, he's kind of omnipotent, acting as a kind of sentinel, and it certainly took a bit of the load off of me.

I know that this was one of the first things shot out in Universal Studios Orlando. Were there any kinks they had to work out? They weren't building the studio around you guys, were they?

Not really. I was really impressed with it. That's a wonderful complex. Now what we had down there, well, the first thirteen episodes we shot out in the actual swamps around Orlando, which was miserable. First of all, the swamps didn't look like the dark miserable swamps you associate with that character. So, they got smart. On the lot, next to the stage, we were working on was an open field and somebody got the idea to build the swamp on this area. So, they did and it was ten times more effective than the real swamp because you could control the lighting, or shoot a scene inside, then move outside and it took ten minutes as opposed to three hours to move the company from the lot to a location. It was learning process, but it was much more effective having the phony swamp.

Can I ask you about the weird turn the series seems to take in the middle. Didn't they get rid of the young boy, Jim Kipp, a main character?

I think you're talking about Jess Ziegler who played the young kid in the first season. When we got picked up for season two, I think he was still in. The way they wrote him out was kind of a shock to me and everybody else except for, I suppose the writers. They had him abducted by a child stealing ring from South America. Well... that's a hell of a way to meet your demise!

Yeah! I mean, I was just a kid watching this show and it may have been the last time I saw it. He was in a cage in the back of a truck, and they just took him away. That always blew my mind. Do you know what led up to that very strange decision?

I think it was mentioned that he was alright, but I'm not quite sure. Well, they decided to make a major turn. With the first twelve episodes with Jess they wanted to appeal to the younger audience. Then somebody said, well, you've got to understand we had USA, Paramount, and Universal's voice in this series, so somebody said we had to get back to the original character, lose the kid, and make it darker. But that's the way it works.

What have you been up to the last couple of years?

Not much, bouncing around, enjoying retirement. Forty years of a very fulfilling career, I'm very happy with it, very proud. I did some good work and did some bummers, like everybody else. I've been extremely lucky, made a good living, and never had to do anything else. I consider myself very, very fortunate.

So you've retired, that's awesome. Ever get a chance to get out there and meet fans, maybe show up at conventions?

I look forward to it, I enjoy people. I had an attitude, but I had some wise mentors when I was young. It's easy when you start working to get a little cocky, but I always had guys around who'd remind me that when you meet your fans to remember that they're the ones who sign your checks, ultimately. They're the ones who watch your product. I always keep that in mind.

It must be fun meeting all the people, like myself, who grew up with _Swamp Thing_.

It is, it's flattering. I've never been one to have accolades showered on my head and feel comfortable about it. It was a job that I happened to do, and I hope I did it reasonably well. That's enough gratitude, knowing someone appreciated it. If I could give you a half-hour escape, then I've done my job.

Well, *Swamp Thing* has always been a favorite of mine. I love *Return of Swamp Thing,* when I was a kid they'd run it on cable all the time…

Now be honest, you loved Heather Locklear!

Hey, everyone loves Heather Locklear! Now, that movie didn't get the release that the original quite got, not sure why, but I only remember seeing it on cable. Did you have any idea what happened to the release of the second film?

Well, the first one really got good critical reviews! People sent me the reviews from all over, and they were very positive. Here, you're dealing with a population of people who want to see it be reasonably close to the comic book character and I think the second was such a departure that it didn't work as they expected it to work. Heather was so hot at the time that I think they thought her presence alone would have been enough to help. I think when they got to the series, they thought they had to go back to the original.

Kind of like what Wes Craven brought to the first film?

Yeah, well Wes really got into the character.

And how was Wes to work with back then? Working on *Swamp Thing* at that time maybe he was a little out of his element since he never did revisit comic stuff, but he did do a great job on that film.

Wes was a great guy. He's very internalized, a deep thinker, like a scholar, which he is. He was trying to get into the characters' heads rather than strictly play it by the book, which a lot of directors do.

And it seems like that movie was a little ahead of its time too because I don't think there really had been a comic adaptation that took its character that seriously at that point.

It was unusual.

How'd you handle that heat?

Well, it's a state of mind. I accepted the job; I knew it'd be miserable but you try to balance it. Stay wet, get a production assistant to spray you down, and drink lots of liquids.

Did it help you stay in character at all?

Eh, not really. When I wasn't working, I was going over the script that I was supposed to do.

So, do you have any crazy stories that you can remember about when you were making the movie? Anything dangerous ever happen while you were in the swamp?

Ah, sure, but you know, it's not particularly funny, I guess. It was so miserable, not just for me, but for the whole company, when you're working in the middle of the swamps in summer in the south. I wish there were one instance… well, stupid things do happen. Like in the first one with the make-up, they had appliances all over my face and my lips, but every time you started to do dialogue, sweat would build up, loosen the glue, and in the middle of the scene my lips would fall off. By the time we got to the series, all around my mouth was my own skin, all around my eyes was my own skin.

Oh yeah, he's got that kind of ridge over his mouth in the second!

Well, again, nobody had done a show where a guy had to work twelve hours a day and it can't just work that way because make-up is make-up, people sweat, makeup falls off. But we learned!

Had it been intimidating at all on that first film, having to carry a movie for the first time?

That's intimidating for a while, but if you survive, the movie survives, and everyone can do their job. The only thing with being the lead is if something happens to you, the whole movie can go down. That itself was kind of intimidating. But you do what you can. My fear was just being able to retain it all.

Thanks so much for your time, Dick!

GUNNAR HANSEN

Interviewed by Mike Cucinotta (3/08)

Over thirty-five years ago, outside of Austin, Texas, a group of filmmakers and actors accomplished something remarkable. With a shoestring budget, little in the way of experience, and conditions that were almost unbearable, they combined their talents to create *The Texas Chain Saw Massacre*. Gunnar Hansen, fresh out of school with a Masters in English, was chosen to perform the role of Leatherface, one of horror's most frightening, disturbing, fascinating, and enduring characters. Gunnar spoke with us recently about the original's making and legacy as well as his role in an upcoming horror satire titled *Brutal Massacre: A Comedy*.

What's the earliest horror film you can remember?

The first horror movie I can remember was *Frankenstein*. I lived in a small town and the movie theater in the next town over was all second run. So I was at the movies with my family and they had previews for *Frankenstein* and it terrified me. Just the previews! I think the scene where the woman is at the makeup mirror and Frankenstein is at the window, and every time the lightening flashed it would project his shadow on the wall and she didn't see it, that really got me scared. So that's the earliest I can remember and after that it was really—well, on Friday nights down in Texas there was what was called *Shock Theater*, it was a horror movie show, or as we said it in Texas, "Shock The-ear-ter".. It just showed really wonderfully bad horror movies like *The Crawling Eye*, *The Deadly Mantis*, and *Them*. Of course, I loved *Them*. It was wonderfully scary. I love that movie.

The first film of yours I wanted to talk about was your most recent one, *Brutal Massacre* from Stevan Mena. How did you get to know Stevan? Also, I heard you were a very big supporter of his first film *Malevolence*. How did that come to your attention?

I met him and he asked me to take a look at his movie, so he sent me a copy. I really liked it. I thought it really had a few things that you weren't seeing in the latest crop of horror movies. It had that real 70's feel to it, versus that super-slick stuff that was being produced that didn't have much scare to it. They were screening it down in Massachusetts and he asked me to come down, so I did, and he introduced me at the screening and I said a couple things about why I liked it and that got us in contact.

So, how soon after that did he start talking to you about a role in one of his films?

Pretty soon after that because by the time *Malevolence* was out and released onto home video, we were talking. I think I was down in New York for something and we had lunch and coffee out in Long Island. He talked about his next project, which he thought would be the sequel to *Malevolence*. We talked about the possibility of my being involved with that. Then I was surprised when he called me for this [*Brutal Massacre*] because I didn't know it was in the works and that he was interested in comedy or would think of me for comedy.

Yeah, it came as a surprise to us too when Stevan announced he'd wrapped on a film and it was a comedy. What was it like doing comedy? I don't think we've ever seen you in a straight-up comedy before.

I really loved it. I'd done a little bit of comedy before in a film called *Next Victim*, which unfortunately has had problems and not been released. It was an anthology film, and I did the wraparound story. It was my first chance to do a comic role, and I really enjoyed it so when he told me it was a comedy, I thought it would be great to do.

What did you think of the character Krenshaw?

Well, I guess it might be... I don't know if I should say, but I could identify with him. (laughs)

Really?

Well, I know people like this. I hope I'm not like him, but he was very real to me, I've met people like this before. So, what I really had to do was work on how he might be dressed, what was his manner, and how did he speak. In fact, I had created such a caricature of him that at the first rehearsal, Stevan said I might have to bring him down. (laughs)

It's interesting with Stevan and you doing comedy, and actually, the whole cast that was involved, because I don't think we've seen them do comedy before, but it all works very well, *Brutal Massacre* is very funny. What do you think it was that really got everybody to work so well?

Well, that's hard to know. That's like asking me, "Why was *Chain Saw Massacre* so good?" Well, it read funny, the script was funny, so my expectation was that the film would be funny. I mean, certainly everybody was really good at it, I mean, David Naughton was just dead-on and dead pan. There was nothing broad about the way he does it. And Ken Foree, his character was just absolutely hilarious and sad. I don't know what it was. I was going to say it was great conditions on the set, but actually, we froze to death!

I don't know, everybody worked hard, everybody was in a good mood. There was no tension on the set, it felt like the shooting just moved through very smoothly, and in my limited experience with comedy, I think that's an important thing.

Now, you've spent an entire career in independent horror, which is what *Brutal Massacre* is about, how true to the making of a low budget horror movie does *Brutal Massacre* come?

Um... I suspect it's quite accurate, in fact. The one place I thought they underplayed was with the financing. They could have made a whole movie about financing and the kind of difficulties you go through and the kind of interference you get from producers and money people. I've worked on films that could have fit beautifully in the film. For example, a producer who showed up on set while we're getting into makeup with a singer who he wants to sing in the movie and who wanted the trailer because he was going to record her. I've never been in a situation quite like in the movie where someone like Krensaw showed up and really screwed things up, but I don't doubt for a second that it happened.

Was there any film you worked on that reminded you of *Brutal Massacre* or any other film you worked on that might be similar to events that happen in this movie?

Well, it's hard because most movies I come in, shoot for a day or two, and I'm gone. So, a lot of the dynamics I don't see. So, I think...maybe *Murder-Set-Pieces* might qualify a bit. I know he [director Nick Palumbo] had a lot of problems. Well, *Chainsaw Sally*, there were times when I think he [director Jimmyo Burrill] was very frustrated with things that were going on. I know there were investors in that movie who were absolute dreams, but there are investors who make it a real challenge to make a film.

Another interesting thing about *Brutal Massacre* is it features a lot of guys that you've maybe shared a room or table space with at the horror conventions over the years. What was it like finally getting to work with these guys?

Well, I thought it was really fun. The sad part is that I know Ken very well and then we were never there at the same time, which was too bad because I would love to have worked with Ken directly. But certainly, working with David Naughton such as I did was a thrill for me because I loved *An American Werewolf in London*. Ellen Sandwiess and the others from *Evil Dead* were great because that's another movie I really enjoy. David and I didn't know each other very well, but we had been at a couple conventions, so we'd talked and of course, the *Evil Dead* ladies, I knew them a little better because I'd seen them at shows and gone over to their table. It's fun when you have known people because it makes the work a lot easier if nothing else. These are already people I like, so that makes it fun to work, but also if you know them then working with them is easier, you know what to expect. And I think David is just an unrecognized comic actor.

Yes, he's really, really good at this. I can't say I was surprised, he's been very funny before, but I don't think he's had a role like this in a really long time. Now, I looked at your IMDb profile and you've done a lot of these smaller films. Anything else that sticks out that you've enjoyed working on?

It's really funny because it's been accelerating. I didn't do any film work at all again until '87, I just turned everything down, I wasn't interested. But yes, a film that I worked on that was just a great pleasure to work on was *Apocalypse and the Beauty Queen*. It was difficult shooting in that it was shot outside of St. Louis largely in an unheated building in February, beginning of March, but that was a movie I really enjoyed working on. Of course, that was the movie where the producer showed up with the singer...

Oh wow...

But I really enjoyed it. Here was a movie where the crew was great, and I really had a part that was of some significance. I mean, usually I'm asked to come in and shoot a day and then I'm out, and because of that I don't get a lot of interaction. But *Apocalypse* was great just because I was there for an extended time and really got a chance to work on the film and get to know the crew and other actors. That was also a film I was pleased with, and it wasn't a horror movie. It was nice to work on a film where I was asked to play a dramatic role, you know, versus a killer. You know I started out playing the killer, then I was playing the killer's dad, then the killer's grandfather, and it was nice to do something outside of the genre.

What got them interested in you for the dramatic role?

I don't know what it was. I don't know why they approached me. I mean, I'm grateful. Well, the guy, Jim Shulte who was the writer, I had met him years ago. He was the person who made the contact, so I suspect Jim said, "You should hire Gunnar." I think it must have been Jim's doing more than anything else.

If I can ask, because I know this is one film that generated a lot of controversy, and that would be *Murder-Set-Pieces*. We actually interviewed the director, and the film was a big nightmare for him. What was your experience on that? You did a small role in it...

What I really liked about that was, even though I had a small part, boy was that guy real to me. He was written in a way that was convincing, so I really enjoyed playing the Nazi mechanic. I can see why it was so difficult to shoot. I think that the subject matter is extremely controversial to shoot, and you have to try to shoot it without permits. There was the scene where a young girl dies, you know, and doing it in a public park. How do you get away with that? If I recall there was tension between the director and the DP in the scene that I was shooting, which was too bad because it created a time problem.

We were shooting in that sort of golden light, and stuff wasn't getting shot fast enough because there was some disagreement between the two of them. It was too bad. The effects guys on *Murder-Set-Pieces* were great, they were the Toe Tag guys. I think it's just a shame that they worked so

hard and then for the released version, so much of their work was cut out of the film because it was too extreme.

What about Nick? Because he took a lot of heat for that movie. He took a lot of heat before that movie even came out. What can you say about him?

He's fine. He was always easy to work with, I'd known him on and off because he'd approached me years ago about taking a look at one of his films. We'd been in contact on and off when he was interested in doing a film called *Sinister*, which I went down to New York and shot a trailer for. He's a nice guy. It's unfortunate he takes this heat because... if you talk about Nazism, does that make you a Nazi? No. And they think he's a misogynist because he made this movie about violence against women and to me, that's just primitive thinking on people's part. I mean, can you not separate the message from the messenger? Apparently not. I think it's really unfortunate that people have given him so much heat for making this film. If anything, it should have generated discussion about films like this, but apparently, from his reports to me, people are talking about what a sick character he is, and when you meet him, he's normal.

Yeah, he's a nice guy. We sat down for an hour with him to let him give his side of the story. Why do you think people who follow horror movies and who love horror movies reacted so strongly to that film, in such a negative way?

Well, is that the people who were reacting?

There'd been a blackout from some horror publications. We're not here to glorify violence, but it's not about that.

That's one of the arguments that drives me crazy when people start banging on horror movies. They talk about being irresponsible and my answer is: Don't talk about irresponsibility with horror movies because horror movies show you the consequence of violence. I don't know what it is. The thing about horror movies is that the rules don't get broken. One of those rules is that anyone who is pre-pubescent is never in danger. For example, in the movie *The Gate*, which is a very suburban horror movie, the kids disappear one by one, and they're all eleven, twelve years old. But as soon as the first one is supposedly killed, I lost interest in the movie because I realized they couldn't be killed because it broke the rules. I knew nothing was going to happen to them.

Well, in this movie the little girl isn't safe, and she does get murdered, and I think right there is a big trigger that they get upset about. The other thing is it may have shoved in people's faces the one thing they like about horror movies and it's hard for them to face. And I don't want to characterize all horror movies this way, but a certain characteristic in horror is they have a strong sexual content. A lot of horror movies in the 70's and 80's were sexual cautionary tales where the more promiscuous you are, the sooner and more horrible you die. There's this insertion of sex and voyeurism with violence. What he does is put it to the extreme and put it in your face. And if you're a person who thinks that's titillating then I think it's a little bit horrifying to have it really, really made clear to you, in the extreme, what you're doing. Maybe that's what it is. People are frightened by what they see because they're looking at themselves.

Ok. So, let's ask you. When you're not working on films what do you do?

Sit at home and watch television... (laughs) Oh, you mean in reality? Well, I do a lot of writing. Writing has always been my primary line of work. So after *Chain Saw Massacre*, I did this movie *Demon Lover*, which was this really bad film directed by an incompetent director Don Jackson that I never got paid for. I just thought, "This is insane, why am I involved in the film business?" So, I turned everything down. I was working as a magazine writer. I also did whatever writing came along. I did a church history, I wrote advertising, whatever it took. Then in '87 when I got back into films, when I did *Hollywood Chainsaw Hookers*, I made a shift, and I started writing different things. I did some screenwriting, I've written some documentary films, some I also produced. I don't do any magazine writing anymore. Right now, I'm working on a drama script, which I hope to take out to LA and start pitching in the spring.

How did Fred Olen Ray get you out of acting retirement for *Hollywood Chainsaw Hookers*?

That goes back to *Demon Lover*. When I did *Demon Lover*, Fred was a friend of Don Jackson, and I met Fred out in Michigan when we did that film. I hadn't heard from him for a while and, out of the blue, I get a letter from him asking if I'd be interested in coming out to LA and doing a movie. So, I called him and my first reaction was, "No, I'm not going to do this." Then I thought, "Well, why am I saying no?" So, I called him and we talked about it and went out there and shot the film. It was a whirlwind, it was great. I flew out, I got to LA on a Friday night, got to his house at one in the morning, got up at 6am and started shooting. And I hadn't read the script.

Really?

Well, I told him that I couldn't really agree to do the film if I hadn't read the script and he sort of hemmed and hawed and then said, "Well it's in re-writes." And I took that to mean that there was no script, and he wasn't going to bother to write it, you know because the chainsaw gag only works if I'm in the film, and he wasn't going to write it if I wasn't going to be there. So, what I said was I'll come out and read the script when I get to town and, if it is what you say it is, then I'll sign the contract. So, I stayed at his house, got the script, read it that night, got up, signed the contract, and started shooting. I had no rehearsal time, but that doesn't matter with Fred. (laughs). We just went on set. It's just a funny experience, because at the beginning he would say things like, "Ok, stand in the window and look menacing." And I'd do that. Then he'd say, "Ok, stand in the window and look angry." Well, it's all the same expression! Then he'd say, "Ok, in this scene, you're going to walk in and here's your line..." Well, I had absolutely no sense of the character at all. By the third day of shooting, I was finally caught up enough that I knew my lines ahead of time. But we shot that movie really fast. He shot that in seven days.

Get out...

Yes, what he did was have me come out on Memorial Day weekend. We shot my stuff Saturday, Sunday, and Monday. I took the red eye home, and he shot for the next two weekends. And the reason he did it that way was because he had been called by some producer to save a movie that had been shot and edited but didn't work. They wanted him to come in and shoot some additional footage and recut the film, and it was on 35mm. So, one of the conditions of doing this was that he could have the equipment, the cameras, and the lights on the weekend when they weren't shooting. So, he had these three weekends to shoot the film because he didn't have to pay for the equipment.

Well, he does so many films, he must work fast...

He's so funny because he told me he was shooting one movie and they had a scientific lab, a set. So, they finished shooting at something like 8pm at night and the crew was coming in at 8am to break the set down. He thought, "Well, I have twelve hours," so he called Aldo Ray and said, "I'll give you a $1000 if you come down and shoot all night long." So, while Aldo is driving over there, Fred is writing dialogue, and he said he didn't even know what the film was going to be, no idea what he would use this in, so he just wrote some generic dialogue that he could put into any movie.

And every film, a classic. But seriously, *Hollywood Chainsaw Hookers* does have its cult following, mainly because of the Virgin Dance of the Double Chainsaws.

Oh yes, and I tried to deliver that line like I was Ed Sullivan (laughs). It's funny because there's this guy Danny Peary who wrote this book on cult movies. I picked up this book and I looked at the entry for *Hollywood Chainsaw Hookers* and it said something like, "When you see Gunnar Hansen's acting in *Hollywood Chainsaw Hookers* you'll see why they refused to give him a speaking part in *Chain Saw Massacre*."

Ooooh....

I was so insulted that I put the book down.

Well, you did fine, for a movie that was shot in seven days that you didn't even have a script for. What can we ask you about *Texas Chain Saw Massacre* that you haven't heard before? I guess, you know that movie has come out on DVD about five times over the last few years...

I was just looking at my bookshelf over the desk and I've got one... two... three... four... five... six... seven different boxes of it. I've got an English version, a Swedish version, a German version. It just keeps being re-released, but I think after this metal box set, the Dark Sky box, I don't see how they could ever out do it.

They almost all have great making-of features, and there have been so many making-of features made about *Texas Chain Saw*. What do you think has people so fascinated about the making of this movie?

Well, they want to know what happened, they're trying to figure out how this movie turned into what it did. I always think it's a happy accident. A movie is more than the sum of its parts. You couldn't have had this movie without Tobe Hooper, but it couldn't have been this movie without the actors, without the dedicated and extremely talented crew, and it couldn't have been the movie it is without the miserable conditions we shot it in. There are people who would like the world to believe they are the reason this movie is what it is, but I don't believe that. It's all of those things coming together. I think all of us were a little surprised when we saw what came out of it.

Was it all just a serendipitous experience for everyone?

Yes, but I don't mean that it was a bunch of clowns that got together and said, "Let's make a movie, Andy." Everybody

there was dedicated to what they were doing. It was the first time I'd been in a situation where everybody was really good at what they did, and everybody was giving their best. I was fresh out of graduate school when people are mostly just screwing off, and so suddenly to be working in an environment where everyone was doing their job well, and they all knew what they were about was a thrilling experience. There was an enormous amount of talent that went into the making of that movie. I don't mean to make light of that at all, but it was a combination of all those talents in some sort of accidental way, and the conditions of how this movie was shot. I didn't know what we were going to get because I'd never worked on a film beside being in a student film.

When did you realize, "We made something."

I think it was a year after filming ended, when they were getting ready to release the film. There was a press party in Dallas, and so they flew me out for the day and as part of that, they screened ten minutes of it, and... I was amazed at my reaction, which was that my heart was racing. Even though I knew what was going to happen, there was no surprise for me in the scene they showed but my heart was racing because everything was timed so well. Everything was so beautifully paced, and it looked so good. It wasn't a pretty movie, but it looked so right. That was the first time I realized we had something. Then once the movie was released it was pretty clear. I went with a friend of mine to show her the location where we were filming.

We were standing on Quick Hill Road, which is north of Austin, and on one side was the *Chain Saw Massacre* house, and on the other side was the Franklin house. We were standing there by a fence looking at the Franklin house and this carload of teenage boys pulls up and they come walking up to look at the house and one of them turns and says, "That's where they made that movie!" That's when I knew, that if these kids were going to make a pilgrimage to see where we made it and they referred to it as "that movie," you know, that means they assume everybody knows. The wonderful thing was all this indignant reaction, I just loved that, you know like Johnny Carson getting up on his high horse.

Carson had something to say about it?

Oh, Johnny Carson was outraged, it was wonderful. He stood up and ranted angrily about how dare they give a movie like *Chain Saw Massacre* and "R" rating, that it should have been an "X." The Philadelphia Enquirer ran two full page stories about how angry the audiences were at *Chain Saw*, that they were throwing up in the theater and demanding their money back. Then right in the middle of all that, Rex Reed wrote a review that said it was the scariest movie he'd ever seen. So, all these things came together. And that's what started me on this irritation of the self-righteous people who think that horror movies are evil.

Why do you think that reaction came about for this movie? People always say that you look back and it's not graphically violent...

It's not graphically violent but it's extremely violent emotionally, and it's a brutal movie to get through because it's so exhausting. It's so visceral and you really feel what's going on. I think that's the reaction to it.

People get on me about this but not very long after *Chain Saw* came out, *Raiders of the Lost Ark* came out. A movie aimed at kids and it was much more graphically violent than *Chain Saw*. But it was a big-budget movie, it was slick, and it was mainstream so nobody is going to complain about how frightening or gory it might be. Now, I wasn't offended by the movie, I enjoyed it tremendously, but what offends me is people won't raise a peep about a movie like that. It doesn't occur to them to complain. It's very easy with a movie like *Chain Saw* to complain because there's no money behind it, you're not offending the industry and it's counter-cultural because its message is threatening. With *Raiders*, the message that confirms everyone's everyday values, whereas *Chain Saw* doesn't say that. *Chain Saw* says evil is brutal and in the world it is unpunished.

Was it the timing too? I saw this great documentary, *The American Nightmare*, that tried to explain the climate, the post-Vietnam era?

(laughing) Well maybe, but you have to be a little careful. As a former academic, let me say that academics love, after the fact, to tell you what something was about. And I hear people say *Chain Saw* is about the collapse of the American family, or it's really about Vietnam. And my answer is: No. *The Texas Chain Saw Massacre* is about *The Texas Chain Saw Massacre*. There is always a subtext, and there are many subtexts, but the movie is about itself. I don't think anybody was thinking, "Let's make a movie about the collapse of the American family." At the same time, I think you're right when you say it came out of its time.

During the film I had the chance to sit down with Tobe. I remember one long conversation with Tobe and Kim Henkel and I asked them, "Where did you come up with

this?" And Tobe said, "Well, there's this guy, Ed Gein, in Plainfield, Wisconsin. Ed inspired the idea of the mask and the bone furniture. Everything else, we made up." So there goes the story that this was about Ed Gein. He said, "We made a list of everything in horror movies that scared us and we wanted to get every one of them in the movie." Now in that statement there's no, "We wanted to get everything scary in the movie while we talked about the collapse of the American family." But obviously, the film resonates with people. I mean, this is thirty-five years after we filmed this...

And it still comes up...

People are still taking about it. So, obviously it affects people, and it affects them in the sense that it must push some buttons. I think what it is that it's so realistic, psychologically realistic, that it does something to people's fears. It triggers a fear. It comes home for people when they watch this movie and all these years later it still does that to people.

What's it like to live with the legacy of it all these years?

It's something I never expected. My hope for the movie was that a few years down the road, a few hardcore horror fans would remember it. If that were the case, to me, it would be a wonderful success. I've never been interested in a lot of attention, I'm very shy, and I never thought of myself as having a public identity, because that's just so far away from who I was. So, it's been a big surprise, and very enjoyable. It's almost a perfect sort of circumstance because as famous as *Texas Chain Saw Massacre* is, it's famous only in a certain way, and you never see my face in it. So, nobody knows who I am. I mean, if I'm around horror fans they know, but I walk down the street, and nobody recognizes my face. They might know my name, but I'm anonymous most of the time and I can be un-anonymous when I go to a convention. And I've had enough of this taste of it to realize how difficult it must be for people who are actually famous. I always thought maybe my gravestone would say, "Gunnar Hansen: Nobel Prize for Literature," but it's going to say, "Gunner Hansen: He Had His Own Action Figure!"

Special thanks to Stevan Mena!

KEITH GORDON

Interviewed by Rob Galluzzo (3/08)

I'm watching *Dexter* and am surprised to notice the name Keith Gordon listed as this episode's director. Could it be? The same Keith Gordon that made his acting debut in *Jaws 2*? Played the lead in John Carpenter's *Christine*? Was in Brian DePalma's *Dressed to Kill* and the comedy *Back to School*? Sure enough! Keith Gordon started his filmmaking career by acting but made the shift to directing almost twenty years ago. We figured his diverse filmography warranted closer scrutiny. So, we tracked him down and he was more than happy to talk to us! Read on!

First and foremost, what are your earliest recollections of the horror genre? Do you remember as a kid the first film or films that scared or had an impact on you?

That's an interesting question! There were a bunch as a kid that scared me, but I'm trying to remember the earlier ones. Some things that scared me weren't even traditional horror. I remember seeing a lot of science fiction stuff as a kid, like *Fantastic Voyage*, the scene where Donald Pleasence gets eaten at the end by the giant white blood cell really scared the hell out of me! I don't think my parents let me see true horror stuff. They'd let me see campy stuff like *The Blob*, which probably when I was four or five, I thought was scary enough. But I don't think I saw real, serious, heavyweight horror type films until I was more into my teens.

I remember seeing *Halloween* when I was seventeen or eighteen and I thought it was a really scary movie, but it wasn't the same as being a kid where you have those things blazed into your mind. It's funny, those films that scared you, you look back at them now as adults and you go, "That scared me?" (laughs) I remember *Star Trek*, there was a monster that they had in the end credit rolls, it was a still photograph and it was the scariest thing to me in the world at seven or eight years old. This one alien face. Why? I don't know! But I had nightmares about it. I don't remember seeing what we consider traditional horror as a little kid. Doesn't mean I didn't but there's nothing that leaps to mind in that category.

I grew up in the 80's, so there was a plethora of things to watch. And you look at a lot of these films as an adult, and some of them aren't as scary as you remember!

Oh, it's amazing how that changes over time. I even find as an adult, things that I found scary twenty years ago that I don't find scary now, and there are probably things that I find scary now that I wouldn't have found scary twenty years ago. I think depending on where you are in life's journey, it can really affect what scares you.

You were sixteen and already acting in plays when you got cast in *Jaws 2*? Is that correct?

Yeah, but not a lot of plays. I spent the summer at the National Playwrights Conference at the Eugene O'Neill Theater where they do a series of staged readings. They're not full-on productions of plays, but stuff by major American playwrights who have stuff that they're still working on. So, I'd spent the summer up there as an actor doing a couple of plays. And I'd also done a guest spot on *Medical Center* of all odd things. Those were the only two professional credits I had before I got the job on *Jaws 2*.

Was it both intimidating yet exciting to be a part of the sequel to *Jaws*? Because at that time, I don't think sequels were all that common! *Jaws* was the type of movie that'd be re-released in theaters!

Sequels were certainly not common then the way they are now. They existed, but they were the exception, not the rule, and it was the sequel to the most successful film of all time at that point! I guess it was intimidating. I didn't go in with any illusions, because I thought the first one was fantastic and very scary. That was a film that scared me, but again, I was already a teenager, so it didn't scare me in that way. It didn't give me nightmares, but I thought about it when I'd swim in the ocean! I didn't go into *Jaws 2* with any illusion that we were going to compete with the greatness of that (original) movie.

To me, I was just excited as a young actor because it was a part in a real movie and a chance to work on a film and learn about it. I was already at that point interested in filmmaking. So, I thought I'd get to be on a movie set for a couple of weeks, which actually turned out to be months and months and months! (laughs)

It was ten months or something?

It was really absurd, because between the rehearsal, and bringing us all to sail, and then shooting with John Hancock, and then firing John Hancock, and then keeping us all on location while they got a new director, and then being in a location that no longer really made sense. Because as the fall came in, every hurricane came right through where we were and would destroy sets, and knock things down, and the shark would sink, and we'd sit around for a week while they dragged it up from the bottom of the ocean!

I ended up spending ten months on the film, which if it happened to me now again, I'd probably lose my mind, but as a sixteen year old, what a great adventure! It was really exciting and fun, but I didn't think we could compete with the first film, and I don't know if anybody ever really could. I mean, I think everybody knew that the first one was a classic. We were making a sequel that we were hoping would be good and would stand on its own merits. But you know? With the possible exception of *The Godfather Part 2*, I can't think of any sequel that ever lived up to the original. I think people, if you get them to be honest will always acknowledge that, even if they're working on them.

Yeah. You mentioned before the change of directors on *Jaws 2*. John Hancock was the original director, he got fired and the producers brought on Jeannot Szwarc. They really re-worked the script when they changed directors. The rumor is that the original script was a lot darker of a film. Did you remember any of the differences between the original script and the one that got shot?

It's funny… in some ways I think the differences may have been exaggerated in terms of tone. I mean, it was very different in terms of specifics of incidents or characters were developed differently. I guess the Roy Scheider character went through some darker moments. Although, I think him getting fired was actually added in the new script. I don't think that was in the original script.

I don't think he got fired. So, in some ways, you can argue the final script was darker. I think there was more violence in the original script, there were more shark deaths. But frankly, there was more violence in the script that we shot than in the final edited version!

I was a kid when I saw *Jaws 2*, and it's kind of a mean-spirited movie! I consider it in the vein of a "slasher" flick of that era! The killer, "Jaws" gets scarred in the beginning of the movie, he ate people relentlessly, and you just felt, "Well, there's another kid gone! I can't believe it!"

In the film, the deaths turned out less horrific. I was sort of disappointed, because I would go and watch all the dailies as someone who was interested in filmmaking and I thought that there were shots that were far scarier and more disturbing than what they ended up with (in the final edit). That may well have had to do with what rating they were going for or whatever. I know when I saw the final film, I thought "Wow, there were way scarier shots than that one!" So, I think there was a toning down that happened to avoid getting an R rating and to have a bigger audience.

I recently re-watched *Christine* with the commentary track that you did with John Carpenter, which by the way, is one of my favorite commentary tracks.

Oh thanks! We had such a blast doing it.

What was it like getting together with John Carpenter to revisit that film for the commentary, twenty years later?

Well, first of all, I hadn't seen John for really quite a few years, and it was really nice to see him again because he was someone that I loved working with. That film has really warm memories in my heart. It was maybe my favorite film acting job ever… Yeah, it definitely was. There was nothing I've ever done on film that was that much fun as an actor. And that was primarily due to the way John ran the set, and his infectious enthusiasm for what he was doing and for the genre, and for telling these kind of stories. So, it was really nice to see him again and to talk with him. And it's funny, because I had heard a rumor that it was one of his films that he wasn't happy with or proud of or whatever.

So, it was kind of nice actually to do that commentary with him and sense that he was happy with the film and proud of it. And he did feel it fit in his canon of work. It was a film that I always felt fondly about. And it was just fun to share the old stories and have memories come back. I think it's a really cool film. I don't think of it as a flat out horror film in the sense that I think it's got its tongue very firmly in cheek, which is why it does work as well as it does. I think if you try to do that film without a sense of humor, you end up with *The Car*. You end up with a film that seems kind of more goofy, because it's pretending not to be goofy. (laughs)

Hey, some people consider *The Car* a cult classic! (*editor's note: like Mike!*)

Some people probably do! But to me, taking an absurd concept and treating it with humor, ironically you can bring more fear to it. Hitchcock did it with suspense. And I feel like that's what John did with *Christine*. By sort of doing things a little over the top or with a sense of humor, in a funny way, it could be more scary because we weren't saying, "Believe this is true!" We're saying, "Let us tell you this fun ghost story." And then suddenly, you can get an audience to go with it in a way that they might have resisted had you tried to be self-serious about it.

It's one of my favorite Carpenter films! And there's things in it that still hold up. The sequence of the car fixing itself is still amazing to me.

And done in an era where it couldn't all be done with CGI! It's funny, I think of a generation seeing that stuff today and probably just assuming it was all done by some computer, but you couldn't do that back then! They had to physically create those effects, and that's what impresses me looking at it. Is that John had to, on a moderate budget, it wasn't a big budget film, find ways to physically make it look like the car was repairing itself and not allotted to some composite or computer station somewhere to create that for him.

A lot of hard work and ingenuity went into it, and a lot of tests. I remember they re-did things numerous times, those specific shots until they got them to where they thought they worked well enough. It was really a lot of effort put into making those specific effects come off.

Yeah. But the final result is film history right there!

Yeah, and look, I'm old enough that I'm old-school. I love physical effects! I always feel nine times out of ten, when I see CGI effects, I go "Oh look, a CGI effect!"

You usually can always pick it out and for me, it totally takes me right out of the movie.

That's certainly how I feel. The generation growing up with it might feel differently. I'm really a fan of, in any kind of movie, whether it's horror or action – when things are really done, they just look cooler. But hey, that's me. That's what I grew up with, that's what I'm used to.

Oh, I totally agree with you there! One of the other interesting things about *Christine*, you did the movie back in 1983. How familiar were you with the work of Stephen King? Because around '83, that was the cusp of when they were finally starting to adapt a lot of his work into films. I don't think there were a tremendous amount of Stephen King movie adaptations at that point.

There had been a couple, but not a lot. There were a couple of things done for TV. I certainly feel old, because I'd have to go look on IMDb to see what the exact order of things were. I don't think we were the first with *Christine*, but there certainly had not been as many of them.

So, were you familiar with *Christine* the novel, or just Stephen King in general when you got involved with *Christine* the movie?

I was somewhat familiar, but I'm embarrassed to say I was not widely familiar. I didn't read *Christine* the novel until I knew I was going to be working on the film. So, once I knew I was going to be working on the film, I of course, immediately read the novel. But I had read some of his short stories, and bits of pieces of his work, but it wasn't like I was a big fan or was reading a lot of that stuff. Although at that time, to be fair, I probably wasn't reading a lot of anything!

That was a time in my life where I was such a movie obsessive that I was seeing every movie that came out, which meant that I had very little time to read novels. So, it wasn't like I was avoiding Stephen King, I wasn't reading anybody else either! I was probably only reading things that had directly to do with the work I was doing. Mostly, in terms of taking stuff in, I was doing it by going to movies constantly, and going to film festivals. And probably seeing ten movies a week! It was not the most literary period of my life. So, Stephen King was left out, but no more than everybody else! (laughs)

Looking back now at *Christine*, what would you consider your favorite scene in the film? Something that you might be proud of workwise? Or just something that perhaps stands out from the shoot?

God, it's an interesting question, because there were so many things I remember fondly in the film. In some ways, some of my fondest memories were not stuff I was in!

Because as someone who was interested in filmmaking, it was so interesting and fun to have the pressure off just to watch John work! Like, the scene where they blew up the gas station?

I just remember being out in the middle of the night, in the middle of nowhere watching them do first the car crashing into the wall, and just being blown away by the bravery of the stuntman! I don't care how much stuff you're wearing. Driving a car into something driving thirty-five, forty miles per hour was pretty insane to watch up close!

And then coming out with the car on fire! A guy was in there driving that thing!

Yeah! And then blowing up the damned gas station! It was amazing to me. I just remember driving out way into the middle of nowhere for that, and just sitting and watching and talking to John and asking him questions. So, I loved that as a filmmaking fan.

Because when you're acting, you're busy being nervous about your own work and the stuff you're doing. On those days, I could just sit back and relax when I wasn't working and just enjoy the spectacle and the complexity of what they were doing. In terms of the acting scenes, probably my favorite was the stuff with the parents. You know, the scene where I turn on my dad and strangle him and say "Fuck you" to my mom.

Yeah! How often do you get to curse out your parents?!

Yeah, it's such a primal fantasy to really turn on your parents. And that was really a fun scene to do. And in general, all of the "bad" Arnie scenes were really fun. John would sort of encourage me; he'd sort of say, "You can't go too far. Over the top is good here." So, he gave me a great deal of license to just try things.

The visits to Dennis in the hospital were really fun to shoot. Just all that stuff was fun to shoot. One thing that wasn't fun to shoot, although it's not the version that was in the final film, and we mentioned this on the commentary, the scene where John Stockwell and I are driving in the middle of the night, and I'm drinking the beer and throwing the cans out the window. That was originally done – the first way John tried to shoot that was by basically bolting a false half of a car onto the front of this Mac truck, and we really were going ninety miles per hour down the highway! It was scary as shit! Because basically, this thing felt like it was going to fall off at any second. And if it had, we would have been just gone. We would've been swallowed up by the truck

that was pushing us. So, that was really scary! (laughs) We ended up shooting the real scene, with what's called "poor man's process," where it was all shot on a stage and nothing was moving at all, in terms of the version that was used.

But really, every day was fun on that show. Harry Dean Stanton is such a great actor! So, that scene with him in the parking lot was really fun to do. Because he gives you so much to work with, and he'd do something a little different every time, and that would push me to do something a little different every time. Really, it would be a long list of favorite scenes, because I have a lot of good memories.

In terms of your work as an actor, it's probably my favorite performance of yours. That character just had such a fantastic arc that it must've been such a blast to play every spectrum of Arnie Cunningham.

Oh sure! Well, it's Doctor Jekyll and Mister Hyde! And how rare it is that you get to do that! To play a character with that much range, and to do it with a director saying don't be afraid to be too big and a little operatic and over the top. It gives you so much freedom. Usually on films, you're so nervous about looking too big or hammy or extreme. But having a director say, "Go ahead. For this movie, it's fine." That's a very rare and special thing to do.

One of the things you mention on that commentary was that working on *Christine*, and even on *Dressed to Kill* with Brian DePalma, even though they were jobs, you considered them paid internships for filmmaking.

Well, absolutely! The thing was, when I was a kid, I was a film nerd. I made really bad Super 8 movies, so I was always interested in filmmaking as a possible ultimate thing to do in my life. To get to work with directors like DePalma twice and John Carpenter and Bob Fosse, it literally was a paid internship. They were all in their different ways very kind about my interest in what it is that they did, and my desire to hang around on the set, even when I wasn't shooting to ask a lot of questions. They could've easily said, "Shut up and go do your job!" But they were never like that.

They were always willing and happy to take the time to explain what they were doing and why they were doing it. What film school could be as good? Here I was getting paid to be there and having real top rank directors explaining in a real way how and why they were doing what they were doing. There's no way a classroom experience could replace that, so I was thrilled. And I was lucky enough to have guys like Carpenter and DePalma who were really kind and giving of their time. Again, they did not have to be anywhere near as nice as they were about the fact that I was asking them questions every twenty seconds about why they were doing what they were doing.

Well, you've been directing now for almost twenty years. And one of the things I found to be a pleasant surprise was to see your name credited as the director on several episodes of *Dexter*.

Oh, yeah!

It's my all-time favorite show on TV right now.

Mine too!

In fact, you directed what I consider the most tense episode ("Truth Be Told") of the first season, which made me go buy the DVD boxset!

Wow! I'm flattered! A lot of TV, some of it is the luck of the draw what episode you get to direct. I got the second to last one (of season one) where everything was building to a climax! It's funny, because it's not like a movie where you get to read the material ahead of time and choose what you want to do. Basically, they just call and say, "Do you want to do the show?" And you get whatever episode they need to slot somebody into. But with *Dexter*, I saw the pilot!

Normally, I haven't been somebody that really chases TV, I mean, I've done some TV. Basically, TV is a great way to pay the rent, but generally it's the kind of thing where if they call and ask me, and I think it's a decent show, why not? This was the first case where I saw the pilot and said, "I want to work on that! That's just cool!" So, I basically said to my agents, "Just get me in at Showtime and let me talk to them!" And I really went in and said, "Please, please, please just let me do this show! Because it's so great and I just want to be a part of it, and I get it, and I get the style of it."

And I'm really glad that they said yes, because I've done three of them now. One the first year and two the second year, and it's really a fun job! If you're going to do TV, you want to do a show that you would want to watch anyway. Doing TV, if you don't love the show, then it really is a job. But working on something like *Dexter*, it's so much fun, because it's something I would be sitting at home and watching! The actors are so good. The writing is so good. The other directors are really good. It's also that rare situation where there's no schmuck! (laughs)

Most jobs, especially TV with the strains of TV and the hard hours of TV, there's at least one actor who's really cranky, or at least one producer who just seems to be there to make your life miserable. (laughs) But *Dexter* doesn't have any of that. *Dexter*, all the people are so cool. They work really hard to not let the hours get insane. A lot of TV shows shoot fourteen, fifteen, sixteen hours a day as standard operating procedure. And what happens is, the actors burn out, the crew burns out, people get angry, people get tired.

On *Dexter*, they make a real effort to keep the days reasonable in length. And I think consequently, it keeps the whole tone of the show really positive. And someone like Michael C. Hall, who's carrying such a burden as an actor, doesn't burn out. You know, the way he would if they were doing normal series hours. And it's really a pleasure to work on, but it is, it's just a cool, well written show.

How was coming back for season two?

This year was fun (season two) because the episodes I did were earlier, so I didn't know how the year was going to end up! They were still working things out! The funny thing about TV is, while you're shooting episode four or five, they don't necessarily know everything that's going to happen in episode twelve. So, it's a little bit challenging for the actors and the director because you're kind of making decisions without really being sure where it's really heading.

But it's also cool, because you get to be a part of the mystery along with the audience! They'll tell you in general terms, "This is what we think might happen." But they were very close-lipped this year, because apparently there was a lot of debating and working out going on, even while shooting about weather Doakes would die or not. All those things, I think were on the table until really late in the game!

Not for nothing, *Dexter's* second season has got to be one of the best sophomore seasons to a show ever.

Well, here's to hoping they can do it again! Because I certainly told them I would be happy to come back and do more of them. I hope they can be as creative (with season three) and do as well.

After you saw the pilot, but before you got your episode, did you familiarize yourself with the character more? There are obviously novels by Jeff Lindsay that the show is loosely based on. Or did you just follow the show as a fan?

I just stayed with the show. Because basically, in talking to the producers, they said they wanted to try to give the show its own identity. Again, if you're doing a movie and you've got tons of time to do tons of research, then I would've also sat with the book. Like if I was directing a feature of the book, obviously I would spend a ton of time with the book. But with TV, you only have so much time between when they hire you and when you start, I felt it was more important to study the episodes that they had done already.

I was coming in late in the season and I didn't get hired until not long before I did my episode, so I really thought it was important to get familiar with what they had shot, what the early episodes looked like and really study it shot by shot. Really look at the other shows, especially the pilot, which established the whole tone of the series.

And really look at where they were putting the camera, where they were putting the lights, what kind of camera movement they were using. Not that you slavishly imitate it, but I do think when you're doing TV, there's this sort of dual responsibility. On one hand, you want to bring something to the table and it's great on a show like *Dexter* where they don't want you to just follow their rules, they want you to add something as a director, but you still want to stay true to the DNA of the show they've already created.

You don't just want to do something that won't fit in. I spent most of my time just trying to get as familiar as I could with what they'd been doing and also spending a lot of time hanging out on the set, so I could watch how the actors worked. TV's such a funny thing because you're coming into something that's already a living organism. It's already going and you're walking into it. It's like becoming the kid who comes into school mid-way through the school year!

I was always fascinated by that idea. When you're directing a feature length, you're there from the beginning to develop this whole thing. But this is TV with a cast and crew that's there every week and you, the director, are the revolving factor!

Absolutely.

So, does that make it more difficult?

Oh, it definitely makes it more difficult. Certainly, a different type of challenge as opposed to doing a feature. You learn to deal with that, and one of the things I try to do when I'm directing TV is to really try and spend some time on the set before my episode, watching how people all work together, so you're walking in with some sense of, "Oh, Michael likes this kind of direction. And Jennifer (Carpenter) likes that kind of direction. And the DP works like this." If you're trying to do that all on your first day on the set, that's really hard.

But if you watch how other people are working, you can get a pretty good idea of what works with each person. And that to me, as a director, is a big part of your job. You're kind of like a psychologist. Really your job is in a lot of ways to figure out a way to help people to do their best work. And that's going to be different for every person involved! So, just observing beforehand really, really helps. It's not always possible, but whenever I can, I try to spend at least a few days on the set beforehand just to familiarize myself with the way people work. And also, physically familiarize myself with the set!

When you're doing a feature, you're very involved with the production designer and designing the sets and what they're laid out like, and what kind of shots you might want to do. When you're doing a TV show, all the sets are already built. So, sometimes I love to go spend hours on the empty set and sit in Dexter's apartment and think, "Ok, where are some places a camera can go here? What are some things you could do here that I haven't seen people do here yet?" And that's also real important.

I love the idea of you sitting in Dexter's apartment and making these decisions! (laughs)

It's kind of funny, and it is kind of creepy because you can end up all alone in these big empty sound stages with one or two work lights on. Especially on a show like that, there's definitely a little creepiness inherent in it. It's kind of a fun back of the neck tickle you can get in those situations.

Obviously, we're *Icons of Fright,* but *Back to School* is one of the only films as a kid that I stayed and watched in theaters, and when it was over, I stayed in my seat to watch it a second time in a row.

(laughs)

It's the only movie I ever did that for. I loved Rodney Dangerfield. I saw him do stand-up about a year before he passed. I was just wondering if you could share one good Rodney story from working on *Back to School*?

Well, it's funny because Rodney was not really an actor, he was a stand-up. So, he was used to thinking in those terms. And one of the things I think is so impressive in that film, and that director Alan Metter doesn't get enough credit for, is really helping Rodney work as an actor, not just a joke teller. You get caught up in his character. And I remember going to rehearsal with Rodney, and his stage act is very precise. Very planned.

So, we were sitting at this table, we were rehearsing one of the scenes, and Rodney said to Alan, "When we do this scene, what side is he going to be on?" He meaning me. And Alan said, "I don't know yet Rodney, we don't even have a location yet." "Well, I need to know! What side is he going to be on?" And Alan says, "I don't know? In my imagination, I guess maybe on the right?"

At the time, I was sitting on the left. So, then we started rehearsing the scene and Rodney spent the whole time talking to the right where there was an empty chair rather than talking to me, because he was so used to trying to get the physicality down of what he was going to do, that he didn't realize, oh when you're acting, you actually have to really look at the other person! So, it was very funny, because it was just not what he was used to! And Alan, I thought did a masterful job with him of getting him to do something he was very uncomfortable with, which was at times be vulnerable. You know?

Rodney was very comfortable with doing the Rodney-shtick, but the few moments in the film that he has to be softer, sadder, I mean it's not a big part of the movie, but I do think it's a part of what makes the movie work is that there's a human being underneath the wackiness. And Alan really had to work with him to get him to feel safe enough to let that out.

I agree, every comedy that has a little bit of heart behind it is usually the main reason it ends up a success.

Yeah, and that film without it really wouldn't have worked. And I think Alan deserves a lot of credit with that film.

It's funny, because with that film, there's odd coincidences that fit into your overall career. Adrienne Barbeau was your stepmom in it, and she was married to John Carpenter, whom you worked with on *Christine*.

Yes.

And Robert Downey Jr. was your co-star but later was the lead in *The Singing Detective*, which you directed!

Absolutely.

It's neat how *Back to School* ties into your other work.

Yeah, I mean, the funny thing is the business isn't that big, and if you're in it long enough, you find a lot of those coincidences. You end up working with people again, and paths re-cross. It's a funny business that way. That's one of

the wonderful things about it is it is its own community. Yeah, it's all true. It was fun to work with Adrienne, who is a complete sweetheart, although we didn't really have stuff together really in the film. But just being around her, I had gotten to know her and really liked her when she was with John. So, it was neat to be in something with her again. And getting to work with Robert again that many years later in that different context was also pretty wild!

What do you look for when it comes to picking the projects that you want to direct? Because they've all been fairly different.

It's funny, it's very, very, very chemical and visceral. The thing I compare it to, when I teach, it's like falling in love. You can date a lot of people. And you can even date some people that are really cool, and you know they're great people, but you just don't get that feeling in the pit of your stomach where you're flipping out with them, you want to get them naked and you want to spend the rest of your life with them.

It's kind of like that when you're reading material. It's very visceral. I've read some scripts that I knew were really, really good scripts. But they just didn't speak to me in a personal way. And I've read other scripts that I knew were problematic, or books or whatever that I thought there's difficult stuff in here that isn't right yet, but I get this. I know how to tell this story. Usually for me, a big sign is how much I see it in my head (like a movie) when I read it. Whether it's a book or a script. The things that I fall in love with, usually even on the first reading, I'm getting images in my head, I know just how the scene should feel like. What the music would be like. And that's a very… again it's like dating! You might well end up marrying someone that's really different from what you thought you would be with, but somehow that person just spoke to your soul, and I find that's the thing with directing. It works the same way for me. So, it drives my agents insane!

Because there's no pattern, there's nothing I can say, "Look for this!" The only thing I can usually say is, "Look for originality." The thing that doesn't usually excite me is if we've seen that same story told that way five times before in the last five years. Even if it's done well, I usually feel like, "We've seen that movie." But there have been fabulous movies and movies that went on to be huge successes that I read and went, "I'm not the person who should do this." So, it's not an easy question to answer, because it's an emotional response. It's not an intellectual thing. People have pointed out to me, "Well, I notice this theme that runs through all your movies." Yeah, well it may, but I didn't think that. I wasn't thinking that when I fell in love with the material.

I think that's a wonderful analogy, the idea of falling in love with something and figuring out what kind of relationship you're going to have with this particular one.

Then, of course, there's the fact that it's so hard to get these kind of movies made! More personal, independent movies. It's the luck of the draw on what gets financed! I've had plenty of different projects that I've loved just as much that have never seen the light of day. So, if some of those projects had gotten made, and some of those that got made didn't get made, you might have a very different take on me as a director. And it would all be the luck of the draw of where the financing happens. People always think of me as very serious, and yet one of the projects I spent years on was a pretty wild comedy that I'd fallen in love with, but that we could never quite get the money to make. Had that gotten made, it would've changed every perception of me as a certain director. It's so funny how that happens. For every one movie that you get made, there are two, three, four that you spend a year, two years, five years on and somehow, they never happen! So, it's an odd thing that way too.

Do you consider yourself a genre fan? Is there anything you've seen in the past few years that you liked?

I'm somebody who's more a fan of creepiness, rather than horror per se. I love the innocence of certain things. I thought *The Others* was really, really cool.

Oh, Alejandro Amenabar was the director of that! His first two Spanish films *Thesis* and *Open Your Eyes* are among my all-time favorite foreign films.

That kind of filmmaking I find much more exciting than some of the straight forward "slasher" horror that's become more common. I love things that leave me with a creepy feeling. Sort of with an unanswered question. That's just what seems to speak to me.

What would be among your favorite films that fall under the category of the horror genre?

Well, certainly *The Shining* is a film I love. And I know a lot of people don't love it as much as the book, but that movie blows me away, as I think of it as part horror, part comedy, part social satire. That's a movie that I've rewatched constantly. Same goes for a lot of John Carpenter's films. I think that *The Thing* is a brilliant movie. Then there's things like *Escape From New York* that aren't horror, but that I love. Same with Hitchcock. I mean, is *Frenzy* horror? I don't know. Not really, but kind of?

You mentioned Hitchcock and one of my favorite movies is *Psycho*.

Well yeah, I love that too, but is it a horror movie? I think it's a great, great movie. Horror is a funny word, because some people mean it much more literally. In a kind of ghost, goblins or "slasher" kind of way. I think of it more as part of the suspense world, and I love suspense movies. *The Exorcist* is a brilliant film. There are movies like *Wages of Fear*. It's suspense, but it's not horror in an obvious way. I don't know when I'd ever been more scared in a movie theater though! I like movies that take my breath away and make me wonder what's going to happen. I don't like films that try to derive the scares from cats jumping out of a closet. That turns me off very quickly. Something like *Don't Look Now* is a brilliant, brilliant horror film.

The craft that went into the filmmaking of those movies, *The Exorcist*, *Psycho*, even John's early movies like *Halloween*, I feel like that's missing today. The ending bit of *Don't Look Now* still scares the crap out of me!

But it does it because it's within the context of a story where you've built up to that. Now a lot of horror that I've seen seem to be based on short term shock scares, rather than build up. To me, making me jump isn't really scaring me, you're just hitting my knee with a hammer.

Scaring me is making me think about something and making me have an image that's going to last and that I'm going to carry with me. So, for me, as a film goer, that's much more exciting. Yeah, you can show somebody getting their guts cut open and pouring out and you're going to provoke a visceral response. But to me, that's kind of easy. Anybody can do that. But make me get invested in a character and get involved in the way that you do with Donald Sutherland in *Don't Look Now*, so that when that ending happens, it has meaning beyond what you'd think.

It's when it has these layers that it becomes such a powerful genre. At its best, it's what our dreams are. Horror speaks to things that go beyond literal logic and into the realm of dream logic, and I think that's fabulous. I think DePalma, at his best, gets you really involved in a different level than just the gross out level. All the best suspense and horror filmmakers do that. I think when Wes Craven is at his most interesting, he's got a lot of stuff going on. To me, that's the real key difference.

NEIL MARSHALL

Interviewed by Rob Galluzzo (3/08)

If you're a devoted genre fan, then like us, you've probably been following the career of writer/director Neil Marshall. After all, his first three films to date offer interesting ensemble casts, usually set in unique locations. From *Dog Soldiers* to *The Descent* to his epic *Doomsday*, we chatted with him about all things horror!

Neil, what are your earliest recollections of the horror genre? Do you remember the first film or films to really scare or have an impact on you as a kid and open you up to the world of horror?

It was really a combination of things, but my earliest recollection was being five or six years old, and being woken up by my dad, he took me into the living room and sat me down in front of the TV, and said, "There's something on TV that you've really got to see!" And I thought, "What's this going to be?" It was *Frankenstein*. It was Boris Karloff in black and white. I was instantly hooked! I was terrified, but I was just instantly hooked into that world of horror.

I assume from that point on, you were a horror fan?

Very much so. My uncle had this big book all about horror movies and it was full of all these amazing photographs from all the classics. *The Wolf Man* and *Phantom of The Opera*, all this kind of stuff. It was full of monsters and creatures, so every time I used to go over there, I always used to look at that book for ages. And my dad and my uncle were both artists, so they always used to draw me monsters and castles and all kinds of stuff like that. So, I think I was absorbed by it and surrounded by it in those days. And then I started to discover it for myself with the advent of VHS in the early '80s. And people started getting those tapes, watching whatever was available. At that time in the UK, this was prior to the "video nasties" scandal.

A lot of people here in the U.S. aren't familiar with exactly what the "video nasties" means. Can you talk a bit about that? It was a lot of notorious movies that were banned in the UK, correct?

When the video market started up, it was basically just a free for all. But instantly, the independent video rental stores caught on to the fact that everybody wanted to see horror movies, and this allowed them to put more and more material in the shops that could never be shown at the cinemas. And there was lots of material out there and it was cheap. So, stuff like *Cannibal Holocaust* and, well all the classics, basically. (laughs) And a whole lot of shit as well, a lot of bad stuff was pretty much all they had to offer. So, yeah, I saw *Zombie Flesh Eaters* and *I Spit on Your Grave* and a whole bunch of other stuff then. Then this government compound came down and there was a list of forty films drawn up, which were going to be banned. Some of the ones on the list, the majority of the ones on the list were pure exploitation shit. But, unfortunately amongst those films were things like *The Texas Chain Saw Massacre* and *The Evil Dead*. We couldn't see those films anymore either. Luckily for me, I was able to see those before they were banned. And then throughout the 80s, while they were still banned, it was quite a pride to get VHS pirate copies of these films. Just to watch *The Texas Chain Saw Massacre* and stuff like that.

Wow.

I was a film student by then, so it was quite an adventure to do that. But all the time, I was going after horror movies. That's what it was all about.

What was the pivotal moment where you made the transition from fan to filmmaker? A lot of filmmakers often say it started with a fascination for special FX make-up and how it was created. What was it for you that made you realize people make movies and you could too?

Um, I went to see *Raiders of the Lost Ark*. I think it was the very next day, the making-of was on TV. And I just saw what an adventure it was, and what fun it was making that film. And every facet of it just fascinated me and I decided then and there that I wanted to direct movies.

Let's talk about *Doomsday*. What were the origins behind the project? How did you choose to make this particular story your follow-up to *The Descent*?

Well, *Doomsday* was always going to be a big project, it could never be done cheap. So, although it's been sitting on the shelf for four, five years as an idea, there was just no way I could get the budget together to make it before *The Descent* had come out. The backer of *Descent*, Rogue Pictures, asked me what else I had. And I said there's this treatment I have called *Doomsday*, and I showed it to them, and they said, "Ok, we'll try to find the money to make this. It'll be small, but we'll do our best." And they commissioned the script, and we took off from there.

The idea itself when I first came up with it was a few things. This was about six years ago when I first came up with the story. Where I lived at the time was near Hadrian's Wall in the U.K. I came up with this thought, what's an area that would exist where Hadrian's Wall would have to be rebuilt? I mean, in its day, 2000 years ago, Hadrian's Wall was like The Great Wall of China. It was this huge wall that stretched right across the UK and separated Scotland. I thought what could possibly happen that this exact scenario would happen again? And that's when I came up with the idea of a virus, and quarantining a whole section of the country.

I was inspired by things like the Berlin Wall, and the walls on the West Bank that they built, and also Chernobyl. There's no wall around Chernobyl, but I just saw some photographs and articles about that, and seeing this world that is basically empty and deserted for ten years and what it looks like, I was just fascinated by that concept. So, all of these things fell into place to create the *Doomsday* idea. Also, I had this image in my head of futuristic soldiers facing off against evil knights on horseback. It's like James Cameron by way of Terry Gilliam or something. (laughs) How could I make that happen that wouldn't involve time travel? So, all these things came into place. What if this quarantined area of Scotland had been left deserted for so long that any survivors there kind of regressed and turned into these savages and tribes. And utilized things that remained there, like suits of armor from castles and museums and things like that, just taking them for themselves to live a medieval lifestyle…

That's pretty awesome! Just so you know. (laughs)

(laughs) Well, it just kind of grew from there.

In your film, the virus is referred to as an "infection" which causes the quarantine. What is the "infection" in *Doomsday*? Because I saw the front cover of the new *Fangoria*. It's absolutely disgusting! I want to know what the hell that is?!

It's called the "Reaper" virus. But unlike too many other viruses in movies these days, it doesn't turn you into a zombie, it doesn't turn you into a mutant. It kills you! And it kills you pretty quick, but it kills you in a pretty horrendous way. Obviously, you get all these fistulas and sores and scabs on your skin, then you start bleeding from every orifice, and your insides basically liquidize until you die.

Oh, that doesn't sound good at all.

No, it's not a good way to go!

Doesn't sound that way! Looking at the trailer and reading what I have so far, it seems like it's got little elements of films I grew up loving. Films like *Escape From New York* and *The Road Warrior* and *The Warriors*. And I see little bits of all those. Was it a conscious effort to let your influences shine in *Doomsday*? Because they just don't make movies like that anymore!

That was precisely my point, and I've worn this on my sleeve ever since I came up with the project. It is an homage to those movies. There are so many people on the internet who seem to say it's just a rip off. I've never said that it wasn't! And it's not a rip off. I mean, it's paying tribute to those movies, and it has elements of them in it, but it certainly doesn't match any one of them or all of them as a whole. When you watch the film as a whole, you'll see it's vastly different from those films. But there are little sequences and moments in the film that will remind you of them.

That's the nature of doing an homage! It's no more a rip off than saying *Hot Fuzz* is a rip off of *Point Break* and those kinds of movies. It's an homage. It's paying tribute. So, yeah, my view was that no one was making films like that anymore, and that's what I loved when I was growing up. I loved the gritty realism, the stunts, the action. It wasn't CG heavy, and I loved the characters. It was just one of those ripe ideas worth revisiting. A post-apocalyptic environment.

Obviously, this is your biggest film in scale. What were the differences between going from *Dog Soldiers* to *The Descent* to now this? It looks huge! Did doing those first two movies give you the confidence to tackle something on the scale of *Doomsday*?

Oh absolutely. My whole theory is that if I'm making a $3 million dollar movie, I want to make it look like a $10 million dollar movie. And that's what I did with the previous two. For this one, we had a $25-26 million dollar budget, I wanted to make it look like a $50 million dollar movie. I don't see any point in just working to your budget, I think you have to try to push the envelope all the time. And put as much on the screen as possible. I loved the scale of this. I loved it!

I really got into doing the elaborate action sequences and choreographing all the mayhem and chaos there. Doing it in South Africa enabled us to do it in a much bigger scale then we would've been able to, because we could afford more extras and more stuntmen and more gadgets and more camera-gear. Just everything we could sort of throw into the pot to make it look as huge as we possibly could. I wanted to make an epic movie.

You just mentioned you shot this in South Africa, what was it about that location that it fit your film aesthetically, as well as financially?

Well, we were incredibly lucky. Primarily, it was a financial incentive to go there, but we wouldn't have been able to do it had it not matched the locations we were looking for. Because of the nature of Cape Town, it's quite old, and it has some old buildings in it, we were able to double London and Glasgow there. We were probably able to get away with a lot more because it's at night.

And then, the countryside outside of Cape Town looked remarkably similar to the Highlands of Scotland. A bit sunnier perhaps, but it does look very, very like it in its geography. So, we were able to double the whole of Scotland as well. You can do so much more there. They let you close major highways for weeks on end. We shot a big action sequence without any major problems. They're incredibly film friendly. And we just got so much for our money there.

How important was casting for this particular piece? Because you've got actors like Malcolm McDowell and Bob Hoskins; I love these actors. And I assume you do too! You're probably a fan of their work too.

Oh yeah.

What was it like working with actors you've admired?

Well, the great thing about a movie of this scale is that it's not so big that you have to cast a star name in it. What I did, and what I was able to do, was cast an ensemble of really, really high quality actors. A few of them that are familiar to audiences or might be familiar to audiences of my films. I was lucky enough to get Malcolm McDowell and Bob Hoskins in there, they're both seasoned pros. They're just so much fun to work with because they know what they're doing! They don't need to stick with it anymore, but they do it because they absolutely love it.

So, they made my job a lot easier because they were so helpful. And I was a little bit daunted working with people like that for the first time, because I've only ever essentially worked with unknowns before. So, yes, a little daunting at first, but they just made it easy. And I also managed to get people like David O'Hara and Alexander Siddig in the movie, some of the guys from *Dog Soldiers* and a couple of the girls from *The Descent*. It's just like a big family reunion with that lot, you know? They come in, but what's very important to me and to them is that I'm not having them come in and just repeat their performances from previous films. I'm only interested in them working with me again, and vice versa, if it's new characters and we can do something different. We had a lot of fun.

What's interesting and what seems to apply to all your films so far is you always have these big ensemble casts. There's the group of soldiers in the *Dog Soldiers*, then the group of girls for *The Descent* and now this. What kind of rehearsal process do you have when it comes to preparing a group of people to work on your films and what are the challenges of directing an ensemble?

Yeah, *Doomsday* was on a scale so different from anything else. The most I'd dealt with before were eight people, and we had something like fifty speaking characters in this movie. So, it's a totally different kind of thing. I don't do read-throughs. We did very little rehearsal, we just talked an awful lot about it. And then, block it out and ham it out on set, which seems to work ok so far!

With the first two films, because they require the work of an ensemble cast, do you cast the first person first and then try to build the rest of the cast around them? How does that work? What's the casting process like when you're trying to find the right group of people to take part in one of your films?

You try to get a bunch of names together and you see

which ones are going to make the most interesting group. You're looking for difference in characters, difference in looks. Difference in style. You don't want to cast everyone that's the same height and has the same build and works the same. So, there's any number of reasons but there's that combination, and there's also who's available, who you can get, who's interested in being in your movie. There are so many facets to casting, it's quite a lottery. But eventually you work through it, and you get the cast that you want, and we got an absolutely amazing cast in this.

I absolutely love *The Descent*. The *Icons of Fright* crew and I got to see an import of it before it made it over here to the States. I remember sitting in the theater watching *Batman Begins* for the third time and getting a phone call from Jason Alvino in the middle of it, interrupting me to tell me that he'd just seen the best horror movie of his adult life, and it was *The Descent*. He told me I had to come over right after *Batman* to check it out…

(laughs)

I loved it! One of the weird tweaks you had to do for *The Descent's* release here in the States was altering the ending a bit. I prefer the original ending. I believe you do too. In retrospect, what do you think of that decision to alter the ending? And also, I know it was partly because of the "testing" process here. I know you've had to test *Doomsday* as well. How weird is that to have to "test" your movies here?

Generally speaking, I hate the testing process! But it's a double-edged sword. You can benefit from it as well. If universally, the audience thinks, "Yeah, it's good but it could be a little bit better," then maybe they've got a point, so maybe it's worth listening to them. It just depends entirely on what they say. It's such a tricky thing. I love it and I hate it. I mostly hate it. (laughs) It's a nerve-wracking experience and I trust my own judgment to it much better. With *The Descent*, the only difference was the change at the ending. That was the only difference.

And the reason for that was, at the time, I wasn't really allowed to say it, because Lionsgate didn't want me to. But the truth of the story was that Lionsgate did test it in the States. They tested it with the original ending on. And then they had the idea of cutting it a little bit so that basically Sarah ended up out of the cave at the end of the film, and they tested it again and it scored much better! Now, they couldn't cut the film themselves, they had to come and get our approval to cut it. So, we thought about it for a while

and we said, "Ok, we'll let you cut it, as long as you give us the widest possible theatrical release. We want a minimum of 1,000 screens." And at that point, there was no guarantee we were even going to get a theatrical release at all. But they said "Ok." So, we agreed to do it and cut the ending on the basis of getting a wide theatrical release, which we got. And I knew all along the U.K. ending would be seen on the DVD, one way or another.

So, it was never going to be a big secret. And it helped them, it got released on the DVD, so it's fair for everybody to see it. And the rest of the world has seen that ending as well, as I wanted it to be seen. So, I figured it was a good deal to make at the time. By that point, the film had already been out for a year in the U.K., so for me it had already proven itself and the audience that I primarily made it for had already seen it, so it wasn't such a big deal. I didn't feel like I was betraying my artistic integrity by doing that.

No, it sounds like you got the best deal out of it! And we diehards in the States had already seen the import. I still paid and went to see it on opening night regardless!

Exactly! Then it becomes a talking point. It was an odd one, because the only difference is it means Sarah's physically out of the cave, but it's no less ambiguous than what we had, and it's certainly not a "happy" ending with that.

(laughs)

It is a strange way to cut it but whatever. The process with *Doomsday* has been… interesting? Enlightening? The response to it has been great. So, I've been happy, and we didn't have to cut anything out of it.

Good! The thing I love about all of your films is they're always set in unique settings, or at least settings I'm not used to seeing in the genre. With *The Descent*, where the hell did that come from? Are you a cave diver?

No! I'd never do anything as stupid as that! (laughs) I don't remember why; I think I saw some documentary footage from cave diving. I literally couldn't believe a horror film had not been set in a cave before! I mean, it's dark. It's scary. What more do you want?

And the whole claustrophobic angle of the first act, you already had people long before the creatures showed up!

Yeah, yeah, certainly! I figured two out of ten people would suffer from the claustrophobia, and it turned out more to be eight out of ten people. I really hit a nail with that one and people really were freaked out by that.

It definitely freaked me out! Then you throw in bat-people or whatever the hell they were supposed to be to up the ante! One of the most interesting things about *The Descent* was the whole look of the film, the way you lit it and really exaggerated the green light and the red light, etc. I'm curious if you can talk about your working relationship with your cinematographer Sam McCurdy, who's been with you on all your films? How do you two both establish the look of each film?

Well, we have an excellent working relationship, we've been working with each other for fifteen years now. What's great about that is that we have a real shorthand about what it is we're trying to achieve, which helps us work fast on set. We don't want to repeat ourselves either, so we don't want to just make the same films again and again. The look we came up with for *The Descent*, we set ourselves a challenge, a good year or so before we actually made the film. We said, "I only want light in the cave from sources that the girls take with them." I didn't want beautiful shafts of light coming in to make it look gorgeous.

That doesn't exist in a real cave, I wanted to make it like a real cave. If you're not shining a torch in there, it's pitch black. And if we can get that across, we thought it would really enhance the claustrophobia, but also the fear factor, because you don't know what you're going to see when you turn your torch to the right or left! Anything could be there. And I just thought that made it so much scarier.

On *Doomsday*, we wanted to go for a much bigger scope and scale for that movie. So, we did it in 2:3:5 ratio and we tried to film it in an epic kind of way. But we had a lot more toys to play with on this shoot as well, because the money was there for the steady-cam and just more gadgets. We had a lot of fun with that. We have a great working relationship and it's just always a pleasure. I think Sam's actually threatened to strangle me if I attempt to do a film without him.

(laughs) Cinematographers don't get enough credit for helping with the overall look of a film!

No, no, and a wise point. Sam didn't get the BIFA for *The Descent*, probably because it's a horror movie and they look down on that kind of thing, but I think he did a splendid job on that movie.

How much involvement do you have in *The Descent* as a franchise now? Meaning, obviously *The Descent 2* is in the works with your *Descent* editor Jon Harris directing. How much say do you personally have in what happens with *The Descent 2* and beyond? We were always curious why filmmakers like Wes Craven have little say in what happens with the *Nightmare on Elm Street* franchise when he created that character and series.

It's dependent on the producers involved. Certainly, in the case of *Dog Soldiers*, in order for me to get that film made, I had to sell all my rights in it to the producers so they would fund it. They weren't going to fund it unless they owned the rights to it. So, that was what I had to do, and as such, I made the film, but I have no right to that material or that story or those characters or anything anymore. So, they can go ahead and do *Dog Soldiers 2* without me, which they've been trying unsuccessfully to do for ages.

The Descent is exactly the same story. The production company owns the rights to it. But they're a bit more sensible than the *Dog Soldiers* guys, because they presume that if they want to do a sequel, then it's better to have me attached to it than to not have me attached to it. So, I'm not actually attached to it at all, but I am looking over shoulders and things like that. Because Jon's directing it, he'll ring up every once in a while, and ask, "What do you think about this? What do you think about that?" And that's about as much involvement as I have. I'm too busy at the moment to do more. But we'll see.

Going back to *Dog Soldiers*, I always wondered what your connection was to the characters of your movies. Like before when I asked you about cave diving for *The Descent*. Do you have any military experience? Because you've got an authentic military unit in *Dog Soldiers*!

My dad was in the army. My granddad was in the army. And I think if I hadn't ended up making films, I would've ended up in the army myself. It was just a desire on my part to capture a British military unit as authentically as possible. Especially when facing off against such a fantastical enemy. I thought it's going to work better if they look as real as possible and behave as real as possible. I did a ton of research about that to get it right.

What about the look and design of the werewolves? Because they look fantastic! They're the type of werewolves I remember as a kid, only exaggeratedly tall! What were you looking for with the look of your werewolves in *Dog Soldiers*?

I was looking for my idea of a perfect werewolf, which to me is a perfect hybrid of man and wolf. I was always deeply unsatisfied with the one in *An American Werewolf in London*. And *The Howling* ones look great, but they weren't on screen for very long. So, I kind of liked the way that they walked on two legs, it was always scarier that way. With the production designer, I told him to make the set so small that the werewolf couldn't fit in. I didn't want him to fit into the set. I wanted him to have to bend over to get through the door. I just thought that would make it much scarier.

Yeah, and definitely more physically imposing! Recently, there's been rumors that you took meetings on *Conan* and *The Wolf Man*. Do you consider those types of films dream projects? Would you want to try to tackle an established property in the future and give it your own spin? Or would you prefer to continue making original films like you have been doing?

Um, I think in an ideal world, I'd just prefer to continue making my own original films. But sometimes it's not easy to get those off the ground, and it's easier to get something that's pre-established. Something like *The Wolf Man* was a long shot. And I kind of felt that I would've been happier had I been there from the beginning and started it from scratch. Because the way it's set up now, it's only five or six weeks away from shooting. It would be going in and filming with somebody else's crew and somebody else's cast and using somebody else's storyboards. It'd be like vicariously shooting somebody else's movie. So, I didn't think that was going to be a good idea. But I wouldn't mind revisiting the werewolf genre.

Lastly, what non-horror films inspire you? What are among your favorites that you consider influences?

Oh, well other than *Raiders of the Lost Ark*, *Jaws* and *Close Encounters of the Third Kind*? That's the holy trinity! (laughs) I love Sam Peckinpah films, *The Wild Bunch*. I love John Boorman's films, *Deliverance* and *Excalibur*. I love westerns, *Rio Bravo* and *The Professionals*, Richard Brooks *The Professionals*. Fantastic movie. I like Ridley Scott's stuff, *Alien*, *Legend*, *Blade Runner*, *Gladiator*. I think he's just a fantastic filmmaker. I like all sorts of stuff!

Thank you so much for your time, Neil!

Thank you!

FRIGHT NIGHT
REUNION PANEL

TOM HOLLAND   **CHRIS SARANDON**   **WILLIAM RAGSDALE**   **JONATHAN STARK**

AMANDA BEARSE   **STEPHEN GEOFFREYS**   **JULIE CARMEN**   **TOMMY LEE WALLACE**

On March 8th, 2008, writer/director Tom Holland, Chris Sarandon (Jerry Dandrige), William Ragsdale (Charley Brewster), Jonathan Stark (Billy Cole), Amanda Bearse (Amy Peterson), Stephen Geoffreys ("Evil" Ed Thompson), Julie Carmen (Regine Dandrige), and writer/director Tommy Lee Wallace were all brought together for the first ever *Fright Night* reunion in Dallas, Texas for Fear Fest 2. *Icons'* own Rob Galluzzo moderated the historic event and now, with the kind permission of John Gray, *Pit of Horror*, and the *Dread Central* crew, we present to you the complete transcription of the panel! Read on *Fright* fans!

Rob: First and foremost, why don't we start with Mr. Holland. Tom, obviously you started out as an actor and later became a screenwriter. You wrote *The Beast Within*, *Psycho II*, and *Class of 1984*, a few of my favorites. Then you made the segue way into directing and *Fright Night* was your first directorial film. What was it about this story that made it the first film you wanted to direct?

Tom Holland: *Psycho II* was an enormous sleeper hit. And this was the first film where I had sufficient credibility in Hollywood to be able to direct it. And I have also – this is truth now, so I'll try to be tactful. I had a film after *Psycho II* and before *Fright Night* called *Scream for Help*, which I thought was so badly directed that directing *Fright Night* was self-defense. (audience laughs) In self-defense, I wanted to protect the material, and that's why I started directing with *Fright Night*, because the previous script that I had written had turned out so badly. So, that's the story.

Rob: What made you decide on a vampire tale? Because I assume you're a big fan of vampire films, and for a lot of us here, *Fright Night* is one of our favorite vampire films, so what was it that you decided on this for the story?

Tom Holland: I had the idea of a horror fan who loved the *Friday Night Frights* like I did when I was growing up. They used to have on the independent channel, whatever town you were in, they'd run the terrible sci-fi, horror movies on Friday night. And you'd fight with your parents and everything else, and you'd stay up until eleven o'clock and you'd watch it. And that was how my generation grew up. And *Fright Night* is my very, very affectionate memory of that. So, I thought the idea of a gonzo horror fan becoming convinced that a vampire lived next door, which of course no one would ever believe him, and it was true. I just thought it was deliciously funny, and what I had always wished would happen to me! (audience laughs) I carried the idea around for a year and I could never work out the story. And then, and I don't know how, I thought of the Roddy McDowell character Peter Vincent! And the minute I had that the kid went to the *Fright Night* horror host, I had a story! And it just sort of jumped in my head finally after thinking about it for a year, like the entire script was there. And I wrote it in two or three weeks. I'd been thinking about it for a year. I had the idea forever, but it was Peter Vincent that gave me the key to the story.

Rob: Can we go down the line and each person explain how *Fright Night* came about for you, your initial reactions to the script, and how you became involved?

Chris Sarandon: Um, the script was sent to me, I remember very vividly. I was living in New York. My agent said that someone was interested in the possibility of my doing the movie, and I said to myself, "There's no way I can do a horror movie. I can't do a vampire movie. I can't do a movie with a first-time director." Not a first-time screenwriter, but a first-time director. And I sat down and read the script, and I remember sitting at my desk, looked over at my then wife and said, "This is amazing. I don't know. I have to meet this guy." And so, I came out to LA. and met with Tom (Holland) and our producer. And we just hit it off, and that was it.

Tom Holland: He took a chance. He took a big, big chance.

Chris Sarandon: On a very, very fabulous script and on a very talented guy, and by the way, Tom essentially sat there and described the entire movie to me in our first meeting. He said, "Ok, it's going to open with this shot, and then this is going to happen." He had the whole thing mapped out in his head. I thought, 'Wow, I don't have to worry about this guy! Let's go to work.'

William Ragsdale: I was working I think in a hardware store in San Francisco. (audience chuckles) Not the same situation! (audience laughs) My imaginary agent called and said, "We have this thing." (laughs) Kidding. I had just gotten out of acting school in San Francisco, and I had met a woman who was a casting director. Long story, she had a friend that was an agent in San Francisco, and they were casting the movie *Mask*. And she said, "Do you know any kids that might be right for this role of Rusty in *Mask*?" So, she said, "I have this guy who might be a possibility."

So, I came down and I met with her and Peter Bogdanovich and that didn't work out. But, a few months later, Jackie Burch tells me, "There's this movie I'm casting. You might be really right for it." So, I had this 1976 Toyota Celica and I drove that through the San Joaquin Valley desert for four or five trips down for auditioning. And in the last one, Stephen was there, Amanda was there and that's when it happened. I had read the script and at the time I had been doing Shakespeare and Greek drama, so I read this thing and thought, "Well, God, this looks like a lot of fun. There's no… iambic pentameter, there's no rhymes. You know? (audience laughs) Where's the catharsis? Where's the tragedy?" (laughs) I ended up getting a call on Halloween that they had decided to use me, and I was delighted and about a week, ten days later, I was on *The Three Stooges* stage shooting *Fright Night*.

Jonathan Stark: Yeah, I remember when they sent me the script, I thought I should give this director a chance! (audience laughs) No, it was my first thing, my first film and I was, "Ok, ok. I knew he had to be a big guy, so I kind of had that covered." And I actually put pads in my shoes and put like five shirts on to look as big as I could. Back when I was actually thinner at the time. And I go in there and I read this scene where Billy Cole has to throw off the detective, and I thought, "Gee, you know, if I was trying to throw off a detective, I wouldn't be evil. I'd be as funny as I could be." So, I threw this stuff in, and Tom was thrilled. After that, he said "Hey thanks, you're great." So, six months go by, I don't hear a thing and every day I'm calling the casting director, "Hey Jackie, do you really think they want me?" (audience laughs) "They really want you!" "But nobody's called me!" But he was true to his word, and he used me and God, I think it was one of the most fun things I've ever been involved in, and that's my story.

Amanda Bearse: I was doing a movie with Stephen Geoffreys where we were boyfriend and girlfriend. It was originally called *Wendell* and then it became something called *Fraternity Vacation*. (audience cheers) Oh, I kept my clothes on, OK? Every other chick in the movie? Whatever. Um, I went through the audition process, as did a lot of other actresses and Jackie Burch was lovely. I had not been in the business for very long. I had not been in Los Angeles for very long, this was a very new experience for me.

This was a major motion picture. This was Columbia Pictures, and this was a huge, big deal. And yeah, she was very much my champion and that was the process as it often is. You go in to audition and you get called back and called back and low and behold, I got the film. It wasn't until right at the end, or maybe even after, Stephen and I realized, "Oh, we're going to see each other next week on this other thing!" So, that was kind of cool too, to have a familiar face there, and off we went.

Rob: Stephen, it seems she told your story for you! But what were your initial reactions to the script?

Stephen Geoffreys: I actually met Jackie Burch, the casting director by mistake in New York months before this movie was cast and she remembered me. My agent sent me for an audition for *Weird Science*. And Anthony Michael Hall was with the same agent that I was with, and she sent me by mistake. And Jackie looked at me when I walked into the office and said, "You're not Anthony Michael Hall!" and I'm like "No!" (audience laughs)

But anyway, I sat down, and I talked to Jackie for a half hour and she remembered me from that interview and called my agent, and my agent sent me the script while I was with Amanda in Palm Springs doing *Fraternity Vacation*, and I read it. It was awesome. The writing was incredible. Sometimes you read a script, but this one, I just got this really awesome feeling about it. I read it and thought I've got to do this. I called my agent and said, "I would love to audition for the part of Charley Brewster!"

"No, Steve, you're wanted for the part of Evil Ed." And I went, "Are you kidding me? Why? I couldn't…" (audience laughs) What do they see in me that they think I should be this? Well anyway, it worked out. It was awesome and I had a great time. And it's great to be here with everybody again.

Rob: For Julie (Carmen) and Tommy (Lee Wallace), how'd you both get involved with *Fright Night 2*? Tommy, how familiar were you with the first movie when you did the second? And did you go back and look at it?

Tommy Lee Wallace: Um, I was a fan of the first movie, enjoyed it and laughed a lot. But a little bit of time had gone by. It seems like back then, sequelitis hadn't quite swept the movie nation.

Rob: I think the first was 1985 and the second was 1988?

Tommy Lee Wallace: Something like that. A little bit of time had gone by, and when the opportunity came up, I thought, "Cool. That sounds like a blast." So, my friends over at Vista Pictures, it was kind of mutual, about the time I was thinking about calling them, they called me and I thought, "Alright." I went to see Tom (Holland). I wanted to get his blessing. And kind of get the torch properly passed. I think the only advice you gave me, Tom, was something like, "Just don't get too serious about it. Make sure it's fun. It's got to be scary, but it's got to be fun too." I took that seriously. And that was it.

Rob: And Julie, your character (Regine Dandridge) is technically the sister of Chris's character (Jerry Dandridge) from the first film. How'd you prepare for that and what'd you think when you first got approached about *Fright Night 2*?

Julie Carmen: And this is the first time I'm meeting Chris!

Chris Sarandon: Actually, I came to the set once.

Julie Carmen: Oh, ok.

Amanda Bearse: (To Chris) Obviously, you made an impression. (huge audience laughs)

Rob: Wow.

Julie Carmen: I had never done a horror film. I had probably never seen a horror film. Things were coming in twos. I think this film was sent to me because I had just worked for the man who owned Vista. I did a movie with Raul Julia and Armand Assante called *The Penitent*, which was done in New Mexico and then went off to do *The Milagro Beanfield War* also in the area. All of a sudden, a vampire film showed up, and not having any horror in my background, I looked at it as a whole new challenge. And we were very blessed to have a brilliant, brilliant costume designer Joseph Porro and a choreographer Russell Clark, and I have to say just in honor to Russell, he choreographed the vampire dance, and he passed away in 2002, so it was a great loss. He was an extraordinary choreographer.

Tommy Lee Wallace: I do want to say that the casting of Julie had everything to do with Chris's performance in the first one. Chris really set the bar pretty high for gorgeous vampires, you know? (audience applauds) And so, we wanted to hold on to that tradition as we went along. The original Dandridge was dead, of course, as he got killed right and proper by Charley Brewster and Peter Vincent.

Rob: Oh, it was a sequel, you could've brought him back somehow!

Tommy Lee Wallace: (laughs) Well… to finish that thought off, we wanted to make sure that we kept that high standard and in came beautiful Julie.

Audience Member: Peter Vincent, was he a tribute to Peter Cushing?

Tom Holland: And Vincent Price, yeah. What I paid homage to was AIP and Hammer. And Peter Vincent was Peter Cushing and Vincent Price. That's what I was doing exactly.

Audience Member: And what was it like working with Roddy McDowell?

Tom Holland: Oh boy. Yeah, everybody will… (pause) I don't really have anything bad to say about Roddy. Roddy was a walking oral history of Hollywood. He had started out as a child actor at 20th Century Fox. He did *How Green Was My Valley* for John Ford. He was a little boy in that, eight years old. He may have received an Academy Award Nomination for that?

Chris Sarandon: Yeah.

Tom Holland: So, Roddy literally grew up in the business, and it's terribly difficult to transition from a child actor into an adult and keep your career going. And that had been the biggest problem in Roddy's life and solving that was a huge accomplishment for him. Roddy was everybody's friend. He was friends with people who could help him, and he was friends with people who could do nothing for him. He was friends with the silent movie stars that were still living at the Motion Picture Home, as well as people like Elizabeth Taylor. He had the gift of friendship. And he was famous for having Friday night dinners at his house, on Wednesday and Friday nights actually. I attended a few. I met Vincent Price at Roddy's house.

(audience wows)

Tom Holland: Yeah, I mean, because *Fright Night* is really the expression of the ultimate fan, which is me! I think that that's one of the reasons that it grows in people's estimation because it touches the fan and that was me, and I felt that way about Roddy, and Roddy knew all the stories. When 20th Century Fox was closing down and being taken over by Sony, he walked me through MGM, through the old MGM, and he would say, "On this stage, this movie was made, and this happened, and so and so had an illicit affair in that dressing room over there." (audience laughs) He would take me through the underground where they ran all the electrical cable and the gas lines. That's also where they stored the nitrate film. It was still there. Hollywood has no history. Modern Hollywood and probably even Hollywood forever. It is really of "the now" and about the grosses of "the now." Roddy kept the flame burning for the talented people who had come and gone. He still loved the people who were the actors and actresses who were the stars of the silents.

And I never met anyone quite like him. He got work by his friendships, but he also loved the business. I met Phillip Dunn there and some other people that some of you younger people here wouldn't know or probably care. Walter Matthau and his wife, Lee Remick, as she was dying of brain cancer. To go to Roddy's house was to get a vision of the business in terms of generations, especially with the actors. Along with that was a mean, waspish tongue that would cut you to ribbons in a couple of sentences too! (audience laughs) He sort of took an eternal interest and he sort of helped me, because this was my first film. And he made it a delight for me, and he protected me. So, he was a wonderful guy. (huge audience applause)

Rob: For William, since we're talking about Roddy, I loved all of your interactions with Roddy. You have so many great scenes together. What do you remember about the shoot and working with Roddy McDowell?

William Ragsdale: Well, two things about what Tom said. I went to a few dinners over there too, and one time I sat next to Lauren Bacall at one of them. I was nervously asking, "Can you pass the potatoes, please?" (audience laughs) But the greatest part of Roddy's house, for me was his toilet! Because you go into the toilet by the front door and as you're peeing, there's Laurel and Hardy's bowlers that are up in front of you on the wall. Also, Buster Keaton's bowtie and stuff like that. It just… takes concentration to pee in that environment! (laughs)

Tom Holland: And one autograph after another of everybody who had ever been anybody.

Chris Sarandon: Every great movie star in Hollywood history. It was really, really awesome.

William Ragsdale: But he was really great! And really generous. And I had grown up on the *Planet of the Apes* stuff and on *Night Gallery*. He was a real icon for me, and for him to be as available, generous, and fun as he was, was great. His tongue was, as Tom said, pretty amazing, and he said to me once, (in Roddy's voice) "I like you so much. I don't know why!" (audience laughs) He was great. He was wonderful, and his comical timing was great. Someone had told me that he had done those *Apes* movies, and he was really covered up. His face was gone, except for his eyes, and so he sort of learned to communicate with his eyes, and learned the technicality exactly.

Audience Member: Was there ever any discussion of having Amy (Amanda Bearse) or Evil Ed (Stephen Geoffreys) in the sequel, *Fright Night Part 2*? Because you guys both survived.

Amanda Bearse: Ok, from Roddy and the parties… to the sequel! (laughs) I recall, and maybe somebody can help me out here, maybe I just made this up. I thought there was one script that was read. And that was thrown out. Maybe

I made it up, I thought I was there? A reading of a sequel script and I was in it. Anybody?

Tommy Lee Wallace: That would've pre-dated my arrival. When I got there, I was certainly a fan of the original, and most certainly a fan of these two guys, so my expectation was that there might be some continuity, but somebody had made a decision, and you'd have to go back to Vista Pictures and the executive staff to get answers on that.

Amanda Bearse: Well, these things happen. It's just the nature of the beast. And really, maybe I should've been more personally offended, but I was just glad that there was a sequel. I did have another little job that lasted a while, and I was grateful for that! (*Married With Children*)

(audience laughs and applauds)

Amanda Bearse: Thank you. Thank you very much. But it's the story that dictates, and the thing about the script for me, there was such an obvious learningness. Tom knew this lore, and that was just rich all throughout that first script. So, I just assumed it was the plot, the story, what needed to happen, and it happened.

Audience Member: This is slightly off topic, not about *Fright Night* but this is for Amanda. Do you still keep in contact with the Bundys?

Amanda Bearse: Who?

(audience laughs)

Amanda Bearse: They're around somewhere. No, yeah, we see each other here and there. But it hasn't been a situation like this, which is really, truly remarkable about not only this evening, but this weekend, to have us all gathered in the same place and it's a gift. It's great. (audience applauds)

Audience Member: I'm sure you all knew *Fright Night* was a great film just from the script, but was there any point where it first hit you that, "Wow, this is even bigger than I expected it to be?"

Chris Sarandon: The first time I saw the movie with an audience in a theater in New York City. I was sitting in the back of the audience, and they went crazy. And I thought "Ohhh, hang on here. What's going on?" Yeah, this was a real audience picture. And that sort of cemented it for me.

Tom Holland: I remember Chris telling me a story about a very famous boxer stopping him… tell the story if you remember.

Chris Sarandon: Sugar Ray Leonard. I was walking out of the Beverly Hilton, some hotel someplace and uh, literally, I'm walking across the driveway to get my car and somebody grabs me. And I go, "What? What?" And there's this great looking African American guy standing there, and he says, (in Sugar Ray voice) "Man? I looove that movie! (audience laughs) *Fright Night! Fright Night!*" And I thought, "Well? We've arrived." (audience laughs) Sugar Ray Leonard.

Jonathan Stark: I didn't go to the screening because I was terrified that I sucked! (audience laughs) So, I went to New York City to hang out with my friends, and they said, "You got to go see it!" So, I go "Ok." They take me down to Times Square to see it. Now, back in the 80s, Times Square was a lot different. But to sit in the theater, and hear, "Oh my God, Billy Cole! Look out!" The entire time! (audience laughs) It was the wonderful screening experience. I was so glad I was actually there instead of watching it in Hollywood. To hear those people scream and warn every other actor on the screen. (audience laughs) It was great.

Rob: And for Jonathan, I've been dying to know, and maybe you or Tom can answer this, but what exactly is Billy Cole? Is he a vampire? What's his story there?

Jonathan Stark: You know, I have no idea! (audience laughs) I'll defer to Tom on this one, he told me today I was a modern day Renfield, but Renfield didn't melt. (audience laughs) He was human. So, I'm going to let Tom talk about this one.

Tom Holland: Renfield. Well, that's who Billy Cole was. I thought he was half-human and half-vampire. He hadn't crossed over yet. So, he could be Jerry Dandridge's alter ego/helper. He could exist during the day and in daylight. That he had been bitten, but enough blood hadn't transferred.

William Ragsdale: Someone asked me today, "Is there anything about the movie that you realize now?" And I said that the people that watch it over and over again, the fans, they see things that we don't see or that we didn't see. And they make all sorts of connections and analogies and stuff. And one of the reviews made a connection between Jerry and Billy having this homoerotic relationship, and I

remember reading the review going, "It's a vampire movie, what are they seeing in this thing?"

Jonathan Stark: Well, Tom, before we shot the thing, we had a week or two of rehearsal. I don't really do movies anymore, so I don't know how much of that is around, but I'm guessing not a lot. Chris and I really worked on the characters a lot. And I remember one scene where I'm washing his hand when he got stabbed with the pencil. Tom's like, "Kneel down in front of him." "Huh?" (audience laughs) "Why?" "I just want you to kneel down in front of him." (audience laughs) "Ok." So, when I watch the thing, I'm like… "Oh my God!" (huge laughs from audience)

Tommy Lee Wallace: Vampire movies have to keep rewriting the rules, otherwise we're still stuck back in what Bram Stoker invented for us. So, the idea that this guy could hang out in the daytime, I think everybody wants that sort of thing. I did a movie, a sequel to *John Carpenter's Vampires* and you want to keep inventing stuff, like blood transfusions, the cause of the blood transfusion is that they could stay out for a little while during the daytime, so you could shoot a couple of scenes and surprise people. I love the fact that Billy Cole could hang out in the daytime. It's sort of the adept I think of Chris Sarandon's character.

Rob: For Amanda and Chris, there's a couple of sequences between the two of you, for example the dance scene in the club. But then also later when you bite her and turn her over, there's a lot of subtleties in your performance, almost being hesitant about hurting her. I was just wondering how much preparation you both had for those two scenes considering how well they both played out?

Amanda Bearse: That was more in the moment as I recall. We did have the luxury of this rehearsal time; it was quite magnificent. We were on these bare soundstages in the studio, which has a lot of history that Roddy shared with us, where we ended up coming back to shoot the interiors of the film. Um, but we were there with just a table and chairs and it was just really raw bones and great stuff. But there's some moments that just play out in the moment. They have very much to do with how the shot is set up and their intimacy. Those were more, as I recall, in the moment. Oh, the director remembers…

Tom Holland: That is Chris Sarandon. Chris wanted to deepen the character. Chris did not want just a black and white, "The vampire is bad." It was Chris's idea; I know he was asking for shades in the character. But Amy's portrait, that was Chris's idea. And once you had that Amy looked like a lover from the past, then you're doing the Bram Stoker Mina. She was Mina, ten generations now. So, I put the portrait in that Charley discovers when he brings the policeman in to look at the house, and you know that Amy looks like someone he was in love with, God only knows how long ago.

And then I put the portrait again up in the house in the bedroom when he seduces her. And that gave him a sadness to play, and you felt the same kind of emotion come through when he offered his hand to Evil Ed. And he said, "You're different," but, "come with me and you'll never be, nobody will ever mock you again, or beat you up or make you cry." And that was following that line through. That came out of Chris's desire to have the character, the vampire, be deeper than the one I wrote.

Chris Sarandon: Also, it seems to me that, going along with what Tom was saying and also Amanda, we were all looking for what was deeply human about all of these people. That we weren't just after scaring the hell out of people, we were also after making them feel for these characters so that when something did happen to them, the audience is involved in some way. That way you have a stake, pardon the expression, in the outcome. And those were the things we did in rehearsal. One of the things that Tom insisted that we did, for instance, is that we all do very detailed biographies of our individual characters and we sat around and discussed them, and we talked about the ramifications of those decisions that we made for ourselves in terms of the inner relationships of the characters.

Tommy Lee Wallace: I want to put a footnote on that, but when Tom mentioned, "Come with me," it made me think of Brad Fiedel's magnificent score, which we amplified in *Fright Night 2*, but wow. What a fine dimension he added to the whole thing.

Julie Carmen: Another thing we were influenced by, I don't know what year it came out, but Lestat, Anne Rice's *Interview with the Vampire* novel came out right before. But I was really blessed to be able to read that and what hit me was the 2000-year-old nature of the character I was being asked to play. And what do you do to keep the spark alive and basically entertain yourself through this extended life cycle? By enjoying the little, tiny subtleties of interacting with people. One of the things I really appreciated in Tommy's script, within a 2000-year cycle, there aren't the same prejudices that we may have just in an eighty-year-old cycle that we may have. There was an opening up, what our society in terms of fear of homosexuality or fear of different races, there was just an opening up and I think Regine was very open to the Belle character, who was more transgender/African American, and I just appreciated that opening up.

Audience Member: Tom, I just always wanted to find out, that whole sequence we were talking about earlier, about Jerry and Amy, the dance. What was brilliant to me, here she was at fifteen, sixteen and she seemed to grow up over the course of the entire dance.

Amanda Bearse: It's a seduction, it was the beginning of the seduction.

Tom Holland: We changed her hair style.

Amanda Bearse: And the music shifts.

Tom Holland: And we also changed the blouse.

Audience Member: Well, for a first-time director, it was so brilliant.

Tom Holland: Well, thank you, but I had a lot of help. In order to show her awakening sexually to him, as they dance, I sexualized her with a change in hair style and a change in blouse. It goes from a cotton blouse to a clinging silk blouse.

William Ragsdale: She starts controlling the relationship there a little bit too. She says yes and no at different spots that he's just kind of available for her.

Tom Holland: These were all things that we discovered through the rehearsal process. I don't know if… it was such an extraordinary opportunity. I don't know if you can ever get anything like that again. How many days did we have, did we have a week?

Amanda Bearse: Maybe two?

William Ragsdale: Part of the equation was that Tom was

an actor for years and years before that, so in terms of the process, he respected that process of it.

Audience Member: It doesn't seem very difficult to get you guys all together right now. How about another movie?

Tom Holland: That'd be great.

Tommy Lee Wallace: Talk to the boss.

Tom Holland: Once again, we care, but Hollywood doesn't. It's like trying to get them to release a box set or getting the information to get them to do a behind-the-scenes. I have a luncheon later this month with a gentleman who is the head of Sony Screengems to discuss uh, a sequel and or remake of *Fright Night*. Now, they never called me. This is how it works. They've done three scripts trying to find a way to remake it, and apparently one script has been worse than the other. And so finally after a year and a half and three scripts, I finally have a luncheon meeting. But nobody would've thought to give me a ring before they started the three scripts!

Audience Member: Have you thought about releasing a special edition of it in Europe?

Tom Holland: They own the rights, though. Columbia, now Sony owns the rights.

William Ragsdale: And Tommy (Lee Wallace) called me about two or three years ago. I live in New Orleans part of the year, and he called me and said, "You know, an interest in *Fright Night* has come up, but what's the problem, you keep saying no to scripts." And I said, "I've never seen a script! To any sequel." But the rumor was that I had been turning stuff down for years and years, but I've never seen anything. So, it's that sort of dysfunctional line of communication that informs everything.

Tom Holland: What they tried to do was throw the story out, change the script, and set it in an amusement park. That is what the last writer told me, and I said, "That sounds a lot like Tobe Hooper's *Funhouse* from 1982 produced by Mark Lester," which somebody finally told the powers that be that that's what it was. (audience laughs) Then they decided they better call me in for a lunch, so we'll see.

Jonathan Stark: If there's a sequel, just a thought, maybe these two are married now (points to William and Amanda), have a family and move in next door to the old vampire's home. (audience laughs)

William Ragsdale: You're a producer, he's a director. We're available!

Julie Carmen: I have a question, how many of you here have seen *Fright Night 2* on the big screen? Raise your hands. Three, four, seven, eight people. Ok, how many have seen it on TV? Ok, most of you. Do you know the history of why none of you saw it in theaters? I'll tell you the history. We made it and it was being released by New Century Vista, and the opening per screen average was between six and seven thousand, which was terrific in those days, and that weekend, the head of the distribution company, Jose Menendez was assassinated by his sons. (The Menendez brothers) So, the whole distribution company went into a tail spin and their product kind of floated. And they pulled everything and tried to regroup from the inside. And then when someone figured out they had a good film on their hands, they sold it to whatever it was, Cinemax or HBO. Then it really found its life in video. I was just curious how many people had seen it on the big screen because it had a very short release and that's why.

Audience Member: Are we ever going to see a special edition of *Fright Night* on DVD?

Tom Holland: I will plead the case. I will plead the case at the end of this month. Once again, my experience is they pull out the numbers, and they tell me how much it would cost to produce and how much money they could make and...

Audience Member: They put all that other crap out! (audience laughs)

Tom Holland: Why did they spend three scripts and three writers and a year and a half trying to do *Funhouse*? (audience laughs) Just call Tobe Hooper and he can remake it!

Jonathan Stark: I was talking to Tom, and I reminded him that Roddy had fifty hours, maybe a little less? This was 1984, he had his video camera, and he shot all this behind-the-scenes stuff. He was goofing around with the actors. I mean, I'm sure it's somewhere! But I'm going to try to track it down if I can and see. (huge audience applause)

Rob: Tom, was there ever anything deleted from the film or is it pretty much what you set out to make?

Tom Holland: No, that film is what I set out to make. That is it, scene by scene, word by word. It was an amazing experience, and nobody messed with me! And I thought that was how it was going to be from now on. (audience laughs) Little did I know.

A quick story and for those who may have a memory, *Fright Night* was the small film at Columbia that year. They were focused on what they were sure was going to be their big hit. It was called *Perfect*. It starred John Travolta and Jamie Lee Curtis. (audience laughs) Ok? And that was where the money and interest was, and they were so fixated on that, they left me alone. And the big sleeper hit of that year for Columbia was *Fright Night*. Nobody knows anything. (audience laughs)

Rob: Question for Stephen. One of the most significant scenes in the movie is the death of Evil Ed. You turn into the wolf and Peter Vincent stabs you. But the thing that's so interesting is that, in most horror films, death scenes happen so quickly, and that one is very prolonged and painful. It's a horrible death. Even Roddy's reactions to your last breath, it's something that stands out. Can you tell us what you remember about your death scene?

Stephen Geoffreys: Yeah, and this goes with the question a long time ago about how I felt like when I first saw it. It's one thing when you're there on the set making it, and then when I saw it for the first time put together with the sound, it just, I could not believe how incredible it looked. And that scene, with the stake, I guess that was shot in post-production after everybody had left. It was agonizing. It was almost inhuman, the stuff that they put on me. But you know, it turned out great, so it was worth it. So, yeah. Does that answer…? (laughs) (audience laughs)

William Ragsdale: The pathos of that moment. Usually that's the heroic moment, when you kill the beast. And in that moment, there's so much sympathy.

Stephen Geoffreys: Yeah, and I remember, it was really difficult thinking about what was happening. It was really hard, I remember. Not just the physical part of it. But it was pretty intense. Yeah, it was crazy. Thanks.

Tom Holland: Special word for Stephen Geoffreys. He took chances. He was big. He scared the hell out of me! And it

worked! The character choices he made, they were very, very great character choices. He was the one that was the farthest out. Everybody was wonderful, but special kudos to Stephen. (audience applauds)

Audience Member: Is there any special reason that only Chris turned into a bat? Whereas Evil Ed was the wolf?

Tom Holland: (pause) None that I can remember. (audience laughs) No, what you do is you break it down and look at the special effects and you choose. We did the bat already when Jerry jumps off the balcony of the house. And the shadow, which is an optical, turns into the bat, then you go to the puppet. So, we'd done the bat. So, therefore, we did the werewolf with him. It's as simple as that.

Audience Member: There was a comic series back in the 80s for *Fright Night* from Now Comics. I think Evil Ed was a main character. Anybody have any input on the comics?

Tom Holland: I'll tell you what's happened, that's sort of amazing. *Fright Night*, and God bless you all, but its reputation continues to grow by leaps and bounds. And I was recently contacted about re-releasing the novelization and I informed Tor Books that I intended to do that. And I think the legality of it is they have six months to respond. And I also did the same thing with the comics. Because there is growing fan interest, I'm going to try to resuscitate both the novelization and the comic books.

(huge audience applause)

Tom Holland: I had separated rights because it was an original, and it was the deal I made with Vista. I don't have the rights to the movies, the studio does. But the comic books and the novelization, I do and I'm going to try to resuscitate them.

Audience Member: First of all, I want to thank each and every one of you for being here.

Chris Sarandon: Thank you for having us. (applause)

Audience Member: I don't know if any of you have experiences, or remember your first vampire movie? Seeing it as a kid, or what affected you?

Tom Holland: I will tell you, the genre was dead. The last vampire movie before *Fright Night* was *Love at First Bite*. (huge audience laughs) It was a farcical comedy with George Hamilton. When they do farce, it means the genre is played out. It is exhausted. For two or three years, there were no vampire movies and *Fright Night* resuscitated it. And as far as I know, there's never been another lag since '84 and *Fright Night*. So, the first one I saw was of course… *Dracula*.

Chris Sarandon: Yeah, the first one I saw was the original Bela Lugosi *Dracula*. Stunning movie.

William Ragsdale: I saw that one too. (laughs) Yeah, I was sort of the next generation I guess, and then I grew up on *Count Yorga* and those guys, the real Hammer guys. I grew up in south Arkansas where it's real hot and humid, so the theater was a real refuge. Yeah. And *Yorga* and *Phibes* and all those guys, grew up on them.

Jonathan Stark: I was never a big vampire fan. But I can remember when I was younger, my mother used to drop a bunch of us guys from the neighborhood off at this crappy theater. Give us money for candy for the whole day. We'd watch like three double features, and they were always Hammer films, and they were unbelievable. They were just exactly what a twelve-year-old boy would want to see. Lots of cleavage and lots of blood. (audience laughs)

Amanda Bearse: *Dark Shadows* came about… (audience applauds) Vampires are sexy because of their humanity and I think that's what part of the allure of this film. It's very sexual content, some of it more overt than others. And then the humanity is also the humor of the film, which to me is what makes it such a unique piece. But vampires, when I was a little kid, they were my horror. They were my bad dreams. But I think it's because there was more reality to that, that humanity and that is, was that close to who I was is what made it more terrifying. So, it was more the bad dreams I had than *Dark Shadows*, but *Dark Shadows* was cool.

Stephen Geoffreys: This movie was pretty much the introduction to me of this type of thing. I wasn't a fan of horror type movies before this, but where I'm from in Cincinnati, they had this talk show host, his name was the Cool Ghoul. And he was totally like a Peter Vincent type character, and I just loved the silliness of this guy and the over-the-top kind of weirdness of it.

Julie Carmen: I remember the first time I read Bram Stoker's *Dracula* and the permission that it gave people in a Victorian

era to be sexual. But I do also have to mention Catherine Deneuve in *The Hunger*. (audience applause)

Tommy Lee Wallace: Everybody remembers that spectacular moment in *The Wizard of Oz* when it goes from black and white to color. Well, there's another movie that that happened in and it's *The Return of Dracula*. And in *The Return of Dracula*, there's a big moment coming up to this open coffin with this woman inside. There's this big stake and a hammer and, when that hammer comes down, it goes to color with all this cleavage and blood! (laughs) That was my favorite. (audience laughs)

William Ragsdale: I want to add one thing, my grandmother grew up in Appalachia. She didn't know what a vampire was. So, she hadn't seen a movie in ages, she went to see this movie and she was like, "Well, why did you hate the neighbor so much?" (audience laughs) "Why did he bother you so much?" I didn't see him drink blood, but the assumptions are everything!

Audience Member: Julie. I speak for every man here that ah, you can draw my blood anytime. (audience laughs)

Julie Carmen: I say thank you!

Jonathan Stark: Can I just tell one thing? Anecdotes. Two quick things. I remember the scene where Chris is hit with that final sunlight, where he goes, "*Argghh!*" (flails arms about) (audience laughs) I remember that day so vividly in my mind because he kept doing it. It's like, "Let do another one 'Arghhh!'" (audience laughs) And he was on this thing where the camera would go down with him, and literally after five times, he looked at me and he goes, "Can you believe this is how I make a living?" (audience laughs)

Julie Carmen: You know, the advocate in me has to get people activated here, but if everyone were to email or hand write a letter to someone at Sony and just say "Hey, bring back all these people in *Fright Night*." Bring Tom and Tommy, they'd have to fight it out who's going to direct. (laughs) It makes a huge difference in Hollywood to hear from fans.

Special thanks to John Gray and the crews at *Pit of Horror*, and *Dread Central*!

PSYCHO REUNION PANEL

TOM HOLLAND

HILTON GREEN

CHRIS HENDRIE

ANDREW LONDON

LEE GARLINGTON

KURT PAUL

JULIETTE CUMMINS

DONOVAN SCOTT

KATT SHEA

MICK GARRIS

CYNTHIA GARRIS

On April 25th, 2008, *Icons'* own Rob Galluzzo debuted twelve minutes of footage from *The Psycho Legacy* documentary at the *Fangoria* Weekend of Horrors and followed it by moderating the first ever *Psycho* reunion panel featuring veterans from all four original films. From *Psycho*, this included assistant director Hilton Green, who would later produce the first three sequels. From *Psycho II*, this included Tom Holland (screenwriter), Andrew London (editor), Lee Garlington (Myrna), and Chris Hendrie (Deputy Pool). From *Psycho III*, this included Kurt Paul (Mother/Stunts), Juliette Cummins (Red), Donovan Scott (Kyle), and Katt Shea (Patsy). And from *Psycho IV*, this included Mick Garris (director), Cynthia Garris (Ellen Stevens), and Kurt Paul (Raymond Linette). Below is a complete transcript of the now legendary panel. You're in for a treat that even "Mother" would approve of!

Rob: Let's start with the original. Everyone has a memory of when they first saw *Psycho* and the influence that it had on them. So, starting with Hilton, you were the assistant director on the very first *Psycho* film. What was it like for you to see the movie for the first time? Do you remember your reactions to the film after having worked on it?

Hilton Green: Yes, by the way, it's an honor to be here, but yes, when I first looked at *Psycho*, the first cut, it was just a plain old movie. It was pretty flat, because there was no music in it. And you can't realize what the score of *Psycho* did to that movie. After putting the music in, it just blossomed and became very, very scary. So that was my first impression of *Psycho* and no one that worked on it at that time ever realized that it would have the legs it did and become a legend.

Rob: Mick, you told a story in *The Psycho Legacy* about seeing *Psycho* for the first time with your siblings when you were very young?

Mick Garris: Yeah, we saw it at the Drive-In. The Reseda Drive-In by the way, for any of you that remember that grand and glorious place! But yeah, I was very young, there were four Garris kids and we were all in the back of a '57 Chevy Wagon. And it was the perfect place to do it. By the way, that's the Drive-In that *Targets* took place at, the Boris Karloff, Peter Bogdanovich movie. Um, and so my family went to see it and, in those days, horror movies were thought of as kids movies.

And this was anything but a kid's movie. So, we were all in our pajamas and watching it, and the most effective scene that I remember, being seven years old, was the reveal of the corpse of Mrs. Bates. I talked about it in the clip there, "Mrs. Bates! Mrs. Bates!" Touch it and it turns and there's Mrs. Bates' corpse. And it horrified my sister so much that we would always tease, "Deedee, Deedee... Mrs. Bates! Mrs. Bates!" (laughs) So, that's the most memorable thing about my first time.

Rob: How about you, Kurt? Do you remember when you first saw *Psycho* and how it impacted or influenced you?

Kurt Paul: My mother would not allow me to watch it. My best part, remembering it, I worked with Tony [Perkins] on a couple of things before *Psycho II*. So, when I worked with him on *Psycho II*, he said, "Listen, darling, you're going to wear the dress and play mother." And I said, "What am I going to do?" "You're going to kill people." I go, "I can't do that." And he says, "Sure you can." "Who's going to wear a dress?" "Well, I've done it!" (audience laughs) Just going around, honest to God, just watching people on these films, there was so much talent.

To be around the original A.D. on *Psycho*. And just working with great people including Robert Loggia, and then somehow, I was lucky enough to go from *Psycho II*, *III*, *IV*, and actually play the crazy kid at the beginning of *Psycho 4*, Raymond Linette, it was just a dream come true. I got lucky and played Bates on *Sledgehammer*, *Bates Motel*, etc. Bates, Bates, masturbates. (audience laughs) I just got lucky, and because people like Hilton were there, it was all a dream come true. And what you're doing is brilliant, to keep people remembering this great thing. Everybody is wonderful. Nobody here has aged. (laughs)

Rob: If you, the audience, haven't seen the sequels, I hope you will go out and rent them now. I hope I influenced you to do that! Chris, what were your earliest recollections of seeing *Psycho* for the first time?

Chris Hendrie: I believe I saw *Psycho* in 1962 in the Warner Theater at Worcester Academy in Worcester, Massachusetts. (audience applauds) And uh, I saw it with my best friend actually, Tom Holland! He saw the same show. We were both terrified, and he ended up writing a wonderful script (for *Psycho II*) and I'd like him to describe his first reaction, which I think is the important one.

Andrew London: I was eleven years old and I saw it at one of those cavernous movie theaters that don't exist anymore that had stars in the sky and clouds. It was so big that when the audience screamed, which was quite frequently, the echo went on forever and I think that movie changed the bathing habits of a generation. (audience laughs) Because everyone was convinced, "Did she really lock the door when she went in there?" I remember how it affected me, I remember after that always peeping out of the shower as a kid! It was a great! It wasn't that far afterwards that we were thinking of ways to pay honor to it. (with *Psycho II*)

Tom Holland: It's hard to imagine now that *Psycho* was a sizable event in film. It changed horror, it changed the intensity of the experience. You saw montage, at least I did, I saw montage like I'd never seen it before. You have to remember up until then, we were looking at Hammer Films with Christopher Lee and we were looking at the AIP stuff with Vincent Price. And all of a sudden, *Psycho* comes out and it all changed. So, everything, where you are today is because of *Psycho*. It changed the language of film and that was because of Mr. Hitchcock. (audience applauds)

Rob: Juliette, do you remember seeing *Psycho* for the first time?

Juliette Cummins: Gosh, I was in bed scared! I remember it raining the first time I saw it. I was maybe sixteen or seventeen and I just knew, I knew that this was a master. This was huge to watch this, what Hitchcock had done.

Rob: You had mentioned to me previously that you're a big Hitchcock fan. Was *Psycho* your introductory movie to Hitchcock's films?

Juliette Cummins: *Psycho* was the first that I had seen. And then when Tony hired me for *Psycho III*, I watched everything, just to see what he was brought up with.

Rob: How about you, Lee?

Lee Garlington: I was only like what, five or six when it came out? Seriously, I'm not lying! But I was in Junior High, it took a long time for things to come on TV, so I think when I was twelve or thirteen, *Psycho* was going to be on TV. We had like eight girls spending the night and I lived in Chicago at the time. And then Senator Percy's daughter was stabbed to death and the show was cancelled! We were devastated! Eight girls with no horror movie!

So, I actually never saw it until I got hired to do the second film. I thought I should probably see the first one! My claim to fame though, number one, *Psycho II* was my absolute first acting job I'd ever done in film or television, so it was the most thrilling four days of my life. And number two, I was the handwriting of "Mother!" Do you remember? They had like ten of us submit what we thought mother's handwriting should look like, and I was selected. It was a big deal! (audience laughs and applauds)

Donovan Scott: I think I was about thirteen and really into Ray Harryhausen more than anything. And I wasn't really into adult drama kind of movies. I was still doing fantasy. But the interesting thing at my theater was you couldn't go in to *Psycho* until the ending was over. You could not go in late to that movie, and so I was very curious why that was happening. In my theater, they really would not let you in!

Rob: And that's how they do movies ever since. Because back then, you could walk in and out of movies, they'd show news reels and things like that before the feature, so you can pretty much walk in anytime during the day, catch half a movie, and stay to catch the first half. But *Psycho* was the first movie where they forced you to go from start to finish. Technically, that's the way we watch movies today. We go at a set time, and that was pretty much the first movie that did that.

Donovan Scott: The other enticement for me was that in Ray Harryhausen movies, they used a lot of Bernard Herrmann music, and I loved Bernard Herrmann's music. And when I saw that that was on the bill, as well as the fact that I couldn't go in late, I had to go see it, and I was Hitchcock hooked after that.

Cynthia Garris: I'm trying really hard to remember! I know I saw it first run on Hollywood Boulevard because I grew up in Hollywood. But really all I remember was my little brother being able to get even with me for all the rotten things I'd ever done to him, by laying in wait for me every night when I went to take a shower. He'd throw the shower curtain down over and over again! I eventually just stopped taking showers and took baths. (laughs)

Rob: Katt, do you remember seeing *Psycho* for the first time and how it affected or influenced you?

Katt Shea: Yeah, I do. It was on a really small little TV set, and I was a very young kid, and it was amazing that it had the power that it did even on a little TV set! I would run into the shower and run out as fast as I possibly could. I just realized that *Psycho III* was my last acting role, and I went on to direct after that. It was great, because Tony was very generous about letting me ask the D.P. (Bruce Surtees) all kinds of questions. It was a great movie to have as my last.

Rob: Why don't we talk about how everyone got involved in their respective *Psycho* movie? Katt, you told me a funny story about how they brought you down to the backlot of Universal to audition for Tony?

Katt Shea: Yes, the casting director brought three actors down to audition for Tony and he had me audition with a bush. So, it was one of those nightmare auditions that you hear about where he'd say, "No, no. Don't say the words to me. Talk to the bush." I guess that was the big test.

Rob: I guess if you can act with a bush, it makes you a good actress!

Katt Shea: It was very flattering, he hired me right away. He said, "You have the part, but I have to read those two other girls." And that had never happened before, so that was kind of exciting and wonderful.

Rob: Cynthia, what was it like to work on *Psycho IV* with Mick, which was one of his early films?

Cynthia Garris: Well, I slept with the director, of course! (audience laughs)

Mick Garris: They all do! (laughs)

Cynthia Garris: Actually, it was really thrilling because this was my first speaking role without special FX make-up all over my head.

Rob: She's the creature "Zanti" in *Critters 2*, Mick's first movie, folks!

Cynthia Garris: That was my first role! He gives me all the best roles and kills me off in every movie. It was really exciting and intimidating because I was working in the little booth with John Landis, who can be very intimidating, even if you're good friends with him! He's still intimidating. And um, it was just very exciting to have Anthony Perkins around, although I didn't work with him. He was around a lot, and it was incredible.

Rob: Donovan, when you did *Psycho III*, you told me a story that Tony actually had remembered you from a commercial and asked you to come in to audition?

Donovan Scott: Yeah, my career was on a roll at that time, and I was starring in several movies.

Rob: *Police Academy*, folks!

Donovan Scott: *Police Academy*, *Sheena*, there were a bunch of them at the time. My agent called me and said there's a few lines in this movie, *Psycho III*. And I said, "Come on. If it's just a couple of lines, I'm really not interested." And he said, "Ok, I'll call and tell them to tell Anthony Perkins that you don't want to go in." And I said, "Wait a minute. Who's doing it?" They said Anthony Perkins is directing it and he wants to cast it and he wants to see you. So, I said, "OK, I want to go see him, I want to meet him, it doesn't matter what it is, let me go!"

Nine years before, he had seen me in a play at the Cannon Theater called *Zenboogie*. It was a rock musical, and in all the commercials, it was just me as a Buddha laughing as the credits would go up. And he called me in and said, "Listen, I'm building the suspense, and I remember your laugh and I love that laugh and I want you to do that laugh before this death in the bathroom." And I said, "Ok! I'd love to do it!" He talked to me for an hour and a half. And it was truly his passion for the film that made me want to do that, because I never would've done that. I didn't think these films were going to be that good, but they were fantastic! But the passion that he had just talking to you about it was hypnotizing! You couldn't say no! He would've been great in *The Godfather* as well.

Rob: And Lee, for you *Psycho II* was your first gig, and you've done many since, but you told me that you've worked with plenty of directors, but doing *Psycho III*, Tony Perkins was your favorite director?

Lee Garlington: Tony Perkins was my favorite director who ever lived. Just bar none. And I've worked with a lot of directors and for me, when I did *Psycho II*, I had a tiny part. I'm Myrna "the mean waitress." That was my billing, "Myrna the mean waitress." And Tony? I thought he was a little odd on *Psycho II*. He was sort of in his own little world. But *Psycho III*, when he was the director and they brought my character back, I'm telling you, very rarely do you find a director who equally works well with the crew and with the actors. You usually get an actors' director or a crew director. And a lot of times for first time directors, there's four categories.

They're either really good. They're overwhelmed and being pushed around by the first A.D. or the D.P. Or they're dreadful and they're trying to micromanage everything. I guess that's only three categories. (laughs) And Tony would literally, the guys would be laying track for the camera for two hours, and he'd walk in and say, "You know, I don't think we're going to do that." And they'd go, "Yes, sir!" Nobody growled, nobody complained. He would say things like – I had a scene, and he goes, "You're about to have a date with a guy you've had a crush on for seven years. Go." The scene had nothing to do with that, but that was what he wanted to be feeding me while I was doing the scene. And he would just know exactly how to talk to you. And I'll just say one more little thing, my favorite thing is, Tony – I could never call him Tony. If I met Robert DeNiro, I would not call him Bobby! It just doesn't seem right. So, I always called him Anthony Perkins because that was his name. "Anthony Perkins, can I ask you a question?" (audience laughs)

He did not like people who pandered to him. He was not interested in sucking up. And I remember, the few days I would work, he'd go, "Lee, Lee! Come sit here!" And we would argue about everything! Every movie he thought that he had done that he thought was great, I thought was terrible. We'd argue about music and politics, and he was just so much fun. He just loved to communicate, and he had such a sparkle and he was absolutely one of the most fun directors. I don't think I've had as much fun with a director in all my life as I did with Anthony Perkins, and that's who he is, Anthony Perkins. (audience laughs)

Rob: Juliette, do you recall your audition for *Psycho III*?

Juliette Cummins: Oh my God, my audition was really cool! I walked in there naked and he said, "You're hired!" (laughs) No, just kidding! I walked into the audition, and I knew Tony was going to be there, but it didn't really phase me. I was so new at acting and I had just walked in. I will say that the moment I walked in, it was kind of like *Vertigo*. Tony was sitting on the chair, and it was almost like the camera pulled back as I walked in. He just put out his hand and smiled and introduced himself. And he said, "Let's work." I didn't know who he really was at the time that I auditioned.

And I didn't really care, I just did the work, and I remember I flipped him off, gave him the bird in the middle of the scene and walked out the door. And I left, I didn't come back into the room. My agent called me and said, "Where are you?" I said, "I'm in my car, I'm going back home." "You didn't even go back in?" "There was no need to! The scene was over! I didn't know I was supposed to go back

in!" (laughs) And they said you got the job. He was funny. You guys don't know that he was so funny. He was a little bit dark, but he was very passionate about what he did, and he really loved life. He loved every second being on the set. And he loved actors and loved people. He loved what he did. Yeah, and I loved him. He was a really neat person.

Rob: Tom, you were obviously a huge fan of the original, and a huge fan of horror. You had a history with director Richard Franklin before writing *Psycho II*, didn't you?

Tom Holland: I had written *The Beast Within* and uh, my God. Richard read a spec script of mine and we met and by some miracle I got the job. Because, finally after years of struggling, I got my first movie produced, *The Beast Within*, and it hadn't been a success, so I hadn't been able to get a job in a year. It's true. Richard loved my writing, and I worked harder on that script than I ever worked on anything else. We knew we were going to get killed by the critics. So much of it was self-defense! We tried to build on the original. I read all the original reviews to *Psycho*, which by the way, were God awful.

That movie was attacked so viciously in 1960, I still have the reviews at home. I'm going to pull them out at some point. I dissected the original and looked at every loose end that I could, and I wrote the sequel off of that. Richard asked me for visual set pieces. He wanted to echo shots that Hitchcock had done, not only in *Psycho* but also in other films. And we designed scenes, like the Meg Tilly looking through the peep hole. There were so many. There's a silhouette cut out of Hitchcock in one of the points of view of the bedroom. We put that in, because Hitchcock always made appearances in his movies! Andrew, next to me could probably speak to this better than I can, because it's now hard to remember. But I wrote that script and we designed the shots. So, I was writing into his wanting to echo Hitchcock in the visual set pieces. And Richard was a student of Hitchcock's and when he was a student at USC had lunch with Hitchcock?

Andrew London: Richard and I went to USC in 1967. And um, we did our first film together in Australia in 1974. He came to visit here in 1979 with his co-producer on a film that he was trying to get off the ground called *Road Games*, which eventually was made with Jamie Lee Curtis. My job was a sound editor on *Coal Miner's Daughter* and we were mixing it when he came to visit, and I introduced him to Bernard Schwartz, who was the executive producer on *Psycho II*. Bernie was the producer on *Coal Miner's Daughter*.

From that point on, Bernie went on to produce *Road Games* and called Richard when *Psycho II* was about to get off the ground. The odd thing was, at the time, I was working as a sound editor, Bernie Schwartz promised me that if I didn't do the editing on *Psycho II*, that I would do the sound editing and when I finally got the picture as an editor, I ended up doing the sound as well.

Rob: Chris, how'd you become a part of *Psycho II*?

Chris Hendrie: I knew the writer! (laughs)

Rob: That's a good in!

Chris Hendrie: Actually, I had just come out from several seasons at the Dallas Theater Center and met Richard Franklin at Tom's house. He had just come in and they were talking about the film, and Tom said there might be a part for me, and he asked Richard if I could get a part, and he said sure. There was one of the deputies.

I think Jackie Birch was the casting director, so I went and read for her. Richard said you look great, you have theater experience, we'll cast you in the movie. So, I was all of a sudden right in the middle of a huge, wonderful project, and I was thrilled to be a part of it. And also, double-thrilled because Tom and I had been friends since high school. I've been in several of his movies, and I've always felt very touched that he'd asked me to be in them, and I've also had a very fabulous time. So, thank you, Tom! Appreciate that. It was a thrilling experience to work with Tony Perkins. And Richard Franklin was a very subtle, beautiful director and I think he did a fabulous job.

Rob: Kurt, you played "mother" in *Psycho II* and *Psycho III*, then you played Raymond Linette in *Psycho IV*. You also played Norman Bates in *The Bates Motel* TV pilot. What do you take away and remember about working on just about all the *Psycho* films?

Kurt Paul: I sound like I'm repeating myself, but we were surrounded by great people. What a learning experience. When I worked with Tony, I watched him work and most of the time, we'd be at the house running lines and such. When we did *Psycho III*, the one he directed, I worked with him because he worked with a very talented man named Bruce Surtees. I learned so much from watching him work. When I was lucky enough to do that *Bates Motel* TV series, it wasn't brilliant, but it was fun with Bud Cort. And the *Sledgehammer* thing, it was like a walk in the park. It wasn't even a stretch. I was blessed.

The greatest thing was when I was at the house after dinner, and I was running lines, this part, this Raymond Linette, I said I can do that. He said, "Well, I can't help you, you have to audition for these young men." George Zaloom and Les Mayfield. Great kids who produced *Psycho IV*. I wasn't playing Tony, but just honest to God, was just blessed to be watching a great actor who cared. He'd have me go up and find out the name of the coffee boy on the set. He'd walk up to him and say this is great coffee, it's a pleasure to meet you, if there's anything I can do for you, let me know.

Tony was the most givingest man in the world, that's my experience. If I was out of line, he would let you know it, just like Hilton would. They were both great men to work with and I was just blessed. (audience applauds)

Rob: Mick, your friendship with John Landis helped you get the gig of directing *Psycho IV*, correct?

Mick Garris: It did. It was a very awkward situation, because Tony had directed *Psycho III* and it was not a theatrical success. And he wanted to direct *Psycho IV* and the studio didn't want him to and, in fact, refused to allow him to do that. So, here I come, you know, fortunately I'd been a writer for Steven Spielberg for a while (on *Amazing Stories*). The only film I had directed at the time was the timeless classic *Critters 2*. (audience applauds) And I guess because it had a number in it, I was qualified! No, it was very difficult because I was very young, and Tony wanted to do it.

But fortunately, he and John Landis were friends and John and I had been friends forever, and so John talked me up really well. I was working at Universal at the time, and he had talked to Hilton as well. John and Hilton, of course, had worked together on many movies together at Universal. So, I had to kind of tap dance. I had to earn Tony's respect, which is very difficult to earn when you're much younger and you're new at the job and trying to prove yourself to an icon. Trying to prove why you should be there running the show to someone who had been the star of three previous incarnations of that.

So, there were some conversations that we had that were very complicated. I would say something like, "I don't really want to go much into camp." And all of a sudden it turned into a forty-five minute sort of defensive conversation about, "What do you mean by camp?" and bristling at the term. He was... the most complicated actor I've ever worked with. I learned a lot from him, and there was a lot of great stuff, and a lot of stuff that was really difficult for me but helped me grow in a tremendous way because of the challenge.

Audience Member: This is a question for Hilton and Tom. While you conceived *Psycho II*, were there many scripts written, and did you by chance contact Tony Perkins first to see if he'd be interested in the project?

Hilton Green: As far as scripts being written, no. There weren't many. But you couldn't make a *Psycho* without Tony Perkins, so that came first. We had to get Tony to agree to it. And before I would do *Psycho II*, I went to Mr. Hitchcock's daughter, Pat. I wanted to get the OK from the family because I was very close to Mr. H and I would never do anything that I thought would offend him. So, I went to her and told her what the studio had in mind, and would she mind, and what does she think her dad would say? And she was just wonderful and gave the green light to all of them, and that's how I got involved.

Audience Member: A follow-up to that last question, was there ever any talk of doing an adaptation of the Robert Bloch *Psycho II* book?

Tom Holland: Yeah, there wasn't a script, there was the book. The Robert Bloch book did not serve Norman well. And I say that tentatively because Robert Bloch is also God. I mean, if Hitchcock is God in the movies, Robert Bloch was to so many horror writers. I sat on a panel with him, so I don't want to inadvertently insult him, but it was not – the book that he wrote, the sequel, was not suitable for the movie because it didn't have a part for Norman that you would've liked to have seen.

Or that Tony would've liked to have played. Also, the original *Psycho II*, and Hilton can probably speak to this, was a cable movie when we started out for Oak Communication, which was a cable company down in San Diego and they were financing. My memory, and Hilton can correct me, but my memory is we didn't have a feature film to begin with, we were going to be a cable movie.

Hilton Green: That's true. And that's where they started when Universal wanted to do it and I got involved. Bernie Schwartz came in on it from the Oak people, and that's how we all got started.

Tom Holland: The script, I didn't realize, did you have Tony before the script was written?

Hilton Green: We had to have. Yes.

Tom Holland: Ok. My memory was that what happened, they announced that they were doing *Psycho* again with Tony and all of a sudden, the worldwide interest from the press was so overwhelming that somebody a Universal said, "Hey, maybe this is more than a cable movie," and they decided to do it as a feature film.

Hilton Green: You can never do a *Psycho* movie without Tony Perkins…

Rob: … as the remake has proved. (audience laughs and applauds)

Audience Member: It must be hard after the home run that is *Psycho*, was there anxiety coming up with that movie? *Psycho II*?

Tom Holland: Yes, yes and yes. (laughs) That's why I worked so hard on the script. We knew we were going to get savaged just stepping out. Tony knew that too. *Psycho II*, we were very serious, and everybody was trying to make a good movie. They did it for nothing over on the studio backlot. Maybe Hilton will remember, but the cost for the studio was something like 3.8 or 4.2 (million).

Andrew London: Actually, I think the original budget was three and a half and when Jerry Goldsmith came on, it went up another quarter of a million. (laughs) It was such a low budget movie for the studio. We shot it in thirty-one days. There was only one shot in the movie that was off the Universal lot and that was an establishing shot of the courthouse at the beginning of the film. I think that partly for that reason and partly because you (Hilton) were there, they left us completely alone.

Hilton Green: It's interesting you're mentioning numbers. I budgeted and scheduled the original *Psycho* for Mr. Hitchcock and before we went into production, it was a number that the studio thought was a little low and um, with Mr. Hitchcock's name on it, but the original budget for *Psycho* and it came in at that price was $780,000 dollars. We shot it in thirty-three days.

Tom Holland: I'll give you another fact and I may be wrong about this, but worldwide *Psycho II* made $90 million dollars. And through Universal's accounting, if Tony Perkins hadn't sued Universal, I never would've gotten my $35,000 deferment, because they had it in the red. They made it for $4 million, they made $90 million worldwide, and by their bookkeeping, it was in the red, it still lost money!

Hilton Green: I'll top that one… (audience laughs) I had a piece of it, but I still don't have a nickel back for that feature!

Rob: Well, it appears we're out of time here. (audience wants one more question) Ok, one more question?

Audience Member: For Rob. Can you talk about making this documentary, tracking down all these great folks. What is going on and what is the status of this project? And do you go beyond the franchise?

Rob: To summarize briefly. I started this documentary project independently with one of my best friends John (Torrani), who was crazy enough to go on this journey with me. (audience applauds) It's not a lavish crew, it's just me and him going to each and every one of these people's houses, and they've all been really, really great about it. Um, right now, I'm hoping to finish it by the summer of 2008. I just contacted Diana Scarwid from *Psycho III*, so she should be in it, and hopefully Henry Thomas from *Psycho IV*. So, I'm still trying to get the last few people and I don't want to jinx it, but yes, there is interest to complete the documentary and I can say you'll all be very satisfied because it will bring a lot of interest to all four movies again.

Audience Member: Well, thank you!

Rob: Thank you. And thank you everyone for being a part of this panel.

LARRY FESSENDEN

Interviewed by: Mike, Rob, Jason, and Adam (7/08)

Who is Larry Fessenden and why do people keep trying to kill him? You might've heard of his company Glass Eye Pix, with which he's directed four films and produced a number of others, including Ti West's *The Roost*. Knowing little about Larry, aside from his many acting roles where he's often killed (Jodie Foster did so last year in *The Brave One*), the *Icons* gang caught his directorial efforts *Wendigo*, a psychological creature feature, and *Habit*, an allegorical vampire film set in New York. They then met Larry in the city for drinks at Bar A-2 where he'd written most of *Habit*.

Rob: What are your earliest recollections of the genre?

Well, without a doubt, it was watching the Saturday afternoon horror movies. *Chiller Theatre, Creature Features*. They would be on every Saturday, and it was my favorite place to be in our kitchen where we had our black and white TV and I just saw a lot of bad movies! *Curse of the Faceless Man* and some that I'd never been able to re-find. *The Crawling Eye* was a really strange and unusual horror movie. And of course, I saw *Frankenstein* and *Dracula*. So, yes, I'm totally a product of the Universal era.

I was thinking recently about doing a *Fango* convention, because honestly, and anyone that knows my work will concur, I'm just not interested in gore. I don't associate gore with horror. I associate monsters with horror primarily. I love *Wolf Man* and *Frankenstein* and *The Creature from the Black Lagoon*. I like some of the spooky atmosphere from B-movies. I never liked *The Mummy* with Karloff, I thought it was too boring. I liked the ones with Lon Chaney Jr. and Tom Tyler! (laughs) In other words, I really had an appetite for B-movies and all those old black and whites.

Rob: It's safe to say that those were the types of films that fed your imagination and influenced you?

Absolutely. And *Famous Monsters of Filmland* was the magazine you would buy in those days, even more than *Fangoria*, which I think started a little later. There were all kinds of weird offshoots of that. And then *Creepy* and *Eerie* were large format comic books. Then I read *Werewolf by Night*, which I've gone on record saying that I want to

make the movie of that! No one's interested in what I want to do, meaning the studios! (laughs) Those were my horror influences, but ultimately it was always my own perception of life. I always took the dark view of everything. Every dark corner was filled with untold horrors. It's funny, I've never analyzed it, but I came from a comfortable situation, but I was always aware of the potential horror in every corner.

Rob: You've written, you've directed, you've acted. I think the first thing you went into films for was acting. What led you on that particular path first? How did you get fascinated with the way films were made?

I entered film only knowing the acting. I knew of Karloff and Lugosi. And then I saw the movie called *Man of a Thousand Faces* starring James Cagney as Lon Chaney. That hooked me into this whole other world, which was sort of the realist dramas of Warner Brothers, starring James Cagney. He played gangsters and did a couple of musicals, but anyway, it was always about the actors.

As I got older, now we're in the 1970's, I was obsessed with Jack Nicholson and Robert DeNiro and Pacino and Hoffman. I particularly remember back in 1976, there's one shot in *One Flew Over the Cuckoo's Nest* where he has his hand on the glass, and this just shows how naïve you could be in those days, he had his hand on the glass in one shot facing this way, and then facing the other way he had his fingers in another formation, and I realized, "Oh, they must've shot the whole scene from one side, and then they must've moved the camera and shot it from another end." So, that's how wonderfully naïve you could be about movies.

In '76, I was already a teenager and that's when I started understanding movies. There was no *Premiere* magazine, there were no making-of DVD's, there was no VHS, there were no ways to know.

What I would do with movies is I'd record them on a cassette tape, and I would listen to them, and to this day that's why I love sound, because I was aware of the rhythms of foot falls, a door opening, the sound of a creek. All of that is how I heard movies. Even when I was older, I recorded *Jaws* on a cassette tape in the movie theater! And I thought it was the most illegal thing I could possibly do! (laughs) I would sweat at the anticipation! I'd sneak in with a cassette player and record it, and as a result I know that movie by heart. And many, many previous movies. I always say, I'm the last generation where film was so precious like that. That was the way that you could even have ownership of something. There were two books on *Jaws*. *The Jaws Log* by Carl Gottlieb and then another one that had extra cool pictures! But it was all about the little, tiny things! That's what *Famous Monsters* was. There were dozens of pictures, like remember that image of the woman from *The Reptile*? She has this reptile face? That image, you could look at that for hours and feast on it because it was seared into your brain! I grew up in this notion of single images. It's a much more precious experience. It's nobody's fault that they're born in this generation. But the amount of media, even that my kid is taking in at the moment, is mind-blowing!

Rob: I miss that! I remember as a kid always seeing this one still from *Evil Dead 2* that's just not in the movie and I'd always think, "What is that scene? Where is that scene?" What's the mystery behind this one image?!

Absolutely! That was another thing! I would always see one picture and think, "That's not where the camera was!" And I'd be so confused! Because I didn't realize that they just had a photographer on set, so you think, "What am I looking at?" Honestly, I wouldn't trade that for anything, other than I'd probably connect with a modern audience more if I wasn't from this time and sensibility. Everything was very potent to me, and in a way, so was life itself, which is why I saw everything as a threat and as very scary.

Rob: You started out acting, so was the transition into writing a natural one?

Ironically, it was *Cuckoo's Nest* again. I was acting in high school; I went to a prep school actually and they had a great theater program. I would always be putting these shows on. I saw *Cuckoo's Nest* and I read it, and I thought

the book is so much better. And then I read the play, and the play sucked. (laughs) So, I was determined to write the screenplay of the book! So, I wrote this fucking 180-page thing and I cast all the cool people from the school. And I was still young, so I cast all the seniors and everything. And I put on that show, and it was a huge success. None of the teachers came, but all the kids came, and it was sold out and it was a big thing! So, in a way, I was already interested in writing and directing to some degree. Then I got a Super 8 camera and realized that where you put the camera determines how you tell the story. Once again, it was just a little homemade revelation. I didn't watch a commentary to hear that! I didn't learn about editing from commentaries, I figured it all out in my own slow, methodical way. I started shooting Super 8 movies, and I became obsessed with editing them. In those days, where you made a cut was the hugest decision you could make! Because you're cutting this tiny little thing and you have to put the band-aid on and then you have to clean off the sprockets, and then you go "It's two frames off!" So, you have to peel it off, put that back and cut it again. It was a matter of pride if your film didn't jerk through the projector. I was thrown out of my prep school and all I wanted to do was go to NYU, because in those days that was the only film school.

So, I brought my Super 8 movies that I made, I showed them, and I got in on the strength of them, although I honestly think it's because my parents paid full tuition! (laughs) I had made fifty Super 8 movies by that time, only a few of which are worth still showing. They would have us in the film school making 16mm movies, which was great. You had new equipment to work on, but what I realized was there was a whole video department upstairs that wasn't being used by anyone! There was no one up there! I thought I could make sync sound.

So, then I started making feature films. I made *Habit*, the original version. The original movie is seventy minutes long, and the irony is most of the movie is me being sick, because I was already having life-threatening panic attacks at that point. So, I made *Habit* and video was just this great revelation. I was just a con man. I would get the equipment every single week and I was always editing in there, out until the last minute of them turning off the lights. I got to know all the proprietors, and I would go to these classes, and I'd end up doing so much work that they'd say, "You don't have to come to class, but if you come in every month and teach the class, that'd be great!"

So, we had a TV show on public access, which was a great thing. And it was everything from me in drag to doing a cooking show, to a couple of horror episodes.

Then I did *Habit* around then. And then I directed a two-and-a-half-hour caper movie called *Experienced Movers*, which is totally zany. And then I was in this neighborhood working with performance artists. I started making money by editing people's reels, actor's reels and so on. That was in the old days. Steve Buscemi was in the neighborhood; I edited his reel. Mark Boone Junior, his stand-up partner. So, I got to know that whole community and it was just this very vibrant time here.

In a way, it derailed me because I just started getting involved in the "scene" and with playing music and doing videos with people and working with performance artists, which is how I became a very prolific editor. But I wasn't really making the "move to Hollywood" or even to indie film. That's the other weird thing, the structure, the ambition, the drive wasn't set up the way it is for a kid now.

Rob: In *Habit*, there's a scene with a photographer taking pictures of naked girls on stairs and you just mentioned working with performance artists. I just was trying to figure out what went into shooting that! Because you've got a photographer and a group of naked girls on the stairs in the middle of New York!

Well, also where would that image come from, and that's exactly the point. You're following up on what I'm saying. That guy is a friend of mine, who's a photographer and that is his oeuvre, which is huge Rubin-esque women. He would place them on classical architecture, and he'd shoot a lot of them in New York as well as other places like Chicago and Philadelphia. They're beautiful black and white photos and they're huge! They really are gorgeous. When I was a kid around 1981, a friend and I were doing some illicit drugs and wandering around New York as one did in those days, and I came upon a series of things. It was the trippiest night!

We were sitting in this one place and this homeless guy came up from this box and said, "Who's that there!" And that used to be in *Habit*! I cut it, because it didn't work so well. But then the next thing we stumbled upon was Marty Scorsese shooting *Raging Bull*! Can you imagine?! (laughs) Right outside of the Copacabana on 57th Street in Manhattan. It was the scene where Joe Pesci smashes the guy in the back; there was Marty, there was this cab, and there was a guy we'd never heard of, Joe Pesci, smashing a door and my friend and I were like, "This is wild, man!"

So, for *Habit*, I wanted to create that same kind of dreamy night that keeps on going. One weird incident after another. Instead of coming upon a film shoot, I thought we'll come across Nelson's shoot and there'll be these weird naked women! How weird would that be? So, that's the origin of that scene.

Mike: You said you were caught up in a "scene." Your character in *Habit*, Sam, you really don't know what he's up to. Is he an artist? He seems so distracted from what he's supposed to be doing.

Exactly, and that was the scene in the Lower East Side. Everyone was sort of an artist, or they were living this kind of creative lifestyle, but very likely they were just a drunk, which is that blurred line. In *Habit*, he works at the restaurant, but his friend makes this comment about him having money and that's sort of the whole idea. Unfortunately, Sam is lost, because he has no need to have further direction. There are huge paintings by his girlfriend, so he lives with an artist. (The other girl.)

And the other guy is so theatrical, the guy who plays his friend Nick (Aaron Beall) actually had a theater down here called Todo Con Nada on Ludlow when we filmed and in my own mind, I just imagined that he was that kind of a guy; I don't really show that he's an artist. In the original cut, Nick, that character is actually performing at the Halloween party, some crazy thing. So, you're a little more aware that he's actually a performance artist, which accounts for his absurdly theatrical nature, the way he communicates.

Rob: *Habit* is my favorite realistic vampire movie next to *Near Dark*. I hold them both in high regard. What was it about that story that, of all the shorts and films you made before, that was the one you decided to remake into a feature?

Because it's truly autobiographical.

Rob: So, you hold it very personal, *Habit*?

Yeah, it's very personal and I say on the making-of that I would make it again as a forty-five year old! And it could be more horrifying, because he'd be married, even have a kid. So, he'd be putting even more people in jeopardy with his self-destruction. We'll see! I don't know if the nude scenes would be quite as exciting! (laughs) But the real answer to the question is that it remains my personal testament about living on the edge of alcoholism and fighting off demons of insanity. Which has dogged me my whole life. And feeling I'm… it's very personal. The panic attacks and just feeling basically out of control. And as much as I have a relatively stable life, I'm just a couple degrees away from that guy still.

Rob: The thing I love about *Habit* is it's so New York. It embodies what it's like to live here. If I ever wanted to give someone an example of what it's like in New York, I'd tell them to watch *Habit*!

It's funny, because the colors of New York really are red, green and the blacks of night. And the yellow of the endless blur of stuff. I do agree. I feel pretty great about the look of that film, and of course it was a great shoot. Just a seven-person crew. Frank Demarco was the DP and it was just seven of us in a tiny car and we'd drive around. A lot of the footage was stolen without permits, and when we needed permits to stage that car accident, we did that on the up and up. That was the last time they had the Ferris wheel at the San Gennaro festival. Which they still have, but now they sell tube socks and "I Love New York" t-shirts whereas then, it was more authentic.

Rob: I wanted to talk about casting Meredith Snaider in the role of Anna. It's the one and only film she did, and I think she's a terrific in it! I thought I read somewhere that she now works as a social worker?

Yeah, and she's a mom too!

Rob: And a mom! So, what was it about her that she was right for Anna? Did you know her previously? Why did she only do that one role in film?

Dayton Taylor was my producer, and it was really just he and I that made *Habit*. And we put an ad in *Backstage*, it said, "Some nudity, frank sexual vampire movie. Lower East Side. No money." (laughs) And uh, we got a stack of envelopes believe it or not! That's the beauty of New York. Me and Dayton were sitting in a pub somewhere and we pulled up the first envelope and opened it, and I pulled out the picture and said, "We have our vampire!" It was the first picture I pulled out and basically, I just wanted that androgynous look. I felt she was so beautiful in her picture. She was also staring right into the camera; it was a really good head shot.

Adam: You even say in the movie that she looks timeless.

Oh yeah! Everything about it. She had this kind of slightly feral female look, which is exactly what I had in mind. Naturally, we auditioned her, and she really started to haunt me. I worked with her a lot, she was not a hugely experienced actress. I mean, she was in acting class and in school. She was a very young girl, but we did a lot of stuff together and sculpted all the sex scenes, and had a very honest relationship and it was just a really great experience.

Honestly, I think a lot of the opportunities that came as a result of *Habit* were scumbags asking her to do nude stuff, and I think it was a little disappointing because she wanted to be an actress! Just in general, acting is an incredibly hard gig. And she drifted away from it. I have seen her since, and I run into her. She's a mom now and a social worker. She was always into psychology. So, she's like a real person! But how cool is that that there's one video on her shelves that she can show her kids or… maybe never show her kids. (laughs) Yeah, I think she's great and I still get inquires about her on the internet. Because she's got a one-sentence bio! It's funny, once again; it's about the over-information we live with. If you withhold information, people go crazy! "Who is she? Where is she?"

Mike: Do you think that helps *Habit's* reputation? The interest in this woman who played that character?

Rob: Maybe she's a real vampire!

Well, that's what's appealing. It does feel like she just visited this movie and just disappeared.

Rob: Well, this is something interesting that I wanted to talk about. I read an interview where you said all your films are pretty much metaphoric…

Absolutely.

Rob: …And that you hope that people take them that way. Whereas for me, I like to take them literally! I like to think that Anna was a vampire for real!

That's fine with me!

Rob: I like to think there are ghosts in *The Last Winter*. So, is that OK with you that I'm taking your films literally?

Absolutely.

Rob: I feel that this is the way you intentionally craft your movies. The scene I love in *Habit* is when Sam is confessing to his friend that he thinks his girlfriend is doing all this crazy stuff with him. You can think, "Well wait, maybe she's a vampire," or "Dude, you just hooked up with a really crazy New York chick!" I love that it can go either way. I tend to lean more towards the fantastic.

And in a weird way, so do I. But there's a part of me that won't allow myself that. That's been the reality of my career. I don't want to explain it. I live everyday with ghouls and goblins haunting my peripheral vision, and that's absolutely real but I know it's also totally subjective. It's just me! Everyone else is like, "What do you mean, Larry? Everything's normal!" You don't understand. I've been dealing with my whole life that sort of specter of death and disease and decay! (laughs) That's just the way I seem to perceive it.

So, my films are very deliberately the two things. I guess what I'm saying is that reality is incredibly subjective. I was just listening to this woman on the radio today talking about schizophrenia. Those people are diagnosed and experiencing hallucinations. You know, I'm not sure about the brain! But who's to say that I'm not right on the edge. I always wonder how my brain might be working!

Adam: You just might be slightly more perceptive to the point where it's overwhelming.

Well, exactly. Or whatever my synapses are doing. They're just putting things together in a different way. You can say it's slightly hysterical or slightly delusional and so on. Bottom line, I'm an "artist" and therefore I see things differently. I'm sure Guillermo Del Toro sees visions when he looks out. The real point in *Habit* and every other film is that those monsters are absolutely real to the people that are experiencing them, and therefore they are real! Their reality is subjective. It's your subjective truth. In the same way that some people can go through tremendous hardships and rise above it by denying the suffering they're going through. I don't know why I'm bringing up that example.

But someone who can overcome torture, or live in that abject poverty, I admire those kinds of stories, people dealing with extremism. So, my basic premise in all these movies is your reality is your mind and what you're perceiving. As far as *The Last Winter*, I don't think the world's going to come to an end because little weird demons are going to come out of the earth. I think the climate is going to collapse and human civilization will crumble. I don't blame the demons, but I think those demons are there for us. And that's what it'll feel like, because human beings apply meaning to reality. That's why we have Greek myths or the great religions. People are telling stories to make sense of physical reality. Those are my issues.

Adam: *Habit* was about how reality is so subjective that you can never completely see something from somebody's point of view. And how terribly lonely that actually is. You started talking about mythology and religion. That's what spoke to me the most in *Wendigo*. The boy gets his

little totem and through that Native American story, that's as close as he can get to rationalizing what horrible random things actually happen in the world. That's as close a comfort as he can get at that age and it's probably a good thing.

You just said mankind needs those kinds of stories to make sense of things. We're living in a world that wants to be spiritual, but it's very false spirituality and a very need-centered spirituality. I agree with the principles and idea behind the order someone can get from embracing organized religion, but the downside is it often turns into spiritual navel-gazing. It's like, "Well, there's me and my group and we have the answer and you don't, so we have the upper moral high ground." So, I do feel that your movies are very spiritual while distancing themselves from traditions.

I have often tried to quote Joseph Campbell. It's a very complex idea, but he says, and this is what my movies are about, "Something can be true and not true at the same time." Which is to say that the parable of Jesus can be a truth. Jesus or whatever your myth is, that can be a truism. A truth that's so strong that you live your life by it. It doesn't make it true. And it doesn't need to be true to be truthful and that is exactly what Joseph Campbell has said and I've always embraced that idea.

Beyond that, my answer to spirituality, and the reason I detest world religions is, yes, I'll say that on record, they are incredibly human-centric. Narcissistic. For all the endless talk about a higher being, I see no reverence for nature, no reverence for the world around us. I see only rules and laws made by men, and stories about men fighting men, putting men down, I see nothing that impresses me in the Christian religion as it is broadcast to our modern society. We all know that every religion has a tiny, tiny pocket of actual decent people in it. But they're often very hard to find. I have essentially contempt for religion. I'm quite proud to be on the Atheist website. (laughs)

Adam: The good of which religion promises, I feel you do embrace it, especially what we see in Native American culture's worldview in your films. Like the ideals are what you'd embrace about them, not elements that drive one inward or against someone else.

I believe very passionately in a reverence of something outside of yourself. A higher moral person and for a sense of community. A lot of people say, "If there's no God, why would you ever do the right thing?" I find that the most contemptible of all thinking. The idea that God is a policeman.

Adam: Meaning the only reason you do something good is from the threat of punishment?

Yeah. "How can there be morality without God?" The whole point of morality is it's a pact, that is what civilization is. It's just a deal. You know what? I won't kill you. I won't kill you today because I want your beer. That's already a leap of faith.

Mike: What about the way your characters in your films perceive reality and your experience with panic. You mentioned before you experienced panic attacks. And as someone who's seen how that alters your perception of reality, and how that can be terrifying, what have you experienced that you've brought to your films?

I just have my own set of eccentric anxieties. And when they take hold, I'm fully convinced that I'm about to drop dead. Then you have this internal battle of like, "Am I really going to take the effort to go to the hospital and go through the role of being diagnosed and sent home in shame that I'm completely fine?" Which has happened to me. So, then you start going, "To what degree do I really feel like I'm about to drop dead?" It becomes this endless guessing game. I've said to my doctor, either I have a heart condition or I'm insane! And I don't know which one would be better! But I feel like a lot of people suffer through these things. Look at how much drugs are on TV. I feel it's an appropriate thing to represent in a film to show a sympatico with the rest of the world. I suffer from anxieties on every level in different things and I do express that.

      Most of my characters are not heroic, strong characters. Mind you, I have tremendous admiration for rising above your own fears, and I would hope to show that in a film as well. I come from a point, in dealing with my characters, that everyone is deeply flawed and basically kind of winging it. There's no such thing as an expert. And I have great admiration for those people that actually are experts and are great leaders. I'm a huge fan of the Shackleton story. He's the guy who led his team out of the Arctic. I'm fascinated by political leaders with integrity and all those kinds of people because it's a very, very difficult world. It's hard to be truthful. We all want to tell little lies, so we seem a little bit stronger, a little bit cooler.

      I'm always interested in that with my characters. Like the dad in *Wendigo*; he's scared of that hunter guy. He wants to be strong in front of his kid. Is he doing the right thing with the kid when he plays the monster? Like what's his problem? Is he making the right choices? But then he's really sweet when he talks about mythology to his kid, there's an honestness there. Honestly, *Wendigo* has some flaws, but there are things about it I think are very beautiful, and that's great. When he's talking about mythology to his kid, moments like that, that's what I like about that movie. Sure, it didn't make it to the top ten list of "gore" films. (laughs)

Mike: In a lot of your films, the characters are working themselves into a frenzy. There's nothing to be afraid of, but you're afraid for them. The way you shoot their reality, it is very dreamlike, it's very unusual. I can relate to it! Having this weird anxious anxiety! Rob knows this about me! (laughs) I get all worked up all the time!

I make movies for nervous people! (laughs) I make horror pictures for nervous people!

Jason: From *Habit* to *No Telling* to *Wendigo* to *The Last Winter*, we're here in New York, you talk about being a New York filmmaker, yet all your films seem to get further and further away from New York! Or more so from civilization! Each film seems to get more and more isolated. Is that a conscious effort on your part?

I don't think so, but it's interesting that… I'll say that location means everything to me. I really try to absorb a location when I'm doing a movie and capture whatever that vibe is. I made *Last Winter* in a remote place because I wanted to be where there was snow; and then the oil theme came to my mind and that's why it was set there. But I'm not trying to get further and further from people. But it is funny, I was going to make *Habit* before *No Telling*, and then a series of events came up, but in a real way, that's the order, it should've been *Habit* first. All I really feel is that every location is part of the personality of the film. It's another character.

Jason: For example, here on the East Coast, we get all four seasons, we get snow, we get heat. But when you were thinking about writing something like *The Last Winter*, it was almost like you wrote a location and dropped the characters in the middle of nowhere. Is it because we live here, in New York and are surrounded by it all the time? The idea of mental escape?

I love reducing things to one of the four elements, and it's true, *The Last Winter* is just one season, one color, one vibe.

Adam: You even reduced the environment even further! Several people die and then the complex burns down. The two people with two opposing points of view are then in the middle of a white void: absolutely, literally nothing. That's what it takes for them to start pulling together.

Rob: Is it true that that was your first mental image you had for *The Last Winter*, which in turn inspired the whole thing? I thought I read that you had this image in your head of two people from different religions and races in the middle of nowhere.

That's exactly right. I wanted the actor that tortures Marky Mark in *Three Kings*. Cliff Curtis. He's a great actor! I imagine him with someone else, because I wrote it after 9/11 and imagined it'd be a Muslim guy. But there's a famous Kurosawa movie called *Dersu Uzala*. And it's about a British colonialist and he's being navigated through nature by this Native guy. I love the idea of someone having knowledge being able to have more power than the guy who has power. Because in the wilderness, the only thing that will keep you alive is your understanding of nature. It has nothing to do with your standing in society. So, that was sort of the beginning thought, as you said, very reduced. And it was a matter of figuring out how to get them there.

Rob: You've lived with *The Last Winter* for a while now. It's been two years since you completed it. How does it feel that it's finally going to be out there?

Oh, I'm so excited. It comes out on DVD July 22nd, 2008. It's been a long journey and it's been fun, no real complaints. Just impatience! Because among other things, I am passionate about the issues. You can argue that this is a pretty relevant time for it to come out! It's about oil shortage, it's about drilling in ANWR where they're talking about drilling again. Once again, not solving any of the real problems, which is that we can't count on oil anymore.

So, it's perfectly contemporary and it is an irony if you're liberal politically. You've been reading about this shit fifteen years ago and the public is barely catching up. Yeah, I wrote a book on environmental filmmaking in 1992, and I have a whole thing about global warming and it's something we have to deal with. It's not that I'm so clever, it's just that I'm reading that kind of information, and the rest of the world is reading some other kind of information. I'm excited about *The Last Winter* coming out, there's a great, pretty funny making-of…

Rob: Which is longer than the movie itself, right?

It's longer than the movie itself! It's two hours of truly "fly on the wall" stuff, what it's like to make the movie, and you see us figuring out and planning stuff and things not going well, and things going well. All the characters are very vibrant. We're really in the middle of the process and it's fun. It's not going to be for everybody because it's not dry interviews.

Rob: This is arguably your biggest film. Was it the hardest to shoot and make compared to your previous films?

Yeah. It had the most challenges. Every film is hard, because you're trying to keep the quality up. I have a friend, and he observes, and he might've been quoting another person, but making a film is to make as few mistakes as possible. There are so many decisions to be made! Every costume. I just did this episode of *Fear Itself*, every costume, every single thing. "This napkin? You want this napkin?" And you think, "Umm, yes, yes, I want that napkin."

But then you've just committed to a black napkin. And you get on set and there's a black table and you're like, "Oh my God! I made the wrong choice! It should've been a red napkin on the black table! Oh fuck! I'm fucked!" (laughs) And maybe you can switch it out, but you can't always switch it out. Every decision matters and there's only one person they ask that question of. The fucking director! So, you can talk about TV is really about producers and whomever, but no, at least from my experience, it's the director.

Jason: I absolutely love *The Last Winter*. It was on mine and Adam's Top Ten list last year.

Oh, thank you!

Jason: I saw it in theaters with my girlfriend and when it was over, we were just sitting there. She likes films, but not the way that we look at it, and…

Are you saying you got laid because of *The Last Winter*? And that's why you love that movie!

Jason: No, no! (laughs) I just thought it was a perfect film. I don't know what it was about it, but there's a line in *The Last Winter* that says we're basically grave robbers of the earth. I thought that was one of the most brilliantly written lines in any recent films I've seen. It capsulated the whole film into that one sentence. It seems now with M. Night's *The Happening*, this new eco-thriller trend, did you know it was going to eventually curve into that sense of the environment being the victim, and we're the monsters?

My whole opinion about that is that is how I feel. It's never been a calculated notion. I mean, *No Telling* is technically an environmental horror movie as well. It's about pesticides and whether we should experiment on animals and what is correct and so on. I do believe, and I've said it before, that these will be the themes of the next generation of horror movies, because the fucking world is collapsing! I don't know if you've noticed, but all this flooding that's been going on? Hello! If you read the old tracts about the problems of global warming, one is going to be flooding.

All these tornados? How can it be that there's tornados in the news every fucking three weeks? It's just so crazy! So, what's going to happen is that the world is going to start to destabilize, and people are going to start telling stories about that. It's a natural thing. They may have it as "mother nature" being avenging, or they may have it as be about people running out of supply, or how their neighbors are starting to prey on them. I think 2012 is supposed to be a big date. I don't buy into that stuff, but I think 2012, I wouldn't expect the world to end in 2012! (laughs)

Adam: Well, I'm reading *The Monster Show* right now. And *The Monster Show* analyzes horror movies pretty much from when they started making them up to until around the 80s it seems. And it shows the perfect examples of how all the horror movies, even the crappy ones, the fun B-ones we grew up with. They all reflect something…

Mike: That's why horror in the 90s was so boring? What were we upset about? (group laughs)

It's funny you say that. It's true in a way. I think the "torture-porn" tradition makes perfect sense under Bush. I also think zombie movies are popular because our soldiers are coming back wounded and battered, and there's this post-apocalyptic trend that will keep on happening. I mean, they've been making those movies for a long time, but I think they're going to take a new urgency. And then things like *The Happening* and *The Last Winter*.

Adam: One of the things that freaked me out, and you expressed this so well in *The Last Winter*, is that everything's not going to just go overnight. It's not like you flick a switch off. People don't worry about the nuclear bomb because if a bomb goes off in Manhattan, the mentality is, "Oh, I'll just turn to dust, I won't even feel a thing. It'll just be over." But it's probably not going to go like that. It's probably going to get to the point where everyone you know gets cancer at forty. People will still live; it won't all turn off like a light switch.

The image in James LeGros' last scene in *The Last Winter*, in his mind, it's his last chance to go home. And that's why I feel that film is so deeply sad, because no matter how much we clean up-and there's no reason to stop and go into apathy, we can at least improve things or hold off decay; but we'll probably never, even if everybody joined hands and did everything, get back to the environmental purity of hundreds of years ago. Or even 100 years ago. The species that died are never going to come back, there's always that sadness. That's the other thing, I'm interested in the melancholy of horror.

Adam: And Jeff Grace's score for *The Last Winter* really hits that.

Rob: It's one of the best scores in a genre film in years.

That's great. I'll tell Jeff you guys said that! I just read the opening chapter of *Lovely Bones* yesterday. It was sitting on set, and I started tearing up. It's about this girl who's murdered in the opening chapter. We all know that Peter Jackson is going to make that film, so it'll be fun to see how he handles it. But she narrates it and she's in her version of heaven; that's the theme of the book. But she's like, "So then I died, and I don't know why I made that decision to go with him into his weird hiding place. He seemed like such a weird old man. I'll never understand why I made this choice. And I remember when he took my hand…" The idea of this series of vague thoughts, "I should have not done that." And then he's lying on her and raping her and she's thinking back, "I remember feeling so bad, and I felt sad for my mom." Anyway, what I'm getting at is it's the poignancy of horror that I find interesting. I'm not interested in the modern fetishizing of, "Hey dude, did you see when his brain was like… coming out?" In real life, when that happens to your friend, to your family, to yourself, that's not your reaction! So, what's happened to our horror entertainment that people are so into that stuff?

Even *Night of the Living Dead*, which is a very violent movie and I love that movie, it was the horror that I responded to, not the spectacle. I don't care what the FX guys can do, I'm more interested in, "How would that feel? What would your reaction be to that?" I still see horror as cathartic, and I think maybe that's different from kids now or certain types of audience members. I don't know what they go to horror for, it's more like a porn thrill, you know?

Jason: Do you think they're really afraid of something like *The Last Winter* or *Lovely Bones* because it's the truth of what's happening?

People are afraid of the truth. That's the sad reality. People don't want their buttons pushed. They want to go in and be entertained.

Jason: It's like people like having their blinders on, whereas the rest of us when we do see a film with an impact…it's like *The Last Winter*, why the fuck isn't everybody talking about this movie? Why isn't everyone covering this movie?

Well, the fact is that so many people find that film deeply annoying. Same with *Wendigo* and so on. Which is fine, I understand. But also, it's very, very endearing that you would take it the opposite way. I can't even tell you what that means to me! It means I'm not insane. It's funny, it goes back to the anxiety thing! "*I'm not having a panic attack!*" (laughs)

Jason: After I walked out of *The Last Winter*, I wasn't talking about the film, I was talking about you! I thought, this guy is thinking exactly what I'm thinking. It made me think, "Wow, I'm not crazy either! I'm not the only one who wants to see these films!"

I always say that not a lot of people like my movies, but the people who do like them are so relieved that they exist. Because they're like, "Oh my God, that's how I feel!" About the relationship of the genre to their reality. The real scary things in life. The feeling of insecurity, feeling that you can't count on things. Look how we failed with Katrina! Does that ever get under your skin? That in fact, the "heroes" aren't going to be there for you? There's nothing more terrifying. You grow up thinking there's heroes, "good guys," the government, whomever, "these systems work. It's the modern world, we know how to deal with this stuff." Then you realize, shit, nobody's funded this stuff? There's no real plan? That's why George Bush's America is so scary. Because they are not interested in helping you. They couldn't fucking care less!

Mike: I'm really relieved that films like yours exist. But do you think something like *The Last Winter* gets swept under the rug a bit because the real world is so challenging and scary? To play devil's advocate, are you sure people don't want to see or be challenged when they get enough of that in real life? You don't need a horror movie when you watch what happened with Hurricane Katrina, for example, do you?

My notion of the arts is that they are cathartic and you're actually working through something and you're communicating and so the sad reality is what you're saying. People have put the arts into another area. They are diversions. Real escapism. I've always objected to the notion of movies as entertainment and yet I still love Fred Astaire movies.

Mike: Those were made in a very challenging, difficult period in history. Look at horror during the 60s, what was popular? Hammer films and crazy monster movies were popular. This wasn't stuff that was challenging people and maybe today, it's just too much.

Adam: Were those entirely studio pictures though? Because then you had indie directors like George Romero.

Mike: Yes, but that was later in the decade. Works like Larry's will probably now start to turn people around. It's eight years of garbage and people are finally starting to turn around. It took that long?

Jason: Even the theme of escapism though, and the thing that I find strange is I think there's plenty of room in art for an aspect of just pure escapism.

I agree.

Jason: For example, my comfort food of movies is *Ghostbusters*. I watch that movie like, twice a week. I fucking love that movie…

You want to know my comfort food? It's the *Jurassic Park* movies. I just love to watch the fucking dinosaurs! Even the new *Godzilla*. The American *Godzilla*, just because I like to watch those little guys run around. (laughs)

Rob: You may be the only one with that *Godzilla*. (laughs)

I probably am! It's probably the worst movie ever made. But the way his tail sweeps across the third story, I can watch that over and over! (laughs)

Jason: Even the escapism films that we enjoy are superior to what we're considering escapism now. It's like lazy escapism. They're not even putting effort into the art that's meant to be fun! I don't understand that.

Well, one thing that's happening with movies, and I knew this was happening. In 1978 when *Halloween* was popular, I thought, "Oh, this isn't good for us," because Hollywood finally realized, "Oh my God, we can make low-budget horror movies and make money!" And I feel it's very perverse that the studios are making all these horror movies. They're really just cookie-cutter films that are directed by very talented rock video guys, so they have this pizzazz to them. But I don't know why they're being made, whereas horror movies used to have a broken spirit behind them, there was somebody trying to get at something, there was somebody that was tortured by something, there was a sense and an authentic feeling to a lot of movies. *Let's Scare Jessica to Death*, some of these movies are so freakin' weird. *Phantasm*. What's going on with that movie? Whereas now, you see *The Grudge 2*! Number 6, the fifth remake from a script by so and so. I don't know what I'm seeing anymore? What does this mean?

Mike: *Let's Scare Jessica To Death* would be the perfect double-feature with *Habit*.

(laughs) It's just a weird fucking movie, right?

Jason: As a filmmaker, you decided you weren't going out West. You were staying here because the only way you could do what you wanted to do was if you stayed here and did it yourself.

Rob: I thought that I read you're being courted by Hollywood types for things here and there.

Well, yeah that's true, but nobody's telling me to move out there and I don't think that would happen. It's too sunny! (laughs) There's no seasons! In the end, I need to be around certain trees and a certain type of landscape and that's what feeds me. I'm not going to move anywhere anytime soon. It's fun to take some time away from home and that's its own education, but I wouldn't move to LA.

Once again, it's a world only about filmmaking and business, and that is not what feeds the artistic mind, and I don't claim to be a great "artist," but I claim to need that nourishment that comes from hanging out with people, cooking and barbequing and drinking beverages and reading and being in nature that makes sense to you. Having the seasons. I can be courted by Hollywood, but they know I'll just be visiting and not coming out there for good.

Mike: What don't they get about New York? Because we've heard the phrase "those weird New York guys" about us!

Well, you appear not to be playing the game. And I have these two agents that I really like and I've always told them from the minute we started together that I was going to be confusing to them. And indeed, they do think and talk about movies in a certain way. It's a great collaboration because I just tease them and they tease me back, but the fact is we are thinking about these things differently. I really believe that

movies have a – it takes a year to make a movie. *The Last Winter* has taken me up to five years to live with that movie. It has to matter; it has to be about something. It's a struggle, you don't necessarily make good money doing it, certainly on the low budget stuff I've done. You're doing it for another reason, and it has to matter.

Don't get me wrong, we're just finishing up *I Sell the Dead* and that's a movie about grave robbing in the 18th century! This movie has no social message. I'm not talking about social messages; I want to make that clear. But then it's about vigorously being about entertainment. It's about one man's vision. Some crazy Irishman! It's not something I conceived of like, "How can I make money? Oh, I'll make a grave robbing film." No. It's about, "Let's follow this crazy dream and see where it leads us!" And it's all about the aesthetics. It's just a crazy aesthetic soup of crazy recollections and Irish storytelling and some funny actors. It's nothing but total entertainment.

But you walk away, and it hopefully feels fulfilling because you've seen something that's handmade. It feels like it's really been put together by a bunch of crazy people and that, in itself, is nourishment in this day and age, when everything is just market tested and market researched. I was going to say I had a great experience on my *Fear Itself* episode, but I swear to God, the last week, I've gotten so many fucking notes, just whittling away at anything that was unique about it. And now I'm just fucking tired of it! Just let it be what it is! I don't care what you expected it to be. I came in under budget, I came in on time. It's a wonderful performance by Doug Jones. Let the thing have some life! I don't care if it makes sense to every fucking viewer. Let it go!

I found the whole thing to be quite charming. It's almost like summer stock. They cycle these directors in, they each do a weird little episode and on it goes. It's kind of like Scareflix.

Adam: This was a pre-existing script for *Fear Itself*, right? How was directing a script from someone else?

That was fun. I did a lot of work on the script just to make it my own.

Adam: I don't know what it's about yet, but does it follow the themes of your previous movies?

If I told you what it's about, you'd laugh. It's a fucking Wendigo movie! Can you fucking believe it? They sent me the script and said, "There's only one weird thing, Larry. It's a Wendigo story." I was like "Fine. I'll be the go-to guy for that!" Talk about remaking *Habit*, I'll also remake *Wendigo*! Um, but it's a different take on it.

It's by Drew McWeeney and Scott Swan, who wrote for Carpenter and as you know, my episode was meant to be for John Carpenter. And it's funny, because back in November when they were first talking to me, they said, "Oh and John Carpenter's making a Wendigo movie." And I said, "Oh my God! Well, I have to be in it, because I'm your go-to Wendigo guy!" Little did I know I'd be actually directing it. It's totally unrelated to my own film, but it's a freaky story. I really liked the structure of the script and that's what I stuck with. There's a basic premise, which I tried to bring out that was already in there. I think it's cool; it's got a strong sense of location. I'd actually be curious to hear what you guys think and whether it does actually relate to my other films. I don't know what it is.

Adam: I know Doug Jones has some prosthetics in it, but it's rare we get to see his face like this.

Doug is fully performing in this. I think he's going to be very prominent as Abe Sapien in the new *Hellboy* because I know he demanded to use his own voice. He not only has no facial make-up, he's also naked in my film! (laughs) So, it's all Doug Jones, all the time. It's really beautiful and he's a great character. It's got all these macerations.

Adam: He's got this great Chaplin quality, and it comes out in all the creatures he does. I'd love to just see him be him, because I think he can still bring all his talents to that.

And he's oddly unique and specific in this, but I suppose one can start analyzing his different performances. His involvement alone makes it interesting. Even that, I had to pitch to the network. I had to beg them because they had no idea who he was. But he is unparalleled, he's awesome. I'm so honored to have worked with him, especially at this time where I think he's really blossoming into the limelight, because Abe Sapien is a huge element of the new *Hellboy*, and I think it would be a great time to be associated with Doug and I'm just so happy for him. Out of the blue, I'd never thought about casting him and I don't know where it came from, but I must say, and I rarely say this, it was one of my best ideas I've ever had. (laughs)

Rob: You said at the *Fangoria* convention that you're essentially just using all of Del Toro's cast now. (laughs)

Yeah! (laughs) Now, I just have to cast the chick!

Rob: It seems like you've got a lot of films in the works with Glass Eye Pix and Scareflix. It's nice to see a bevy of East Coast filmmakers making these types of films. What can we look forward to from your film company? What are you excited about?

Well, I'm very personally involved with *I Sell the Dead*, because we spent two and half years on it. I got Ron Perlman to be in it. My producer, Peter Phok, got Dominic Monaghan to be in it. It was a great shoot. I was in it, so I still do love acting. It was a great character, and I love the setting. I love writer/director Glenn McQuaid. It's a charming movie and unexpected in the marketplace. I have no idea how you guys will react or how anyone will react to it! It's such an odd bird. But to me, it's a cozy blanket. Who wouldn't want to watch this on a Sunday afternoon? So, there's that. And I'm excited about Graham Reznick's movie *I Can See You*, which is more out there but a true example of my insistence on supporting auteurs. Ti West, of course, has made an extremely eccentric movie called *House of the Devil*. It feels like it was made in another time.

Mike: Well, AJ Bowen's in it and we love that bastard!

Yeah, AJ Bowen is awesome in it. I know you guys have been a supporter of his.

Adam: That's the thing you were talking about before about the singularity of visions. There's no subtext in *The Roost*; it's a killer bat picture!

Yeah. But to me, the subtext (in *The Roost*) is the pacing. There's something incredibly subversive about Ti's pacing and he takes that to a whole other level.

Adam: But you are still seeing someone's singular vision. It's a popcorn picture, but it's not a generic popcorn picture.

Yeah, that's the point. Nobody likes a lecture. My movies happen to be a little sociopolitical but that's just my tick. The fact is what I find more interesting is unique filmmaking and unique artistry and that's what I'm interested in supporting. Then Jim McKenney's movie *Satan Hates You*, which is out of control. That movie's completely insane. We just filmed yesterday a scene with the Devil, and two incredible bosomy succubi and smoke machines. It's insanity! I'm in this one!

Mike: But do you survive?

(pause) No. (laughs)

Rob: Is it true that there's a video clip of all your on-screen deaths?

Yeah, yeah! We showed it at the Two Boots Pioneer Theater one year, and the only reason I haven't put it on YouTube is that one of them is from Ti's movie *Cabin Fever 2*, so we'd be sued by Lionsgate in a second! My beloved collaborators on *Fear Itself* and every other movie I've made! I did a movie with JT Petty. A twenty minute film…

Adam: Was that the short prequel to *The Burrowers*?

Exactly, and that's called *Blood Red Earth*. That'll be great. It's as cool as *The Burrowers* in my opinion. It's the same creature presence, but it's sort of in a Native American setting. It's really cool, very, very atmospheric. JT's awesome.

Adam: Did Lionsgate come to you asking you to produce these prequels for JT's movie as a backstory?

My old comrade Douglas Buck, who made *Sisters* and, of course, *Cutting Moments*, he hooked me up with JT. I think JT wanted a local film company to do his stuff. It was interesting because I had an association with JT's cinematographer Phil Parmet because he shot *Animal Factory*, a Steve Buscemi movie that I'm in. So, I knew Phil, who also shot *The Devil's Rejects*, and actually I tried to get Phil to shoot *Sisters*. So, I've always been a huge fan of Phil's. The idea is to have as big a community as possible; and Doug is up in Canada doing his stuff. He's got a new project he's working on and that's very exciting.

I'm mostly interested in community. I'm not talking about factory farming. I'm talking about little farms that produce the vegetables locally, and that's what kind of entertainment I'm interested in. Not just huge slaughterhouses and huge fields and fields of vegetables that have to be sprayed with pesticides in order to grow. I'm talking about little communities that are filled with like-minded people and everybody is like, "Hey, let's put on a show!" And then the idea, with DVD, you maybe can get distribution for those kinds of projects and just keep people on edge. You don't know what you're going to see when you watch an unknown little independent movie. You go to the multiplex, you know what you're going to see. You have no idea what your entertainment's going to be if it's been brewed in a local economy.

Rob: What's next for you in terms of writing and directing?

I'm going straight to Hollywood and selling out as fast as I can! (laughs) No, I do have a big Hollywood project that may

or may not happen. I keep withholding saying what it is, but one day I'll just spit it out to all of you guys because enough is enough. I was recently in Mexico writing, and I would like to go back there and make a really down and dirty western/horror/apocalyptic picture. That's something I would like to do. Then I have a beautiful non-horror picture I would love to do. Tom Waits and Ron Perlman as brothers.

Rob: Wow!

Ron wants to do it; I just have to talk to Tom about it! That would be the most beautiful thing. I finally get to make my musical! Ron Perlman as a lounge singer. It's awesome! Fuck horror, this movie will make you happy! And I don't make those kinds of movies often! But I love this script and I'm going to try to get that out there as soon as I can, I just need to give it a polish and get it to Waits!

TUESDAY KNIGHT

Interviewed by Rob Galluzzo (7/08)

We were fortunate to speak candidly with actress Tuesday Knight, who took over the role of Kristen Parker from Patricia Arquette in *A Nightmare on Elm Street 4: The Dream Master*! We asked Tuesday about her experiences facing off against Freddy Krueger in the Renny Harlin directed *Nightmare*. She also talked about returning for *New Nightmare*, the "almost-made" Madonna bio-pic, and what it was like appearing on *The X-Files*!

First and foremost, what are your earliest recollections of the horror genre? Do you remember the first films to really scare or have an impact on you? Left an impression on you when you were a kid?

The Exorcist! That freaked me out! I remember I had to sleep in my parent's room for a week after seeing it.

I still have trouble watching *The Exorcist* now as an adult!

Uh-huh! It freaked me out, and then I became friends with Linda Blair, and I still can't get it out of my head. (laughs)

Would you say you became a horror fan back then as a kid or did it take a little while for you to revisit the genre?

No. I'd say that *The Exorcist* scared me to death. I think when I first became a horror fan, honestly was when I saw the first *Nightmare on Elm Street*. That's when I started getting into watching them. After *Nightmare on Elm Street*, I wasn't into doing them per se, but I definitely became something of a horror film buff and I would look at a lot of those movies.

Let's go back to the beginning. Tell us a bit about the origins of your acting career? Because I know you did both music and acting, so which came first and was one outlet meant to nourish another, so to speak?

I started acting when I was younger, and I did a lot of funny shows like *Mod Squad* and *The Brady Bunch*. It seemed like a whole different world. But then once I got to be around eighteen, nineteen, I really got into music. Music was my thing. Oh, also, my dad (Baker Knight) was a musician and

a songwriter. So, as a kid I was always in our living room with Ricky Nelson and Frank Sinatra and performing for these people. It was just a really nice audience, and I had no idea who these people were. (laughs)

Well, that's quite an audience to have!

Well, I didn't really know them yet! They were just my dad's friends. Do you remember the band *The Rascals*? They were in there too. So, just from being young, I really got into singing, and then I think until I was about twenty-four, twenty-five, it was all about music. I did a record deal with CBS and another one with Epic, because the first one that I did, they didn't like the producer and I did. If it was me now, I would've said "Too bad, that's what you're getting, 'cause that's the me that I am! That's the music I do!" But that wasn't what I did. I was young, and they said, "Well, we want to make you more into this Cyndi Lauper, rock 'n' roll Madonna thing." So, they took me away from my producer and my band, so everyone hated me and then I did a second record.

But right when that second record had reached a little bit of success and one of the tunes was in the top five dance hits on the charts, I had the audition for *Nightmare on Elm Street 4*. I knew when I got that role, it was going to be between that role or going on a tour. And I thought, "There's no way I'm passing up Freddy Krueger!"

***Nightmare 4* was literally the peak of Freddy-mania. That was as popular as it got. Do you remember what your audition was like for the film?**

Oh totally!

And you were a fan of the series prior to your movie?

Oh, yeah. I remember they told me I was going in for Renny Harlin and that they were trying to replace Patricia Arquette. When I hear something like that, I either go the route of not trying to look like the actress at all and doing my own thing, or I go in quite like them. So, I went in a lot like her. I watched the prior movie and saw what she was doing, although I think I brought my acting to a more elevated state. (laughs) I mean, I love her! I thought she was good; I was just trying to maybe bring more color to it.

So, I went in like her and Renny basically hired me on the spot, which was really insane, because I'd never had that happen. It was literally my second job in film. The first one was *General Hospital*, but this was my first film, and I thought "Oh my God!" The second day (of auditions), we picked the other people to go alongside me, which was Lisa Wilcox and I picked Andras Jones. And Brooke Theiss. And Toy Newkirk.

He had me read with all of them, and he'd ask me, "Who do you think was good? Who do you feel you worked best with?" And so, I picked them. There was a girl who was really, really good who was also trying out for Alice, and … all I can say is damn. (laughs) This other actress was really good, and she looked like Andras, so it would've looked like they were brother and sister. But there was something about the hiddenness and the pretentiousness of Alice, something that Lisa had that was a little more shallow; you know how Alice is just a little more introverted with her own things going on? Her dreams and her imagination? She comes off as reserved, non-social.

It seems you didn't have any intimidation of taking over the role of Kristen Parker from Patricia Arquette? Considering how fast they made *Nightmare 4*, once you got started, did you try to mimic what Patricia had done before, or did you not even have time to think about that and just played Kristen your own way?

Well, in the beginning I was looking at her and watching what she had done, and I was watching for what she brought to the character. But from then on, I just dropped it and brought myself to the character. That's what I do when I work anyways. Back then, I was new, and it was ok for my agent to say, "I want you to go in and just be like Patricia Arquette so they'll hire you!"

But Renny really wasn't like that. He wanted someone that looked like her but would also do something different from her. Maybe be a little bit more stronger, bigger, or just different. So, once I showed him the way I was going with it, he let me go. And Patricia Arquette, I ran into her at a Blockbuster once and she came up to me and told me what a good job I did!

Oh wow! I always wondered what she thought of your take on the character!

Yeah, that was really cool.

I know that *Nightmare 4* was locked down to a set release date in August of '88. Was it a fairly fast production?

It was, but it was such a heaven-sent thing for me, because when I was done shooting, I said to Renny, "I'm a song writer. And if you give me a day, I'll write something for this movie." And what I did actually ended up being the title song. (laughs) It was really fun! I went to the studio with my partner. We literally spent three hours on the song, came out, drove it over to the office and Renny came down with Rachel Talalay, and he said, "Ok, play it for me." So, I opened the car doors and blasted it, and he said he loved it, freaked out and took the tape. And I really didn't know where the song was going to go in the movie, so when I sat down at the premiere and saw that it was the title song, I was stoked!

That's awesome! To have your first big gig be a *Nightmare* film and then to be doing music, and have your song be the opening track to the film, that's just so cool!

The only bad thing about it was that they really screwed me. They didn't put my song on the album! They did not put me on there because it would cost them more money, and they knew I was sort of new to it, so they basically just took the song. I just now got a copy of it, if people go to my fansite, I can send it to them, because I've never really had it myself! That was crazy. That was really not cool. I obviously didn't know what I was doing at that point, and they fooled me with some sort of contract that made it so that they didn't have pay me anything for it.

Wow. Well, you have to take some consolation that at least it's there in that movie forever.

At least it's there in that movie forever. You're right. It was in God's hands and that's how it was supposed to be. So, I just take that as an amazing blessing. I thought it was awesome.

I spoke to Ken Sagoes about a year ago for *Icons…*

Oh, I love Kenny!

I know on *Nightmare 3*, a lot of those kids got preliminary time just to hang out and get to know each other. Did you guys have anything like that on *Nightmare 4* where you got to know the rest of the cast before shooting?

No. We really didn't get a chance like that. It was set over in Simi Valley, so we'd meet over there to do our scenes. There wasn't that advantage. And usually there is something like that like if you're going out of state to shoot something.

Well, 'cause you're all stuck together in the same hotel!

Yeah, but we didn't get anything like that on *Nightmare 4*.

What about Andras Jones, who played your boyfriend Rick? How'd you guys prepare for your cinematic relationship together?

Well, you know, we started going out for real, so that kind of played its own part into the life of it.

You guys dated during the movie?

Yeah, while we were shooting it. Uh-hm. (laughs)

***Nightmare 4* was shooting just as a writers' strike had begun and I know there were various changes and multiple drafts of the script. Was this challenging for you and the actors? Do you remember any radical changes?**

No, not really. Everything from the original script was kept. The radicalness might have been more on how to shoot it and what to do with it. I think for the actors, it was script changes that were pretty much relative. There were a few action things that were tough on me, because I got hurt on the film several times and no one seemed to care about it! (laughs) Either the stunt person wasn't there or whatever it was, there were a few times where, I really hurt my eye on one scene. And I'm on this catwalk for another scene, I did this thing and hurt my leg. By the end of it, I was just so exhausted, because at the time I was working on *General Hospital*. Two jobs, which was not too bright! But when you're that age, you think, "Well, I have two jobs! I'll just never sleep!" (laughs) Then you get sick! So, I was passing out a lot. The last part of the shoot was very hard for me.

I wanted to talk a little bit about working with director Renny Harlin? Because this was so early in his career, and he obviously went on to direct several high profile movies after *Nightmare 4*.

It was only his second feature because he had done *Prison* before *Nightmare 4*.

Right, *Prison* was his first film. The stories on the DVD about him and Bob Shaye not seeing eye to eye in the beginning of *Nightmare 4* are pretty hilarious. I was wondering if you had any stories you can share about your experiences working with Renny Harlin?

Renny and I worked together amazingly. We really got along great! Everyone thought Renny and I were sleeping together the entire movie. (laughs) And I found that out later. But I was like, nope, one guy and it wasn't even happening there. But Renny was overprotective, and I think a lot of people didn't like that. I got along great with all the guys, because I'm a tomboy and I was friendly and open. And Lisa (Wilcox) was not like that. We couldn't get her to come talk to any of us. Um, Renny didn't really care for her that much. Renny was very professional, very creative and really had some cool ideas for Freddy. It was so neat to see these different ways that he was having us do things, because he was trying to make a film here that we wanted to make be the most successful *Nightmare*, which is what it became! He really put some cinema into it. Just something that was not in the other ones. Especially *Nightmare 2*, which I didn't like very much. He really added a lot to this one, and I think he was really patient with everybody.

I have a funny story about Renny. We were getting ready to do this scene on the beach. So, I was going to wear that little Hawaiian bathing suit. Renny was like, "We've prepared your wardrobe for you, so once you get it on, we'll double check it and get ready!" So, I said, "Yeah, no problem." I go in there, and literally, this bathing suit was about as big as a band-aid! It was like one string of that Hawaiian suit. So, I come out and I'm like, "Um, Renny? Are you kidding me? I can't walk out like this!" And he goes (in Finish accent), "Oh Tuesday. Oh Tuesday. It looks so wonderful with your buttocks! It looks so real, it's lovely and everyone will love it! It looks great!" (laughs) And I said, "You are crazy! You better sew me on a little skirt, right now!"

This lady had to come in and sew that little skirt on! That was one thing. And he also did it with one of my other costumes, this night shirt? It's the part where I'm sitting on the window of my house lighting a cigarette, while trying to stay awake. If you look in the scene, the shot only goes up to my waist, so it looks really good in that shot. But then he wanted me to wear it while I was running, and while I was running the thing was blowing up to my chin! "I can't do this!" (laughs) It was really funny, and he was such a funny guy. I had a blast with him!

Again, going back to the peak of Freddy-mania, I remember hearing a story from Howard Berger from the FX team about the beach scene. I believe he said by the second day of the beach scene shoot, word had got out they were shooting a new *Nightmare* movie in that spot and hundreds of fans showed up and surrounded Robert Englund's trailer hoping to get a glimpse of him as Freddy. Do you remember any of that from the beach day?

Yeah, I was in the trailer when it happened! It was insane! I was talking to Robert at the time, and I said, "This is so frightening." But he was like, "This is just what happens, the fans love Freddy." Their love for him was almost tipping the trailer over! (laughs) I was saying, "I know that they love you, but could you tell them not to tip over the trailer?" (laughs) So, he'd open up the top, the skylight and would say, "Hey guys, be cool! Don't tip us over!" I mean, I'd go in there and talk to Robert about the TV series, *Freddy's Nightmares*.

Yeah, it took hours to get that make-up on, so I figured he'd have plenty of time to chat then.

Oh yeah! I had make-up on too. We were doing the beach scene, and they had this one scene, I can't remember why? But they had a prosthetic of my chest where I had boobs with no nipples on them! To this day, I wonder, was this for Renny's home? I don't know what it was for. They ended up just taking it off me and doing whatever scene it was for a different way. It was just so weird that he wanted me to sit up with boobs with no nipples!

I don't know, maybe it was a wacky nightmare idea or something?

Exactly! I think it was one of those ideas where it was like, "Ok, we won't do that." (laughs)

You played "Elm Street's last brat" and you have a fairly memorable death scene in the first half of *Nightmare 4*. What do you remember about shooting that boiler scene?

I know I got really hurt in that scene, I'll tell you. You know the scene where I'm at the table with my mother and she'd given me sleeping pills. Which by the way, Brooke Bundy who played my mother was great and such an amazing actress. I love her and we became good friends. Um, ok, so I fall through, and I end up on the ceiling?

Ok, obviously you know that was shot on the floor with slates going up on the wall. I had to climb over those at least seven times. I swear, the whole insides of my thighs and my legs were black and blue! It was crazy! Then I had to

come down and fight with Freddy! That, however, was just so amazing and so surreal for me. It was a dream come true! I had my convictions, I knew what I was doing there, and I knew what I wanted out of it, but working with Robert (as Freddy), it was just… really heavy!

Robert as a person is just so amazing, and so full of character. But when he gets on that outfit, it scares you! Even though I know it's Robert underneath there! He gets into it and he's so funny. The way he does Freddy is so brilliant. I mean, Freddy is funny! (laughs) Freddy has a really good sense of humor! So, he was just walking around me in that Freddy way, and we started doing the scene and it got really heavy. We had this face-off, and it was just awesome. I had a great time. Robert and I get along so, so well.

It's so funny, you meet Robert and he's just such a nice guy that it's hard to imagine him as that terrible character!

Oh, I know! And what's kind of a drag, unless you're working with him, you don't get to speak to him a lot because he's so bombarded with fans! And some of the conventions we've done together, it's kind of hard because he's always surrounded! A few years after *Nightmare 4*, about three years later, he was working on another project and I saw him there and we started talking and he said, "You know something, when I went to Japan and did my little Freddy tour, people were more excited to see you!" (laughs) I said, "What?!" He goes, "Yeah. Here I am, the one there, and all these pictures up on the wall are of you!" How ironic is that? That really made my day. And it's funny, because now in my present life, my jewelry is really big in Japan.

You're huge in Japan! I love it!

They like blondes! Or anyone that looks like Madonna! (laughs)

Correct me if I'm wrong, but I thought I read somewhere that you were once going to take part in a Madonna bio movie, which I thought was a fantastic idea, because even back from *Nightmare 4* I thought you had a striking resemblance to her.

Actually, what happened; the real story. I did a movie called *Mistress* about four years later with Robert DeNiro and Christopher Walken. It was this great ensemble, and I was this new kid on the block. It was just amazing to be able to work with all the people on that, who were all so nice and so wonderful to me. What happened was we had had the premiere for *Mistress*, and a group of people were hovering around me after the show and they said Madonna had sent them from Maverick. They were calling her Mo, which was her nickname then. I had no idea what that was! "Who's that?" (laughs) "Um, Madonna?" "Oh, OK, I've heard of her!" (laughs) And so, through the beginning of my acting career, I really struggled because I'd always hear, "No, she's great. We really love her. But she just looks too much like Madonna."

So, here they said, "We came out to look at you. And Madonna's going to freak out when she sees you." Basically, they were scouting me to play her, and after that night, the company hired me to play her. So, we did get together and we did start, and did some stuff together. I got to do some of the tunes, which was really great. And then, they decided it just wasn't time to do a bio film, because she was only probably in her early thirties at that time? So, to do her life story up until that point, it would've ended her story at thirty-five when there was so much more she was going to do, you know what I mean? So, they decided to do it in another ten or so years or whatever it was. Regardless, it was great. I was happy anyway to be involved in it. Because let me tell you, Fox offered me the role of Madonna in their portrayal of her story, and I passed because there's no way I'm going to do something without Madonna's ok and without her there sitting next to me. She was great though.

I actually have a funny story about first meeting her. I went to Warner Brothers one day to audition for a movie called *Desperately Seeking Susan*. And it was her part. So, it was funny, she walked in, and I was walking behind her, and my assistant goes, "That's Madonna." And I went, "Oh God. We're dressed alike!" And my assistant said, "Yeah, you guys look alike!" So, I thought, "Oh no." So, she walks in and then I came in. She saw me and started making these lewd masturbatory moves to me, as if they were supposed to scare me or freak me out or something. Well, I did them back to her. And she just thought it was funny and really cool. Later on, when I told her that that was me, she was blown away. Because she remembered it, but as a whole other girl. She said something like, "Wow, fucking you would be like fucking myself." And I go, "Yeah… but better." (laughs) She's really so sweet and has a huge heart, but the thing with her and even someone like DeNiro, people are just so afraid to go up to them just to say hi.

You did later end up working with Madonna for her recent video *4 Minutes* and her tour, right?

Oh, with the jewelry? Yeah. There was always some kind of connection back to her. Luckily. And it's always really a joy and exciting to do something with her.

Well, sure, it's Madonna! I can only imagine what this must've been like, but, what was it like to see *Nightmare on Elm Street 4* for the first time on the big screen?

It was so amazing, I just couldn't believe it. I just remember running down the stairs after I got the part, sobbing and saying to myself, "I can't believe I got the part!" So, when I sat down and they started the New Line logo, and then my song started, I was so thrilled. It was crazy and I was on cloud 9 for the entire movie. It was so surreal. There I was, and what was so cool was that at the end of my song, it goes right into the *Nightmare* music!

Like they mixed it right into the last note! I thought that was so cool! I felt like I'd finally made it. It was really awesome! And when I started getting calls from people telling me my song wasn't on the album, I got to say, I didn't take any action against it, because it was like you said before, this is the way it turned out. I have to watch out because most times I'm overly giving. And I really need to stand up more when I think something is wrong.

But with that one, I just felt blessed to be in it, and to have the title song was a dream come true. The whole thing was amazing! So many things came out of that experience. I have to say, Lisa Wilcox was not one of them in the beginning at all. Our relationship was a whole other thing. That was something very different from the very beginning when I met her. The other people I remain good friends with, Kenny, Toy, Rodney.

I had such a good time talking with Ken (Sagoes) for *Icons* last year. I mean, I grew up on the *Nightmare* films, so for me, it's such a treat for me to talk to you guys!

Ken said in one magazine that he liked working with both of us, Patricia and I, but that I filled her shoes fine and that there was nothing lost, there was more gained, and that he really got to know me better. And so that was cool. Of course, Rodney (Eastman) hated me on the film! (laughs) I tell him that now, and he goes, "I did not! I did not! I loved you!" And I'd say, "You did not, you hated me because I wasn't Patricia!" Because he and Patricia had a love affair on the set of *Nightmare 3*. So, when I came in, he was like "Ok, that's not her!" So, I tease him about it now giving me such a hard time then. But he's really cute.

You got to come back and do a bit part in *New Nightmare*!

Yeah, boy was that shocking! Wes, I can't believe what he said about me in the commentary! It was so sweet. Our meeting was so brief before and I knew he liked my performance. I think he thought *Nightmare 4* was the next best one to the one he did. But for *New Nightmare*, he picked me out for that scene, he didn't ask anyone else (from *Nightmare 4*) to come back! And I couldn't believe it!

It's a cool scene because you get to see some characters from the first movie there too!

But I was looking for Andras or even Kenny or Rodney! They were the *Nightmare* guys, those two!

I told Ken this, I like *Nightmare 4*, but I pretend the first twenty minutes never happened because as a kid, I was just so upset that they killed him off.

I am too! I am too. I hated that he died in the movie. Those guys (Kincaid and Joey) should've gone on longer.

What do you remember about shooting *New Nightmare* and reuniting with people you worked with on *4*?

Well, it was weird for me because I was united with people I didn't work with. I didn't know the people from the other films. But Heather (Langenkamp) and I got along immediately. We were hanging out a bit and she was so, so great. I was waiting to see other people from my film, but there was no one there, and I didn't understand why. I found out later when I listened to the commentary, Wes says, "Tuesday Knight. What a great actress. And what a trooper. I had to have her back." That is so strange to me! Because we only met a few times, and it was always really great when we met, but I had no idea.

How much involvement did Wes Craven have in the fouth film when you did it, because at that point, I thought he was just a producer on the series and just kind of overseeing it?

None. Nope. I had just met him at a function for New Line and then he came to see *Nightmare 4*. But I was very shocked, and I felt really honored on *New Nightmare*. Andras is always teasing me about it. "Oh, nobody else got a call! But Tuesday did, because everybody likes Tuesday!" (laughs)

Well, I'm so glad you were kind enough to open up with us, Tuesday. I mean, I grew up on the *Nightmare* films, and while I love horror films, I'm just an avid fan of all kinds of films.

Like me! I love every genre of movies too.

I love all movies. But I have a special place in my heart for the horror genre because it was a very important part of my upbringing. It was something that was always there for me.

I love it too! Have you seen a movie called *Dead Silence*?

Yeah, of course! James Wan directed that one!

It's awesome! Oh my God, I love it. Heather (Langenkamp) did an effect on it.

Oh, that's right, because her husband is David LeRoy Anderson, the FX guy!

That movie, I had no idea with that ending! It fooled me completely! And also, that woman, Mary Shaw? She scared the shit out of me! I can't even watch the menu of the DVD! Have you seen *The Gravedancers*?

Yeah, of course! Mike Mendez directed that one!

Oh my God, I love that one too! Those directors are doing great movies. *Gravedancers*? That smiley face?! And in *Dead Silence*, I cannot take it when Mary Shaw is on the stage! And the little kid finds the puppet under his seat?

Let's talk about *X-Files* because you did an episode. I love *X-Files*, but I honestly only consistently watched the first four seasons and then after that, I'd catch random episodes. So, you were in "Trevor", which was a Season Six episode. What was that experience like? I hear David Duchovny is a prankster on set? Is that true?

Uh, he is, and he is wonderful. But the woman is a nightmare!

Gillian Anderson?

Yes. She was the nastiest woman I've ever worked with on anything. I almost walked off, and the reason I didn't was because of David, because he was such a doll. And of course, the money. They were giving me good money to do it. Gillian was like, "Oh, you're the guest star this week? I don't sit with guest stars. No, I'll only talk to children guest stars." I mean, unbelievable. I'm in a scene with her, and we're walking out the door and it was really cold where we were. So, I just say, "God, it's really quite chilly." And she looks at me and goes, "I have no idea what you think is chilly or what you're talking about. Or any concept of you." And I just looked at her, nodded and said, "…Great. Ok."

Rob Bowman directed your episode, and he directed the first movie, right?

Yeah, Rob Bowman was very informative, and he really knew what was going on. I thought it was very strange that during our scenes, our takes, Gillian was never getting directed. Ever. I thought that was weird, because Rob would go up to David and talk to him, give him direction. I was wondering what was going on. It turned out, Rob doesn't direct Gillian anymore because she's too difficult. She has to be on the show because it's her show and people love her. But at that point, she just was doing everything the way she wanted to. That was fine with David because he basically just works off of what she would do. David and I were having a really fun time though, because the woman who's house we were shooting at? She had baby pigs. (laughs) We loved them! But every time we'd go to see the baby pigs and turn the lights on, they'd start squealing because they were afraid of the lights! We'd say, "We're not going to hurt you! We love you!" (laughs) There was another time we were all sitting there together, and Gillian literally had her assistant move her chair away from me and David and the other guest stars.

Well, that's Hollywood for you! Or… Vancouver.

It totally is. She was very much like; she had an army sergeant thing going on. She was chain smoking cigarettes. And pacing a lot and everybody was afraid to go up to her except for the little boy! The episode was called "Trevor" and the kid who played Trevor, she loved him. They were holding hands and singing songs, but she didn't like any of the other people! (laughs) It was weird, and it's hard when that happens. I think, as an actor, I have worked with lots of big actors. I've had the good fortune to be in ensemble pieces with great actors. I got to do Billy Bob Thorton's movie, *Daddy and Them*, which was packed with great people.

And I always go in there thinking, "*I'm so lucky to be here.*" It's really disheartening when the person you're working with or that you know and really enjoy watching just turns out to be a nasty person. It really ruins it for me, I have a problem with that. People that I've met that just treat other people poorly. There's no excuse for it. There's no excuse to treat anyone badly on a shoot. A carpenter is no less important than an actor. Everyone's doing hard work. Oh my God, they do so much! On *Mistress*, at lunch, I'd get in trouble because I didn't want to go get food before the extras! They make us go up in front of people that are waiting to eat, and it isn't cool. It always just hurts me when people don't treat other people nicely. I don't like that.

In closing, in retrospect, how do you look back on your experience doing *Nightmare on Elm Street 4: The Dream Master* and being a part of that legacy? How has it affected you personally, especially now looking back on it?

Well, looking back on the film and doing it was really pleasant. It was great and I have some really great memories. There were some difficult times, but I wouldn't change it for the world. I mean, what a great, great opportunity! I still think it's one of the greatest things I've ever done, and it is. All in all, it was a really wonderful experience, and I felt so lucky and thrilled to death to do it. I'm really grateful and glad to have been part of it.

JEREMY KASTEN

Interviewed by Rob Galluzzo (8/08)

Icons recently spoke with director Jeremy Kasten about his film *The Wizard of Gore,* which is based on the 1970 cult classic Herschell Gordon Lewis original of the same name. Jeremy's update boasts an impressive cast lead by Crispin Glover, Kip Pardue, Bijou Phillips, Joshua Miller, Brad Dourif, and Jeffrey Combs. On the basis of the film's beautifully bloody opening five-minute scene, which plays out to Black Heart Procession's "The Old Kind of Summer," we knew immediately that we had to talk to Jeremy.

What are your earliest recollections of the horror genre? What do you remember as a kid being the first thing to open you up to the genre?

I was really young. When I was four, I saw the 1923 Lon Chaney version of *Phantom of the Opera* and it fucked me up! Because I wasn't old enough to make the distinction between black and white and color or silent film and sound, it just was a scary movie! And it got under my skin and gave me nightmares and fucked me up! And about six months later, I was attacked by a dog and had my face virtually torn off, I almost died...

Oh my God!

It was a horrible, horrible incident. And in my mind, that weird part of you that can already relate to the monster? It already existed for me. *Phantom* had that sympathetic *Beauty and the Beast* element to it. He was in love with the girl, but he was too ugly. And all I thought was, *"Now I'm the monster."* I remember waking up in the hospital and seeing my reflection for the first time. My face was covered in stitches. I had 550 stitches in my face. Just seeing my reflection two days after I turned five, I was eaten by this dog! And something in my mind just snapped where I thought, "I'm the monster. I'm going to be that scheming monster in the basement!"

No wonder you make horror movies now!

Right?!

That's quite a traumatic thing to go through, especially at that age. Because of that event, did you become a fan of the genre and continue to relate to the monster? Things like *Frankenstein* and the Universal monsters?

Absolutely. There's that, and also, growing up in the 70's, horror was really, in the same way it was in the 50's, it was everywhere and in a very acceptable kind of way. It didn't strike me as a kid as being movies for weirdos or geeks or whatever. It was just movies for young people. Young people saw horror movies. That's what it was in the 70's! And so, I remember being, as I think we all were, fascinated by the films I couldn't see as much as the films I could. Sneaking in to see *Alien* in seventh grade, I remember thinking, "I can't believe I'm seeing this movie." That movie messed with my head! Even the movie poster to *Alien*, remember that?

Oh yeah, the hovering egg!

Just the way it looked, and the font, and the way the title treatment was laid out with all the space between the letters! And the tagline, "In space, no one can hear you scream." Just looking at that poster in those days scared me! They don't make horror movies like that anymore where you really don't know who's going to live and who's going to die. That's what's extraordinary about that movie. Forty-five minutes into that movie, you still have no idea who the protagonist is. That's amazing.

That'd be difficult to pull off now.

They wouldn't let you! They absolutely would not let you.

It's so funny, you just mentioned the poster to *Alien* and the impact it had on you. When I was a kid, I used to frequent the "mom & pop" video stores and just be so fascinated by the covers of all the horror VHS titles! I'd stare at them and just imagine what the movie was like.

Same. Think about this… that's gone! And here's how to make a million dollars tomorrow. I love Netflix. And as much as I love Netflix, that experience that we had either looking in the newspaper for what was playing at the drive-in, or the sense of walking through the video store and looking at the shelves, that's gone, man! When I go to Netflix, I'm usually going off of a list of things people have recommended to me. I'm typing stuff in. But somebody has to invent whatever that is, that sense of discovery for online browsing.

What was the point that you developed your interest in the way films were made? What was it for you?

I had a best friend in the first grade whose parents had a Super 8 camera. Now, any kid can use a video camera or iMovie, all those tools are everywhere. But back then, it was more like being a ham radio enthusiast in 1975. I finally thought, "Whoa! The film, I physically understand. Once you get back the cartridge that you'd have to develop through your drug store, you'd get it a week la*ter, and you'd have film.*" That physical manipulation of it, I loved. I loved to draw and I loved to act and I did a lot of theater growing up. I'd also make music, but the way that film brought that all together, the way you could draw on film to make a monster, or if you could time the tape recorder just right when you would start the projector, you could add sound and music. All of that coming together in a really kind of basic rudimentary way was appealing to me. So, I started making movies really young and I'm sure part of it was the make-up effects and making monsters and doing stop-motion, but I think psychologically I always had nightmares growing up.

And there was something in me about putting them on film, to try and show the weirdness of it? Before I did drugs (laughs), showing the psychedelic experience that nightmares are. That was really appealing to me, and I made some weird films! Not like "art" films, but just trying to show what it was like to have dreams where you go into the back of your closet, and it'd be a tunnel that led into something. I'm sure it's because of *Phantom of the Opera*!

Let's talk about *Wizard of Gore*. How'd you get involved with that film? Because I remember hearing about *Wizard of Gore* shortly after *2001 Maniacs*, and both are remakes of Herschell Gordon Lewis movies.

Well, it's funny, you talked before about the VHS art and going to the video store. We had that "mom & pop" video shop in my town too, and there was a time when my mom had to go in and tell them, "He walks like… two miles to get here. He has permission. Let him rent whatever. Stop making me come in." (laughs) At the time, those shelves had like forty horror movies and a dozen Herschell Gordon Lewis movies. It seemed like everything of his came out all at once! I didn't make the distinction at all about what these movies were as opposed to *The Thing*. They were just other horror movies. I also knew, because I'm from Baltimore, the John Waters connection to Herschell. So, I understood the kitsch factor of John Waters, but I also thought, "This is important! It influenced John Waters!" So, I always thought, even since I was a kid it'd be really cool to redo Herschell's movies. And in fact, I would've loved to have done what Tim Sullivan did with *2001 Maniacs*. Not in the same exact way, but the story of the Southerners getting revenge.

So, you were always a fan of Herschell Gordon Lewis?

Grew up with his movies, loved his movies. And talked for a long time about doing different takes on a lot of his movies. I wanted to do five remakes of his movies! *The Attic Expeditions* was such a hard experience that we started thinking about how we could make a movie where the money would come together more easily, and the remakes seemed like a good idea. This is way before the rash of remakes. And doing a remake of a movie that I don't think anybody would get fussy about. It's not like it's *Psycho*. I don't know why they remake certain movies. Ok, *Amityville Horror*? Fine. It's not a very good movie. It could be better. But *Texas Chainsaw*? Why? But with Herschell's movies, and Herschell will be the first to admit this and he has, *Wizard* deserved to be revisited. All of his movies have such a great germ of an idea that's unexplored in some ways.

Wizard of Gore the most, because it's so fucking strange! It doesn't ever really make sense! So, we talked about doing a bunch of remakes, and Zach Chassler, the screenwriter and I were already working on a couple of other projects together, and he came to us with two pitches, one of which was this post-punk neo-noir downtown LA loft district take on it with the magician in a kind of Iggy Pop mode. Like that nasty icky David Blaine kind-of really cocky magician, which was great. And the other take he had was this Vegas, over-the-top homage to Siegfried and Roy illusionist kind of thing. And we went with the punk-rock version. And ironically when Crispin Glover came on board, he sort of brought back all that Siegfried and Roy stuff without even knowing that he was taking the two ideas and glomming them together. So, that's how it happened. Zach pitched us the idea, and we loved it. It made sense!

And it did everything I wanted it to do, which was take Herschell's movie, keep the germ of the idea and go someplace really different with it and be very contemporary about it. And it's my goal to try to make horror movies that have a regard for them as cinema and high art. I don't mean to sound pretentious! I spend a lot of time with dear friends lamenting about when you could make a movie like *Don't Look Now*. And that was a genre picture then!

That movie still scares the shit out of me.

It's a perfect film, perfect film.

That's not pretentious to say! I mean, look at how horror films are regarded in places like Spain. It's a well-respected genre elsewhere!

That's why movies like *The Orphanage* are not coming out of America. That's why the smart shit isn't ours at the moment. Nobody with the money, nobody with the real "studio" money wants to think about genre pictures in those terms.

Let's talk about casting Crispin Glover in the movie, because you hear *Wizard of Gore*, you think, "Ok, they're remaking that." Then you hear it's Crispin playing the lead and immediately you have to see it! How'd he come on board? Was he a fan of Herschell's films?

We went to him. We offered him the role; we sent him the script. He was one of the first people we went to, because it was a lynchpin to the project kind of casting. And Crispin read it and then watched the original and called me and wanted to talk about it. His thing was he felt the movie was very different from the original, but it was important for him to have the mind-fuck element from the original, which was strangely completely at odds with what I wanted to do, which was make a complicated mind-fuck movie where you absolutely know what happened at the end.

Because I had gotten so much shit for *The Attic Expeditions*, I want to make mind-fuck movies, but I don't want to make movies that piss people off. It's a hard line to walk. I understand *Jacob's Ladder*, but it seems like a lot of people get very angry when they watch *Jacob's Ladder*, so I have to account for the fact that I don't mind it, but some people do. That was one of the hardest things to balance. Crispin's desire to make the movie Crispin-ish and my desire to make the movie satisfying. That's not to say he couldn't have made it a satisfying movie, but I had to balance that.

Well, Crispin has a very different kind of sensibility if you've seen his movies like *What Is It?* But regardless, great casting and I'm glad Crispin is in it. But dude, fucking Joshua Miller! I was so pleasantly surprised to see him in this movie! I love *Near Dark* and *River's Edge*. How'd he get involved?

Joshua came in and auditioned, which is amazing, right? I have no idea how that happened because I don't think that he's out there auditioning for much. I think that Erin Griffin, the casting director probably thought of him, called and asked if he was available, and Joshua was willing and able to come in and read. And I was floored! I mean, dude, his dad's Jason Miller! Plus, he's directed a feature of his own. He's written a novel. He's a really dialed in, smart guy. And also, kind of Hollywood royalty in the way that interests me, you know what I mean?

I'm still blown away by how good he was in *Near Dark*.

Unreal, right? To answer your question, he came in and auditioned. I had seen more people for that role, and he was the last person at the end of five days after reading people for that role. I had seen so many people and really knew that I wanted something different, but I didn't know what. I tried everybody that was a "character" and then Josh came in and he's not any of those things, he's just Josh. But that's what makes him so interesting. Him and Zach Chassler, the writer, hung out a bunch. So that he could spend time with Zach and Zach's got a laconic New Yorker quality to him that I think Josh picked up on.

What about Kip Pardue? Is the tattoo on his neck real?

No! That's so funny! Herschell called me after he watched the movie and that was his only question.

His only thought was, "What's up with the neck tattoo?"

It was like my dad being like, "All your friends have tattoos?" and being confused by that! No, it was make-up. We applied that to Kip every day. Kip was Erin's suggestion as well. I'd never seen much of his stuff. He's pretty and a good actor, but there was initially nothing about him that made me think, "Oh I have to work with Kip Pardue." But then I went out to dinner with him and he's an incredibly intelligent, really, really interesting guy. And he's got a darkness to him.

Sometimes you meet people, and you can just see their soul a little bit. Look, I'm a director going out to dinner with an actor. He'd read the script. He knows what I'm about, I know what he's about. I'm sure he wanted me to know that about him somehow. That he had something interesting and dark. He understood the movie in a way that very few people would have, and that really appealed to me. Nobody sees this kind of character, it's a hard thing to do. Someone who wears vintage suits all the time!

I love that about your movie though. Yes, it takes place now, it's very contemporary, but there's something very vintage feeling about it. It feels very noir. Was that a conscious thing for you?

Yes. Absolutely. LA is where noir is so grounded and born in so many ways, and I think there's such a deep tie with downtown being the link. I was inspired by people moving back to downtown Los Angeles, and the tie between the noir of the 40's and the post-punk world of now with people taking back the city. I wish I could say something very flowery about the political climate then and now and how there's a parallel, I'm not sure that's so, but there's definitely something to be said for people taking this city back and how weird that is. How weird to a city that was once so vibrant with department stores, and now these department stores have sat abandoned for seventy-five years, up until recently when they started becoming lofts or places where people would put on punk rock shows. That's what downtown was about for a long time.

What about Bijou Phillips? She's got a genre history with _Hostel: Part II_ and she did _It's Alive_.

Bijou is definitely a lot to maintain on a set, but what you get in exchange for that is that when you're rolling, she is so there and so present as an actor. Look, making movies is hard work and it's hard for everybody. I don't pretend to understand how actors' brains work. I try! And I care deeply about their process. There are moments when people ask you things on a set like, "Why do I go over here?" But that's my job! My job is to answer those questions. And answering, "Because I said so," isn't a good enough answer to get someone to commit to that performance. So, for people on the set, the DP, the other actors, the Suicide Girls, it looks exhausting. Because everyone's standing around while you're explaining to Bijou why you want her to put her purse there and walk over there. Because you already shot the other part of the scene two days before. I don't mind, even if it's exhausting because it's my job. A harder thing though, and I'm just being perfectly honest here, is that I never really knew if she or Crispin had read the script. I know that Crispin never read anything other than his words. There were things that Crispin couldn't know about what was happening in the movie!

(SPOILER) He was very clear that he couldn't be the person who wasn't pulling the strings. There was a whole lot more where Jeffrey Combs and Crispin shared the stage, and Jeffrey would wheel things out for Crispin and turn things on and be the assistant to the magician. Crispin couldn't do that. Crispin did not want to share that space, which I understand now seeing the movie. It's not an ego thing. It's a Crispin thing, a movie thing, and a good instinct. But, there was a lot of stuff where Crispin explained the movie at the end a little bit more, and that all had to be written out. There was a scene where Kip goes backstage and finds Crispin held together by braces and he's huffing on the tetro, and he can barely move and he's falling apart. And you realize he's an addict to the tetro and somebody else is behind it, and Crispin is trying to get himself together to do his show. At that moment, there was this "sympathetic monster" thing that really appealed to me. All this interesting stuff, and it also made the movie make a lot more sense. Crispin could not do that scene.

So, a lot of stuff got written out that he couldn't do that would've maybe grounded the film a little bit more. When he'd ask questions about things, I'd have to be really careful not to say, "because the geek is in charge" or "because you're being manipulated," because he would short circuit. He had to be in charge! It's not that I was lying to him, he just didn't want to know. He was sort of saying "I'm giving you the tools for directing me, but don't tell me what's behind the curtain, because I can't perform that way." So, it made it difficult to direct him. **(END SPOILER)**

Similar with Bijou, I don't think she understood that her character was a whore! Because… I'd start to say it and she'd get her back up. Well, because Bijou doesn't want to do those kinds of roles anymore! You're making a genre movie, no matter how big it may feel to the fans, it's a tiny movie. There's not enough money, nobody's fed. Nobody's making their rate, you're begging people to do you favors, all that! It took me years to get the movie made! While you're making the movie, it all feels like this precarious balance like it could all shut down and go away at any moment! Bijou could freak out, walk off the set and suddenly your movie would just stop! And yeah, you can sue them or something, but the movie's over! It just ends. So, you constantly have to keep things in line. That was hard for me, that level of vague manipulation where she'd say, "Well, how do we know each other?" And I'd have to say, "Well, you know, you knew each other because you were… his sex partner… but in a way… kind of like… a prostitute… a little bit!" And she'd be like, "But I'm not a prostitute! I'll tell you right now, Maggie is not a prostitute." And I'd go "Ohhh, ok."

She had to be able to put it all together when she's getting punched and abused by Kip's character!

Here's the funny part about that. If you watch that scene, and I don't mean to blow it for you, but that's not Bijou! She answers the door, and then she swaps out. By that point, her and Kip could barely be in the room together. To be perfectly honest, they did not get along. So, I didn't even want to put them in that situation! It's one shot, she answers the door, and then she's done. Then, the double comes in and gets beat up. So, until she went to the premiere, I don't know if she knew what the movie was about. But she likes it! Big supporter and she's been really good about it. She wouldn't lie, she has no reason to and she's very clear when she says things, but she really loved the movie. But I don't know if she got it until she saw it. But then again, maybe this was like one of those Crispin things, where she could only know certain things. Who knows? Actors are so complicated!

It's funny, you mentioned Jeffrey Combs before and I didn't recognize him in the movie until the very, very end! Which is a testament to what a great actor he is...

Really? You really didn't?

I really didn't know it was him! In fact, was it him? Or another actor for most of it?

No! It is him! That was him the whole time!

Because I saw his name on the box and kept thinking, 'Where the hell is Jeffrey Combs in this movie?!' It was not until he speaks in that one scene that I realized it was him.

That's great! I'm done! (laughs) I feel like I did what I was supposed to do in the genre! I made Jeffrey Combs unrecognizable! That was the goal! This was our third film together. As long as I have something to give Jeffrey, I will always work with him. The only reason he's not in *The Thirst* is because Mark Altman didn't want him in the movie. When we were developing this script, I went to Jeffrey, and Dan (Gold) and Dan (Griffiths) and Zach and all sat down and had lunch with Jeffrey, and I think we were just developing the idea, we hadn't written it yet. Jeffrey and I talked already about him doing roles where no one knows it's him, and letting him go in directions no one's seen him do.

I think he's so immensely talented, and that people sometimes pigeonhole him. He could've been an actor in a whole different way, but he's a genre actor. And one of the most important lessons he taught me on my first movie, which I'm perfectly happy to live with because all I've ever wanted to do was make horror movies, is you dance with the one you came with. And he's ok with that. But again, by the same token, after that first movie, I promised him I'd never make him play a "mad doctor" again.

I had to do that on my first film, but I'll never ask him to don a lab coat in one of my movies again. (laughs) So, he and I and Zach really conceptualized the character of the geek together, and Jeffrey's idea was that he wouldn't speak until the end, and he'd be unrecognizable. He designed the costume and the look. I think it's the third movie he did with Autonomous, the FX guys. They had a rapport with him and got together early on to start sketching ideas. Designing noses, and the beard and just going over every detail. Him and I have a shorthand. It's easy, because it's Jeffrey.

We get on the set and it's more like playing. I don't have that weight of, "How is this going to go south?" Look, if I made another movie with Bijou, it'd be a totally different experience. My first movie with Jeffrey was a lot harder because he was the star! He was the big guy on that movie. And so, it was just a different vibe afterwards. By our third movie, I could say three words to him and it's a half hours' worth of attention I'd need to give Bijou.

Another interesting thing is that the "Suicide Girls" appear in this and it's their first movie appearance ever. How'd they get incorporated into the world of *The Wizard of Gore*?

When Zach finished the first draft of the script, it had the victims just like in Herschell's movie that were all female, but in Zach's movie apropos to modern exploitation film, they're stripped naked, and Montag does whatever he does...

And they're all from Jumbo's! (*We're talking about the strip club 'Jumbo's Clown Room' on Hollywood Blvd in Los Angeles) I literally just went there for the first time the other night.

How great is that?! For me, as someone who's from the East Coast but who's fallen in love with the seedy underbelly of Los Angeles, to have Jumbo's give me the rights to use the name and the logo, it's just so cool!

It is, and it's funny, I literally was there the night before I sat down to watch the movie! So, hearing the mention of it was surreal for me having just been there!

It's a magical place! So, yeah, I should mention, it doesn't seem like a big deal now (having the Suicide Girls) and post what Eli Roth did last summer, but I've been making this movie for a long time, and the idea of having nudity and violence in the same frame when we were trying to finance this movie seemed like a much bigger deal. But the "Suicide Girls" seemed like such a great tie to that. I had just discovered the site; it was 2004 and I thought it was awesome! It was the hot girl that you wanted to see naked from across the room at a punk rock show! There she is! She's naked on the internet! It's just a brilliant business and I got it right away and I thought these are the girls I wanted. This is how I'm going to do this.

Plus, they added to that perfect noir-punk rock meld that the movie has.

Totally, it seems like it gives it a backbone in a way. Now, we're on the verge of it seeming like, "Oh God, the Suicide Girls?" If we waited another year for this thing to come out, people would've written it off. Like the Pussycat Dolls now versus three years ago. You think, oh that's kind of intriguing, that sounds dirty! Now they do fucking ads for Bally's Fitness, you know? So, I joined the site with the plan to get them to do the movie, but I really had to become a part of that world and that community. My assistant editor who's one of my best friends now was head of the SGA, the Los Angeles group where you meet up. Over the course of this very Machiavellian manipulation, it became my world. I would say a good portion of my friends now I met on a porn site! That's so fucked up! But it's great!

The DVD version that's out now, the "unrated director's cut" is your definitive version of the film. For starters, I love the opening. Love the piece of music that plays over the opening and the credits, and I love that it kind of comes up as a score element throughout the rest of the film. How'd you find that song?

When Zach was writing the script and I was tossing off ideas, I'd say things like, "Don't forget that this location should be a department store, because I'd been to a punk rock show at a department store when I first moved to LA!" Someone had put together a stack of CD's, so I was constantly listening to early goth and punk stuff, but with a certain vibe I was looking for. I knew someone who was really into music, so I told them "Here's the vibe of my movie, make me a stack of CDs." And there was one song I kept coming back to and I thought it was so, so amazing!

And I listened to it every day on the way to the set. It's called "The Old Kind of Summer" by a band called *The Black Heart Procession*. It's just an amazing song. I kept thinking, "I'm going to use this somewhere, it's got to open

the film." But then as an editor, your instinct is to go against what the director wants to show him something new, but I was cutting the film myself. So, I cut the main titles to a different piece of music. And as soon as I was through my first assembly, I thought it was pretty good. I then tried a different piece and yeah, it was cool too.

I tried five or six other really good opening pieces of music. They were all good, but I put on that song, "The Old Kind of Summer" and it was as if the film came alive to me. It was tragic and heavy and mind-fucky and muddled and intense! All these things that I wanted the movie to be. It set it up so well. Then when we finished that cut, I sort of got removed from the process of editing the film, and got the cut taken away. And had it manipulated and just got marginalized towards the end.

It was all I could do to not speak my mind, because I felt one misstep, and I was going to be cut out completely! It was this horrible feeling! Like, your baby is being torn from you and so you put up with it so you can be around the baby still! It's really hard to explain if you haven't been through the experience, but it sounds like you understand completely...

Well, when producers get involved... here's the analogy I'd say it's like. It's like going through a divorce, but you don't want to say the wrong thing to piss of your wife/soon-to-be ex because you still want to see your baby!

That's exactly what it's like!

You know you're not going to get along, but you bear it for the kid.

And you think, "Oh my God. She's crazy! She's really crazy! (laughs) I just have to wait for everyone else to figure it out and I'll just not say anything for now!" I mean, I remember at one point standing in the editing room and saying, "Well, we should at least just call about that Black Heart Procession song. It might be inexpensive. We haven't even tried!" And the guy looked me in the eye and said, "We're not using that song. I don't like that song." And it was poking at me! He knew it was going to get at me! It was so weird. So, there was no money to do this director's cut. We did it on a borrowed Final Cut Pro with borrowed drives. It was like so surreal! The movie's huge and there's a hundred people on the set! And anything you need; cup of coffee, press your shirt, whatever to like... two dudes in a depressing room, eating Taco Bell. (laughs) Pick up shots and inserts are like that too. Where the movie is huge and then it goes to two people with one light and a flashlight trying to get that shot of the hand unlocking the door or whatever! And with the post on this movie, it was totally that.

So, with the Black Heart Procession song, I had to track down the band! A friend of a friend, his brother is friends with the lead singer. So, I went to a show, introduced myself, handed him the DVD and said it would mean the world to me if I could use it. I just wanted him to see that it was meant to be in the film...

And it really is.

Thank you.

The opening with that music is so awesome.

In the end, I became friends with *The Black Heart Procession* and I'm directing a music video for them, so it all worked out beautifully.

So, what else is in the "director's cut" DVD that's different from the original festival cut? What can fans look forward to on your DVD cut of *The Wizard of Gore*?

I'm going to tell this story as succinctly as possible. When I got to the point where the film was taken away, the argument was that this movie does not need to be gory. "Stop trying to make it gory, Jeremy!"

Even though it's called *The Wizard of Gore*? (laughs)

I mean, it's not called *The Wizard of Creeping Dread*, dude! (laughs) That's so weird! They knew what they were financing! No, come on! You aren't the ones the fans are going to tear apart on the internet! If you don't see the bad guy get killed in an at least mildly gory way, you fucked up! Making a movie is such an exhausting experience. The money runs out. I'm sure that the financial considerations were such that they didn't want to try anything anymore, they just wanted to get it done, which is what happened. Look, we opened at the LA Film Festival and it's not like the original cut of the movie couldn't have stood on its own. To a large extent, people liked it, it got good reviews. But I always felt there were these critical parts missing. I would say sixty percent of the music is new in the movie on the DVD. The score was never right, and I was never given the opportunity to make it right. And by way of example, and this is really important, someone was getting made fun of for releasing a "director's cut" that was only a minute different if you look at the total running time, but it was a point of pride with me to release a movie that was not thirty minutes longer than

their movie. Its thirty seconds (length-wise) difference, but my cut I extracted scenes that didn't work and pieces that were boring.

And it's just a more paced, more exciting thing. And what they did was just take little pieces out and made the movie kind of flat. So anytime Crispin or Jeffrey or Brad Dourif laughs maniacally or has a crazy look or does something that's a great moment, they'd be like, "Well, nobody's talking here, we can take that out." But what you end up with is a flat movie. You need those moments! Those moments are the moments that make the movie! So, it's a more special movie. It's got more Crispin and less Kip. It's got more gore. There were effects shots that were never completed...

It's got wonderful music and a great score!

Thank you! The first score was good! He did a great job. There just wasn't the time given to it to finesse it the rest of the way. I was lucky, Steve Porcaro did the score, and then a composer came on named Eric Powell from a band called *16 Volt* that Joe Bishara hooked me up with. Eric came on and what he essentially did was took the score that was two-thirds of the movie, essentially the last two reels has a lot of new music. For the beginning of the movie, the score would be good, but it just wouldn't go along with what was happening. So, Eric would score on top of the score and shape it to the movie, and it helps enormously.

You mentioned talking to Herschell Gordon Lewis before, so he has seen the movie. What does he think of your take on *Wizard of Gore*?

He was really nice about it. I think he was surprised at how artsy it is. (laughs) Because it's not an art film, it's a horror movie. Herschell's movies are somewhat campy, but retroactively so. At the time, they were not meant to make you laugh, they were meant to make the girl sitting next to you scared and cuddle up to you, that's what drive-ins are for! Tim's approach for *2001 Maniacs* was to play on how campy they are now, very much the opposite direction I went in, and I think Herschell was surprised by our movie. Um, I couldn't quite tell what he thought! Because he's such a polite, lovely man. He really is awe-inspiring in every way. And so, everything he said to me was incredibly sweet, but I also wasn't sure if he was surprised by how different it was, and maybe as the creator of these characters and of this world, a little bit disappointed that it's not beat for beat his movie, just modernized. It's a different story, it's just got the elements of the source material.

You have to figure that he gets a kick out of the fact that these young kids that were fans of his are now getting the chance to redo his movies.

That's for sure. And he's been a huge supporter of that from the beginning. I met him in '97 at a *Fangoria* convention in New York.

I was there!

Were you? I was in the middle of making *The Attic Expeditions* and we were still raising money for it, and Tony Timpone was so cool and let me come to do a presentation for it. I was a kid and doing anything I could to raise financing for that movie. And I met Herschell at that con, and I said, "Look, someday I want to remake one of your movies." And he said, "Well... I wish you all the luck in the world with that!" Because he doesn't own any of them, so to him it's more of an ego boost, I'm sure.

I love your movie and I love Tim Sullivan's film *2001 Maniacs*. I love them both for different reason, but I really think they would both make for a great double feature.

Agreed!

I would love to see *The Wizard of Gore* and *2001 Maniacs* on the big screen, double feature...

I don't think anyone would like that more than me and Tim! (laughs) If you can imagine the two of us doing the Q&A afterwards?! That sounds like the most fun I could have ever! I would love that! And to be clear, I feel the same way about Tim's movie. I respect the hell out of him. I'm in no way saying that there's a right way and a wrong way to tackle Herschell's stuff. Thank goodness there's two different approaches! If we were just doing the same thing, it'd be boring! Hopefully the next person that does a Herschell remake goes in a totally different direction.

It's great that your movies exist, but hopefully people reading this will also go back and rediscover Herschell's movies as well. They're definitely worth rediscovering.

Absolutely!

Special thanks to Arianne Schrodel and Jeremy Kasten for his time!

MICK GARRIS

Interviewed by Mike Cucinotta and Rob Galluzzo (9/08)

Mick Garris got his start much like we did here at *Icons* by interviewing filmmakers for magazines and his Z channel show *Fantasy Film Festival*. He then went on to write for *Amazing Stories* before directing *Critters 2* and *Psycho IV*. He would eventually team with Stephen King more than any other filmmaker on projects such as *Sleepwalkers*, *The Stand*, *Riding the Bullet*, and *Desperation*. He also created Showtime's hit series *Masters of Horror*! It helps that he's probably the nicest guy in the movie business, which is why he agreed to speak to us about all of the above!

Rob: First things first, what are your earliest recollections of the horror genre? As a kid, what memories do you have of what opened you up to the world of what's scary?

Well, the first thing and I've told this before was that my mother, when she was very, very young, like two years old or something, one of her first movies was the original *King Kong* and it so terrified her that she just never got over it! So, *Son of Kong* was coming on television when I was really young. So, I remember we had a TV and then another one on top of it for some reason. And my mom wanted to make sure that it was a very careful family viewing experience so there wasn't any terror that would occupy my brain for the rest of my life.

She didn't realize it was a good thing. (laughs) And so we're all watching, there were four of us Garris kids, we were all really young and we were all born within five years of each other. And my mother and father sat down to watch *Son of Kong* in a very protective atmosphere with us. But *Son of Kong* is a comedy. It's not a scary movie at all, even though it has a giant gorilla! But that giant gorilla is my first memory of my step into the world beyond the real world. And so that was like, "Wow, this is great!" After that, it was the Universal horror movies that played all the time on Channel Five when I was a kid.

Rob: And you and your family used to go together to the drive-ins all the time, right?

We went to the drive-ins to see *Psycho*. I saw *Psycho* for the first time at a drive-in, the Reseda Drive-In, which is no longer there anymore. But it wasn't that long ago that it

finally shut down, but it's where they shot the scenes with Boris Karloff in *Targets*. That was the neighborhood drive-in that we would go to. We'd bring in our own popcorn because it was too expensive for us…

Rob: Even then?

Even then!

Rob: So, it's safe to say that you had a general interest in films from a very young age.

Absolutely!

Rob: So, what was it that made you segue into really searching out how the people behind these movies made these films? What led to you doing the public access interview show?

It wasn't public access! It was on the Z channel, a paid show. People often make that mistake but there's a very large distinction between the two.

Rob: Sorry, sorry! Well, the record is straight now!

Anybody can do a public access show, but this was paid TV! Well, at first, I wanted to be an artist and a cartoonist. My father had gone to art school and had talent in art, and I inherited some of that ability to draw. But I never really followed up on it, because once I started to write at age twelve, writing took over my interest in drawing.

Then I became a rock n' roll musician, when I was like fifteen years old and the singer in a band at around eighteen years old, writing songs. I've always watched television as a kid, movies and cartoons and television series, and all that stuff. When there were only four or five channels to choose from. It had always piqued my interest, particularly the "ultra real" or the "beyond real" supernatural things, horror movies, cartoons, etc. So, my writing took that approach, that's what I was most interested in. My writing kind of went that way, and then I thought I would try my hand at screenwriting.

I was a journalist as well for underground newspapers and school newspapers. At that time, underground newspapers were a big deal. They were the alternate press, and they were very political as well as into more alternate arts, music and film. So, I started writing about music as well and started doing interviews, and that was always fascinating to me; the creative process. The creative process was always something that particularly fascinated me. The more I wrote, the less I started to write fiction, and the more I started to write screen material, and became more interested in doing that.

And so, I was doing interviews for newspapers and magazines and all these things, and started writing for the Z Channel magazine, which was the first paid TV channel, before HBO. When I was writing for that magazine, I proposed to the editor of the magazine, who was also a program director for Z Channel at the time, that we do something, a serious version of those horror host things that came from my youth. Start with a fifteen minute interview before the movie with the person who made the movie. And it was really fun and successful for the channel.

Rob: A lot of them have surfaced recently. I mean, the one on the *Videodrome* Criterion release with you interviewing John Landis, John Carpenter and David Cronenberg is fantastic!

And a bunch of the *Masters of Horror* discs have them!

Rob: Right! There's even an episode on the bonus disc of *Masters of Horror* Season One.

Yeah, that has Steven Spielberg and John Boorman. I think it's probably really boring.

Rob: I'll have to show that to Mike, because *Exorcist 2* is one of his favorite movies, Mick.

Mike: I love that movie!

It is the most underrated movie!

Mike: It's wild! It's nutty and insane!

It is! And I like it! I did an interview with William Friedkin, and he was so insulting about the makers of *Exorcist 2* and the fact that we dared show *Exorcist 2* and have those people on, that the Z Channel thought, the legal staff thought it might be libel and they never ran that show.

Rob: Wow!

So, there is a great "lost" *Fantasy Film Festival* with William Friedkin. I was on my honeymoon when they said they needed to redo it and I couldn't redo it, so they ended up just not doing that show. That's a little scoop that no one knows about. An exclusive for Icons of Fright! (laughs)

Mike: Right! ICONS EXCLUSIVE! William Friedkin doesn't like *The Exorcist 2*! (laughs)

(laughs) I don't think there's any mystery about that! But anyways, he was so nasty about it that it never got on the air.

Mike: Scorsese loved it.

Really?

Mike: Yeah.

Well, interesting enough, Martin Scorsese doing a remake of *Cape Fear*, and this is after we did *Psycho IV*. He's the only other person to re-score the Bernard Herrmann music for *Cape Fear*, and it was after we had done it for *Psycho IV*. Nobody had ever done that before! So, I would like to think I influenced Martin Scorsese! Who, by the way, directed the first script I ever had produced.

Rob: Oh, which was an *Amazing Stories* episode!

Right. Which I'm not credited for, although it was a page one rewrite.

Mike: You wrote *Mirror, Mirror*? That's my favorite *Amazing Stories* episode! I just got chills!

Well, Joe Minion got credit for it, but he wrote the first draft. For a number of reasons, it needed rewriting. Because of the network, because of Spielberg's tastes. Because of what

Scorsese wanted to try. And I was a story editor for the series, so it was a page one rewrite, every word.

Mike: It's one of the scariest things I've ever seen.

(laughs) Thanks!

Mike: It traumatized me! Even today, I watched it recently and it's still terrifying.

Oh good, good! Yeah, Sam Waterston's great. And you know who the monster is, right? Tim Robbins! So even though it's uncredited, that was my first produced script.

Rob: We were just talking about *Mirror, Mirror* because we did an article on the "Scariest Television Stories" to coincide with *Fear Itself*. And that was Mike's number one choice. Can you summarize your experience working on *Amazing Stories*?

Well, it was the greatest film school in the history of the world. The opportunity was given to me because I was doing a documentary on *The Goonies* up in Astoria, Oregon. They had just started shooting and Spielberg was there, and I was introduced to him. And he said, "You must do a lot of these things?" And I had just started to really commit to writing, trying to do it full time. I left doing publicity at Universal to do it full time. And I said, "Well, I don't do much now, because I'm trying to make a go as a writer." "Oh, really?" You never want to tell someone, "I'm a writer! Here's a script in my back pocket!" But he said, "Oh really? We're looking for writers on this new series I'm doing called *Amazing Stories*."

My agents had known that and so fortunately his readers had really liked a script I'd done, and they gave me an opportunity. I was the first writer hired to do *Amazing Stories*, an episode. I wrote it in three days. I turned it in, they really liked it and asked me to do another one right away. And so, then before I'd even finished it, they called me and asked me to be the story editor. So, here I am, a story editor on *Amazing Stories*, never having had this job before, never having been paid to write before for screen material, and now I'm writing scripts directed by Bob Zemekis and Joe Dante and myself and Peter Heinz and all these people. Going to the set, there's Clint Eastwood directing an episode. Here's Steven Spielberg directing an episode. I learned so much, not so much on the set, what I really learned about filmmaking on the set is how much filmmaking takes place before you get to the set, and off the set.

With Scorsese in particular, he would clear the room of everyone except him and the actors when he was rehearsing a scene. And this is on television, you really don't have time to do that! Although, *Amazing Stories* had a rather elaborate budget. And so, then he would bring in the DP and the first AD and then go through it with them. But to just talk with Scorsese about what changes he wanted in the script, I think there was a car chase sequence, a stunt sequence in the original script, and he said, "You know, I'm not very good at this kind of stuff. Maybe we should write around it?" What a great window into an amazing filmmaker! One of the great filmmakers of all time, to be at his beck and call, writing what he wanted.

Mike: Your experience on *Amazing Stories* had to have laid the groundwork for going into your anthology series, *Masters of Horror*?

Absolutely.

Mike: What'd you take with you from your experience there when you were putting *Masters of Horror* together?

Well, I don't like series television and I don't watch it. *The Office* is the only series I watch that has a continuing cast. I don't have the time or the inclination or the interest to get to know that family every week and to go back. I'm not addicted to *Lost*. I'm not addicted to *Heroes*. Where you miss a week, and you miss the show. I like movies! I like a story that's told all in one, and the *Amazing Stories* experience was something that really - it was just the kind of television that was my ideal. It was a little half hour movie every week, but not tethered by quite the financial restraints, although there's still quite a bit of financial restraint doing a Steven Spielberg series as it was. But not as much. And yet, it also proved that anthology and network television do not go hand in hand, because the way television has developed over the years and over the decades is series television or reality television.

And even that, you have a cast that evolves. So, in the case of *Masters of Horror* and later *Fear Itself*, it was just really reflecting of the taste for horror, it was strictly a horror series. But within the confines of horror, it was varied. *Amazing Stories* could be animated one week, it could be kid oriented, it could be science fiction, it could be a thriller like *The Amazing Falsworth*. That was really broad, and too broad for an audience to catch on TV, but on Showtime? First of all, *Masters of Horror* was financed by Anchor Bay and not Showtime. Showtime licensed it for a very small fee.

It would've been made if there was a network or not, although it helped to have a network. Showtime's audience is so small that you could be a big hit, and we were the number two show without any advertising for two years, just by being good and by word of mouth. And *Fear Itself*, although I was not involved during the production and I left because of the writer's guild and didn't go back for a number of reasons, many of them over network TV and horror not being able to really mix, it showed that the audience for network and commercial TV doesn't really want an anthology.

Mike: With *Masters of Horror* premiering on cable, that definitely freed that series up a lot, right? It was originally going to be a DVD series?

Yeah. And it still was. We made it exactly the same way, with a little bit of input from Showtime. They had five rules that we never thought of breaking anyway. And even so, *Imprint* never got shown. It didn't break any of their five rules, but it was just…

Mike: What were some of the rules?

No violence against children. Uh, no male frontal nudity. Um, no sexual relations between kids. You know, some things none of us intended on breaking anyways.

Mike: How did *Imprint* not end up being aired if it didn't break any of those rules?

Well, because it's so intense. It's hard for me to watch!

Rob: Well, the thing I loved about it was it became the episode that you had to see.

Exactly.

Rob: I remember all of us at Icons screening it together and we were horrified the whole time!

And the first version was seven or eight minutes longer! And that was almost all in the torture scene. (laughs)

Rob: As Jason Alvino from our site said, when Billy Drago is the least scary, weirdest thing in your movie, you know you've got something intense! (laughs)

(laughs) Absolutely!

Mike: How'd you get all these names together for *Masters*?

Rob: I love the original teaser poster that had George Romero and Roger Corman, who obviously didn't get to make episodes.

They always intended to do it!

Rob: Is the story with Guillermo Del Toro true? Did "masters of horror" come from him offering all you guys to sing happy birthday to a dinner party at a restaurant?

Well, there was a table next to us having a birthday party, and so we all sang happy birthday, and Del Toro said, (in Spanish accent) "The masters of horror wish you a happy birthday!" (laughs) So, he gave us the unofficial name. It was a joke! It was a self-disparaging joke! The so-called "masters of horror." But it was the perfect name for the series, and it gave it a validity that just a standard horror series wouldn't. And it's also – I came up with the title for *Fear Itself* when I was still involved with it. We still intended to have these guys. But it also easened the burden of having to deliver thirteen big name directors, which they didn't really pull off.

Rob: I've only seen a few episodes of *Fear Itself*. Stuart Gordon's *Eater* is really good.

Stuart's is really good. *The Sacrifice*, the one that I wrote was changed a lot. But it was pretty well received and that's what I hoped it would be.

Rob: As New Yorkers, we were glad that Larry Fessenden got to do one.

I think he's incredibly talented!

Mike: Now, if *Masters of Horror* was the number two show on Showtime, why make the switch to NBC for *Fear Itself*?

Masters was very successful for Showtime, but Showtime did not finance the show, they paid a small license fee for it. The first season, Anchor Bay was owned by IDT. They were sold to Starz. Starz bought IDT entertainment and Anchor Bay, and Starz is a much more corporate organization than Anchor Bay was at the time. They had people that were interested in the immediate bottom line. And although it took them almost a year to make their decision, we thought we were going forward with a third season. They backed out.

Immediately, Lionsgate, who was one of the first groups we took *Masters* to and wanted to do it, but didn't act as quickly - Lionsgate said, yeah we want to be involved. They actually had it set up at HD net and it was the perfect fit. They wanted something with similar variety to help their channel. You know, they have Dan Rather and then some movies that people don't know about, but that they release day and date in theaters. It fell apart because they also wanted theatrical distribution rights for the same fee. When that happened, I thought, you know, we did two years of groundbreaking television with Showtime, maybe it's ok to end it at this. And then Lionsgate sold it to NBC. But NBC, of course, didn't want to look like they'd inherited a series from another smaller network.

So, they wanted a new title, so we renamed it *Fear Itself*. When NBC wanted to do it, I contacted all of the filmmakers and said, "Look, Lionsgate and NBC are going to do this. I don't think I want to take part in this, because I don't think it could be what we intended," where the filmmakers have final cut and total creative control. And almost all of them bowed out with the exception of Stuart Gordon who said, "No, just stay on, we should do it. See what we can do! *Twilight Zone* was done for regular television and *Alfred Hitchcock Presents*." Well, people's ideas of entertainment were different then too. And it became very clear during the process after we developed a bunch of the scripts that they were looking to make something more familiar and not something groundbreaking. Even though a horror anthology would be groundbreaking. And people like Stuart Gordon did make some good stuff, but it was the guys who were first that got the least interference. As time went on, and I wasn't involved so I didn't see what went on, but from what I heard, it just got worse and worse.

Rob: That's a shame.

It is. But *Masters of Horror* will always be there. We did two years of that, twenty-six films, all of which I'm really proud of. Whatever the fans have to say on websites and IMDb and stuff, we did some really great shit.

Rob: It's funny, because it's been a couple of years since these have been on, and I was just re-visiting the first season on DVD. And not that it'd been so long that I didn't remember them, but I appreciate them now. I think they're pretty good!

I think what happened was fans got so spoiled by Season One, that Season Two, I think most of the filmmakers outdid themselves with their second films, but because they were second, it didn't have the impact of, "Holy shit! Look what's on Showtime! We got Joe Dante, Stuart Gordon, Tobe Hooper, John Carpenter, Larry Cohen, Dario Fucking Argento! Takashi Fucking Miike! Doing a one-hour TV show for American television! And doing it with

no interference!" Interestingly, Miike and the producers in Japan were hugely disappointed that it didn't air here, and they would've been happy to make cuts. But we didn't want them to! (laughs) And Anchor Bay was really cool about it. And the other thing about *Imprint*, Walmart sells forty percent of the DVD's sold in the United States. And Walmart wouldn't carry it. So, it wouldn't run on Showtime and Walmart wouldn't carry it.

Rob: That's actually a pretty cool thing to say though!

But how cool is Anchor Bay for doing it anyway? It is cool to say that, and it's hard for me to watch, but the filmmaking is beautiful and fantastic. It would've been interesting to do it in Japanese with subtitles.

Rob: I love the episode, but that's my one critique. I wonder if it would've worked better had it been in Japanese with English subtitles.

Well, the thing is most of the Japanese cast did it phonetically. They didn't speak English! And I was in the room where they're doing these rehearsal sessions. We had an American coach in there with them. It was tough! The dwarf character? It was really tough for him to talk. English is a very tough language for Japanese people.

Rob: I couldn't speak Japanese phonetically! (laughs)

The next one that we did with Norio Tsuruta, *Dream Cruise*, it was a small cast but virtually all the Japanese on that one spoke very good English.

Rob: We were talking about this on the way here, but we forgot you wrote *The Fly 2*! We fucking love that movie!

I tried! I've learned to say, "thank you very much." But there was a lot of rewriting done and I was really proud of the original *Fly 2* script. It was political, it was about anti-abortion and all this stuff. It got changed a lot. It was turned into a teen horror movie by the studio, which was very popular at the time.

Rob: It was very gory!

It was very gory, but Chris Walas, the director was a make-up FX guy! So, he leaned in that way anyways.

Rob: All that stuff with Martin Brundle growing up and discovering his father's work, it's all brilliant stuff.

I share credit or blame with the Wheat brothers and with Frank Darabont for that. Because that's where Frank and I met! I left to direct *Critters 2*.

Rob: And you wrote *Critters 2* as well?

David Twohy wrote the first draft, then I did the drafts after that. It's a movie I'm proud of. It's not something that everyone would love! It's a sequel to a low-budget rip-off of *Gremlins*! (laughs) But as that, I'm really proud of it! There are really good performances, the photography and the FX are good. For a $4 million dollar movie?

Rob: I remember seeing it in theaters as a kid and being blown away by the little Freddy Krueger cameo. (laughs)

Oh yeah, yeah. My favorite little funny moment is when the "critter" ball rolls over the farmer and reveals the skeleton. That's a funny bit.

Rob: Was it challenging working with a ton of "critter" puppets? I mean, now it would be all CG. I miss the old days of puppets!

You know, I didn't want my first movie to be an FX movie, and so my first movie is not only an FX movie, but a really cheap one and with lots of kind of effects! Opticals, as well as puppets and puppets that look like puppets! It was really hard, but the Chiodo brothers were great though. They were really great. We had a really good time doing it, I have to say. I remember running back and forth to shoot second unit, and the tabletop of miniatures with the critter balls. It was really hard, but it was really fun.

Rob: It must've been fun just to kill them. Like the one with the tire?

Oh yeah! That was my Warner Brothers cartoon gag that I put in there. Same with the critter that had the eyeballs that go BOING! That's my voice going BOING! (laughs)

Rob: Let's talk about your relationship with Stephen King. The first thing you did with him was *Sleepwalkers*. That was the first thing he specifically wrote for the screen. You must've worked very closely with him on it?

Not at first! He had written the script, and I had met on it at the studio and Stephen had director approval. It was a great meeting, and they said, "Ok, there's a formality of another meeting that we have to do, then we'll get you

working." Well, they hired the other meeting. That director got hired. He went and re-wrote horribly the script that King had written. Arrogantly re-written a script that King had written to turn it into this stuff with the planet of the "sleepwalkers." Nobody liked where he was taking it, and what are you going to do? Rewrite it so much that you lose Stephen King's name? The purpose of doing it! After I had not gotten the job, they came back to me a couple of months later and wanted to meet with me. I didn't realize that at that lunch meeting, they were starting me that day. They didn't tell me that was happening, but they hired me that day and put me in an office. So, I worked at putting back as much King into the script as possible and did a rewrite myself with that stuff. And I had not met King, but he'd seen *Psycho IV* and that's the reason he approved me!

Rob: Well done!

Yeah, he really liked that film, and didn't expect to. Nobody expects to like a film with four in the title! Especially based on one of the great films of all time. So, we didn't really work together so much as just over the phone. I would have an idea, and I'd say, "Would you like me to write it?" And he'd say, "Well let me give it a shot." And the next day, in the fax machine would be a few pages of great stuff! The only scene I can really take any kind of credit for is the mirrors scene, which was cut to shit to get an R rating.

Where you pan off the mirror onto the clothing on the floor and pan across them making love, and in the mirror is what they look like as sleepwalkers. That was something I had written. And when the film was done, the ending didn't really work, and King told me, "You know, I'm not very good at endings." (laughs) That was news to me!

He came up with a new ending and I said, "Since we're doing a new ending, can we please add an opening scene that explains the sleepwalkers?" People were kind of confused about who the sleepwalkers were and what they did. And so, I wrote the Mark Hamill scene. "Look, we're going to do a week of shooting, this will be half a day, just let me do this and start the movie with a bang." And so that's what we did. But I first met King on the set for his cameo.

We had spoken on the phone up until then. He came out to do his scene with Clive Barker and Tobe Hooper, and that morning I was eating my granola on the set and broke my tooth! This was up in Franklin Canyon and my dentist was down here on Ventura Blvd. So, I had to rush down here, get a brass temporary cap on my tooth and go back up before King arrived to shoot his scene, along with Barker and Hooper.

Rob: That's so amazing. To be doing one of your early films and to be directing King and Hooper and Barker all in the same day.

Yeah! It was fantastic. And all of them have become really good friends, all of whom I've worked with several times.

Rob: I can't even begin to imagine the complexity of tackling *The Stand*…

Neither can I! (laughs) It's the hardest thing I've ever done, and I hope it's the hardest thing I will ever do.

Rob: How did you get involved with it? King wrote the script for this too!

King wrote the script, it was going to be a film project for years, they were going to do it as a two part feature film with George Romero. For like fifteen years, they were planning on doing it as a feature. And then, ABC came to him and asked if they could do *The Stand*. They bought *The Stand* from him to do it as a mini-series. And he thought, you know? Maybe this is a good idea. It's such a big book. To break it down into movies, it just hasn't worked.

Rob: Was this before or after the mini-series of *IT*?

This was after *IT*, which was done right around *Psycho IV*, because Olivia Hussey had worked on both, so that was 1990. We shot *The Stand* in 1993, and it aired in May of 1994. At first, I think they went to a couple of feature guys, big name directors all of whom didn't want to do television, and Steve said, "Is this something you'd be interested in if we get this going?" "Are you kidding?" I did have those thoughts too. I had finally broken into features, and the idea of doing television, I was hesitant about it… but it's *The Stand*!

So, when they finally went forward with it, King asked for me to be the director. The script was delivered to my doorstep, all 460 pages of it. I remember looking at it when I got home thinking… "What the fuck?" (laughs) First of all, reading it and having to do it quickly! I did one script a day just so I could give it the attention of the four scripts. Yeah, it was massive. I mean, how do we do it? The producers were known for doing very cheap films, very low-budget films. King had been partnered with them on other things before. When you have a project, you just figure out a way to do it. Give me parameters and we'll figure out how to do it within those parameters. We shot it in 16 mm to keep budget down. Saved maybe $300,000 dollars we didn't have.

We shot mostly in Utah, because it's a right-to-work state and had a lot of locations we could use. So, we shot one day in the Mohave, we shot one day with a 16 mm second unit camera running around Maine. We shot a couple of days in New York. We shot a week in Pittsburgh, where we shot most of the New York stuff. And we shot a couple of weeks in Nevada for the Las Vegas scenes. It was just so big, you could never, ever see the light at the end of the tunnel. It was a 100-day shoot. And the first thirteen weeks were five day weeks. The last seven weeks were six day weeks.

Rob: Wow.

Almost nobody shoots six day weeks anymore. It used to be common practice on location to do six day weeks because what else are you going to do? Well, for a director, five day weeks are seven days weeks, but six day weeks are eight day weeks! (laughs) It just was so massive that some of the parts were even cast on videotape while I was on location. I would sometimes go on a location that I'd never seen except in pictures before we got there, because it was so big! It's 100 days of shooting.

Mike: What's going through your head during all of this?

Well, the first thing is getting the script so it's great. So that you trust the script. Then you have to forget about everything surrounding you. All you can think about is what you're working on now and what leads in and out of it, and then just trust it if it works for the picture.

Mike: How do you stay focused on all that with four scripts and shooting out of continuity?

Well, you have to. You just have to, that's all there is to it. You have a continuity person with you, you have your assistant director with you, and each department is trained to focus on the progression. This takes place over the course of a long time. Originally, we had cast Diane Lane to play the Shawnee Smith part, and she would've been great! But what we didn't know was that she was pregnant. And she said, "Well, wouldn't that make an interesting facet of this character?" And I said, "Yes, but we're shooting five months apart from these two scenes!" (laughs) "They're five months apart! It takes place over a long period of time too so we can't make you pregnant the whole time either." So, everything impacts on everything else.

We originally hired Moses Gunn. He was going to play the judge. We weren't going to get Ossie Davis to play with Ruby Dee because they're so often teamed together, we thought it'd be great to get her to do this on her own. But Moses Gunn had come to us very ill. So, he was getting better, we shot one scene in the train station, that giant scene where everybody's in the train station gathering and Stu Redman's up front and they vote him to be the leader. Well, Moses Gunn shot just one shot of him in there, and he never got over being sick. He had the flu and pneumonia. We replaced him with Ossie Davis who was fantastic, and right after the film was done, Moses Gunn died.

So, the shoot was an eternity. Plus, all the post-production was done in New York. I was living in a hotel! I lived away from home for a year on *The Stand*. So, it was rough! But Stephen King was on the set for at least half of it, off and on. It has an amazing, wonderful cast with whom I became really good friends. So many of them are people I still see and am close to and still cast all the time.

Mike: How was Stephen King on the set of *The Stand* and what were some of the things he interacted on?

It was like a toy train set for him. It's like the greatest train set. Never once did he ever say, "You know? You should do this." He was very respectful and trusting. He just wanted to be there and watch. And I would often go to him and ask him, "How about a line for this or that?" or "What do you think of this or that?" But mostly, he was just there to have fun and to watch. You know the scene out in the middle of nowhere where there's a line of cars and you see the city burning in the background and Adam Storke has his guitar there. Well, Adam Storke is all by himself playing guitar and singing *Eve of Destruction*. Well, me and Steve and Adam were all playing guitar and singing *Eve of Destruction* in between takes! (laughs)

It was just great. But it was the hardest thing. The weather was always exactly the opposite of what it should've been. It was the bitterest winter there in a hundred years. And so, when it was supposed to be sunny and clear, it was raining and when it was supposed to be raining, it was snowing. It was just bitter and difficult. I have a very light nature, but I got really cranky. Not with other people! Just the circumstances were incredibly difficult. Everything I had done up until that point was very small scale like *Sleepwalkers* or *Psycho IV*. Even *Critters 2* seemed like a huge movie to me, and then along comes this scene where we've got 600 extras out on the Vegas strip. It was enormous! And it didn't stop! And it didn't get any easier, it just got harder.

We spent the last days in Las Vegas. It was rough, but it was also so great. It was such a great script and such a great book. We knew we were doing something special, but we never thought that it would become the monster that it became. Supposedly it was the most successful mini-series ever. It had fifty million people a night watching, and more every night of the four nights. They just added on. It became the water-cooler show. It was the *Jurassic Park* of television.

Rob: Anytime it's on cable, I have to watch it.

Mike: At the age I was when that hit, it was a big thing.

It was huge, it was huge. And everywhere you'd go, there were billboards. It was the one time when I was involved in something that was a phenomenon.

Rob: And you're responsible for my crush on Molly Ringwald. I never really had a thing for her like most people did in the John Hughes movies! But you dyed her hair jet-black, and I gained an instant crush!

I'll tell you, she had done a movie for my friend Tom McLoughlin, a TV movie about someone who had gotten AIDS called *Something To Live For* and she was just amazing in it and really great. Because all I thought of was the John Hughes movies too and we cast her because of *Something To Live For*. She did a great job.

Mike: There's another version of *The Shining* that you did with Stephen King. Obviously, Stephen was never really happy with Kubrick's version. So, when he decided to do *The Shining* again, what was the original intention? Did he come to you and ask you to direct?

What happened was after the huge success of *The Stand*, ABC came to him and said, "What do you want to do?" And *The Shining* was what he wanted to do. He wanted to do a version of the book! Books and movies aren't the same thing, and he knows that. But part of the deal was that Kubrick had the rights. Kubrick got paid a lot of money for the rights to that. He got a million and a half bucks for the rights for us to do this. And part of the Kubrick's deal was that King could not say anything critical about his movie…

Rob: Although we all know what he thinks!

He's on record all over the place on it. We weren't remaking the movie. We were doing a mini-series, a novel for television.

Mike: So, you never really had the pressure of remaking Kubrick's film?

No. As much as I love the Kubrick film now, when it first came out, I didn't like it at all, because I went in there with the highest hopes for one of my favorite books of all time, and it wasn't that book. So, I didn't understand it as a Kubrick film, but I really didn't like it as adaptation of my favorite book.

I went in there naively thinking, "We're not doing anything to do with the Kubrick film. We're making a mini-series based on the King book written by King!" And it was the best script I'd ever read. It was a fantastic script. In a lot of ways, even better than *The Stand*. So human, so emotional. I was naive, because it didn't even strike me until this moment… The very first person I talked to was Gary Sinise, asking if he'd be interested in playing Jack Torrance before it had even got finalized. And he said, "You know? I'd be hesitant about stepping into Mr. Nicholson's shoes." That's when it first struck me! We went through a lot of actors who wouldn't do it, because the first line of every review was going to compare it to Jack Nicholson.

Mike: So, what about the final product? How do you look back on the experience of *The Shining*?

One of my favorite things I've ever done. First of all, the production values, we were in one place for most of it. Well, a couple of places, a stage, a hotel. So, I was able to really use some filmmaking that I wasn't able to in *The Stand*. *The Stand* was guerrilla filmmaking, and I did everything I could, but we were rushed and on a much tighter budget with so many locations and so much cast that we were trying to just get it and put as much art into it as possible. But in the case of *The Shining*, I was able to really build some dread. I think that some of the filmmaking in there was much more sophisticated in the like. And I know a lot of fans, because Kubrick had made *The Shining*, they were going to hate it no matter what.

Plus, it was made for television. But I'll tell you, that last hour? It would've been rated R had it been theatrical. It's scary and it's violent. I have a hard time watching violence against women. And directing violence against Rebecca De Mornay wasn't easy! But it's one of my favorite things that I've done. I had a really great, great experience. The producer was terrific. King was there for probably two thirds of it. He was writing *The Green Mile* at the time. And every time he'd finish it, I'd get a stack of pages and would be able to read it before it ever got published.

Mike: Any update on your next adaptation, *Bag of Bones*?

We are very close to happening. We have a great script by Matt Venne. He wrote *Pelts* for Dario Argento. It's a really good script, we're about to go out to studios, but we've already done some location scouting, so we're real close. It's one of the things that I'm most passionate about. I love that book. And I love the idea of a passionate ghost story. There have been a few in the past but not like this.

Mike: What is it about that one in particular?

This one, it's just all about imagination and loss and heartbreak. I had lost my brother. I had lost family members to death, and the feeling that they leave behind; this one is about death and rebirth. It's about passion, it's about romance. It's about things that aren't necessarily the *Fangoria* reader's favorite thing, but it's a grown up really scary ghost story. I love it.

Rob: Can't wait! Thank you again for talking to us, Mick!

TOMAS ALFREDSON

Interviewed by Rob Galluzzo (10/08)

One of the best movies we've seen this year is the Swedish vampire flick *Let the Right One In*, based on the novel by John Ajvide Lindqvist. So, when *Icons* was offered a chance to sit in on a round table interview with director Tomas Alfredson, we happily accepted! The following is an interview that took place in New York with several journalists present, all fielding different questions. We are presenting you with the entire transcript; questions from *Icons* are noted. Beware of mild spoilers.

Vampires are very "in" right now with *Twilight* coming. You have *Let the Right One In* being remade for American audiences, and people are dying to see that. There's also *True Blood*. Why is the vampire craze starting up again?

You know, that's really strange because I started working with this three years ago and nobody was talking about vampires! So, it's some kind of synchronicity as they call it. I really don't know. Maybe vampirism has something to do with the "animal" inside of us. Maybe it's something that's been suppressed, held down inside of us, that has to come up every twenty years. I don't know really.

What was the inspiration for *Let the Right One In*?

I was very stuck by the very unsentimentally told story about the bullied boy. Because I had some periods when I was a teenager being bullied. So, that was the first thing that struck me the hardest. And then it was this very original blend with this supernatural thing. I didn't have any specific interest in vampires or vampirism before, so that was totally new to me. And that was the biggest, hardest thing for me. To find the solutions, how to stage those things.

What made you decide to choose the main character, having it be the story of Oskar, a twelve-year-old boy? It's rare in a vampire film the kids are the main characters.

Before we started shooting, dramatists asked me "Who is the main character, the boy or the girl?" And I would say they are both the same character. The boy and the girl, they are the same person. The light and the dark side of the same person. But what was your question?

Why'd you make children the main characters?

Well, that's the main story from the book. From the beginning. That was not a choice for me.

Well, because it's based on the novel.

Yeah, it's based on a novel.

So, being based on a novel, what were the wrinkles in adapting this novel, making these decisions in terms of making it into a film for you?

Well, we had to make some big choices of things we had to cut out. The biggest thing that we left out that the character Håkan, the older "blood" supplier for Eli, he was an outspoken pedophile in the novel. So that really gave another tone to the whole thing. That's too often used as an emotional special effect, without taking responsibility for what that really is. It's a really complicated thing to debate on screen, I think. So that would've disturbed the story a lot to have that.

Did you envision in your mind when you developed Eli as a character that she was always looking for a replacement for him? Or was that an accident?

No, that's up to you to decide, really. There are a lot of things in the film that are up to you to decide. And that's the sort of style of it. My point of view is that it's a happy ending. They leave this country and live their own lives as they want to, but it's suggested as Oskar being the new blood provider, if you want to think that.

324

Rob: I love the movie, I think it's very beautiful. And when I tell people about it, obviously it's a vampire movie, but you can take the vampire element out and I see it as a movie about two twelve-year-old kids falling in love with each other, which is why it's so beautiful. So, how difficult was it finding the right child actors to play these "adult" themes? They were both fantastic and it's rare that you see kids acting at that caliber, so how hard was it to find Eli and Oskar?

It took almost a year to find them. It was very hard. And my ambition was to have, as I said, the same character. Two sides of the same character. So, they were not only required to be a good boy and a good girl, but they were to be the perfect match as well as a couple, and as well as being two sides of the same coin. That was really complicated. These are two extremely strange and intelligent children. They're very quiet. A lot of integrity.

Rob: And this was their first ever film experience?

Yes, yes.

What was particularly "Swedish" about this film? Because what I was thinking, if you see *30 Days of Night*, it of course exploits that seasonal setting. And in this film, you get that feeling of the dark season and the darkness there and the personalities of the people. I think there's something uniquely Swedish about this film that perhaps another vampire film wouldn't be like or another film wouldn't be like. Can you speak a little bit about that?

Maybe it could be the amount of silence and talking through silence. Swedes are very quiet, sometimes. And not answering a question is also a way of answering a question. Or turning your back to somebody is also a form of communication. So that is something quite special and Swedish, I would think. The idea of silence, and the things that you suddenly hear in a silent community.

Tomas, everyone's talking about the recently announced remake of *Let the Right One In* from *Cloverfield* director Matt Reeves. I wanted to know how involved you will be and if they're going to try to "Americanize" it and make a lot of changes?

I'm not involved at all.

At all? I read it's something you're not happy about.

Well... it's sort of... it gives you some sort of feelings of

jealousy, of course. I have been dancing with this material for three years, and now somebody else is doing it. But you have to put that aside and just wait and see what they come up with. And maybe they'll find other things in that book that could be interesting. It would be very sad if they made a copy of this.

Well, I imagine it won't be as violent and perhaps they'll make it PG-13.

Excuse me – why three years? Why did you have to wait three years?

Well, it was very tough to finance. Yeah.

Getting back to this discussion on the remake, what do you hope they will do? Go more his direction or her direction?

I don't know. I would be very happy if I was surprised.

Rob: Would you be receptive if they reached out to you and asked for your advice on the remake?

No.

What about a sequel? That almost should motivate you!

(laughs)

Is he going to stay with her until he's old?

I think they go out in Europe, eating people, having fun.

Did you have any people in mind that you were glad they were killing?

(laughs)

Were one of those boys that got killed a model for someone that tortured you?

(pause) No. (laughs)

Nobody was cast with that in mind?

No, no.

Rob: This is more of an observation and a question about how you feel about this. For me, I didn't think the horror came from the vampire girl. I was more terrified of what kids will do to other kids when adults aren't looking. Those were the scenes that affected me. How much of that came from the book? And how'd you balance making those scenes just as suspenseful as say the vampire attacks?

I really cannot tell, but I think it comes from the book and my own experiences from childhood. But yeah, that's very hard to tell. That's a common commentary. That people are as terrified of the "horror" parts as they are of what people do to each other.

Did you pretty much stay close to the book when doing the film?

Yeah, we picked out this love track out of the book, and I think it was very true to that.

And how did you discover the book? Was it something that was popular in Sweden?

No, a friend gave it to me. One of the producers-to-be. And usually, I hate when people give me books or films, because I really like to discover that for myself, but I read it. I don't think you should do films from good books either, but there are exceptions.

You've done a lot of other films. How alike or different is this from your other films which people here are not as familiar with as they will be with this one? Can you tell me what was the difference in your process with this film as opposed to your earlier ones?

Well, the process is the same. I'm mostly famous for doing comedy. Black comedy. And drama television. But for me, the process is the same. It's all about telling stories. It's not funny making comedy. And it's not scary making horror. It's all about taking it seriously and telling stories. And showing your heart (in the material).

Well, you said you weren't a horror fan. Have you become a horror fan? Are you looking to read more or watch more horror?

Yeah, maybe. It's very interesting to explore what scares us, I think. I don't get so much scared these days anymore. The things that make me scared are thinking of my children being hurt or murdered or something, but I'm not scared when I go down in the basement or I'm not scared when

I'm sleepless. These are feelings that come from childhood mostly. And fear appears before the scary things happen. So, it's all about finding what those fantasies contain. So, when I was studying before this film, I was watching a lot of Renaissance painters and looking at what they do for the eyes when portraiting people. There is a lot to learn from the old masters with how they treat eyes. For instance, there is an artist called Hans Holbein, who made fantastic portraits of people in the mid-1500's and there is a very famous portrait of a young British prince. It's a close-up and he has a red robe and a crown on his head, and he is looking underneath the spectator, which is really, really spooky. I have worked very actively with eyes in this film. With eyes not seeing each other, with eyes out of the eyeline. So, it's a lot about eyes that makes a scary, creepy feeling.

I was curious about sound design and how important that was for you, because it was so vivid and strong with each sound. Do you have a sound designer you generally work with?

Well, we had worked together once before but I had this very clear vision. It's like with visual framing – it's very much about what you have in the frame, but also what you do not have in the frame. What do you take out from reality or from this specific world? And it's the same with sound. It's not so often that sound editors work with this so much with framing out sounds. Because if you put out specific sounds surrounded by silence, they really mean something. They really do something with your mind. You really have to be picky with what you pick out to make those specific sounds. You really put them into close up, but it's very interesting how that works. I really wanted to tell this as close as possible to the boy Oskar. To hear his own breathing, his own tongue moving in his mouth. We even had a microphone put very, very close to his eyes to hear his eyelids open and close. It really gives you a lot of contact with the character when you hear that. Especially if you remember in the scene when they're lying together in the bed. There are a lot of human sounds that are extremely subtle. But they bring a lot of life to it.

What particular audience were you looking at when you made this film?

Oh no, no. Never. That's not my work. That's work for publicity people.

What kind of decisions did you make in how much you wanted the vampires to feel vampiric or not? It's

interesting how much violence you put in and didn't put in, whether we were going to get a sense if there were fangs or not. Things with the skin. When she was lacking the blood, she started to look more decaying. What was involved with your art direction? Your thoughts on that?

Well, there is a lot of CGI in this film. I think over fifty CGI shots. And it's a fantastic toolbox to use, but it seems like almost everyone is using it too much. If there's a car explosion, it seems like the car has to explode for three minutes and has to be the biggest car explosion you've ever seen. And it's not good for the material or the reality to it. So, we tried to hold back on that as much as possible. You can do so much with those effects in a subtle way. For instance, changing the size of the eyes by ten percent. Just make them ten percent smaller, and nobody could tell what you have done, but it's really spooky when someone suddenly has little, smaller eyes. In one scene, they were bigger and so on. People cannot really pinpoint it. If you make a car explosion for four minutes, everyone will know it's fake and why.

Would you be interested in taking on a Hollywood project? Have any Hollywood studios approached you to make an American film?

Yes, I've got a lot of calls from the studios and from agents and from people trying to hire me for projects, but that's a very big thing to do to change workspace, and to change your life around you and your language. It would be very interesting to do, but it'd really have to be the right project with the right timing.

Would it necessarily be horror?

It could be anything that's good! Or anything that I could feel I could come up with something. It could be any sort of genre.

Are you working on anything at the moment?

Yeah, I'm working on Royal Dramatic Theatre in Stockholm with a comedy group. Yep. It hasn't got a name yet but it's opening in August. We're seven people writing it together. And three weeks ago, I opened with *My Fair Lady* in Stockholm, so I do different things.

I assume it's in Swedish?

Yes! In Swedish!

Going back to the film, do you feel it's for a specific audience? Do you feel it's for teens, do you feel it's for adults, is it for everybody? Also, in terms of the R rating, do you think it's going to limit anybody? Do you feel like violence is over judged in America?

Ok the first one was who the film is for? I really don't know. These are questions for marketing people…

Well, your personal opinion. Would you let a kid who is thirteen see your film?

I have a son that's thirteen and I let him see this because obviously this takes a lot of space in my home. I had explained to him a lot about how it's made and so on, so I let him see it.

Was he scared?

Yeah, but he was mostly scared of the tormenting bullying parts rather than the horror parts. But maybe, I wouldn't let someone younger see it.

I thought this was violent but not like *Hostel*. Have you ever seen *Hostel* or any of these "torture-porn" movies?

No? Are they popular?

Yes, the *Saw* films are.

Ah, yeah. I just read about it. It never interested me.

So, what's the rating system like in Stockholm?

I think it's rated for fifteen.

What would you do if you met a vampire? Have you ever thought about meeting a vampire?

(long pause) Uhh, yes I did. I tried on the internet before we started shooting, I tried to get in contact with vampiristic people. And nobody answered. (laughs) But there is some sort of interesting thing with the obsession of blood that must come from the animal side of ourselves. If I met a vampire? I would pick up my garlic hot dog, because I wouldn't want to be a vampire myself.

Rob: In terms of the shoot itself, were there any scenes or specific moments that were difficult or challenging? Or was this a smooth film to make?

No, it wasn't smooth in any way. It was really tough because of the temperature mostly. And working in the dark with children. That was really tough. It was like minus thirty Celsius, I don't know what that is in Fahrenheit?

That's cold!

(laughs) It's like having somebody shouting in your ear, and I destroyed two fingers.

And you didn't shoot this in Stockholm, right?

No, it's set in a suburb to Stockholm that most Stockholmers know of, but most of the exteriors were in Luleå, the very North of Sweden.

You said you tried to meet vampires. What do you think of those people that worship vampires and want to be them? There are people who get fangs and really want to be like this. This film made it so realistic that it made it feel like a possibility.

Well, I can say that I love people who make their own choices and who can be whatever they want to be without hurting anybody. So, as long as they're not biting people, I really like people when they do what they want. (laughs)

Are you going to stay away from horror for a while now?

No, I'm going to bite any project that's interesting, so it could be horror or a comedy or something very boring! (laughs)

Would you do another vampire film though?

Why not? As long as it's good and interesting.

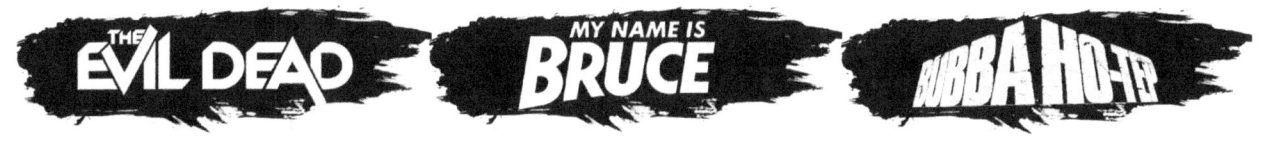

BRUCE CAMPBELL

Interviewed by Mike Cucinotta and Rob Galluzzo (10/08)

Bruce Campbell is a man that needs no introduction. Genre fans know and love him for his portrayal of Ash in the *Evil Dead* trilogy. But now he's back with his latest directorial effort *My Name is Bruce* where he plays B-movie actor "Bruce Campbell," recruited by a small town to save them from a monster. We got to chat with him about shooting his latest movie in his home state of Oregon, the future of *Evil Dead*, and his past filmography including *Bubba Ho-Tep* and the underrated *Running Time*. Read on for our chat with the man himself Bruce Campbell!

Mike: Hey, this is Mike from *Icons of Fright* and also on the line is Rob, my partner on this fine online publication.

Rob: That's me right here, Bruce. How are you?

Good, how are you?

Rob: Good! Well, first and foremost, thanks so much for taking the time to talk with us. We're obviously big fans.

Well, ya gotta get the word out, you know?

Rob: (laughs) Yeah. Funny thing, we know you live in Oregon and we're friendly with one of your neighbors, the lovely Adrienne King!

Oh yeah!

Rob: Who I believe has already seen *My Name is Bruce*?

Yeah, she saw it at a little sneak preview we did in town. She's just up the road, as we say.

Rob: Yes, yes, and she spoke very highly of you when we found out you two were neighbors.

Well, she is an actress.

Rob: Let's talk about the beginnings of *My Name is Bruce*. You had written the book *Make Love The Bruce Campbell Way*, and now you've got the film *My Name is Bruce*, both of which have a sort of satirical look at yourself. For the

movie, was this an idea that was brought to you? Was it something you came up with? Or maybe a bit of both?

Mark Verheiden, who wrote it, pitched it to me with his partner and friend Mike Richardson who's with Dark Horse Comics. And those guys are old pals from the old days. Kind of like me and Sam Raimi in the Detroit area, those guys were old pals back in Portland. And so, I'd worked with Mark a couple of times through comics. Mark Verheiden wrote the *Evil Dead* comic that Dark Horse produced, so there were a lot of tie-ins for us. And we liked each other. So, they pitched this idea, where Mark explains it's kind of based on this old comic book from the '40's where the movie star Alan Ladd was kidnapped to fight pirates. Because they thought he was a swashbuckler and he could take care of this. So, he thought it'd be fun to do the same type of deal, only upgrade it to a B-movie actor who's known for fighting monsters or whatever and have him kidnapped to fight a real monster in a small town. Of course, it turns out to be a terrible idea.

(laughs)

Because the Bruce Campbell in the movie is a jerk, moron, idiot, and he can't do anything. It's a big learning curve of how a movie hero learns to be a real hero. Or attempts to, anyways.

Rob: Was it a given that you would direct this? Because I figure acting and directing would be a lot of hats to wear.

My producer knows the lower the budget, the more I want to do. If I'm going to make a low, low budget movie, then

I really want to have control over it, and not have all these assholes involved. I don't want a lot of chefs involved. So basically, it was me and Mike Richardson who were the only guys to make any decisions on the whole thing. And that was great. It was really nice to be able to have one partner, and we just hashed stuff out, and the movie is what it is. Not the product of a committee.

Rob: I've seen you at dozens of conventions, Q&A's, book signings, etc. over the years, and I know that you often have funny encounters with fans at these events. Did you cull any real-life convention experiences and inject them into *My Name is Bruce*? How much were you able to put in with writer Mark Verheiden?

There's one sequence in the film where everything I got was almost verbatim from fans. Every word out of their mouth is something I've heard verbatim. And my responses in the movie are more like how I would want to respond. But in real life, you have a little bit more tact or you're going to be filling up blogs the next day. Ya know? "Bruce Campbell is an asshole!" So, this movie was my protection shield. I can hide behind the character. The Bruce Campbell in this movie is the actor I would've become if I had stayed in LA for ten more years.

Rob: Wow. And that's not the first time I've heard something like that.

Yeah. I bailed to Oregon, and it saved my life. So, this is more of a satirical look of what could have been.

Mike: What are some of the differences between Bruce Campbell the actor and Bruce Campbell the character?

The real Bruce Campbell does not drink whisky. Uh, I do not feed my dog whisky. I do not live in a broken ramshackle trailer in the desert and leave my dog for months at a time alone. Um, what else? (laughs) Just about every other non-comparison you can make. … but it's because I'm serving the story, obviously. The story is, even if you remove me, my name from the equation, it's still a story of a guy known for playing X, Y, and Z, but in real life is not anywhere near it. It's the story of how he attempts to potentially redeem himself.

Rob: You joke in the trailer about having shot a movie in Bulgaria, a few actually, but this one you got to shoot in your home state of Oregon.

I shot some of it on my property.

Rob: What were some of the biggest differences for you in directing this film as opposed to *The Man With the Screaming Brain*? Home field advantage?

Home field advantage is everything, because everything is normal. I know where everything is. I know where the hardware stores are, I know who I can get to play all these different parts, and because it's not Bulgaria, I can bring them up to my property and use 'em and shoot 'em. I can capitalize on all the local things that are available. Anywhere from cheap building products to open land to build a town on. I could create it exactly how I wanted it. It was having that control. Whereas in Bulgaria, anything can change at any day. You could get kicked out of a location at any time because of greed or corruption. It's a weird society there. The people are great, but they're in a horrible transitional period in their lives. They break in capitalism, but the roads aren't fixed and shit's all bombed out and there's packs of wild dogs. It's just kind of a crazy, a little-bit of a lawless place. It's a great place. I'd go there to hang out, maybe. But I don't know that I'd make another movie there. Because I need stability! When you make a movie, you need control over stuff. We wound up getting control in Bulgaria; we wound up taking over an old Soviet military compound, and clearing trees away that had grown up since communism fell, but we made it into a studio, a backlot. So that Bulgaria itself couldn't invade. So, in Oregon, I just wanted to have as much control as possible. It was great. It was a huge difference. Everybody spoke English.

Rob: In… Bulgaria?

No, in Oregon. Well, at least most people.

Rob: I read that your DP on this was Kurt Rauf, who worked as a PA on the original *Evil Dead*! So, you've known him since way, way back…

A long time. A lot of people in the movie are people that I've known for a long time, or people that I've acted with for a long time. And they're either people that I've never acted with, or people that are old cronies. (laughs) So it was fun. We really cast a lot of locals. The lead actress Grace Thorsen (Kelly Graham) is from Medford, Oregon and the lead kid is local. So, it's fun. We're going to have a hometown premiere in December (2008).

Rob: What I think is really cool, and you did this with *Man With the Screaming Brain*, is that you're doing a tour with the film. Rather than opening everywhere at

once, you're going from town to town. How's the touring experience for you? Getting that immediate reaction?

Yeah, it's just a good old-fashioned tour. You know, whenever a band has a CD to sell, they have to tour. And as guy who wrote a couple of books, guess what? You want to sell books, you better tour! And so, that's really the long and short of it, you gotta tour. But also, I enjoy it. I love car trips. We're doing it all by car. It's just a great way to get out there. 'Cause look, I've been in Miami during the dead of summer for the last six months. I'm ready to see a mountain. Maybe I'll change my tune going over the Rockies, but I do like it. I like seeing these towns again. And frankly, it lets you know if anyone's out there paying attention.

Rob: Are you surprised by the ever-growing fanbase for you? Obviously, a lot of people know you from your genre work, but every time I see you at something like a book signing, I'm surprised by the variety of fans. It's either young kids or older fans. What's that like for you?

Well, it's nice. I've actually been around long enough that I get the second generation now. I've had a lot of fathers come up and go, "Hey, I want you to meet my son Ash. He's now a big fan of the Evil Dead movies." And so, they've passed it along, so now it's a generational thing. But also, weird stuff happens now. We just got picked up for a third season of *Burn Notice* on USA, and so, I'm finally getting, "Hey, aren't you the Burn Notice guy?" And I'm like "Oh, OK!"

Rob: I'd seen *Evil Dead: The Musical* here in New York and I know you came out for the first couple of shows. I love the show. I was always hesitant of the idea of anyone other than you portraying the character of Ash, but that actor Ryan Ward is fantastic as Ash! He's a really, really good actor…

He's terrific, and that kid has worked harder than I ever did on the original movies! (laughs) Because he's got to go through the whole experience every freakin' night. And sometimes even matinees!?

Rob: For years now!

He's got the thousand-yard stare, because he's got the hardest gig in show business! I agree though, he's done a really, really good job and he's a sweet kid, and I hope he goes far. Now the gag is in his life. People will go up to him and be like, "Oh, you played Ash!" (laughs)

Rob: Well, the thing that I realized seeing him portray that character is that we're at the point where Ash goes beyond Bruce Campbell. He's a horror pop culture icon. The Van Helsing of the 21st Century. I mean, girls dress as Ash at horror conventions now!

(laughs)

Rob: Obviously, you couldn't have possibly imagined that would happen when you made the first film, so how do you feel about the fact that this character you created has spawned a life of its own?

It feels good! Because as an artist or an actor or a filmmaker, you never want to bomb. We were blessed that the very first thing that I ever did really caught on. Overseas first! It wasn't really huge here. It took a while to grow. Ultimately, it led to a second and then a third. You can never really have any idea. But what our goal was, we wanted to get our investors their money back. Part of doing *Evil Dead 2* was to get some claim. *Evil Dead 2* finally broke them even and got them into a little bit of profit after six, seven years. Now, they've made a bagful of dough, so now we're fine. Here's what it was. We wanted to be able to go into our local multiplex where we had seen *The Poseidon Adventure* and actually be able to see our own movie there. And that was great. We did that!

We got some popcorn and just sat in there. It was like a Saturday matinee. There weren't that many people there and we just watched the movie, only it was our movie. That was the biggest deal for us. I felt like we succeeded right there. It was like the *Rocky* thing. We just wanted to go the distance. We wanted to raise money, actually shoot a movie and actually get it into a theatre. That was huge. Right then and there. So, today's expectations, people are trying to make a certain amount of money every weekend! We were happy to get into a theatre.

Rob: I wish I could go back and tell you that you'd have multiple action figures based on your likeness years later.

(laughs) Yeah, and there will be a new one for *My Name is Bruce* coming out.

Rob: Really? That's cool!

Yeah, it's a full sized one, like the Ash from *Army Of Darkness*, only it's from this movie. You can either put a whisky bottle in his hand, or his dog's bowl, because his dog's name is Sam 'n Rob, or *If Chins Could Kill*, the book. He can hold the book as well.

Rob: Is that a Dark Horse related thing?

Yeah, it'll be most likely Dark Horse, because they have a whole merchandising deal. It's a logical place to use them.

Rob: Dark Horse is mainly known for comic books, but they've in recent years branched out into movies. What was it like working with a company that was somewhat new when it came to making films?

Well, Mike Richardson has actually produced a fair share of movies, so he's been around. But I think he wanted to just have fun on a low-budget scale, because I don't think Mike likes all the chefs. Same as me. We just want to be our own bosses. And so, Mike was able to find a deal out there that financed our movie when basically it was only Mike and I that had any control. To me, I don't care what the budget is, that's awesome. That's what I'm looking for is that control. It's all about creative control. And so that situation worked out really well. Mike is a great partner, and also, very tall. Mike's very tall.

Rob: (laughs) Well, let's talk about Ted Raimi because he plays two roles in this movie!

Three!

Rob: Oh, three roles!

Mike: Were Ted Raimi's roles written for him? Or did you cast him afterwards?

We knew we needed these characters in the movie. The movie was just written first. And then I went, "Oh yeah, Ted could play that guy. Oh yeah, Ted could play that guy! Oh yeah, he can play that guy." We got more bang for our buck that way. We brought him into town, that way he didn't charge any more per diem for more roles. (laughs) And Ted – Ted and I are old pals. With Ted, we can dick around a lot. When you're shooting things quickly, he gets it, he's from television too. He knows the pace of things, and we like to be able to fool around with things and make shit up, so it allows us to do that. This movie is a weird combination of old cronies of mine versus people I've never worked with before that were local in Oregon. So, it was a foreign combination. My leading lady had never been in a movie before. She's a babe, by the way, so keep your eyes on her. They always find these starlets in the small towns!

Mike: You mentioned television. Was the pace accelerated on this film when you were shooting it? Was it like a television production, schedule-wise?

Pretty much. We shot it in twenty-three days, so we had to sort of get at it and get it done. But fortunately, because a lot of my pals have worked in TV, the hardest thing was getting all the local crew to figure that out. Because it really is a certain pace that you have to hit. And it's a maintain pace. There's really no relief of "Oh that scene is done, let's take a fifteen minute break!" There was never that. "Oh ok, that scenes done. We're setting up over here. Bring that dolly over here." Not run and gun, because I feel in order to get something of value in twenty-three days, you've got to be planned. You have to plan out how you want to shoot it and how you're all going to make it work.

Mike: And the local crew, were they green? Or were they ready to go and experienced?

They were mixed. Like my sound guy was an Oregon guy who was absolutely fabulous. I'd use him again in a second. Just salt of the earth, right there, ready to go, pleasant demeanor and delivered good sound. We used mostly production sound, because I'm a big fan of using the sound on the set, if you can. Because it's the original performance. There's nothing like it. And then other people, we brought some people down from Portland, and they actually copped a little bit of a big city attitude, and I said, "Wait a minute. Let me get this right. You're from Portland, right? I used to shoot in Los Angeles, so what's your problem?" (laughs) So, it's weird, we had a little bit of weirdness going on, but all in all we had a great crew, and I brought in a cameraman that I've known since the *Evil Dead* days, Kurt Rauf. So, you have to fill it out with people that you must have and then try to invite some newcomers and have some fun.

Mike: What about directing yourself as yourself? That's some sort of crazy meta experience. It has to be.

That was definitely weird. That's the weirdest thing of all. But it becomes unweird though, because in my head, as an actor I'm still playing a role. I'm playing the part of Bruce Campbell. So, in my head it's actually not Bruce Campbell, because I know who that Bruce Campbell is. So, it actually wasn't that hard to play, because I'm not playing myself. I'm playing "Bruce Campbell," a horrible, warped, distorted version of myself. So, it wasn't really hard, because I still had to figure out how he wanted to play a scene or how he would act with his fans, and it wasn't how I would. It's how this character would.

Mike: Was there anytime you found yourself slipping into Bruce Campbell, yourself too much? Or was the script just so far removed from that.

It's pretty far removed. There's not a lot where I would go, "Wow, I just felt like myself in that scene!" (laughs) Because, he's such a moron in the movie that I hope I didn't feel like myself!

Rob: And you also have Ellen Sandweiss, your *Evil Dead* co-star, playing your ex-wife in the movie!

Exactly! I wanted all of them. I wanted the other two ladies. And the other two ladies were going to play other parts, but they were concerned about union issues, because we made this non-union. And so, they didn't want to be tortured by that. I tried to get them all, but I'll get them back in the next one. I'm going to try to get Freddy and Jason for the next one too.

Rob: Nice, nice. But I think you'd kick their asses though.

No! But I'd cast them as a farmer and a rancher or something. You know what I mean? It would be completely not them.

Rob: Oh, you mean Robert Englund and Kane Hodder?

I'd get Robert Englund, and he'd play the guy who pumps your gas at the gas station, ya know? And Kane Hodder, I'd make him a pharmacist. (laughs)

(laughs)

You know what I mean? Then I think we got something!

Rob: Well, is it too early to start talking about what you're doing next? Another film? Another book? Television? I know *My Name is Bruce* is not even out yet, but there's already rumblings of a sequel? Is it even feasible to think about that at this point?

Here's a quick rundown of all the *Evil Dead* stuff, because I know it keeps coming back. Like a bad check, ya know?

Rob: Just note that we did not mention *Evil Dead 4* once!

Oh no, no, no! I appreciate that, and I know it's a pre-requisite. It's important because people do ask about it, so you do have to let them eventually know to what extent we even know about them. And the bottom line is this. Um, I think when Sam is ready to do it, we'll all just check our

schedules. He got involved in this massive *Spider-Man* franchise and it seems like it's still continuing. So, who knows? Who knows when the hell anyone will be able to get into another *Evil Dead*. But I think we both desire to do it. It's just really scheduling more than anything.

Because I'm under contract now for five years for USA to do this show, and they just picked up a third season. So, we're just all busy. And as far as a remake goes, there's nothing for me in the remake, so I wouldn't really be involved other than being a producer, because… what am I? The old guy at the bait shop? "Hey kids! You be careful! That place is haunted!" "Oh, shut up, old man!" Ya know? And they drive off into the woods.

Rob: Well, we were just talking about *Evil Dead* with our friend John Torrani last night and he would like to see a sequel with your daughter "Ashley" taking up your mantle, since girls now dress as Ash at the horror conventions! It could even start with a close up shot on your face and you saying, "Give me some sugar, baby." And then it pans back, and you realize it's you in the kitchen asking your daughter to bring you some sugar…

Hey, that's as valid as any idea. Valid as any. Truth be told, I think if all of us really, really felt we had to jump on those movies immediately, they would've been made. So, it's a combination of timing and drive.

Rob: What about the *Evil Dead Musical* movie? The producers of that show recently announced a desire to make a movie version. Didn't you originally help those guys get the rights to do the musical version of *Evil Dead*?

Yes. Well, we didn't discourage it. They were pursuing to do that. I think it's an issue of… Look, if there was already a play of it, as long as you just kind of document it and you could show that in movie theatres as a midnight thing, then it's its own beast. Because it's already so different. I don't think there will be any issues, but we'll see what happens. We'll see what happens.

Look, when we made the first *Evil Dead* movie, it's now 1979 when we made it, we're coming up on thirty years. We never really thought of this stuff. So, you can't always plan for it. So sometimes people go, "Why is *Evil Dead* a musical? A movie? What?" They're always confused. Because everyone thinks there should be sequels and remakes. But I don't know? Should there always be? We never planned it when we did the first *Evil Dead*. We really only did the sequel because our second movie *Crimewave* bombed, so we were like, "Crap. Let's make a sequel." (laughs)

Rob: And by the way, *Evil Dead 2* is my all-time favorite horror movie.

Yeah, it's a cool little movie. There's no question. But… (laughs) I don't remember where we were going with that…

Rob: I was asking what was next? If you were going back to television or another book?

I'm going to go back to television in March to do the third season of *Burn Notice*, because we are the number one show on cable, baby.

Rob: Congrats, buddy! Congrats.

We're up twenty-five percent over last season, so we're growing like a weed. So, I'll do that and hopefully I'll make another movie in the Fall of '09. That's as much as I can plan. And I'll tour all this Fall. I'm going to twenty-two cities.

Rob: We're going to try to catch you in New York.

Yeah, I really want to be in New York City, Halloween at the Midnight show of *My Name is Bruce*. That'll be interesting.

Rob: I saw *Bubba Ho-Tep* when it premiered in Chicago, which I believe was the first screening of it. And it's one of those films where everything just works. It's got one of your best performances, an incredible score by Brian Tyler, Ossie Davis, Don Coscarelli. Because it's so rare that that happens on a movie. Was that the main reason that the sequel just never came together? A matter of, "Well, we got it right the first time. Why mess with it again?" Obviously, Lansdale never wrote a sequel in short story form, so you would've been treading new waters there had you done it…

Yeah, and that may have been the problem. If you don't stick with the original pieces, it's hard to get something that's going to be like the first one. So, here's the real long and short of it. Don and I could not agree on an approach and on the story. And the elements I disliked the most, he actually liked the most. So, we realized that was a pretty big divide. And we didn't want to jeopardize a friendship over this. Because ya know… I don't want to play that game of keeping him from making it. He can certainly make it. It's his to do. If he wants to make ten of these, go baby, go. But for me, I have to know why I'm on that set, and I have to know why I'm there. And I have to enjoy being there.

Rob: Well, you nailed it with *Bubba Ho-Tep*, so I'm not heartbroken that there won't be a sequel, when we have a really great first movie.

Yeah, it's ok. I'm ok that there isn't a series. Some things happen, and that was a glitchy one that just came to a halt. We had to just let it go.

Rob: A friend of mine recently became a huge fan of your work, and I ended up lending her one of my favorite films you've done, *Running Time*, with Josh Becker. How do you hold that film and experience in your filmography?

Oh, I think it's a very groovy little movie. I would recommend that movie to everybody. I think it's a tight little thriller that's got a great cinematic twist to it, and it's more energetic. The fact that it's planned as one shot is pretty bold shit for a movie that cost $110,000.

Rob: Have you spoken to Josh Becker about putting it out again, because I believe it's been out of print for a while?

Um, I have not. I don't know what his deal is with Anchor Bay, but I think they still have it? I just got it on Amazon.

Rob: Really? Ok. (*Note: It is still available on Amazon!*)

It had a legitimate release through Anchor Bay and they tend to keep things alive and in visibility. But maybe it is harder to get. But yeah, that one I totally endorse.

Mike: Do you have any particular favorite version of the *Evil Dead* DVD? Because we own every one!

I get a little wearisome over DVD extras. Because now as a filmmaker I feel burdened to entertain people even more. Like *My Name is Bruce*, when it comes out on DVD, it'll be out in Blu-ray in February and it's going to be gorgeous. But because we also have a beautiful hour long making-of doc about making that damned thing, I feel pressured as a filmmaker now to do as much for the DVD extras as I do for the movie! And so, personally? I prefer to just take the disc. Pop it in. Play the movie. Turn it off. I'm that kind of guy. I'm not a bells and whistles kind of guy. Because to me, it's about the movie, it's not about the extras. That's just me.

Special thanks to RJ Millard and ToddZeller!

2008-09
THE LOST INTERVIEWS

TOM HOLLAND

KATT SHEA

DAVID J. SCHOW

TOM HOLLAND

Interviewed by Mike Cucinotta and Rob Galluzzo (8/08)

By the time we sat down with Tom in June '08, he'd already been a big supporter of *The Psycho Legacy* doc and also participated in the first ever reunion panels for both *Fright Night* and *Psycho*. And so, he was a lot more candid with us about his career, past and present. We talked chronologically about his work up until *Child's Play*, but he really wanted to break and continue another day. We never got to conduct "Part Two," hence why I think this interview has been "lost" this entire time! But it's still a great discussion, mostly on his rarely spoken about acting career, and a perfect time capsule of this moment with Tom Holland!

What are your earliest recollections of the horror genre? What films do you remember kind of having an impact on you and introducing you to the world of horror?

It's almost cliché to say now but *Psycho*. But what I really remember as a little kid before that were the William Castle films. That's what I remember. Then I remember growing up with AIP and with Hammer. But the one that I knew was different and that changed everything was *Psycho*. There's no two ways about it.

When did you first see *Psycho*?

I saw it at a boarding school called Worcester Academy in Worcester, Mass. Where I was imprisoned in my sophomore year in high school. And I saw it with my buddy Chris Hendrie, who is in *Psycho II*. And it had me under the seats. But that had an intensity. Compared to the Vincent Price stuff. What came close to that? *Curse of the Demon* was a progenitor of the modern horror films. But that gives you a sense of it. You can see the potential in some of the Val Lewton stuff. Maybe the *Leopard* film? And maybe the one where it's a William Irish novel. William Irish was a pseudonym for... Who wrote the original short story, *Rear Window*? Cornell Woolrich. But there's one where... You can see the form building. *Phantom Lady*. Robert Siodmak directed it. And it's also by the same author from one of his novels. And it's a gal who's trying to help her lover who's in prison for murder and trying to provide an alibi. And she's going out with the lover's best friend who works in an architectural firm. And of course, she doesn't realize it, but

we do. The best friend is the murderer. And she gets closer and closer to the real murderer. Of course, she puts him in greater and greater danger. In other words, you start to see the suspense. You start to see the structure of what will be the modern suspense horror film. You can see it coming on in the 40s and the 50s. And if you have enough film history. But I also point out, because through you, at that seminar down at *Fangoria* when Hilton Green was there, who was the first A.D. on *Psycho*, he said they all went to see *Psycho* without the music. And they said, eh, okay. (laughs) I mean, I thought that was sort of a stunning kind of admission. And I wondered if I would have thought that. If that Bernard Herrmann score wasn't there, what would I have thought?

It was the same story with *Halloween*. Everyone thought the movie didn't work until he did that score for it.

I did not know that.

And that's the thing. It's like *Psycho*, *Halloween*; music is very important for those specific films.

Well, now I listen to *Halloween* and it sounds very thin to me. The basic three-chord thing I think is wonderful. But now it sounds so thin to me that, of course, twenty-five years ago it didn't. But that's sort of interesting.

Your career has followed interesting paths in terms of being in every aspect; acting, writing, directing. But the first thing you did was act?

I apprenticed at Bucks County Playhouse in Bucks County, Pennsylvania. And I was in love with film, but back in those days, they didn't really have film schools. They had theater departments. They had them at Carnegie Tech and Northwestern. And that's what I found out when I apprenticed at Bucks County. What I found out was about acting teachers in New York. And I started then when I was like, fifteen or sixteen. I found out about acting classes in New York. And then the next year after I finished high school, I started going to New York and taking acting classes. And then I found out your two best schools were in a consortium at Carnegie Tech and Northwestern. And the graduate level for theater was Yale. And I had accepted both at Carnegie Tech and Northwestern and went to Northwestern. But I was never that interested in theater. What I was really interested in was film. And I shot a 16 mm short film at Northwestern. And nobody had a film department. And you used a cold splicer, and you wore white gloves. And that's how you put it together. And then I went to New York to be an actor because there just wasn't... There wasn't any "in" to being a director. I didn't even know movies were written. There was no sense of screenwriter in those days. I'm talking early 60s?

Did they do a lot of film work in New York at the time? Because it seems like now the thing is, LA is where you go as an actor for film. New York is more for theater.

But the way it worked then was you had to go to New York and be a theater actor to prove your bones before you'd come out to LA. And I went to New York, and I worked and did soap operas. I was the lead on several soap operas and had some phenomenal experiences. I got mobbed at Shea Stadium at the *Beatles* concert in 1966. And my wife will still talk about it. It scared the hell out of me.

Andrew London told the funniest story when I interviewed him for the *Psycho Legacy*, where he said he came into a meeting, I guess his first meeting for *Psycho II* and saw you and immediately recognized you as Tom Fielding from all those TV shows! So, he immediately recognized you from the TV stuff you did.

That's right! Because there was another Tom Holland in the Guild. Henry Fielding was popular at the time, and Tom Jones, yeah it was Tom Jones. But I was never comfortable not using my real name. I was put under a seven-year contract at Warner Brothers by Harry Warner. And I was out at Warner Brothers. I had to go to court to sign because I was a few months shy of eighteen or something. They

were just making *My Fair Lady*. They were just finishing it. The *Camelot* set was still standing at Warner Brothers. So, I mean I saw the last gasp of classical Hollywood. I have a perspective on all this. Now it all started to change. And then I was going back and forth, working in New York as an actor, and working out here. I came out here and did the Chrysler Theater. *Out On the Outskirts of Town*, written by William Inge, starring Anne Bancroft. And I was the juvenile in it. I was the other juvenile. And Jack Warden was in it. And Frank Corsaro directed. And backing him up, because he was a stage director and not experienced, was Sidney Pollack. Sidney, I think had just done *The Slender Thread*. In New York, I was close to and palled around with Al Pacino. I had the original part in *The Tiger Wore an Orange Necktie*, which was a play about dope addiction. And that was at the New Dramatist Guild.

And then I came out here and was working out here. And the part was finally done on Broadway by Al Pacino. And he was in the play with me. And Al was just a terrific guy, and obviously a terrifically talented actor. I went back and forth for a time between New York and here, because everybody back in those days put down LA. LA was the town without a good restaurant, and without culture. And everybody from New York was a snob. Plus, everybody, you know, still? (laughs) But less so now. There's a very evolved culture here now in LA. When I went to see Bill Malone's film on Friday, we passed, I don't know, four or five clubs. It was Friday night. It was like ten o'clock when I got out of there. And I could not believe the maître d's, the valet services, and the people stepping up dressed to the nines. Beautiful girls. I mean there's obviously a huge club scene now. On Vine and Hollywood Blvd. Hollywood is exploding. And that place was a pit all my life until recently.

Anyway, I was more interested in acting on a film. So, I made the move out here. And started working here. I got in The Actor's Studio. This is when Lee Strasberg was still alive. Must have been '68, '69. And I was sitting, I would go in there and listen to him. And from there, I got into playwright's wing. I started doing plays. And what they had there was they had the playwright's wing at The Actor's Studio. This was on De Longpre in Hollywood. And playwrights would put up their one-act plays. And they would direct them. It's very much what you're talking about now with short films. And all of a sudden, I realized that writers were directing their own material. And I became friends with Jim Bridges. And Jim was doing that. And I think Jim had never directed at the time. But he had written the *Forbin Project*. And he gave me the idea. He said, if you write, it's a great way into directing. By then, I knew I wanted to direct. And I was more interested in that than I was in acting. But if there were film schools, I probably never would have been an actor. I just didn't know how to get to it. Then around that time, you had guys like John Milius breaking in. And then, all of a sudden, writing original screenplays was a way to get into directing. So that's what I started doing. And that took me about five years. And then I started to work.

What was one of the first things you did? *The Beast Within*?

That was the first thing. I think it was the first movie that was produced. *Initiation of Sarah*, which was a movie of the week, which was the first jiggle show, as they said at the time. That was ABC. Well, that's where they threw the girls in the fountain and got them all wet. And they came out with wet t-shirts. And you could see their nipples. And there was a lead article in the Sunday LA Times calendar section, which was a big thing then, about all the outrage throughout the country. You could see nipples beneath the t-shirts. It was Morgan Fairchild. I did the *Model Shop* with Jacques Demy.

I was friends with Harrison Ford. Same generation. And Harrison was the one, out of all those guys, who were working. He's the one who broke out and became the biggest star. Out of every group, there seemed to be somebody during that period that had luck. Of course, Harrison was supposed to have been the lead in the *Model Shop*. That's who Jacques Demy wanted. Columbia wouldn't take him because he wasn't a name. And instead made Jacques take Gary Lockwood, who was one of the two stars of *2001: A Space Odessey*. And Harrison was so pissed off, I think at some point he told somebody off at Columbia that he was under a seven-year contract and got fired. And then he became a carpenter for ten years. And then he started to get work with Francis Coppola and that turned into *Star Wars*.

I've probably told this story before. This is a true story. It was about six months before *Star Wars* opened. And I ran into Harrison at a party. And he had a beard. And he had a big gut from drinking beer. And he was really pissed off and angry because he'd done the sci-fi movie. It was probably a piece of shit. But he couldn't get any work. And he was going to have to go back and start carpentry up again. And he built the hot tub for Colin Higgins. He was the director that did *9 to 5*. And he was just generally pissed off. He was probably about thirty-one, two, three. We all were. He was a little older than I am. And then *Star Wars* came out. And he was the biggest thing on the planet. But the point is none of them had a clue. They did not have a clue what they had with *Star Wars*. I don't know whether the director did. But sure as hell, the actors didn't know.

Probably the most obviously talented actor I'd ever seen was Al Pacino. And he was a stage actor. His body language. He communicated so much about what the actor was feeling internally. He was so obviously talented. So many film actors work here to here. I did *A Walk In The Spring Rain*. I was the juvenile in that with Ingrid Bergman and Anthony Quinn. I mean, I worked a lot. And then I transitioned into writing. The last time I worked professionally was 1982 in *Winds of War*, which was a big mini-series that Dan Curtis directed. But during the seventies, acting became a way to make a living to support writing as I tried to transition, and I'd gotten that idea from the playwrights in the Actors Studio.

When did you do *The Incredible Hulk*?

I think that was 1976 or 1977. I was the guest star on that. The guest star villain.

You were the pre-Martin Kove evil Sensei from *Karate Kid*. (laughs) What was it like working with Bill Bixby and Lou Ferrigno on *The Hulk*? I used to love that show so much.

I knew Bill Bixby and I don't remember how. But I think we dated the same girl? I knew him from *My Favorite Martian*. I did an episode of *Combat!* When I was down in Dallas at the horror convention, some fan showed up with a bloody script. They had a copy of the *Combat!* script. Now that's out there apparently. I'm going to be able to turn on the TV, flip the channel and watch my hairline recede. (laughs) So, I did it all. I like to say that I've been a hot and cold success and failure... In almost every different aspect of this business in my life.

That's shaped you as a person and artist.

It's shaped me. It's how I learned. My orientation was acting. From acting to writing and from writing to directing. I think if I had come up in a different generation... I would have gone to directing right away. I like to think... I hope you agree with me... Generally, the acting is very solid in my material. And I think that's because I know how to direct actors. I've always had a terrific rapport with them because I was an actor. I also think the hardest creative task is writing. That is the most difficult. You don't know terror until you face the blank page or blank computer screen.

Was *The Beast Within* based on an original story or book?

Harvey Bernhard, the producer of that. He was also the producer of the *Omen* series. He bought a book title. The writer hadn't written the book yet! So, Harvey hired me to write a screenplay based on the title. And he didn't have anything. He didn't have an outline or anything else. Just the title. The book was written after the movie. I don't think it bears any resemblance to the movie.

Where did you come up with this idea? This bookish creature that runs around? I remember the poster as a kid. I thought it was a werewolf movie. Just from *The Beast Within* title and the kid. But it's far more horrifying that this kid becomes a giant locust.

What was happening to me... I was writing this stuff in the 70s. Everybody thought I was nuts. They replaced me on *Initiation of Sarah*. There was another writer on it too. I was writing stuff where... I had the girls being cursed in the sorority, turning into pigs and donkeys. That's a horror film. I was doing the stuff that we're doing now. I was doing it in the 70s when nobody else had that kind of sensibility. *The Beast Within* is an example of that. That's the first time, or damn close to it, that anybody was doing rubber effects and bladders to make them blow up.

It's known for its special effects.

That was what was in my head. That was way ahead of the curve back then. People really thought that I was crazy. What I was writing was too far out for them. Somehow, I got that. That's the first script all the way through. But the movie was not a success. And I couldn't get a job for a year. Then *Psycho II* arrived and changed everything.

When did *Class of 1984* happen?

That was a success. But that still didn't seem to change anything in terms of paying work for the majors. This is now 2008. We're in a very interesting time. We're in transition time. The old model, the majors may be dying. Or at least they're losing their monopoly. My whole life, all I've seen is the independents crushed by the majors. There's been attempt after attempt. They either buy them out or they strangle the distribution avenues. They eventually somehow dominate the business. Somehow, *The Beast Within* slipped through. Somehow *Psycho II*, *Cloak and Dagger*, *Fright Night*. But I think that's because they were always... I think I got into the system working for the majors but on the very, very low end. And they weren't paying attention to it. I think if they paid attention to it, they would have been horrified. But anyway, *The Beast Within* was what... I mean, you could do that script right now and it would be very correct in terms of the effects. Except now you could do them. Back then you couldn't do the effects that I had written.

That was kind of like a weird drive-in kind of movie. Which studio did that?

I think it was UA.

It had that AIP kind of feel to it. Is that what you were aiming for?

It was very bloody. It was about this kid. What was interesting about it to me was the kid had a monster inside of him, which was an allegory for all kinds of things. And he was building this mold where he was going to slough off the human skin. And at the same time, he's falling in love with this human girl. And he was trying to keep himself from killing her. I mean, there's just all kinds of interesting stuff.

Now, *Psycho II* is obviously a very important script in your career. And one of the things that I wanted to bring up about it was, obviously, your relationship with Richard Franklin. Because I think before *Psycho II*, you had met him because of a sword fantasy movie you wrote?

I wrote something called *The Crystal Tower*, which was everybody's favorite original script of mine. Carolco bought it and made an overall deal with me. And we tried to get it done. And just as we were getting it together to get it done, they went bankrupt. And the script's been tied up in their bankruptcy forever. But that script, *The Crystal Tower*, now it seems like a familiar tale. But it certainly wasn't then. It's about a boy who hears voices and the voices are calling him Arthur. He doesn't understand what it is. And he finds this drunk, this homeless bum who claims he's Merlin and claims the kid is Arthur reborn, and that the war with Mordred and the witch Vivian is about to begin again. The kid, and everybody, thinks he's insane. Then, of course, things start to happen. That was not there. Now I don't think you can get a modern Arthurian tale done because they've done five million of them and they're all Saturday afternoon specials. But then, that even predated *Excalibur*.

And was Richard Franklin attached to that?

No, people loved that script. They loved *Cloak and Dagger*. *Cloak and Dagger*, by the way, is just a terrific... I mean, I can say this now. *Cloak and Dagger* was a better script than it was a movie. And Richard directed that. With *Psycho II*, Richard fulfilled that script totally. I mean, the movie was as good as that script. *Cloak and Dagger*, his son was autistic. They discovered that Davey was autistic. I wrote it for Davey, and I called the kid Davey. But he was dealing with all kinds of schools and medical things while he was directing. They didn't know very much about autism then and they thought it was curable. So, he was going crazy with his wife and flying all over the country while he was trying to direct the picture.

You had a close relationship with him on *Psycho II*. I can only imagine what it was like for people to read the script to *Psycho II* for the first time. What were the reactions at the time?

Contrary to what Hilton (Green) says, they did not have Tony Perkins until I wrote that script! That is why the movie was slated as a TV cable movie. They didn't think Tony would do it. He had said, no, I'm not interested. And that was because of the Robert Bloch novel, which was, I don't want to say… terrible, but it did not create a sympathetic Norman Bates.

Did you ever read it? I know you didn't read it then, but did you ever read it after?

No, I didn't because I didn't want to interfere with the writing of *Psycho II*. But when I wrote the screenplay and all those people read it and said, 'Hey, it isn't bad?' And they gave it to Tony and Tony said yes. And then things began to change. And Universal, once again, they didn't know. And this goes to your documentary. Generally speaking, large organizations are bureaucratic. They are not pro-creative. You have things happen like what happened to you on the *Psycho* documentary. There is no individualism. There's nobody taking responsibility. There's very, very little thinking. And there's hardly any thinking outside the box because you get killed for it. So, you only get the safest, most routine kind of reaction. What got me into that? So even when they got Tony Perkins, it was still a fucking cable movie. It was a brilliant fucking script. I've never written a better script.

Is it the one you're most proud of?

Well, no. *Fright Night* is terrific. *Cloak and Dagger* is a terrific script. Not as good a movie. He really fucked it up. He fucked it up because he cast Dabney Coleman. They should have cast Kevin Kline. Dabney was not a sympathetic father figure. Dabney couldn't pull off the human heart and warmth. But that was the fault of that movie. And Dabney was insisted on by Tom Mount at Universal. He said, you either cast Dabney or we won't make the movie. But they didn't know what they had with *Psycho II*. But then even when they had Tony, they were still thinking of it as a cable

movie. And then you had the announcement that Tony was coming back to play Norman Bates. And the amount of media interest was just fucking phenomenal. And it was worldwide. And that's when they started to think, 'Oh my God, maybe we have something.'

So, they were literally dragged, kicking and screaming to release it theatrical. When they had no intention, you had to knock them off the side of the head with a two by four. Because they can't change. Once they're set on a course, everybody follows orders. And there's no reward for deviating or thinking outside the box. And so, you have a business that can't act or react quickly to changing circumstances, which is what we're in now. Talking about the digital revolution, or the potential digital revolution, I can't tell you how many Hollywood professionals and major players are telling me that there is no future on the internet. Or if there is, we'll be long dead before we see it. But that's because it's so threatening, I think, that they may very well be true. But I mean, there is a… The town is reactionary, and the town doesn't want to change. They don't want to learn new business patterns. And everybody's afraid of their wonderful income being cut in half or more. It's just really interesting how a corporate organism reacts to competition. Because what everybody tries to do is monopolize and remove threat, remove risk. It's about removing risk and killing anything that's potential risk. And we're in the middle of that.

Your difficulty is that what the DGA is trying to do is inject all their people into this new digital thing?

Yeah, because they're going to kill me. I wouldn't do better if I signed that. And what the DGA is saying is that if I do anything digitally for profit, then it has to be DGA. Well, if I do an online pilot, which is how they interpret *Driven*, (Tom's unreleased noir pilot starring his son Josh Holland) because it looks like a presentation, then I can work with non-DGA or not pay DGA rates. But it's crazy.

Then it's time for innovation.

Totally. Totally. I mean, see, everybody's threatened all along the way.

I don't understand how anything gets done around here.

Well, but it's just the majors who do it. They don't want the independents. They'll either crush you or buy you out.

Back to *Psycho II*. It was huge, which no one expected. What else was out around the same time for context?

I don't think we had any horror competition. We didn't have what you have now which is where you counter program movies for the weekends.

Here's a rumor I'd read somewhere. Was it true that Universal was so satisfied with your script that they went back to Robert Bloch to ask if he'd consider changing his *Psycho II* manuscript, and turn it into a novelization? And he was pretty pissed off about it. (laughs)

That… sounds familiar. He'd written a sequel that was such a downer if you were a Norman Bates fan.

It's an interesting novel, but you couldn't have made a movie from that book. In the book, Hollywood is making a movie called *Crazy Lady* based on the events from the first novel, and the director happens to resemble Norman Bates? Very bizarre. What was some of the groundwork that you were going for when you were writing *Psycho II*? The original is Hitchcock, so there's that pressure. How do you even approach it? What's the first thing you think of?

One of the qualities that made the first one so impactful was Tony Perkins created Norman Bates, who is this serial murderer you loved. That you feel sorry for. He has this terrible duality where you want to Mother him, even though you know he's going to turn around and kill you. So, you wanted to keep the audience feeling sympathy for Norman. Because that's the perversity of it. And in order to do that, I had to come up with a concept that in some ways absolved Norman. And that was that he was released after years of trying to get himself back to normal mental health. And the vengeful relatives decide to drive him mad! As their vengeance. And he's fighting desperately to hold onto his sanity as all these murders are happening all around him! (laughs) And then, of course at the end, you find out that he's mad as a hatter as your tag! But up until then, he's so sympathetic and desperately trying to stay sane!

And you want him to! This is 1982. The time of *Friday the 13th* and *Halloween* sequels. You could easily have gone the cheap route here. Norman escapes from the institution and goes on a slasher rampage. Did anyone ever push you in that direction?

No, but we didn't have respect for those films you just mentioned.

I think also because everything you guys did was so under the radar, it's not like anyone was paying attention or there was some kind of expectation.

We were a cable movie. They made it for nothing. They left us alone! It's only when they started paying attention to me that things got terrible.

You had told me your method was to map out every scene on index cards, correct?

Yes, because what Richard did, Richard Franklin gave me a six-week course on Alfred Hitchcock. We ran every Hitchcock film. We looked at individual set pieces. And we were trying to create or duplicate; Hitchcock had three to five visual set pieces per film, and we were trying to do the same thing. We used the same shots. The girl looking through the peephole. And the eye coming up on the other side of it. Those were Hitchcock set-ups. We were working so much off of them and yet we had to remain honest, which was, everything logically had to fit with the first one.

What I love about it is, yes, it could be as clean cut as Mrs. Spool was the killer and killed everybody. But I love you don't know for sure. Maybe Norman did do one of them? Maybe it was Mary? Maybe Lila Loomis? It's vague enough that it could've been any of them at any time, or it could just be all Mrs. Spool.

I can't remember specifics, but it wasn't Norman. I know that I set it up so that it definitely wasn't him. But at the end, he goes mad and kills his Mother! I can't remember if Mrs. Spool did all of them or if I set one up that maybe Lila did one of them.

I feel that Lila would've been nuts enough to murder someone! One of my friends recently watched *Psycho II* for the first time, and you would only pick this up now, he immediately figured it out because you named the girl Mary Samuels, which is the name Marion Crane goes by in the first film…

He caught that?

Yes! But in 1982, you wouldn't had to have seen *Psycho* a lot to pick that up in a theater in 1982!

What a memory on that guy! (laughs)

Us horror nerds today pick up everything! (laughs) Now, what came out of *Psycho II* for you?

It started getting me all kinds of writing jobs. As the jobs kept coming, I became viable as a first-time director.

How were you able to pitch *Fright Night* to be your directorial debut?

I wrote it as an original spec. And I went in, and I sold it.

And was the deal always, 'I wrote this, and I also have to direct it.'

Yes, it always was. Because I had a terrible experience. I wrote this script that was just great called *Scream For Help*. The movie was unreleasable. Now we're older and it doesn't make any difference, but Michael Winner directed it. And Michael just didn't have a clue how to make that kind of movie. Nice enough fellow. But it was unreleasable. And I said I can't go through this again. It was a brilliant fucking script. It was *The Stepfather*! About two years before *The Stepfather* came out. We just missed it. So, with that, I thought as a director I couldn't do any worse. It was an act of self-defense.

At this point, you had been involved in films for so long, what'd you pick up that prepared you to direct your first feature?

I learned from all of it along the way. And I knew so much. There wasn't very much that I hadn't done. I don't know how to put it, but… I knew a little bit about what everyone does on a film set. I don't know if I could do any one of them, but I sure know how the whole thing works and comes together. I know where I'm not supposed to cut!

How about getting Roddy McDowall in *Fright Night*?

Roddy was a terrific human being. And such a sweet, sweet man. He was just very supportive, protective, and a good friend. He introduced me to a lot of old Hollywood. I'd go to his house where he'd host these dinners; he would have a Wednesday night for straight people and a Friday night for gay people. He had two dinners a week. I met Vincent Price and his wife at Roddy's house. I met Walter Matheau with his wife. I met Lee Remick. I met John Schlesinger, the director of *Marathon Man*. I met Philip Dunne who was a huge writer in the 30s and 40s at 20th Century Fox. I met the guy who was the head of press relations for David O. Selznick. I met the director of *Three Coins in a Fountain*, Jean Negulesco, at Roddy's. Just everyone.

Roddy was a walking history of Hollywood. He remembered everything and would not write his biography. He knew everything. We walked MGM as they were closing it down where he had been a child actor. He took me underneath where all these pipes were, now it's Sony, but that's where they had all the nitrate films stored in racks all right next to where they had the utility pipes running underneath. He showed me where Katherine Hepburn met Spencer Tracy. You may not even know who these people are! Well, you guys know. But to me, they were Gods! We had movie stars! You've got… I don't know what you have now. I grew up when movie stars were movie stars. It was the classical system when I was growing up as a kid. I was seeing the last gasp of Hollywood. Jean Negulesco, I went over to his house in Beverly Hills. He was married at Howard Hawkes house! His wife was best friends with Slim Keith? It was the entre into a world that I had looked at. I came from a small town in upstate New York. I grew up reading fan magazines, and looking at films like you did. And all of a sudden, I'm there. Every time I went over to Roddy's I was hoping to see Elizabeth Taylor!

(group laughs)

He really did it. He went out to the Old Age Home, the Hollywood Motion Picture Home, and would visit the Silent Movie stars that were still alive. He was out seeing Mary Astor after she'd lost her mind. These are the famous Hollywood stories. It's like in Benedict Canyon, going up Easton Drive, at the end of it, you come up to the house where Harlow spent her married night with Paul Bern, who worked at MGM and after he couldn't get it up, he killed himself. And it's that house. That famous scandal. I mean, I was into that kind of thing. I don't know why, but I adored it. Roddy was everybody's best friend. But the way that Roddy worked as an actor, that Roddy was almost a professional friend. He agented himself by being friends with everybody. But if he didn't like you, God help you. He had a tongue. And I don't know what was wrong with him, but he had a series of young lovers, and he could never hold onto them. They were long term affairs, but he wasn't leaving them, they were leaving him. And I never understood why. I could see the tongue. He was just wonderful though. Things would happen like that; I would be on the set….

He's such a fascinating guy.

He knew everything! He knew all the oral history. He used to say that Hollywood has no history. He was the keeper. Like in *Mad Max*. He was the guy that kept it all in his head. He would not write it down and I do not understand why. And he wouldn't have a memorial service, and I don't know why. But anyway, among the things that happened, I'm walking around, shooting the very beginning of *Fright Night*, and at the time I smoked two, three packs of cigarettes a day for forty years. And I'm walking around drinking black coffee and smoking cigarettes, and Roddy, he said, "*You know, you've got to really be careful, because that's how Noel Coward went, but he was just fine, and then one day he started to cough, and then it was just straight downhill after that.*"

He knew Noel Coward, from what was the high gay society, and then the generation after Roddy was what Tony Perkins represented, and Tony's best friend was Stephen Sondheim. Tony's great love was Grover Dale, who was a famous choreographer of the time, and something terrible happened, they couldn't get it through their heads, and Tony decided to go straight, and went through a long period of analysis, trying to convince himself he was heterosexual. There is a famous love story with Grover Dale. Roddy had stories like that about the generation before him, the Forever Amber, who was the female star, she burned to death in a hotel fire, oh God, Darnell, Linda Darnell, I think, he said she was the most beautiful woman he'd ever seen. He said Howard Hawks was a compulsive liar and could never tell the truth about anything. He said John Ford was absolutely wonderful and totally irascible. If you looked at him wrong, he'd take your head off. He was like that with everybody.

I mean, he would go on and on about the stupidity of Hollywood. He couldn't get them to revive the *Planet of the Apes* series, but he talks about how God awful it was with the guy who was the producer on that, always trying to get the next one out of the studio, right, and how horrible it was to get the sequels done, and yet one sequel after another, they kept saying, 'Well, that's my last one, it's not going to make money,' and it would make a gazillion dollars. He was full of stories like that.

Plus, he had this huge respect for Darryl Zanuck, it's a generation before me, so it's two generations before you, but I mean, I just remember getting together… I wish I could remember the director's name, but he directed *Three Coins in a Fountain*. I met him, when he was in town, and his wife was Slim Keith's best friend, and Slim Keith was one of the crowd with Barbara Paley, which were women who lunched, which was the group that destroyed Truman Capote, am I ringing any bells with any of this stuff? I had dinner with them, and he had bought a house from Glenda Swarthout, or Linda Swarthout, who was a huge opera singer, when they were young, and I sat there with him and his wife, and they must have been like eighty-five at the time, they

had retired, and he directed, I think, one of the segments of *The Longest Day*, they had retired to Marbella, in Spain, and we walked around this house in Beverly Hills, and he told me about the parties there, and Garbo stood there, and Robert Taylor was over here, madly in love with her, and I mean, it was fascinating to me. It was David O. Selznick's press agent, head of publicity for David O. Selznick, one of his best friends, and he was there telling David O. Selznick stories about how he couldn't stop gambling, and how, what he went through to have the affair with Jennifer Jones.

And I just sat there with him, this was the kind of world that Roddy opened up, and if you didn't love film, and old film history, it wouldn't have meant much to you, but Roddy at the same time was like that about the silent film stars, when he'd been a boy. John Nicolesco was the one that I met at Roddy's house, who had me over to his, where I started to meet all these other survivors. God, some of the people, that's probably been the best part of being in the business, is the people I've met, and not the younger people, the older people.

How'd you meet Chris Sarandon for *Fright Night*? You didn't meet him through Michael Winner, did you?

No, no, you know that he blamed Michael Winner for destroying his career.

Ah, because of *The Sentinel*, right?

That's right.

Yeah, he spoke quite frankly about Michael Winner when I spoke to him.

Never got over that. He was on his way to being a movie star, and he really felt that, and I think also *Lipstick*. You know, really wrecked him. Because Chris is a really talented actor.

You met Chris for the first time on *Fright Night*?

On *Fright Night*, yeah. And I had to convince Chris to do it, because I was a first-time director, and he was so badly burned because of things like Michael Winner.

And Michael Winner directed your last script.

And destroyed it. Just destroyed it. And yet, Michael Winner did some of the great, trashy action films of the 70s. He did *The Stone Killers*. He did a couple of westerns that were pretty good, I think.

What about the *Death Wish* movies?

Well, the *Death Wish* movies was how he destroyed *Scream for Help*. He destroyed it because the *Death Wish* movies, what worked for him was cutting dialogue. And so, he figured if he cut dialogue and went down to just action, that would make a successful movie. Wrong.

So, Chris came in and just auditioned.

Well, he auditioned. He was just fabulous. And then I had to convince him. I had to jump through all kinds of hoops trying to convince him that I knew enough to do it. The secret to that was we really rehearsed for two weeks. That was the secret.

Did he begin to trust you?

Yes, I think because, at the very least, he knew I knew how to block scenes. You see, what I do, because of the theatrical background, is that I can take a scene. If you have a dialogue scene, an acting scene, I can put it on the speak and make it work and I can block it. And I can get it so it's working. It goes beyond that. The problem is if the writing is any good. This is what you do first. Then you look for a master. You look for the camera angle that gives you the physical orientation and hopefully where you can see the whole thing all the way through. And then you go in for your coverage. If you start shooting your coverage first, like your master, you will almost always screw up. But if you can't put the scene on the speak and make it work, you're fucked to begin with. So now if you're doing something that's just visual without any dialogue, you still have to do that. You see less and less scenes where they can stand on their own, where the camera should be unobtrusive. And one of the reasons you get a camera that jerks off so much and calls attention to itself with the cutting is because the acting scenes aren't there where the character and the drama of the situation draw you in and you want a camera that gets out of the way. But you don't get that in scripts a lot.

You mentioned meeting Vincent Price at Roddy's house…

Wonderful man.

Did you ever tell him that you homaged Peter Vincent after him?

I don't know. What I remember is he was failing in those days and he and his wife were lovely and all I remember is he was a terribly refined man. He was an art collector of huge proportions. He was a cook of great distinction. I mean, you met some of these people and the refined sensibility was what blew you away. I'm so coarse compared to them; my sensibilities are so blue collar.

It's funny because we interviewed another filmmaker this week named Jeff Burr. I'm a big fan of his. And his first movie, Vincent was in it and his producing partner and him got his address, and just waited outside his house.

Who was that now?

The director's name is Jeff Burr and his first movie is called *From a Whisper to a Scream*. And he walked up to Vincent and apparently just waited outside his house. They literally just knocked on his door and said, "Mr. Price, we have a script for you." And he's like, "Oh come on in," and invited them in for fifteen minutes and chatted with them. He eventually ended up doing the movie. But that kind of thing just doesn't happen anymore.

What a lovely man. I think those stories are fascinating. I still find myself falling into that when I'm around John Landis actually. Because Landis has those stories. He used to have lunch with Alfred Hitchcock.

Hitchcock apparently went to the movies every week?

He ran a movie in his screening room every week.

I know him and Landis had a conversation about *Dressed to Kill*, the De Palma movie that's essentially a rip-off of *Psycho*.

He didn't like it.

We did the reunion a few months ago for *Fright Night*. So, Columbia wasn't really paying attention to you while making it. You do the movie you wanted to do, and then it became a hit. And now, some twenty years later, it's a cult classic. Are you surprised by the fan base for *Fright Night* now?

Mm-hmm.

What was it like for you to reunite with everybody back in Dallas a few months ago?

That was wonderful. I mean, really heartwarming. First time, it was just terrific. I remember Guy Mackle, who was at the studio at the time, all of their big high-profile projects had failed. He jokingly but ruefully said, 'God, it's going to be horrible. The best thing I'm known for during my tenure is Fright Night.' He said that to me. (laughs) I think *Fright Night* has become an intergenerational movie. Because it's warm-hearted. It's a loving look by a fan at the AIP and at the Hammer movies. It's still a funny idea.

It's one of those rare movies that while the adult horror fan can enjoy it, it's the type that's almost safe enough to show kids.

That is the surprise and that's why I think it's carried down to the generations. Because parents watch it with their children and it's safe to be able to do that. Because you don't have massive amounts of murder and mayhem.

Do you have any thoughts on how the vampire genre has shifted or changed since then?

No, not really. Tell me about the books. (He means the *Twilight* books)

Let me tell you right now, they don't want to put vampires into a *Fright Night* remake. When *Twilight* comes out, Sony's going to change their mind.

I was going to ask you, what do you know about *Twilight*?

It's going to be huge. It'll bring vampires back. Every ten years. 1985, *Fright Night*. 1995, *Interview with a Vampire*. And now, another ten, twelve years later, we've got *Twilight*. Every ten years, the vampires come back.

Well, it also shows you how long these things take to cycle. I asked Alan Dabio to shoot *Fright Night*. And he turned it down because his cousin was the woman who wrote *Interview with a Vampire*. And he was so sure in 1984 that it was just about ready to be done.

KATT SHEA

Interviewed by Mike Cucinotta and Rob Galluzzo (8/08)

We had never been in touch with Katt Shea until Mick Garris had suggested her for *The Psycho Legacy* immediately after we had interviewed him. Within hours, she welcomed us into her home and immediately became a big supporter, going so far as to accompany us to *The Psycho Legacy*'s LA premiere. After having several private conversations about her incredible career, first as an actress and later as a director for Roger Corman, we knew we had to get her to go on record for a trademark *Icons* chat! For the first time ever, here's our "lost" interview with Katt Shea!

The first question that we ask everybody is what are your earliest recollections of the horror genre?

You know what comes to mind? *The Creeping Terror*. That was a really, really bad movie. Let me think of something better. (laughs) See, I love Larry Cohen movies. His Mutant Baby movies really made me happy.

It's Alive!

It's Alive! (laughs) *It's Alive* made me really happy. Because they're hilarious, and they're great, though. See, that's not a bad movie. That's actually a very good movie, and it's great. And *God Told Me To*, I really liked. I've told him before (Larry Cohen) that I'm such a fan. Oh, *The Exorcist*. *The Exorcist* is a great movie. *Carrie* is one of my favorite horror movies. Of all time. Absolutely. Without a doubt.

Oh, is that the reason you jumped at the opportunity to do *The Rage: Carrie 2*?

It was such a natural thing, and it was so easy for me to go right into. I identified so much with Sissy Spacek and the character of *Carrie*. I was the kid in school that got made fun of, so...

Did you ever talk to Brian DePalma about *Carrie* when you worked with him as an actor on *Scarface*?

You know, isn't that funny? No, I didn't really have a chance to talk to him (about *Carrie*) because he was just very intense working on *Scarface*. I mean, I talked to him about the movie. It was funny, I was in this particular scene in the

nightclub where everyone gets killed. And I forget what I said to him exactly, but he had just gotten done shooting the scene, and I said, "I think that's the scariest thing you ever shot." And he said, "I know, I'm standing here," but it really freaked me out. And he was like, so happy about that. He was like, "Yeah, really? Really, tell me more. How did it freak you out? Where did you feel it?" It was like, wow, that was really... It was nauseating to be in that scene. Everybody's mowed down. And it's never been that way for me before because, obviously, in *Psycho III*, I get my throat slashed and everything. It was like no big deal. That didn't affect me at all. But the scene in *Scarface* did.

What are the origins of your acting? Because obviously you've written, you've directed, you've acted, but that was the first thing that you kind of pursued in film. So, do you remember what it was that kind of started your interest in acting?

Well, I was a writer, and people kept saying, you should be an actor. (laughs) Like, you're very expressive. You're crazy expressive. So, I studied acting to be a better writer and to be a better director. I didn't actually know I wanted to direct then, but I was studying acting. I was directing in the acting class. I was actually the only one directing in the acting class. So, I was doing more directing in the acting class than acting. But then I started to go out on auditions, and I took the cold reading class, and then I started booking jobs. And I felt like a complete imposter, you know. I got an acting job! How weird is that? What do I do now?

How difficult was it in the beginning? Because I know you worked on some Roger Corman films.

It was really hard until I sort of developed this method, this auditioning technique, to cold read; to get me out of my head so I would be really relaxed in the auditions. And then I started booking jobs. But I learned it from this friend of mine who taught it, and now I teach it. It's these exercises that really get you out of your head, that I could go in and I could just deliver. I mean, that absolutely worked.

I sympathize a lot with actors. I have actor friends, and I know one, for example, said that she had read something and went in on an audition, and not that she blew it, but from reading it, she had it a certain way in her head, and then she acted it that way, and then on the spot, the director's like, *"No, I kind of want you to read it like this."* And she's unprepared because she's like, wow, I had it so set in my head.

That's what I do in this class. I have them do all these exercises with it, so they're doing it a hundred different ways in the class, so then if they're directed, they can just do it. And it's fun. They don't have any preconceived notions. So that's really powerful.

What was one of the funnest gigs for you in the beginning of your acting career?

Oh, I did this movie called *Preppies in Manhattan*. It was really fun. Because the part I played was this really bitchy preppy girl, and I had an accent and everything, I gave everybody hell, and I was a complete bitch. And I based it on Katharine Hepburn. It was so much fun. Really fun to be in character.

***Psycho III* is a very prominent film in your career. You were a big fan of the original *Psycho* movie, but this also was your last acting gig. And this is where you met Michael Westmore, who in turn really helped you get *Stripped to Kill* made…**

He helped get my first movie made. I mean, you just don't know these things. It's such serendipity. But I did know at that point that *Psycho III* was going to be my last acting gig. Because I really wanted to direct *Stripped to Kill*. It took me a year to convince Roger Corman to let me do *Stripped to Kill*, but he had already said yes by that time. I'm pretty sure, because I think by the time I was shooting it, I knew that that was going to be my last acting job. I was just done. Because of the difficulties, an actor's life is really rough. I just wanted

to move on. Especially when someone (Anthony Perkins) is putting you in an ice chest with real ice, throwing you out the window and dragging you around in a rainstorm. And joking about it the whole time. (laughs)

So, what'd you pick up from working on *Psycho III*? Bruce Surtees was the cinematographer and very open to a lot of your questions?

He was very helpful. He would explain how he did things. He was shooting really low light, and I asked him what kind of film he was shooting and what kind of lenses he was using and things like that. He was very open. I was careful to ask him when there wasn't a lot of pressure on. But he was really great that way. And because he knew I was interested; he would offer information too. He would just say, see how this light's falling over here, something like that.

Michael Westmore made a fake prosthetic set of breasts for you on the set of *Psycho III* and that's what you showed to Roger Corman to officially convince him that you could definitely pull it off? Was that how that happened?

Well, he didn't actually make them. I told Roger that Mike would make them and Mike wrote a letter saying that he would do it for the cost of materials and that they would be totally realistic. He had already won an Academy Award for *Raging Bull*. When Mike says he can make something like that, you're convinced. And Roger's big objection was that we couldn't fake it. We couldn't make a man come off as a woman in the movie. It would not be possible to do. Because this was before *The Crying Game*. It hadn't been done yet. *Terror Train* actually did it, but she didn't have her clothes off. She was well covered the whole time. But I didn't know that at the time. I'd never seen *Terror Train*. So, I didn't even have that to refer to. I couldn't even say but look what they did. I didn't know anything about *Terror Train*. So, I was kind of going on faith. And he went on faith.

Where did that story for *Stripped to Kill* come from? Because you had that script for about a year before you got to finally make it, and it was the first thing you decided you wanted to direct.

I went to a strip club. I lost a bet. Oh, I lost a bet with my writing partner over mussels. He said mussels were poisonous at a certain time of year and I didn't know that. And I said, no way. Am I losing the bet? And then I had to go to a strip club. And he knew that would be really horrible for me and I wouldn't want to do that. So, I had to do it. I paced up and down. And he goes, '*Forget it, you don't have to do it.*' And I said, '*No, I'm going in.*' And then, of course, they thought I was an off-duty stripper. So, I sat down, and I just started watching the acts and then I fell in love with them. People don't know that stripping is like this. This is awesome. They were swinging around the pole. You never saw a pole in a movie before. I'd never seen a pole, period, or people swinging around on it. So, I just thought, you know, these people are artists. They're real artists. And this is their outlet. And I want to make a movie about it. I want to feature that in a movie.

What do you remember about your first directorial experience? Once you were shooting, was it smooth?

No, no one took me seriously at all. They just saw a girl. I was twenty-seven or something. And I looked like I was twenty. I probably looked like I was eighteen. I never looked my age! So, they saw a teenage girl walk in and went, "You're not the director." Any girl walking in, they would say, "You're not the director." I remember going to a meeting with a special effects guy and everybody's sitting around and I'm going, "Well, let's start the meeting." And the special effects guy said, "We're waiting for the director." And I said, well, I'm here.

Did you feel that at some point they eventually gave you respect by the end of the shoot?

Oh yeah. Well, probably two days in because I was a tyrant.

What came about because of *Stripped to Kill* for you?

Actually, *Stripped to Kill* was really big.

Which I'm sure made Roger happy.

Yeah, it was the number one movie in Europe. I want to say in France, but I'm not sure. But it was the number one movie. So yeah, and Roger was shocked by how much money it made. He was never going to work with me again after *Stripped to Kill*!

Really?

Yeah, because it was too long. And I was being an artist. I was being really artistic and he didn't like that. And it was way too long. So, he was really mad at me. He was never going to speak to me again. And then *Stripped to Kill* made all this money and then he said, "Do want to make another movie?" (laughs) The next movie I did was *Dance of the*

Damned. So, he had a set, and he asked us, my partner, Andy Rubin, to come up with an idea to shoot in this set and it was a haunted house. Nobody wanted to use it. So, we came up with that it would be the vampire's house and then he would meet this waitress who really wants to kill herself and they're going to come together and he's going to experience the day through her and he's going to give her the perfect death experience. Because she's suicidal. So, it was a great idea really. I still think it's a great idea. I'd like to remake it. But anyway, we changed the whole set all around. We completely made it into this modern Frank Lloyd Wright influenced house instead of the haunted house with cobwebs. And we made a nightclub, and we made the movie on two sets. The house, the vampire's house. Have you ever seen it?

Possibly on cable?

It really got lost. Because of the timing. Virgin bought it and then they went under. So, it really got lost. I really like that movie. I really like the story of that movie. *Stripped to Kill 2* is on DVD. Isn't it? MGM originally put it out.

I remember when *Poison Ivy* came out. The thing that I remember standing out was Drew Barrymore because if I recall correctly, I don't think anyone had seen her as an adult actress yet. Everyone remembered her from *E.T.*, and as a child actor. Then she did this movie *Poison Ivy* and had grown up with all this tabloid history behind her. Here, she's playing this scandalous character having an affair with her friend's father, which blew people's minds in 1991. How did she get involved?

Yeah, it was a big deal for her to do that movie, and nobody knew what she looked like anymore. I just remember one day the girls came over to rehearse, Sarah Gilbert and Drew, and they were out in the driveway, and someone drove by and they stopped and said, "You're Sarah Gilbert," and Drew was standing right next to her. And they didn't recognize her. And they said, "Can we have your autograph" to Sarah. And they didn't even recognize her. She really didn't look like she looked as a kid. She really didn't. But how did she get involved? She auditioned. Simple as that.

You also had Tom Skerritt in *Poison Ivy*. What was it like working with him?

It was good. It was good working with him. He came over to my house too. He came over to meet about it and read the script. It was very hard for him to do that part. Very, very difficult.

He wanted to do it, but it was really hard. He had kids. It was hard for anyone to take that role.

Was there anyone else interested that came in that didn't want to tackle it because of the subject matter?
Sam Shepard. Sam Shepard couldn't do it.

Were you surprised by the success of it? Because, I mean, it made people look at Drew Barrymore in a whole new way. I know she started working heavily right after that movie. And it spawned a bunch of sequels!
People have said to me recently that it's a classic. And I'm like, really? (laughs) Wow. Cool.

Any movie that you can see at the video store that has two and three sequels, I think automatically makes the original a classic.
Well, that's cool! I'm really happy. I'm really happy about it. That's all I can say. I didn't expect anything. I got a retrospective at MoMA. Are you kidding? (laughs) I was thirty-four and I got a retrospective at MoMA. It's like a lifetime achievement award. I'm done. You don't have to do anything after that. Maybe you have to pay your bills. It's like everything's cool now.

Poison Ivy **was at the height of** *Roseanne,* **right?**
I wrote it with her in my head. (Sarah Gilbert)

Really? That's interesting. Did you see it with her character on *Roseanne?*
Yeah. Not so much her character on *Roseanne,* but who she really is. You can tell from her character on *Roseanne* who she really was.

Was there ever any pressure for her to not do it? To do a film with adult themes while working on a family friendly TV show?
No, her mom is really smart, and she read the script, and she really liked it, and she had seen some of my other movies and so she was incredibly supportive. Barbara Gilbert. Really smart woman who wanted Sarah to do it very much. The only thing that was threatened was she was supposed to smoke in the movie and her mom said, "Well, she can't smoke." But it was a point in the movie and Sarah really smoked in real life, only her mom didn't know she smoked.

So, I made Sarah tell her mom she smoked so that she could smoke in the movie but then her mom got really mad. So the line that's in the movie, she says, "It's okay for me to be a lesbian, I just can't smoke" came out of Sarah's mouth. She was like, "It's okay if I'm gay, but I'm not allowed to smoke." So that ended up in the movie.

What was next after *Poison Ivy?*
It took a really long time. I did this movie called *Last Exit to Earth.* I had to go back to Roger Corman after *Poison Ivy* because nothing happened. Nothing came through. Everybody in town met with me and wanted to work with me and everything like that and nothing happened. That's Hollywood. A lot of people say that's Hollywood for women, but I won't go there. So, I made a really low budget movie for Roger, and it wasn't very good. It had its charms, but it honestly wasn't very good and there just wasn't enough money. He had lowered the budget so much and he thought I could work magic with anything, and I finally couldn't. He had taken too much money away from me and I couldn't work the magic that time. So, then *Carrie 2* came along, which was wonderful for me, not so wonderful for the director before me.

Had the kids latched onto the original director? (Robert Mandall) How difficult was it stepping into it?
Yes. They didn't like me. They didn't want me. I had to win them over.

Did they start shooting it with the other director? So, you came in really late in the game?
He cast them, everything. He'd rehearsed with them, he'd cast them. He shot for two weeks with them. He got fired and I walked in. Yes. But luckily, I did *Poison Ivy.* So, it's like every kid on it was like, "Well, she did Poison Ivy. Okay, well we can't hate her too much!" (laughs) But they did hate me for a little while.

Did it ever go on record why they fired the original director or did they just not like his direction?
It was just creative. Honestly. They just didn't see eye to eye.

Did any changes happen in the script when you hopped on board? Were you able to interject anything?
Yeah, I had to because there were some things in the script

that I just really didn't think worked. I got there on a Thursday, and I was shooting on Monday. So, they would not shut down because it would cost too much to shut down. And I really wanted them to shut down so I could do a rewrite of the script. So, I had to do a really quick pass on the script. And the problem was the actors were not exactly warming up to me because I was juggling so much. The DP I met on, I think, Friday night. He flew in. I picked him from his resume, and I picked him by accident because I thought he shot *The Wall*. *Pink Floyd's The Wall*! He shot a different *The Wall*. But he flew in to meet with me and I said, "I loved *The Wall*," and he went, "How did you see it?" And I went, "What do you mean how did I see it? I've seen it like fifteen times." He goes, "It's not out yet." And I just went, "Oh shit." But we got along really well, and he shot magnificently. I think *Carrie 2* is magnificently shot.

But the thing was I was juggling so many balls in the air I wasn't paying a lot of attention to the actors who already didn't like me. And I had a scene with Dylan Bruno where he's in the locker room and the coach is berating him and he makes him pull down his pants and there was some nudity involved and Dylan said, "I'm not doing this." And I said, "Okay. We have to talk." And I knew what was wrong. It was because I wasn't paying enough attention to him. And I said to him, "I will pay a lot more attention to you if you do this right now." I said, "You will get my attention." And he went, "Okay." And he went and he pulled down his pants. And I did pay attention to him.

What about Amy Irving? She was the only person that returned to the first movie.

She knew what she was doing! She didn't really require a lot of directing, to tell you the truth.

It's weird because *Carrie 2* is one of those, dare I say, hybrids, a sequel and a remake. It's essentially retelling the original story, but it is a continuation of what happened in the first movie. So, as one of your favorite De Palma movies was it exciting for you to take a crack at this or was it more like you didn't even have time to think about it?

No, I just knew it was dangerous. I mean, obviously, you can get crucified for something like that.

Was there a rush to make a release date?

Well, they had a lot of things set but it was mostly about money. They had put a lot of money into it. And they lost a lot of money on the switch over. So, I had to actually reshoot everything and stay on the same budget. I didn't get any extra money. So, it was almost kind of like going back to do a low budget movie that cost $20 million which is unfortunate because I probably shot it for $5 million, probably. A lot of money went down the drain. Maybe it was more than $5 million but not by much.

Well, we obviously enjoyed what you did with it. Had you been on board earlier for pre-production, do you think you would have made a slightly different movie?

Oh God, yeah! It's weird though because the movie has such a feel of my movies. I mean, it's really crazy. And I wonder about that. Why does it have such a strong feel of my movies when I had to do everything so fast. I don't know. It's really funny. But it does feel like one of my movies. But I know it would be very different.

How did they get you as director?

Jeff Kleeman did. He was a fan for a long time. He was a big fan of my film *Streets* with Christina Applegate. I had a lot of fans from *Streets*. Lots in Hollywood that were just crazy about *Streets*. And I love that movie too. But Jeff Kleeman brought me in and then Lindsay Duran was the president of United Artists. And she championed me. And then Frank Mancuso was the President of MGM. And I met with him very quickly. I mean, I was hired in a day. It just happened so fast. They were looking for somebody who could save a really bad situation and do it on a shoestring. Essentially. So that was really the thing. I was known for doing things that looked like they cost a lot more on a really low budget.

What was your relationship like with Emily Bergl, the lead of *Carrie 2*. She's following in Sissy Spacek's shoes, in one of her most famous roles; having to emulate that and at the same time add something new to it. And on top of that, she worked for two weeks with the previous director that hired her!

It was hard. I really had to, you know, romance her and make that work. Yeah, that was hard. I think that was very hard on her.

She was so good. I love the tattoo thing, by the way. Was that your idea?

It was in the script, actually. It was in the script, but you know, I worked on it so that it would be raised up first. Those kinds of things are really fun to work on.

What about the conversation about the band Garbage in the diner? Was that just the script thing?

It was in the script.

I was kind of hoping you were a Garbage fan, and you threw that in.

You know, the writer though, I have to say, was a huge *Poison Ivy* fan and he told me he was completely inspired by *Poison Ivy* and the dialogue and the kids. The reason that movie has such the vibe of one of my movies is because the writer was already in it. The writer had done that. Who knows, maybe Jeff wanted me to direct it from the beginning. And something else happened. I wouldn't doubt if that were the case. I wouldn't doubt that at all. Because Jeff had been trying to work with me for years. And here was this writer that was inspired by *Poison Ivy*, and somehow, we all ended up there. I read the script twice before I started to shoot it! That's unheard of! And the second time, I was doing rewrites. It was the second pass of me reading the script, I was telling the writer some scenes that needed to be cleared up. So, I'm shooting a script, and I don't know the script.

It's amazing how it all came together though!

And then I'm trying to figure out how to shoot it so it's really interesting, and different. The last guy got fired for the way he was shooting it, so I'd better shoot really well! (laughs) It was a hard job. It was not one of the easier jobs. Donald Morgan was such a fantastic DP. And he was on fire, and he was on fire because I was such a risk taker. When I told him an idea I had, he just went, "Holy shit! You're kidding. Wow, I'm in heaven. Let's do it." It was really cool. We did that black and white stuff. We're shooting this dream sequence, and the shot where Emily's face comes right down onto the windshield. I shot these pieces, and I had this whole thing worked out how I wanted to do this. And we lost our place. The script supervisor didn't keep track, or too many things were going on, and Don was almost in tears and says, "I don't know where we are, and we can't do the vision you had for it." And I went, "I don't care! OK, just shoot it this way, and then that way, we'll do some black and white, and somehow, we'll cut this all together." And he was like, "You're insane!" This is going to be so much better than what I first thought, and it was. That was awesome. When she hits the windshield and we cut to the black and white, it was great, and it wasn't at all what I had in mind because we lost our place. But that's filmmaking!

DAVID J. SCHOW

Interviewed by Mike Cucinotta, Rob Galluzzo, and Jason Alvino (8/09)

David had become a great personal friend and *Icons* supporter shortly after we interviewed him for *The Psycho Legacy*. This was one of those rare occasions where most of the *Icons* crew were in LA together! Rob, Jason, and Mike all spent a cool August night getting candid and hearing, in some cases for the first time ever, David's accounts on *Leatherface, The Crow*, and even his *Creature from the Black Lagoon* with Guillermo del Toro. This interview had been long thought "lost," until now!

Rob: All of us here at this table have a memory of when we were introduced to the horror genre. Do you remember what your earliest recollections of horror were? Both in film and literature?

I don't think there was anybody who, during a certain period of time, encountered dinosaurs and didn't immediately want to become a paleontologist when they were little, and that kind of relates to, flash forward a couple of years and you get to the *Creature From the Black Lagoon* and you go, it's a dinosaur animal. Hey, this kind of fits. I didn't read Edgar Allan Poe until I was in high school, and even then, it was audio recordings. It took me a long time to get to the print, to the text version, but it's kind of a two-pronged answer. One answer is scholastic books in high school used to sell horror anthologies, but why did I get those horror anthologies? Because even earlier, when I was a little kid, I saw monster movies on TV. Specifically, my first cogent memory of watching an entire monster movie on TV was *The Mummy's Tomb*. I've been a big *Mummy* booster ever since. People who argue he's too slow don't get the idea that he's inexorable. While you sleep, he's catching up with you.

They used to have a kind of a *Shock Theater* thing or a *Chiller Theater* thing on TV, and this was during a time where you didn't have instant access to anything that you wanted to see, and the more you wanted to see something that you'd heard about or read about in a monster magazine, the more of a Holy Grail it became. So, you would obsessively scan *TV Guide* looking for the magic word, which was melodrama, which meant "monster movie," and you would literally go to school all week waiting for Friday or Saturday to come around, because if you didn't, that makes it what? That makes it a religion, because you have specific hours,

you have rituals, and you have practice, and you have to keep the faith, because if you don't stay up until 11:30 on Friday night, you miss seeing *I Married a Monster from Outer Space*, because that might be the only chance you ever had. This is difficult to explain to people now, where you have instant access, but there was no bulletin board, there was no internet, and everybody felt that they were together, once you had been exposed to - I just gave you eight sentence fragments in a row, that's pretty good. (laughs)

Once you had been exposed to something that supported that, like monster magazines, because the chances of meeting somebody else in your town who was into the same stuff were pretty slim, but the monster magazines gave you an idea that there was one kid in each town who was doing the same thing as you were, and that was the unofficial community. But yeah, having written a whole lot of prose stuff, still, my first exposure was to movies. The first movie I paid to see twice was *The 7 Faces of Dr. Lao*. *The Time Machine* had a profound effect on me, because I went to see it on a double bill with *Tarzan in India*, and I missed the beginning of it, and so I sat through *Tarzan in India* to see *The Time Machine* again, wound up sitting through *The Time Machine* a second time, and by the time I had to walk home, it was dark. This was back when kids could walk home by themselves, and that was pretty creepy. Then I saw *Planet of the Apes* at a drive-in, and I was doomed. That one, I went back the next night and saw it again, with my older brother, who was driving the car.

Rob: Nowadays, we have access to things like video and DVD, but you really have to love a movie to go see it again

and again. I can't remember the last movie I paid to go see more than once.

Well, I actively lobbied people to go see *Downfall* when it came out, the Hitler movie, the one that didn't win the Oscar that year. It was the one with Bruno Ganz as Hitler, because that was just such a good movie. But, again, you've got to read subtitles, and we're getting more and more people who can't read, period. When George Lucas was making *Star Wars*, 20th Century Fox came back, and they said, 'Well, you have a scene in this movie that has aliens speaking in a subtitled alien language, and we can't put that in the movie, because what if the kids can't read?' And it's like, well, they can have the kid next to them explain it to them. Now it's a cliche, it's a convention in alien movies that they speak in a subtitled alien dialect.

Mike: You said it's like religion. Is that how you feel when you see a movie you want to see again and again? Is it comparable to what religious people would call a spirit?

It is a religion. It's my church. It's like Stations of the Cross, basically. You do these little rituals. You watch the movies where you can. You try to be responsible to your genre. Have you ever heard of people being responsible to the comedy genre? Are there that many websites on the internet for comedy movies? Yeah, we actively proselytize for it. There's a protective group instinct. There is a definite feeling of them and us.

Mike: We try to marry our own. (laughs)

Yeah. You try to mate within your horror species group. It is very much like a religion. I would rather have that than the kind of conventional religion shit they tried to push down my throat when I was a little kid. The more you look at it, the weirder it gets because it is exactly like a religion. Especially when you didn't have all this access and you had to actively participate or motivate yourself to go out and get it. That makes us exactly like those guys on the corner with the Bibles waving them in the air. Maybe a little more polished, I don't know. The more you look at it, the more you look at horror film fandom, the more it is like a sub-religion. Maybe we're a cult instead?

Mike: It's like Jason likes cannibal movies and I like supernatural movies.

You're like the Protestant. You're the Catholic. I think it's as valid as any religion. In fact, I think that fans of this stuff could find more to defend their faith with because our faith is based on stuff you can demonstrably point to and say

that's real or go look for yourself. Where every other religion is based on well, you just have to believe it. Now, somebody came up and said, well, you just have to believe there's a movie called *The Mummy's Tomb*. (laughs) No. I would go find it and see it and then I would go, I know there's a movie called *The Mummy's Tomb*. It spoke to me.

Rob: Your place has a pretty extensive *Creature From The Black Lagoon* collection. Did a collection for this particular stuff start early on? Were you collecting *Creature* stuff since high school?

No, because you have to remember when this started, there weren't that many things to collect. Franchises and stuff pre-*Star Wars*, nobody understood how merchandising worked, so the stuff didn't exist. What did exist was kind of tentative, and also when you're a little kid, you tend to gravitate toward the things that are available. So, you would do things like get 8mm films of this stuff or there might be like a little Marx plastic figure or something like that. But it was also containable. It was within the limits of your allowance or whatever job you had that made money. I mean, these things cost pocket change. I have a *Frankenstein*, *Dracula*, *Frankenstein*, *Wolfman* and *Creature* Pez Dispensers that I bought when I was a little kid at a drug store for pocket change, literally, that are by my reckoning $450 on eBay for the *Creature* Pez. This was unimaginable.

But there also wasn't that much stuff to collect and as you collect stuff and also as you grow up and you're now working at a job, you can now go out and enable that if you catch the collecting bug because what are collectors but archivists of this stuff? It's another way of promulgating the religion because what if everything else is wiped out? Well, my collection will still exist, and I am the archivist of this stuff. This particularly came into its own during the era of videotape because everybody that had a videotape of a movie acted in some way as though that was the only copy. What if this was the only copy left? Well, then I'd have it. That kind of thing. And I could show it to other people. And I think part of the reason, the impetus for collecting in the first place is that you can show it to other people. And if that's not spreading the faith, what is?

Rob: And that was the thing with video… Video was the first time that people could actually keep this movie. It wasn't like, "*maybe* Psycho *will play again in a couple of years at some screening or whatever.*" Video was the first time that we could actually physically buy and own and show people these movies that we grew up on.

Well, there used to be a big thick book called the *Encyclopedia of Film*. It came out about a quarter century, thirty years ago, something like that. And when Betamax first came out, there was a friend of mine who got fourteen of them and two television sets and literally recorded every movie that was on TV with the goal of checking them off in the *Encyclopedia of Film* until he had all of them. And some of those betas now are movies that still haven't been released on DVD and will never be released on DVD until somebody scans them. And again, he's being an archivist. *Video Watchdog* correctly calls 1980 the dawn of video time. Yes, video cassette decks existed before that, but if you went to rent videos, there was maybe a hundred titles you could rent. It takes time for this stuff to penetrate through to the point where you get a video store where you have thousands of titles. Then video goes down, DVD comes in, and they only have a hundred titles. And then the DVDs gradually accumulate. And then you look backwards at the video store, and you go, but they still have 860 movies that aren't on DVD.

Jason: It's like Blu-ray right now. There's not many.

Right in the 90s sometime, basically when video was going full stream and it was ready to be deposed by another medium, there was a friend of mine who came over with the VHS of *Frankenstein* when it came out. And he said, you know, I love that I can hold this in my hand, that I can put it in and play it anytime I want to, and I wouldn't take this away from anybody. And then being an old school guy, he looks at me and he goes, but you know what? This is too damned easy. Meaning that we really had to fight for every inch because it wasn't all just out there waiting for us to grab. It wasn't out there in the first place.

Mike: We always talk about this when we go to the horror conventions with the rise of the internet. What's there to ask of somebody in a Q and A that you didn't already read on the IMDb or in fifty other interviews that they've done? The access is everywhere.

And then people are asking questions too, under a circumstance like that, where they already know the answer to that. They're just asking to demonstrate the level of their recent reading and not to find out anything.

Rob: So, you got into the horror genre as a writer first and foremost.

Through prose writing, yeah.

Rob: So, what kind of initially led you to film stuff? I mean, obviously, you were always a fan of film. So, what was it that pushed you towards that world?

Well, I got magnetized more toward it than actually pushed myself, because I always thought that if you were to do enough books, eventually somebody would want to option something, and that's how you get in. And in a way, that sort of came true, because Mike DeLuca was a big fan of this stuff when he first started at New Line, and he, in fact, was a fan of my short fiction, and called me to write, at that time, *A Nightmare on Elm Street Part 5*, which turned out to be *The Dream Child*.

And I went in, and I met everybody at New Line. Mark Rudetsky was just starting there, Rachel Talalay was just starting there, and Mike DeLuca were all development people at New Line when I came in. They didn't even have credits on films at that point. And they wanted me to do this movie, and I pitched them a treatment that I wrote called *Freddy Rules*, which they said, 'Great, we want you to write this movie, go across the hall, give me your social security number, oh, and one more thing, we need to see a script you've written.' And I got busted, because I was the only jerk in Hollywood without a script in his back pocket already, and I did not get that job.

Rob: Wow.

And so, Mike and I began hanging around Sun Studios in Sun Valley where they were shooting *Freddy's Nightmares*, in a studio literally the size of this dining room. Boy, those shows must have cost a whopping five, six bucks each to produce.

Mike: And they don't look it. (entire group laughs)

And you know, you had CJ Strawn out there doing his best to make the sets look different, and CJ's design approach was to have lurid odd colors on the walls and rooms and stuff, and CJ worked on all the New Line movies of that period, so there was like the CJ period where you can see his design in effect. And we bugged the producer, Jeff Freilich, and finally, you try to write these elaborate things out. This is a story about, da-da-da-da-da, and they go no, no, and ultimately, I'm sitting on the couch in Jeff Freilich's office, and I said what if Freddy was somebody's dream date? What if somebody really wanted to go to the prom with Freddy or go on a date with Freddy? And he goes, 'Sold!' And it was late in the first season, they had one slot left and it was literally the last show of the first season, and I wrote the teleplay for that show.

It was directed by Gerald T. Olsen, who had been a producer on movies like *Rapid Fire*. He shot the second unit on *The Hidden*. The scene in *The Hidden* where the car hits the guy in the park and breaks the windshield and he goes over the top? Jerry shot that. And so, he shot my show. And the day that I turned the first draft of that teleplay, which was called *Safe Sex*, into New Line, within twenty-four hours, I was hired to do their next horror project, which was *Leatherface*. Kevin Morton, who was one of the producers, came up and said, 'What would you do with… Leatherface?' And I said, 'Well, same thing I did with Freddy, except you wouldn't let me.' So, now we're off and running.

Jason: Did somebody try to date Leatherface? (laughs)

Yes, absolutely. And to this day, in the two *Chainsaw* movies that I've written, the two things that producers will not allow is, one, Leatherface on a motorcycle, which is in both scripts, and two, you can probably guess the second one.

Rob: Anything to do with Leatherface and sex?

Kind of. Naked Leatherface.

Rob: Naked? Whoa! You want to take it there?

Naked Leatherface. Had him in both scripts and couldn't do it.

Rob: So *Leatherface* was before the *Critters* movies?

Yes. *Leatherface*, I did three drafts, one I actually wrote in Texas at Joe Lansdale's house in the basement. And Joe's a good buddy; brought me a hat from the local soft shop with a severed Barbie doll arms and legs glued on it. It's downstairs, I still have it. And I sat there and on Joe's incredibly primordial word processing thing, did the second draft of *Leatherface*, actually in Texas, which is the closest this movie ever came to Texas.

Rob: Before that, if I recall correctly when we spoke to Jeff Burr about it, he said they already had a script and from his recollection, it sounded like what Kim Hendel ended up doing with the next sequel.

No, what happened was Kim was in on the initial meetings because he was a rights holder. I actually had a meeting with Kim Henkel at New Line. Kim wanted to do an idea, which wound up being the plot of the fourth movie, based on the prom. Kim made a very passionate argument about 'What is the most important event in a teenager's life? The

prom!' And I thought, 'Kim, maybe not now. It's not that important.' But he had written his script but there was no other *Leatherface* script except for the three drafts that I wrote. And in the middle of me writing these three drafts, guess what happens? They bring *Nightmare 5* back to me. The movie I couldn't get hired to write has now gone through Bill Wisher, Les Bohm, who hated it so much he wanted to put a pseudonym on it, and did, and several other writers. It comes back to me for a dialogue rewrite while they're shooting it. And so, it's like, the dialogue is all there. Please, help us fix the dialogue. And so there was literally a guy coming to my apartment in Hollywood and taking pages to the set because I was typing on an old IBM.

Jason: This might be a stupid question, but…

We could probably handle a stupid question at this point!

Jason: At this point in time, you were a published author. You had books out that these people could go to the bookstore and buy with your name on it. Like, books that sold copies. You obviously knew what you were doing in the writing department.

Yeah, but what makes you assume they would go buy them and read them?

Jason: Let's say they didn't read them. Let's just say, if you were like, 'Hey, my name is David J. Schow, I'm a published author. Sure, I can write a screenplay for you.' What was in their mind the thing preventing you from writing that screenplay? That you didn't have a screenplay?

Yeah, they just wanted to know I could mechanically do it. In that form.

Jason: So, when you did the *Freddy's Nightmare* episode, was that the first time you ever tried to write a screenplay?

Yes. But see, the thing was, at the time I collected scripts. And all through that time, remember, I'm working on the *Outer Limits* book. And I had multiple drafts of every *Outer Limits* episode ever written. Plus, I collected film screenplays. I spent a lot of time working on *Alien* articles for things like *Cinefantastique*. And I had every draft of *Alien* up to that point. And I was a huge fan of it. And it's one of those movies that knocks you out. When I went in to see that movie when it was finished, I knew every single thing you could possibly know about *Alien*, and it still knocked me out. When was the last time that happened to you? So, I had scripts on my shelf. I took them down and just copied that format. And that's how I learned how to do it. There was no workshops. There was no college. I'm a college dropout. There was no handlers or anything. I just approximated that form. And I did it well enough that when I handed it to them, they go, great, write our next movie. The books didn't get me anywhere.

Jason: I guess the thing I'm leading up to is… because you were able to mechanically do something, they were like, okay, write our next movie?

They just wanted to make sure I could write a script, literally.

Rob: They came back to you for *Nightmare 5*, which sadly, ended up one of the least successful…

It was the most compromised *Nightmare* movie, ever.

Rob: What was your initial take on it?

I don't remember. I'd have to look at *Freddy Rules*, but I remember it had a thing in it called the Coma Pit, which is an even worse part of the dream reality that you can't get out of. I'd have to pull the treatment out to say more because I haven't looked at it in a long time.

Rob: Going back to Leatherface. And Kim's script…

While I'm writing *Leatherface*, Kim had his script that he ultimately made into the fourth *Chainsaw* movie, and then they brought *Nightmare 5* back. The irony is that Jeff Burr, when he did *Leatherface*, followed the script dialogue-wise so little that there's actually more of my dialogue in *Nightmare 5*, for which I get no credit, than there is in *Leatherface* for which I get sole credit. It's like I had to write that script without knowing who the director was. I didn't have any interface with the director until we're shooting the movie. So how much could there be? There was no time to do anything.

Rob: That was the one *Chainsaw* that they did here in L.A., so once Jeff Burr was on board, did you go to set and talk with Jeff about what was going on?

Yeah. Only briefly because he was so harried and he was under so much pressure and Jeff had this habit of taking the script pages for the day and he would fold them up like a Chinese fan until they were like a little cylinder about this thick and he would just fold that and unfold and you could always see him grasping this little stick of script pages

walking around the set and we were shooting right between *Tour of Duty* on one side and *China Beach* on the other side. So, there's Hueys going over all the time. So, it was kind of like being in Vietnam and there were a lot of rattlesnakes. There were a lot of rattlesnakes on that set because the grips would get them and kill them and put them up on the food board at the catering truck and the snakes just kept getting longer and longer on the catering board until they were just gigantic horrific rattlesnakes.

Rob: Did New Line give you criteria for what they wanted in their *Leatherface* movie because obviously they had Freddy Krueger, and I think they had just obtained Jason Voorhees. There were little elements that just felt so much like the *Nightmare* franchise. For example, I love the opening but it's, of course, reminiscent of how Freddy made the glove at the opening of the first *Nightmare*.

That's intentional because the only mandate, once I told them the parameters of what I wanted to do, which included stuff like the monster truck with the skin bra on it, the fact that something that's more in a minor key in the film that they don't really pursue is the fact that they kill or they capture animals and tag them with this jewelry to sort of define the boundaries of where their working area is. So, once you find one of these animals, you're inside the chainsaw zone.

Another thing was, and this was something Jeff didn't fully get, but Leatherface has an entirely adopted family. They're all from different places and they've all unified into this one group because nobody else is like them. And we figured Grandpa at that point was so old he'd have to be dead, so we just made Grandpa into a kind of a mummy and that's his head right up there that Howard Berger gave me. And the other thing was that everyone in the family was missing a body part that had been replaced with a substitute made out of chromed bones. Originally, Leatherface's leg brace was supposed to be made out of chromed long bones. I know Jeff hated the brace, but it was like that also because he injured his leg.

Rob: Were you aiming to make a more direct sequel to the first one or did you take the second into account as well?

Only into a minor key because the phrase "the saw is family" comes from the second movie. And insofar as the leg brace, the saw is family, yes. But the only mandate from New Line Cinema was we have to make a franchise out of *Leatherface*. Hence, especially the beginning, him putting the mask on was very consciously predicated on Freddy putting his glove together.

Jason: When they first said to you, "What can you do with *Leatherface*," were you like, "Holy shit?"

Rob: Was it something you even gave thought to? I mean, I'm sure you were a fan of the original. And it's like, here's this iconic character in this famous movie. What would you do with it?

I went away and tried to think up some odd things to do with him and then came back and talked to them, with the truck, the family. The way he looked which was specifically a mask made out of seven or eight different people. Where it was very visibly stitched together. Where you had one skin color here and another skin color up here. But then I also had him in a biker jacket and a tutu at one point. Because remember, Leatherface from the original *Chainsaw* is in drag for half the movie. Nobody has ever nailed this idea or likes it. But he wears dresses, folks! So, they didn't particularly like that part.

But strangely enough, if you get the laserdisc of *Leatherface*, there is a commentary by me and Greg Nicotero that was done roughly eight years after the movie came out. And they didn't port it over to the new DVD. And I'm dying to know what I said. Because it was a lot closer to the production and I need to get somebody that can make me a disc of the laser disc. So, I can hear my own commentary again. Because it has more detail because Tim Lucas wrote it up in *Video Watchdog* when the laser disc came out and he wrote a paragraph in there about how if they had stuck to the descriptions of Tink and Leatherface in the script, Tim said we would have had two really formidable monsters, and it just got kind of sanitized. Partially due to the severe shooting schedule. Partially due to, they had Jeff spinning in circles for the whole time. And partially due to the fact that some of the ideas were just so berserk they didn't want to deal with it.

Rob: I actually remember picking up a comic book adaptation of it from I think North Star Comics.

Yeah, it was done right after. Ed Gorman did most of those. Was it Ed Gorman? No, Mort Castle.

Rob: But what's funny is you get writing credit on the comics. Did you have anything to do with it?

Mostly with the first issue. They asked me what I thought of this, and it actually used lines and dialogue from the script and everything and then it dovetailed away with the second, third and fourth issues. But the first one is pretty close.

Rob: So, this movie was the first of several things you wrote that got compromised in production?

Let's jump back to *Freddy's Nightmares* for a second. First teleplay that I ever wrote got produced. First feature that I ever wrote got produced. And I wrote the teleplay that was too sexy to broadcast. And the *Chainsaw* movie that was too offensive to release. The *Freddy's Nightmares*, they ended up cutting eight minutes out of the show! I don't know if you've ever watched eight minutes of film go through a Moviola, but it's like a week and half. And it's like, 'We can't show that on television! We've got to put something else in there!'

So, we had to dash in and write at the last minute something to cover eight minutes of missing footage, because there was a lot of carnage in that show, and a lot of nudity, oddly enough. And I have dailies to this day, we have one shot that they didn't even dare do, which was, basically our teen lead is having a dream in which he's sleeping with the goth girl chick who wants to go with Freddy as a dream date. As he is - how can I put this delicately - having an orgasm, Freddy comes out of the guy's chest, spits his heart into his face, and delivers a line.

Now, during the five, six day shooting schedule, we're shooting this at eleven o' clock at night… We had a rubber body. With an X in it. Robert's underneath, comes out. Spits. Does his Freddy line, laugh. And we took it like, four times. So, every time he comes up through the chest, he has more slime on him. And organs and latex and shit. We get the dailies and during – Freddy comes up through the guy's chest, spits his heart out, and the camera moves down. Frame Robert, just like this. He delivers his line. But when the camera tilts down, the pecks on the chest are like this. And it looks like Freddy's head is coming out of someone's ass. (laughs) Which I thought was an even better idea! Man, it took three hours to do all that. They cut that.

Leatherface misses its release date, which was November and got pushed to January, which is a movie dead zone. All the advertisements and marketing had been done for October-November, so we were dead. We didn't have the opportunity to replace anything in the movie with new stuff that was shot to be softer, because again, when you go to the studios and argue that now the narrative doesn't make any sense, they go 'Narrative? It's about a guy with a power tool!' I'm sure Jeff would've liked that opportunity. I'm sure that even left to his own devices, he could've come up with some kind of band aid that would've made more sense than just cutting, cutting, cutting, because the art of cutting films is you have to know when to stop cutting before the movie bleeds to death.

Mike: Are they really this condescending towards these movies? That it's just people with power tools?

On a certain level, I think so. You have more ability to object or reject a studio thing if your movie made money. At the time, New Line was looking to refresh the whole *Texas Chainsaw Massacre* thing and make it into a franchise. And so, this movie has even more on it to produce results. And it didn't. Jeff tells the story about reading the trades to see what it was behind when it opened, and it was very depressing. It opened in eleventh place. But it's like getting a bad review of anything. You're not going to get a good review on *Variety* for a *Chainsaw* movie! So as far as that goes, that attitude that you're talking about is correct. Horror has always been a ghetto. It will always be a ghetto. Because when you do things in horror movies that are effective, they are stolen by mainstream movies, to the point now where we'll give Anthony Hopkins an Academy Award for being a psychotic cannibal in *Silence of the Lambs*, which they'll say is "not a horror movie, that's a thriller. That's a suspense movie!"

Horror, as a result, is the front line of where things are done in movies. When you have elaborate FX for deaths and you advance that forward to the point where somebody in *Die Hard 2* can kill a guy by shoving an icicle through his eye and through his brain, or in *Under Siege* when Tommy Lee Jones gets a knife in the forehead, that's horror movie tropes bleeding into the mainstream. But they very rarely bleed through as horror films. The guys that write and direct those films are watching horror movies to see what to do next! It's a curse at the same time. You're always going to be limited by the fence that's on your genre if you're writing horror. Or you can turn around and write a thriller that has horror perceptions in it and hope that'll help distinguish that movie and make it seem more intense.

Rob: When they were shooting *Chainsaw 3*, they had the rights to do another *Chainsaw* within a year or two? There was a small window with the rights, but they were planning to do another one. Did discussion of what the fourth movie would've been ever come up with you?

We didn't talk about it. I think by the time we could've talked about it, the option was already gone.

Rob: Were you surprised at all when seeing the final version of *Leatherface*? Because Jeff Burr, for example, said he didn't know how the movie ended when he saw it!
Neither did I! The original ending of the movie is Kate Hodge walking off as the sun comes up onto a road, hitchhiking, trying to catch a ride, but knowing that she's dying. Because she's been in the pool of toxic dead bodies, and she knows she's got a septic infection from that. So, she's going to try to make it as far as she can before she drops. Which is kind of a depressing ending. (laughs) All of those other endings, I had nothing to do with.

Rob: I still love the movie!

But you see, that's just it! If you work on a film like this, you know from the inside how it got compromised or couldn't be what it is, and someone comes up to you years later and tells you that's their favorite movie, they're not wrong! Because your window of experience was completely open to something different at that time. The reasons that you like this movie are completely different than our conditional reasons for not liking it. So, there's a little piece of me that doesn't like it, but there's another piece of me that has to love it, because it's like my first born. It's my child and I still love it to death!

Rob: Anything else from *Leatherface* stand out?

At the time, they had to manufacture Leatherface's saw for that movie! They were the longest blades that had ever been put on a chainsaw and they cost like three grand each to make. One of the reasons you write is you get to see them build all this stuff!

Jason: Where was New Line in terms of Freddy while *Leatherface* came out? Because I feel like the franchises were all starting to lose popularity. Or did they think people would just come out to see any Freddy movie?

I think they started to reconsider after *Nightmare 5*.

Rob: Well, because right after that, they killed him!

And remember, DeLuca wrote the script for *Freddy's Dead*! They felt like no one else can do this, we got to do it in house. And he actually did it, which makes him one of the few producers out there that has actually written a script, which is another reason I cut Michael a lot of slack. He wrote *In the Mouth of Madness* for John Carpenter too. New Line's approach to the franchises was actually a groundbreaking kind of thing. It's exactly the business model that Platinum Dunes is using now. It was a little ahead of its time, I think.

Mike: Maybe if they'd gone a little deeper for more classic, if they would have been considered a more classic monster at the time, they could've had another couple franchises.

We were talking, even at that early period, we were talking about monster rallies. We were talking about putting Freddy and Jason together, or somebody else. I mean, because it's the same thing that happened at Universal in the 40s. It's like, well, we'll put two in one movie, and that'll work, you know. And everybody wrote *Freddy vs Jason*, including me.

Rob: Really?

Yeah, I did two drafts of it in 1996, right before Rob Bottin got it. And Goyer.

Rob: What were some of your ideas about combining those two franchises? Because I read an article where everybody had a different take on that. How did you get over the hump of putting those two together, considering they're in different backdrops?

I thought the way to do this movie is you make it one-third about Freddy, one-third about Jason, and one-third about a new character that you'll bring in, who was in my draft, the head of a Freddy cult, who, on the theory that Freddy had been so thoroughly destroyed, at the end of the last movie, that bringing him back was a very elaborate process. And in a parallel story, you have Jason at Crystal Lake, who is resurrected with the heart of the female lead's boyfriend stuck into Jason's chest, so that he can combat Freddy in and out of the dream realm.

The one thing that I was really proud of was a scene where they have to go get Jason and bring him back to Springwood or Springfield or whatever. But the three people in the car with Jason, sitting there in the passenger seat, get hungry and they have to go through a drive-thru restaurant to get food, with Jason sitting there in the car. And then later, they have to put Jason down into the dream realm so he can grab Freddy. Then they wake Jason up and he brings Freddy back into the real world with him. And this happens at a dream realm version of Crystal Lake where you discover Freddy tried to drown him when he was a little kid. And they have to wake Jason up by sticking him with his own machete. And they wake Jason up and Jason and Freddy come back in the car and all of Crystal Lake comes too. And so, it floods out of the car in this big warehouse. That was like the big scene in that one.

And I have no idea what the other drafts were like. It was fun while it lasted. But it was... I don't think it was anywhere near getting done when I wrote it. It was just... It was one of those legendary things. That was kind of the difference because you have an automaton, like a killing machine, and then you have this wisecracking... One of your monsters has dialogue and one doesn't. What is that? That's *Frankenstein Meets The Wolfman*. Of course, originally,

Frankenstein had dialogue. What would Jason say if you gave him dialogue? It's like, stop it. But that was *Freddy vs Jason*. There was more to it than that. I just didn't recall off the top of my head.

Rob: Well, I would like to jump into *The Crow* if you don't mind. It's one of my all-time favorite movies of ever. I can say that proudly. The thing is, if I'm remembering the time period correctly, there weren't really a lot of comic book-based movies. I mean, the *Batman* series was happening, but they never let that get nearly as dark as something like *The Crow*.

Jason: *The Crow* was a perfect movie for that time. The soundtrack to the movie was... That was the time where we were both really into horror movies, really into... That kind of music. I remember going to the theater. I saw it at the Franklin Movie Theater by myself in the afternoon and all black and being all gothy.

Rob: So, I guess my question is, considering the time period and what was going on at the time in films and the idea that comic book movies were not really taken seriously unless it was *Batman*, how do you approach adapting this comic book, this graphic novel, the stuff that James O'Barr did?

Well, I have a question for you. Would you call it something like the difference between... I don't know that this is the first one. I would say *The Crow* is an early example, but I don't know if it's the absolute first. The difference between... And we'll see if you perceive what I'm talking about. The difference between a comic book movie and a graphic novel movie. The comic books grew up and became graphic novels. They're making comic book movies, but that's *Batman*. We've got to do, like, Tim Burton's *Superman*, we have to make it into Americana mythos.

Rob: Graphic novels are what comic book fans took seriously. And that's what I mean is *The Crow* was the first one that took a comic book property seriously. It was dark. It was true to the original source. It's just like the comic. Whereas, I mean, *Dark Knight Returns* was already around, but if you look at the first *Batman* now, it's nothing like that really.

I think it was a different focus. And you have to remember that when we were doing... The first exposure that I had to *The Crow* was in the middle of doing *Critters*. Uh-huh. And

Leonardo DiCaprio. I swear to God. There was a producer named Cotty Chubb who worked on *The Crow* who I knew from getting called to do a project with Penelope Ferris called *Deadly Metal*, which we had several meetings about, which was basically about a band that eats its groupies. But working with Penelope was lots of fun. I mean, because she's a riot. And so, we met. This movie ultimately never went anywhere. Cotty moved on and joined Ed Pressman. Alex (Proyas) signed up to direct *The Crow* based on a rewrite. And so, we all sort of met there.

Cotty called me in because he'd known me from *Deadly Metal*. And he assumed there was some kind of rock and roll, black leather connection to this stuff. But when we first got *The Crow*, when John Shirley did his first draft of the script for *The Crow*, the comic wasn't complete. And indeed, the comic wasn't complete even when we finished shooting the movie. We only had the first three issues. And we had a set of incomplete pencils for four and five. So, there was no ending. We had to come up with the arc all of that because in the comic book, there's something like seven or eight guys in that car that rape Eric's wife. And I'm going, 'Wait, maybe we need to reduce the number a little bit.'

But we spent about a year and a half, off and on, trying to figure out the various problems of graphic novel versus a movie somebody would watch to see. Because if you've read the graphic novel of *The Crow*, which is straight out of James O'Barr, it's like the guy dies, he resurrects, he's very sad, he's very mopey, he says lots of poetry, shoots a lot of heroin, plays the guitar, kills a bunch of guys, shoots some more heroin, kills a bunch of guys, plays the guitar, shoots some heroin, kills some more guys. And it was very in your face, and it was very violent.

And ironically, O'Barr had illustrated a short story of mine before we ever came together on *The Crow* for a magazine called *Horror: The Illustrated Book of Fear*. He illustrated a short story of mine called *Blood Rape of the Lust Ghouls* and that was where I first saw his drawing style. And so, he was vaguely familiar to me when we came out of *The Crow*, but they showed me the material and it was like, take what you can use. The original drafts of the script had a talking bird in them. I took one image from one panel of the comic and made him into the Michael Berryman part, the Skull Cowboy, that got cut out ultimately. But it was a lot of R and D for nothing but it was fun while it lasted. But to your question, your question again was specifically how do you approach adapting that graphic novel. It wasn't even finished.

Rob: I didn't realize it wasn't even finished…

We couldn't just call James up on the phone and go, so how does it end?

Rob: Plus, the fact it was so personal to him.

He was intuitive. It's like, I really don't know. He's following his muse. And you have to admit at a certain point that you're not making a comic. You're making a full-fledged movie that lots of producers have input on. We need this to be this, and we need certain things to be certain ways because now we've got one, two, three, four producers, Alex, me, and the comic all in sort of a circle trying to figure out a compromise of how we could do it. And it took a hell of a long time. We did a ton of drafts and it absorbed just a huge amount of time. We did whole arcs in the script that got developed and then developed more and then abandoned. One thing was, we had an Asian bad guy in an early iteration of the script that does a lot of things that Michael Wincott does in the finished movie. And Brandon Lee came on and it was like, 'What's with the Asian bad guy?!' And I thought, 'Oh God, you're right. Boy, that was stupid. Let's get rid of that.' And so, it was things like that. Brandon contributed heavily to the script. I have a picture of Brandon rewriting a page of the script with Jeff Amato. So, when Brandon signed on, it was shortly after Alex joined up.

Rob: Did that change the direction of it? Because if I'm not mistaken, I think James O'Brien said that producers were coming at him with things like, we can get Michael Jackson and make it a musical or something really far-fetched and weird like that. Did you deal with that?

Well, remember that John Shirley's original script was written when they thought Julian Temple was going to direct it, the guy who did *Absolute Beginners*. That would have been a completely different movie. When the director comes on, that helps snap the project into focus. When you get your lead, that snaps it into a lot more focus. It's enormously influential on how you do the script because now you have a face and a body to put on that character. One thing I like to do is get headshots of people. When I was laying out *The Outer Limits* book at a print shop on Sunset, it was one of these places that does headshots, and they have a big bin of all the headshots that they did. And I would go through that bin and find people I thought looked sort of like the characters we were trying to write for *The Crow*. And I would put them on the wall. I'm going, that's the face of that character until we cast it. And these were totally unknown actors. These were people right out of the bin. But if you can put a face on it, it's a lot easier to work on the script.

Once we got Brandon, all we had to do, basically, is just set up the next meeting or the next phone call. Because he would pore over the script. It's like this whole thing, I don't know, this, that, and everybody gets a vote. That's kind of the most liberated period of writing the script is pre-production. Everybody has an equal say. And as a committee, if we're all sitting here working on a script now, we can vote down an idea or we can say, yeah, that's something worth pursuing.

And there were tons of ideas like that that came and went. The number of bad guys increased, decreased, how evil they were, what they looked like. David Patrick Kelly was responsible for coming up with ninety percent of how his character looked. And we had to stop him. We had to pull him back at a certain point because he wanted to be entirely covered in burn gel. You know, all of a sudden, fire was his thing. So, he wanted to be glistening with fire retardant the whole time. But if you look closely at the finished film, his hair is still that way. It's full of Zel gel or something. And he came up with the tribal markings on his head and the fact that he wears his high-heeled boots, which he used to run in to work up a sweat before each take.

Every actor, I can't say there's a single actor that didn't come on that didn't expand a character enormously from what we had in the script because in the script you're limited to a sketch, or you're limited to a couple of traits and you've got to count on the actor to carry it. If you get the opportunity, which we did on *The Crow*, you get the opportunity to sit down with the actor and say this in my mind is what this character is about, and you can't put that in the script because it would be a page-long description. But you can give that to the actors as kind of overtime. It all influenced. I remember I had dinner with Ernie Hudson, and I said this is this guy's history. This is when he got married. This is when he got divorced. This is what happened to him. And he would go, I got it, I got it, I got it.

Jason: Is that some of the fun stuff for you as a writer?

Oh, it's a lot of fun. It's like frequently you just don't get a chance to do it because modern script writing, working on projects now, it's like a one-way process where you don't get to be on the actual production. And in the case of *The Crow*, we worked on this for a year and a half. Then we went to North Carolina for six weeks of pre-production. Then we got two months of shooting. Then we got everything. I was there for everything, which is rare. As a result, I'm all over this damn movie. I did hand inserts. I did knee doubling. I'm about six different dead bodies in the shootout in the boardroom. One shot is my legs. One shot is my arm sticking out.

Rob: The uncut version of that scene, by the way, is unbelievable.

I love the work print version of that scene because it just seems to have more little things like when Jeff Amata gets shot, you see this cloud of blood behind his head, this mist that hangs in the air, or you see it better. In the work print, I always thought that him running along the rooftops was rhythmed better to the Nine Inch Nails song in the work print than it is in the movie. I got so used to watching the work print, which we temp tracked to *The Last Temptation of Christ* and *Dead Can Dance*. I got used to watching it with that music, so the score still sounds funny to me. *The Last Temptation of Christ* fits that movie perfectly, musically.

Rob: To be sensitive about how I ask this, how much did Brandon's death affect the outcome of what you guys were originally setting out to do?

Oh totally, because there wouldn't have been a movie. After the accident, Alex said, "I'm not going to finish it, we're just going to shit can the movie."

Rob: How far along were you at that point?

Three days of shooting left.

Rob: Wow.

But unfortunately, it was all character stuff with Brandon's character. Stuff where he spoke, specifically stuff before he gets killed in the movie. So, we had to then figure out ways to cover it, and so the movie was dead. They flew to North Carolina, they shut the movie down, it was a very, very bad scene. Unless you've lived through something like this, it's like you have no idea how bad it got. Then, everybody's kind of sitting around in their individual places waiting and waiting and waiting. Six weeks go by and two of the actors went up and talked Alex into finishing the movie. Because the theory being, we can put Brandon in the ground, or we can put Brandon and the movie in the ground. If the movie stands a chance of standing as any kind of legacy.

We all know, from working with Brandon, we know what he would want. We're pretty sure that he would say, 'What are you out of your fucking mind? Finish the movie.' By all means, which is the only reason we went back. And so now, we have this kind of huge sense of mission, going back to do it correctly. But we've got to cover scenes that we don't have our main character for. Which is how we got the scene with Sarah in the loft talking, and the cat is walking around, she's talking to the empty room. Originally, Eric was in that scene. And we said, what if it's her talking to the empty room? And somehow it comes out as a better scene, strangely enough. He shows up at the end of the scene. But what was the effect? It was totally, totally crippling. John Landis knows what this was like. I know what it's like. Alex knows what it's like. And the actors over there know what it's like. But very few people.

A lot of people feel like they own *The Crow*. Because it was a huge part of their childhood, and they tried to find out everything that they could about it, and everybody started websites, and everybody's in this competition to be the biggest *Crow* fan ever. And they're making all these assumptions about what the people on the movie, or the actors on the movie, would have wanted or would have done or something. And again, man, if you weren't there, shut up. But no, there was no movie. There was no movie. There was no movie. And we had to live with the idea that... Because we'd been shooting steadily for two months at this point. And then we'd have to go, if that was all for naught...

Rob: Wow.

And then we jumped at the chance to finish it. I mean, a lot of people, a lot of the crew came back for no money just to finish it. It was that weird. I mean, we had the most bonded crew in the history of motion pictures. I remember when Clyde Basie, the medic, turned down $100,000 from *The Inquirer* for an interview or something. We were all totally behind Clyde. It was stuff like that.

Jason: You wouldn't have that now.

Yeah. And so, something changed, right?

Rob: Well, there's one scene I was wondering about. It's the scene where The Crow kills T-Bird. You don't really see The Crow except from behind, and he doesn't say a word. And it's just effective because he's like, I know you, but you can't be you, you're dead. And it ends with the flames that form The Crow silhouette. It turned out damn beautiful.

Now, that's the scene we shot after the accident with Jeff Cadiente doubling Brandon. All of that was scripted. Everything that happened in the car, and it was scripted that way. But I think that you're probably right. I think that probably Eric had some dialogue in there that's not there anymore. Because that's the way we shot it.

Rob: It was effective that he didn't say one word to this guy, but yet the guy knew exactly who he was, what he was there to do, and what was going to happen to him.

I remember when we torched the big crow outline because we actually did that on a sound stage. It's actually, you can't tell, but it's indoors. And it looks like it's out by the dock, which was on the other side of town from where we were shooting. And that was one of the, symbolically enough, that was one of the last shots of the shoot with him sitting prior to the crow outline.

Rob: And one of the most imitated ever since.

Yeah, have you seen *Daredevil*? (laughs) When I first saw the posters for the Joker in the latest Batman movie, *The Dark Knight*, I went, *The Crow*.

Rob: That's true. I didn't pinpoint it right away until the black under the eyes and it definitely had a very *Crow*-esque look to it. One thing, I read a really interesting article a couple of years ago, and if we want to go off record on this, we can. I know Alex has really wanted to do kind of his own special edition of *The Crow*. I don't know if there's some kind of discrepancy with one of the producers? Alex had all this great material that he wanted to contribute to it. And then one of the producers wanted more control over the special edition because he was doing the fourth *Crow* movie with DMX, which never ended up happening, thank God. Alex has never gotten to do his DVD of it or something along those lines.

I don't think he wants to recut the movie. I think he just wants to get a chance to do his commentary and feature all the behind-the-scenes footage on *The Crow* I shot with my giant JVC video camera. We had all this footage and Mark Rance contacted me about using the footage because he was busy doing background on the first disc of *Dark City* and then we, subsequently, all sort of rejoined on the special edition of *Dark City* later to do the commentary and stuff. But I had all this footage, and we had all these features and, in fact, we even had EPK stuff shot on the set.

But Alex was loth to participate in a lot of this stuff just because he had very strong feelings about the movie, understandably so. And Mark was one of the people who was instrumental in kind of talking him out of the box and saying, 'You know, some time has passed and maybe we should get some of this stuff down for posterity.' And we sat down and did our audio tracks. We have a commentary track with Alex, me, Alex McDowell, the production designer, Darius Volsky, Derek, the DP, and Simon Merton, the art director. And so, we had this entire track.

But one of Alex's conditions for participating was that he had approval on all the supplements. And Alex, at that time, they were doing a special edition of the first movie and a special edition of the second movie and the third movie, the first two sequels. And Alex's argument was that Jeff Most, as a producer, was more present on the other two movies and he didn't want a lot of input from Jeff or presumed veto power on the supplements on the first movie. He wanted them to go in more or less as is. And Jeff didn't like this. And so, when he said, well, I'm going to assert myself, I'm going to assert my right to prevent this from being done in this movie, Jeff did, then Alex just said, well, I'm out.

So, we lose the 90-minute thing we had cut together of my behind-the-scenes footage, because I swing with Alex. We lose that commentary. We get the commentary from Jeff and John, essentially, in its place. And nothing's been done with it to this day. So, it's just Alex had the power to sign off on whatever was on that disc and he asserted that power, which he had by contract. People later tried to deny that he even had that ability, but he had signed documents from Dimension giving him that. And they decided to swing with Jeff. So, it's like one of these days somebody will see this stuff.

Rob: Do you have that 90-minute behind the scenes cut?

Oh, sure. I have an hour cut. I have a 90-minute cut. Nobody's going to see it unless they have private showings with no cell phones kind of thing. Because somebody videotaped my sizzle reel I made out of that and put it on YouTube.

Rob: Really?

Yeah. I did a five-minute highlight reel of some of the stuff that I'd shot and showed it in San Francisco and somebody videotaped it off the screen up there, which is why... I cut it to "Paint It Black" by the *Rolling Stones* and that's why the audio is missing from YouTube.

Rob: Is it still on YouTube? I would imagine that got...

You can't get rid of it. Once you scotch it from one place it pops up in another place. We were very cagey with the footage. We wouldn't leave it with anyone anywhere because, if you have a post house and you're doing this stuff, someone will leak it. And the fact that the only versions of some of the footage that exists are these horrific ninth generation

video dupes, because we were pretty able to keep a lid on it because it's ours. Technically, it's mine. Nobody has a right to do anything with this stuff except me and Alex. So, one day, and I'm saying this now on what, the fifteenth anniversary of the movie. Before we die, maybe get a version with supplements out there. Our supplements. Well, I told Alex, I said, 'Well, you know, we could do a bootleg audio commentary on *Icons of Fright* if you want to. Why not?' I also told that to F. Paul Wilson because he and Doug Winter and I have done a commentary track for *The Keep*, which is very illuminating.

Rob: We don't have to go into our personal feelings on the *Crow* sequels, but...

I haven't seen them.

Rob: Really?

No.

Rob: Well, essentially the biggest problem with them is they're just remakes of the one that you've done.

I understood that the Tim Pope one was really beautiful to look at. I saw about five or ten minutes of it, but I haven't watched the sequels. I did watch the first episode of the TV show.

Rob: I totally forgot about the TV show!

The Crow show. And the one with Mark Dacascos because the first episode is a remake of the movie. And I called Alex up right after that and he goes, he goes, 'Really, what did you think?' And I said, 'Imagine a broad daylight, missionary position, Hawaiian shirt version of *The Crow*.' And he just laughed, and I don't think he's watched it to this day.

Mike: On the show, wouldn't he get angry and the Crow makeup would appear on his face? Wasn't it like the *Incredible Crow*? *The Incredible Crow*.

Rob.: Didn't you work on a *Creature From the Black Lagoon* remake with Guillermo del Toro?

Oh, very briefly but it wasn't that much work. When Guillermo was up to do *Creature from the Black Lagoon*, he called me into a meeting in his office while he was working on *Blade 2*. Which was the first place I met (Tim) Bradstreet. And flat out, he goes, 'I want you to write it.' And we set up a series of meetings with Gary Ross at Universal where we could never get to the meeting. It was always moved. It was always canceled. And finally, Guillermo, half out of frustration that we could never get these meetings and half out of the fact that the window had passed, and he had just moved on, then he was off it. And he was off it. I was off it.

Guillermo's idea, which was different from a sort of long-standing idea that I had for a *Creature* remake which was based, actually, on an old book outline that I had and never used for anything. Guillermo's idea, which I thought was a great idea, was to shoot a period Victorian. And I said, well, you know what that is, I said in the meeting staring at him across the desk? I said, 'You know what that is? That's *The Lost World*.' That's Sir Roxbury or whatever his name is in the book with his giant elephant gun and these guys with these cameras that are these big, big box cameras and stuff going into the Amazon for the first time. And finding out that the Creature is not the monster of the first movie, but he's actually kind of venerated as a demi-God type figure. So, he has people that enable him, and he has a whole culture built around him, which is our job to destroy.

I think the thing that appealed to Guillermo the most was the idea to do the whole thing period. And I was willing to swing with that. But we never got to develop it. We knew one thing, when we went into the studio, they'd ask, "Well, can it be modern day?" Well, we should have a story as a backstop for when that comes up. Inevitably, if they force it away from what he wants to do as a director, they run the risk of him walking off the project. We never got that far. This is before he was the Guillermo we know today.

Rob: You adapted your own story "Pick Me Up" for *Masters of Horror*, right? The one Larry Cohen directed?

Yeah, when Mick was doing the first season of *Masters of Horror*, he came to me and said, 'I want you to adapt that story of yours.' Boy, that was a kick. That was the first script that Larry directed that he hadn't written. And will probably be the only one! Plus, I got to be on the set for those. Here's Larry Cohen asking me how to do stuff! That was a thrill. Plus, if you follow Larry around, the guy is independent filmmaking personified. He would race from one monitor to the other, he doesn't watch monitors, he doesn't watch dailies. He would get the discs of the dailies and hand it to the showrunner and say, "Here, go watch these and tell me if any of it is good!" He would watch a scene and say, print take one, and print take three. And he was dead on, every time. He doesn't waste time. He stays five feet away from the actors. And he really engages the actors. And just watching that guy work was just miraculous. He was just all over it.

And boy, that was fun. It was Larry Cohen!

Rob: I love Fairuza Balk!

And we had no idea we had her until I got to Canada and Mick called me on the phone saying, you're never going to guess who we got to play the girl. Never in my wildest dreams did I think it'd be her! She was great. Michael Moriarty is a unique guy! He's really weird and I like him that way! But when I was writing that script, I was hoping that we could cast Michael Ironside for that part. But if you get Larry, you get Michael! But I had never seen that interpretation in my head. But as I'm watching Michael do it, I thought this is good! Michael came up with the thing where we warms the cigarette with the lighter before he lights it, he's full of character stuff like that. Six weeks before we shot, he had been in this hellacious bar fight! He got the shit kicked out of him by four guys, which is why he's limping in the show.

Rob: For *Texas Chainsaw Massacre: The Beginning*, did they come to you because of *Leatherface* or…?

Actually, they were partnered with New Line and (producer) Mark Ordesky called me up and gave it to me. I thought, 'Oh God, we're back in *Chainsaw* land again!' We worked for seven months on the script, trying to give it a dynamic that the other films didn't have, and trying to explain all this stuff. Where does Hoyt comes from? It was all for naught. Because the original script they didn't want to do was by Sheldon Turner. And Michael Bay had sent out a rather infamous memo, it was actually a smart, sharp memo – he goes, making movies is too damned hard to devote all the time and energy to something that's not right in the script. It's like, I'm not going to do this script. It's like, 'I'm not going to do this script.' So, we had to rethink it and replot it, and it didn't matter because when they got to Austin to shoot, basically, they called Sheldon back. As kind of punishment for not rewriting the script when they wanted to. This is just my guess.

But, uh, you know, Sheldon had six, seven months earlier, he's got five, six projects going on and he's going, no, I don't want to, I don't want to write *Chainsaw: The Beginning* again. I've got other stuff to do. This is just my speculation. But six months later, they're shooting and it's get your ass down to the set. I could tippy-toe through that movie, which I have not seen, by the way. Uh, I could tippy-toe through that and, and the scripts, because we had to arbitrate. And I'm going, yeah, I invented that, I invented that, I invented that. But the process of arbitration assumes what everybody accounts as their own creation differently. If you write a first draft and it has a scene set in an alley, any draft, any scene set in any alley, anywhere, is credited to you. No matter what happens in that scene. Because you came up with the word, the alley.

And it proceeds, as a little mountain of Tinker Toys falling apart, it proceeds from that premise until everybody basically gets screwed on credit, which is how arbitration works. Which leads to me complaining about it on the deleted part of the audio commentary. So, you can't win, you know. It's like even when you tell the story, it's like, nah, we're cutting that explanation out.

Rob: So, you've never seen it, so you don't really know how much of your stuff got in there.

I've never seen it and then weirdly enough, I went back up to Vancouver and Lee Tergesen, who's in the movie, as the biker, who didn't exist before I wrote a biker into the script, is up there playing the the lead in the *Masters of Horror* we're shooting up there for the second season. So, it's like, I saw you were in something else I wrote, oh yeah, what's that? And *Texas Chainsaw Massacre: The Beginning*. Silence. Okay, next topic. So, I don't know whether it was good, bad or indifferent. They kind of tend to look alike, even to the posters that they're doing, where everything is just kind of got that post-industrial, decayed, brown, sepia tone look to it. And it's like, every time you have a mad killer set up with a slaughterhouse somewhere, and you see all the rusty tools and stuff. Wouldn't you like to see one that's nice and sparkly clean, where the fluorescents aren't flickering all the time, and you can actually see what you're doing.

Rob: I didn't mind the Platinum Dunes *Chainsaw* remake; it was a lot better than I thought it was going to be.

It was okay, but it's a completely unnecessary movie. But then again, how many movies are really necessary?

Rob: Last question on *Texas Chainsaw*, I've always loved your opening scene pitch that they didn't use!

Oh, yeah. This is me pitching it verbally to Michael Bay on the set of *The Island*. No pressure or anything. We go down, and he was shooting... the beginning of *The Island*, they shot it in what used to be an aircraft plant in Downey. 500,000 square foot set. I mean, it's a city. Unlike *Freddy's Nightmares*, which shot in a closet, it's like... It's everywhere. Functioning elevators and stainless steel, and everything. And Michael's over by the elevators, and he's like, ah, action! Cut! And then he and I run over into the corner and do this, waving our arms and talking to each other for five minutes,

and he runs back to the monitor, action!

And, uh, the two things I pitched to him were the idea of the beginning of him being found in the slaughterhouse dumpster. Basically, there's a horrific obese woman working a meat line, stamping bogus USDA seals on detained meat. It's like Lucy and the Pies, you know, and she gets this gas pain, and it's actually her giving birth, and the horrible little baby just drops out on the slaughterhouse floor. But in order to keep the rhythm of the line going, she just reaches down with a meat cleaver and cuts the umbilical cord and throws him in a dumpster. And he's scavenged out of the dumpster, and it's one of those red dumpsters that they used to have in the meatpacking district in New York, where they had the red trash cans. And people who are so poor they have to scavenge food out of the dumpsters, opens it up and takes him, and that's Luda Mae, basically, as a younger woman.

And then the other thing I pitched to him was the title sequence, which was designed to cut some time after the baby's taken out of the dumpster. There's a steer skull sideways in the dumpster, and you hold on the skull. You hold on the skull for so long you begin to wonder what the hell's going on, and then the dumpster lid goes up, and the skull flies out of the dumpster and lands in a wheelbarrow full of offal. And you realize you're seeing film being projected backwards as some guy tossed the head into the dumpster. And so, you see the guy walk backwards with the wheelbarrow into the slaughterhouse, and you follow that skull through the slaughterhouse process backwards, the de-hiding pit, the bleeding pool, until it's a whole cow at the far end. So, the skin goes back on. The blood goes back in until you see this nice little cow. Little mouse cow face looking up at the camera like this. Reverse angle of just a silhouette of Leatherface, who's now nineteen, and you just see his shadow, and you just see him swinging the sledgehammer back like this, and it crunched, and it goes to black, and then you start modern day. And that's how you cover his teen years. He's just working in the slaughterhouse. Michael Bay got excited about it!

Rob: What could and should have been!

2009

DEREK MEARS
JEFF BURR
ROB ZOMBIE
JOEL SILVER
SUSAN DOWNEY
DAVID LESLIE JOHNSON
JAUME COLLET-SERRA
VERA FARMIGA
PETER SARSGAARD
ISABELLE FUHRMAN
MARCUS DUNSTAN
PATRICK MELTON
JORDAN LADD
PAUL SOLET
GLENN MCQUAID

DEREK MEARS

Interviewed by Mike Cucinotta and Rob Galluzzo (1/09)

We were given the chance to chat with actor Derek Mears who dons the infamous hockey mask of Jason Voorhees in the upcoming Platinum Dunes relaunch of *Friday the 13th*. Since our time was limited, we thought it'd be fun to get YOU, our faithful *Icons* readers involved. So, we asked him questions submitted by you guys. Below are Derek's responses to YOUR questions! And for the record, for a guy portraying one of the most iconic movie maniacs, he's easily the nicest interview we've ever done here on *Icons*. Read on!

Hey Derek! Normally for *Icons of Fright*, our interviews tend to be more extensive and cover the entire career of who we're speaking to. We will do that interview with you soon enough! But for now, since we're limited on time, we thought it'd be fun to have fans send in questions.

Oh, that'd be fun! This'll be a blast!

And don't worry, the fans sent in good stuff…

Question number one: "Why do you feel it's ok for you to ruin the Jason character?" (laughs)

(huge laughs) No, no! That's definitely not in there! Let's start with Seth from Houston, Texas. He asks, "Is the new movie a sequel or a remake?"

It's more of a retelling or a relaunch. Kind of like what *Batman Begins* was. The mythos of Jason exists. In my opinion, it's the best parts of *2, 3* and *4* from the original series pulled out and told in a totally different story.

Justan Carlson from Davenport, Iowa would like to know, "How awesome does it feel to be the first Jason to not have to walk after victims? Fully running is how it should be."

(laughs) Completely, completely awesome. (laughs)

From Brian in Houston, Texas: "Being that this movie was shot in Austin, how do you think the surroundings of Texas will fare against the previous movies?"

I think it'll be great! Especially the way that cinematographer Daniel Pearl shot it. One thing's for sure, I can guarantee you it'll be the most beautiful looking *Friday the 13th* film you've ever seen.

Wow, and you're a die-hard horror fan, so it must've been cool to work with Daniel Pearl who shot the original *Texas Chain Saw Massacre*!

Oh yeah, I learned a lot from that guy.

Renna from San Jose, California wants to know, "I know the first original film had Jason Voorhees' mother. Will the new film feature a glimpse of his mother?"

From what I hear, yes, we did shoot the scenes for that. There was a controversy online for a while where no one was sure if Mrs. Voorhees would be in it. I, myself, have not seen the final film yet, which is driving me crazy! (laughs) I've only seen what the fans have seen online for the trailer and the one TV spot. I hear there's another TV spot with Jason on the roof, but I haven't seen that yet. I'm like, '*I remember shooting that, I want to see that!*' What I've been really impressed with on this film is that the producers, Andrew Form and Brad Fuller, have been looking at the fan feedback to influence what they're doing on the film. Once it got out there that Mrs. Voorhees wasn't going to be in it, that she would only be talked about or referred to, the fans got up in arms. And now from what I hear, they put Mrs. Voorhees back in the film, which is awesome.

Oh great! You can't not have Mrs. Voorhees!

Oh, I completely agree!

Johnny Nash from New York would like to know, "Did you use any inspiration as Jason? Example, Kane Hodder? Or any other Jasons?"

No. I mean, I've seen all the films, I'm familiar with all the actors that have played Jason before me. I've basically used the script that Mark Swift and Damian Shannon wrote, and I did my own character from there. I had to put what I had known before about Jason to the side to try to discover new aspects of him. So, once I created my character, there are times in this film where for certain takes, I don't know if they're going to use them or not, but I did some homages, a tip of my hat to some of the guys before me. You might watch the film and say, "Wait a second… was that a Ted White head tilt?" Or "That guy totally moved like CJ Graham for that moment!" So, I don't know if they'll use any of those takes, but just out of respect for the guys that came before me, being a fan of them myself, I put in little things here and there. But all and all, the character is all my take.

From Chuck, An American Psycho in London: "I would like to know is it hard to play a character that doesn't talk or even have facial expressions?"

It's not really tough at all. It's funny, because the common misconception is, "Oh, being that you can't see your face, you can put anybody in the mask. It's just a guy in a mask. It'll be fine." Which I completely disagree with. To me, acting is acting. There's no sub-category where you're a prosthetic actor or a masked actor. We're all actors, and if you're in the right mind set in the character of the particular scene you're doing, whatever you do is going to transcend and go through that mask and be captured on camera. So, I'm mentally in a state of hurt and I'm extremely angry as Jason. Someone destroyed someone that I love, and I want to take my revenge out on them. You really have to own that and be in that moment! I don't care what's in front of your face, if you're in that moment, it's going to come through. You're going to be able to read it. If you think, "Oh, I have a mask on and nobody's going to be able to see what I'm actually doing," you're going to lose the intensity. You're not acting then.

From our reader Doug from Inverness, Florida: "What is your favorite kill in the new *Friday the 13th* movie?"

There's a scene, there's a photo out of it where Willa Ford is out in the lake and I'm standing by the side of the lake in the middle of broad daylight. That sequence is my favorite in the film. But it's weird though because we shot it two different ways. One way is more of a psychological kill which I really, really dig. And the other way is still good, but it's a little more violent. I don't know which one they're going to use because I haven't seen the final product yet. I don't know if I can give anything away since I haven't seen it. (laughs)

Do you personally have a favorite kill from the entire franchise? One that sticks out for you?

Oh yeah, man! It sounds kind of cliché, but *Part 7*, the girl in the sleeping bag and Jason slamming it against the tree.

It's a classic!

I love that. It's so good!

Jim Corrupt from Liverpool UK: "Your machete seems a lot bigger than the other Jasons. Are you more badass?"

(laughs) It's genetic. That's why my machete is bigger.

(huge laughs)

No! I didn't really have a say in it. I just kind of showed up and they were like, "*Here you go!*" Handing me the machete. (laughs) Am I more badass? I don't know…

Come on, let's just say that you are!

I think you guys are going to have to be the judge of that. Let's let the fans be the judge.

Our staffer Adam Barnick has a question for you. "Your Jason seems like he could be the most thoughtful and cunning of the bunch. Can you speak about how Marcus Nispel worked with you on the character, directing Jason? Did he approach you just like one of the other characters?"

Completely! That's what we talked about the whole time for this part. I was really blown away listening in on the interviews with the producers and Marcus. They've said, "What's different about this role is we've actually hired an actor to play Jason as opposed to a guy in a mask." I've made my living as an actor for eleven years and I'm part of the cast. We all hang out and see each other which is amazing.

For the intelligence of the character, that comes from the script by Mark Swift and Damian Shannon. They wrote him that way. They wanted to make him more of a character for this one, rather than just an entity. A lot of our long, long talks as a group were about trying to base Jason in reality. Make him a character and make Jason scary again. Because as the series went along, although it was great, it got campier and campier, and we became less and less afraid of Jason. We're trying to tie back in to give you that "Oh shit" feeling when you see Jason on the screen.

You just reminded me, our staff writer Danny Price from Australia didn't have a question, but he just wanted us to thank you for making Jason scary again.

Oh, man. That's so awesome. It's really a team effort. I'll take the thanks for everybody. In my opinion, Scott Stoddard who did the make-up FX and designed the new look of Jason and applies all the make-up for Jason. He's in the trenches with all the blood and guts and torn limbs and severed heads. I mean, he's a fan of the series and he's fifty percent of Jason. I always use the analogy that I'm in NASCAR. I'm the one that gets to pilot the crazy car, but he's the one on the headset that can see the whole track and will tell me if my tires are low, or telling me things like, "Hey, the camera is not picking you up on this angle. If you lift your head up a little bit more, you can show off this side of the face and it looks really cool in the shadows." He's really an amazing, amazing artist, and he's really passionate about this film.

What can you tell us about the teenage characters in the film, because as the series went on, not only did Jason get campier, but also the teenage characters. How are these characters compared to the other *Friday the 13th* victims?

It's wild, when I first read the script, I was talking to my wife Jenny and I go, "This is crazy, because I really care about these characters!" And the comedy that was written into the film, it wasn't like the cheesy campy "Here's my set-up and punch line! Not so funny, but more stupid!" This is legitimately funny. And there's been talk on the internet where people have heard this movie is funny. And they think it's not supposed to be funny. What I want to clarify to some of the fans is that there are aspects of the movie that are funny, but Jason himself is never funny. He's always dead serious. But there's little bits of humor to the film that come as a release from the tension. The tension builds to such a high level that you need little bits of humor to relieve that tension.

But all the kids in the film, you generally like them. And I was blown away! I had become so close with the cast members. We all genuinely liked each other. We got to know each other so well. There are scenes when you see these talented young actors so committed to what's going on, to the reality of this horrified situation, you see them crying and screaming. I'm off camera listening to them, and I'm emotionally attached! I'm worried for them. They'll cut, and some of these characters will still be in the moment and trying to wind down from what just happened in the scene. They'd still be crying and trying to come back down to reality. And I'm really, really excited to see what the final product is for this film, because from what I saw on the sidelines, these guys are seriously talented actors.

Derek, thank you so much for your time! We really appreciate it!

No, no. Thank you guys so much for the interest. I really appreciate it. And please, for you guys and the fans, if you see me at a signing, come up and say hello!

Special thanks to Gemma Cacho!

JEFF BURR

Interviewed by Mike Cucinotta and Rob Galluzzo (3/09)

Words cannot express how much I love *Leatherface: The Texas Chainsaw Massacre 3*. When I was roughly fourteen, I waited outside my local theater until someone pretended to be my "guardian" and snuck me in. And from then on, I followed the career of director Jeff Burr with great enthusiasm. Throughout the 90s, he directed sequels to *The Stepfather, Pumpkinhead,* and *Puppet Master*. I eventually discovered his underrated anthology debut *The Offspring* aka *From a Whisper to a Scream*. Jeff was kind enough to sit down with Mike and I to candidly discuss the above movies and more. We got the full scoop on making *Leatherface*, heard stories about Vincent Price and Terry O'Quinn and got the real story on *The Devil's Den. Fright* fans, this is one of our finest interviews!

Rob: What are your earliest recollections of the horror genre? As fans, we always remember what introduced us and opened us up to the genre, so what was it for you?

Actually, one of the first movies I can remember seeing in a theater was a double feature, and really, it's not a horror film, but it was *Frankenstein Conquers the World* and *Tarzan and the Valley of Gold*. It was my brother's sixth birthday party, so I was dragged along when I was four. And I just have vivid memories of both those movies. I'm sure that was a big influence just because it was such an amazing thing to see. A giant monster and a giant kid with a big forehead in *Frankenstein Conquers The World*. (laughs) The first horror film I remember in a theater really getting me was *Equinox*, and it was a double bill with *The Blob*. I was probably around nine years old, around 1970, it was a double bill re-issue and *Equinox* just scared the living crap out of me! I love that movie still to this day. So, that was a big influence, and then around the same time, we had something called *Shock Theater* with a guy named Dr. Shock (and Dingbat) who was a hilariously bad horror host, but they showed the original *Thing From Another World*. That just scared the crap out of me too! Of course, all the *Frankenstein* movies. They had the horror package of all the *Frankenstein* and *Wolf Man* movies, so those were big influences too from very early on.

Rob: So, it's safe to say that from a very early age you were a big fan of the genre and followed it?

Oh yeah, absolutely! And then, the other thing that really happened kind of concurrently was, and it's so cliché, I saw my first issue of *Famous Monsters of Filmland*. The cover was at a supermarket, and I'd never seen the magazine before and, boom, there it was. Just the fact that there was a whole community of people that made these magazines. There was another one called *The Monster Times*. I never subscribed, but I would try to get them. They had very spotty distribution, so it was just amazing to get a copy when you did. All of those were big influences.

Rob: Did reading some of these magazines like *Famous Monsters* introduce you to the behind-the-scenes of movies and how these things were made?

Oh yeah!

Rob: Where'd your interest in how films were made begin?

That's interesting because I really don't know. The only thing I can say is that my parents acted in community theater, so I would go see plays with them in it. It was a cool feeling to go to a play and see them or see behind the stage at how the play was done. So, I guess that did have an influence. Like so many people my age, my grandfather gave me an 8mm camera that he didn't use anymore for home movies. So, I did the home movie thing, and it was a natural thing, just like kids now with digital cameras. You just start screwing around in the backyard. Eventually making little movies. Ninety-nine percent of the people who do that, there is a point where they get interested in other things, but for me it always stuck. So that was kind of the progression.

Rob: So, what was it like at the very start of your career?

Well, same way it is now in terms of, the one thing, I swear to God, there is in some ways no difference in making Super 8 movies in the backyard and making professional movies. You bring kind of the same things to bear. And the fun is still there. But of course, there are differences. But it's more similar than dissimilar to make a Super 8 movie with your friends and to make an independent horror movie. Because really, the first movie that I did, *The Offspring* (aka *From a Whisper to a Scream*), it was really working with some of the same people that had worked on my Super 8 movies and shooting in my hometown, so it was very different but it was also very similar. With my Super 8 movies, like with most people, they started small and then they grew. Each movie got more and more elaborate, or I would try different things and it all led to features.

Mike: For your first feature, you have a terrific cast! You've got Susan Tyrrel, you've got Vincent Price. How'd you get them for your first movie? Nowadays, you see a lot of classic horror stars coming in for a lot of independent movies. But you got one of the most classic of all horror stars at a completely different time.

And we didn't have a lot of money! One of the things that happened was Courtney Joyner who co-wrote the movie, he knew this director, Steve Carver. So, I would occasionally go over to Steve Carver's house. Every Thursday, he would have a gathering. And that's where I met Terry Kiser and R.G. Armstrong, people like that and Oscar Williams. And really, everything worked in concert. Oscar Williams was a writer/director who wrote *Black Belt Jones* and did *Five on the Black Hand Side*; great guy. He actually got us Rosalind Cash. It was one of those things where we were talking and then her name came up and it was like, "Oh I love her. Rosalind would be great." And he said, "Well I know her! Here's her number." So, he made the call and introduced us.

So, with Terry Kiser and Rosalind Cash and Susan Tyrrel, we literally just got them directly from friends. Clu Gulager was a friend of Susan Tyrrel's, so one thing led to another, and we assembled the cast that way. And Vincent Price, that was literally Darin Scott, the other producer, and I just going up to his house. We found his address, went up to his house, knocked on his door and gave him the script.

Mike: Wow, really?

Yeah! It was hilarious. All we had was his address from a celebrity address service, which they don't do anymore because of stalking laws and whatnot. Anyway, so for fifty cents, you could buy addresses, so we get this address and that's all we had. We had the script and a note. We park on the opposite side of the street to his house. So, we get nervous and we're sitting in the car saying, "Well, how do we know it's his house?" "I don't know. You got to go up there!" "No, we both got to go up there!" (laughs) And as we're babbling and trying to talk each other out of doing this, a mail truck pulls up, the postman gets out, knocks on the door, the door opens, there's Vincent Price. So, A) we know it's his house and B) we know he's home, so we have to do it. So, we pull up, we wait a little bit, we knock on the door, he answers! And, "Gee, Mister Price! We're filmmakers and we have this script, and we really love you!" (laughs) You know, he had every right to say uh-huh, grab the script and just close the door. He actually invited us in, he spent about fifteen minutes with us and couldn't have been more gracious. He said he would read the script and get back to us. It took a while to put everything together, but several months later he was on the set.

Rob: That's amazing!

It's a much more complicated story that I don't know if you want to get into it. It's convoluted but what happened really, the real story, what I just told you is absolutely true, but here's the curve in the road. He read the script, and then he called two days later and said, "Well boys, it's pretty good and I like it. And I like you guys, but I just don't know. I don't know if it's for me. I've been trying to not do horror films." So, it wasn't a true no, but it wasn't a ringing endorsement either. So, we're thinking, what do we do? We had shot the movie and continued editing, and then I kind of forgot about Vincent Price because I assumed he was not going to do it. Why? I don't know, but in my head, I thought, "You know who would be great in this movie? Max von Sydow." And why him? I have no idea.

So, I call up Max von Sydow's agent, Walter Kohner, so he reads the script and says he wants to meet me. I go in for a meeting, and he says, "Max will not do this movie. I can tell you. But I have the perfect client for you. Vincent Price." (laughs) So, I make no mention that we contacted Vincent several months earlier, and what happened was the door opened again, we got a dialogue open with Walter and it came down to Vincent wanting to see a little bit of the movie that we had done. So, we set up a screening of a rough cut. He sees it on the big screen, we showed him the most tame episode we shot and he agreed to do the movie. That's really how we got him. It was a total fluke!

Rob: And that ended up being one of the last things he did, right?

He announced during the making of the movie to the *L.A. Times* that it'd be his last horror movie. Nothing to do with the movie. At that point, he had a chip on his shoulder for being known for that only. He'd done so much other stuff. He ended up doing the movie, and I believe he did three more movies after. *Edward Scissorhands* was his last movie. He also did the voice for a Disney movie around the time.

Rob: So, when I was a kid, I wanted to see *Leatherface: The Texas Chainsaw Massacre 3* so badly, that I waited outside of a movie theater until a couple would pretend I was with them so I could get in. Because I was underage at the time!

That's great, that's great!

Rob: I'd do that all the time, because I had no one to take me to horror movies as a kid! So, I'd wait outside for every new horror movie and ask some older guy to just pretend to be my older brother! I'd say, "I'll pay for my own ticket. I'll sit far away from you. I just have to get in to see this movie!" So, I got into Le*atherface* and for a fourteen year old kid at the time, I was blown away. I absolutely loved it.

Aw, thank you.

Rob: I know it was hell to make! But I loved it back then and I still do. How did you get that gig? Because it seemed *Leatherface* was a very hectic movie! I know Peter Jackson was attached at one point and maybe another director? So, how'd you get involved?

Here's what happened. I had done *Stepfather 2*, so my agent at the time Bobbi Thompson at William Morris, she said, "Hey, I can get you a meeting on the new *Texas Chainsaw Massacre* movie." I thought 'Great!' This would've been around May of 1989, and we had just finished *Stepfather 2*. So, I have a meeting with Michael DeLuca and Jeff Schectman, who was an original producer that ended up dropping out of the movie. They had a script then, so I read the script and gave them my impressions. And… that was it. That was in April or May of '89. Didn't hear anything more about it. Then at the end of June, I get this phone call from my agent saying, "New Line wants to meet you about *Leatherface* again."

I have another meeting and they offer me the job essentially. So, I'm thinking, stupidly, "Wow, they must really want me!" But what they told me then was that they'd hired a director and he'd worked on it a little bit, but he had to drop out because of contractual reasons with 20th Century Fox on the TV show of *Alien Nation*. It was a guy named Jonathan Betuel. He did *My Science Project* and some other stuff. But he dropped out, and I was their next choice. I had the weekend to mull it over and I decided to do it. But I was operating under the delusion that they actually did want me. And what really happened, which I found out later, was I was the only director that they kind of would accept that agreed to do the movie.

In other words, they'd offered it to several people, including Peter Jackson and they were really high on him, even back then. This would've been after *Dead Alive*, I guess? I'm sure there were others, so I'm probably being charitable when I say I was tenth on the list. I was thinking they liked my work, or liked my take on it, or whatever. That was kind of the way I entered it. It was two and a half weeks before production started, so we were casting and doing everything else. But a lot of stuff had already been done, like the house had been constructed. Which I thought was a mistake.

I think one of the biggest mistakes of the movie was the idea of shooting it in LA. And that was one of the first things I said, "We have to shoot in Texas!" And they said "No, we've already built the house." So that was not even negotiable, the fact of shooting it in Texas. And I think to date, it's the only *Chainsaw* movie that was shot in California. There were a bunch of things like that I couldn't change as the director, but I knew it going in. It was an odd thing, because I'd never really replaced a director before…

Rob: Now, didn't they have a release date locked or something like that?

Well, here's the thing, what they had, they were working backwards. They had a release date locked. And the theaters were already booked, and it was set for November 3rd, 1989. It was basically set for around Halloween. So, all the theaters were booked, and they'd promised the movie, so that was the whole thing. It had to be finished by then, so they couldn't really delay it. Or spend any more time in prep.

Rob: So, they never contacted Tobe Hooper or anything?

No, I think Kim Henkel was involved initially? There was another synopsis I read on the initial sales sheet they gave me that they took to Cannes. I bet you it was much more like *4*. I think there was a prom? Was there a prom in *4*?

Rob: Yep.

So, I think that's what Henkel was going to do, but he dropped out very early on, and I had nothing to do with that development and I don't know how they arrived at David J. Schow. I think he'd done some *Freddy's Nightmares*. One of the first things I said was that I would love to contact Hooper, just tell him what I'm doing. Not necessarily to get his blessing, but I just thought it was an obligation. I had done the same thing for *Stepfather 2*. First thing I did was I called Joe Ruben, the director of the first *Stepfather*, because a friend of mine had done *Dreamscape* with him. He was very gracious when we spoke about *Stepfather*. So, I felt I had to do the same thing with Tobe Hooper. But they (the producers) said, "Contractually, you cannot talk to him." They had no contact with him at all. It's all to do with the Vortex limited partnership or something.

Rob: Did you ever talk to him afterwards?

Yes. And that's hilarious. (laughs) The only thing he ever said to me about the movie, because we talked about a whole bunch of other stuff. But I went out to breakfast with him. I don't remember how this all happened. But the movie came out in January of 1990, so this was around March 1990. And uh, the first thing he says to me as we sit down for breakfast, he goes, "Jeff, I got to tell you. I went to your movie opening night, and it was such a strange experience walking into that movie knowing I had nothing to do with it." And I said, "Well, Tobe. It was strange for me too, man!"

Because I saw the movie for the first time in January in Tennessee and I literally did not know how it ended, even though it had my name on it. So that was a very strange experience to me! We never got into the actual movie. I'm sure he hated it. But we never got into if he liked things about it or anything like that. But again, he was very gracious, and I've since met him several times.

Rob: Did you have anything to do with the infamous teaser trailer they did for that?

No, that was literally done before I was hired. Here's the thing! Literally, when I signed the deal to make the movie, the next Friday, I went to see *A Nightmare on Elm Street 5: The Dream Child* opening night at the Chinese and the teaser for *Leatherface* was playing with it!

Mike: Ha! They hadn't even made the movie yet!

No! I literally just signed to make the movie a few days earlier and there's the trailer for the movie I'm making!

Rob: It must've been surreal!

Yeah, yeah. Unfortunately, it was a midnight show I went to, and it wasn't a full crowd. But the audience that was there went nuts! So, that was kind of a cool thing. It's very much like the trailer to *Friday The 13th Part 8: Jason Takes Manhattan*. It's a very similar trailer in the sense that you think it's one movie and then boom, it's not.

Mike: What about the look of *Leatherface*? It looked more glossy than the previous movies.

I don't know if it's my style or anything, but one thing a lot of reviewers said was, "They obviously had more money than all the other ones!" And I would say, "No, we didn't! We had nothing!" At the time, it was a $2 and a half million dollar movie. And something like $700,000 of that 2.5 went to Vortex. They got the rights to make that movie and one more by a certain date. It wasn't like we had a lot of money, and it was less than a thirty-day shoot. It was a relatively low-budget movie. Again, I felt because we couldn't go the totally "gritty" way, if I was left to my own devices I would've shot it in 16 mm, but it was a much more corporate movie.

Mike: Right, it had that feel to it. I mean, it was New Line! It was very much a New Line movie.

Yes, in a lot of ways. It really was. So, there's good production value, and a good sound job.

Mike: What about this actor, Ken Force?

Ken Force! There are two misspellings on the poster! Ken Force (Foree) and Tom Hudson. Tom Hudson is Toni Hudson in reality. It's bad enough there's one mistake on it, but there's two! Unbelievable. But Ken, it was my choice to bring him in because he was in *Dawn of the Dead*. And he was just a blast to work with. I loved him. He was great.

Rob: One of the things I always liked about the *Chainsaw* series, unlike the Freddy franchise, Leatherface was totally different in each movie. He looked and acted different, maybe because of the actors that played him. But I always loved R.A. Mihailoff's version of Leatherface.

I think R.A. did a great job. I'd known R.A. for a long while. He was in a student film of mine at USC. And I thought he was the perfect guy to do it. But again, I felt I should talk to Gunnar (Hansen) first. So, I called him up and offered him the role. Also, the thought was if Gunnar comes back for the third one, then it's a true sequel on some level to the first one whereas the second one was a diversion. But New Line would only offer him scale, which to him was a big insult. So, he didn't want to do the movie, which I totally understand. So, after that, I thought R.A. would give it his all and he gave it his all and was a great guy to work with.

Rob: Billy Butler and Viggo Mortensen are both in this and weren't they roommates at the time?

They knew each other then, yeah.

Mike: What ever happened to Viggo Mortensen? (laughs)

I don't know! I wished him the best. But, no he was great…

Rob: And I had heard that his first audition didn't go all that well? He had a bad day or something?

Well yeah. I brought him in because I had seen him in *Prison*, which a friend of mine had written. And I thought he was great in that, and I thought he was a really interesting guy. I knew who he was, so I brought him in. The problem with the casting on this, there was always Bob Engelman there, and sometimes DeLuca. So, there were other chefs in the kitchen, you know? It wasn't that his audition was bad, but New Line had a guy that they wanted. Deborah Moore, the executive in charge of production had a guy that she really thought highly of, and he actually was cast very briefly as Tex.

Then he booked a very high paying commercial that would've conflicted with the first day of shooting. So, I said you have to pick one or the other, because I need you totally there on the first day. So, he chose the commercial. (laughs) So, I was able to get Viggo, so it all worked out. And Viggo, just like everyone else in the cast was always there, ready to go and had great ideas. Just a joy to work with, and I'm not just saying that. I can guarantee his approach to stuff now is exactly the same as it was then. He's just so committed and he's such a really good guy. All the family members were great.

Rob: I love that you gave Caroline Williams from *Chainsaw 2* a little cameo as the news reporter!

Yes, I did! Because I had just worked with her on *Stepfather 2* and it was so weird that I was going from that to *Chainsaw 3*, and she had done *Chainsaw 2*. So yeah, I had to get her in there.

Rob: I think you even say in the commentary on the DVD that maybe her character got so screwed up from the events of *Chainsaw 2* that she became a reporter.

Well yeah! She was a radio announcer in *Part 2,* so in my version of it she was a marauding journalist trying to track down Leatherface. The thing I didn't like in the movie, in terms of conceptually, which there wasn't really an answer to, was the similarity of this family to the original family. Was there a direct connection? We should've just said screw it all and just done something completely different. Because you have the old grandpa, so there's enough similarities where it gets confusing. Was this supposed to be relatives of the original family?

Rob: I always thought Alfredo was actually the Hitchhiker from the original!

Yeah! There are too many similarities.

Mike: I like to think they're just an extended family of nut jobs all over Texas!

Yeah, but are they literally related? Or is it birds of a feather coming together? Is there a swingers newspaper that they subscribe to? (laughs) "Wanted: Old guy that sucks blood!" So that always irritated me because it wasn't thought out as well as it could've been. The leg brace was probably a bad idea too.

Rob: Well, that was because Leatherface saws his own leg at the end of the first one though, right? That's what I always took it as.

Well, it was continuous of the second. He gets injured in the second movie? I can't remember, but I think there was a more catastrophic leg injury. The leg brace was a continuation from that, which at the end of the day I thought was a mistake. Because it decreased his mobility. Cool sound effect though!

Rob: As a huge fan of the film, I must've bought it a dozen times over the years! There are so many different cuts of it. I bought the original VHS, which is the theatrical one. Then a few years later, they came out with another VHS version that was "unrated," but there were scenes missing from it from the theatrical, and even more bizarre was that they edited out the OJ (Simpson) joke. Did you know about that?

I did know that! And I have no idea why!

Rob: There's one point where Alfredo calls Ken's character OJ, and I think the "unrated" VHS re-release was when the trial was going on. I watched it back then and remembered there were a few new scenes, older scenes missing and then they totally removed the OJ joke!

Exactly, I have no knowledge of that. (laughs) Literally, I had no contact with New Line for years. The first time I went into New Line's office after making that movie was in 2003 when we were doing the Special Edition DVD.

Rob: Wow. And for me, I've owned it so many times, including the work print…

That work print would be the closest thing to some kind of so-called "director's cut" on some level. What happened was, it was just a cursed project basically, all the way around. The timeline was we cut a version of the movie. We had a test screening, which is what they always did with their horror movies. They had a research test screening in a mall in… Glendale or Burbank. In the valley. So, that's the first time that Rolf Mittwig, who was the head of foreign sales, saw the movie. It was the first time that Sara Risher saw it all put together and probably the first time Bob Shaye saw it too for that matter.

They're all in attendance, and the movie plays pretty good. It wasn't thunderous, but we could see where we could improve it. What happens is there's a meeting afterwards and it gets better numbers than *Nightmare 5* and some other stuff. So, they're not ecstatic but they're not unhappy in terms of the numbers they were getting. But there's a pow-wow afterwards and Rolf Mittwig from foreign says, "I cannot sell this movie anywhere. It's going to get banned in every territory. I cannot sell this movie." Everybody panics. Sara Risher hates the movie and is very offended by it. She thinks it's sick and offensive and uh… (laughs)

Mike: It's called *The Texas Chainsaw Massacre*! What'd they think they were making?

But also, have you seen the first two *Texas Chainsaw* movies? You know what you're getting into! So, Shaye goes, "Well, ok, I'm coming to the editing room tomorrow and we'll work on it." So, Bob Shaye comes into the editing room, and this would've been late August, and literally, it was so painful, he'd say, "This goes, get it out. That goes, get it out." And a lot of it was the gore and some other stuff, some little bits. So, I think the movie is getting emasculated then. So, we finally agree on the cut, and we submit it to the MPAA, while we're still mixing the movie, doing the sound work on the movie.

Because of the release date, they concurrently submitted to the MPAA while we're cutting the negative of the movie as well. So, the MPAA, the first pass on that, Richard Heffner, the head of the MPAA at the time, calls up Bob Shaye, apparently, this is what I was told and said, "There is no way this movie is going to get an R rating. No matter what you do with it, there's no way." So, panic ensues, they start chopping and literally we're chopping the negative. Because they want to keep up the negative, because they were going to be making release prints right away to meet this deadline.

Mike: And the MPAA was coming down hard on horror at this time.

And the other thing, I really do think this made a difference. The title itself. The second *Chainsaw* film went out unrated. So, I think that had a psychological effect. Basically, *Leatherface* was submitted eleven times. After each submission, more stuff was cut out.

Rob: Does the MPAA even tell you what to cut out?

No, they do not tell you. They say "the overall tone." Well, the overall tone, then that means we did our job! You can't really cut down a tone. The other problem was that because of the release date, we were actually physically cutting the negative of these shots. We didn't have digital masters, we just cut on film, so they never made a protection of the shots. They could've made protection IP's, an inter-positive for each effects shot for later in an unrated release or something. But it didn't exist.

So that's why yes, there is an unrated version of the movie, it's not the "unrated" version that it would've been, unfortunately. It was crazy! Literally, it's getting written up in *Variety* every day. William Friedkin was doing preliminary sound on *The Guardian* at the same sound place we were at, so I would see him every morning. I was a big fan of *Sorcerer* so we'd always talk about that. Finally, one day he comes up to me and says, "Man… what is in your movie?" (laughs) "I got to see this thing. What is in your movie that I'm reading about it every day?" Turns out he was a huge fan of the first *Chainsaw* movie, and he had actually gotten Tobe Hooper some development deal at Universal in '86.

So, it was written up in *Variety* saying, "Will this movie ever get a rating?" I don't know if it was a record at the time, but it must've been. Submitted eleven times?

Rob: It delayed the release date at the time, didn't it?

Here's what happened. It's unheard of. At a certain point,

we realized we were never going to make the original release date, not because the movie wasn't finished, but because we couldn't get a rating! So, after that, we finished the movie and everything kind of shut down. The movie was mixed and basically finished, and I was let go. I was upset. Right around that time, they had a test screening, which I didn't know about, in New York. Again, this is what I was told so I don't know if there's more to the story, but the Ken Foree character got high ratings at the test screening, so they wanted to keep him alive for the next movie. So, they shot this ending with this guy, Michael Knue, an editor who had done a lot of New Line movies.

So, he shot that new ending where Ken Foree shows up with a band aid. (laughs) They cut down the chainsaw to the head thing, but anyways, they did that without me, and I had no knowledge of it until after it was done. Finally, when it did come out during the dumping grounds of early January, I didn't know how the movie ended! I literally bought a ticket to the movie back home and watched this movie with my name on it. I called DeLuca earlier and said, "Well, look, all this shit's happened. Call it the MPAA's movie. Don't call it my movie. I want my name off of the movie."

The problem with that was, the first reel of the movie had no changes. So, they'd already printed up 1,000 copies of that first reel. That's why the "Directed by Jeff Burr" credit is still there. That was the last words I said to DeLuca. "I want my name off this movie! … Hello? Hello?" (laughs)

Rob: Well, I'm glad your name is on there.

It was just a bad combination of all those things. It came out in January, and they didn't advertise it at all. I saw some TV spots of it, which I'd love to see again, but I don't think they ever did a trailer other than the teaser one. I know they did TV spots that said, "the most controversial horror movie of all time." I was like OK. I hated the poster. A picture of Leatherface with the chainsaw? OK.

Rob: I've been dying to know this since I was a kid. I saw a picture of R.A. Mihaloff getting make-up put on his face before putting on the Leatherface mask. Did you ever shoot anything revealing Leatherface's face?

No, we didn't. Never did. Never did. A reveal? It was discussed, but there was nothing like that ever shot.

Rob: Finally! Put to rest. Do you think *Texas Chainsaw 3* now would have an easier time securing a rating considering what's out there now?

Oh my God! Whatever original cut, let's say the test screening cut of *Leatherface* would get an R rating now. Absolutely. *CSI* has more graphic stuff now! Unless there was a political reason, because of the series. I mean, it really is one of the most infamous titles of all time. A lot of people take offense just because of that. But yeah, I can't imagine it not getting an R. Also, at the time, another thing to consider, New Line was a true independent. They had not been bought by Time Warner. And when they got bought by Time Warner, and became a true studio with studio backing, you have more clout. You know what I mean? No one would ever articulate that, but it's true. Yeah, it'd be a whole different thing now.

Rob: Because New Line at that point had both Freddy and Jason, did you ever get the impression they were trying to make him the next Freddy or Jason?

Oh absolutely! Not necessarily him, but the film, absolutely. The whole idea was the *Nightmare* movies may have peaked. It was another horror franchise. Anytime anyone uses the word franchise for a movie, it's over. Nothing good can come of it! Because you can't just concentrate on making a good movie, and then worry about it as a franchise. Because if you worry about maybe doing this in *Part 1* and then maybe this in *Part 2*, it's a bad way to think.

Rob: Let's talk about your experience with *Stepfather 2*, which is a movie I like tremendously.

I'm kind of an independent filmmaker at heart. And *Stepfather 2* was my first movie where there was a corporate structure around it. But in retrospect, they were ok.

Rob: Weren't the deaths in *Stepfather 2* amped up to be a bit gorier?

That was a weird thing, because it was just a made-for-video movie. ITC, the company that made it, was going to start a new division of direct to video titles. Very much how Dimension ended up doing direct-to-DVD sequels recently with Dimension Extreme. This company did *Zapped Again*! That was another one right after ours. That was the plan. They decided they liked the final version of the movie and decided to try to sell it. Miramax bought it! To my knowledge, it was sight unseen, they bought it for a lot of dough. There was a test screening of the finished movie. That's the only time I met Harvey and Bob Weinstein. I believe it was the first time they saw the movie. And they were livid! The movie played, it got a good response, and got good numbers. But they were just livid, because they were expecting something with mucho blood! They were expecting a totally different movie. I remember they were out in the lobby like these two big school yard bullies saying, "What the fuck? What the fuck? Where's the blood?"

I'm kind of defending what I had done, but they were asking, "Who the fuck are you?" This was before they were "The Weinstein's," before they released *Sex, Lies, and Videotape*. They bought the movie, put it out theatrically, but they cut a little bit out and they added some badly done blood effects. Badly done, because Terry O'Quinn refused to do it. Really, they were meaningless, so that was irritating.

Mike: *Stepfather 2* is interesting; it's really got a much different tone then the first movie. It's a little broader than the first.

Definitely. My brother and Darin Scott were the producers, so I had a cocoon of support. We had different ideas, and there were things we wanted to do. When we were writing and working on it, it was not a given by any means that Terry O'Quinn would do it. Not at all. We were praying for him to do it, but it wasn't absolute that he would do it.

Mike: Was he interested at all?

Fortunately, they paid him a fair amount of dough and he agreed to do it, but it was one of the things I asked the original director Joe Ruben when I called him. "O'Quinn is so good, I can't imagine the movie without him, but did you have a second choice? If you couldn't have gotten O'Quinn for the first one, did you have a second choice, just for curiosity's sake," I asked him. And he goes, A) Don't make the movie without him and B) Yes, I had a second choice, and it was Art Hindle, a Canadian actor from *The Brood*.

Rob: And the original *Black Christmas*.

Yeah, *Black Christmas*. That was his second choice.

Mike: What about the casting of Meg Foster?

Well, it was a very low budget movie, so that role was always going to be scale or close to scale. They were hard lined for that because they had to pay O'Quinn a fair amount of money. So, we interviewed, and I met with all these wonderful actresses. I wanted Kay Lenz. She had done a ton of stuff. She did Clint Eastwood's second directorial movie *Breezy* and she was a real interesting actress, perfect for the role. Lovely to meet and had good ideas about the script. Then one executive thought she wasn't classy enough,

because recently before that she had done a Roger Corman movie called *Stripped to Kill*.

Rob: Oh, Katt Shea's movie!

Yes, Katt Shea wrote and directed that one. This one executive thought she wasn't classy enough because of that movie. We end up settling on Season Hubley, whom I've always liked. So I had dinner with her, she agreed to do the movie, but in the negotiations, all her agent wanted, and this is very fair, because this is a direct to video movie, if it shipped more than 50,000 units or 100,000 units, something huge like that, she wanted a bonus of like $10,000, which at that point, if it shipped more than that, we'd all be heroes!

Everybody would've made money. They did not go for it, so at the last minute, she dropped out. So then, the producers said we'll get Meg Foster. It was a last-minute thing. They paid her a fair amount of money and they thought she was a classier name than Kay Lenz. She had done a movie with O'Quinn, I don't know if they had any scenes together but it was a movie called *Blind Fury*.

Mike: She was mostly acting against Rutger Hauer in that.

Yeah, so anyways. She gets cast at the last minute and I really didn't want her. Not that I wasn't a fan of hers! I loved her in several movies. Thematically, what O'Quinn wants is something very traditionally, blandly American. Like middle-American. You had Shelley Hack in the first one, who's kind of a bland American attractive beauty, but not intimidating and not really out of the norm. And Kay Lenz is definitely in that sweet spot too. Now, Meg Foster visually, you can't get around it. She's striking and call it any euphemism you want, exotic. Strangely beautiful, or beautifully strange. And I thought she was totally wrong for the movie.

She gets cast at the last minute, and she's an experienced enough actress to know that she was cast at the last minute and so I think there was a little bit of insecurity there. I wasn't as experienced of a director at the time to pick up on that and realize that, and I could've been more supportive of her in the beginning. So, that's how she was cast, but as I say, I think she was miscast in the movie, not by any fault of her own at all! But she was great to work with, but it was also a weird time for her, because she was making that transition from leading lady to character actress in the sense that she had just turned forty. It was tough for her too. She was good to work with, but irritatingly miscast. Just the reason they thought one person over the other was stupid.

Rob: What about Jonathan Brandis, who was in a lot of great movies at the time, *Stephen King's It* and *Neverending Story II*? Unfortunately, he's no longer with us.

Which is shocking to me! I had run into him a few times since we made the movie, and he was a great actor. He was so cool to work with. I remember, it was down to Brian Austin Green, Jonathan Brandis, and one other actor. I thought Brandis was really interesting and had… not a haunted quality, but let's say a sensitive quality. He was perfect for the role, and his parents were great. They didn't strike me as traditional stage parents; they were just genuine down to earth people. He was very committed and intense with his role and O'Quinn loved him too, they had a nice bond.

Mike: For O'Quinn, this is one of those roles for an actor where they get to play these two sides to a character. *The Stepfather* is kind of like Norman Bates, where he has to be really normal, and then also really sinister. He stepped into that so well on the first movie, did he need anything to get back into that for *Stepfather 2*?

Ok, what we did have, and I didn't even ask for it really, was three days of rehearsal with O'Quinn. Paid rehearsal, which is almost unheard of on a low-budget movie. So, we got a chance to know each other a little bit and bond. He's one of those actors, which is my favorite kind of actor, where you can joke with him, but as soon as you're needed on set, he's instantly in character and just knocks it out of the park.

Once you yell cut, he's back to picking up a story he was just telling you about his high school football days or whatever. So, he was just a really great guy to work with, I'd love to work with him again. I tried to get him in a couple of other movies and we either couldn't afford him, or the schedule wouldn't work out, but I'd really love to work with him again because I loved him to death.

Mike: He's one of the reasons I couldn't trust anything during the first season of *Lost*!

He won the Emmy, which was so cool, and he totally deserves it, because he's incredibly talented. We talked about the character in those rehearsal days and he told me about the stuff he had done on the first movie, so it was certainly more O'Quinn. It was almost like a TV thing in a sense. It was like being a director coming in to an already established character. We tried to give him different shadings, but it was really his interpretation that came through. In retrospect, it's certainly broader than the first, but that's always the problem with doing a sequel is that the surprise is gone. If you've seen the first movie, you know the character.

Mike: Did he contribute? Did he want re-writes or offer suggestions?

Oh, he did! I was worried about that quite honestly, because let's face it, if there was an 800-pound gorilla on the movie, it was him. They could do it without Jeff Burr, but they couldn't do it without Terry O'Quinn. So, I was worried that he might wield that as some actors would as a contentious power thing, but never, he never did. He always had ideas, but he would never say anything like "It's got to be this way or no way at all." With the third movie, *The Stepfather 3*, I guess they offered him to write it, direct it, produce it, whatever he wanted, and he didn't want to do it. If he had that in his mind, he could've absolutely done his own movie.

Rob: I've never seen the third one.

And the weird thing is that Season Hubley, who dropped out of *Stepfather 2*, is the lead of *Stepfather 3*. It was a weird rounding of the circle! Guy Magar, the director of *Part 3* called me up and did what I did, "Oh hey, this is Guy Magar and I'm directing *Stepfather 3*." So literally I got the same call I'd given to Joe Ruben! (laughs) And the first thing that Ruben said to me was, "Sequel? We killed that son of a bitch!" So, I kind of said the same thing to Guy, just for a laugh.

Mike: Well, they brought him back!

Rob: And they're bringing him back again for the remake of *Stepfather*!

Now, what I was told about the remake was that it combined certain things from the first two movies. But yeah, remaking *Stepfather* is going to be crazy. But for the third one, Guy asked me the same thing, if I saw another actor for the role of the stepfather because he knew he wasn't getting O'Quinn. I was curious about the movie, but I think I only saw the first fifteen minutes of it, but I did think the composer who worked on *Stepfather 2*, he weaved the music from the first and the second into 3, so there's not clips from the second movie, but there's a musical homage so that was cool.

Mike: So, after doing *Stepfather 2* and *Leatherface*, what brought you to Charlie Band over at Full Moon to do the *Puppet Master* sequels?

I had done an independent movie, a labor of love called *Eddie Presley* in between and some TV. Quite honestly, I needed a job. I had worked for Charlie Band years before on a movie that didn't get made for Empire called *The Vault*.

I got paid for it, worked on it for three or four months but nothing really came from it, and Empire kind of collapsed. So, then I got a phone call out of the blue in January of 1993 and it was Charlie Band who asked me to come in for a meeting on Monday. I hadn't talked to him in years! So, I came in, and it was presented to me that, "OK, you're going to do four movies for me and we're paying $25,000 for each movie so you'll make $100,000, but you really won't make $100,000 because the first two movies you're going to do are really one movie so I'm only going to pay you $25,000." (laughs)

(laughs)

But still, it was cool! It would be four movies and I get to go do this crazy movie in Romania called *Oblivion*. It sounded good. He was going to direct *Puppet Master 4* and *5*, but it was called *Puppet Master: The Movie*, because they were going to do it as a feature for Paramount. The first Full Moon theatrical feature. That was what it was! And so, what they did was they had split the script that they were going to use for the feature in half and then padded it out so you now have two movies that could be done for much less money. It was originally going to be the *Puppet Master* feature that he was going to direct. So, he couldn't direct the two movies so he got me.

Never say never! I vowed never to replace another director again, and not have a long prep and here I am basically doing almost the exact situation I had on *Leatherface*. So, we started shooting three weeks after I got the job. At the time, it was really like a TV studio, so they had the same people on staff. The same director of photography for most of the movies, the same production designer, a lot of the same crew for each movie, so it really was a machine. So that was a very short shoot for the two movies, but it was a fun experience. The scripts truly made no sense to anyone. To anyone!

Rob: Well at that point, the *Puppet Master* series had redefined its continuity. *1* and *2* are in continuity. *3* retold the original story, so *4* and *5* were following the continuity of *3*.

Yeah, *3* was more the prequel in a sense, and this was after that. They forgot all the Egyptian sort of stuff and now it's like this Sid and Marty Krofft demon in the underworld that's wreaking havoc! (laughs)

Rob: Was it difficult to do *Puppet Master 4* and *5* together on a tight schedule AND deal with the puppets?

That wasn't so difficult on that level. It was difficult because it was such a short shoot. And to try to get around certain people who had done so many movies for that company. Just like on a TV episode, they'd be hesitant to do something different. It'd be like, "Well, we didn't do that on *Trancers 2*." "Well, you're doing it on *Puppet Master 4* and *5*!" (laughs)

It really was like making one movie, like a mini-series, it was a very quick shoot. Of the two movies, I prefer *5*. But most people prefer *4*. *5* is goofy and… *5* had the promotional team at Full Moon, Dan Schweiger and Dave Parker, they affectionately nick-named *Puppet Master 5* "Hall Walkers." Because *Sleepwalkers* just had come out and half the movie is guys just walking down halls. (laughs)

It's a little dull, but the cast in *5* I like. Ian Ogilvy was great. Charlie Band's dad Albert was always around, and I loved him. He was great. A guy that truly loved film and loved being on the set, so he was always fun to have around. All the Full Moon movies were under-budgeted, and the promotion was more important than the movie! But what was cool was they'd always make a print of the movie to show at Paramount. They would have a big screening there. It was a good experience because quite frankly it got me back into professional filmmaking in a sense. Because in 1991-1992, I was working on *Eddie Presley* and just finishing that up, writing some stuff, so to have a professional job as a director was a good thing, it came at a good time for me.

Mike: You had one more sequel to get through after this…

Rob: And I like this sequel, damn it!

Most people hate it and I know what you're talking about. I've gone on record, and I'll say it, *Pumpkinhead 2: Blood Wings*, I think it's my worst directing. Why, I don't know? Ultimately yes, I'm the guy to blame, but I think purely for me, it's my worst directing job.

Mike: What do you think went wrong there?

Everything really. Again, it was replacing a director and coming in on such short notice and not being involved in the script development at all. I found out later, Krevoy tells the story on the *Pumpkinhead 2* DVD that basically he lucked into this. He had a script that was a horror film and literally someone said, "Can you make *Pumpkinhead 2* and get it started in ninety days" or something like that, and he said, "Yes, I can!" And what he did was took a script that he was developing for a horror movie and just retooled it somehow into a *Pumpkinhead* movie overnight.

Rob: That happens a lot.

To the people that wrote it, they're big TV writers now, but then they had no real affection or affinity for the genre. It was a really, quite frankly, not a good script, but it had to be shot within a certain date to retain the rights. Again, all the wrong reasons to make a movie. People think it was a thought-out sequel to the first movie, and it was not at all. It was not designed as a sequel to the first movie, script wise. It was not designed as any continuation; it was a completely different movie that they just added Pumpkinhead to. Structurally, it's very much like a Stephen King type story. I just feel that it's not so, not so good…

Rob: You had a great and interesting cast! I mean, Soleil Moon Frye, aka *Punky Brewster*. It was the first time I'd seen her as an adult. Andrew Robinson was in it. Cameos by Kane Hodder, R.A. Mihailoff, Linnea Quigley.

Actually, Linnea was hired before I was, because Krevoy had met her at the Dylan Dog festival in Milan, Italy and had never known her, and she was being honored at the festival, so he thought she was this big, big star. "*Oh, we got to get Linnea in the movie!*" "*Yeah? I think we can get Linnea!*" But yeah, I've always liked her.

Mike: Was Stan Winston involved at all?

Not at all.

Mike: Did you feel the need to make that call to Stan?

Yes! It's like a recurring thing. It was a contractual thing where I couldn't talk to him, though. My thing was call Stan and see what make-up stuff there is. Is there anything from the first movie we could still use? But no. I wasn't allowed to. I will tell you the end of that. Years later, many years later in 2003, I'm at Sitges Spain for a film festival and Stan Winston is being honored there for a lifetime achievement award. So, I'm in Spain at the bar in the hotel where the festival is. Stan Winston is alone at the bar. Just looking around. I think, "Ok, I just got to go up to him." (laughs)

So, I go up to him and introduced myself, and I go, "You know as a matter a fact, I uh…" and I was being self-evasive because I recognize the faults of the movie, but I continue, "I knew the production designer of the first movie, and… I directed the second movie." And he looked at me and didn't say a word to me. Just looked at me and took off. I don't know if he was jetlagged or what! What I had heard was that he was genuinely pissed that a sequel was made. And I believe it! (laughs)

Rob: You should've went up to him and just said, "*I made Pumpkinhead 2. Sorry.*"

(laughs) Yeah! It wasn't like, "Hey, we got a lot in common! You did one and I did one!" I was a big fan of his work, of course, and wanted to say hello. Maybe he'd just arrived or something, but that was my one and only contact with him.

Lastly on *Pumpkinhead 2*, it was great working with Andrew Robinson and there is some stuff that I'm happy with, some set pieces that are ok, but there's one thing that always pisses me off, and I folded too quickly on it. I designed this sequence to be a split screen sequence. Even if I had to pay for it myself, I should've just kept it, because you would've talked about that sequence at least, even if you hated the movie. It could've been really cool. It was the scene with R.A. and Linnea and Pumpkinhead is stalking the cabin. It would've been very cool and to this day, it pisses me off that I didn't make it happen.

Mike: After that, you did *Night of the Scarecrow*, which on the early days of the internet, I remember people being very complimentary of.

Some people really like that movie and I'm proud of a lot of it. It's very action packed for the last fifteen minutes of it. And that was the highest budget I'd had since *Leatherface* really. It was like $2 million. That movie… it's not that it died, it's just that nobody saw that movie. The problem was Republic, the producers that made it were a team, Steve White, with Barry Bernardi. And Barry Bernardi had done a lot of Carpenter movies. During the making of the movie, they split. So that was problem one. Then Republic, the company that co-financed it, went through a management change and basically went out of business.

Mike: It's not on DVD!

No, it's not on DVD, I don't think it's out foreign, because there's a bootleg of it that Dave Parker got me at a convention but all it is is a bad transfer off the VHS.

Mike: I remember I caught it and liked it very much!

Well, did the world need another scarecrow movie? The answer is no.

Mike: Are there enough scarecrow movies should be the question! Because there's a terrible series of them out now.

The weird thing on that movie too which just mystifies me is that the poster for it, for the video release is really cool artwork! But the actual video box is not that! I don't understand it! The poster is really cool but it's not what's on the video box. I just don't get it.

Rob: Can you talk a bit about *The Devil's Den*?

I can talk about whatever I want! It's America, man! (laughs)

Rob: What's the true story about *The Devil's Den*?

What happened with that movie, again I got a phone call out of the blue and it was this guy John Duffy who had produced some movies that friends of mine had done. It was really a traditional meet, "Hey, read the script, tell us what you think." It was written by Mitch Gould, who had written one of these Steven Cannell series of million-and-a-half-dollar horror movies. Anchor Bay put them all out. So, it was intended to be one of those, but Cannell didn't want to make it, so John Duffy and Mitch Gould ended up raising money and putting it together with New Arc Entertainment, which was a part of Anchor Bay and Starz Media. So, they hire me to direct the movie.

Mitch Gould is a stuntman, so he wanted to be the stunt coordinator/second unit director and that was part of the deal going in. Wouldn't be my choice, but ok. It was an eighteen-day shoot, very low-budget. So, we're casting the movie and you look through all these lists of names. So, we end up with Devon Sawa and Kelly Hu, at the very last minute. They wanted Kelly very badly in the movie. I was thinking there were a lot more interesting choices, but they wanted her and paid her a lot of dough. She really didn't want to do the movie. She was basically… it was basically paying for her to be there every day on the set.

I'm not saying she was unpleasant. She was civil, but you knew underneath the surface that she thought it was all bullshit and she didn't want to be there, which was disappointing. Uh, and they treated her like she was Grace Kelly or something. Devon was cast at the last second. He was cast practically by Anchor Bay. I like him a lot. He was a very inventive actor and a lot of fun, and great in many ways to work with. He gave his all to the performance, whereas Kelly was reading the script maybe five minutes before she did her scene.

Rob: Well, you got Ken Foree in *Devil's Den*! So, it must've been great to have worked with him again.

They had Ken in mind even before I came on. Starz liked him so that was almost a done deal from the beginning. He did a great job on the movie. The rest was cast traditionally through auditions. So what happened during the production of the movie, Mitch, because he had written it was very protective of the script, and he was the second unit director and it was such a quick schedule where what I would do is shoot a set, and I'd have a list of shots to do when we went to the next set that he was supposed to do. He would never do the shots that I gave him. He would do his own stuff, which was totally irrelevant to the movie I was making. That was problem one. So, we wrapped the movie, we shot it in eighteen days. It comes in under budget and on schedule. And we started editing. It was a quick editing schedule, so I show a cut of the movie to Mitch, and he goes, "Well, let me work with the editors for a day," which I'm not happy about but I placate him. And in one day, he makes some of the stuff just so much worse. So then, it's right around Christmas, he was supposed to come in the next day for us to talk about how the cut is going to proceed.

And he doesn't show up. The producer shows up and says, "Mitch feels that he needs to take over the movie." So, I'm like, "Why does he feel the need to take over the movie?" "Well, he just does." "OK. Well, where is he?" The producer says, "Well, he feels if he shows up it'll weaken his position." (laughs) I'll always remember that! The upshot being, he took the movie, got a new editor and spent eight months re-cutting the movie. We only had three weeks to do it! Eight months to re-cut the movie, and he totally re-cut it. Literally, there is not a single edit that was in the original version. And every line of his script, every word of the written script, is in the finished movie, which is unheard of! There's always stuff cut out! To either make it play better or play faster. Every word of the script was in the movie. He was completely protective of that original script. And as it turns out, how he was able to do this was that basically he was one of the main investors of the movie, which I did not know. So, he was really the power behind the throne when it came to that. He was so adamant that it had to be his script.

There was some fun stuff in there, but it was basically a *From Dusk Till Dawn* low budget knock-off, really. So, the way to have fun with it would've been to make it as quick and wild as possible, and it kind of just lays there as it is, in my estimation. I thought the sound job on the movie was just dreadful. He had scored it a totally different way. Because it was re-cut, I thought I'd use a pseudonym and take my name off the movie. I gave them my pseudonym, and I also said in the making-of, if I was in it, just cut me out. So, it's Mitch's movie in the sense that it's his cut, and it's awful.

Rob: Well, I'd like to see your cut!

And not to say that my version is a classic! It's just fun. It's a fun bad movie versus a bad bad movie.

Mike: Any happier experiences lately?

I'm really cut out to be an independent filmmaker. I don't know, it's just my view of what a director does and what a film editor is supposed to do bumps against a lot of what people think directors do nowadays, I guess. I do want to do another horror movie, but I do want to make it on my own terms and make something that really can do something. Like *Devil's Den*, no matter what you do with it, it's still going to be a *From Dusk Till Dawn* remake. So, my goal is to make another horror movie eventually and whatever fans I've had have always been very loyal and supportive, so I want to do something that will justify their faith. My career so far has been very checkered, charitably if you can call it checkered, and there were a lot of misguided projects, but the older you get you want to do better things.

Rob: Is it true you're working on a documentary right now too?

Yes, one of the things I'm doing now is a documentary on TV directors from the 50s, 60s and 70s. Guys that have done a lot of TV movies and who have IMDb pages that are a hundred entries long! Some of those guys are amazing. They're in their 80s and they're still so energetic and passionate about what they've done and what they're doing. Those guys inspire me. We're still interviewing people for it.

Rob: I caught a little bit of *Straight Into Darkness* recently on cable and I thought it looked absolutely beautiful.

Oh, thank you, thank you. That and *Eddie Presley*, those are two that I'm very proud of it. Along with *The Offspring* (*From a Whisper to a Scream*). These are more representative of what I want to do and am capable of doing. The frustration for me is to not be able to be allowed to put the creativity you know you have on the screen, for various reasons. That's the frustration.

Mike: Can you talk a bit about David Warner in *Straight Into Darkness*?

Warner was great! I adored working with him. He was hilarious off the set, totally professional and old-school. And totally committed. We only had him for a week, so it was a very tough shoot. He was totally committed to the role, had great ideas and brought so much to the table. I was a fan of his anyways, but as a director it was amazing. This particular movie had very difficult shooting conditions in Romania. It was miserable! But he was great, and I mean, what a face! He has an amazing face.

He works all the time, but I wish people would allow him to do more high-profile jobs in America. He should be turning down stuff! And maybe he does, but he moved back to England. We talked about *The Omen* a bit. (laughs) And Linda Thorson, even though we had a problematic relationship in the beginning, she was really cool too. She was on *The Avengers*. That movie's representative of the type of stuff I'd like to do. I'm not abandoning horror films or anything! I love horror movies, but the next horror film I do independently, I want to do something that I can really shake people up with and get a chance of really breaking out.

Rob: We'll be first in line!

ROB ZOMBIE

Interviewed by Rob Galluzzo (5/09)

A few months back, *Icons of Fright* was invited down to the set to see the making of Rob Zombie's eagerly anticipated *Halloween* sequel *H2*. With three days left in the tightly scheduled shoot at the time of our visit, it was difficult for Zombie to break away to chat about his intentions with the latest film in the *Halloween* series. Now in the midst of post-production, he took a quick break from editing to fill us in on how the project has evolved since last we spoke to him.

One of the things I really appreciate in the new *Halloween* is the fact that you're the first filmmaker in the entire series to actually treat Michael Myers as a character. What exactly were the origins of your story for *Halloween II*? Was it the idea of getting to portray Michael as a character this time around? Or was it a chance to do a lot of the stuff you weren't able to on the first movie? Or maybe a combination of the two?

I guess a combination of the two. The main thing that made me excited about *Halloween II* or *H2* or whatever the fuck we call it... um, was just that I was over the baggage of whatever John Carpenter had done before. That baggage was gone. And I could pick up the story from where I left it and go anywhere with it. I felt that where the movie ended, truthfully, with the last movie, the character of Laurie Strode is kind of a boring character. But I thought by the end of the movie when she's covered in blood, and she shoots Michael that she becomes much more interesting. So, I was very interested to follow the path of what would've happened to her after that night. And how she would be. And how Sheriff Brackett would be. And how Michael would be.

The characters were all interesting to me, but now I could really get away from worrying about Michael coming home to Haddonfield and establishing who he is, and I could really focus on very character-oriented details with these people. That's what I really liked about it. It's totally fresh, it's totally different. It's not like anything we've seen before, and I think it makes for a much deeper movie. It's kind of like what I did with *The Devil's Rejects* from *House of 1000 Corpses*. The first one was kind of cartoony, here it is, and then I thought for the second one, OK, well now we can really do something with these characters.

Which is why I like *Rejects*, because it kicks off running right off the bat.

Yeah, so this is kind of the same thing.

Now that you don't have the remake baggage with this entry in the series, and you don't have to follow the story beats that Carpenter had established in the original, what was your working relationship like with Tyler Mane on this one? Was it a different approach for Tyler playing this version of Michael Myers this time around? Did you have more freedom with him on *H2*? You guys know each other fairly well, so obviously you have a rapport as friends, but what was the working relationship like for this film?

Well, the working relationship with Tyler – Tyler is great. What was great about this movie in general was that now I was friends with everybody and that goes a long way to taking things to another level. When we made the first movie, I just met Malcolm, I just met Scout, I just met Danielle. I didn't have a real deep rapport with them. But then, two years later, you're friends with people, you know them, you can take things to another level that sometimes you just can't get to, because you just don't know the people well enough! You don't have the time, unfortunately. The way they schedule movies now, you don't have the time to get to know people and get to rehearse with them, it's like you're just thrown in there. Sometimes meeting people literally for the first time, on set, on the day that you're working, which really sucks!

Because you don't get to know them in a way that you know how to push their buttons or get their strengths or their weaknesses, you're just not aware of it. This time, with Tyler and with everybody, it was much better. What I felt with Tyler last time, it's easy to underestimate what he did. Like, you have a guy, he's not talking, you're putting that mask on him. We're pretty much taking away all of his tools as an actor at that point. (laughs) And I still think that he conveys a lot. And in this movie, what I tried to do was strip away even more of those restrictions with him, so that he could make Michael more of a full-blown character. To me, that's what's interesting. I know some people think, "Oh, Michael should always be the Shape. He should be this mysterious figure in the shadows." I figure, well you've got eight movies of that!

Exactly, and this is your version of Michael.

Let's do something different! And for me, growing up, the movies I grew up on, like *Frankenstein*. The monster was terrifying, but there was a soul of some sort to the monster, no matter how brain damaged he was. That's the way I always sort of saw Michael Myers is telling it like it was *Frankenstein* or something.

One of the things I loved that I saw on set was the new half-mask; the idea of seeing part of Tyler's face and Michael Myers face at the same time. It was something Wayne Toth was explaining to us about how you just wanted to do something different. You said, "I love Tyler's face, we should show more of Tyler's face." The reason I like it is because it looks like the mask is peeling off and there's almost no real difference between Michael's actual face and the mask. It's still just as blank and expressionless as the mask is. Very creepy looking.

I think what's going to be funny when people see it, I know that people think they know what it looks like, but when you see it in the movie and the way it's lit, it's just like you said, you almost can't tell the mask is missing. It blends into his actual face in such a weird way. It doesn't look like the *Phantom of the Opera* where it's half human, half mask. Because Tyler's skin is all cruddy and the mask is cruddy. We definitely have the same mask in the movie, and then we have the sort of crumbling mask. It's almost like, I wanted to make the mask significant. Because in the other movies, the mask is just a random mask. Michael broke into a hardware store and stole that mask; it doesn't mean anything. There's no significance to it, it just happens to be a cool mask he's wearing. But I've always tried to make it that it's significant and you can see in this movie as the mask deteriorates, so does essentially Michael Myers psyche.

Scout Taylor-Compton had a lot to do with Laurie Strode in this one because you gave her a different character arc. When we spoke to her on set, even she said she had no idea what she was in for until she read the script on the plane. What are the biggest differences with Laurie Strode on this movie as opposed to the first one?

Well, the biggest difference was that Laurie Strode in the first movie was the good girl who gets into this bad situation. And then we find out Michael Myers is her brother. In this movie, she is the survivor of a horrible event. Her parents are dead, her friends are dead. She's battle scarred from it all. So, she's much, much, much darker of a character and what I wanted to do, what I thought was interesting, in the first movie, it was more like Annie Brackett was outgoing and Laurie was a little bit shy.

They both survived a horrible event. People's personalities change after a horrible event. Some people become withdrawn, which (in *H2*) became Annie, and some people get that sort of "Fuck it, I don't give a shit" attitude about their life, and they get kind of the exact opposite. And that's where I took the Laurie character. She's sort of out there. She's re-inventing herself with a new set of friends and a new way of acting and being. And you know, you wonder through the whole movie is her state of mind deteriorating because she's related to Michael? If you have a sibling that's psychotic, do you share those same genes? That same state of mind? Did the craziness manifest itself in Michael Myers when he was ten, but it waited until she was eighteen? That's what I found interesting about it.

One of the things I saw on set that got me really excited were a lot of these dream sequence scenes and characters. I love some of the stuff I saw that you and Wayne Toth had put together for those sequences. On top of the fact that you're incorporating a lot of Halloween, the holiday, this time too.

I wanted the movie to have a lot of visually surreal imagery too. That was one thing, the last one was very much like Michael in a suburban neighborhood. That's pretty much what you get. That's what the *Halloween* world was, but with this one I just wanted to take it further and be able to just trip it out and have some stuff that if I showed you certain stills from the movie, you would think, "What is this? Some classic gothic horror movie? How does this figure in?" That's what was really interesting for me was tying all these bizarre worlds together and just trying to take it to a new level visually and giving it more elements of classic horror, so people don't go, "Oh, it's a 'slasher' movie because it's a guy with a knife." I wanted it to be something more than that.

Plus, I really wanted to add more Halloween, the holiday myth to it, so it was much richer in that vibe.

You're giving us stuff that we've never seen in the *Halloween* franchise before, which is why I was excited to get glimpses of some of that stuff on set. As far as other characters in the film, I did a panel last month at the LA *Fango* with Brad Dourif whom I'm a huge fan of. There's one moment in the first film that just sums him up. It's the moment when Sheriff Brackett finds Annie battered and bruised. His reaction, he's just so good in it. He expressed at the panel that he had a lot more to do this time around in *H2*. So, what's Sheriff Brackett like in this *Halloween*?

Yeah, Brad really was able to in this film – that really goes back to what I was saying before. Certain people and actors are easier to get to know than others, and Brad is… a little trickier to get to know. So, on this film we could take what we were going to do together much deeper, and it was easier to get an incredible performance from him. He even said it, "Thank you for kicking my ass the whole way through." Because he is spectacular in this movie. He really understood the role of the single dad with the daughter who's got problems. He really embraced it. He wasn't just the Sheriff. He wore the scars from his life on his face too, because in this one, yeah, I left his hair long, gray and scruffy, he's the Sheriff who is over it. He's very, very tired. Life has beaten him down, he's done in. And Brad really, really embraced the role and really ran with it. He's a key figure. He's not a background character. He is a complete leading force in the movie.

That's great because I always enjoy Brad and his take on Brackett, and obviously I assume he can't be too happy that Michael's back, so I'm curious to see what you do with him. One of the other things I wanted to talk about was that you had a new Director of Photography on this movie, Brandon Trost, who also recently shot *Crank 2*. You used Phil Parmet on your previous two films, so what was the look you were going for with Brandon on this? How'd it differ from your working relationship with Phil?

Well, me and Phil had a great working relationship on *The Devil's Rejects*. I love Phil, he's a great guy. We really worked well together, and I feel we really accomplished what we set out to do on that movie. But just… sometimes you can't explain why things go good and you can't explain why things go bad. Something on *Halloween* just didn't click anymore. We kept butting heads. Not getting along. It just basically ended our relationship, for whatever reason. What I was trying to accomplish was not happening and I was not happy. It was just a mess. *Halloween's* a funny one, because *Devil's Rejects* was just one of those movies where everything went right all the time. *Halloween* was one of those movies where everything went wrong all the time. If it could go wrong, it did go wrong.

Halloween II was one of those movies where everything just went right. It's just weird, it just happens, and you can't explain why it happens. *Halloween II* looks awesome. And it shows in the movie, because when things are going right, it just clicks. Brandon was great! I met with a lot of DP's and I just clicked with Brandon. He's kind of young and willing to do anything. He doesn't have pre-conceived ideas about, "Well, that's not how you do it." He just had a way of working that's exactly how I like to work, and I just wanted to make the movie more dirty and gritty and real. For me, I thought *Halloween* got a little too glossy.

And some of the grit that I thought was essential to the horror wasn't there for me. It always kind of bothered me, so for this one I wanted to take it back and make it more like, you're watching it, and you feel like you're watching a real thing. In the aftermath with Laurie in the Myers house with the police where you feel like you're watching a documentary. And it's really disturbing that way! Because you get swept up in the reality of it. What if Michael Myers and all of this was real?

When I was on set, I caught Malcolm McDowell as Dr. Loomis pulling up in a limo, fresh from a new book tour. Did this guy actually go and write another book and exploit the events of the first movie?!

He's rich and famous and loving every minute of it in this movie. That's why… the Weird Al Yankovic thing, that's why that came into it. I wanted a scene that was the epitome of where Dr. Loomis went. I thought, what could be better than having Dr. Loomis on a talk show like a Jimmy Kimmel type show, and he's sitting there on the couch with another guest just trying to talk like he's a serious doctor, when he's a complete Hollywood phony. And that's when I was like, who could we get that would be such a recognizable person to people that would be the complete opposite of who a serious "doctor" should be sitting with? And that's when Weird Al came up, I thought perfect!

He's a huge, completely recognizable celebrity, but you cannot sit there and try to be a serious doctor of psychology with Weird Al Yankovic at your elbow. And it worked out great. I know it seemed ridiculous when the news broke, but when you see it in the movie…

Well, I love Weird Al! (laughs) Did you know Weird Al beforehand?

No, I didn't. It was just one of those things that came up. Chris Hardwick, who's playing the talk show host, I was like, "Chris, I need to find somebody that is that sort of personality." And I knew Chris knew TV people and I knew he was friends with Bob Saget, so I was thinking, "What about someone like Bob Saget?" And he was like, "What about Weird Al?" And I thought, "Weird Al. Yes!" He called Weird Al and he said, "Fuck yeah!" Got on a plane and was there the next day.

That's amazing. (laughs)

Yeah, it was awesome.

One of the things that's come up over the course of the last several years, people always ask you if you're ever going to do a director's cut of *House of 1000 Corpses*. Is that something you're even interested in doing at this point? Would you rather leave it as is? Or would you want to tweak it one day?

It'll probably never happen, just because… I don't know. (laughs) It's sort of sitting there and I don't know if there's really the demand for it, or if I'd have the time for it. Who knows? You never know. Maybe in a couple of years when it's the tenth anniversary of that movie and if I have time, and Lionsgate feels like putting up some money to do the edit, we'll do an edit.

I don't know if the current version of Lionsgate would want to do it! (laughs)

Yeah, Lionsgate's very much changed in the last little bit. It's a totally different company.

Before you started this movie, you finished your last record and put it on the shelf to concentrate on *H2*. So, is the record still set to come out at the end of the summer? Are you going to jump right back into touring?

Well, we'll probably put the record out in September and go out on tour. Yeah, that's the plan.

Well, thanks so much for chatting. I don't want to keep you, because I want you to finish editing *Halloween II* so I can see it! So, thanks so much for your time.

(laughs)

I genuinely appreciate what you try to do with your films, and I know you talked with Tim Sullivan about this last time. Guys like me and him are just happy that there are new horror flicks coming out! I try not to be as judgmental as most critics, because after all, it's just entertainment. And it's all meant to entertain.

That's cool, and Tim and I talk about that all the time, like, "When did everybody become… such a dick about everything!" (laughs) It's unbelievable, anytime you put anything out there, it becomes "and here's 900 people saying why it sucks!" (laughs)

(laughs)

Even though they don't know what it is and they haven't seen it yet. And it's just… I don't know. It's a weird culture. People take everything… That's the thing. Once something is said, it just becomes law, even if it's completely unfounded! You can't put the cat back in the bag once it's out. And every rumor starts with just somebody saying, "I heard THIS." I remember someone recently said, "I heard they're going to computer generate Daeg's face onto the new kid." I'm like, "You heard that?" What kind of super technology do you think we're working with here? It gets so silly.

The point being, I appreciate the films you've done so far.

Well, thanks man. It's good to hear that.

I'm sure we'll cross paths soon enough. Best of luck to you on all of it.

Cool, right on man. Take care.

ORPHAN PRESS JUNKET

JOEL SILVER   SUSAN DOWNEY   DAVID LESLIE JOHNSON   JAUME COLLET-SERRA

VERA FARMIGA   PETER SARSGAARD   ISABELLE FUHRMAN

I'll admit I was slightly intrigued by the poster for *Orphan* the first time I caught it. I couldn't help but stare at this oddly photoshopped image and try desperately to figure out exactly what was wrong with Esther? Needless to say, whatever they did to the image worked because it got me to stop and examine it. But after that, I honestly didn't have high expectations for yet another "evil child" movie. However, because my expectations were low, *Orphan* actually ended up exceeding them and I left the theater more than satisfied by the experience. It's a fairly solid little horror movie that definitely earns its R rating and delivers on some truly genuine shocking twists.

In May 2009, *Icons* was invited to sit in on a series of roundtable interviews with various people involved in its creation including producers Joel Silver and Susan Downey, writer David Leslie Johnson, director Jaume Collet-Serra and actors Vera Farmiga, Peter Sarsgaard, and Isabelle Fuhrman making her screen debut as Esther. The following is a series of quotes from the hour-long interview session. Enjoy! - Rob

On the origins of the story and co-producer Leonardo DiCaprio:

Joel Silver: Appian Way is Leonardo's production company; they had really come up with the idea for this movie and it was a horror movie they wanted to make. And he had sent off the script and Warners had read the script and thought this might be a great vehicle for us at Dark Castle to jump into. We met with Leo and his business partner, and we felt that it was a great idea. Susan worked with them very closely to bid off the script and with the movie itself.

David Leslie Johnson: At the very beginning, the project was developed internally at Leo's company Appian Way, and one of his executives Alex Mace wrote a treatment for it. They basically were looking for a writer to adapt the treatment and get a fresh take on it. They only gave me the first three pages of it. Basically, the beginning of the story, the family dynamic, who the characters were, and Esther comes to the home. Now what happens? So, I sort of took that, came up with the ending and worked backwards to match up with the story they had and pitched them that and that's sort of how it came to be.

On casting Isabelle Fuhrman as Esther:

Susan Downey: It was pure old-fashioned casting. We put a bunch of kids on tape, and she just popped right out. And it was interesting because if you do read an early draft of the script, the description of the little girl is the complete opposite of what Isabelle actually looks like. She was supposed to have pure white skin, and blonde curly hair. It wasn't her look, but she was so good in her audition and just stood out from all the other kids that it was a no brainer.

Joel Silver: Leo was making a movie in South Africa, *Blood Diamond* actually, and the way that you can cast now, there's websites with protective locks so you can put up video of all the people testing for a role. Leo called me early one morning and said, "I saw this girl and she's fantastic!" We hadn't even seen it yet because he had been ahead of us in time, and he just said, "She's the one. She's the one." He was very specific about that because being a child actor himself, he was very conscious of what that does and what that is and he was always concerned that this girl not be affected by the process. He was very conscious that she be very focused and not given too much information about things in the movie that might hurt her future.

Isabelle on portraying the character of Esther:

Isabelle Fuhrman: I read the script, and I talked to my acting coach about the character, and he helped me figure out different things I could do, because each person has different things. Some people bite their nails. Some people run their fingers through their hair, or scratch or itch. So, I was thinking about different things I can do that would make Esther different from me, because she's totally different from me. I like touching my hair, and I don't do it all the time, but I do run my fingers through my hair, so Esther I thought maybe would do something a little different. A little more swing in her step and she'd be a bit more girly because of her secret. I went to lunch once with Vera and we were at a restaurant. I kept watching all these women, they kept looking at me like, why is this girl staring at me? I was watching them for how they crossed their legs or tilted their heads. Or how they grabbed for their water. I was watching Vera a lot on set, and it all just helped and worked. On the day, it all came into place.

Susan Downey: The thing with Isabelle is she's got great parents and they're really smart. They're incredibly supportive and with any movie you do, you always have a teacher on the set as well. You just kind of talk them through it to a certain point. You're always conferring with the parents and with the teacher about what is appropriate and not. And what's great, we saw this when Jaume was working with her and the other kids, there's certain things you can explain in a somewhat adult way, and there's other things you try and you see it's just so above their experience level and you're like, "OK, just imagine that your sister just stole your toy." (laughs) You know? You have to really boil it down for them. But I think with Isabelle, she's incredibly smart and very articulate. Her parents are the same way, so it made it very easy.

Isabelle Fuhrman: I had a dialect coach during the entire filming (in the movie, Esther has a thick Russian accent), so he'd come into my apartment where I was staying in, and we'd go over the lines in the accent and we'd try to get different sounds. Like the W's are different. My mom's Russian, so I watched her a lot. Foreign people move their lips a different way. We tend to move our lips fully when we say something like "show." But Europeans keep their mouths kind of closed, they're not very open when they talk. (Gives example.)

Well, my usual day was, I'd get my hair curls and then I got into my dress, I would go, I would transform into her, and I would go about my day being her, being Esther. And um, something clicked. Every morning, I would put on the dress and it clicked, time to perform.

David Leslie Johnson: When I first started writing the script, it was sort of one of those things that you can fall into with the evil child is how are all these adults being outsmarted by this child? I wanted to go into it thinking she's just really that smart. She's Hannibal Lector smart. She walks into a room and sizes everybody up and she figures out, 'OK, I know what your weakness is and what your weakness is' and I don't want anybody looking at me. I want you looking at her. And being mad at each other so that I can do what I want to do. That was the idea.

On the appeal to this story and the character arcs:

Susan Downey: It was very much in the writing. It was very much in the script that we had originally received and then continued to work on and develop. The characters that we got from the original material in terms of Kate's backstory and John's backstory or for the little girl, just everyone, there was such a level of consideration that you often see more in dramas than in genre pictures, so we were fortunate to be able to have that as a starting point and to continue to develop it. Which then when we brought Jaume on, that's what really appealed to him. He's one of these directors that grew up on the great horror movies of the 70s, the ones we always reference in our development meetings that we hope to achieve and you never do. Or you, you know, you keep looking for that. He continued forward with what the script already brought to the table, and it allowed us to get actors excited and involved who furthered that and continue to elevate the material.

Vera Farmiga: For me, when I consider a script there's always a sense of wanting to defend the character and I had that with Kate. The appeal of the script for me was trying to understand miscarriage grief and at a time when I was desperately trying to get pregnant and wanting to be a mother. So, there were issues in there that intrigued me about it. I spent a lot of time on websites for women who've gone through three trimesters and then suffered miscarriages and I was completely moved by it. The shock, it's an intense grief and the recovery from it. The body heals before the soul does, so I saw that in my character and wanted to explore that.

Peter Sarsgaard: Well, I immediately felt very comfortable around Vera. There's usually a 'getting to know you' awkwardness. But from the first day, when she busted her lip, we were fine. It was also the only accident I remember happening on the film before cameras rolled.

Vera Farmiga: I wailed into Jaume and cracked my nose.

Peter Sarsgaard: And got a bloody nose! With playing these characters, you feel them out and they're from your own life and they're from what you're sensing coming from that place, and it's fairly subtle, so it's those kind of things that just happen.

Vera Farmiga: We have a chemistry and we've known each other for ten years. We have had the same manager for a decade.

Peter Sarsgaard: We didn't go back and write the story of our lives together, no. But the alcoholism, we talked about that stuff.

Vera Farmiga: Sure, this is a highly dysfunctional relationship that they have. I think how she first deals with the shame and pain and guilt and bereavement is to turn to alcohol. This is a man who just puts bandages on these bullet holes, he doesn't really deal with things in this relationship and the grief is really what drives her to drink. She spends the whole film recovering from that. She feels tremendous guilt for her daughter.

How does *Orphan* compare to other "evil child" movies:

Vera Farmiga: I did something similar, but not many people saw *Joshua*. I had a great time with Sam Rockwell and the only really similar thing is that there's a mother in distress, but I really don't feel that my career's in danger of being pigeonholed. And the story was radically different for me. I look at the character and what her trip is, and I found this really complex. It's a complex grief, trying to get over a miscarriage, and the dysfunction of this family. I have to say, what really got me, the secret of the film, I had never read anything like that before and I wanted to be a part of that, but I wanted to make sure that whomever would be a part of that as well could make it work. As soon as Peter's name was brought into the mix, I said '*I'm in.*' We'd been trying to find things to work on over the course of a few years.

David Leslie Johnson: Even when the *Bad Seed* was made, it was a taboo subject. At the end of *The Bad Seed*, they have to break the fourth wall and say, "Oh, look here's the actress, she wasn't really bad and she didn't really die." (laughs) It's such a bizarre ending! I don't remember ever seeing a movie like that where they actually had to say, "It's OK everyone, the little girl's fine." So, it was definitely, I think, more taboo then and I think that was sort of – it sort of broke a barrier of what you could or couldn't do certainly. But I think that the idea of children being scary has always been there. Because there's something very primal about the need to protect children, so when you turn that on its head and you make the children, the child the bad guy, it's violating everything that you feel. They are meant to be innocent. And there's another aspect to it, and I don't know if this is real or not, but there's obviously a need to nurture kids and protect kids, but on some level, I wonder, kids also are reminders of our own mortality in a way. Ultimately your child kind of looks like you, grows up and acts like you and ultimately is here to replace you. I don't know if maybe that's one of the reasons that it persists as a horror sub-genre, maybe.

Jaume Collet-Serra: The idea is for people to see the movie and have them think they know what this movie is going to be like, but it's not. So, right now with the poster and the trailer, a lot of people are feeling like they've already seen this kind of a movie, but I don't think that's true. So, hopefully the movie will have an opportunity to grow with word of mouth.

Isabelle Fuhrman: This is an evil character, and most evil characters are male. Not many evil characters are female. There's *The Good Son*, *The Omen*. There was *The Exorcist*, but I never saw that movie and I probably never will because I'm freaked out by the head spinning around! (laughs)

A journalist asks, insensitively, if Isabelle, now twelve, is ready for "*America to hate her?*"

Isabelle Fuhrman: (pause) I'm totally different than Esther, and if America hates me then I've done my job! I'm supposed to make everybody hate me, but at the same time, I hope they feel sorry for her, but at the same time think, 'Whoa I feel sorry for her, but she's so mean!'

On what's next for producers Joel Silver and Susan Downey and Joel's appreciation for comic book properties:

Joel Silver: *Lobo* (based on the DC Comic character) is the one I'm really excited about doing one day, hopefully soon. I've always loved graphic novels. We bought *Watchmen* and *V For Vendetta* in the late 80s. I lost *Watchmen* over the years; I wish I hadn't, but I've always been interested in graphic novels. When I read *Watchmen*, it changed my view of so many things, it was the first time I read a graphic novel really like that. So, look we made *Richie Rich*, before so I've been involved with comic book stories for a long time. *Predator* might as well have been a graphic novel. Obviously, it wasn't but it read like one.

Joel Silver: With *Watchmen*, Look, I love Zack Snyder and I love his work and I think he's very talented, but the script that we developed was I think better than the movie they made. I thought there were some really good ideas we came up with. I know he stayed very close to the original material, but he made some changes anyways. I think it could've been a more satisfying movie. But you make the best movie you can. I think Zack made a great movie though and I don't want to minimize what he did, but at the end of the day it was more tuned to just the big fanatics of *Watchmen* as opposed to a broader audience that didn't know the original comic book. As far as *Lobo*, we've got a script for *Lobo* we like. And when any of you see *Avatar*, the technology is genius. It's fantastic. So, it's time. I think it's structured now as a PG-13 movie, but I love it. I want to make a good *Lobo* movie and it's a great character.

Susan Downey: We all have high hopes for *Sherlock Holmes*, that it will be a big fun action version of it, and I actually think we got there. It maintains the integrity of people who are *Sherlock Holmes* fans. It's smart, there's a great history at the core. I think Robert Downey Jr captured the essence of Sherlock. I think Jude Law is going to surprise people in his portrayal of Watson. I don't think we've seen Jude do something, in my opinion, that's as fresh and solid as this performance. He's really, really great. Rachel McAdams adds a wonderful splash as Irene Adler and so I think we're going to satiate the people who are old Sherlock fans and see that we're doing it right, and for the next generation who hasn't really read those stories, I think they're just going to enjoy the ride.

MARCUS DUNSTAN & PATRICK MELTON

Interviewed by Rob Galluzzo (7/09)

The Collector is the directorial debut of Marcus Dunstan and genre fans should take note. This indie flick was written by Dunstan with Patrick Melton, the duo who have scripted not only the *Feast* trilogy, but also *Saw IV, Saw V* and *Saw VI*. (They've just been tapped to write *Saw VII*!) We got the chance to chat with them about all of the above, including the humble beginnings of *The Collector* prior to its premiere last night. Read on for our exclusive chat with Marcus Dunstan and Patrick Melton!

Where did the story for *The Collector* come from, chronologically, for you guys? Was this something you wrote after *Feast* but before *Saw IV*?

Marcus Dunstan: This was actually written before *Feast*!

Patrick Melton: This started as a short film. To go way back, when I was in film school, I had to come up with ideas for short scripts for this Kodak endowment thing, where Kodak gave LMU all this money to make a short film and so Marcus and I had written *Rolled Bones*, which was the first script before *Feast* in 1999. And so, we brainstormed together, and we came up with this short script and it's called *Thief*; what if a thief broke into the house of a serial killer? We wrote the script, and it didn't get made for that thing, but afterwards, we decided let's make this on our own and Marcus wanted to direct it. It was going to be a ten-minute short, but then we won *Project Greenlight*. So, then it went on hiatus.

Well, you guys were busy for a couple of years after that!

Patrick Melton: Right after (the first) *Saw* came out, everybody wanted that million-dollar idea. Like, a horror movie that you could make for under a million dollars, and you can make it in a contained location with a high concept. We had this idea and we ended up pitching it in a meeting to these guys who ended up producing this. They bought it in the room, with the agreement that Marcus would direct it. We finished the script, but the problem was the company

said they didn't have enough money, so they were going to go halves with another company. Marcus didn't have an appropriate reel, so we couldn't sell him as a director. So, the company gave us $5,000 to shoot the trailer to the movie, which would be stylized to show off Marcus as a director. So, we did that. All the Gulagers helped. John Gulager shot it. Clu Gulager was in it, Diane Goldner was in it, Tom (Gulager) was in it. It came out really good, and we started taking meetings showing people the trailer along with the script. Bob Weinstein ended up seeing it, watched the trailer, closed the door to his office and said, "You're not leaving this office until I get this movie." So, we sold it to him. A year or so later, we started shooting in Shreveport, Louisiana with Marcus directing, and we finished it. Edited it for about a year and then they watched it. (Marcus starts laughing) And said, "We love it! But... we don't have any money." Because all their money was in *Halloween 2* and *Inglourious Basterds*...

Those pesky movies that no one's going to see!

Patrick Melton: Right! So, we said, "What if we bought it back?" And they said sure, as long as you give us what we spent for it then sure. Mickey Liddell watched it, really liked it, bought it back and here we are.

Now let me ask you; I know very little about the movie beyond the initial premise. And you had this story for a while, but the general misconception is obviously, you

guys have done the *Saw* sequels, and *The Collector* has "traps" in it. So, what can you say to genre fans that don't know anything about the movie? How is this different from what we've seen in *Saw IV*, *Saw V*, or *Saw VI*?

Marcus Dunstan: The difference between this and *Saw* is we're coming from a point of a thriller intersecting with a horror movie. *Saw* has always taken place within the horror realm and has embraced that. Whereas we wanted to take James Caan from *Thief* and have him accidentally break into The Tooth Fairy's house from *Manhunter*. (Both Michael Mann movies, by the way!) Tactics to catch a cat burglar in your home, if you're not going mano a mano from scene one, it involved setting up some kind of snare. Perhaps setting up some kind of compromising position for that thief to have to endure. So, we kept this as close to the vest and what you can really make from anything already in your home as possible. These things, if they are implements used in the movie, we built them ourselves in the living room. If you see razor blades? I cut my fingers on them for real to make sure they worked. And it's just based on very intimate fears, things that are around your home, because we didn't want these to be specific elaborate traps at all. We're trying to create a villain that is the land equivalent of a shark. If you go into the water, a shark might get you. If you're on land, you're on this killer's territory and everyone's vulnerable.

Patrick Melton: The big difference too is the tone is very different. The *Saw* movies are wonderful because they almost seem like you're going into a different world with the heightened reality, while this one, we tried to keep it more grounded with things that are in your house. Things that can be put together quickly that aren't sort of too fantastic.

It's kind of like Nancy at the end of *A Nightmare on Elm Street*. Rigging the booby traps!

Patrick Melton: (laughs) That's so funny you say that.

Marcus Dunstan: I got to say one thing. You've got to stay through the credits on this one, because we've rewarded the person that does! A little something extra.

In terms of *Saw*, you guys have both gone on record saying that *Saw VI* is one of your favorites, and probably the best one you've done. It seems you guys went into *Saw IV*, *V*, and *VI* with an overall story arc. Now you guys are doing *Saw VII*. So, is it interesting, challenging or different to start from scratch with *Saw VII*? Or are you continuing

some of the threads that appeared in your trilogy?

Marcus Dunstan: A lot of *Saw IV* and *Saw V* really hinged on *Saw VI* coming together. And the way *VI* did, it recharged our batteries creatively. *VI* recharged us and it gave us new ground, which we hope to mine more horror from.

Patrick Melton: What we were really trying to do was, we finished *VI* and we were done with *VI* before we even started thinking about *Saw VII* to be honest. *VI* ends and we wanted to end that arc from *IV*, *V*, and *VI*. Those three, *IV*, *V*, and *VI* all make sense tying the stuff from the first three as well. And it ends! You could leave *Saw VI* and say, "OK, I'm done, I'm happy, I'm completely fulfilled." Now, with *Saw VII*, we're definitely turning the page a bit. It's a new chapter. But you'll see, and we can talk more in depth when you see *VI*, but you can where it's going to go, but there is definitely a closure at the end of *VI* and with *VII*, it is the beginning of a new trilogy. It's the third trilogy for the *Saw* films.

Is there any criteria going into *Saw VII*, either from Twisted or Lionsgate, or are you guys free to go whatever direction you want?

Marcus Dunstan: No, there's always been a bible and a canon and an ultimate end game for them, so we have to respect the rules that have been established, and we have to respect the tone. Other than that, it is earned. Earn the audience.

You're both writers, and now Marcus is directing, but you also made a fun little cameo in Adam Green's Halloween short film *The Tiffany Problem*. Any chance we'll see you acting in front of the camera again soon?

Marcus Dunstan: (laughs) Based on my appearance in front of that camera, I think I'm going to have to do a little changin' before I make any more appearances! (laughs)

I seriously just want to thank you guys for *Feast*. That first movie was probably one of my favorite genre pictures since *Evil Dead 2*. Just the same kind of energy, so I'm always indebted to you guys for writing *Feast*!

Marcus Dunstan: Aw, right on! We didn't want to let any Gulagers go untouched in *The Collector*. Diane Goldner's in it. John Gulager helped us with some shooting. Tom Gulager was the second unit director when we were shooting for twenty-four hours a day! Clu Gulager recorded some beautiful narration for us. So, everyone from the family is in this one.

This is more of a fan to fan inquiry. *Hellraiser* is up next to be "rebooted" and there have been several writers brought in and you guys were amongst the bunch to take a crack at it. What was your take on it, and what's made this new *Hellraiser* so difficult to crank?

Marcus Dunstan: The treatment for it was beautiful, and what it did was, it just gave scale to what was only hinted at in the darkness and the shadows of the first entry. We didn't want to go back and repeat that story, if at all possible, because that first story was wonderfully told. So, it wanted to grab darkness and appreciate it much like a *Pan's Labyrinth* would. And Pinhead's become more than just that ending guy that gives a few lines. He's become a figure in horror cinema, so we wanted to respect that, and re-announce that and make it bigger. The problem with that first treatment? It was too darned expensive. It just was.

Patrick Melton: Our thing was… everyone knows Pinhead. You show Pinhead, people know exactly who he is. The average person, they may not know exactly which movie it is or they may not have seen a *Hellraiser*, but they know him. We were trying to build up his backstory and make him a true supervillain. And so, a lot of the story had to do with fleshing out his backstory, which is revealed more in *Hellraiser II*. We were combining elements of one and two and building up Pinhead as a bigger character. Because not only in his past life, but also in the time he's spent in hell. Giving him an end game, an end goal, and making him much more active as opposed to just torturing people. I don't know, it was just maybe too much minutia for Dimension. At the end of the day –

Marcus Dunstan: Sometimes when you're a fan of a movie, you want to put a hell of a lot more in it than necessary. You want to see the dream version of it, when… maybe it needs to be sheer, severe and slick. And that might ultimately be the *Hellraiser* that comes out. I don't know.

Besides *The Collector* and *Saw VII*, what's next? Anything you're excited to tackle?

Marcus Dunstan: Well, I'd love to direct an adaptation of a graphic novel called *Deal With The Devil* by Mike Miller. It's just a brilliant bad-ass plot and I think it would make one hell of a movie.

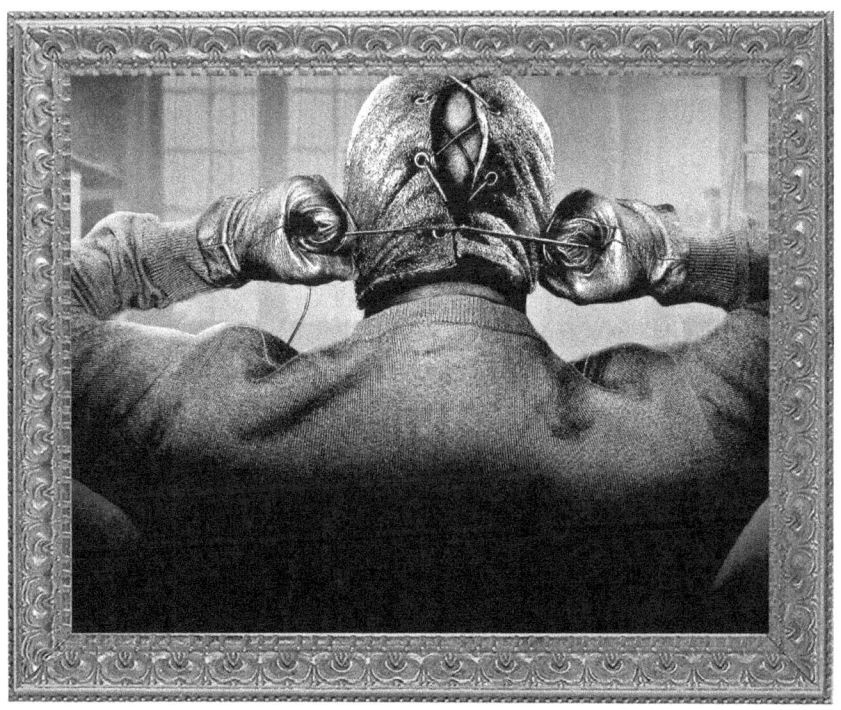

JORDAN LADD

Interviewed by Rob Galluzzo (8/09)

It's kind of hard not to crush on Jordan Ladd when you're sitting across from her and spending about five minutes just talking about the forgotten art of making a "mixtape." But here we are and with limited time, we jumped right into her experiences portraying Madeline, the mother that would do anything for her baby in *Grace*. No stranger to the genre, Ladd also worked with another first time director on a little movie called *Cabin Fever*. We chatted about the challenges of tackling such a complex and emotional role, working with Paul Solet, and shooting in Canada.

What were your initial reactions to reading the script for *Grace*? You've done some genre stuff in the past such as *Cabin Fever*, so I'd imagine you probably got offered a lot of horror stuff after that. What was it about this that made you return to the genre?

I've had a fairly strict "no horror" policy after *Cabin Fever*, not that I don't like the genre! By default, by working in it, I've become a fan. Because all the filmmakers I've worked with supply me with the genre movies that they dig. For *Grace*, it was really a compelling piece about a woman's love gone wrong. How loving too much can be self-destructive and it was something that in my own personal life I was exploring anyway. About self-preservation and not over nurturing people. So, it really spoke to me. And of course, when I read it, I didn't want to like it. I didn't want to have to do it. But I got to page seventeen and I was already working, unbeknownst to me, I'm already working on the character in my head. I got to the end of the script, and I thought, 'OK. I have to meet this guy. Because I want to say no. But if I say no, and somebody screws this up, squanders this opportunity, or somebody gets it and I look and think shoot, why didn't I do this?!' (laughs)

So, you just had to meet the guy who wrote this script?

Yeah. I needed to meet him, and I just needed to know, do you need to tell this story, because there is carnage and suspense and these moments that ensue out of your allegiance to this story OR is it that you need a story because you love the gags? Does this story supply a reason for you to hack people up and use lots of blood and all that stuff? There's a difference to me. I can't work on something where there's a body count

or a lot of blood, just for the sake of it. And he told me that was just a part of telling this story. That was a big thing for me. We sat down for what I thought was going to be a thirty-minute meeting, and we sat for four hours until his car got towed! We talked about love gone wrong and excessive love and self-love and family dynamics and co-dependency. And I was amazed that someone, a man could write something so sensitive and then speak about these subject matters, because it's rare to come across that just in life, someone who's engaged in relationship dynamics. So that was really the clincher, meeting and talking to Paul. We had a good rapport going and a real understanding of who these people were, specifically my character.

Although I was hesitant to take it because I'm not a mom. I've never given birth; I don't know how that is. I didn't want to get it wrong. And he assured me that those feelings are universal, I mean I've never had a kid. And he said, "Well, I've never had a kid either, but I was able to write this. We're going to figure this out together. Both of us as non-moms. You can do it!" We really went to those places and unfortunately, I had to live there for a while, which was uncomfortable. But I needed to do it. I needed a place to get those feelings out, because they existed inside me. Every actress brings something to a character that they can really purge their soul into. This gave me permission.

What's interesting about this movie, unlike most genre stuff, this really focuses on the characters. There's no particular "villain" in this movie. Of course, we're sympathetic to your character Madeline. But at the same time, I understand the motivations of Vivian or Dr. Sohn

or Patricia. Everybody in this film wants something they can't have. They each want what's best for the baby. Was it difficult to find who Madeline was for you? Did you incorporate people you knew to play it?

It was not difficult to find Madeline at all. Madeline was finding me! As soon as I made the decision in my mind that I was going to do this project, I became flooded with ideas, where I started sleeping with a pad and a pen next to the bed. I was surfing the internet a lot. I read a lot about Sharon Tate and what kind of mother she would have been, had she had the opportunity. And I mean, that's a very dark notion. But she was a reference point for me.

Had you seen the short film version of *Grace* before this?

No, no…

Did you avoid it because obviously a different actress (Liza Weil) portrayed Madeline in the short and you didn't want it to interfere with how you were going to play it?

No, I didn't avoid it! I wanted to see it and Paul said, 'You can't see it. It's got to come from with inside you.' There was one moment where I unintentionally felt influenced by it. I had seen the making-of the short film version of *Grace*…

By Adam Barnick! Who by the way, says hello…

I heart Adam Barnick so much! He's such a rad dude! I had seen his making-of from the short. It really gave me more of a sense of what Paul's set would be like. Liza (Weil) obviously had a take on Madeline, and it was a very strong take. Paul, however, said I shouldn't watch the short, so I watched the making-of.

And there was one shot that he kept from the short specifically that I had seen in the making-of, which was where the camera travels over Madeline's body right after the car accident and she's bleeding. I had a big day, I had my headphones on, and I'd been balling my eyes out all morning, not talking to anyone. There were maybe one or two days where I had to shut everyone out and really be in that character. And so, I'm doing all this preparation, I get to set, I'm crying, tears streaming down my face, I'm laying in the bed. And all of a sudden, I feel the camera traveling above me, and I'm visualizing Liza! I'm comparing what I'm doing to Liza, and everything just stopped for me.

Thank God, he didn't show me what she did, because I would subconsciously feel that I wasn't honoring that or that I wasn't good enough. I'd feel as if my allegiance wasn't to her performance, and that would've been really complicated for me to even approach this when someone else had put their signature on it already. I still haven't seen the short! But I'm curious to see it now since all is said and done. (laughs)

It was necessary for Madeline to come from inside me and for me to not have a point of reference other than my own imagination and my own heart. I used Paul's script for things to draw upon. Madeline just started chasing me down, I was non-stop all night. I'd call Paul saying 'What are you doing to me? I'm up all night, scribbling ideas!' (laughs) He was doing the same thing.

You've worked with first time directors before, obviously Eli Roth on *Cabin Fever*. What was the experience like with Paul as a first-time director compared to your previous films?

Paul was a really interesting first-time director and I honestly can't compare him to anybody. Eli Roth was so different as a first-time director. It's apples and oranges. For neither one of them did it seem like it was their first project. And technically it wasn't, they'd both worked creatively on shorts before. So, they were both comfortable on the set. But they're so enormously different. *Grace* was an intimate story, Paul's more of an introvert. Eli's an extrovert. That was a lot of fun, it was a big party for *Cabin Fever*. *Grace* was very serious. Somber for me a lot of the time. Sometimes we'd joke around, of course, but underneath it all, it was a tough piece of material. With someone as sobering and serious as Paul, he kept it in that place for me, so it was interesting. I can't compare them! They're so different and the stories are so different.

I've heard about the shoot in Moose Jaw, Canada. Adam Green's told us a few stories about bar fights? You, however, are absent from all these late-night tales. What were you up to when you guys weren't shooting?

I stayed in Regina! So, I had to drive an hour and a half to work every morning. It was simply because I was in Regina already, I had unpacked my room and my dogs, and my dog's toys and my stuff and my groceries. We had six-day weeks, so when everyone did the move on a Sunday, I just thought 'I'm not going to make it. I need to sleep the whole day and do laundry' and I didn't make it. I just stayed behind and slept when I could! That's why I'm not included in their escapades in Moose Jaw!

PAUL SOLET

Interviewed by Rob Galluzzo (8/09)

Icons has been with *Grace* since its inception and over the course of the last few years, we've really gotten to know and see filmmaker Paul Solet's passion for the genre. We had the chance to sit and chat with Paul briefly about the long road that brought us here, as well as the current state of the genre. Considering our familiarity with him, we just jumped right in.

I wanted to talk a bit about the style of this movie now that I've finally seen it! I think this is the best compliment I can give you – *Grace* doesn't seem like the debut of an American independent filmmaker. It felt very much like a well-crafted foreign film, that... just happens to be in English. I know that you personally like a lot of foreign films, especially the work of Chan-wook Park. Did you draw from foreign influences or reference them during the making of *Grace*?

Well, there's definitely artistic references and film references for the movie, but that's not the sort of vocabulary that I really used on set. It's never really, 'Well, I want it to look like this,' it's more like, 'Well, let's look at this.' Like, 'I love this.' It's more sort of the core idea of this style of storytelling which is let's cut the bullshit. Let's strip it down and really slaughter every scene we can. There's no cute horror beats in *Grace*. My whole goal was to create a world that was authentic enough and consistent enough that you don't have an opportunity as an audience member to leave. To check out by going, 'What a great scare there! That's a horror moment!' Yeah, there are scares, but if we have people passing out at the screenings, then we're doing our job viscerally. And that is hugely important to me. I would not downplay that.

The movie needs to operate at all levels. There can be no willingness to settle for anything short of a fully functional film. Emotionally, intellectually. Again, I've said it before and I don't want to get too precious about it, but film should function spiritually. You should leave a film and think, 'What the fuck just happened to me?' (laughs) If you forget the movie when you walk out of there, then I've lost. I lost.

That much you accomplished! After seeing the movie, I knew I had to think about it. Because there were things I didn't know how to feel about. But the fact that a day later, I still wasn't sure how to feel about certain characters proves that the film worked. For example, there's technically no "villain" in the movie. There's no one you dislike, every character has their own motivation and need for something in this movie. I was pretty much torn on my feelings for everybody...

That's the point! Look, I'm glad to hear you articulate that and I'm really glad to hear you were torn. This isn't the usual thing. To be perfectly honest, I think too frequently, filmmakers are underestimating their audience. They're saying, 'Let's make a villain and let's make a good guy.' And the reality is much more interesting. Reality is, there are no black and white areas and everyone thinks that they are right. Everyone can explain to you why what they're doing is the right thing to do.

And that's much more interesting, it's much more challenging, and it might be much more challenging for an audience because it's sort of a new thing. But the reality is there are no villains in this picture. I think about it as an actor would need to. The guy playing Dr. Sohn needs to know what his motives are. You don't play a villain. An actor who plays a villain, you know what they are? That's a bad actor. Seriously. A villain? "I'm the villain!" No. An actor needs to know their motives and they need to believe in them.

Well, everyone's got a little good, and everyone's got a little darkness in them. My idea of a villain is someone who lets the darkness show a little more...

I think they're all different kinds of villains and all different kinds of ways to play them, but the term "villain" is just irrelevant. What drama is motives in conflict. That's where drama happens. That's why people squirm in *Grace*. That's because drama is happening. And it's not like it defines expectations. I have no interest in giving you what you're expecting. I won't do it! I don't care, that's not interesting to me. There's enough shit out there that's doing that. What's the point?

I'm being completely serious, you know me. I come at this stuff as a fan first. When I feel manipulated by a film, I get infuriated! (laughs) I'll leave a movie cursing and screaming, and it's ridiculous! But my initial reaction is I become infuriated, and then I become excited. I become excited about, 'OK, let's step this up.' I feel like we can't just sit around as fans and bitch if we're not going to do anything to solve the problem. You don't need to be a filmmaker to be doing that, to be moving towards solving that problem with the horror genre. Like, as a fan, go see the movies that are doing the things that you want them to do. Go support the movie! I have no opinion about remakes, you know? John Carpenter's *The Thing* is amazing. Are you going to tell me remakes are all shitty? That's just stupid. It's a black and white thing to say. But when you have a movie, a real genuine film that's doing all these things that we're always complaining about films not doing, for us not to be supporting it whole-heartedly is a travesty. And beyond my emotional reaction to it, the practicality of it, the reality of what that does, you're just going to get more shit. If you want the same old shit, so be it. You're not going to like *Grace*. Go see any number of other horror films.

This has been something that's been with you for a long time, but it's finally playing in theaters and in festivals. How does it feel to finally see this thing after this long road? I mean, you just went to Korea to show it! What's that experience been like for you considering everything that's led up to it?

I could not be more gratified with the reception of the film. We shot this movie very quickly with no resources. When we started talking to people about this movie, they'd say, 'This movie can't be done in twenty-four days. Can't be done.' And we were like, 'OK, twenty-four days? Let's do it.'

Then they were like 'Twenty-two days, twenty-two days to do it.' And we were like 'Egh, whatever, it is what it is. We'll make it happen. We'll make it work.' Then it went down to twenty days. We figured we'll be in LA, we'll call in every favor we can. Then we hear, 'Well, it's eighteen days. And you're shooting it in Regina, Saskatchewan.' (laughs)

Nine days in, the tax incentives got screwed up and we only had seventeen days! You end up doing one to three takes at that point. But we went in prepared. We went in with enough passion. This was a crew in rare form. This was a family thing. You had people coming early and leaving late and not charging for that. This was some magic shit here and that shows on screen.

My conscience is completely clear with this film. Of course, I see things and think I wish I had done them differently or I wish I had more time to do that, but I know deep in my gut that there's nothing more that we could've done with the resources we had to work with. And I'm really proud. I watch this movie with every single audience. I don't walk around outside and make phone calls. I watch the audiences watch the movie. I've seen it with eighty audiences from Utah to France to Scotland to Korea to everywhere. And it goes over the same in each one. It really hits the beats, it really does. The most reserved audience, a Korean audience that is so polite and calm and quiet, it really fucked them up! It really did!

(laughs)

There is nothing more gratifying. And dude, you've been with this thing since day one. Without you and *Icons of Fright*, this thing wouldn't have happened. It's a great example that this isn't just a filmmaker's universe. The guys that run the sites, the filmmakers, the fans, everybody, this is our genre! This does not go down in the comedy scene. Those guys spend time trying to one up each other. That's not how we roll! That's not how the horror crowd does it. This movie was possible because of all of us.

GLENN MCQUAID

Interviewed by Adam Barnick (8/09)

"Recreate 19th century England and Ireland in modern Manhattan with stars, stunts, and practical FX!" This directive might give some emerging indie filmmakers heart attacks, but not writer/director Glenn McQuaid. *I Sell the Dead* finds grave robbing partners Arthur Blake and Willie Grimes (Dominic Monaghan, producer Larry Fessenden) awaiting their executions for their criminal lifestyle. A holy man (Ron Perlman) arrives to take Arthur's confessions, and Arthur spins his macabre coming-of-age story; but who's conning who? *Dead* is a hoot, its decomposing tongue planted firmly in cheek.

What are your earliest memories of the horror genre?

In the late seventies and eighties, BBC2 ran a series of late-night horror double bills. They always showed a black and white classic such as *The Beast with Five Fingers* followed by something in color, like *Race with the Devil*. So, from very early on I developed an obsession with horror. One of the first videos my dad bought was *The Wicker Man*, so I have a very strong connection with that film. I was very much aware of film makers like Freddie Francis, Terry Fisher and even Ken Russell from a very young age. It wasn't until my teens that I really became aware of what people like John Carpenter and David Cronenberg were doing and how far they were taking horror. *Rabid* was my first Cronenberg film and it felt dangerous to me, and I loved it! At the same time, bands like *The Virgin Prunes* and *Throbbing Gristle* were coming out and challenging everything I was being taught by the schools and church, it was a very exciting time.

Tell me a bit about how your upbringing in Ireland influenced the stories you're interested in telling.

My schooling was through the Christian brothers in Ireland and, though I met a few of them that were cool, most of them were twisted arseholes. So for a lot of my education, I just tried to keep myself entertained to get through it all. I escaped into comics like *2000AD*, Stephen King, Clive Barker, and as I mentioned earlier, horror films. Storytelling was also a big part of my growing up. My family and all the family friends are great at reminiscing and telling stories, it's a real gift and a dying art and I was eager to explore the craft of it with *I Sell the Dead*.

I'd read about particular styles of Irish storytelling that deliberately involved pulling the audience's leg. Though it sounded like it relied on the charm and imagination of the storyteller to not have the audience mind that they were being misled, which to me, feels just like this movie and Blake and Grimes. They're total con men, but big-hearted and so fun to be around, that I don't mind if they're stretching the truth. Plus, the unreliable narrator always makes for storytelling you have to pay close attention to.

I love the idea that you are in the hands of the storyteller and never sure exactly what to believe. Everybody embellishes their stories and even memories to some extent. My childhood memories of films are always challenged when I see them again as an adult, over the years I had somehow added subplots and characters that never existed. My favorite novel is still *Dracula*, not because of the story, which I love, but because you are in the hands of so many different story tellers and you have to give yourself over to all of them to piece together and appreciate the bigger picture.

As a kid I saw television trailers for films like *The Shining, Dead and Buried* and *The Amityville Horror* and I would make up my own story lines for them. I actually convinced people I had seen the flicks and spun them my versions of the stories. I was always caught out when people saw the actual movies, but I was obsessed with getting there first with my stories.

How'd you come to work with Larry Fessenden and Glass Eye Pix? Can you tell me what you contributed to them and what you learned/took away from working on them?

My background is as a visual effects artist, I used to do effects and design for television commercials in the States and in Ireland. The checks were great, but I wanted to make the jump into filmmaking before it was too late. I met Larry at the wrap party for Jim McKenny's *The Off Season*. I had already seen *Wendigo* and was a fan, so I offered to help him out on any of his future projects.

Our first big collaboration came with Ti West's *The Roost*. I headed up a small team of artists and we created the CGI bats in that movie. I'm very proud of the work we put into that movie, I think the bats really add a lot to the finished film. I then went off to help Larry film *The Last Winter,* in Iceland. That was an amazing time. I got to see Fessenden working with his actors and crew; he is a force of nature on set. I was hired as the visual effects producer but when I got there, Larry gave me a small crew, shook my hand and told me I was the second unit director! So, I really learned a lot during my time on *The Last Winter*.

Were you urging Larry to consider you in the Scareflix lineup from the start or did you fall into doing *I Sell the Dead* more organically?

I pitched Larry several ideas, none of which he was too enthusiastic about. One of them was called *The Father and Son Weekend*, about a scouting trip where the kids turn on their fathers, but it did not go down too well! It wasn't until I suggested I expand my short film *The Resurrection Apprentice* that Fessenden really perked up. I think he waited for the pitch that I was truly excited about.

I wrote *The Resurrection Apprentice* as an exercise in tone. I wanted to create a tiny little drama set in the universe of Hammer Horror. I was reading books like *The Italian Boy: A Tale of Murder and Body Snatching* by Sarah Wise and a book on Gallows speeches from eighteenth-century Ireland, so the story was a sum of all my interests at the time. We shot the short in Jersey City of all places!

What was enticing to you about this project? The dynamic between the mentor and the boy? The mood/aesthetics?

Character is probably the most important thing to me as a writer. Without solid characters, I think everything else will just fall apart. When I was finished with the short film, I felt I had so much more to explore with the characters. I love the mentor/boy relationship and without Willie Grimes and Arthur Blake, there would be no *I Sell the Dead*. I think a year after finishing the project, I decided to jump back into the world, which eventually became *I Sell the Dead*.

Once you had nailed the feature's narrative, and knowing you had to deliver on a smaller budget as a Scareflix production, did you pull back or just write what you wanted to see and plunge ahead?

I really just wrote what I wanted to see at the local cinema. I figured we would shoot a lot of the movie on green screen, and I could use matte paintings and CGI to create our environments, so I tried to let my imagination run wild. Of course, the production turned out to be very different than I imagined and we were lucky enough to shoot in great locations with some incredible name talent.

I remember *The Resurrection Apprentice* having a subtly comic premise over how 'matter of fact' they are in their jobs, but thought it was much more somber overall. *I Sell the Dead's* tone is much more gleeful and rip-roaring, like it's had a few pints and wants to top its drinking partner's tall tale with its own. What made you decide to take a lighter, comic approach?

When I finished the short, I felt it was a little stiff and maybe took itself too seriously. As I mentioned, it really is a tiny little drama set in a spooky world, not much of anything happens! When I showed the finished short film to people, I realized how badly I wanted to incite a bigger reaction from the audience. And so, when I jumped back into the world, I really had the goal of entertaining people in mind.

Showing my work to audiences has been a big learning experience for me, I really do keep them in mind when I write and direct. As I wrote the feature, I also tried to keep myself giggling and that made it a pleasure to write. I think it's possible to create a movie like *I Sell the Dead* and not go comedic, but I felt that the comedy allowed me to be more absurd with my characters and even my direction.

Once you knew Daniel Manche and Larry Fessenden would reprise their roles, how did you go about bringing Ron Perlman and Dominic Monaghan into this?

I had worked with Ron Perlman on the set of *The Last Winter* where we were all cooped up in Northern Iceland for a few weeks. Also, Larry and Ron are quite tight and so we approached Ron quite early.

Dom came on board a little later and his casting was really the brainchild of my producer Peter Phok. Peter brought an amazing ambition to the project when he came on board. It was quite a ride trying to get these two actors on the same set, they are both very busy people, and we were blessed that it all worked out for us in the end. All of the actors were very gracious to work with and wonderful collaborators. As a first-time filmmaker, I couldn't have asked for a better cast, it really was a dream come true.

How did your visual FX background contribute to the ease (that's a relative term) of telling this story? Were other areas more of a learning curve?

Having a background in visual effects probably helped out more in prep and post than on set. I storyboarded and created a few animatics for the movie but a lot of that had to be thrown out due to the crazy nature of low budget production. I think the biggest learning curve for me was getting the hang of creative camera coverage and blocking. If you look at the first scenes I shot (*The Resurrection Apprentice* scene) and compare them to the last few days of photography (the whole vampire scene), you will see a development in confidence and style with the camera.

I would think the two biggest expenses/areas of research and concern after casting were costume and production design. What kind of work went into your costuming?

I worked very closely with my costume designer David Tabbert; I had built up a fairly large visual diary for all of my collaborators and I had a very specific look for each of the characters. We have a fair amount of night photography in the movie and so it was always a fine balance to have these characters in the right dark fabrics without losing them to the black of the night. I referenced the costumes in John Badham's *Dracula* as well as a bunch of Hammer films.

I don't think a lot of people know you shot nearly the entire film in and around New York City. Tell me a bit about how you pulled that off?

We originally thought we were going to shoot in a studio and use a bunch of green screens but thankfully we moved away from that concept. Most of the studio spaces we investigated were too expensive anyways and so the entire Glass Eye Pix office went out location scouting. We scoured the five boroughs and came back with all the amazing locations that you see in the movie. Staten Island was the gift that kept giving, we eventually shot over half of the movie there.

The tavern in the movie is actually a bar in the east village called The Scratcher, we completely changed the look of it and turned it into our grave robber's refuge. The locals were quite taken with the new vibe! I wanted to prove that it was possible to make a period movie on a low budget in NYC and I think we showed that, it's just not easy!

I was lucky enough to have an incredible art department. My Art Director, Beck Underwood, was an absolute powerhouse and kept everything steaming ahead, my production designer David Bell came up with some great concepts that really explored the world I had created. Certain locations, like the tavern, required a ton of art dressing and design but others, such as the execution square, already had so much production value that we really just came in and carefully dressed them with a killer Guillotine here and a vintage cart there. I think the use of fog also really helped.

Were you thinking of Angus Scrimm in his part from the beginning? Other than the obvious nod to genre fans in what his character needs, I was thinking 'This is the other role Angus was born to play.' He'd fit right in in a Dickens adaptation here.

I was always hoping to work with Angus. He's been in a few Glass Eye Pix productions in the past and so I knew I had somewhat of an in with him. I met him in LA to discuss the project and he came on board soon thereafter. For an icon of horror, he really is an incredibly kind and warm gentleman!

You had an unusual production in that you had to put it on hold for a few months halfway through due to *Hellboy II*. Can you talk about that? To me it almost feels like an ideal way to make a film, assuming it's easy to get everyone back; you can shape what you already have and learn from the first half of production.

We actually held off for six months! At the time, I really resented the halt in production. I wanted to have it all wrapped so I could get stuck into the edit, but in retrospect, it really helped to have the break. My best work is from the second half of the shoot. I learned so much from the first round that I came back stronger and more prepared for the remaining shoot, but it was quite tough knowing I only had half a movie during the break.

I remember some painted/stylized backdrops mixed with live-action through the film. Is that a nod to the matte paintings in classic British horror films that influenced you? I also felt it gave the film a more literate quality, like the characters were stepping through the pictures in a novel.

Those shots were a nod to the art of storytelling. I wanted them to be stylized in a way that felt theatrical and broad. They were also ways for me to get back into the cell where Arthur is telling the stories, bookending his stories in a way.

For your villains/criminals, it's appealing that Arthur and Willie are the most 'innocent' of the lawbreakers in the film. I know a lot of press discusses the supernatural beasts they encounter, but I found the human monsters even more intriguing. Tell me about where the House of Murphy came from; and I have to geek-question; is Valentine's mask a tribute to *Eyes Without a Face*?

I'm a big fan of *Eyes Without a Face* and so the design of Valentine's mask was a nod to that movie. The idea for the clan, believe it or not, came from Jennie Livingston's *Paris is Burning*! I love that documentary; I love those fierce legendary children running around New York City forming their own "houses." I just took the idea to its next logical step and formed a house with supernatural grave robbers - The House of Murphy!

As for the supernatural cast, any particular visual influence in how you approached each kind of monster? I notice more of a tribute to past films in the shooting approach, production design, etc. and not the creatures of yesteryear. Do you have a favorite creature in the story?

The zombies are my favorite. My approach was to have them be more whimsical and curious than people are probably used to. I figure we've seen them every other way so why not tweak them a little. I referenced *Shock Waves* to the makeup guys; I wanted them waterlogged and dripping with seaweed.

How have festival audiences reacted to the film?

The response has been really great; it's given me a lot of confidence as a filmmaker. I've learned so much by showing my work to audiences. Not everybody is going to like this movie and some of the reactions have been negative, but for the most part, people are getting it.

I saw you do a Q&A where you mentioned writing a new film that wasn't a sequel to this, but that you would probably revisit this grave-robbing duo in the future. Can you tell me any of your plans for upcoming projects?

I am writing the further adventures of Grimes and Blake but that will hopefully go to comic book form before anything else. It's a collaboration with Brahm Revel who has already adapted *I Sell the Dead* into a comic, which will be coming out on Image Comics in October. Other than that, I am writing a few other projects. I really want to get something off the ground in Ireland as well as get another horror film going over here in the States. Either way I really want to have my next step as a writer / director be a bold move.

Any words of wisdom for filmmakers working towards that first feature, now that you're on the other side of it?

It is so important to take the time and think outside the box with your coverage. The camera really is your paintbrush and there are so many paint-by-numbers directors out there, if you want to make a career for yourself you really have to step up and tell your stories with confident strokes. That to me is the most exciting thing about film making and where the heart of it lies. Also having a solid vision and being able to articulate it in a timely manner is an absolute must.

2010-11

DARREN LYNN BOUSMAN
MARCUS DUNSTAN
NICK PRINCIPE
FRANK HENENLOTTER

DARREN LYNN BOUSMAN

Interviewed by Rob Galluzzo (9/10)

Considering director Darren Lynn Bousman's impressive body of work, which spans multiple *Saw* sequels, the rock musical *Repo! The Genetic Opera*, an episode of NBC's *Fear Itself* and the upcoming remake of *Mother's Day*, it's a surprise that we never got him in the hot seat for an extensive *Icons* interview. So, with the launch of *Massive Hysteria*, we decided that he would make for the ideal interviewee to kick things off in style! Bousman invited me over to his place for our career spanning chat, which took place in between sips of extra strong coffee with the sleazy "giallo" cult classic *Strip Nude for Your Killer* playing on his TV in the background.

What are your earliest recollections of the horror genre? Do you remember the first films to really impact and scare you?

Well, my brother was huge into horror when I was a kid and he had a lot of old EC comic books, and so it started with me reading all his old EC comics, which then led to me reading his *Dracula* comics. It's funny, because it wasn't a slow step into it, I basically dove in and the first movie he showed me was *Henry: Portrait of a Serial Killer*. And I was young! I was probably ten or eleven.

Here is my first horror memory. I was at pre-school and they had a lock in one night where basically all the kids were going to stay there overnight and the parents were going to pick them up the next morning. I woke up around midnight and all the workers were watching *Friday the 13th*, so I walked in and must've been there for at least two kills before I started bawling. I immediately started crying and they knew they were in trouble at that point, so they quickly ejected the VHS, quickly put something else on and then said to me "You didn't see that!" I'll never forget the memory of them trying to tell me that I didn't see what I thought I just saw. It was one hundred percent *Friday the 13th*.

Those two things really kind of fucked me up – *Friday* and *Henry*. And then the next one my brother showed me, which at the time my mind couldn't even process, was *Cannibal Holocaust*. That didn't do anything to erase those earlier memories. Then I backtracked into finding the things most people start off with like the Lon Chaney stuff. But it started out pretty hardcore.

No wonder you make such unpleasant films! (laughs) At some point, you're on a steady diet of these movies and you start to realize that there are people that were behind the making of them. So, when did your interest in the way films were made begin? And did you know right away that was something you wanted to do too?

The movie that I can go back to and remember that impacted me to the point where I wanted to go research it to try and figure out why I felt the way I did about it was *La Bamba*. I was a kid in grade school and *La Bamba* came out and I remember it made me so sad. Up until then, no movie had really made me sad. I'd been disgusted by movies, but no movie had ever made me sad. And I remember that was the thing that made me want to watch more and more movies. One of my best memories was going to a video store, which used to be such a cool thing. My dad would say, "Alright, it's Friday night, let's go get some movies." Just looking at the walls and walls of VHS tapes. It's kind of become so impersonal going to a video store now. They have ninety-five copies of the same movie and then maybe seven copies of something else. Back then, that was the most awesome thing being able to go to the video store with my dad. I saw *La Bamba* and I wanted to see other movies with those actors in it. At that point, Lou Diamond Phillips had just done *Young Guns*. The boxes of VHS tapes were so amazing, but then when you see the boxes in the horror section, those boxes were just so fucking awesome.

And so, it became a thing that my dad let me rent pretty much whatever I wanted to rent. There were no restrictions outside of hardcore pornography. I remember my parents took me to see *The Crying Game*. I was way too young to see *The Crying Game*, but I was mesmerized, so by that point, they let me rent whatever I wanted to rent. So, every Friday night, we'd rent a scary movie, then a comedy. I watched *A Nightmare on Elm Street* with my dad. That's how it all started for me, having these Friday night VHS viewing parties.

I really miss those days. Going to the video store and being so captivated by the amazing box art, especially for horror movies.

I buy movies based on titles these days. Like this movie playing now, *Strip Nude for Your Killer*. That's all I needed to hear was that title and I'm like "SOLD!" But I remember the bad-ass VHS boxes from all the movies, you never knew what you were going to get. You'd see like, *Monkey Shines*, and you'd see the monkey on the front cover and as a kid think, that's going to be awesome! I can't wait. But it was also a bonding experience with my dad. Every October, I would have the biggest party that everyone wanted to go to, and I thought I was all bad-ass. Meanwhile I was probably kind of a douche. (laughs) But the party was that we would go to all these haunted houses together. In Kansas City, haunted houses were huge. People spent millions of dollars to renovate these downtown warehouses and open them for two months. When you show up, there are lines that wrap around several huge city blocks. It's a huge festivity and there were always like ten or eleven of them downtown. People would come over and we'd watch two or three horror films, and then we'd all go out at midnight to downtown Kansas City for these haunted houses. So, I have this very nostalgic feeling for that and it all revolves around horror, which is why I never really grew out of it.

When did you first officially dabble in filmmaking?

I made my first thing in middle school. I'll never forget it; it was called *Midnight Sons*. And I used *The Doors* as a background soundtrack. The thing that was cool was that it didn't turn out terrible. I realized that music saved how bad anything else was in the movie. You could put *The Doors* over anything, and it'd be cool. I did that and it was a bank heist; us thirteen-year-olds trying to do a bank heist and make it look cool. (laughs) That was the first thing that I did, but I was writing way before that. The first story that I ever wrote was for a seventh grade English class. And my dad is my hero in so many different ways, but I'll never forget this; I wrote this story called *Cabin 9*. I remember when I was in fifth grade, I was already reading Stephen King, I

was reading *The Shining* then. By the time I was in seventh grade, I was well versed in Dean Koontz and King and I knew horror.

So, I wrote this short story called *Cabin 9* and got an F on it. The teacher said it was plagiarist. The teacher said, "You plagiarized this, there's no way that a twelve-year-old kid wrote this." I called my mom crying telling her they gave me an F and why. I'm sitting in the middle of class, and I hear my dad coming down the hall. "Darren! Darren!" He seriously opens the door up and he goes, "Are you the English teacher? I'm Mister Bousman. You're going to come talk to me in the hallway right now." My dad began to berate the English teacher telling him, "I sat there and I watched him write that story. You have no right to accuse him of plagiarism." So, I got an A. The teacher apologized to me in front of the class. So, that was my first thing that I did was writing these horror short stories.

The story as I know it in terms of how you got Twisted Pictures attention for *Saw II* was that you had this script circulating for *The Desperate*, which eventually became the basis of *Saw II*. So where were you in your career at this point? Because by then, you'd already directed the stage version of *Repo! The Genetic Opera*, right?

I had directed the *Repo* show by then. I moved out to LA in 2000. Right off the bat, I thought I was going to be ok because I got a job on *The X-Files*, immediately. Day one being here, I got a job on that show. And I was working all the time, making pretty good money. But then I was fired, because I quickly got upset. Seriously, I was a bitch. I was getting coffee; I was standing in a corner making sure that no one walked through it. It was just making me mad, it had nothing to do with filmmaking, and I guess at that point I had delusions of grandeur that I was this amazing filmmaker, and they could all go fuck themselves. I got bitter and angry, and I was kindly asked never to return. There was a two-month period where I didn't work at all. But I am a great talker in the room. Or maybe a great bullshit artist. (laughs) Put me in any room and I can get people excited.

So, I talked myself into a development exec position at a place called Hallway Pictures, which was a completely urban based company. They did *Shaft* and *Why Do Fools Fall in Love* and I was somehow able to talk myself into that company. I was fired after they realized I was just some white dude from the midwest that doesn't know shit about urban comedy. Then I was fired from *Van Wilder* where I was told, "We've done research on you. You've been fired from every job you've had." I was actually told, "You are never going to get a job in Hollywood. You're done." And

I went through a six-month streak where I couldn't get a job. I couldn't even get a coffee job. I couldn't get shit. And so, I got fed up, I got angry and I finished this script that I'd been dabbling in called *The Desperate*. I labeled it after I was finished with it because that's exactly what I was, I was desperate. Desperate to prove that I was a writer, prove that I was a director. And the whole point of it was just me being angry, it was my way to vent. That script went around for about a year where various different people tried to get it made but couldn't.

Eventually, this guy said he was going to make it for a million dollars, said he was going to let me direct it, but said that he was going to co-direct it with me. He was kind of a shady dude. I had already went out looking for DP's and I had met David Armstrong, who had just finished as a cinematographer on *Saw I*. He looked at it and said, "Do me a favor. Give me twenty-four hours and don't let anyone else read this." David brought it in to Twisted Pictures and twenty-four hours later, Twisted Pictures made an offer to me. It happened very quickly in the realm of *The Desperate* becoming *Saw II*, but it took me five years to get from the point of coming out to LA, getting shitty jobs all over the place to actually being on set shooting *Saw II*.

When Twisted picked it up, did they always intend on making it *Saw II*, or were they thinking of making it its own film as *The Desperate*?

Again, one of the things I've learned about Hollywood is that filmmaking is ninety-five percent politics and five percent creativity. I basically strong-armed myself into directing it, because I was attached to direct *The Desperate*. It was its own independent film; it wasn't part of a franchise, so they didn't care if I directed it. Then when it turned into *Saw II*, my contract said, "The Desperate *or any variation thereof*," and so when they changed it to *Saw II*, I legally was still attached to direct it. They were really cool though. They let me do it and it's crazy how it just takes one instance for everything to change. I'd been out here doing the same thing for years and years and years and in one instance, everything changed.

At the time of *Saw II*, you didn't really have a director's reel that catered to horror, so you went out and shot the short film *Zombie*, which is on the DVD for *Saw II*, right?

I actually shot *Zombie* twice. The first time I shot it, it turned out really, really bad, so I did it again. I shot the original *Zombie* about six months prior to that and I just threw it away. It was so bad. But when they told me I had to have a short film to show them, we went out in two days and shot

it, edited it and re-did it. It's still a bad short film, but it was something we did in an afternoon that showed them that I could direct. And again, at that point, I didn't know if I wanted to be a director, I knew I wanted to be a writer. Up until college, I was an acting major. Eventually I dropped acting and went into filmmaking.

When *Saw II* came out, it was still the beginning of that franchise. At what point did you realize that *Saw* was becoming bigger than any of you ever thought it could be?

Even when *Saw II* was done, no one knew that it was going to turn into a franchise. First of all, I was in pre-production up in Toronto on *Saw II* before *Saw I* came out. There was about a two to three week period where I thought I was going to be fired off of *Saw II* when they realized how big *Saw I* was. At that point, Lionsgate had no idea that *Saw I* was going to do what it was, and here I am, a first-time director out there and they've got a huge franchise on their hands. After *Saw II* was finished, they wanted to put it straight to video. And there was a huge chain of emails that were sent around saying, "Are you insane? This is not a straight to video movie." And luckily it ended up going theatrical and *Saw II* made more than *Saw I* did and at that point, I think they knew we had a franchise here.

The turnaround on all the *Saw* films is very fast, but how soon after you did *II* did you know you'd be back for *III*?

Here's the reality of Hollywood and it's sad. You're only as good as the last movie you did. Example – Oren Peli, the director of *Paranormal Activity* can go out right now and he could make *National Treasure 3* and be given $100 million dollars or Daniel Stamm who did *The Last Exorcism* could go out and do the next James Bond movie. Why? Because right now, he has a massive fucking success on his hands. When *Saw II* came out, it was a massive fucking success. It blew records. When *Saw III* came out, it blew records. I could've done pretty much anything at that point. The deal with the *Saw* films and why I stayed with them was first off, it was such a great experience. The crew, Lionsgate at the time, everyone was just awesome. On top of that, it was a guaranteed release date. There was a guarantee that it was going to come out in theaters one year to the date. No film has this. Look at *Mother's Day*. It's sitting on a shelf right now and probably won't be released for at least another six months. Because most films don't have release dates. I didn't want to be in a situation where I finally had done something, and I didn't want to wait for the next thing to take two years to come out, so we signed on for *Saw III*.

And *Saw III* was a lot more creatively liberating for me, even though I didn't write it, I worked on the story for *Saw III* probably more than I did for *Saw II*. And of all the *Saw* films that I did, it's my favorite one because it's the most emotional, it's the most character driven, it's not necessarily the best one, but in my mind was elevated above what some of the other films are. It was crazy. It happened so quickly. I did *Saw II* and went on a press tour for that. I was in Japan; I was in Germany. I came back, it was released and then I was on a plane three weeks later to shoot *Saw III*. So, at that point, it wasn't like *Saw* had opened up and made a billion dollars and I got a million offers. That's not what happened. *Saw II* wasn't out yet, it opened, I was doing a press tour and three weeks later, I was on a plane to do the next one. So, I think maybe if there was a lag in between there, I probably would've done something else. But I'm glad I didn't. I'm glad I did *Saw III*.

Your intent was to not do the fourth film, I remember initially you were going to walk away after *Saw III*. Obviously, there's a lot of little nuggets and teases in *Saw III* of things that would eventually be explored in future installments. So, I'm just curious, now that we're up to the seventh one, how far in advance were you guys thinking of certain plot threads. There's the quick flash of Betsy Russell, the thing with the letter, emphasis on Hoffman in that one scene…

It was important for me to put those little hints in, because in my favorite franchises, the films connect. They're not afterthoughts. James Wan didn't have an afterthought for what *Saw II* would be. He wasn't thinking of that, he just wanted to make the best *Saw* film on its own. That kind of shot us in the leg in a lot of ways. With *Saw II*, we hoped it would be a franchise, so we started putting little things in there. I don't like movies that fit in a box. I don't like every question being answered, in fact that kind of makes me mad. My hope would be that you don't answer questions because then it gives you something to talk about. There's nothing fun to talk about with a movie when you know what everything was. So doing the letter was on purpose. What could we not answer for the audience to have them talking about it? We had our own interpretations what all these answers were, but we didn't want to tell anyone because again, we wanted people to talk about it. I think that's what makes movies exciting. So, when we started *Saw III*, we specifically had five or six story points that we weren't going to answer. So yeah, it was set up. Did we know what the end of the franchise was? No, I don't think anyone could say they really did. Maybe on *Saw IV*, we started thinking

where it would inevitably go to, but when we did *Saw III*, we did not know where *Saw VII* was going to go. Ask Mark Burg though, he'll probably say differently. (laughs)

I remember when you came back on board for *Saw IV*, you were quoted as saying the thing that made you want to do it was that the script by Marcus Dunstan and Patrick Melton had a twist that totally got you. What exactly was the twist that brought you back?

Do you know what it was? I think for *Saw IV*, I love the idea that something was happening parallel. Everyone's always looking for a twist now and it's like a magic trick. You go to The Magic Castle, and I don't care who you are, you're always trying to figure out how the magician is doing it. I think with *Saw*, by the time that *Saw IV* came around, I was looking for the twist. I thought I knew exactly what it was going to be. And then when it got to the point where it was happening parallel and simultaneously as *Saw III*, that was not something I was looking for. So, to me, that was exciting. The problem with *Saw IV* was that way too many things were going on in my life at that point. *Saw II* and *Saw III* had both been huge successes and there I was getting offers to do other bigger films. But all I cared about was making *Repo*. The deal was they were going to make *Repo* right after *Saw* ended. Pre-production for *Repo* was pretty much backed up against *Saw* and so on a given day, I would get fifty emails for *Repo* while I was doing *Saw IV*. And it became a nightmare. In retrospect, I would've done it differently. *Saw IV* was kind of a fog.

You're notorious for saying that a lot of *Saw IV*, including the sets, went into *Repo*.

Yeah, yeah, it completely did. (laughs)

I've heard a lot of rumors regarding the original casting on *Repo*. Are you able to talk about that at all?

Yeah, originally, Anthony Stewart Head was always my original choice. He was the guy that I wanted from day one when we first started going after people, but he's not a name that if you say to an "executive," they'd recognize. When you say he's in *Buffy the Vampire Slayer*, then they know who he is. They wanted a name that would sell foreign. So, the name that we all agreed on at that point was Patrick Swayze. Patrick Swayze was cast. He was actually rehearsing with us, and he left the project about a week or two before we started recording the music. At that point, I was left with no Repo Man. It was a blessing in disguise though because I was able to go back to the producers and say, "I want Anthony Stewart Head." I launched a campaign for this guy and here we are a week before we have to record this album and we have no one, so they allowed me to bring him in. Luckily, he loved the project, and it became serendipitous after that. Originally it was Swayze. He was great and he had a great voice. Patrick was really, really nice. We talked numerous times. He was in the recording studio every day. But it all worked out with Anthony Stewart Head.

And by the way, I really like *Saw IV* a lot…

You're the one! (laughs)

Well, stylistically as a director, I like it! I love the progressions of your transition shots from *Saw II* and on. By the time we got to *Saw IV*, it was just absolutely ridiculous all the transitions you were doing!

I know, I know. On *Saw IV*, I got more creative because I didn't care. I really didn't care. When I did *Saw II*, it was the first film I ever did, and that was my one shot, I could've fucked it all up. In *Saw III*, they knew they had a huge franchise, so everyone was looking at me under a microscope to make sure I didn't kill the franchise. By the time *Saw IV* came around, I didn't give a fuck because I'd proven in *Saw II* and *Saw III* that I could do it, so people left me alone. And so, we tried some radical things. That twist is pretty insane if you think about it. We had to go back and rewatch it to make sure it worked. People had to be ambiguous; they had to say things that meant two different things. The transitions, you only see about half of what we shot. Not even in the director's cut! We shot some insane things that they were like, "Come on, Darren!"

This is my favorite one and I think they put it back in the director's cut, but this is a funny story. There's a scene in *Saw IV* where Jigsaw is next to Betsy Russell's bed and he's holding her hand and then he says something to her and throws down the watch. When he stands up, Betsy Russell is in a different outfit on the other side of the room talking to Strahm, in the interrogation room. It was a very complex thing where we built a hospital set next to an interrogation room and we had walls moving. The best was it was so subtle yet so complex that it confused Mark Burg. He was like, "What the fuck just happened?" They spent a tremendous amount of money to remove a reflection of Jigsaw in the interrogation mirror, because it blew his mind. "It's going to confuse our audience!" It's still in the movie, kind of, but what we shot was way more elaborate.

Even the color scheme on *Saw IV*, I always thought stood out. In particular, the autopsy at the beginning where everything looks like it's black and white except the red from the blood when they cut Jigsaw's body open. Was that a stylistic choice?

Regarding the color schemes, *Saw* always had that greenish thing that's in all of Jigsaw's scenes. So, we decided in the autopsy, Jigsaw is dead so there would be an absence of color. Because if you look at the *Saw* films, everywhere that Jigsaw touches or is, is green. It's always got a green hue to it, so we wanted to do something different when we went into the autopsy, because again Jigsaw is dead and he's passing it on to this guy.

Obviously, a lot of people talk online about this; what kills or traps have you shot that you weren't able to use, or that didn't make it into one of the films?

The glass case in *Saw IV* and we actually shot the whole trap scene. I loved it. They loved it and they wanted to put it in *Saw V*. And it made me a bit upset, because why would you hold something that would work great for *Saw IV* just to use it in *Saw V*? Let's make *Saw IV* great, then worry about the traps for *Saw V*. They cut it out of the movie, and it was a big fight. But yeah, they cut that scene. There's a lot that we almost did – probably the most upsetting trap to me, which was a nightmare, the one that almost made me have a nervous breakdown – it was the most complex thing, the couple pulling the rods out…

The rods through the pressure points.

Right, that was a real thing that we read about. A guy had a pole through him, but they knew if they pulled it out, the artery would've broke and he would've bled to death. So, they had to leave the pole in, cut it, cauterize it, and then slowly pull it out. So, we got this great idea from that. We didn't have the trap worked out as to how we would do it. We were already shooting *Saw IV* by that point. And so finally I put my foot down and said, "This is what I want to shoot, we're going to do it!" And then we realized how complex it was, because there's no poles there, it's all green screen stuff. Then having a 360 shot and realizing we'd have to put poles in there afterwards? It was a nightmare. I had a breakdown and started crying on the set, because my head hurt too much. (laughs) I couldn't figure it out. It was towards the end of shooting. Also, while shooting *Saw IV*, mentally, I was not in a good place, because on *Saw IV*, and I think they've done it this way ever since, they shoot all the dialogue up front and then they shoot the traps at the very end.

So, on *Saw IV*, it was four weeks of people fucking talking! And I remember calling Peter Block and saying, "Dude, we're making a mistake. I'm on week four of Betsy Russell talking!" That's why I added the glass box scene, which was never in the script. I added it at the very end of the shoot because I thought we needed something else that was cool. But yeah, I had a lot of mental instability on *Saw IV*, because I was concerned that the script was going to turn into a talking movie and when it comes to *Saw*, that's not what the fans pay to see.

We also had a different ending that Lyriq Bent and I wish we shot. I really believe that if we got to shoot the ending we wanted to do, it would've done something huge for the movie. What Lyriq and I planned was to do the opposite of what the twist was. We wanted him to actually figure out what he was supposed to do, because the whole thing about *Saw* is that nobody ever realizes what they're supposed to do. He didn't realize that he was supposed to let Eric Matthews go. What if he did realize it? What if he didn't open the door? Again, make the twist being something different. He actually didn't do it. He stops at the door, he breaks down crying, doesn't save him. He gets up and sees Agent Strahm with the gun. Strahm sees Lyriq with the gun, thinks he's Jigsaw and just shoots and kills Lyriq there. That would've been fucking awesome, and people would've talked about it. We ended up not shooting it and only shooting the way it ends now, but I'm really upset because I think it would've been a whole lot more dramatic if we did that. Actually, I wish I could just go back, and re-shoot *Saw IV*. (laughs) Maybe they won't make any more *Saw* films after *Saw 3D*, but they can let me re-shoot *Saw IV*.

(laughs) You mentioned in the *Saw IV* commentary that you shot at least an additional five minutes of scenes after Hoffman walks away at the end. What was that stuff?

They used it for *Saw V*. It's funny, there's actually a lot of the stuff I shot in *Saw VI*. It used to end that after Hoffman walked out of the room, he walked downstairs, got the little girl out, they walked outside, blankets were thrown over them, she was put into an ambulance; there was a whole section of them leaving the warehouse, but we ended it there. It's a better ending where we ended because we ended on a high note. But yeah, we shot quite a bit more.

Obviously, you got Donnie Wahlberg to come back as Eric Matthews for two more of the *Saw* sequels. I remember when *Saw IV* was going into production, rumor had it he really didn't want to do it. And even after it came out,

rumor had it he wasn't happy that he did it. I wonder if you could shed some light on that?

He was so mad at me. (laughs) He won't even talk to me right now! Donnie and I became really good friends after *Saw II*. Donnie and I had a run in on the first one we did together while we were shooting. Like a massive run in where I think he was ready to quit. Because here I am, a young fresh filmmaker to him doing *Saw II* and I always busted his balls about being in *New Kids on The Block* before I really knew him. So, I think he was pissed at me, and then one day he got really upset. It was really early on, and I think it's because I didn't know what I wanted him to do. And eventually Lyriq Bent came up to me and said, "You cut a scene together. Just show him a scene. Let him know that you know what you're doing."

So, I called Donnie and Dina Meyer over and I showed them a scene. I do a lot of weird shit that might not make a lot of sense to people. A lot of what I do on the *Saw* films is what's going on in their head. So, there's a scene where Donnie's standing at a fence, and I go, "OK, Donnie stand at the fence, don't make any emotion, just stand there and don't do a thing. OK, now punch the fence! OK, now scream like a tiger." And he's like, "What the fuck? I feel like an idiot!" "Donnie, just scream like a tiger!" And then I'd say, "Donnie, stand there and jump up and down. Turn the camera on and off." He's like, "What the fuck am I doing?" So, I showed him that finished scene, it's actually in the movie, and it's cool because it's what's going on in his head, so the minute he saw it cut together, he was like, "I'm sorry. I get it now." And ever since then, we became really good friends.

I called him back for *Saw III*. He didn't know if he wanted to do *Saw III*. And I'm like, "Come on!" He's like, "but I ended on top in *Saw II*." "No, no, come back to *Saw III* for like a minute." "Alright, I'll come back but I want to be in and out in a couple of days." And then when I called him on *Saw IV*, he said no. I played the guilt card on him. "If you don't come, they're not going to make the movie and blah, blah, blah." And he's like, "Fuck!" He was so angry at me, but he flew in, and did it and I think the entire time he was pissed at me. (laughs)

He did kind of go out like a bitch in *Saw IV*.

That's what he was saying! "I'm crying. I'm a fucking bitch up here! Why couldn't you let me die in the bathroom!" (laughs) Yeah, it was pretty bad.

What's it been like for you having been with *Saw* for three films to now see the subsequent sequels as a fan?

It's a little weird. *Saw V* is a weird movie, and this is no disrespect to director David Hackl. I think they churn them out so quickly that *Saw V* was not as fleshed out as it could've been. I would've done *Saw V* differently. I wouldn't have done some of the choices that he did, that's not to say that what he did was bad at all, it's just that I would've done it differently. It didn't seem to connect and there were things in it that I just didn't get. I really, really, really liked *Saw VI*, the one Kevin Greutert did. I think it revived the franchise a bit. I think I was the one that was like jumping the shark in *Saw IV*, I was like jumping in mid-air and then it ended. And David Hackl had to continue my jump. And Kevin Greutert brought it back a little bit. I think David is a great director and he's a great production designer and I'm looking forward to see what David does next. I just wish they would've spent a little more time between the movies and fleshed out those stories a little bit better.

Well, by *Saw IV*, the series became episodic, much like a television show and they purposely didn't answer all the questions raised and that frustrated fans. It felt like things kept being saved for the next movie and that doesn't make for a satisfying experience for the fans on the current movie.

It does frustrate people. And at that point also, *Saw* became so huge, that instead of going back in under a microscope and making sure that everything made sense and questioning if this would deliver to the fans, it was like, "We're fucking *Saw*! We're awesome!" That's the problem anytime anything gets big, you start to believe the hype. You can't believe the hype. You have to go back and do exactly what you did on *Saw I* and *Saw II* and *Saw III*, and make sure that you look at everything under a microscope. My problem was I didn't do that on *Saw IV*. I didn't. I was making *Repo! The Genetic Opera* when I was making *Saw IV* and so I learned my lesson. The funny thing is a lot of people like *Saw IV*. I guess something worked in it. I like a lot about it. The hair trap I love. And I do like seeing Donnie's head get squished by those two ice blocks. (laughs) That's pretty awesome.

You got to do an episode of *Fear Itself* titled *New Year's Day*, which started your working relationship with Briana Evigan. So, what was it like going from feature films to tackling a TV show?

That was after *Repo*, and it was while I was still cutting *Repo*. The problem was when I did *New Year's Day*, it was a vacation, it was to get away. I had become obsessed with *Repo*. It became all immersive. I had been for two and a half

years fighting and fighting to get *Repo* made and fighting and fighting to get it released. And so, this *New Year's Day* came up and it allowed me to go on vacation for three weeks and do something else and step outside of *Repo*. It was actually not the most fun experience. Again, with *Saw*, I was in that family, I knew everything, I knew everybody, I knew the story, I knew the world. So that was that.

With *Repo*, I spent ten years trying to get the movie made, so I knew that world, I knew what I wanted to do. With *New Year's Day*, it wasn't that. I flew into a city that I'd never been to before, and it was like, "You shoot in seven days. Here's your script. Figure it out." And it was extremely difficult. The thing with Briana is funny; I have a crush on Briana and she knows it, everybody does. I saw her in *Step Up 2* and I said to my wife, fiancé at the time, my next thing I'm doing, she's in it. So, I called her agent up and said, "I have a crush on your client, I want to put her in this thing." (laughs) So she said sure and flew in and shot the thing. I was like this creepy old man. (laughs)

By the end of this show, we became really good friends, we were hanging out and she was just so down to earth and really cool. I felt bad because *New Year's Day* was on TV so I had to adhere to all these rules, and there were guidelines and restrictions, and I wanted to work with her when none of that applied, where I could actually work with her. So, I thanked her for doing *New Year's Day* and told her I'd put her in the next movie that I do. Luckily, we did *Mother's Day* together.

For a while there, you were rumored to be attached to several remakes, everything from *Scanners* to *Hellraiser* to *Children of the Corn*. Did any of these ever come close to really happening with you as the director?

Scanners was really close. I was stoked about that one. David Goyer wrote the script, and it just didn't come together. David turned the last draft in four days before the writer's strike. Everything during that time just kind of fell apart. Yeah, I was attached to *Children of the Corn*, *Scanners*, *Hellraiser*, *Battle Royale*. Well, *Battle Royale* was more me wishing to be attached to it. (laughs) But the issue, for every one movie I make, there's twenty-five movies I'm attached to that'll never happen. There are all these movies that as a director you never know which ones are actually going to go through. And so, you put yourself on as many as you actually believe in as possible and out of those, one maybe two will happen.

Those were all Dimension movies. I signed a deal with Dimension right after *Saw II*. What makes money is sequels and remakes, so Dimension basically pulled out every remake that they had and tried to get me attached to them. I couldn't wrap my head around *Hellraiser*. I met with Clive Barker. Clive and I came up with a take, which I loved. Bob Weinstein and team did not love it. Here's the thing, the only way I'd do a remake is if the original creator endorses the vision. I wouldn't want to do a remake where Clive Barker would be pissed off or his fans would be pissed.

So, I wanted to meet with Clive and come up with a take together on it. Clive and I came up with something that we really liked, and it just didn't come through. *Scanners*, it was funny because I got to meet David Cronenberg and it was bad ass meeting him, but I went up to him and was like, "Hey David, I'm actually attached to the Scanners remake," and he looked at me and goes, "Yeah, that's great." And walked away. (laughs) He was not very happy about that. *Scanners* just didn't come together. The script was a bit off.

I flip-flopped on *Children of the Corn*. Originally, I didn't want to do it, so I passed on it. And right after I passed on it, I thought, fuck I want to do it. But by then it was too late, I was already out of my Dimension deal. *Children of the Corn* is something I would remake now that I think about it. I had a big problem wrapping my head around the concept of how can a town be completely overrun by children, where they basically killed all the parents and they've been living like this, and nobody knew about it? I couldn't figure it out with today's technology. With cell phones, with PDA's, with laptops, with iPad's. I didn't buy it. And they wanted it to be modern, they didn't want to set it as a period piece. I couldn't figure it out and then I finally did figure out a take into it, but by that time I had moved on.

One thing I thought that was interesting that you mentioned on one of your commentaries was how pivotal music is to you while you're developing projects. I was wondering if you could talk about that a bit? Do you make music mixes when you get a piece of material that you're developing or during the writing process?

It is. I'm writing the script right now for this movie called *11 11 11* and it's kind of consuming my life. I try to write based on a song. I always try to base whatever I'm writing on a particular song, whatever that movie is to me. So, when I wrote *The Desperate*, for example, there's a song by Bright Eyes called "Arienette." If you listen to the lyrics to it and you actually go back and watch *Saw II*, you'll see some exact parallels from it. When I was coming up and we were doing *Mother's Day*, it was the same thing. There were three or four songs I actually played on set, prior to shooting. In fact, Rebecca De Mornay had me play these songs for her in

pre-production on set. I think music moves people, it makes them feel a certain way, it triggers emotions that might have been oppressed. And I think music is the thing that is a character. It will end up being a character in your film. So yeah, I always think when I'm starting a project, what's the feel? What's the music? Is it Tom Waits? Is it REM? Is it Muse? Who is the feel of it, and I'll make a mix. For example, right now there's a playlist on my computer called *11 11*. And it has things like Portishead and The Ditty Bops. It's like weird music with female singers, because it's ethereal. Again, I always do that. I think people take for granted how important music is, especially when it comes to creating art.

You've been really fortunate to work with some amazing actors from movie to movie. Tobin Bell for the *Saw* movies. You've got guys like Paul Sorvino in *Repo*. Rebecca De Mornay in *Mother's Day*. How do you get some of these names to work on your projects? Is it a matter of luck? Persistence? Or maybe a bit of both?

Well, each movie is completely different. I have a list of people, the Bousman repertoire, that will be in everything that I do. Once you're in that, there will always be an open invitation for you to come back. For example, J. LaRose is a very close and dear friend, and he will be in everything that I do. If he wants to be. He doesn't have to be, but the offer will always be there. Lyriq Bent's another example. Tony Nappo who was in *Saw II*, I brought him back in *Saw IV*. He was in *Repo* and he got cut. He's in *Mother's Day*. Alexa Vega is in *Mother's Day*. Again, these are people I connect with that get me. Here's the issue, anyone in the creative field, be it an actor, director, producer, there's stories about you. "I heard he's insane and did this, this and this!" It always sounds bad unless you were there, and you witnessed what caused or whatever led to it. These are people that have been with me from the very beginning that know who I truly am, that the stories aren't real. Lyriq Bent was the first guy to stick up for me when Donnie got upset. Lyriq gets me. Now Donnie gets me. These people get me. And I think it's more fun to work with people that are your friends. And they're incredible actors.

Mother's Day and *Repo* were crazy with the casting. *Repo*, I cast every single person in it. In the very end, everyone I wanted I got. I said I want Alexa Vega. I got her. I said I wanted Sarah Brightman. We got her. Terrance Zdunich was already in it. Bill Moseley was a personal friend of mine, so I went to Bill Moseley. With *Repo*, I probably could've gotten anyone because it's such a weird movie. Actors get the same script over and over and over again. They want to do something different, something that's creative and challenging. So, I lucked out that I got everyone that I wanted on *Repo*. *Mother's Day* was crazy because I had to fight harder to get the brothers more than anything else. I really wanted Patrick Flueger, Warren Kole and Matt O'Leary. The producers wanted big names. It took me three months to get Patrick Flueger who plays Ike. They met with every actor in town and finally they let me have him. My favorite was Deborah Ann Woll from *True Blood*. Deborah comes in and the minute she walks in the door, I said, "You're cast, you don't have to read." She's like, "What?" You're cast! I was such a huge *True Blood* fan, so she was cast right as she walked in.

Rebecca (De Mornay) was hard because there were so many different avenues to go with mother. Originally, we were talking about going with an older mother, like an Ellen Burstyn. Nah, let's go with a more subdued Sissy Spacek like mother. Then we had rewatched *The Hand That Rocks the Cradle* and Rebecca's bat-shit crazy in that one. The problem with Rebecca is she's beautiful. When she came in, we're all like, 'She's hot!' She's not motherly. How do we make her look like we don't want to bang her? I'm sure she'll love me saying that. I have lucked out. But probably that's the hardest thing about filmmaking now is that directors in this genre are stuck in a specific budget range, unless you can cast higher level names.

The problem is that no actor wants to do a movie that glorifies violence or that's fucked up and dark. You're not going to get the high-level actors for that, so it's a catch twenty-two. You have to cast a high-level name or you can't get a high level name in this genre. I'm talking like, to get George Clooney to be in a *Saw* movie or Brad Pitt to be in a *Hostel* movie, it's not the easiest thing in the world. It's a very hard catch twenty-two casting these types of movies.

How have you changed from movie to movie as a director in terms of your relationship with the actors? What have you learned from them on each experience and going into the next one?

I'm more an actor's director now. I wasn't on *Saw II*. I think the biggest change that happened to me, in the *Saw* films, it was all about the cool transitions, the camera set-ups, etc. But with that said, I majored in acting. That's what I wanted to do. So, I came from a place of knowing what they want to hear. Knowing their fears and knowing their insecurities, because I had them when I was on stage. I was doing big theatrical productions. I was seventy pounds lighter and went to the gym all the time. So, I knew to some extent what to say. Also, I'm very outgoing and personable. I go out with the cast, I hang out with them, so we form

these relationships and bonds. With *Repo*, I'm dealing with Sarah Brightman, I'm dealing with Anthony Stewart Head. At that point Alexa Vega, I had just met, and she'd worked with Robert Rodriguez, Martin Scorsese, Joss Whedon. I was forced to talk to them in a way that was all about their performance, because I wanted them to create something that was memorable long after you left the theater.

That translated very much into *Mother's Day*. *Mother's Day* is a success of epic proportions on an acting front, because here's a movie that could've been just genre fare fodder. It could've been any one of these countless horror titles of home invasion. But I think focusing on Rebecca's performance and Deborah Ann Woll's performance and Shawn Ashmore's performance elevated the movie to make it more realistic. Now, I get more out of talking to the actors than I do talking to the D.P. I've used the same D.P. now on three different things. I trust him. He knows what I like, he knows what I don't like. So, I'll talk to him for a second, and trust him to do his job, so that I can go talk to the actors. Because in the very end, they're the ones that are going to bring the performances to life. And great actors can make a bad movie excellent. I watch a lot of low budget films, a lot of terrible movies. The story can be awesome, the camerawork can be fucking great, but if you have a bad actor, I lose interest. I think I'm now realizing the importance of acting and getting those performances out of the people.

Of all the remakes we mentioned, why *Mother's Day*?

I always said I would never do a remake of a movie I actually liked. And I don't dislike the original *Mother's Day*, but it's not a great film. I think Lloyd and Charlie Kaufman would be the first to say that. It had a great idea. It had amazingly horrific, hilarious performances. It was ahead of its time and had social commentary in it, but it doesn't stand up today. If you were to honestly put *Mother's Day* in front of a bunch of cinephiles and say, 'What do you think of this movie?' It's a product of its time. It is what it is. If you look at *Brazil* or *Blade Runner*, those movies hold up. There are things that are amazing about them that you can't possibly make any better. With *Mother's Day*, it was a film I looked at where I thought, OK, I can do something unique and different with this without stepping on Charles and Lloyd's toes and basically tearing their film apart. That was the first thing I said to them. I don't want to fuck with your movie. This is your movie, *Mother's Day* from 1980. I want to do a different version of this movie.

What would happen if that family lived right now and in today? What if we got rid of the comedy approach and did a dramatic approach? Take the same characters you created but take a dramatic approach with them. It might come off as insulting remaking someone's movie… I mean, I guess it's cool because you get money, but if someone twenty years from now came to me and wanted to remake *Repo*, I'd get upset because I put such passion into it, and it had such an impact on my life. That's how everyone feels that spends years of their lives devoted to something. For Charles and Lloyd, that was their *Repo* twenty years ago. So, I didn't want to go through and try to do a carbon copy of what they did. If you want to see that movie, go rent the original *Mother's Day*. But I did like the concept of a mother and her perverted relationship with her sons and the people around them. That's why I picked *Mother's Day* because it was a movie I felt I could do something unique to that wasn't done back then when they made it.

Are you a fan of the other Troma titles?

I am a Troma fan. I have a ton of their movies, and I think they're awesome because they don't give a fuck! They don't care. They just go out, have fun and make their movies. And the problem was, if I were going to do *Scanners* or *Children of the Corn*, I actually legitimately like those movies for what they did. How do you go in and remake a Cronenberg movie? How would you do that? The weight on your shoulders to do something like that is insane. With *Mother's Day*, the fact is that unless you're in the horror community, the majority of people have not seen the original.

I had a really tough time processing your version of *Mother's Day* after seeing it. I liked it a lot, but it's a very unpleasant movie and that's not normally the type of genre film I like to see. While I understand their importance to the horror genre, I'm not exactly a huge fan of things like *Last House on the Left* or *The Hills Have Eyes* or *Funny Games*. Again, while they are good movies, they're all unpleasant experiences. That said, *Mother's Day* is your best film as a director. Of that sub-genre of horror, it's the best of this type of story. And the ensemble of talented actors in this are unlike anything I've seen in a genre film like this.

Well, thank you. I appreciate that. I'll tell you why I think *Mother's Day* is an important film and this is just a side-tracking of the fucked up nature of Hollywood. Staci Wilson from *Horror.com* came up to me after the movie and said, "I don't know what to say. I just feel empty inside." Uncle Creepy from Dread Central, I showed it to him and the next day, he said, "I just want to go in the bathtub and cry." The reason that I love that comment specifically about this film

is that it leaves you with a cold, hollow feeling that when you walk out of the theater, you're either mad, you feel upset or gipped, you just want to talk to someone about it because you're thinking, "What the fuck did I just watch?" That translates negatively when you're going to screen it for a studio because there's nothing happy about *Mother's Day*. There really are no laughs. It's not a fun movie, it leaves you and it rapes you emotionally and then it just ends. I love that because it'll stay with you a day or two after you leave the theater and that's a hard thing to do with movies these days.

Look, I loved *Piranha 3D*. Seriously, loved it. But I forgot about it a half hour after I left the theater. I really, legitimately like Alex Aja's movies, but I forgot about *Piranha 3D* right after I saw it. The same can be said for the majority of horror films coming out these days. You pay your twelve dollars (or twenty in *Piranha*'s case) and when the movie ends, it's over and you're onto the next thing. I want to do films that it's not over when the movie ends. That you obsess over how much you hate the movie ala *Repo*, which there's a fraction of people that spend so much time talking about how much they hate it, or there's a fraction of people that drive hours and hours two years after its release to see *Repo* in theaters. *Repo* was a dangerous film, but it's a film that continues to live on. It continues to live off of other people's hate and other people's love. Those are the movies I want to do. *Mother's Day*, I don't know if it's going to get the same kind of hate it or love it reaction, but it's definitely going to make you upset when you leave the theater and that's what I want. I want people to feel empty when they leave the theater, because that's the thing, you're actually feeling something. That's the big thing with film, the great films make you feel when you leave the theater.

I remember when I saw *Requiem for a Dream* for the first time. For a week after the fact, all I wanted to do was talk about *Requiem for a Dream*. About how disgusted and disturbed and horrific I thought it was. I guarantee after I watch *Strip Nude for Your Killer* right here, I'm done talking about it. (laughs) That's what I aspire to do with my movies. I learned more about filmmaking on *Repo* than I did on any of the *Saw* films, because I saw the importance of how you leave an audience. Forget the movie itself, but what is the experience I as a filmmaker want to have with the audience? And I think when I went into *Mother's Day*, as Scott Milam and I were coming up with the idea, we thought how do we want to leave the audience? How can we accomplish that? To me, it was not about cool transitions this time. In fact, we cut the transitions out because it was too gimmicky. I shot probably my best transition ever and we cut it out. It killed me because it was so awesome. They're on the phone trying to get a hold of mother, and Ike grabbed the phone and he's like, "Lydia! Where are you?" And you see a 360 degree of the house. He grabs the phone and when he comes back, we removed all the walls and we push outside and it's raining outside and she's on the phone. Then we pull back, she walks forward and when he crosses back, the walls are back up in place. It was awesome, it took us a day and a half of choreography, but it got cut. It became too gimmicky. Where *Mother's Day* succeeds is in the performances. I didn't need to do gimmicks to sell the fear, to sell the terror. They did it themselves. Deborah Ann Woll. Shawn Ashmore. Patrick Flueger. All these people sold the performances and hopefully that's what I'm going to start doing more of, selling performances and not just gimmicks.

I know your original cut was a substantially longer cut than this final one, which in itself runs a solid two hours. The thing I grapple with when it comes to this film is if you're going to have this much unpleasant stuff happening, I need a few glimmers of hope here and there to balance it out. In other words, I want to see these people fight back and I think you were able to get that moral balance in your current cut.

It's funny you bring this up because it's the biggest critique the movie gets. The first version of the movie was about four hours and thirty minutes. I shit you not! It was an epic. Unlike the *Saw* films where for DVD you'll add back in twenty seconds here or in *Saw III's* case twelve minutes back in. There are hours that were cut out of *Mother's Day*. Entire characters that were cut out. There was an entire character arch of a guy that shows up at the house that gets killed by mother and Addley. The people downstairs have to grapple with this whole thing. And in the current cut, he's gone, he's not even in there, he sort of is, but we don't show him. What I wanted to do with *Mother's Day*, and I think this is what most people might have a problem with, there are no good guys and bad guys in it. There's no more white and black.

Did you base this at all on fact?

This is based on a true story, which is not a secret. This movie is based on the Wichita murders, which is a script I tried to get made for years and years and years. And the true stories was that these two brothers break into a house on Christmas Eve not realizing that people were downstairs having a Christmas party. They accidentally shoot one of them trying to calm the situation down and they were fucked. They essentially killed them one by one. It was a horrific story, a horrible fucking story. In reading the police

files about it, one person survived it, hearing her testimony of this story is one of the most horrific things ever and I wanted to try to do something that was more akin to real life. *Repo* was completely otherworldly. *Saw* is almost like a comic book when you think about it. I wanted *Mother's Day* to be something that is more realistic in that things like this happen and you can't really pick out the good guys or the bad guys.

The first note I got when I turned the first cut in was, "You need to make the villains villainous and you need to make the good guys great. They need to fight back." The first thing I cut was all that shit out. I decided I'm going to make a choice with this and be ballsy. I have those scenes. I have scenes where the bad guys are villainous and scenes where they almost get out and there's those moments of hope. I got rid of them to make that shade of gray. The whole movie is like a gray overcast cloud with this foreboding sense of dread. I know exactly what you're talking about. You want those moments of hope, but I wanted to wade those out of this movie. It's a horrible thing to say.

It's tough. The balance was there in the cut I saw, but there was a while where I thought the villains were just too much. And I kept thinking, 'Please somebody, do something!' It's a tough movie to balance.

It is, and this is a movie that I will be excited about putting the director's cut out for, because it's so different. It reminds me of *The Desperate*. If I ever get to make my version of *The Desperate*, what was cool was it was real people really killing each other, but they were doing it of their own free will. The purpose of *The Desperate* was people who were desperate in their lives were given the opportunity to have the desperation cured. A man dying of cancer would be given a miracle drug that's not on the market yet if he does this. A child who has been kidnapped by the mob, we'll pay the mob debt off, but you have to play this game. These people willingly sign this contract to play this game and it's kind of like *Battle Royale* where they go to a house and they're all given a weapon and they say one person has to die every hour.

It's a lot more complicated, there are a lot of rules, but to me what was scary was watching a seventy-year-old man kill a nineteen-year-old girl. Not watching the nineteen-year-old get killed, but watching this seventy-year-old man struggle to have to kill her. He's bawling, he's crying, he's apologizing as he's doing it. Forget the blood, forget the violence, forget the girl screaming, it's him apologizing for doing this thing. That to me is true horror.

It's funny you mention that because the ATM scene in *Mother's Day* is what probably affected me the most. And not in a good way!

I'm so sorry! That was the biggest debate for the movie. Keeping that scene or losing that scene and we tested it. The whole reason we did the test screening was because of that scene. Certain people wanted it out and certain people wanted it in. I wanted it in. People were saying it makes you lose compassion for everyone; you can't keep that scene in there. I said 'No, put it in and let's test it.' So, when you do an NRG test screening, they come back to you with a booklet, and the booklet essentially says everything about the movie in the audience's opinion. It says who their favorite characters are, who didn't you like, where does the movie drag, etc. One of the questions is "favorite scene?" "Least favorite scene?"

So, they show it to 400 people. Book came out and for least favorite scene, ATM scene and it says one-third of the audience thought this was the most horrific scene of the whole movie, not needed, blah blah blah. There was a whole page devoted to it. They're like, "See? We need to cut it out!" We flip the page. Most favorite scene? The ATM scene. Over one-third think it's the best scene. So, it was both the least favorite scene and the favorite scene by the audience. That's when you know you have something. When people either hate it so much or love it so much. It was fifty percent right down the middle. So that was awesome and that's when you know you've got something that's going to spark debate, when you touch on something that they both love and they hate. So, it stayed in.

You mentioned your inevitable director's cut for this…

The thing with director's cuts is they're pretty much the same as the theatrical cut. At the end of *Saw III* when Angus comes in with the circular *Saw*, my director's cut was different, that whole section. The term "director's cut" isn't really what it is. You have ten weeks to do a cut of a movie. And at ten weeks, you present your version of the movie. Then you go and you have to show it to the producers, the studios and they give you notes. Fifty percent of the time, you actually like the notes. It's like a clay. I spend ten weeks molding a clay, then someone comes in and pushes the clay however and you like fifty percent of what they do and that becomes your director's cut. Then you keep taking notes and going through the process, and at some point, your version goes this way, and theirs goes the other way. With the *Saw* films, there's pretty much the same version up until the very end. It was usually some small things that I wanted to do, and the producers didn't. So, it's not that different.

Mother's Day is a completely different movie. It's not that my director's cut isn't good. It's just too long. It's an epic horror film where there are entire sequences of Rebecca De Morney that are amazing. She kills someone in the movie and gives this monologue that is so fucking powerful, and I just didn't have time for it. I had to cut two and a half hours out of *Mother's Day*. On the *Saw* films, I usually had to get it down by twenty, thirty minutes. Two and a half had to go out of *Mother's Day*.

Is there a cut you prefer? Will we get them both on the DVD release?

The one that's being screened and that will be the theatrical cut is the best cut and it's the perfect amount of time. If it was one note longer, it'd be too much. The majority of insanity happens towards the end of the movie, I mean, a lot happens leading up to that, but it's so much in that last twelve minutes which is why I think you feel so badly walking out of that movie. In my version, the director's cut version, that end sequence is three and a half hours in. Can you imagine? The performances are awesome and I'm not just saying this. There were some award-winning performances that these actors gave me, but at the end of the day you have to do what's best for the movie. The saddest part is Ike and Addley. Those two guys gave some of the most amazing performances I'd seen in a genre film, and I had to cut seventy percent out of it. Because I wouldn't cut, I'd keep it on them, and they'd just improvise and do these amazing things.

I'm excited for people to see the director's cut – the director's cut is not any better than what you're going to see in theaters, it's just different. Here's the thing – I love *Pulp Fiction*. I love *The Big Lebowski*. Anytime a new edition of those movies comes out, I go out and buy them. Even if there's only one second more to them, I don't care. I'm obsessed and I have to have them. I think you have to love the original cut to want to see the director's cut, because it's just that, expanded.

MARCUS DUNSTAN

Interviewed by Rob Galluzzo (9/10)

For such a nice guy, Marcus Dunstan sure has written some of the most disturbing, disgusting, and deranged movies we've seen lately! He and writing partner Patrick Melton got their big break on the third season of *Project Greenlight*, which chronicled the making of *Feast*. That project became an instant cult classic and spawned two sequels. The pair followed it with *The Collector*, which marked Dunstan's directorial debut, but not before tackling the *Saw* series starting with *Saw IV*. Marcus met up with *Massive Hysteria* for lunch at our favorite Burbank diner where got the full story on how this lifelong passion became a career!

What are your earliest recollections of the horror genre? What were the first things that really scared and had an impact on you?

The first movie I watched through my fingers was *Suspiria*. The first horror movie I saw in the theaters was *Creepshow 2* and my grandmother took me. And the first horror movie that I sought, that I absolutely had to see, was the first *Creepshow*. And that was in a Holidome during a snowstorm in Grand Rapids, Minnesota. And I begged and begged and begged to get the illustrated *Creepshow* comic, which I had read so much that the spine completely broke and I had all the brightly colored Bernie Wrightson pages all over my lap. So, on this night, my sister, my mom, my dad and I all piled into this bed and up came the show and I'd turn the pages with it to match along. I kept saying, "This is coming up!" And our family lived up to the tagline, "You'll never have more fun being scared." That was it! It was just wonderful. I luckily fought and fought and was able to convince them to let us watch *Creepshow*.

How old were you around this time?

Well, *Creepshow* came out in '82, so I was seven. By the time it hit HBO, this was probably '83? For the second one, I was definitely a little older and my grandmother was an ER nurse in the Iron Ranges of Minnesota and she and my grandfather were a wonderful couple. We would bond watching *The Avengers* late at night or *The Night Stalker* and make popcorn. If I had an overnight with my grandma, that meant we could go to the video store. I saw *Dirty Harry*

for the first time with her. So now it came time for us to go to the movies and I told her, "Grandma! We have to see *Creepshow 2*!" She was like, "You're right. We do have to see *Creepshow 2*!" (laughs) This is a woman that was just so wonderful. When I would go get *Fangoria* magazine, I had to get permission from an adult to buy it from the local comic shop and she had walked me in and issued said permission. The same to get this old comic book called *Gore Shriek*, which I think had about six issues.

Talk about shaping someone and giving them a chance, she gave me my first still camera and ultimately out of nowhere on my sixteenth birthday, she presented me with my first camcorder. We didn't have a lot of bucks to go around, but this was amazing. It was a really good one! And I loved it. So then all of a sudden, I wasn't just in front of my friend's camcorder, I had one too so we could start doing shots from two angles. And before I knew it, I just started to sit behind it and watch. It all spiraled beautifully out of control from there. With *Fangoria* again, I was able to get all those rubber body parts from the ads in the back of that courtesy of my grandmother, yet again. She said, "you should probably have these for your battle scene!" (laughs) The last conversation I had with her, she knew that *Feast* was getting made, so that was great. It was one of those relationships where I think every hope of our macabre dark humored days came into sharp focus in that moment. She bowed out from our plane of existence, but knowing I was about to make my first horror movie. That bizarre violent strangeness that was about to happen was one of the best things that could have ever happened and she was so tickled by it. She'd chuckle and say, "Oh Marcus! How'd you ever think of that…" She'd stop herself before saying "…stuff!" (laughs) We quoted her many times in the script for *Feast*. Her way of cursing, which was so staccato and hilarious. That was it, The Iron Range of Minnesota probably did more to shape me than several years I spent in Illinois. My grandparents, people with an open mind and a great sense of humor.

You mentioned getting your first camcorder at sixteen. It's always interesting to me when you realize as a film viewer, "wow, somebody made this." When did you realize what went into films and when did you decide that you wanted to try to do that?

When holding that camera and actually shooting things, there was a delight, an absolute delight in becoming something else and that just evolved the more I did it. When I was a kid, I had terrible acne, so with filmmaking, I could put on a mask and stand behind the camera. But I still could exist because what I made could exist. I was very shy about standing up in front of any classroom. But there was this wonderful teacher, Sue Ellen Rickelman of World History, who said to me, "You know, you could turn in a video for your history report." Not only would I not have to stand in front of anybody, but we can hit the lights off in the class and they'd have to watch a world that I helped influence? I knew that she loved the *Conan* soundtrack, so everything I did had the *Conan* soundtrack on it. And the more violent, the better! They were weird twist movies where like, Cleopatra would have an affair with Ramses. (laughs)

You've been writing with Patrick Melton now for quite a while. What were the origins behind that working relationship? When did you guys meet and decide to become collaborators?

Well, we met when we were both in school at the University of Iowa. It just so happens we had a ton of things in common, besides proximity. We both were projectionists at the movie theater. We both had a love for these puffy VHS box movies that we'd sneak and watch all through our formative years in high school. And while Patrick was definitely on the writing track there, I was getting my hands on new cameras. I was still trying to blow things up and make things that were violent yet entertaining with a twist hopefully. Those years went on by, and suddenly we were no longer under the wing of a university that gave us a curriculum and structure for our life. Now you either pick your parents' basement or an adventure. Patrick was heading on out to California

and a year later I showed up, ended up staying in North Hollywood.

In under a year, I ended up moving into his old apartment while he moved right upstairs. By Halloween weekend, I had completely run out of money, I had nothing left. I was shooting the last of the Super 8 cartridges that I had to make trailers for things that I wanted to do. I was lucky to get ahold of a computer, one that I borrowed from Pat, and I had a ream of paper left and that was it. Patrick had the idea, 'Why don't we try to do one of these low budget movies? We've seen 'em all. Why don't we write the one that is familiar enough to rope them in but different enough to be something that we wanted to see?'

And on Halloween weekend, the first words of *Feast* started to be written… that was 1999. The movie wasn't made for another five or six years, but that was it. It's been ten years now, and since then we've been trying to gross each other out and make each other laugh and shock a few folks along the way, hoping that some night, our little window of the world is going to keep some kid up and maybe he'll watch it through his fingers and be inspired to come up with the next great idea. The next great horror movie always stems from someone who stayed up a little too late watching something they shouldn't have before they were mature enough. Their mind is so fertile that they'll just take it in directions that we could never dream.

That's the funny thing. Right now on cable, kids are catching *Feast* and *The Signal* and *Hatchet* and all the *Saw* movies. Movies that you and a lot of young filmmakers are making. So, the cycle is definitely continuing.

I've had a number of odd occurrences just based on the slightest affiliation with *Saw*. And it's amazing, it became a shared representation of something frightening and shocking and whatnot. When James Wan and Leigh Whannell were concocting it, it seemed to be a reaction to – a dissatisfaction with horror movies at the time. And it was angry and mean and seriously wanted to hurt but be clever and reward the mind. And now, wouldn't you know it, old Ghostface from *Scream* will be staring at us again this April. (laughs) So now that the blood and sincerity and the earnest nature and the twists and turns from the detective stories with adults is offering its final chapter with *Saw 3D*, the clever one about the young folks and the adults and the one with the acknowledgment of a pattern from the decades prior, is back and giving it a new voice. I like that statute of justice, one pot always filling another forming some semblance of equilibrium.

Well, the thing about *Scream 4* is that you have to assume that they're going to acknowledge everything that's happened in horror in the last decade, the same way the first one did. It'll be interesting to see them pull off that balance.

Oh yeah.

Just to give you an idea of how much I love *Feast* – My favorite film of all time is *Evil Dead 2*. Hands down. Everything about it. It's funny, it's scary, it's brilliant and innovative. It made me aware of the camera and storytelling and how movies were made. I didn't follow *Project Greenlight*, so I didn't know *Feast* from that. I heard about *Feast* because I was at a *Fangoria* Weekend of Horrors in New York, and they showed the opening scene, and it blew me away. So, with that said, *Feast* became my favorite horror movie since *Evil Dead 2*. It's just got the same manic energy, the same humor, the same vibe. I can tell you guys were *Evil Dead 2* fans! What was the kernel of the idea, the seed that set that one off?

What John Gulager was definitely able to do, the lineage of his family – yeah there was a lot of *Evil Dead 2* in it, but there was also a lot of *Return of the Living Dead* in it. And both films knew when to be serious. *Return of the Living Dead* let the threat be humorous a little bit, but fortunately in a bizarre way. For example, the "send more cops" line. It was serious for the threat at least, but amusing for us the audience because we knew what was going to happen! Henrietta in the basement in *Evil Dead 2* was terrifying! She was delighted with what she/he was doing, but there was an unapologetic glee to that mayhem. And what was missing from those movies, if I went back to what Pat and I were thinking when we wrote *Feast*, was that nobody reacts the way that people would to these things.

If this happened in my little hometown of 8,000 year-round residents, if it was last call at the local bar? It'd be hilarious. It'd be tragic! But how people would deal with that is the way they'd deal with somebody that just looked at their woman! Oh, and now her head's gone. What are you going to do now? All your weaponry is in your truck and you're too drunk to open it. What are you going to do now? Just that simple scenario, an ape-shit scenario befalling a Midwestern reaction; that was it for us. That was its course. If we wanted to go really deep, we could say it's actually a metaphor for the creatures being Republicans literally devouring the middle and lower class. I mentioned that to one actor and they were like, "Why am I doing this movie?" (laughs) It's actually bigger than that! I reached deep for that explanation. It's about the fun of the shock and the

awe. That's where our idea for it stemmed from, and what Gulager was able to do was keep it serious so the laughs could be funny, and the adrenaline intense. The kernel? Where'd it come from? Just the idea of a guy kicking the door open and saying, "Hey, everybody's about the get their ass kicked!" And then his head's gone.

Then it's a submarine movie and it's just about getting peeks of everything outside of that. That one scene where he comes in and gives that whole speech, that was the one scene that was never touched. It was like OK, if we have a dollar to make this thing, if this scene takes ninety cents, spend it! We'll figure everything else out. Instead, we'll chase an extension cord attached to a body. We've already seen enough of the creature to know it's nasty. So OK, when we're chasing an extension cord, we already know what's at the end of it. That whole movie was a wonderful experience. For Pat and I, there was also a delight in being naïve enough to not have a boundary. There could've been another instinct that was applied when we wrote that. We could've been looking at the remakes of Japanese movies and thought, "We probably shouldn't do creatures, let's do something like that."

But you didn't cater to what was going on in horror then, and I appreciate that you opted to make a creature feature instead. When *Feast* came out, it felt like its own thing.

And yet if you look at the plot, it's *From Dusk Till Dawn*. It takes place in a bar! When we first wrote it, it was supposed to be in a casino. It was supposed to have an entire Micmac burial ground vibe, which would've been way more expensive. I thought OK, you can try to run from it and try to tell people that it isn't similar to that other film, or you embrace it and make examples of why it's different. So, what we wanted to do was start to build a universe out from that. *Feast* is what happens when *Evil Dead 2* hits your bar. *The Collector* was about what happens when a few Dario Argento slashers get loose in a house. So, we're hugging what we love, the movies that kept us up so late and hoping to put enough originality on a spin while acknowledging a framework. The jokes in *Feast* are all about familiar set-ups, but with, "I didn't see that coming" pay-offs. So, the advantage of having something similar to *From Dusk Till Dawn* was you already know what this is. This is people that are going to be stuck, they'll have some flashy personalities and they'll probably all die one by one. You start to set it up so you're like, "Oh, he's the cocky guy. I know he's going to go last – Oh, his head's gone!" "She's the hot one so she's – what? She's smart?" (laughs) We assumed that you'd see it because it's a monster movie, but now you'll really enjoy it if you've seen all these other horror movies, because we're playing on what you know. *Feast* was a great first movie because it was powered by a lot of enthusiasm for everybody that was on that. There was something happening every day that was vulgar, humorous, dangerous or exciting. Every day there was something going on and it kept getting crazier and what a wonderful cast. They were sticky from head to toe every day, but it was a delight to be there.

Since then, Pat and I have been fortunate enough to observe other kinds of horror movies being made, I don't know if there's ever that mad glee like that first time, when that well-endowed creature comes running through the room. That doesn't happen often, and that even brought the most jaded folks over to take a look. (laughs)

One of the most humorous aspects of *Feast* is the opening character stats. Letting you know right off the bat exactly who everyone is, what their probability of survival was in a few lines of text. Was that always in the script?

Yes. And at the time, that influence was plucked really from what I loved about *Three Kings*. It had these rapid-fire intros to characters, which were great. They'd define themselves through actions anyways, but I thought we'd never seen that in a horror film. And you know what you can do with a horror film? You could acknowledge the stereotypes and then lie! Totally acknowledge them and play with it. I love giving all this detail into a character that's dead two seconds later. (laughs) That's funny. And it's also a tough joke to sell to the actor! The studio's like, "Why do we need to know all this about this person?" That's the point. No one ever knows dick about victim number one, but we're going to tell you everything. His hopes, his dreams, he was college bound. He was going to invent the post-it note, but unfortunately, it didn't quite work out.

You mentioned the cast before. Judah Friedlander, Henry Rollins, Krista Allen, Balthazar Getty, Sean Penn's mom Eileen Ryan; all terrific actors. As the writers, how was it for you and Pat to see these people embodying the characters from this script you guys started back in 1999?

Wonderful. They exceeded what we ever could've imagined.

Was Jason Mewes in there the whole time?

That character's name at one point was Sniff. And he was really, really foul, but then all of a sudden, they cast it, and it was Jason Mewes. And it was so unmistakably Jason Mewes. You can't hide that. So, there was a round table discussion and there was Ben Affleck, Chris Moore, Roger

Nygard, Patrick, myself and I believe Mike Leahy and the topic of discussion was punching up the character cards at the beginning. When we got to Sniff. "Sniff's Jason Mewes, right?" I think it was Melton that said, "Why don't we just say it's Jason Mewes?" (laughs) And the whole table doubled over and turned bright red, because all of a sudden it told what the rest of the joke was going to be. Occupation: Actor. Life Expectancy: Has already exceeded life expectancy. So that was a bit of fun when that came together. To think, here's a contest put together product through *Project Greenlight*. And here I was, the guy who went to see *Creepshow 2* with his grandma, surrounded by icons of humor and Oscar winners and my buddy from college and we couldn't believe that they were focusing their massive pull and talent, taking time out of their careers that were miles beyond our wildest dreams, to make a down and dirty offensive creature feature. That was just one of the many charms.

Through that experience on the first *Feast*, you and Patrick have had a wonderful relationship with the Gulagers. What can you say about your initial introduction with them and how your relationship flourished into practically family?

Well, we were honored to learn from them. My first pretty darned serious relationship, I was talking through the rough beats of it with them. Because as a family unit, they're so unique and wonderful and bonded. Their lives I see as a reaction and an existence because of art. The idea of the film, the shoot, the edit, the production, that's when they're at their most alive. That isn't the grind, that's the reward for them. It all boiled down to one moment. During *Feast*, at the end of a pretty rough and tumble schedule, there were three stages up and running. You had the closet here, the corner bar here and the main hallway for where Judah was going to get vomited on. John was running between all three.

At one point, I showed up just to see what was going on and John was in a different room. And the reason nobody could find the entire Gulager family is because they were working, shooting stuff that is in the film, in complete silence, only with a few gestures. No bullhorn, no command. I walked in and saw John holding his own camera, Diane holding the light, I think his brother Tom was pumping fake smoke, and Clu was using his cowboy hat to wave it as John drifted over the De Los Muertos elements of set décor that were provided by Clark Hunter.

And I think they even brought in some from their own kitchen. Sure enough, that shot is in the movie. Sure, the flick's got these good actors in it, but there's this shot that starts to tell us we might be in a horror movie and that's how it was created. And what it represented was like, wow, no one can find them because they're so into it, pulling it off with gentle hand gestures and whispers. I'm endlessly fascinated by how that family's vision sees the world and how they live and thrive in art. It's great. The world is a hell of a lot more interesting with their films in it.

The *Feast* sequels, *Feast 2* and *Feast 3* seemed like a lot more of a collaborative effort, especially with the Gulagers. So, what were your thoughts when the prospect of doing a sequel, let alone two, came up?

That happened at a party, maybe the Golden Globes? A rep from the DVD company came up to us and was like, "*I got to tell you,* Feast *made a shitload.*" We were like, "Yeah, thanks!" We walked around the room and sure enough, another exec from Dimension came over and was like, "Guess what? We're making two more!" And the deal was made in two weeks. The thing is, financially those budgets were very low and at this point, there's got to be a reason to do it. And there were still some middle fingers we had there. By this point, the serious horror movie was still out there, dominating. The PG-13 horror was just getting limp and more limp. So, we thought… no one's killed a baby yet. (laughs)

And so, the true origin of *Feast 2*! (laughs) Because the follow-up *Feast* movies were done back-to-back and on a limited budget, were there things you guys wanted to do that became impossible to pull off? For example, did you ever have a definitive origin for the creatures?

Oh yeah, the creative freedom on the *Feast* sequels was wonderful. The problem with creative freedom and small resources is that something's got to give. The scripts were created, and we worked all the way up to the writer's strike, and then our hands were tied. I could not do anything about it as the budgets for two already low budget movies were evaporating. That was hard. Yeah, lots of ideas and concepts, but thanks to Gulager's passion and his ability to literally pull magic out of thin air, he was always able to deliver those beats no matter what they were. I love that the crew built this actual school bus on a hydraulic lift to simulate the bus actually driving out, but ultimately the completed shots after all was said and done, Gulager bought a miniature school bus on eBay, sand from a putt-putt course, and straws with two home consumer cameras slightly slowed down. I tell you, you watch them all together and you think, "That's awesome." The miniature looks better than the real thing. I just don't know of any other director that would do that! Because the process of seeing your written material

delivered and then, all of a sudden, you lose the resources to make it happen, it can be agonizingly defeating, but no, he went rogue and did it. He made it happen. It was thrilling to watch him do his thing.

John seems to be the type of filmmaker that really cares for the material and will go the extra mile. For example, I love that opening Super 8 footage for the first *Feast*.

And the second two as well. Something like that, so beautiful, so classic and so unique to that project. You write that into the script that we're going to start off with this Super 8 footage, and you'll hear, "Nah, we don't need that." So, he goes and does it anyways and those same people are like, "Now, I love that beginning!" Of course you do. What does a guy have to do? Directors essentially have to go out and pre-make the movie, show it to you and hope that you'll still give them permission to do it again. It's hard. You're always in a fight for creating imagination with people. But at the same time, when there's more and more money at stake, you have to. The act of pre-creating helps you get it right.

Would there ever be a *Feast 4*?

(laughs) Well, there's so many things that we could never get to, so yeah, we'd love to. *Feast 4: On The Floor* was our title! And by that point, it's to embrace literally where no man or beast has ever gone before. The level of offensive would be through the roof.

Were Krista Allen and Balthazar Getty characters ever in your script for *Feast 2*?

Yes, and it was an awesome scene. There was literally another ten minutes of the first *Feast* where those characters were all supposed to come back. Hot Wheels, Bozo and Heroine 2 as she was left named, and it was key scene, we really wanted to do it. But when you approach actors and say, "Hey, remember that movie you guys did for two bucks? Guess what, we're going to do another one and now we can offer you fifty cents! Oh yeah! It's going to be twice as hot and hurt like hell! Come on board!" Unfortunately, everybody involved to my knowledge was willing to make it work, but honestly, I think scheduling really just f-ed it up. You could have one person donating their time here, and another donating their time there, but you really need them all in the same car!

Have you ever heard from Ben Affleck or Matt Damon or Wes Craven on the sequels considering they had such a hand in the first one? Do they even know they exist?

Haven't heard what they thought of the sequels. I think they know they exist? But I don't know so! Talk about directors, Ben Affleck's an amazing director. *Gone Baby Gone* is amazing. I can't wait for *The Town*. When one looks back at the roster of talent that was helping out on that first movie, it's just mind boggling. You could not find more nice, genuine people. They weren't just offering lip service, they really got in there and helped and that was just so cool.

So, *The Collector* was something that you and Patrick had had for a long time. What was it about that story that made it be what you chose as your directorial debut?

In 1999, it was just a short film called *The Midnight Man* and it was very, very simple. A thief breaks into this killer's house. At that point, it was the killer's house and with the killer, it was just a cat and mouse element. So, when *Feast* happened and it opened on fifty screens, played once at midnight and slowly but surely picked up fans. On its initial release, it was tough to then come out with another script that blended humor and horror and was based on observations of other movies. Serious horror was winning. So, we thought 'Do we have anything that we're passionate about that's in that vein? What about the story of that guy that breaks into the wrong house? Oh, that's cool.' That's not a big budget thing and these movies getting a shot are pretty low budget.

It just so happened when we were talking about that idea, Pat and I were on a panel showing clips from *Feast* with a company that was looking to do one-to-two-million-dollar horror movies. We met with them the next week and that was that. In fact, the *Project Greenlight* show captured the first meeting regarding elements of it. We all look like we're nine years old in it now, but that was the humble beginnings. What ultimately became the motif for the killer, the traps and the methods and all that, our initial look for the killer was always based on the Italian giallo slashers. I love that. The black gloves, the sleek exterior. A high sense of fashion for such a depraved mind!

It definitely has that Argento influence.

That's exactly what we were going for, hence the gratuitous shots of hands and eyes and lips. I think there's something almost erotic about something that depraved.

Can you talk about the irony that here you have this story about an Argento-style killer who sets up traps, and then you guys simultaneously start working on the *Saw* sequels?

Yep. Serendipity at its best! That's what allowed us to have a chance to work on *Saw* was our script for *The Collector*. That script was making the rounds before *Saw III* came out, and there was a chance that it would be considered as a potential spin-off or an origin tale or something like that.

In the same way Darren Bousman's *The Desperate* script eventually became *Saw II*?

Yep. Absolutely. But ultimately that wasn't the direction those guys opted to go in because they had a storyline that we could still pick up with this killer. What it did was this; if we walked in with just our script for *Feast* and said, "Hey, we'd like to do a *Saw* movie!" They'd read it and be like, "What the hell? This is a little monster humping a deer head. Saw is about adults and crisis and vices and devices!" When you have a script about a killer late one night who breaks into a house with traps, then you think OK, these guys can probably do a *Saw* movie. So that script helped immensely. But after the fact, *The Collector* script was alright, so Dimension said they'd like to make that! Because of its modest scale, that allowed me to get a shot at directing, which was great. You can't imagine having the good fortune to have a few films get made and then as a writer to get a chance to direct something. That just worked out beautifully.

How much did the influence of working on the *Feast* films have when it came time for you to direct *The Collector*?

Tom Gulager was my second unit director on *The Collector* and was in it. John helped shoot it. He's a great D.P. Diane's in it. Clu did some marvelous recordings for us. They were completely infused with us because they too came from a very grounded, serious place with their filmmaking. John's reel at the time contained some very serious stuff, which was actor friendly but also cool and punk. That mixed with a creature feature worked wonderfully. So, it was a no-brainer when I said I'm trying to do something serious, and character motivated here. Those aesthetics work wonderfully. The idea was a lot of preparation, which battles you select on which days you feel strong. I learned priceless life lessons from the Gulagers.

I'm always fascinated by the process of directors working with actors. For *The Collector*, you had Madeline Zima, Andrea Roth from *Rescue Me*, you had Michael Reilly Burke who once played Ted Bundy! What was your working relationship like with all these people and how difficult was it to get them all?

The casting window was accelerated, and we were lucky. Fortunately, it comes down to having a great casting director and we had Monika Mikkelsen. Nine times out of ten, I went with her first choice. And if I didn't go with her first choice, it was because the person was busy and couldn't do it. But it was phenomenal. I was very open with Monica and told here, "This is my first time. I'm probably going to do a lot of things wrong. Hopefully get some things right too. Hopefully it'll look pretty cool. Would you mind getting me some actors that get that? And won't mind if I stammer a little bit or respond with a curt 'I don't know.'" (laughs)

These folks were great, Madeline Zima in particular. I had never orchestrated a sex/death scene before. She had to be absolutely vulnerable, and she was so cool. To help that moment out, I cast a friend of mine that I knew was married and wasn't going to be a sleaze ball. I think everyone we auditioned for that other part was just a groper. It's not about that! I wanted people who understood the choreography and what the moment was actually about. This was our version of the big car explosion, but we were going to try to do that with suspense.

Being a fan, you know how pivotal the killer is…

The thing is when you see the killer in the film, there are several people playing him. Gary Tunnicliffe plays the killer. Tom Gulager plays the killer. Our great stunt man Steve is the killer a lot. The DP, Patrick Melton is the killer in one of the most iconic shots of the whole show! When our camera pans up and we find the thief and the killer on opposing sides of the same door, that's Melton! We had to tuck his shag underneath the mask but that's him. We shot twenty-four hours a day so actors couldn't always be there, so it was very helpful to have friends don the mask. It could be anybody, and we could tell more story in less time.

Did you do the Argento thing and let your hands be the killers for any shots?

Oh absolutely! Actually, I went ahead and did a more masochistic version of that. When Argento shows his hand, it's beautiful and lovely in these great black gloves. In *The Collector*, my hand is the one that gets burned in the car! I didn't have a fake hand to do it. The scene needed a little more tension, a different thrust. You have to stay in this house, you have to steal this item or… and the "or" reason was there, but the person that was threatening harm I felt should inflict just a bit. So, seeing a thief keep his cool while his hand was on fire was kind of awesome. And the vulnerability to his instrument. So, we had the tightest

lenses we could find. I got real close and we burned my hand for a little while. Sure, it was bandaged up for a couple of months, but we got it! (laughs)

You have to bleed and burn for your art, I guess!

Yes, that moment was my contribution to the hand mythos of the killer.

I'm a big music fan and I love Nine Inch Nails. You've got Charlie Clouser on the *Saw* movies, but for *The Collector*, you were able to get former Nine Inch drummer Jerome Dillon to compose your score. How'd that come about?

I straight up pursued, begged, used manipulation, whatever it took! I'm a big Nine Inch Nails fan. That was it. I thought what was dated about some of the films I liked such as the Italian slashers was sometimes the music would take you out a little bit. Sometimes it's so iconic and perfect that it would burn in and stick with you forever, like the *Suspiria* music. But I wanted to update the soundscape and not the visual. Meaning, let's go back to a time when the camera was predatory, and the music provided, in this case, an industrial heartbeat. Because there's something about that first really iconic cue from Charlie Clouser in *Saw*, "Hello Zep" – it almost sounded like there was a machine turning on when you listen to it and that added an auditory sense of dread.

So, with Jerome, I was hoping to achieve something that had twenty-thirty minutes of silence, and I wanted the music to help us tell a story and I wanted something we hadn't quite seen or heard before. The closest I could come up with as a reference was *Run Lola Run*. It takes a very simple map and complicates it with beautiful character developments, life making decisions and that in itself is an art film, but then it added this bold wonderful soundtrack. At the time, I was like, 'I kind of want to dance to this movie!' (laughs) Watching this vibrant woman kick some ass through town.

So, I thought OK, let's pull from that, and pull from the industrial and my love of all things Nine Inch Nails and see if we can give this thief and killer some personality audio-wise, meaning whenever the killer is at work, it's string-based instruments, whenever the thief is at work, it's synth. So, it's electronic. It's his tech versus this other guy's tech. And just another way to help build the instincts that the killer's supposed to represent, which were threads and silks and all these things and devices and traps that make metallic sounds, but his process was always stuck in strings. Whereas with the thief, the first thing he breaks out is this high-tech equipment and he's from a thriller and most thrillers have synth soundtracks. The slashers I like often have strings, even the *Friday the 13th* movies. It's so good and creepy. Plus, to mention, the soundtrack itself, Jermone was mixing existing cues beautifully.

Another person to call out is Andrew Reed whose band Patient 113 has a song we used in total innocence as first heard in the beginning and then Jerome's retake on it when it's a montage of the deceased added such a sinister vibe to it. I love that mix of raw and polish. Then to have Depeche Mode was a dream for me, because I love that sleazy guitar riff, and it didn't betray anything in the soundscape to have that.

Sometimes, a pop song in a movie can be so loud and brash in comparison to everything else. *Opera* had some pretty heavy metal cues in it. The pacing and the way we were constructing this, if all of a sudden, a death metal beat kicked in, the imagery just couldn't keep up with that at all. That works better in comedy because it's an unexpected element that enhances what you're seeing. If you saw two octogenarians racing for the bathroom and you play death metal, it's different than classical music. Death metal would make us all laugh at that scenario, I think. This was the opposite. Here's a guy that's bleeding from a bear trap, there's a woman with her shirt off, what if we played something kind of sexy? That's disturbing. OK, I've done my job!

You've talked about doing a sequel to that film, but as of right now, how serious is *The Collector 2*?

It's being budgeted right now to be shot this fall with myself returning as director. I believe it's definitely happening.

I remember when *Saw IV* was going into production a lot of writers were pitching multiple takes for what would inevitably be the next *Saw* movie. The task ended up falling to you and Patrick, not only for *Saw IV*, but *Saw V*, *Saw VI* and now the upcoming *Saw 3D*. You had *The Collector* script floating around, but what was the initial idea that you and Patrick pitched to Twisted that convinced them that you were the guys to write the next few *Saw* movies?

Going back to *Project Greenlight*, it's your script against 1,200 others. That was a big, big chance. That was the golden ticket, maybe we could do it. We were lucky. That process was down to two horror scripts. One was ours and the other, this other gentleman. Each of us knew we were going to be getting notes on how to augment our material. We were given twenty notes. We elected to change twenty-one things. The other writer? Was given probably about twenty

notes as well. He wrote back and asked for all the people that distributed those notes to justify each note. That script was gone. So, that's important lesson number one. Important lesson number two was that the existence of *The Midnight Man* script was an example of tone that made it a possibility for us to have a legitimate chance. By the time we walked in for the *Saw* gig, I know it was down to three. This is after we'd written them. Once again, we were in a contest. Our script versus two others.

So, you and Patrick had already written *Saw IV* before officially getting the gig?

Well, this was after several hoops. What I liked about the audacity of that chance, are you kidding me? We can go from six months ago trying to figure out which bill to pay to now having a chance to work on this movie? That'll be out in theaters? The *Saw* franchise? So, the answer is we went overboard. We didn't just walk in with *Saw IV*. We walked in with *Saw IV*, *Saw V* and *Saw VI*. We had this wall painted red, and Pat and I shingled it with index cards taking every character from the past trilogy, every character that we'd like to create and every question that we'd like to answer and built a narrative and a new thrust, which was complete with twists, turns, demises, ideas for traps and whatnot. Whether any of that ever existed beyond that day or that chance, that's just what we were willing to put into it. This was three days of coffee and Mountain Dew, and gum, and borrowed food, whatever we had to do to stay up and take that shot.

So then, we finished that first draft and it's a behemoth. It was too expensive. It's too long, it's got all this stuff in it. Same quote as with that *Feast* script, we entered a contest for a million-dollar production budget with a script that was budgeted at $40 million dollars. (laughs) So we did the same thing. It was like, "We asked for *Saw IV* and you gave us *Lethal Weapon*!" (laughs) Oh, alright, from that point, what it did have, and I think only dissecting the process now, I think we had a really cool hook, and that was the motivator for the plot, meaning a guy's on a block of ice, he's dead in ninety minutes, his friend will do anything for him. That was enough of an engine and not only that, but those three shots (from *Saw III*) with Jigsaw and a woman, maybe that was his love? Maybe that was his wife? We came in with, "Guess what we can do with your flashbacks here? What if you told what happened with that person?" All of a sudden, an entire movie was filling out with all new characters. And then, one thing that we were really, really proud of and that just worked out beautifully was the intimacy of the killer in the *Saw* films at that point, it was on tapes, there was some distance. There was a tape, now he's long gone, and it was a great irony. We thought, wouldn't it be nice to see a healthy, living breathing John Kramer face to face with someone where it wasn't all about punishment, but it was a little bit about anger? He was testing his own morals. Can I not cross the line and deliver or destroy this person? Yeah, I can do that. But they're going to have to go through hell to get back at me. And I loved that. That was a cool thing too to strive for.

Once that engine began, it was really neat that characters that could represent, it was such fertile ground. Every single one of us has a vice, whether we care to admit it or not. And the fact that this kind of philosopher fellow, who's terminal, would like to strap us into a device version of our flaw and set it to a timer and ask us to survive the worst in ourselves, it's terrific! It's like a new age killer and really cool. Plus, that irony that it's a killer that doesn't kill you. He puts you into a bind!

Was there any criteria going in? Because if you look at *Saw III*, you see little tidbits and hints to future installments. Were they always prepping Hoffman (Costas Mandylor) to be the next Jigsaw? Was that mysterious woman (Betsy Russell) always meant to be Jigsaw's wife? How far in advance were they thinking when you guys came on?

Well, what's interesting, once again, is the interpretation of a shot. In *Saw III*, Costas Mandylor walks into a room, picks something up and puts it in his pocket. That's it. It's not like he winked at the camera, it's not like he stabbed someone on the way out. Simply, with music and tone and the juxtaposition of imagery in that room, maybe he's good? Maybe he's bad? Either way, we're interested in what his motive is. And that was cool. The universe was left to spin that in any which direction which was really nice. Um, and as a movie viewer, I knew who Costas Mandylor was. I'm a big fan of that film *The Pledge*. He's a bad-ass actor. Really? We get to invent something for that guy? Way cool. There was a bible that we would work from, but otherwise, we really were able to stretch, create and push, because ultimately everything would come back into place. At that point, three films in, they really knew what they were doing.

As far as the trilogy you guys did, I like *Saw IV* a lot because it's *Saw 3.5*! The interesting thing is I revisited *Saw III*, and you just expected the next entry to be about Jeff (Angus Macfadyen) looking for his little girl. When you guys first came in to do *Saw IV*, was that ever considered as the potential story, the conclusion to finding that little girl? Obviously, we see what's happened to her through

***Saw V* and the post credits scene in *Saw VI*, but I expected a whole movie about that!**

A lot of those things are attempted, but again, it's all out of respect to a timeline. How long has it been since the last one? How vital a component could this character really be to keep the plot going? So, it's one of those elements that, well, actually may be hinted at in things to come.

Because of the speed of which these films are put together, how stressful is it on you and Pat in terms of not knowing if certain actors or characters are going to be able to come back? Because I know on *Saw IV*, it was really undecided up until the last minute if Donnie Wahlberg was going to come back. There was a good chance he was not going to do it. So as writers, do you guys plan for that?

I remember at one point we had three different drafts going for *Saw IV*. We've got Donnie for two days, three days, or two weeks. Or potentially the lead and that was really interesting, because the version where we had him for two-three days, Detective Matthews, there was emotional resonance to him. You wanted to see what happened, because he had so much to lose and so much to fight for and it was Darren's brilliant scene how he outsmarts the shackle in the opening of *Saw III*. It's such a Rambo moment! You want that guy to have his day and have his big bad-ass moment. And I think that it was one of those things that I legitimately prayed he'd come back. I don't think it could've had the same impact without that person. For some fans, I think it was a surprise that he showed up again. I think it was the best version of that. That situation you mentioned could've happened. You wouldn't have had the exact same movie had he not come back, and we would've had to change things so that it'd hit in the same way emotionally. That was a challenge and fortunately it worked out. I don't want to think about if he didn't come back. (laughs)

Just from watching the *Saw* films, listening to the commentaries or seeing publicity stills, sometimes trap ideas don't get used until later entries, or sometimes there will be a still of one that never shows up in the actual film. Have there ever been any traps you guys came up with from the trilogy you did that didn't make it into the film?

Well, the one thing that I do remember being an augmentation and it's never come up so I guess it worked out just fine, but we really wanted to castrate a rapist. So, in *Saw IV*, we have this guy surrounded by all these assorted photos he's taken with all the horrible tapes playing and his choices are to gouge out his eyes or lose his limbs. Well, it was supposed to be stick your junk in a deli slicer or lose your limbs, but *Hostel Part 2* had just come out that summer. And they owned the removal of shlong. You can't do better than that! That bit had to change. So, we thought, well we can't see that so let's take… eyes? (laughs)

As far as *Saw VI*, I think you guys capped out the series so perfectly. So, I'm intrigued by where you can go next with it. The thing I loved about the ending of *Saw VI*, you guys ended it with Jigsaw finally being a full-on villain. Because John Kramer to me, I never really saw as a villain. He was a strong philosopher, he tested people, but he never actually killed them, he thought he was doing the right thing. Amanda was bordering on being a masochistic serial killer, not letting people fairly overcome their traps and was not a likely successor for Jigsaw. But Costas as Hoffman shines in *Saw VI* and he is a bad, bad guy. He's a real villain. So, I love that literally by the end of it, after all the terrible things he does, there is no doubt that that guy is a villain, and you left him with his jaw literally hanging off! I thought wow, the new Jigsaw is totally a horror villain now.

The groundwork was laid out. Where his twist came and what happened to him and how he became in line with the Jigsaw philosophy and how Amanda went off the rails, but it all comes down to this. Hoffman was the cruelest of both worlds. He wasn't afraid to get his hands dirty, liked the idea of the punishment element, but really wanted to focus on using personal elements. That's what was fun. Seeing someone with a very interesting yet dangerous philosophy, now being executed by someone (like Hoffman) with no moral code.

There's that one creepy moment in *Saw VI* where he's listening back to one of the torture traps, and you know he's listening to it strictly because he enjoys it. I'm curious to see how you'll carry that on. Speaking of the seventh *Saw*, *Saw 3D*, it's not a secret that finally after six films and all these fan rumors and speculation, Cary Elwes is back as Dr. Lawrence Gordon. In what capacity has yet to be determined. Did you guys ever attempt to incorporate that character into *Saw IV*, *Saw V* or *Saw VI*?

Well, I think that character represents one of the great unanswered questions of that whole series, and so with this installment, it's time to answer it. And… the answer's awesome. (laughs)

There were rumors that you guys had mapped out a potential new trilogy of *Saw* films kicking off with *Saw 7*, but now this one is being called the last of the series. Is this a combination of all the ideas that maybe at one point could've been a new trilogy?

We were just given the shot to make the wicked go for broke conclusion.

But we've learned from *Friday the 13th Part 4: The Final Chapter*! So, is this really the final chapter?

(laughs) I believe so.

Last year, *Saw* was a big part of Universal's Halloween Horror Nights. They did an amazing maze that encompassed things from all the *Saw* movies. It was funny, I was walking out of the maze as you and Patrick were walking in. What was that like for you guys, just a few short years after being a part of this world to see it literally at an amusement park?

The best part was that my parents were there! And so, we walked through, and they were like, "Did you write that? What is wrong with you? Oh my God!" (laughs) Just hearing that over and over was so funny. That was really cool. It still doesn't feel real! It was double cool to walk behind the director of another house of horrors that he had something to do with too. It was so awesome. As a kid, it would be like opening that awesome present that makes you jump up and down and you don't realize you're clapping. Then when you're an adult and something that awesome happens, you just kind of go slack, because you're trying hard to not show how excited you are. Here I am with my parents who put up with a lot of stuff when I was a kid. Everyone else was playing baseball and basketball, and I was in the basement with *Fangoria* watching *Friday the 13th* movies on USA network where they cut out the nudity but kept in the gore, so I could study the FX at least. While other kids were asking for subscriptions to *Sports Illustrated*, I wanted *Tom Savini's Grand Illusions Book 2*. It was a lot to accept, but they did, but here's my parents, at Universal where there's an hour and a half line where all these little macabre creations that I had something to do with were coming alive and scaring people. That felt good.

NICK PRINCIPE

Interviewed by Rob Galluzzo (10/11)

Actor/stuntman Nick Principe wears his love of horror on his sleeve. Literally – on his sleeves are tattoos devoted to his favorite horror icons! So it's safe to say that he's a die-hard fan, and when he moved out to Hollywood to get into show biz, he did it with one goal in mind – to one day be a monster. Now, he's gotten to do it several times, most notably in Rob Hall's *Laid to Rest* and *Chromeskull: Laid to Rest 2* playing the modern-day icon of fright Chromeskull. We caught up with Nick to talk about his humble beginnings, our mutual love of genre flicks and of course, wielding the blades of Chromeskull for the second time! Read it below!

What are your earliest recollections of the horror genre? Do you recall what your first introduction to it was?

Absolutely! I remember me and my mom were at my Aunt Linda's house and she had a daughter that was around the same age as me, and they had a laserdisc of *An American Werewolf in London*. They wouldn't let us see it, so they told us to go hang out in the basement. So, I was probably 6 or 7 years old and I remember watching that movie through a crack in the door with me and my cousin piled on top of each other trying to get a glimpse. That's probably the first horror movie I remember and what got me into the genre.

I would assume catching that little glimpse of *An American Werewolf in London* made you a fan for life?

Just like any little kid, you want to see what you're not supposed to see. So here's this movie that is entertaining me, scaring the living crap out of me, but yet I wanted to watch more. I couldn't pull away from it. Right from then, that was it. That was it for me. That was all I was interested in watching was horror movies. I was lucky because I always looked older than I actually was, so they'd let me in to R rated movies at the theater and I could rent stuff with no problem. It honestly hasn't slowed down since!

There's always a point for us where we come to the realization of what movie-making is. Meaning, we realize 'Wow, people made this. There's a director, and an FX crew that created what I'm watching'. When did that

happen for you and in what capacity did you want to get into the movie business?

In complete honesty, if I knew all the bullshit that surrounds getting something decent made and the long hours and the time you'd have to spend in the FX shops, like something that'll take 3 weeks to do, and then 45 minutes to shoot – I don't know if I would've gotten into this! (laughs) But I'm glad I did. I think my first recollections of filmmaking were from that VHS tape of Michael Jackson's *Thriller*. And how they had a documentary about the behind the scenes and they had segments on the prosthetics, and they even dabbled a bit with *An American Werewolf in London*, because John Landis directed that video as well. So I remember they were showing all this amazing stuff with Rick Baker doing the make-up FX. I just thought, "Wow". Aside from this amazingly cool world of movies, there's this whole other cool world of making movies. Even at that early age, I wanted to be the monster. I always wanted to be the monster.

I think that "*Making of Thriller*" really influenced all of the genre fans our age. It definitely had that impact on us.

Yeah, for our age group for sure. And to my recollection, that was one of the first VHS tapes that gave you a behind the scenes look at a film; this is long before the days of the DVD special features. For a lot of us, that was our first look at the painstaking FX process.

425

Do you remember your first on-set experience? Did you start out in the business trying to be a stuntman first, or an actor? What was the beginning for you?

Well, again, I'll be totally honest with you. I moved here to California wanting to be Kane Hodder. Basically, I did some research and thought to myself, "How do these guys get cast to play the monster roles? Do they take any big guy? What's the deal here?" I looked into it and it seems they usually hire stunt guys, because most productions don't want to pay an actor to do the acting and then a stuntman to do the stunts, so they just hire a stuntman to do both. So, I figured, alright, if I want to play a monster, I guess I have to be a stuntman! Now, I wasn't just jumping blindly into it. I have a black belt in kenpo. I used to fight very early on in the early stages of MMA where there weren't as many rules. So, I had credentials. I just really focused on that.

But here's my first real film experience. I was actually working at a music store in Los Angeles. I'd only been in LA for about 3 months and everybody always told me that if you see a bunch of trailers and trucks, that means they're shooting a TV show or a commercial or something like that. So across the street from this music shop I was working at, there was this Armenian Church and there were all these trailers set up.

On my lunch break, I just walked over there and ignorantly and blindly, I looked for the first person with a clipboard and a headset. And I went up to him and said, "Do you guys need any help?" And this guy replied, "What are you, a PA?" (production assistant) I didn't even know what a PA was, but I said, "Yes I am." (laughs) So, the guy says, "Well, 3 people called out today, so fill out a W2 and you're in." There was a grip on that shoot that happened to be wearing a Sepultura t-shirt, so I figured "Alright, this guy's probably cool. I can talk to this guy." This guy saved me that day. I went up to him and said, "Listen, man. They just hired me as a PA. I don't even know what that means. What do I do?" The guy laughed and basically said, "Well, if they call your name over the radio, just do whatever they say. Whenever the first AD yells something, just repeat it. And whenever you've got nothing to do, just clean up." So I can only imagine what these people thought when they saw this 6 ft 7 tattooed guy running around like a madman just cleaning stuff up. I got hooked up with a stunt coordinator on that show and now here we are. I never went back to the music store after that lunch break, by the way.

For me, it's always fascinating talking to guys that do stunts professionally because you obviously have to be somewhat of a daredevil. And a little crazy for sure! No

offense! **Do you remember the first stunt you tried pulling off? Do you get scared every time you have to approach doing something dangerous?**

Well, they always say there's a fine line between stupid and crazy. I'd like to think I tip toe across that line often. (laughs) The first stunt I ever did was a fight scene, so I wasn't nervous doing that. But there have been a couple of times where I'll read a script and think "Oh man. Some poor guy is going to have to do that." And then I realize I'm that poor guy! There's about 30 seconds where you question yourself, but then I just shrug my shoulders and say, "Oh I'll make it work."

So, let's talk about the character of Chromeskull! How'd you get that role in that movie? Did you already know Rob Hall beforehand?

Me and Rob met on the set of Robert Englund's sophomore directorial job, a very goofy movie called *Killer Pad*. Rob took that job for the same reason that I did. We both just wanted to work for Freddy. I think Rob and I even discussed that if he showed up to set every day in the hat and sweater and glove, we both would've worked on it for free. So, we met there. My favorite sub-genre of horror has always been "slasher" films and then zombie films and Rob and I had talked about that, and I mentioned that I had worked as a "zombie movement" coach for a SyFy movie called *Dead & Deader*. So we talked about horror movies and just stayed in touch over the years. And then I was at Joe Lynch's *Wrong Turn 2* premiere screening at the Mann's (in Los Angeles) where Rob came up to me and said, "You want to chase my wife around in the woods in this slasher movie I've got going?" And I was like, "Do you even have to ask? Of course! I'm your man!" There wasn't an audition or anything like that. The following Monday I was in his shop getting a life cast done for the mask.

When you went in for that first lifecast, how far along were they in terms of the design and look for Chromeskull? Did they already have an idea for what the mask was going to look like? And discussion about what the mask was going to be?

Chromeskull is something that Rob had in his head for a while, so he knew what he wanted the mask to be. Originally, although he wears a suit, he was supposed to wear a black shirt and a black tie, but I thought we should give him a deranged psychologist look, so we changed the shirt and tie into a turtleneck. The knives are mine. I brought those in. I had taken a bowie knife and put blades on the side and some spikes on the brass knuckles part to make it more like a French knife. That's pretty much my contribution to Chromeskull in terms of what I brought to that.

When it came time to shoot, how collaborative was Rob in terms of what you wanted to do with the character and how the kills were pulled off?

Rob gave me free reign to do whatever I wanted and at best he would occasionally say, "Alright pull it back. Not as extreme." Or "Don't do this." But he for the most part just totally let me go. He'd give me as many takes as I wanted and he was so, so awesome to work for. He really let me make the character my own. I've been quoted before saying this, but again Chromeskull is his son, but he's also my adopted stepchild.

The thing that stands out about the first *Laid to Rest* is the kills, which when you have someone like Rob Hall involved, you have to expect that to be top notch. So do you have a favorite kill from the first movie?

Definitely. That would be Johnathon Schaech's kill. Where I throw the knife into his mouth and rip his face off. That was my money shot. I love that kill and it's definitely my favorite kill in that one.

Anyone that talks to you will realize pretty quickly that you've always been a lifelong horror fan. You had this ambition to play the monster in something and then you finally got to be the monster. I remember you guys promoting the first film at the *Fangoria* Weekend of Horrors here in LA and I recall you talking at the panel about how excited you were just to be on the cover of *Fangoria*. It's just an amazing thing to accomplish. How was all that from your perspective as a fan? Promoting the first feature and getting the cover of *Fangoria*?

Well, you know the deal. You're in the same boat as me. You can say whatever you want about *Fangoria* right now, but back in the day, there was no internet. *Fangoria* was your source of horror movie info. There really was no other place for us to get that stuff. My mom had gotten me a subscription to that magazine from the time I could read up until I could pay for the magazine myself. It's a horror geek's monthly bible. And I remember when they were talking about our movie possibly getting the cover. It's either *Laid to Rest* or *Terminator: Salvation*. So I figured, well there goes that! (laughs) It was nice to be nominated! (laughs) But then a few months went by and I remember someone called me at 5 in the morning West Coast time to tell me I was on the

cover. I hung up! I was half asleep and didn't know what they hell they were talking about. So I went back to sleep and about an hour and a half later Rob calls me up and says, "*We got the cover!*" Me living in my Hollywood state of mind, I still didn't believe it.

I walked into a Borders and there was a stack of them with Chromeskull's face on the cover. I will not lie, I totally cried. No matter what happens for the rest of my life, I will always have that. I can leave this world tomorrow and still be happy because I did what I came out here to do. Anything after that is frosting on the cake. As far as promoting the movie and going to all these conventions? I love it. I love it so much. I love these people so much. You have no idea how much I love horror fans because I am one. So when we talk about these kind of things, I get so excited and the fact that I'm involved in it is even better. Because this is something I'd be talking about anyways and I'd be at these conventions hanging with these people anyways. The fact that I'm in said movie, it just makes it all the better. There is no better fan than the horror fan. There's no romantic comedy conventions. There's no drama conventions… well, actually here in LA, there's always a drama convention. (laughs) But you know what I mean. This is the best genre in the world and I love being a part of it. I wouldn't trade it for anything in the world.

That's awesome, man. And it's great to have someone that loves the genre get to play one of our modern day slashers. A lot of people working on studio horror projects seem to have a lot of contempt for the genre, so it makes me happy when people like you that love it get to do it.

Absolutely. It kills me sometimes when I try to get a job on one of these big studio projects like something like *Predators* – not to take anything away from anyone's performance, especially Derek Mears whom I love and think is awesome. He's a great stuntman and actor and a great human being who also is a huge fan of this stuff. But, I just hate it when they hire someone just because he happens to be big and he's just doing it for a paycheck and it means nothing to him. That's very frustrating. Because I'm not just going to show up, punch a ticket and then leave after 8 hours. If you hire me for a horror gig, I am going to give you heart, soul, blood, sweat and tears.

And you might even tattoo yourself for the sake of a horror movie! That is you getting the Chromseskull tattoo in *Laid to Rest 2*, correct?

That sure is. Ya know what? You want me to do something

for your movie? Ask me. (laughs) Worst I can do is say no. I had already planned on getting a Chromseskull tattoo, but I planned on getting it on my knee, because on my left leg I have all my favorite horror icons. I've got Kyra from *Night of the Living Dead*, I had her sign it and I got that tattooed. I've got Fulci's *Zombi* on me, a random zombie from *The Walking Dead*, Michael Myers, Leatherface and Roy Batty from *Blade Runner*. Some of my favorite bad guys are on my leg and I wanted to put Chromeskull there, but hey – we needed tattoo footage for the movie and the knee wouldn't work out because it was doubling Brian Austin Green's chest. I had a little bit of space left on my back, so we threw it there and just to make it my own, I had them write "Born To Kill" above it.

Very nice! Now, going into *Chromeskull: Laid to Rest 2*, I would assume you had the second film in mind while you were making the first. Did you and Rob have any conversations during *Laid to Rest* on where this story might go?

We kind of goofed around with it, but the biggest thing for us was "How are we going to bring him back from this?" It was a pretty raw dog ending. The one thing we agreed on was that we did not want to go supernatural with Chromeskull for a sequel. I love the fact that he's still a human monster. That makes him way scarier to me. A lot of people don't like this actually, that we're breaking a "slasher" code because he's not disheveled, he's not dirty, he's not lumbering, he's not mentally disabled. Instead, he's very calculated and clean. That's exactly why I like him! He's not like any of the other "slashers" other than the fact that he's silent.

Initially when we were going into it, it was just going to be a one-shot deal. Just the one movie, which is why he got so messed up by the end. But the more and more we talked about it, we just knew we were onto something special on set and we really felt it. So the process turned into how are we going to bring him back? I did a lot of research on the internet, and I found this story about a guy in Russia who was hunting bears and a bear pretty much took off his face from above his lower jaw to his forehead. And they were able to reconstruct a fake face for him to snap on. So right there, we thought OK, there's actual medical proof that if this did happen, someone could survive it as long as there was no brain damage and they were able to immediately get the help they needed. So we went with that.

It was Rob and (co-writer) Kevin Bocarde that came up with the fact that Chromeskull had all these people working for him. It kind of establishes that the guy's a multimillionaire, and for me, him having a crew like that to do

his clean up work was a statement saying that if you have money, you can buy anything including people. You can make people look the other way for a price. If this guy has been doing this for so long and has killed this many people, how does he not get caught? Well, he's probably in bed with political figures, police figures, government. That's how he makes things go away, because he has so much money. That's a really, really scary truth. If you are super rich, you can probably get away with whatever you want in this world and there are no repercussions.

Brian Austin Green had worked with Rob on *Terminator: The Sarah Connor Chronicles* before, so it's cool to have him here in the movie. Can you talk about your working relationship with him? Because he's kind of the sequel's second Chromeskull.

And I gave him no pointers whatsoever on his version of Chromeskull, because he was supposed to be new to being a killer and he was supposed to be awkward about it. The first time he kills somebody is at the beginning of the movie and you can see in his face how much he likes it and wants to run with it. In the film, he's basically my right hand man, my second guy in charge. But then when I get all messed up, he gets it in his head that he can replace me. And Chromey does not like that whatsoever! And it comes back to him pretty badly!

As people shall see when they see the movie!

As far as working with him, to be honest at first I thought, wait, the guy from *90210*? But ya know what? He did a phenomenal, phenomenal job. He's definitely the best actor in the film, hands down.

My favorite aspect of *Chromeskull: Laid to Rest 2* is that I feel Rob has mastered the use of practical FX combined with CGI digital FX. There were spots in there I couldn't tell how certain things were done and it's amazing when you don't notice any digital augmentations. It wasn't until I watched the featurette on the Blu-ray that I got to see how much both practical and digital work went into pulling those FX off. So, what do you think of the way you guys pulled off the FX on this one and what was your favorite gag for Part 2?

I am hands down against CGI at all costs. I can't stand it. It's dominating everything in film, and I really don't like it. But I do understand that sometimes it helps to enhance certain things. But every kill on set for both *Laid to Rest 1* and *2* was done extremely practical and in the later phases would be touched up with minor CG enhancements. For the second one, my favorite kill is actually a 3-way kill when 3 cops try to arrest Chromeskull. It's actually a 5-minute scene where it seems like there might be a cut in there, but at no point did that camera cut. It took us about 3 takes to get that scene perfect. To me, it's amazing. I kill two guys at once, and slowly kill the third guy and it's all in one shot. It's just awesome and I can't believe we pulled that off. There's rarely anything like this in a genre movie that's done in one take.

When I first heard about the sequel, there were rumors that it'd be a prequel and sequel, or that there would be two films, one a prequel and one a sequel. Obviously, this is a direct sequel. But what's interesting is the end of *Chromeskull: Laid to Rest 2* definitely leaves the potential for another sequel. But then there's a scene after the credits that could set up a prequel.

Ah, good job, Mister G! A lot of people miss that extra scene.

How much of that prequel story have you guys worked on? Or is it something we're just going to have to wait for?

I don't know if you'll ever get the full backstory. With the second one, we definitely give you little tiny bits to see where he's coming from, but I personally don't want to know anything about the guy. It's cool to find out about that sort of stuff, but to me it's always scarier if you don't know. My explanation is that evil is evil, and it doesn't need a backstory to exist. Chromeskull's family could've been monkey tamers for all I know and then they did this and that, and that's what made him the way he is. Whatever scenario you want to imagine, that's fine. But if we explain it, nobody's going to be happy with it. So I like holding it open like that and just giving little tidbits of information here and there. But nothing too revealing.

I assume you'd be game to play Chromeskull again if the opportunity arose?

I will do these movies until they send me to space. (laughs)

(laughs) You won't do the sequel in space?! Come on, man!

No, no. I like *Jason X* and all, but that's when you jump the shark. But to answer your question seriously, I will continue to do these movies as long as Rob is involved.

So what's coming up next for you?

I've got a movie called *All Superheroes Must Die* coming out that I did with the Trost brothers, Brandon Trost and Jason Trost. Very, very talented family. Brandon was the DP on *Crank 2: High Voltage* and Rob Zombie's *Halloween II*, as well as the upcoming *Ghost Rider: Spirit of Vengeance*. And he just finished an Adam Sandler movie, so he's in the big leagues in Hollywood. But his younger brother loves I guess what you can call B-movies. The first movie we did together was something called *The FP*, which is getting released by the Alamo Drafthouse's distribution company. If you like avant-garde cinema of independent films, you'll love it. Jason's follow-up film to that was *All Superheroes Must Die*, which is basically about super villains taking over, so the heroes are on a quest to save the world and get their powers back and of course, I play yet another villain in that. There's another film I did called *Madison County*, which is another slasher film that I think fans of that genre will love. The trailer's up on line and we're waiting on a release date for that. I starred in an episode of *Femme Fatales* for Cinemax called "Crazy Mary." I think that airs in January. And one of the biggest things I'm proud of because it's my first real non-make-up role with a lot of dialogue is something called *Nobody Can Cool*. It's a heist film. I'm proud of that one because I did study to be an actor, and technically I am an actor. So hopefully that one will show the world that I can do more than just wear a mask and get set on fire and do stunts!

FRANK HENENLOTTER

Interviewed by Rob Galluzzo (10/10)

As a native of Long Island, I can't help but have a strong affinity for the films of fellow New Yorker Frank Henenlotter. On top of three *Basket Case* flicks, Henenlotter also helmed the trippy yet deranged *Brain Damage* and the cult classic *Frankenhooker*. And he's finally back with his new film *Bad Biology*, co-written and produced by rapper and friend R.A. "The Rugged Man" Thorburn. In a synopsis a bit too X-rated to share, just trust us when we say it's in line with the usual bizarre lunacy you expect from Frank's movies. We had the privilege of sitting down with the normally reclusive filmmaker for a signing at Dark Delicacies in Burbank and chatted about his entire career. (Originally published on *ShockTillYouDrop.com* in 2010.)

Frank! First and foremost, I have to say…welcome back!

Thank you! (laughs)

For a while, there were several different movies you were attached to make. One was *Sick in the Head*, which I believe Fangoria Films was going to do at one point. How did you end up deciding on *Bad Biology* as your new film?

Well, all the others either fell apart or fell through, or there was something in them that I didn't like at the last minute. And what made *Bad Biology* work was the freedom, because R.A. "The Rugged Man" (Thorburn) had the money and he's one of my friends and it was him and I making the rules, nobody else. So, we could just go nuts with it.

Speaking of going nuts with it, it feels like an uncommercial movie…

No, I disagree. I think it's a very commercial movie. It's just not mainstream. Mainstream and commercial are not the same thing.

Then let me rephrase that, it's not exactly a mainstream film. Was that ever a concern going in to make this, or did you and R.A. figure, '*Let's just do what we want?*'

You know, I think it's a very commercial film for people that are sick of the mainstream. That's all. I think it's going to do well on DVD. It's not going to be a favorite of the people who want the same conventional stuff. But that was the point.

I wanted to talk about the casting process for this. Considering the subject matter of the movie, was it difficult to find Jessica? Did you have to say much to convince Charlee Danielson to play the lead?

No, it actually wasn't difficult at all. Just the opposite. Charlee was going out with R.A. at the time. She read the first thirty pages of the script, and she asked us if we would let her do it. She loved the character, and I was thrilled when I heard she wanted to do it. But even then, I tried to spook her a bit and scare her off. And she didn't get scared, thankfully, because she really was just what I wanted. She was absolutely perfect. She's got this fragile beauty, she's like the girl next door. She's not the kind of person you'd expect to star in this film and go as crazy as she does. An absolute delight to work with.

How about the other lead, Anthony Sneed as Batz? Did he audition for this? Or did you already know him?

Anthony, I think, heard about the film on Craigslist. He came to an audition and at the time he looked a little too, well I'm so overweight so I can say it. He looked a little plump. He was a little too healthy. And I said he didn't look like the kind of "junkie" we needed for the character. So, he said, 'Fine, I'll lose thirty pounds.' And this was thirty days until we started shooting. I figured, 'Yeah, right.' And I never thought of him again, but sure enough he showed up thirty days later and lost thirty pounds for the part. I was so thrown by that commitment. I thought if you're really going to drop thirty pounds for this film, then I've got to take you seriously and I did. And he was great.

When did your relationship with R.A. start? Because the first time I remember seeing you two together was for the featurette on the *Basket Case* DVD where you're both visiting the old shooting locations for that film.

When he was nineteen, he was signed to Jive Records and he called me up and asked if I'd do a music video for him. I knew nothing about hip-hop, but I thought, yeah, it'd be great to do it. It was an interesting collaboration at first because I didn't understand half of what he was talking about! Every time he'd say something to me, I'd have to say, 'What does that mean? What does that mean?' Literally, he would translate it to me. And the same thing, I would say something to him and he'd ask, 'Well, what does that word mean?' But we got along fine and had a great relationship. We did the music video for Jive, it was called *"Bloodshed Hua Hoo."* From there, we had a great friendship.

On *Frankenhooker*, you collaborated and co-wrote with former *Fangoria* editor Bob Martin, who also wrote the novel version of *Brain Damage*. So how did your collaboration with R.A. on *Bad Biology* differ from your previous collaborations with Bob on your earlier films?

It really wasn't much different, it's pretty much the same. Collaborating is great because you're playing handball. You're constantly asking, 'Can you top this?' with your partner in it. I think it was the same with Bob and R.A. You just keep going for that extra joke, that extra bit that's going to push it over the edge. I couldn't have done the films by myself. That's how you get good ideas is you work with good people. And Bob Martin was exceptional, and R.A. was exceptional. That's how you do it.

You've got a few cameos and familiar faces in *Bad Biology*. First of all, Tina Krause?

Yeah, she worked on a couple of the videos that I did for R.A. I did a couple of R.A. videos, but just didn't sign my name to them. I used the name Frans Pinky. Just so people didn't think those videos were horror films. She's in one of the videos that's on the *Bad Biology* DVD.

And also, you've got Beverly Bonner, who's appeared in all of your films, turn up in *Bad Biology*.

Yep, yep. She's a good friend and I love having her in the films and she's always good. If an actor or actress makes you laugh every time, why not keep using them? I had (*Frankenhooker*, *Basket Case 2* producer) Jim Glickenhaus do a little cameo also as the magazine editor.

You've also worked with FX artist Gabe Bartalos five times, from *Brain Damage* and on. Can you talk a bit about your working relationship with him over the years?

I love working with Gabe. When you know somebody, you trust them, it makes the collaboration a lot easier because I can talk to him in shorthand. When we create a creature, it's nice because we both feel authorship over it. When it's done, I honestly feel it's mine. He honestly feels it's his. And we're both right. It's really wonderful.

You obviously have an artistic background, so how much time and focus do you and Gabe spend on creating the creatures that are in your films? Because they're always so distinct and unique. You know a creature from a Frank Henenlotter movie when you see it!

We spend a lot of time, but I tell Gabe what I want. He takes and turns that into 3D. He's the guy that spends all the time creating it and nurturing it and building it. Not me. And then I come in at the end and say, 'Well, we can have this or that,' or 'It's perfect.' That's all. He does the backbreaking work on it. (laughs) Some of his ideas are so radical and out there. He's one of the few people I encourage and say, 'Surprise me. Go for it.' And we did! Some of the stuff like "Twister" in *Basket Case 3* was a freak that I just couldn't believe I was seeing when I first saw it.

Basket Case is probably your most well-known film, because it's part of a franchise. Would you be opposed to ever revisiting it? Whether it be a sequel, a *Basket Case 4* or a remake? How would you feel about another *Basket Case* movie?

Well, I'm not going to do anymore *Basket Case* movies. I shouldn't have done *Basket Case 3*. So, I ain't doing anymore. *Basket Case 2* I like and am very happy with.

The ending to *Basket Case 2* is still one of my all-time favorite endings to a horror movie!

I agree! I like *Basket Case 2* a lot. I understand people might not like it because I went in the opposite direction, but I already made *Basket Case 1* and I didn't want to repeat it. I wanted to go in another direction. *Basket Case 3* was a disaster. Less said, the better. If somebody wanted to do a big budget remake of the original, I think it would work. That'd be fine. But there's no point in doing a low budget remake of it because that's been done!

So, you'd be okay with a remake if the right person did it and did it justice, so to speak?

Yeah, of course. Sure.

Frankenhooker is another one of your films that I love. The hooker explosion sequence is one of my favorite things in any of your movies.

Oh, that exploding hookers scene, of all the stuff I've ever done, that's my favorite sequence. I mean, everybody should explode hookers. It just doesn't get better than that! (laughs)

Didn't Gabe read that and initially think, 'Oh cool, we can make this gory,' and you said, 'No, I want them to explode like fireworks!' (laughs)

Gabe's first reaction would be to do blood and gore and I wanted to turn it into a fireworks display. I thought it was more patriotic and more Fourth of July. If it was blood and gore, I don't think it'd be funny. But exploding hookers with the stars and stripes, that was funny. It took Gabe two seconds to say, 'Well, alright!' It was hilarious. And it was also insane doing it! It really was! We didn't know how many explosives to put in those mannequins. We didn't know what we were doing. We didn't know how we were going to blow them up. A lot of it was chance. I remember, we were shooting in slow motion to capture it, but it was fantastic to have these explosions, and it was raining body parts down on us. Just marvelous and an insane way to make movies.

One of the coolest things about Frankenhooker is you've got the great Bill Murray quote on the poster and the box!

Here's the story behind that. Bill Murray was mixing his film *Quick Change* in the daytime, and we were mixing in the same studio in the evening. So, we were overlapping, and he was seeing our stuff and just couldn't be any friendlier. He had all these toys in the place, and he was sharing them, he started watching the film and started hanging out. And then eventually, he was asking, 'Can I see reel two?' and stuff like that. Someone at Shapiro Glickenhaus got wind of it and they started calling his office and asking for a quote. And that really horrified me. Because Bill was being so generous and friendly and all of a sudden, this seemed whorish of us to come out and say, 'What can we get out of this?' I was so embarrassed. He wouldn't return the calls about the quote, and I was humiliated that they'd even ask. He never gave us the quote and that was that.

One day, I'm walking toward the Brill Building where Sound One had their offices and SGE had their offices, and I see Bill walking a couple of feet ahead of me, and I was so embarrassed by them asking him for the quote that I didn't want to encounter him. So, I started slowing down, thinking he didn't know I was behind him. Then he started slowing down. So, I stopped walking, and he stopped walking. And then he went, 'Fraaaannnk?' I have no idea how he knew I was behind him! And I sheepishly walked in with him into the elevator and once the elevator doors closed, I immediately said, 'Bill, I am so sorry. I apologize. I have nothing to do with them asking you for a quote. I'm embarrassed by it. Please, you've been so generous and kind.' And he said, 'Really? You had nothing to do with it?' And I said, 'I swear to God, I had nothing to do with it.' So, he said, 'Okay, I'll give it to you.' And right there in the elevator, he said, 'If you only see one movie this year, it should be Frankenhooker.' And that was the last time I ever saw him.

(laughs) Wow. That's such a great story! Brain Damage is also a fan favorite and visually it's a beautiful movie. Do you still consider it one of your personal favorites?

Oh yeah, it was always my favorite up until *Bad Biology*.

One of the coolest things about Brain Damage is that you got Zacherley to be the voice of Elmer!

The first monster magazine I ever bought was I think *Famous Monsters* number seven with Zacherley on the cover. I grew up watching him on channel nine, *Zacherley at Large*. I was trying to find a good voice for Elmer. I wanted someone intelligent and articulate. I was talking to an agent who handled voice over actors that were distinctive. He mentioned a couple of names and when he got to John Zacherle, I went, 'Oh my God!' It was such a thrill to get him. I was just so in love with the guy. I thought it was almost a shame not to have him on camera in *Brain Damage*, so that's why I had him do a cameo in *Frankenhooker*, so at least we have him in two films now.

He's a great guy and he'd always do the Chiller conventions back in Jersey.

Oh yeah. Just a prince, that's all I can say about him.

FRANK HENENLOTTER (CONTINUED)

Interviewed by Rob Galluzzo (10/11)

A year later, I had the opportunity to speak with Frank again. This time, we chatted about restoring *Basket Case* from the original 16mm negative for the Blu-ray release, his documentary on the Godfather of Gore Herschell Gordon Lewis, as well as his radical idea for bringing Belial back in a *Basket Case 4*!? Candid as usual, here's our fright follow-up interview with writer/director Frank Henenlotter!

Here we are again talking about *Basket Case* on Blu-ray. It looks great! I had a chance to watch it the other night. Is it true that you were just always unhappy with previous incarnations and releases of *Basket Case* and that's what led to this Blu-ray release?

Oh, absolutely. I was horrified by them! I hated them! I shot the film in 16 mm. I remember the film looked bright and was in color. And when it got to theatrical release, the distributor made a dupe negative that was so dark and so murky, it looked like we had no lights. It was awful and I was so embarrassed and hated it. And then, it was projected at 1.85:1, which I should've realized, but in my naivety, I thought if I shot it in 1.66:1 full frame, they would show it in full frame. No, no, no. It looked cropped and so dark when it played. That dark master, not only was used for every theatrical print, but also for the initial VHS releases. So, of course, I hated how it looked. Finally, I was able to do the transfer myself for this Blu-ray. I had the original 16 mm negative. I had a 16 mm print, and we did it from the 35 mm IT, the inter-positive because it was virtually identical to the 16 mm print. So, we had it all there and we kept preparing everything. We kept asking ourselves, 'Is this as sharp as this? Is this as colorful as that?' And I was able to finally make the film look like the original 16 mm answer print. That's all I ever wanted, was for it just to be the film I shot.

You had found the original 16 mm negatives that you thought were lost for a while. Was finding those the genesis of the Blu-ray? Or were you planning one already?

That was definitely it. When I proposed doing an HD version of it to Image, they looked at me like, 'Ummmm.' (laughs) I said, 'Guys, guys. I found the original 16 mm negative.' So that made a difference. We ended up only using the 16 mm negative only for reference because the 35 positive was so well made. I had assumed that all the steps to 35 mm were a disaster. And it wasn't. This was a lot easier doing it in 35. It gave us a lot more control if we had to do anything. 16, by the way, is a disaster because it's an A and B roll print. We would've had to splice it all together. So, it was easier to do it from the 35 IT, but we kept the 16 mm negative there in the studio, so anytime we had a question, we could reference the original and match it. The point was, there's no way I could make *Basket Case* look like it was shot yesterday or anything. There's no way I can make the film look pretty! But I can at least make it look like the film I shot way back when.

The thing I love about it is it is a time capsule of New York in the 80s.

Oh yeah.

When I was a kid, New York was a scary place! (laughs) And *Basket Case* captures that.

Everybody says that, but I was cutting high school and going to 42nd Street back when I was fifteen years old. For a street that was supposed to be so full of crime and danger and everything, I never saw anything like that. Occasionally I'd see a fight in the theater or something. Of course, there were plenty of crazies and wackos. But they wouldn't bother me at all! You learn real fast what to deal with and what not. While the street was full of crime, if you weren't buying hookers or drugs, no one gave a shit! So, you could be walking down the street and someone would mutter under their breath, and if you shook your head no and ignored them, they were already looking past you to the next person. So, it was never a problem for me. I was very comfortable in New York in those days. I was extremely comfortable in the sleaze and cesspool that was 42nd Street. (laughs) I loved it.

When I finally moved into Manhattan, I was there six nights a week. So, I was very comfortable going to those theaters. To me, I would feel uncomfortable when I went to a fancy theater. And I didn't have to go to 42nd Street. A lot of the movies playing on 42nd Street were also playing a couple of blocks away in Times Square in better theaters.

Sure, maybe they cost a dollar more, but I liked the ambiance of 42nd Street, I liked the crowds, I liked the enthusiasm. I just felt very comfortable there.

I knew how scary and crazy it was. In fact, here's a *Basket Case* story about how scary it was. In the film, there's a moment where we shot in a truck and Kevin (Van Hentenryck) is walking past 42nd Street. He passes a porno store. It's a porno store that is in the film, it's got a yellow glow in it, I think. The first take we did of that, a guy in that porno store saw us, he was looking out as we were filming. He came charging out, racing at us and jumped into the van threatening to kill us!

Oh man!

We were like, 'What? Why?' He thought that we were CBS TV. I don't know why. Kevin's the one that talked him out of it. He was like, 'Hey man. We're making a movie.' He goes, 'What? You're not the news?' Kevin's like, 'No! Look at our cameras. We're just making a monster movie.' The guy's like, 'I'm sorry, I'm sorry. I just thought you were CBS, and I don't want them poking around here anymore.' (laughs) I don't know what that was about, but that was stuff that happened in those days.

I'm curious because you've lived with this movie for so many years. When you revisit it, is there anything new that you discover or something that you forgot about, in particular, with doing this restoration?

No, I really know it so well at this point, it's sickening. It's so difficult looking at your old films because you want to go back and fix them. So, no. Nothing surprised me other than how young we all were. (laughs) Once upon a time, I was a thin young man. (laughs)

Now that you've got the original *Basket Case* on Blu-ray, any talk about getting the sequels out on Blu-ray too? In particular, *Basket Case 3*, which I know you're not fond of, but it's become so difficult to find these last few years.

I don't know. I don't own the rights to any of the others, so I don't often know what they're doing until they're announced. I'm clueless. Maybe there will be, maybe not, maybe they're already in the works? I don't know.

Did you have any involvement in the *Frankenhooker* Blu?

No! None at all. I would've liked to have supervised the transfer. I've seen transfers of my other films that I would've

fixed had I been there. But if I'm not asked, I can't fix and that's that. The only thing I knew, I know Synapse was thinking of putting out *Frankenhooker* on Blu-ray. That's the last thing I heard was they said to me, 'We're thinking of putting out *Frankenhooker*.' OK. Then it's done and coming out. Oh well. There was a big gap between we're thinking of doing it and it being done, you know? And meanwhile, I got a phone call from a friend of mine from Scotland who was working on *Frankenhooker*. He was working on the UK version and asked me to do a commentary for it and I said, 'Sure!' So, I did a commentary for the UK version with James Lorinz. But no one asked me about the US Blu-ray until I finished doing that other commentary and I wasn't going to do two in a row. I can't do that. (laughs) It's exhausting doing them. A week later I got asked to do one for the US release and I thought I just did one!

Well, I guess we'll have to get the UK one for your new commentary essentially.

I'll just say I'm lucky I own one film; most directors don't own any.

Brain Damage is probably my favorite of your films. I would love to see that get a nice Blu-ray release.

Again, no clue. All I know is who owns it. I'm not involved in any of that.

You've got the *Godfather of Gore* documentary coming out as well. I feel you've been a champion of Herschell Gordon Lewis' stuff for years now, especially giving his films proper releases via *Something Weird*. That must've been a rewarding experience getting to pay tribute to the man with this feature documentary, no?

Yeah. I don't think anyone needs to champion him anymore because he's well known now. But once upon a time, no one knew who he was. I dedicated *Basket Case* to him and basically no one had a clue who I was talking about back then. His films were very difficult to find. And yeah, through *Something Weird*, that's been the fun of it, putting those movies out. The same time that we put out the *Basket Case* Blu-ray, we'll have *Blood Feast* in HD. *Blood Feast* in HD?! Good lord! And *Two Thousand Maniacs* and *Color Me Blood Red* all on the same Blu-ray! We're probably next going to do *The Wizard Of Gore* and *The Gore Gore Girls* on Blu-ray.

Oh nice!

And it's – it's a bit scary. Because every time you pick up a film can, you can put your ear to it and hear a clock ticking. They don't last forever. Especially films that were independents. There are no dupe negatives, there's no preservation print. There's nothing. There's one negative and one theatrical print and that is it. We went to our negative for *Two Thousand Maniacs* and as soon as they opened the first can of it, we smelled vinegar and it already shrunk. So, the negative of *Two Thousand Maniacs* that was available a couple of years ago for us to use is gone. So, we had to go with the theatrical print. Now we're talking about *Wizard of Gore* on Blu. The print that we used for the DVD, I think, its five or six reels. Reels one and three are also appearing thinner. Fortunately, we've got a couple of prints of that one. But we've only known one print to exist for *The Gore Gore Girls*, so it's kind of a race against time that we continue putting these out and making HD transfers, because they're not going to last forever. I think people should know too when they complain about a print having a scratch here or there, it's either that or nothing!

Well, I'm thankful for the work you're doing on Herschell's films for sure.

It's a pleasure doing that stuff! I mean, who else is going to do high-def versions of his movies?! (huge laughs)

Has he seen the documentary? And if so, how does he feel about it?

Oh yeah. We did the premiere for the film at the Fantasia Film Festival in Montreal, and Herschell was the special guest along with myself, Mike Vraney and Jimmy Malson. We all went down there together. I think Herschell was a little apprehensive at first going into the doc until he heard the reaction from the crowd! The crowd loved it! So afterwards, he was in a great mood, he sang four choruses of *Two Thousand Maniacs*.

That's amazing! Last question, I've heard rumblings you're thinking about doing a really radical *Basket Case 4*?

I mean, I have an idea but it's so radical that I don't know. It's one of those ideas that's either a total disaster or a really good one! You know how you're not sure? Either way, I think it's worth doing. If I shoot myself in the foot, it ain't the first time that's happened! (laughs) And anything that follows *Basket Case 3* will be seen as OK. (laughs) Nothing could be as bad as that.

Well, before they remake it, and while most franchises go to space, I welcome whatever radical idea you have for a new *Basket Case*!

Oh, it really is out there. It really is. So, I think let's try it! I haven't even written it yet. But it's rumbling and I have to finish a couple other projects first and then maybe I'll do it.

Whatever you do next, I'll be looking forward to it. Once again, Frank, thank you so much for your time!

My pleasure!

EPILOGUE
2024-25

PARKER FINN
JON WATTS
DANNY PHILIPPOU

PARKER FINN

Interviewed by Rob Galluzzo (10/24)

It started as a short film and then became a cable streaming exclusive movie before pivoting to a proper theatrical release. Parker Finn's debut feature as a writer/director, *Smile*, became a surprise smash hit for Paramount Pictures. The sequel was inevitable, but the way Parker continued the "curse" in *Smile 2* opened up the world in bold, exciting, and ambitious new ways. We chatted about the continued evolution of the *Smile* franchise, why he wants to tackle a remake of *Possession*, and his advice on how to pitch yourself as a filmmaker to the studios.

What are your earliest recollections of the horror genre? I'm sure there was something you saw that you probably shouldn't have seen a little too young that left an indelible mark and is the reason you're making these movies now!

Oh, you know, I think I have a few distinct memories and it's interesting. Some are from horror, but some are not from horror films. They're just from other films that scared the shit out of me as a kid. I often think about *Poltergeist*. I saw the original *Poltergeist* as a kid and that movie scared the hell out of me. I can't believe that's a PG movie. And everything from the little clown to the tree to all that stuff, I thought was going to happen to me. A moment that I often think back to is the ending of *Indiana Jones and the Last Crusade*, when he drinks out of the wrong cup. Instantly, he ages a hundred years and dies. Something about that stuck with me very hard when I was a kid and I couldn't shake that. Again, obviously it's not a horror film, but definitely lingered with me. I also think about in Tim Burton's *Batman Returns* when Danny DeVito's Penguin is dying, and all that black stuff is coming out of his mouth. It was so upsetting to me as a little kid.

I think that scarred a generation of children!

The first time I saw John Carpenter's *The Thing*. The first time I saw *A Nightmare on Elm Street*. I mean, *Nightmare on Elm Street* is probably almost more than anything else indelibly burned into my brain.

I just revisited it for Halloween season. And that original one, I found a lot of threads of *Nightmare on Elm Street*

that I feel, subliminally or not, are definitely carried into your work. But we'll get to that. I want to know the beginning for you as a filmmaker in terms of, did you start pursuing directing or was there another avenue?

Well, I grew up in northern Ohio, sort of in between Cleveland and Akron. So, the idea of directing was not something that ever occurred to me or seemed like a possibility, but my dad was a cinephile. So, movies were a big deal in my house. And I think early on, I thought maybe I wanted to be an actor because that's what I saw on screen. It's easy to be like, 'Oh, I want to be Harrison Ford because he's Indiana Jones and he's Han Solo.' But I think, definitely special effects, any behind the scenes stuff I could see. I think the filmmakers that I first really started to become aware of were Steven Spielberg and James Cameron and probably Ridley Scott, where I thought, oh, these are voices making these films.

Certainly *Terminator 2* had a huge, profound impact on me. I wanted to understand how they made the T-1000. To me, it just blew my mind. But even further back with Cameron, I mean, *The Abyss* was another one that I thought, how did he do this? I don't understand. I remember having that realization of, 'Oh, they're not actually filming in a lab at the bottom of the ocean. This is a set that was built somewhere.' *Alien* for me. I love *Alien* and *Aliens*. I think I probably think about *Alien* more than I think about *Aliens*.

As a kid, *Terminator 2* and *Aliens* were awesome. They're just action packed and exactly what you want to see when you're young! Now, as an adult, I prefer the first *Alien*

437

and the first *Terminator*. Because I can see, especially the first *Terminator*, that it's a low budget movie and kind of magic that it works as well as it does.

Totally, yeah. And those are huge. And then I'd say as far as thinking about people really authoring films, I mean, *Jurassic Park* was seminal. I had to understand how does this movie exist? I could kind of wrap my head around it. As a kid, I was constantly stealing my dad's camcorder and making shorts, and just playing around with it. And whether I was with friends doing stuff or even with action figures, I remember discovering, 'Oh, I can pause recording and shift the camera to another angle and start recording again. And it's a cut,' that sort of stuff. But the journey to becoming a director felt very far away despite all of that. I was also always writing. My mom was a school teacher and I always had to have a book in my hand. So, reading and movies, storytelling in general, were very big for me. I started writing and realized it was something that I really loved, but movies were always the goal. I just had to figure out how to actually start doing it.

Was there something specific that got you started? Just meeting other like-minded people that wanted to act that made that suddenly possible, because I think this segues into some of the short films that you did.

I feel like I cared about movies and wanted to talk about movies more than people around me growing up in the Midwest. People liked movies. But I really liked talking about movies. I was a major video store kid. And I was also obsessed with the art of media. I love VHS box art, which is an art form; that brief window of laserdiscs where you had fully vinyl sized sleeves of art that were amazing. I was also really into that. I mean, maybe you were the same, but I could spend hours and hours at a video store just looking and reading the backs of boxes. I went to college in Colorado, I was an English creative writing major. And then I ended up coming out to California for grad school. And so, that was my way out here and then, I started making short films once I was in school. That was the first time that I felt like I was doing something with other people versus just something I was doing with friends, if that makes sense.

Totally! I'm in the same camp. I'm from Long Island, New York. I was the one that talked and showed my friends the cult movies I was finding. And I ended up in California, just as we all migrate towards our own! Let's talk about the short that inspired *Smile*, *Laura Hasn't Slept*. What I love is the evolution of that story. Because the short,

Laura Hasn't Slept, to *Smile*, to *Smile 2*, they're vastly different themes and stories that you've evolved. So, with the short film, was that intended to be just be a short; a calling card? Or did you always kind of want it to be a pitch to a much larger feature length film?

It was more of a calling card at the time. I had made a handful of little shorts in school that I never put out into the world. It's a nice way to sort of fail in private. (laughs) *Laura Hasn't Slept* was actually the second short that I pushed out into the world. (The first was *The Hidebehind*) And with *Laura Hasn't Slept*, it was the first time I ever spent any money on a short, really. I mean, everything else, it was always done for $8 and a bag of potato chips. But with that short, I had been writing stacks of shorts along with features and was trying to figure out what made the most sense to show off, what I thought I could do. It was exploring things I was interested in, and it had to pack a punch within ten minutes. What I loved about that short, on the technical side, it allowed me to flex a bunch of technical muscles. And then also, it had a central performance inside of it, which I think is sorely lacking from a lot of like genre shorts. I was interested in this idea of where mental health and the supernatural could meet. Which is sort of where that came from. I was kind of chasing that feeling of… when you first wake up from a bad dream and those first two minutes, you can't quite shake it.

And you feel this panicky sense of doom, even though, your logical brain knows it was just a dream, but your monkey brain thinks, I'm in danger. Which is really sort of ineffable, sort of an ethereal thing. But it was like, 'Can I create that feeling in this short?' So that was all the stuff that I was going into the writing of it with. And I always feel, personally, that shorts should feel self-contained rather than a cynical commercial for something else. Now, if they can do that, but also be a satisfying experience on their own, I think that's really important. So, it wasn't until I was in post-production on that short that the idea that became *Smile* started really drumming up inside my brain. It definitely springboarded me into that, but it wasn't backwards engineered at all.

Right. Well, I love the cast. I love Lew Temple. He's so underrated, but kudos to Caitlin Stacey! I recognized her from the Lucky McKee movie, *Kindred Spirits*, which she did a couple years back. Technically, I like to think that *Smile*, the movie, could be a sequel to the short. I pretend it's the same character and it's just her next step.

(laughs)

Once the short got attention and it became feature length, did it come natural to you on how you would expand it? Were you excited about the ideas and maybe pulling from some of these other shorts that were in the drawer?

I find that shorts and features, when I was writing them, they are stretching very different muscles. I actually find them to be related, but also distinct art forms. I had probably written eight or nine features at that point. So, I had been really immersed in that as well. What was important to me was to take the stuff from the short that was informing the feature, but to leave behind some of the things that were just for the short and allow the feature to be its own thing. Because the way I like to write and how I like to approach horror is to be very character driven and sort of mine everything from the inside out.

So, I had to make sure to, and I always tell this to people when they're thinking about shorts to features is, forget all of your misgiving's about what it has to be. If the short put you in the position to make a feature or if you're going to pitch a feature based off the short, that shared DNA, I think is really helpful in getting people to see what it is, but you don't need to be so beholden to what the short was doing. I think the best shorts are often almost told like a joke. It's a quick setup and then a punchline and you're out, right? So, there's room to really explore ideas as much as sort of tell a quick anecdote. I was planning to write what became *Smile* before everybody started coming and knocking. And then, I happened to have the opportunity to pitch it ahead of time just because the short captured the attention of the town for one week.

The short is so different from what the movie became. If I saw the short, *Smile* is not what I would expect the full version of it to be! It's an evolution. I think that's super cool. Talk to me about *Smile*. You made it as a streaming movie, right? And then it became a theatrical movie. Every filmmaker I've spoken to hates the test screening process, but in this case, it was a major advantage to you because that is the moment that Paramount saw this could be a theatrical release. What was that like from your vantage point? Because you're making it for a specific platform, and then it becomes a much bigger thing, which obviously worked perfectly for theatrical.

Yeah, despite having gone through the process successfully twice now with the testing, I hate it too. (laughs) It's a very stressful process that is incredibly imperfect, but it's also the only thing we really have. So, for now, at least it's the best version to sort of figure out where you're at. And as an aside on the testing process, I think the testing process can

be very useful in a couple of ways. For example, sometimes you're so close to your project in post that you can miss the forest for the trees. So, if suddenly, you test your movie and two characters that are siblings, if half your audience thinks they're in a relationship, it's like, oh, okay, clearly, we were too close, we didn't realize that we're not giving people enough information here and you can address that. Or if you find that half of your audience is fully confused on something in a bad way, that's something to take a look at.

When people are, 'Oh, I wish it would have been this,' or 'I wish it would have been that,' it's that stuff that comes from the test audience that is not very useful. And I wish studios, maybe, would drown that out a little more. Because movies are made usually from a director's taste surrounded by producers. That's the taste you should go with, not with the audience after you've made it. But the biggest thing, especially for horror and for comedy on the other side of the coin, is that when you're sitting in a theater full of 200 strangers who have no bias, you know really quickly if the scares are landing or the jokes are landing, because the audience won't lie. They're either going to be laughing, or they're going to be screaming or jumping or whatever it is. And so, that's a really good thing to know as well, because at that point, you've seen the scare or the joke or whatever a hundred times, it doesn't work on you or the editor or anybody else anymore. You need a group of people who have never seen it before. So that can be very helpful.

But yeah, I mean, that first test screening changed my life, and I am extremely grateful for it. When we made the film, we made it to be able to play on the biggest screens and the loudest sound possible. That was just how I wanted to make the film. And we were hoping at the time, maybe we'll get a festival premiere before we go on streaming. In a theater with an audience. That's what we were chasing. And yeah, when they made that shift, it was incredible. I think there was this undeniable electricity in the audience which then came through in the scores where you could feel like, oh, this is a movie that really wants to be watched in a communal experience. And to their credit, Paramount recognized that very quickly.

You mentioned it yourself, but I love that horror and comedy are the only two genres that elicit an uncontrollable response from your audience. You can't help but yelp or laugh out loud! It's just what happens. Let's delve into the sequel. When I saw *Smile 2*, I told this to Paramount. I'm a pretty well-versed cinephile, especially in horror history. I don't think there is another example in horror history where a studio had as much

confidence in giving a filmmaker ten times the budget, ten times the ambition. I mean, Wes Craven got knocked off of *Nightmare on Elm Street 2*! I'm just in awe. And I think it's worth celebrating that they gave you that much trust going into the sequel. Was it always a given that *Smile 2* would be next for you? And once you got that opportunity, I feel that you were proving, 'Hey, by the way, I can do a lot of genres!' (laughs) And I'm going to show you that in this movie. I could make a big musical number and do drama and comedy and all that stuff. I don't know what my actual question is. (laughs) I guess, how did you convince Paramount to support this huge swing?

Yeah. Well, that was, so I'll answer all those. (laughs) I'll try to. First of all, not ten times the budget. (laughs) We went from seventeen million to twenty-eight million, which is still a big jump. And I am extremely grateful for that. But absolutely, the movie was putting a ten-gallon movie in a five-gallon bucket. So, it feels like a much bigger movie than what we actually had to work with. But I also recognized that twenty-eight million for an R rated horror film is… it's cuckoo bananas. Like, that's amazing. And again, very much like the short when I made *Smile 1*, never in a million years did I expect there to be a sequel. I didn't think there would be demand for a sequel. I was hoping the first movie would find an audience, that people would discover it.

It was opening weekend when the word "sequel" first came up. And I was really unsure because I didn't consider myself a sequel guy. And also, I can be very suspicious of sequels. I think a lot of times sequels are made cynically in success. Right? Oh, the first movie made a bunch of money, and it didn't cost a ton to make. We obviously have to make a sequel. And I think so many sequels, especially to horror films, are rushed. And not made with the same love and care and thoughtfulness of the first one and what made it connect with people. And so, I stepped away because I wasn't sure what I was going to do. Paramount brought me this opportunity to say, 'Do you want to make a sequel? We're all ears about what you'd want to do.' And so, I went away and thought, all right, if I'm going to consider this, and I should because how often in life do you get to create something, and then somebody is asking you to create a sequel to that. I mean, that's amazing. And I wanted to keep in mind what an incredibly special, lucky position that was for me and not just turn my nose up at it because it was going to have a two after it.

So, I went away and any idea I came up with in the first month, I threw out. It came too quickly. It's too obvious. I don't want to do it because somebody else could come up with that idea. I sort of stumbled upon this character that

became Skye Riley, this mega pop star, this very public facing person in this world of hers. And I got obsessed with this idea that I could really jump rails into a different world, keep the connective tissue and the DNA of *Smile* running through it, but to allow the sequel to be a film that truly has its own identity and its own metabolism. And that seemed really exciting to me. I kept thinking about *Terminator* to *Terminator 2*, and any of those sequels that we think about in that way. How do I do that with a horror film? And part of me also thought, okay, I'm going to take this big swing. I'm going to walk into Paramount and I'm going to pitch them this. And there are other movies I can go make, but if they'll let me take this big swing, I'm coming back to *Smile* and I will do it. I will write and direct it. And I ended up producing it as well.

I think that was definitely not the take they were expecting. (laughs) But I think they couldn't deny the interesting approach to it and the unexpected nature of it. And I think they saw what I was trying to do about turning *Smile* into something that invades a character's world, rather than something that felt like it was just trying to continue and excavate the mythology or anything like that. It was like, no, this is a brand-new character study, but it's still going to make people jump out of their seat. It's going to be propulsive and all this stuff. And they said, 'Yes.' And then I was like, 'Oh shit, I guess I'm making this movie!' (laughs) And yeah, along the way, I think there were a lot of questions brought up. And I understand the hesitation. 'Cause there's this question of well, fictional musician biopics usually don't work. And I'm aware of that. And they were like, 'Maybe she could be like a pop star in the periphery of the movie?' And I was like, 'No, no, it is part of her story. We need to build credibility out of all of that.' And bit by bit, they kept just saying yes. So, then we were off to the races to start, I was writing it and then we were prepping it before I knew it. We turned it around very fast. I mean, *Smile 2* came right after the first one.

Amazing. I was at CinemaCon earlier this year when they showed us the teaser, but they didn't tell us what it was. So, we're seeing this elaborate stage show, and I thought it was a Lady Gaga movie or something. (laughs) What is this? So, the twist that it was a *Smile* sequel, I thought that was a great teaser. And also, there's already a level of paranoia that comes from being a celebrity. I thought it lent itself perfectly to that conceit. Which brings me to Naomi Scott (who plays Skye Riley) and, in general, finding your leads because I personally didn't know her from anything else. I thought she was incredible; totally carried the movie and you needed somebody really strong to be able to carry that movie and make you believe that she's a pop star and going through all these traumatic things. And by the way, the same thing with Sosie Bacon in the first movie, she's tremendous. What is it about the casting process for you? Is it an instinctual thing? Is it specific things you're looking for? How do you find the people that will bring forth your vision?

Well, going back to the idea of how I like to use horror to tell a really character-driven story. I really also love to make performance-based horror. So, Naomi carrying the second one, Sosie carrying the first one. It's like, yes, the things that are going bump in the night are very freaky and scary and get you to jump out of your seat. But it's the human being going through it, I think, that really gets under people's skin and makes them very stressed out and nervous and gets them, I think, to sort of relate to and connect with the film so much. And so, I write these very difficult roles to take on for sure. And I'm looking, usually for somebody who is hungry to really prove something. I really want somebody who's going to be a partner in crime and lock arms with me and jump off the deep end with me. I like weird, freaky, big performance shit. And I'm looking for actors who are the same way. Because I think that sort of simpatico can really produce some real magic as far as what you're capturing. I like to try to steer away from casting on type or anything too obvious.

For *Smile 2*... Naomi was Princess Jasmine in the live action *Aladdin*. She was a *Power Ranger*. She was a *Charlie's Angel*. Famously, she was in *Lemonade Mouth* on the Disney channel. And when I first met with her, we were supposed to meet for a thirty-minute coffee and two and a half hours later, we were still just geeking out about, 'Oh my God, wouldn't this be amazing to do together?' And that sort of thing is always what I'm looking for is somebody who matches my level on the other side of the camera. I think casting is so much of the process. Films are so different with different people in lead roles. I try to take it very seriously and I try to ignore any noise. I think a lot of this town thinks in terms of value, which is so liquid and going to change two and a half years later when the movie comes out anyways. Who's the hottest person at the moment or whatever it is for me, who would be stunt casting, who would be this or that? Maybe I'm old school in a way. I think I've been really lucky to get away with it thus far, but I'm just way more interested in finding an artist that I really connect with who I think we could go out and actually make magic together and leave everything else behind.

And by the way, I'm all in for you and Robert Pattinson doing a new version of *Possession*. But again, it's a movie that exists. There has to be some sort of personal connection or something about the material that you feel is reason enough to make it your next film.

Yeah, I love the original *Possession*. One of my favorite films of all time. Before I was making this new version, it was still a film that I would revisit two or three times a year. It used to be… you couldn't even get your hands on it! I bought $200 special edition import Blu-ray like twelve years ago, because I had to have it. And I'm not even somebody who collects Blu-rays, by the way. I think there is something about *Possession* that has always sort of stuck with me. There's something about it that I've always been chasing. And sometimes you don't know what it is, but there can be a particular piece of art that you find yourself obsessed with in a certain way. And I think that *Possession* is criminally underseen, first of all. And I think that nobody is making films like *Possession* anymore, certainly not in Hollywood.

When the rights became available for the first time in forty years, and I was reached out to about it by Roy Lee at Vertigo Entertainment, we went in and secured them. Initially, I asked myself, do I have something that I can do with *Possession* now that will feel really exciting and fresh and yet still honor and homage the original, and it will be able to be a way for me to scratch a particular creative itch that I've had in a way that can be very direct. I'm trying to have a conversation with the original film and be in dialogue with it, but also to offer something new and although I can't say a lot about it at this stage, because it's early days, what I will say is that I can assuage any fears that we are not doing any sort of sanitized, Hollywood, shallow, sharp corners shaved off version of it. If the film gets made, I want people to be like, how the fuck did this get made in Hollywood? I cannot believe this exists. And I'm hoping to continue the goodwill from *Smile 2* and say, hey, I'm genuinely trying to bring something that has studio resources but is really designed with a true genre enthusiast heart at its core.

And I also like the idea that if in making this spiritual successor to *Possession* and releasing it to the world, it will also help shine a light back on the original *Possession*, and people will go and discover it. I can be part of that lineage. That's such an honor for me. It's just something I'm very excited about. It's going to be a batshit insane film. Yeah. It's going to be great.

To wrap up, I've never really asked a filmmaker this, but when you introduced *Smile 2* at CinemaCon in 2023, it was the first time that I'd heard you speak, and you're talking to a room of 3,000 theater owners, which can be nerve wracking. But what struck me was you were very well spoken; you had great confidence. I talk to a lot of filmmakers about their humble beginnings. The one thing I have never asked anyone about is pitching yourself. Because what I thought when I saw you speak was, 'OK, this guy must be really good in a room. He's got confidence. He speaks well.' I assume you have a way of getting your ideas across clearly. How important is that pitching process for up-and-coming filmmakers? What advice can you give in terms of how to how to properly pitch yourself?

I can think of a few ways to approach that. I think that part of a filmmaker, or a director's job, is getting people excited. It's rallying the troops, right? And that starts at every stage of the process. So, that means to get somebody to say yes to an idea, such as producers. And then to get the financiers, studio, whoever it is; to actually take the risk, but you've got to convince them as well. And then also all of your collaborators moving forward; all your key department heads, actors, certainly all of these people. And then in post-production, I mean, post is still fraught with opinions and changes and all this kind of stuff.

But it's about how you, the captain, can steer everybody through all that. So, I think inherently, and that's not to say that it's impossible to make movies if somebody is incredibly introverted and shy and their whole thing is, I want to just make my art and that's that, that's a perfectly reasonable approach. We've seen many incredible filmmakers who've been able to do that as well. No doubt. I think that pitching is really important, and confidence is really important. I don't particularly love public speaking. I, like anyone else, dread it for sure when I have to do it, but I always try to find a way to be talking about something that excites me; something that I feel, truly. And I try to carry that excitement and that confidence forward in that way. I think for up-and-coming filmmakers, when they get that opportunity to be in the room, one thing that's really important to remember is that, especially if you're a first-time feature filmmaker and I don't even care if you're there because of your short film that you're going to try to adapt into a feature or whatever.

I genuinely don't think that, for the most part, 99% of the time, it's not about the concept necessarily that you're selling to them in the room. It's oftentimes, I mean… ideas are a dime a dozen and it's really about… are they excited by your vision. Do they trust you? Because everybody wants to be able to say no, because taking a risk on a first-time filmmaker is an insane decision to make, because you're talking about potentially millions of dollars for somebody

who's never done it before. When you have this whole pool of people who have made features before that, at least they have a track record. So how do you get them to say yes? I think it's to make yourself undeniable. And you want the person on the other side of the table in their brain to think, "If I don't get in the passenger seat of this car with this filmmaker, somebody else is going to, and I'm going to miss out." Right? So really, it's about that confidence. "Hey, I am doing this thing one way or another, I'm going to make this happen." And you want people that are betting on you as the filmmaker rather than betting on some kernel of an idea, because it's not the concept that's going to see the movie through to the finish line. It's the filmmaker and the passion and everything behind it, the ability to get other people invested. I think it's really important, but it's worth remembering what you're actually selling when you get into these rooms is yourself as the captain of the ship.

Yeah. Enthusiasm is contagious and I think when you're genuine and sincere, it's very obvious it shines through.

When you're pitching the concept, I always like to think about it too. People pitch in different ways. And I think being really good in the room is extremely helpful, of course. But if you're the kind of person where that's not where you shine, that doesn't mean that things are hopeless. Because there's lots of people who get movies made that pitching in the room is not their strong suit. But I think if you are somebody who can get over that hump of public speaking and being able to pitch, I always like to think of it as, keep your pitch under thirty minutes, if you can. And pretend like you just saw your favorite movie you've ever seen and you're trying to describe it to somebody else that you desperately want them to watch the movie and you're trying to make it exciting for them. Right? I feel it should be the tenor rather than coming in like you're on *Shark Tank* and you're trying to sell them. It should ideally be practiced, but you want it to feel very casual and conversational. I think that is really important. And again, it's all about that passion, that excitement.

Great advice. Thank you, Parker, for being the first new Icons of Fright interview in over a decade! Best of luck. And I can't wait to see *Possession*.

And I'm honored to be included! So, thank you.

Special thanks to Chris Aronson and Craig Elliott from Paramount. From Parker's team, thanks to Natalie Lieb and Cassandra Bielmeier.

JON WATTS

Interviewed by Rob Galluzzo (2/25)

For filmmaker Jon Watts and his writing partner, Christopher Ford, they didn't think much about their trailer pitch for the faux horror movie, *Clown*. They were just trying to get attention for their work. But it did catch the eye of modern "Master of Horror" Eli Roth and suddenly became a real movie! From there, Watts teamed with Kevin Bacon for his contemplative little indie movie, *Cop Car*, before helming three of the biggest and most successful *Spider-Man* movies Marvel has ever produced! Now, he's set to revive a long dormant beloved horror franchise, this time as a producer, *Final Destination*. We got to chat with him about how fate, and maybe his sense of humor, guided all of the above. Read on!

What are your earliest recollections of the horror genre? Because I think for all of us, we have images and moments from films that we probably saw too young or that have just stayed with us forever. So, what was that for you?

Well, I wasn't allowed to watch horror movies at all. Completely forbidden. Definitely not any R-rated movies, but anything that even seemed adjacent to the horror genre was completely off limits. So, I wasn't exposed to it really at a young age. Except when I accidentally did see something that gave it an even more mentally scarring effect. And the one that immediately comes to mind when you ask that, for me, this is so fucked up. I was a little kid visiting with my family on a vacation in England. I was up late watching, must have been Channel 4 or something? There was a guy who had a midnight movie show and I didn't know what I was watching. It kind of just seemed like a John Hughes high school movie about the rich kids and the poor kids. And it was that film *Society*.

Oh my God. I know how that ends! So yeah!

I can only imagine watching it and thinking this is just a high school movie. And then by the time it gets to that final scene, I honest to God thought I was staring through a portal into hell. (laughs) This is why I'm not allowed to watch horror movies or R-rated movies! And for the longest time I didn't know what movie it was. I remembered it more like it was a nightmare I had as opposed to something I had actually watched because I couldn't describe that to anyone.

It's called "shunting" what they do in that finale.

That's what that's called?

Yeah. I didn't know the term until years later, but yes.

I just, I couldn't, I thought it was not real. Yeah. For the longest time. It wasn't until I finally had access to the internet that I could figure out what I had watched.

Did *Society* turn you off from the genre or make you more curious?

It terrified me, but I think on a subconscious level that prepared me to finally face the fears when I was not going to get in trouble.

Well, I was actually texting with our mutual friend Craig Perry (*Final Destination: Bloodlines* producer) recently about *Cop Car*, which I promise I'll get back to in a minute. But the reason I bring that up is because he had mentioned that you actually teach a course specifically on where to put the camera.

Yeah. I think it's a secret. I don't know if it's advertised. I don't think it's too big of a thing. It's just a little seminar. I do it at NYU. I've done it once. I'm going to do it maybe again this year.

Well, the reason I brought that up is I wanted to know your origin story in terms of filmmaking. I think for a lot of us, we watch movies passively. And then there comes a point where you realize, "Oh, somebody made this… I understand the mechanics behind it. Maybe I could do that too." So, was directing always the clear path in?

Yeah. I became aware of what a director was because of Alfred Hitchcock. I loved those movies as a little kid. And you knew that, 'Oh, the director has a cameo.' I would watch *Alfred Hitchcock Presents* and things like that. At a young age, that was kind of the only director that you could also see in the movie. It was like, 'Oh yeah. Steven Spielberg, Alfred Hitchcock.' I didn't quite understand what being a director meant for a while, but I wasn't going to do any of this. I was going to be a chemical engineer. And then I just started making movies with my friends on the weekends. And in my senior year, I applied for these film school scholarships, total long shot. I couldn't go to film school unless I got a full ride. So, I kind of don't think I actually want to do any more math and science classes if I don't have to, but you know, see what happens. And I amazingly got into film school.

Wow.

It was a very shocking last second pivot for my family. I went away to New York to go to film school. And you would talk about Hitchcock and Spielberg because they're the great directors. But I loved seeing *Ed Wood*. The Tim Burton *Ed Wood*. Because that felt more like on the level of something that I could make, like not the movie, *Ed Wood*, what Ed Wood was making.

Right.

It was *Plan Nine from Outer Space*. That feels like something I could make. You can't watch *Lawrence of Arabia* when you're a 16-year-old kid in a small town in Colorado and think 'I want to do that someday.' But you can imagine yourself making *Glenn or Glenda*. I liked *Eraserhead* for that same reason. That seems like something I could have made. Just in terms of the scope and the scale. I have one friend who will be an actor. I know the old, rundown warehouse that we could use as a backdrop.

Yeah. I love movies about making movies. And I think *Ed Wood* is probably my favorite Tim Burton movie by far. So, let's talk a little bit about *Clown* because the story of you getting to make it is just one of the great Hollywood stories. It started out as a trailer, or a short film sort of

thing. **And then Eli Roth saw it and got involved? I know I'm oversimplifying that. But what was the goal with that? Was it always just to make a short to show what you could do? Or did you have an idea for a feature?**

It was made as a prank. We had a YouTube page where we would post dumb little funny videos that my friends and I made. After we were out of school, we would make them for fun because we were making movies. And one of the jokes was always trying to think of the absolute worst horror movie that you could pitch in a room of Hollywood executives that would ruin your career forever. We would joke around about what that film was. And we just kept adding layers to it. Like, 'Okay, it's about like a man who painfully transforms into a clown. Okay.' And they were like, 'Yeah, and he wants to eat kids. Yeah, great, great.' Just like a Hollywood suicide kind of pitch. And then one day, I think we were all just in a cranky mood because no one was picking up our TV show pilots. No one was reading our scripts. We thought, 'Let's just make the *Clown* trailer and see if we could fool people into thinking it was real.' That was the only intention was a prank to see if our handful of YouTube followers, which was very early days of YouTube, if we could trick them into believing that this was a real thing. And so that's how we framed it. Me and Chris Ford listed ourselves as co-writers along with an actual Hollywood screenwriter whose name we just stole off of the credit block from something else. And then, we all loved Eli Roth because he was another NYU film school guy. And *Hostel*, it was so fucked up and great. We thought if we put Eli's name on it, people would maybe believe it, and it would help sell the prank. And also, it would make people jump to the conclusion that, 'Oh, this goes somewhere really disturbing and dark.' So yeah, we put Eli's name on it. This was completely a prank, and we were shocked and really scared when it suddenly took off and became viral before things went viral. I was genuinely worried when I heard that Eli found out about it and was going to call me that he was going to be mad.

What was that call like? "Hey, we should make this!"
I was like, 'Please don't sue us. (laughs) We were just messing around,' and he was like, 'No, this is a great idea. I really like it. It's a great tone.'

Did you have an idea for a feature?

No! And I lied and I said, 'Of course.' And then, me and Chris Ford flew out to LA to meet with Eli. And by then, it was like a week or two weeks later, we had just quickly put together an outline for what the feature would be. And he was like, 'Great, let's do it.' So, he went and set up some money to make it. Eli had the trailer. He asked, 'Can I use the trailer to try and raise some money?' So, he went and got a little bit of money, and we went off and wrote the script.

Incredible, incredible. You know, it's so funny because I -

Completely a prank. I wish I could look back and say that I had this brilliant strategy. But no, I don't know.

Well, it's funny because I just rewatched it and I hadn't seen it in quite a couple of years. Was it hard for you and Chris to expand that into a script? Because watching it, the story feels so natural. It just feels like some campfire myth. A guy gets the suit. And it turns out that it was actually the skin of some mythological demon. It all feels like it was meant to be. So, was it hard putting it together or did it all just come out?

It was fun. It was like, 'Oh no, are we really going to get away with this?' Yeah, it was fun to write. It's being re-released soon. I don't know if I'm allowed to say. There's a German Blu-Ray specialty company who does special editions of these things. And there's going to be this beautiful 4K remastered re-release.

Is it Turbine Media?

Yeah, Turbine! Ha!

Yeah, I've worked with them in the past! On their *Psycho* boxed set. They're great.

Oh yeah, Turbine's doing it. It's beautiful. There are four custom covers. They made a "making of" documentary where they interviewed all of us and got all this behind the scenes footage. I'm like, 'Oh, this is what it feels like to make a movie that becomes a cult movie.'

Okay, so your second feature, *Cop Car*. Here's the thing about that film. The last 20, 25 minutes, to me, plays out like the sort of scene that Hitchcock would have killed to make. The movie goes along and it's almost a *Stand By Me* sort of thing, following these kids. But it's like pulling back a rubber band that leads to that finale, right? And it's all of the hallmarks of a Hitchcock suspense sequence, which is why Craig told me you teach a class on where to put a camera. So, it all makes sense. When putting that film together, that story, did you reverse engineer from that final suspense sequence? Or did that come naturally

as you were writing that story? You wrote it with Chris Ford again?

That was a script that I wrote beginning to end and then Ford did a pass. But I wrote that in about a week.

Wow.

It was weird. That never happens. I'm a genuinely much slower writer than that. But I had always had this idea about two kids finding an abandoned car. It's a recurring dream that I used to have. I'm in a car with my friend and we're 10 years old and we're driving, and we shouldn't be. Um, and then I pitched it to Ford, and I asked, 'What if it was a police car?' And then he was like, 'Whose police car is it?' And I thought, 'Ooh, give me a sec.' And then I went and wrote the script. So that one just came together really naturally where I knew that all these pieces were on the table. And just waiting for all of those pieces to come together. It sort of naturally lent itself to this crazy, shoot out situation out in the middle of nowhere.

Well, your love of Hitchcock shines through in that final sequence I thought!

It's my favorite kind of sequence in any movie; when you get down to that sort of pure visual storytelling. And that's the spatial awareness, the spatial dynamics of, 'Okay, I know the car is here. I know Kevin Bacon is here. I know the kids are in the back. I know where the windmill is relative to the car,' all that 3D kind of math that goes on. And you're just trying to figure out who's conceived what and where.

Well, and then the girl gets out of the car in the middle of it and you think, oh no, the stakes just keep getting higher. I love that. Well, let's jump ahead a bit. You're a producer on the new *Final Destination* movie! *Final Destination: Bloodlines*. And not just a producer. I think you're the reason this franchise is even back because I know they've been trying for years! So, why *Final Destination*? Did you always have an affinity for the franchise?

Oh yeah. I love it. I've always loved *Final Destination*. Um, I think probably as I'm talking to you, I'm realizing exactly why it's the *Final Destination* movies… just to have that pure cinematic language. To make a sequence. It's a movie that's just sequences, just visual, cinematic sequences with a little bit of plot in between to get you from one to the other. And the first one came out when I was like a freshman in film school. So, anything that comes out when you're a freshman in film school, takes on an elevated amount of importance no matter what. But I just, as a film student, learning about how to put together my own projects, just watching those initial kills. I thought, that's it, man. That's what I love. So, I've always been a fan. My wife and I, one of our very first dates, was to see *Final Destination 5*.

Oh wow.

We accidentally saw it in D box. (laughs) Um, you know, where the seats move around. That was totally chaotic. Especially because that opening sequence is so long. So, you're being shaken around in your chair for twenty minutes.

(laughs)

Um, and then the call came in, I don't know if it came in from Craig (Perry) or if it came in from someone at New Line, but the call actually came in to my wife, who's a producer and was a manager for several filmmakers. They were looking for someone else. She was like, 'Well, uh, they're not available to talk about *Final Destination* ideas, but you know who likes *Final Destination* is my husband.' And so, I talked to Craig pretty quickly after that. And I said, 'I think I can come up with an idea. Let me just see if I can come up with an idea for *Final Destination*. And I'll send it to you. You guys like it, you could run with it. If you don't like it, no harm, no foul.' I think this was during the pandemic. So, no one was doing anything. So, yeah, I said I'll spend my time thinking of *Final Destination* ideas. So, I came up with a little pitch and I sent it to Craig, and he was like, '*Yeah, let's do that.*'

Is there any reason that you chose to produce instead of directing it? Or did you want to give guys like Zach (Lipovsky) and Adam (B. Stein) an opportunity to direct in the way that Eli gave to you?

I thought that I was going to not even be available to do it. So, I just liked the idea of using it as a jumping off point. It's such a perfect opportunity for younger filmmakers to come in and show off what they can do. So, I thought, I was happy to just write a little bit of a story and go back to the thing that I was working on. I was happy to be able to come on board as a producer and help the guys, give them some directorial advice along the way and also learn to work with a different studio that I'd never worked with before. I've never really been in that position. I've worked with such great producers that I thought, you know, it might be nice to try to do that for someone else.

I'd heard, and you can correct me if I'm wrong, but I'd heard that the directors, Zach and Adam, when they were pitching you guys on Zoom, one of the things they did was they had calamities and things happening all around them in true *Final Destination* fashion, which to me is a great lesson. Any aspiring filmmakers out there, you need to just go the full nine yards and really prove yourself!

It wasn't just calamities that were happening around them. Has Craig told you what the pitch was?

No, he just mentioned that.

They stood out. We should include that Zoom pitch as a "special feature" on the digital release or something. It was their final Zoom as they're taking us through their ideas. Um, and 20 minutes of the Zoom was their actual pitch for, what they think the story should be. Ideas for kills. Talking about the different kills in the different films in the franchise and why they worked and how there's always this balance and maintaining the tension and the misdirects and all the things that are great about *Final Destination*. Also, they were talking about the characters' potential, character dynamics that we could take advantage of in the story. Just really doing a great job with a pitch and the whole time they're doing it; they're sitting at a kitchen island. And in the background of the living room, there's a fireplace going. And then, I guess what they had done is they had switched over to their PowerPoint presentation. And then when they switched back, they were still there talking and the fire in the background has spread a little bit. You see an ember pop out and there's sort of something on fire on the wall and everyone else on the zoom is like, 'Oh guys, look at behind you. I think something happened,' and they're… it's such a *Final Destination* thing, right? They say, 'Okay, hold on.' And then they go back to put it out and the fire spreads and we're like freaking out; it seems really real and we can't believe it! And it eventually leads to the ceiling fan above them getting fried with the electrical sparks, and the ceiling fan falls off of the ceiling and chops one of the guys heads off and blood goes spraying everywhere. It was incredible. And it only slowly dawned on everyone on the Zoom what was happening, and we were all screaming like we were in the theater watching a *Final Destination* movie. When that zoom was over, how can you not hire them after that? They won that so, so hard.

How the hell did they pull that off on a live Zoom?! Did they pre-record that stuff?

It was live up until they went to their PowerPoint presentation and when they came back from their PowerPoint, they never actually came back from the PowerPoint presentation. They came back to a pre-recorded message that felt live. Yeah. It was just so impressive. It was such a magic trick and it was; talk about showmanship. Those guys, they can entertain an audience. They're going to do that for the Zoom pitch, just imagine what they'll do for the film!

What's your favorite *Final Destination* kill or set piece from the whole franchise? I know that's putting you on the spot here.

Yeah. I think a lot about… in the first one, the shower. With Tod. (Chad Donella) The string choking him and slipping. Slipping in the bathtub. Because that one is just so, so small and so real and so visceral. I think about that every time I'm taking a shower and it's one of those ones that can just really, really stick with you.

Yeah. I mean, I love them all, but for me, the truck highway sequence from *Final Destination 2*. That's one of the best action sequences of ever.

Oh yeah. The way it's put together; that's a good lesson on second unit directors and what they do as well. I go back and reference that all the time. I think that's such a masterpiece of filmmaking. Oh, and also underrated because it's not a kill, but the almost drowning in the carwash in *Final Destination 4*. That is pretty good. That's an underrated one.

I know that the late, great Tony Todd is in this film, and he's been a part of the whole *Final Destination* franchise in one way or another. I'd interviewed Tony before and he was a great, great guy, and a great actor. I think it feels right that this new movie kicks off in his honor. Any thoughts on working with the great Tony Todd?

I didn't really have the one-on-one time, like Craig Perry and Zach and Adam did. But it was great that he wanted to do it. And there's a poignancy to making a film that's having fun with the idea of death with someone who's really facing it. It was very emotional.

If you wouldn't mind indulging me, I want to talk a little bit about *Spider-Man* with you, because I grew up a fan of horror films and *Spider-Man*. These are the things that molded me and made me who I am! Who was your Spider-Man growing up as a kid? Because for me, I think it was *Spider-Man and His Amazing Friends*.

I didn't have a big *Spider-Man* exposure as a kid. I knew *Spider-Man*. I was aware of *Spider-Man*. Um, I had *How To Draw Comics The Marvel Way* book that I was pretty obsessed with. But it wasn't until the movie, the first Raimi movie that I thought, 'Oh wow, this is amazing.' It was Sam Raimi. I was obsessed with Sam Raimi. I loved, loved *Darkman* as much as I loved that. So, when he made his *Spider-Man* movie and seeing his style translated into that world, I thought it was the coolest thing I'd ever seen.

Yeah. I think I was a little too young when I saw *Darkman* because for a superhero movie, it's super violent! But I loved *Darkman*. (laughs) I saw it three times as a kid in theaters!

And I don't know why as a kid, I was so drawn to *Darkman*. It's because I had those suppressed memories of watching *Society*. Right? (laughs) Something about disfigurement, maybe, I don't know, it was manifesting itself. It was a cry for help, really.

Who's your favorite *Spider-Man* villain? When you got to do your *Spider-Man* trilogy, obviously, the best thing about *Spider-Man* is he's got an incredible villain's rogue gallery, and you got to pick plenty of fun ones for your movies. Excluding the movie versions though, do you have a favorite Spider-Man villain in general?

Um, I, you know, I really liked… I was really thrilled to do Mysterio. Just knowing that we could do such crazy visuals with Mysterio. That was one that opened up the door for a lot of fun directorial choices. I like Mysterio a lot. And I just like that he's a con man, kind of. (laughs) Yeah, that's it. So, just the meta-ness of having a character in a Marvel movie, basically fooling everyone into thinking that he's a character in a Marvel movie. I liked the layers that came with that. But, um, I, I would, it would have been fun to do Kraven the Hunter in one of our films.

Yeah.

Because I liked the idea of someone hunting Spider-Man. I like thinking of Spider-Man as the target. There's so much you can do. He has just the best rogue's gallery.

Totally. Spider-Man and Batman.

And actually, I liked all of them. I was trying to figure out if there was a way to do something with the really weird deep cuts. Like, Jackson Wheel. (laughs) With the big wheel type face. All the really, really weird ones that everyone wants to forget about. Is there a way to incorporate them somehow into a Spider-Man movie?

I always thought they should just do an opening montage of him catching a bunch of those weirdo secondary characters! That'd be a fun way to open one of those movies.

I can say I don't know anything about the next one and I'm really excited to see it without knowing what story it's going to be. Like, to watch it as a fan for the first time in a while.

Well, I'll say I'm the only person I know that still has a home 3D TV. I have all the imports from other countries of your *Spider-Man* movies in 3D. The Mysterio stuff in *Spider-Man: Far From Home* is amazing in 3D. Really, really amazing. I also think I speak for all of us Spider-Man fans when I say that the theatrical experience of *No Way Home*, especially after the pandemic, was just such a beautiful treat. So, I just want to thank you for that on behalf of all of us. Because it came after a very dark time.

When we were making that movie, there was this feeling on set where we thought, are there even going to be movies by the time this is done? It was really… (pauses) there'll never be another experience like that. Making it, finishing it. And then I snuck into the theaters opening weekend just to watch people watch it. And you could feel that catharsis.

Oh yeah.

Yeah, it was, it was pretty special.

We needed it! And I also want to thank you for giving some redemption to Andrew Garfield, because when I first moved to LA, I used to work at Amoeba in Hollywood. And he would come in and he was so nice, so kind, so genuine. And I remember the first time I talked to him was when first he got cast as Peter Parker for *The Amazing Spider-Man*! Before they had shot it. The first movie hadn't even come out yet. And we talked about *Spider-Man,* and he sincerely didn't want to let the fans down. So, thank you for giving him a great return.

He's such a good Spider-Man. He's a great Spider-Man. He just, you know, they didn't get to, maybe, finish what they started. I don't know that much about the actual making of those films, but his characterization of Spider-Man is really great. And there was so much there that I felt didn't get explored. They never got to make the third movie where you got to see more of that and where it went and his emotionality and his ownership of the character and his take on all of it. So, he had all of that as an unresolved, I think, exploration of the character. So, for him to actually get to finish up the story he was telling as an actor, I thought was; that was really, really, really fun to watch.

Yeah, that was awesome. I mean, he's a great guy. He's a great actor. And thank you for giving him his due in that movie. My last question, is anything genre-wise the last couple of years that's impressed or turned you on to any of these newer filmmakers, or do you find yourself going back to some of the horror classics now with an objective eye?

There's been a lot of great horror stuff. I feel like horror is really thriving. People want to go and have that communal experience. I really liked *Talk to Me*. That one really jumps to mind. I've seen a lot of great cool stuff. *Skinamarink* is one that's from another world. That movie is so disturbing and cool. But *Talk to Me*, the way that they took that idea and looked at it through the lens of, 'Oh wait, if kids actually were able to do that, what would they be doing? They'd be filming it and posting it and making it a party game.' And where that goes and the level at which those guys executed that movie, I just thought; it's like the best feeling is to be jealous when you walk out of a movie. And I was jealous. I was like, 'Man, I wish I had done that.' That was awesome. Robert Eggers doing the super, super classical take on *Nosferatu*. I loved that too. I don't know. I liked *Wolf Man*. I just saw *Wolf Man*. I thought that was another really smart, interesting way to tackle the *Wolf Man* story. It reminded me of *Clown*, because he's not a bad dad! He's a good dad trying to do a good job. And he's overdoing it by something that he can't control. I was like, I get it. I made a movie like this too. I don't think *Clown* was at the front of anyone's mind while making that. Hopefully not. (laughs)

Well, I really appreciate your time, and I can't wait to see the new *Final Destination* and anything you do, quite frankly, I'm all in on and excited to see!

Special thanks to Craig Perry!

From Jon's team, thanks to Sarah Pierce.

DANNY PHILIPPOU

Interviewed by Rob Galluzzo (3/25)

At least once every decade, a debut feature arrives from a new filmmaker that commands our attention. In the case of *Talk To Me*, the nightmares came on twice as strong courtesy of directing duo Danny and Michael Philippou! Not since the original *A Nightmare on Elm Street* have I felt so uneasy after walking out of a genre movie. The mysterious plaster "hand" that these kids use to crack the door open to the other side is the perfect metaphor for starring straight into the complexities of death, loneliness, and grief. The brothers have already completed their follow-up original horror feature *Bring Her Back*, which continues exploring those themes of loss. But here, we dig deep to uncover the true-life inspirations of *Talk To Me* from co-director Danny, which until now, he's never openly revealed!

What are your earliest recollections of the horror genre? Because I feel like all of us, we probably saw something a little too young that we shouldn't have seen, and it has stuck with us forever. So, for you, what was it?

My mom was so brutally strict with anything that we could watch. So, our classification here, it's a little bit different. We've got a PG rating like you guys have, and it's designated to low level violence and medium level violence for the PG level. And our mom would let us watch PG, medium level violence, anything like that, up until twelve. She was so, so strict. And anything that would defy that was so exciting to us. So, our dad's… because our parents are divorced, my dad's friend from work would take us to watch the MA-50 plus horror films, which is America's R. That was like the first time that we got to experience a proper horror film in the cinema. I remember those as my earliest memories of rebelling against my mom and watching these films in the cinema. But then before that, I remember the first thing that I ever watched that scarred me or scared the shit out of me was randomly *Alien 3*, which my auntie was playing on the television. My dad's like, "Oh, I don't know if you should watch it." She's like, "Oh, it's a movie, whatever, let him watch it." And I just fucking couldn't sleep! I remember the guy with glasses; the alien was bursting out of him or taking over him. That scared me more than the alien. The fact that it was taking over this human body and it was growing out of it. And then all those images of *Child's Play*. That used to scare the shit out of me as well. The *Child's Play* VHS covers and watching *Alien 3*.

So, at what point did filmmaking become an option? And what I mean by that is, I think for all of us, we watch films passively growing up, but there does come a point where you realize like, oh, somebody made this, whether it's trying to figure out the special effects makeup or realizing that it was a camera trick. What inspired you and your brother to think, "We can do this too."

Yeah, it started with the *Goosebumps* books and R.L. Stine. And the name R.L. Stine, to a six-year-old or a seven-year-old, that was so incredible to me that this one person made all these worlds and all these monsters and all that sort of stuff. So that, I used to obsess over. It was R.L. Stine. That was my earliest, earliest memory. And then, it never really felt like a real job. It never really felt possible. And my parents didn't think it was possible. I remember the first time we started crewing on films in South Australia, it just blew us away that they filmed movies here, because it just isn't really in the culture here as much as it is in the States. So, once we knew that it actually was a job that people were crewing, even just a light on a film, me and my brother were so blown away when we saw a lighting truck for the first time in person. So that was so incredible. We used to crew on movies for free, relentlessly, just putting our hands up to say, literally, you do not have to pay us. I really just want to be on set. That's when we started crewing on films. And Michael got his first paid job on *The Babadook* as the runner, driving around the actors and stuff like that. And even earlier than that was the *Lord of the Rings Extended Edition* box set. So, they had these really in depth behind-the-scenes making-of those films. Oh my God… Peter

Jackson wrote us a letter after watching *Talk To Me*. And it was the best fucking thing ever. And I got so nervous. I didn't write back to him! (laughs) Which is brutal. I feel so brutal. I hope it doesn't come across as rude. I started trying to write something back. But I'm actually too nervous to write anything or to express anything. And then I'm like, I don't want to bother him even. So, I would just shut the fuck up and like, be so grateful for that. But yeah, hopefully it doesn't come across as rude. But that was like one of the best things ever, was getting a letter from him.

So, you guys were working on crew stuff. And then, you'll have to forgive me because I know you through the features, not so much the YouTube stuff you're well known for. But I feel like YouTube became a really valuable tool in terms of figuring out not only how to share videos, but how to make them and edit them and put them out. Is that where you guys cut your teeth, making the YouTube videos?

No, it was even way, way before that. I was obsessed with gore and FX and makeup. We started making stuff when we were nine. We had this series that we made called *The Evil Flamingo*, which was, again, I think of like Chucky and killer dolls and stuff like that. And I remember just at nine and ten doing these makeup effects. *(Note: He pulls up one of these shorts on our Zoom chat screen.)* Byron, that's *The Evil Flamingo* there, that's the doll. That was when we were really, really young. So that was before YouTube, before anything, just making these VHS things. We made seven of these *Evil Flamingo* movies. And then from there, we made this series online with a friend, which was like a ripoff of Buffy called *Tamafi*. And it was our friend Tamani as a Vampire Slayer. Randomly enough, the show went ten seasons as kids, all the way from thirteen up until age eighteen. So, it was ten seasons of the show, and we did six movies. And on the final film that we were doing, this *Tamafi* movie, the big final movie with all of our friends, they were outgrowing it and getting real jobs and not understanding why we're still making this stuff. So that stopped. We didn't finish the last movie. And then I had no way to express myself or make anything. And so, then I started making the YouTube videos.

Was horror always kind of the path for you in terms of the kind of films you wanted to make? Obviously, with *Talk to Me* being your debut feature. Was that the story and idea that felt right to be the first? Or did you want to tell other genres? Because a lot of people, you just mentioned Peter Jackson, I mean, *Bad Taste* and *Dead Alive* were incredible starting points.

The first thing that we ever started writing was actually an action comedy. But it was the first time that I really started getting comfortable with writing again. I wasn't ready to make a feature at that point. It was very early on in our YouTube career, and it was starting to get a bit of attention and traction online. These producers approached us, and we started developing and writing this action comedy film. But we were never in the headspace or in the mindset to completely chase it or make it this full-time thing because we were so caught up in the YouTube world. That became our jobs where we were able to shoot and record this thing for instant gratification online and instant feedback. And experiment with everything from stunts to visual effects to building sets for the first time or working with crew members for the first time. Those early years were a building ground. We were just cutting our teeth so much and learning how to do so much. But yeah, we were writing, but not full-time. And it was always a side thing that we were doing. It helped me get comfortable with properly writing, but it was not until I started writing *Talk To Me* that I thought, 'I have to make a horror film. I have to make a horror film. I have to.' And even the next three projects that we've got that are written are all horror films. I'm obsessed with it. I love it so much.

Now, did this all happen basically because of the pandemic? You're doing the YouTube stuff, but then the world shuts down. So, is that when you pivoted yourself to writing because now there was time?

It was actually a couple of years before the pandemic. It was around 2018 that YouTube started changing their guidelines and the way that the algorithm worked. And they were really not favoring mature content. We just noticed that anything with any sort of swearing or anything with any sort of mature things, they were cutting the reach and cutting out monetization. It became not viable to make; we couldn't really express ourselves on there anymore. You have to really censor yourself. We were loving short form content, which was putting all our energies and efforts into this three to five minute thing. And at that time, YouTube was shifting to be about the watch time. It's about how long a video can be and how many minutes an audience can be watching for. And so, all those changes started happening and I felt really boxed in, but it was really good timing because I also started to feel boxed in by the content that I was creating. I was scared of even having two characters have a conversation. That felt like something I couldn't do on YouTube. I'd be too embarrassed. I felt like something had to blow up. I don't want to bore the audience. That stuff was terrifying. But it was all perfect timing. That's when I started collaborating with my co-writer, Bill Hinzman, on writing feature film scripts. I felt like with all that practice; it was time to attempt to tackle a feature.

I have a very emotional connection to *Talk To Me*, which I'll explain in a bit. But I want to know the origin story because I watched the film with the audio commentary and the basic gist of it is, or at least what I got is, you had had a car accident and there was this moment when you were in the hospital and anxious from the car accident and you held your sister's hand. And that immediately brought you comfort. This loved one's touch just immediately put you at ease. There's just something so deep about that idea. The idea that a loved one can bring you peace through their hands. Was that the origin of this? Was that the seed? How did all these ideas come together for that script?

It's so incredible. Whenever you're writing a horror film, you sort of fixate or hone in on everything that bothers you. I'm trying to put a magnifying glass on everything that bothered me. So, I remember that was a really profound experience. Just, yeah, the touch of someone you love pulling you out of this state of shock was so… it was so crazy how, literally the shaking just stopped. And so, I was sort of thinking that if you didn't have anyone, if she wasn't there to hold my hand or no one was there to hold your hand or give you comfort or just a natural connection between people, if that wasn't there at all, what would happen to me or to anyone? So, there's no one to pull you out, even with mental health or anything, if you fall into a bout of depression or into a dark hole and there's no one there to grab your hand and pull you out of it, you're sort of left down there in the hole. And Mia is sort of rejecting any personal connection. She's rejecting this thing with her dad and he's lying to her to try to protect her, but it's actually drifting them apart. And so, she can't connect naturally with him. And she started trying to force a connection with this other family a little bit. When she comes over, Jade's a bit like, 'Thanks for inviting yourself over.' And is pushing away Mia. And so, Mia starts attaching herself to her little brother; any way to be part of this family. *Talk To Me* became about these forced connections and rejecting the natural connections and holding on to these forced ones. And if you don't have those connections, you start relying on and fall victim to your biases, drugs, alcohol, sex, or whatever it is. You do anything to help pull you out of these things, but it's an unhealthy way of doing it. So, "the hand" sort of represented that. And that was natural in the material in terms of thematically and what the characters

were going through. But originally it wasn't even a haunted hand. It was a Ouija board. And then in later drafts, it was just a haunted object. We didn't know what it was going to be. And then hands and a touching connection was all the way through it, thematically.

And then you find other things to put in. I had another story that always bothered me. When I was nineteen or eighteen, there was a place called Kangaroo Island, which is that run of the South Australia. I was part of this documentary team filming this pilot about Kangaroo Island. So, they sort of dropped us off on this island and we were just talking to the locals and mingling with people, recording. "This person's opening a coffee shop. Oh, this person's got this fishing charter boat". But there was also this really weird underbelly as well, where it was like, "Oh, there's the cat man that peels all the dead cats off the road and skins them and dresses his furniture with cat fur. And he's made a board of cat's faces." A lot of the locals are sort of aggressive towards the wildlife there. And I remember, they dropped me off at some kids footy bonding trip or something. And these kids were literally "children of the corn." They were pinning each other down, shaving each other's head with sheep shears. And they're like, "Oh, let's shave Danny's head." And I was like, "Yeah," just trying to go along. So, I ended up getting my head shaved with these sheep shears. And they're like, let's take Danny to see the 'roos. And then I remember I got on the back of this car, hanging on to dear life, in the back of this pickup truck and they drove out into this field. And there were hundreds of kangaroos on this field. I've never seen anything like it. I was capturing all this footage, and it was this incredible scene. And these kids started running the kangaroos over, driving into them, running them down. And then they would get out and start beating the kangaroos to death. And the kangaroos screamed, they literally… I remember it screamed like a human, this really guttural fucked up sound that I still hear to this day. (pause) That sound bothered me so much that it naturally made its way into the film as well. And then, you know, mental illness runs in our family. Suicide runs in the family. And that sort of made its way into it as well.

Talking to my mom who lost her mom to suicide. And there's this weird thought of like, 'Oh, maybe that was the right thing. Maybe when you're in those things, maybe that was the right thing to happen to grandma. She tried everything, and this was the only thing that would work to stop this pain.' Those are the intrusive thoughts that would happen, or my mom would rationalize it in this sort of fucked up way. And that made itself into (the script) as well. It's a concoction of a lot of little things. Even our neighbors who we watched grow up, their mom would say, "Oh, could you drop him off at school?" And then the intrusive thought of like, 'Oh, what if I crash the car and kill him? And I'm responsible for his death.' Those things as well. Anything that sort of bothers you or makes you express it and put it on the page. Even if it's not a one-to-one analogy, there's hints of it and you integrate it into the characters in this. I guess that's what you have to do if you're right. Analyze really uncomfortable feelings or thoughts or experiences.

Well, you know, for me, if we can, I want to talk about grief because the thing is, I've lost both my parents. I lost my mom right before I saw this movie. And what your film did that I've never seen done successfully, not even in a horror film, but in any film is capture the feeling of grief and how lonely it is. And what I mean by that is what I've learned from my personal experience is sometimes people treat grief like it's contagious. And I felt like, here's Mia, here's a kid that lost her mom in a terrible way. And you'd expect the kids to have a little bit of compassion, but they treat her like it's contagious. Like, oh, her mom's dead. Like, ew, we can't be around her. And I've never seen a film do that. Even when I lost my mom, people were kind, obviously, but not everyone reached out to me right away. It's because they don't know what to say and they don't want to bother you, but grief is lonely. It's lonely when people don't reach out to you or help you. And I think you captured that, the loneliness of grief through Mia in the film, which immediately makes me completely buy that she would do this, that she would want to open that door, that dangerous door to the other side. I mean, is grief another thing that you were thinking about? Have you heard that analogy before?

Yeah. Well, I remember the first time that I experienced proper grief was our grandfather was living with us when we were kids. And so, our parents, my mom, was sort of like a bit away. And then my dad was always at work. And so, he would really, really raise us from ages of seven until thirteen. And then we came home one Christmas morning, and he was dead. And it was the first time that I really felt that. And then thinking back, did we even say "Merry Christmas" that morning when we came down? We never got to thank him in any sort of way. When you're going through this, it really is this internal struggle. And then you feel embarrassed because you bring down other people when you talk about it, especially when you're a kid, but because no one has experienced it, people are uncomfortable with it. And they don't understand it, especially when you're going through high school, things like that. And the natural

thing that happens is you just make jokes about it. It pretty much became a coping mechanism as a kid. So, that was the first time I was like, 'Oh, my friends can't help me here in terms of this thing that you're going through and trying to process.' And family, you feel a bit isolated from as well. It is a really internal struggle for a little bit. And eventually you have to let people help pull you out of it. But that was the experience of grief, it was embarrassing. It was a mood killer. You didn't want to trauma dump on anyone because it would bring people's moods down. I remember there was a girl in school, a friend of mine, who lost her mom. And that's what people would say about her. It was like, "Oh my God, it was like a year ago. And she's still fucking going on about it." That's literally the way that they would talk. And I just remember that very vividly. Because that group of friends were having such a good time. She's literally attaching herself and bringing everything down. And using a mom's death as a reason that we have to fucking invite her to all these things and stuff. So yeah, that was another part of it that I put in there.

Well, to me, that's where real horror comes from, is just the way people treat each other, right? It's a year since this girl loses her mom and people just don't want to be bummed? It just seems like such a horrific, insensitive thing. That's what I took away from it. I wanted to talk a little bit about casting because I did listen to the commentary last night. And well, let me start here. And I hope you don't take this the wrong way. I am so impressed. I'm so impressed that this is your first film. Because basically, for most first-time filmmakers, most would have a tough time killing their darlings or losing scenes. And what impressed me is that you guys, both you and your brother, were so hyper aware of scenes going too long, or when we needed to cut, or how to get the most weight out of the violence, for example, things like that, which I have to believe probably came from all the experiences of making all these YouTube videos and a series. But I was so impressed that you guys could clearly see what this first movie needed. I think the character of Riley (Joe Bird), I mean, could you have cast a more angel-faced kid that you desperately don't want anything bad to happen to? That, I think, is a magic trick for horror filmmakers is here's a character that is so innocent looking that you think, 'Please don't let anything bad happen to him.' And the worst thing happens to them. And it just has a visceral effect on the audience. So, with his scene, for example, you were saying the movie's not that gory. It's two minutes total of gore, but people remember it as much gorier, the same way that

people think *Texas Chain Saw Massacre* as a gory film. And it's technically not, you don't see anything on screen. All this seems like conscious effort on your part, I assume from watching a lot of horror movies, you basically knew what you were doing.

Yeah, yeah. And there's also those collaborations as well. Like our editor was saying, "You don't need this. You don't need this." When we're going through it, I was like, 'We do need this. It's character! It's not all about the action.' That was sort of our defense. Once you start watching with other people, you can feel when people's energy sags and when the point is being made too much. Having those scenes and acting that stuff out, these big conversations with Riley in the car are so good for character. And then Riley sort of senses that she's a bit upset and to brighten up her mood, he turns up the music and they start singing. Coming in on them singing tells that story. And there's already a lived history in the car having acted out those scenes and lived those scenes and talked about those scenes. You can just feel it with their relationship as opposed to outwardly saying it. That was such an interesting thing that we learned all the way through the edit process. And then you always cover too much, you shoot too much and then you peel it all right back. You ask, "What's super fundamental? What needs to be seen? What's better seen instead of said?" That all comes in that editing process. And yeah, the same with the gore and the violence, what's the middle ground? Because we shot some really fucked up stuff. Oh, we wrote some really fucked up stuff. That initial script for *Talk To Me* was so savage! It was really full on, like too full on. So, it's all about refining, refining, refining. Our producer as well helped us find that middle ground. Otherwise, it starts turning into schlock or starts to feel a little bit B grade when you really start pushing it too far into the other direction. Yeah, so it's a part of the collaboration to have all the people around you to help try and find what a comfortable middle Yeah, yeah.

That Riley scene, if it went a little longer, it wouldn't be as disturbing, right? Because then you start laughing at the absurdity of it all.

Yeah. But on the flip side of that, there are certain genres that lean into it. So, I always get excited when I'm like, "There's an uncut version of *Friday the 13th Part 4*?!" Or for any slasher film or a different type of genre, you want to see the gore!

Can you tell me a little bit about Sophie Wilde as Mia? She was such an incredible find for you guys. She's not really a final girl, but she has the characteristics of a final girl. She's like Nancy Thomas from *Nightmare on Elm Street* or even Florence Pugh in *Midsommar*. That's the first time I ever saw her and you just know, oh, she's going to be great. What was it about her that stood out?

Literally, during those audition scenes when she started reading, there were three different scenes that we gave to her. And her range and the way that she was expressing herself, the way she was emoting or the way she was putting this character on screen was like, we've gone through hundreds of tapes at that point. We've talked to so many people. And these scenes and the way that she was acting just blew us away. I could not believe what I was watching. And then the people that were helping finance it were really pushing for, yeah, a name, a big actor. It's like, I can't believe you're even trying to debate what we're seeing right now, because this person is not a star yet, but it's so obvious that they're going to be a star, and they can be a star. I couldn't get over how powerful those scenes were and how much she was able to jump between different moods and emotions so quickly too. If she's like that on the day and on the Zoom, what happens when you give her the space to really, really focus on that scene or that emotion or that part of themselves. She was so down for doing those things, to stay up all night and come to set, not having slept. So, you're at the edge of the edge. She was so down for that. And so down to put herself into the character. It was the best acting I'd ever seen on these audition tapes. It became this amazing thing. If someone else's performance wasn't as strong, you could always cut to Sophie. Because she's given you so much, it's so incredible how much she could hold a frame. Yeah, she blew me away. So, all from those initial audition tapes that she was doing. And you can never expect anything extra from anyone. If you're not seeing it in the tapes, what's to say they can bring it? If they can bring it there, they can bring it on set.

(SPOILER) Regarding the ending, I don't think there could have been a more fitting and inevitable ending to *Talk To Me*. It still gets me! Was that something you had come up with early on and then reverse engineered? Or was it naturally leading there as you were writing it?

Yeah, I think it came three drafts in. And going back and forth with my co-writer on different ideas. He was presenting different endings and discussing. And it was something that was found, yeah, a few drafts in. Because initially it just finished with the car crash. And it always felt like something was missing. And the way that we sort of write is you write just on instinct initially. And I'm passing all these pages of just scenes and ideas and stuff. And he starts really refining it and structuring it. And collaborating in this amazing way where we sort of bounce it back and forth, back and forth, back and forth. And you shape it. You have a draft. And then you go back through it again. And you're like, 'What's not working here? What's there? What can be better? What can we focus on? How can we fix this, change this?' It's just something that happens. The evolution and finding the hand as the haunted object. That's the same thing with finding the ending. It was never initially there. It's just like all the pieces are there. And the last piece of the puzzle is usually those moments. So, for us, it was through the drafting process that that came out.

Well, you got to make the movie you wanted to make. And then A24 picked it up. But you had mentioned on the commentary and on the press junket that there were studios interested in making this, but they wanted you to make big changes. Was there a temptation to do that? To do the studio movie version? Because you guys are young. That's a big break. I mean, I guess how did you fight off the temptation and know that you had to make it on your own? And by the way, I'm glad you did because the movie's perfect as is.

Yeah, thank you. Thank you. It was so tempting. And when you're in that initial position, you're literally thinking, 'Whatever it takes to get this done, I will do it. If they need to have this and that, let's just fucking do it. Like, if this is a proper film, we can get a proper budget. We can do this properly. It'll be in cinemas. They're saying it's going to be in cinemas. They're saying this, they're saying that.' And it was literally through the strength of our producer, Samantha Jennings, making us comfortable with the idea. She said, 'We can do this independently. We can do this on our own. And we can have complete control.' And even at the time, you're sort of like, 'Fuck, I want that.' But what if it doesn't get made? She's so headstrong that she thinks we can get it financed independently that I'm like, 'Okay, I can trust that. I believe it can get done because her belief in it is so strong as well.' And so, it was a really difficult decision to make. But we felt comfortable with her. We started feeling really comfortable. And then once the notes started coming in that were sort of hinting at, oh, maybe it's better if it isn't Australian, or maybe they should do "the hand" in the graveyard and things like that. And it's like, 'What happens in the edit if they've got final cut, and they've got complete control? What happens? We don't get the final say, and that just seems too terrifying.' And on the contrary, to be completely fair with them as well, they gave really good notes too! There were good notes from them as well. But ultimately, it came down to the thing where we were not

going to have complete control. If we make it independently and then sell it. That was the other thing as well. You have to make it and then you have to sell it as opposed to its already sold. It was another big thing. That was so terrifying. But every step of the way, it felt like the biggest roll of the dice. Casting Sophie (Wilde) and losing a million dollars out of the budget felt like the biggest roll of the dice. And us putting all of our fees back in was the biggest roll of the dice. And us, yeah, turning down the studio and doing it independently was a roll of the dice. But I don't know, it was through that trust with her and the comfort of doing it our own way that we pushed through.

Well, I'm glad you did. It was the right way to go. The best independent films of all time in horror are things like _Texas Chain Saw Massacre_, the original _Nightmare on Elm Street_, _Blair Witch Project_, et cetera. _Exorcist_ is a studio movie, but that was William Friedkin! (laughs) He earned his final cut at that point.

He was at that point where the studio was listening to him, right?

Exactly. He could get away with it. You hinted a lot after the first movie came out that there was so much left to explore. I don't really want to know anything, but how far along are you with a sequel? Is there a clear-cut idea of how you'd follow it up or what you'd do with _Talk To Me 2_? I love when people go really crazy in a sequel. I really love what Parker Finn did with _Smile 2_. I thought _Smile 2_ was such a wild swing from the first one. So, where are you at with the sequel?

There are two directions that we could take it in. And so, there were two versions of the script that we were writing. We had two drafts of two very different films following completely different characters, which was a fun thing to try and explore and navigate. And we've honed in on an idea now that we're really, really excited about. And then all the way through _Talk To Me_, I was still writing pages. And so was my co-writer of _Talk To Me 2_, we had 60 pages of what a sequel could look like and could be at that point. So, I definitely know I want to do a sequel. I was so excited about doing a sequel. I just know I don't want it to be next. I didn't want to go straight into it because I wanted to be steeped back into the world when I had a bit of space from it. To really, really process my thoughts, my feelings. So, we've just finished shooting _Bring Her Back_, another horror film. I want to do one more film before _Talk To Me 2_, I think, before I can go back in and really make sure the script is as strong as it can be, and I'm as excited and it feels as fresh as it can be. Yeah, that's where I'm at right now is that we have an outline that we're very happy with. We have pages that we love. We have characters that we love. And it'll be about drafting, drafting, and redrafting, redrafting over the next, it could be three, four years maybe.

All right. Well, look, my request is you can explain some stuff, but don't explain everything. Because I love that the kids literally had no idea exactly where the hand came from. It was just stories they heard. That's how it would be if you found that relic in real life. You wouldn't actually know the origin! So, I love that.

Exactly.

I don't want to know too much about *Bring Her Back* because I want to be surprised the same way I was with *Talk To Me*. But I will ask this; how are you feeling about it? What can you tell me about it without spoiling anything? How are you feeling about this follow-up film that you did?

Yeah, it's still a theme (of grief and connection) that I was really, really interested in exploring. And those experiences are things that I was honing in on, that we sort of hinted at a little bit with *Talk To Me*, but really, really magnified it in this film. So, it's super personal. And it feels scarier to make this because there were no expectations with *Talk To Me*. People were really convinced that it would be a pile of shit. (laughs) And we're like, 'This is scary now, where there's an expectation behind it!' I feel like I would have got too much in my head about it if I waited too long to do anything. So, it was a thing of running towards the door while it was open. And while there was a momentum there, this was a script that we were writing while we had *Talk To Me*. It was something that we had at the same time that was being developed at the same time. And also, it's very different from *Talk To Me* too. *Talk To Me* was a party horror film. And this is different. So yeah, the whole experience, I'm always hot and cold on it. I'm always terrified. And you always feel like you've got to cave to any sort of expectations. You don't want to let anyone down, either. We've worked with Sally Hawkins. She's this incredible, incredible character actor. And we're so scared of making something that will let her down. You're so scared of letting A24 down. So, there's all those fears, there's anxieties. And you just have to trust yourself and trust the material. But every time you make a film, it's the most overwhelming, tense thing. And you always question why you're doing it. And then you get it out, and you'll jump back in for some reason. But it's such a, it can be a soul crushing thing. (laughs)

Well, look, I hope you keep making original films, because I love what you're doing. And I love the voice that you and your brother have. But you flirted with IP. There was a *Street Fighter* movie, apparently. Is there any horror IP that, hypothetically, would be fun to tackle? I feel like you want to do a killer doll movie, maybe? Or do you want to continue doing these original horror stories?

That was sort of the conclusion that we came through at the end of *Street Fighter* while we were developing it. We had to make a choice between making *Street Fighter* or making *Bring Her Back*. And that became a thing as well, really trusting yourself or getting more excited about bringing original visions to life. That's so much more exciting to me than any other IP could be. Again, that was a really big decision to make. Because I actually really loved the people at Legendary that we were working with. They were so collaborative and amazing. And it was another really tough choice to make. It's like, 'Oh, you can make this really incredible, big blockbuster action film,' which is exciting. Or, 'We can go into a house and focus on three characters for a few months.' I think the conclusion that we came to the end of it is, I really just want to make our own stuff. And maybe a book adaptation that doesn't already have an onscreen adaptation. That would be interesting to me, potentially. But remaking anything or doing a sequel to anything, I don't think would be for us. Again, I wouldn't want to let down any original fans. Trusting and building our own stuff is always more exciting.

Right. Well, you said you're a big fan. What's been exciting and inspiring to you in the genre lately?

Oh, my God. There's so, so many films. That's what's so exciting right now is how much horror is at the forefront. It's pretty incredible. And even those really small budget films are really incredible, like *Oddity* was really fun. I like that there is this next gen of horror filmmakers that are coming up, like Parker Finn or Ari Aster. I think these people can be looked back on in thirty, forty years, as the new Wes Craven's. They're the new voices of horror. It feels like we're in a golden age again for horror. I was speaking recently with Leigh Whannell, who did *Saw* and *Insidious*. And he was just saying how impossible it was to get a horror film made at that time, especially in Australia. Now, I just think it's so cool.

Special thanks to Frank Martinez from A24. From Danny's team, thanks to Bob Sobhani and Carly Plasha.

ICONS OF FRIGHT

THROUGH THE YEARS

459

BEN CHAPMAN

CONTINUED

BY MIKE C..

WHAT WAS IT LIKE TO WORK INSIDE THE SUIT?

IT WAS VERY COMFORTABLE. THE FOUNDATION OF IS LIKE A ONE-PIECE BODY STOCKING. IT ZIPS UP THE BACK. IT WAS LIKE A LEOTARD. SO WHAT THEY DID WAS, EACH PIECE WAS MOLDED SEPARATELY. THE LOWER PART FROM JUST BELOW THE KNEE DOWN, THE FEET, WERE LIKE BOOTS. THEY CAME UP TO THE KNEES. THEN THEY'D ZIP OF THE BACK AND SNAP THE DORSAL FIN CLOSED. SAME FOR THE HELMET. THAT'S IT, IT'S VERY SIMPLE. BUT IT TOOK A LONG TIME TO GET INTO. ABOUT 2-3 HOURS...

DID YOU HAVE TO DO A SCREEN TEST IN COSTUME FOR THE STUDIO TO APPROVE?

NO, WE TOOK SOME PHOTOS, BUT NOT REALLY A SCREEN TEST. HE WAS VERY TOP SECRET. WHEN THEY WERE CONSTRUCTING HIM NOBODY WAS ALLOWED IN MAKEUP. THEY DIDN'T WANT ANYONE TO SEE WHAT HE WAS GOING TO LOOK LIKE UNTIL THE DAY THEY RELEASED HIM.

WHY WEREN'T YOU CREDITED IN THE MOVIE?

THE REASON THEY DIDN'T CREDIT, AND THIS IS CRAZY, IS THE STUDIO WANTED TO GIVE THE IMPRESSION, THE ILLUSION, THAT IT WAS A REAL CREATURE. IF YOU SEE THE ORIGINAL FRANKENSTEIN, BORIS DOESN'T GET CREDIT. IT'S A QUESTION MARK IN THE CREDIT. I LOOKED AT THE STUDIO AND ASKED IF THEY THOUGHT THE PEOPLE WERE THAT STUPID, AND THEY SAID,"YOU'D BE SURPRISED WHAT PEOPLE BELIEVE".

WHAT DO YOU THINK KEEPS THE "CREATURE" ALIVE, AFTER ALL THESE YEARS?

THE STORY STILL HOLDS UP TODAY. THE STORY IS ABOUT TRYING TO FIND OUT WHERE MAN CAME FROM. WHEN YOU PLAY THE MOVIE TODAY IT'S STILL JUST AS INTERESTING. ALSO, JULIE AND MYSELF WANT TO THANK ALL YOU LOYAL FANS OF "THE CREATURE". WITHOUT ALL OF YOU, WE WOULDN'T BE SITTING HERE AND THE GILLMAN WOULD'VE BEEN BURIED AND FORGOTTEN A LONG TIME AGO. JULIE SAID IT, "YOU KNOW WE'RE SET IN STONE NOW." AND IT'S TRUE, WE BELONG TO THE UNIVERSAL FAMILY. YOU KNOW WHEN THEY SHOW FRANKENSTEIN, DRACULA, WOLFMAN, YOU SEE THE GILLMAN. HE'S THERE FOREVER. WE'RE VERY GRATEFUL.

BE SURE TO CHECK OUT THE ENTIRE BEN CHAPMAN INTERVIEW AT:

WWW.ICONSOFFRIGHT.COM

ICONS OF FRIGHT INTERVIEW

THESE ARE PAGES FROM THE ORIGINAL *ICONS OF FRIGHT* MINI MAG HANDED OUT AT THE CHILLER CONVENTION IN 2004

HIGH TENSION CONTINUED

I AM HAPPY TO SAY THAT HIGH TENSION IS A WELCOME RETURN TO TRUE HORROR FILMS OF YORE, WITHOUT ALL THE UNNECESSARY BELLS AND WHISTLES. A SIMPLE STORY, A FEW WELL-ACTED CHARACTERS, AND GORGEOUS CINEMATOGRAPHY MAKE THIS ONE KILLER MOVIE, PUN INTENDED. IT IS, UNABASHEDLY AND UNASHAMEDLY, A SLASHER MOVIE. THAT'S IT. NO OBSCENE BUDGET, NO INTRICATE SUBTEXT, NO HEAVY-HANDED SOCIAL COMMENTARY... JUST MAN KILLING PEOPLE BECAUSE HE CRAZY. BASIC PLOT: TWO COLLEGE GIRLS GO ON A STUDY RETREAT TO A FAMILY FARM IN THE COUNTRY. THIS IS EVIDENT FROM THE CORNFIELDS. THEN, FOR THE REASON EXPLAINED ABOVE, SOME CRUSTY GUY IN A SPOOKY TRUCK COMES A CALLING ONE NIGHT AND GOES FUCKING BUCK ON THE WHOLE FAMILY. SCARY-ASS BUCK! OUR CUTE FRENCH HEROINE SEEMS TO SLIP PAST HIM UNNOTICED, BUT HER FRIEND IS CHAINED UP AND TAKEN AWAY IN AFOREMENTIONED SPOOKY TRUCK. CUTE FRENCH GIRL THEN TRIES TO SAVE HER FRIEND FROM CRUSTY GUY AND MANY GALLONS OF BLOOD ARE SPLATTERED UNTIL THE BIG FINALE WHEN EVEN MORE BLOOD IS SPLATTERED! THEY MUST HAVE USED ALL THE KARO SYRUP IN FRANCE FOR THE ENDING SEQUENCE ALONE FOLKS.

NOW DON'T GET ME WRONG, THE FILM IS NOT WITHOUT A FEW TWISTS AND TURNS (ESPECIALLY THE OFT-DEBATED ENDING), BUT AT IT'S CORE YOU HAVE A 98 MINUTE VERY BLOODY FREAK OUT THAT DOESN'T SHY AWAY FROM INTENSE TERROR. AFTER YEARS OF CINEMATIC SPAM, THIS ONE DELIVERS THE GOODS LIKE A TRIP TO THE OUTBACK STEAK HOUSE ON PAYDAY.

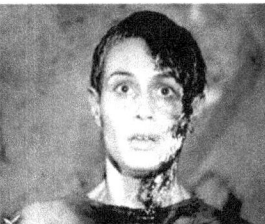

DIRECTOR ALEXANDRE AJA HAD DONE A FANTASTIC JOB OF CREATING A CELLULOID TIME MACHINE THAT TRANSPORTS US, IN SPIRIT, BACK TO THE EIGHTIES. NOT IN A CAMPY WAY, MIND YOU... IT'S OBVIOUS HE HAS A LOVE AND RESPECT FOR THE GENRE. HE REALLY CAPTURES THE HORROR IN THE ACT OF KILLING, NOT JUST THE SPECIAL EFFECTS AFTERMATH. THERE ARE SOME TRULY CRINGE-WORTHY SCENES THAT ARE PLAYED WITHOUT EVEN THE MEREST HINT OF HUMOR.

CONTINUED

ICONS OF FRIGHT REVIEW

THE VAULT OF THE FORGOTTEN AND OBSCURE
BY JSYN

ALTHOUGH THESE OVERLOOKED FOOTNOTES OF MOVIEDOM HAVE BEEN LOST IN THE ANNULS OF FILM HISTORY, THEY STILL EXIST IN THE MEMORY OF OUR CINEMATIC SUBCONCIOUS!

SOME ARE HITS. MOST ARE MISSES. BUT EVEN THE FAILURES ARE SO SPECTACULAR, THEY CANNOT BE DENIED!

DO YOU DARE ENTER THE VAULT OF THE FORGOTTEN AND OBSCURE???

CHOPPING MALL /1986/ D: JIM WYNORSKI
TEENS OF THE EIGHTIES HAD THREE LOVES: SHOPPING MALLS, KILLER ROBOTS, AND CLEAR SOFT DRINKS. THIS MOVIE HAD TWO OF THOSE THREE. ADD GRATUITOUS NUDITY AND YOU GOT YOUSELF A PARTY!

FRIGHT FACT! THE CAST BOASTED GENRE FAVES LIKE BARBARA CRAMPTON, MARY WORONOV AND DICK MILLER!

THE PROWLER /1981/ D: JOSPEH ZITO
HEY A SLASHER MOVIE WITH GORE FX BY TOM SAVINI! THERE WERE ONLY THIRTY-SEVEN OTHER MOVIES YOU COULD SAY THAT ABOUT IN THE YEAR 1981.

FRIGHT FACT! DIRECTOR JOSEPH ZITO IS RESPONSIBLE FOR SOME OF MY FAVORITE 80'S MOVIES, MOST NOTABLY FRIDAY THE 13TH: THE FINAL CHAPTER, INVASION U.S.A. WITH CHUCK NORRIS, AND THE DEFINITIVE DOLPH LUNDGREN FLICK RED SCORPION.

HUMONGOUS /1982/ D: PAUL LYNCH
THE TV SPOT HAD MOVIE TRAILER GUY SPELLING OUT THE LETTERS, "H-U-M-O-N-G-O-U-S!" WITH HIS SCARY MOVIE TRAILER GUY VOICE. THAT WAS IT FOR ME, CRAWLED RIGHT UNDER THE BED I DID! I THINK IT WAS ABOUT A GIANT MOGOLIOD CANNIBAL STALKING NAUGHTY TEENS ON A DESERTED ISLAND. NEVER SAW IT, BUT I GOT THE GIST OF IT FROM THE MOVIE POSTER.

FRIGHT FACT! I JUST CHECKED IMDB AND THAT'S EXACTLY WHAT THIS MOVIE IS ABOUT! WOW!

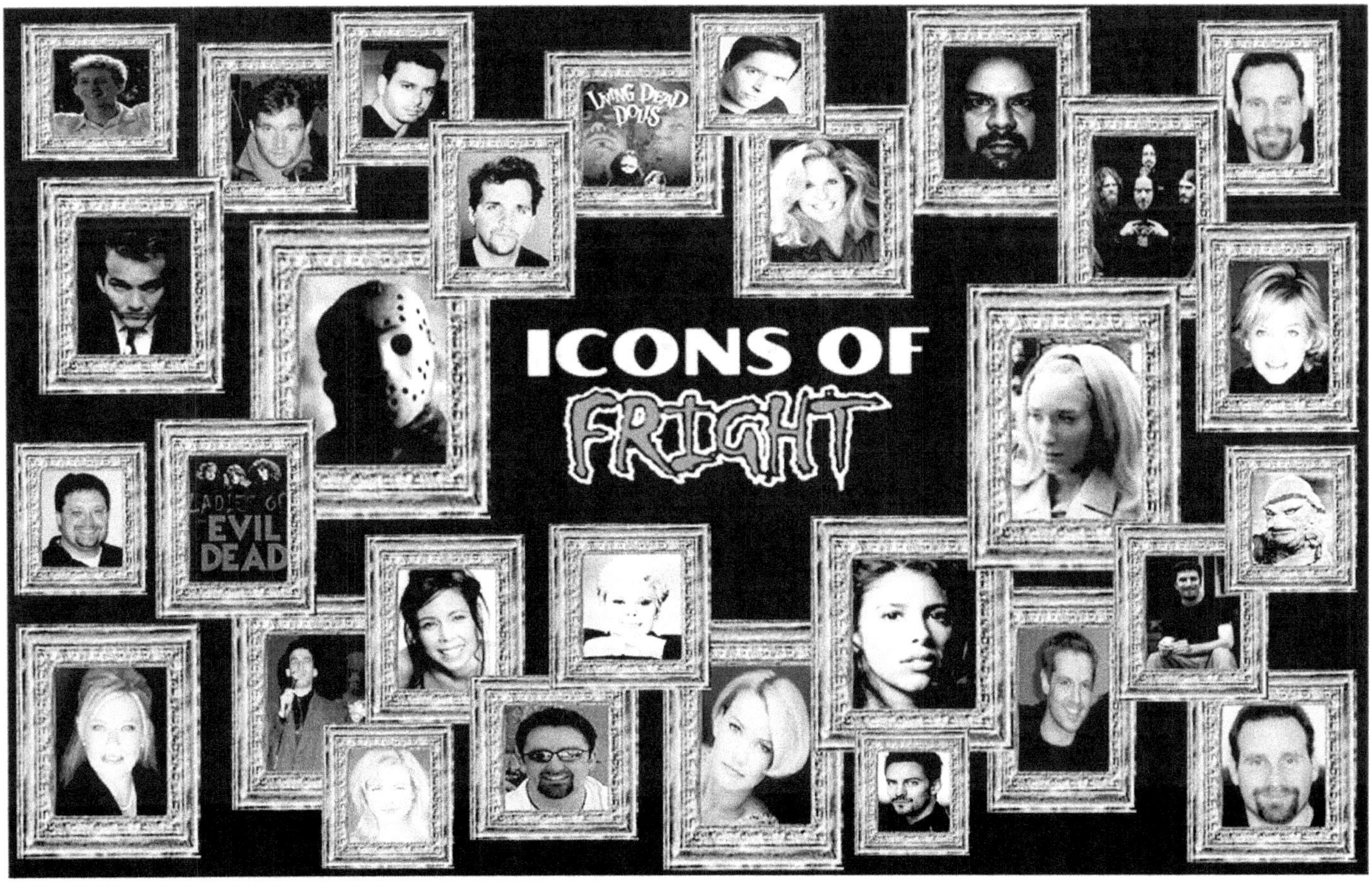

ICONS OF FRIGHT

IN MEMORIAM

BETSY PALMER

GUNNAR HANSEN

LAR PARK LINCOLN

JEFF BURR

HILTON GREEN

CHRIS HENDRIE

BEN CHAPMAN

ZELDA RUBENSTEIN

DICK DUROCK

ACKNOWLEDGEMENTS

The authors wish to extend their sincere thanks to our friends, families, and contributors who supported *Icons of Fright* throughout the years:

Eric Alvino

Dan Berghofer (aka Danny Price)

Ted Bohus

Elliot Brodsky

Paula Burr

Steven Ciancanelli

Bob Clark

Kevin Clement

Nathaporn Delahousse

Beth Puttkammer Dereli

Jonathan Ehlers

Paul Ehlers

Preston Fassel

Judah Friedlander

Juan Galluzzo

Rudy Galluzzo

Michael Gingold

Michael J. Hein

Heather Hillen

Tom Holland

Ian Holohan

Mike Kerr

Bethany Kivin

Kevin Klemm

Rich Koz/Svengoolie

Neil Marshall

Stevan Mena

Vincent Minichiello (Technoweenie)

Alisa Phongluangtham

Craig Perry

Lawrence Raffel

Scott Reynolds

Will Rot

David J. Schow

Bill Shafer

Victor Solnicki

Terri Stamper

Tony Timpone

Dante Tomaselli

Guillermo del Toro

Spooky Dan & Tammy Walker

Special thanks to Joe Maddrey!

And to Dustin McNeill for making this book possible!

MEET THE FRIGHT CREW

MIKE CUCINOTTA

Mike Cucinotta is the co-creator of *Icons of Fright*. He works as a video marketing editor with clients that have included AMC's Shudder and Warner Archive. He gladly and proudly has accepted his seat at the table with Martin Scorcese and Pauline Kael in vigorously defending John Boorman's *Exorcist II: The Heretic*. Mike currently resides in Brooklyn, New York.

Mike dedicates this book to the memory of his mother Denise Cucinotta. He thanks his partner of twenty years, Mark Alonzo, for his endless support and love.

ROBERT GALLUZZO

Robert Galluzzo is the co-creator of *Icons of Fright*. He's also the director of the documentaries *The Psycho Legacy* and *Analog Love*, and producer on the Shudder original *Lucky*. He's contributed to *Blumhouse, Fangoria, FEARnet, Shock Till You Drop*, and co-created the horror podcasts *Shock Waves, Killer POV*, and *Dexter: Wrap Up*. He currently resides in Los Angeles, California.

Robert dedicates this book to the memories of his parents Salvatore Robert Galluzzo and Benita Maria Novello-Galluzzo, and also *Fright* friend and supporter Kristin Wicks.

JASON ALVINO

Jason Alvino is an award-winning screenwriter who has worked in film for over twenty years, first as an accomplished special makeup effects artist before shifting focus to screenwriting full-time. He has developed original projects with notable producers and directors, including the theatrically-released horror thriller *Itsy Bitsy* (2019, Shout Factory) He is based in Long Island, New York.

Jason dedicates this book to Shem Andre Byron.

ADAM BARNICK

After starting his film career with the Fangoria-distributed horror short *Mainstream*, Adam has directed music videos and multiple documentary featurettes. As an editor, his clients have included Paramount Pictures, Village Roadshow Pictures, Arcana, Mattel, IFC Midnight, ArieScope Pictures, and Glass Eye Pix. He is currently in post production on *TURN*, his first short horror film in several years. Adam now resides in Vancouver, Canada.

Adam dedicates this book to Frank, Elaine and Jesse Barnick; his wife Sharai, aka princess shredder, Pizza the Real Dog, and Sean Kane & Bryan Stauss, who he watched many horror movies with.

If you enjoyed this book, consider other titles from

HARKER PRESS
PUBLISHER OF SCARY GOOD BOOKS